Racing the Silver Arrows

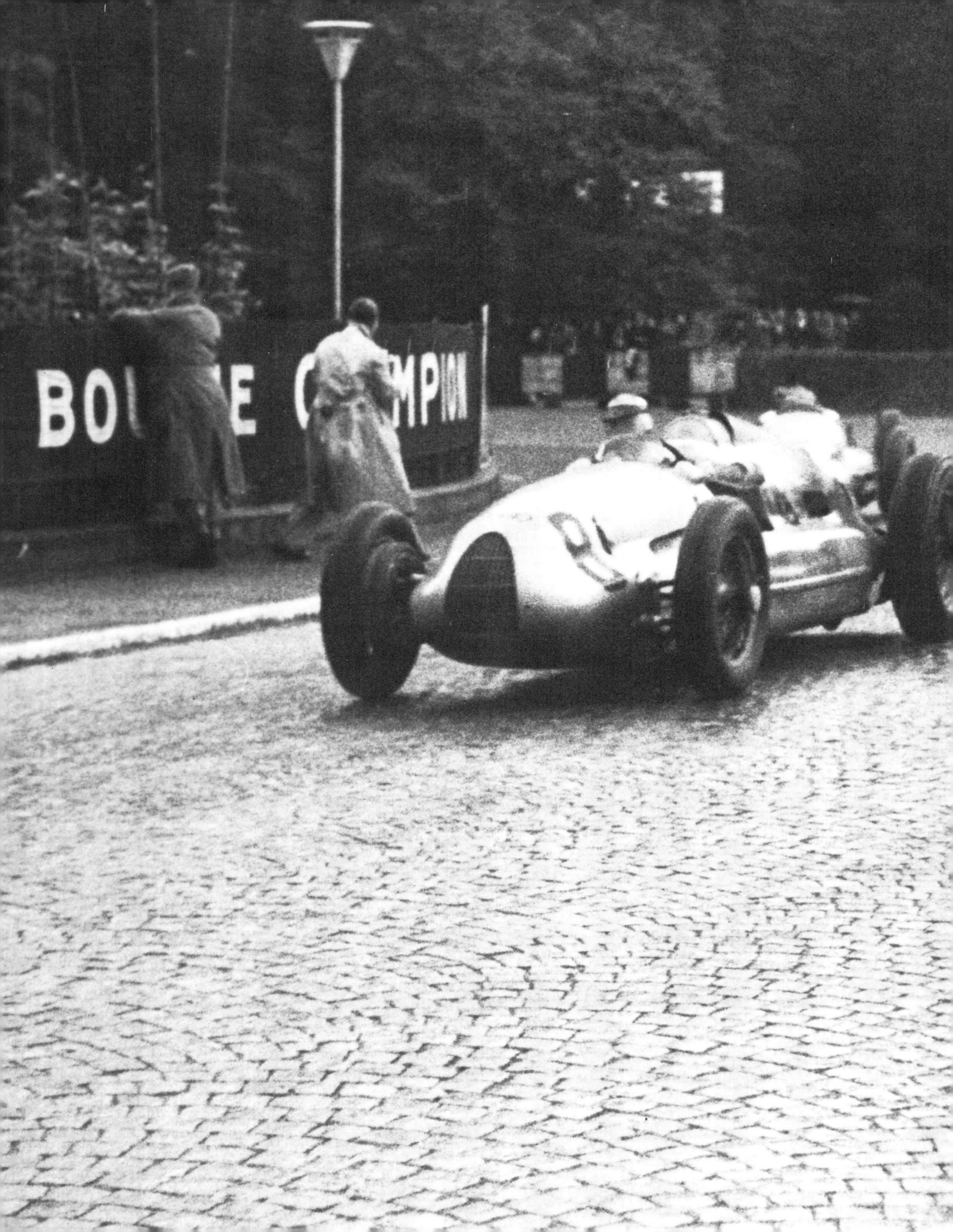

RACING THE
Silver Arrows

MERCEDES-BENZ VERSUS AUTO UNION

1934–1939

CHRIS NIXON

OSPREY

For my mother,
Linda,
and in memory of my father,
Nick.
With love

Published in 1986 by Osprey Publishing Limited
27A Floral Street, London WC2E 9DP
Member company of the George Philip Group
Reprinted late 1987

British Library Cataloguing in Publication Data
Nixon, Chris
    Racing the silver arrows: Mercedes-Benz versus
    Auto Union 1934–1939.
    1. Automobile racing—History   2. Mercedes
    automobile—History
    I. Title
    796.7'2   GV1029.15
ISBN 0-85045-658-4

Designer Gwyn Lewis

Filmset and printed by BAS Printers Limited,
Over Wallop, Hampshire, Great Britain

Contents

Foreword

The Grand Prix has always been the highest form of motor racing, since it involved cars which were designed in every way for maximum power. With these cars a special road circuit became the scene of races in which the best racing drivers in the world competed.

Before World War I the Grand Prix of the Automobile Club de France was *the* major car race of the year. The race was held on circuits formed by public roads, and involved far greater distances than is the case today, for instance. The first Grand Prix of all took place in 1906 on a 103 km (64 mile) circuit in the Le Mans area, over a total distance of 1236 km (767 miles)!

In the time between the World Wars, this distance was reduced to 500 km (311 miles), but the races were still held on road circuits, i.e. on roads such as a normal motorist experienced in everyday driving. The Grand Prix car was at that time the most efficient possible road car in terms of its suspension, engine and transmission. This was to be the case until well into the period after World War II; it was not until recently that races started to be held mainly on short, track-like circuits. Then as now, however, the drivers operated constantly at the very limit.

I think the greatest time was from 1934 to 1939. This is understandable, since it was then that I had the opportunity to take a major part in the great battles of the so-called Silver Arrows. I had succeeded in rising from a racing mechanic (I was Chief Mechanic for Luigi Fagioli) to the ranks of the topmost Grand Prix drivers, with Mercedes-Benz. Just then, the war ended my career, when I was at the peak of my form. In 1939, I became European Champion, driving for Mercedes-Benz. Although I was able to continue racing after the war, and even achieved some success, the electrifying atmosphere of the contests between Mercedes-Benz, Auto Union, Alfa Romeo, Maserati, Delahaye and others was never to return.

In *Racing the Silver Arrows*, the Englishman Chris Nixon recalls the great days of these cars; his descriptions bring back to life the exciting races of the years 1934–9. For that I thank him and wish him and his book every success.

Hermann Lang
European Champion, 1939

Hermann Lang passes the pits and grandstands in the rain on his way to victory in the 1939 Belgian Grand Prix—and the European Championship

Acknowledgements

It's difficult to know where to begin in thanking all the people who helped me put this book together, but it's probably fair to start with all those in the Daimler-Benz Press Department, Archiv and Museum in Stuttgart who were unfailingly courteous and helpful on my many visits to that fascinating place.

For their Memoirs of Mercedes-Benz and Auto Union I am most grateful to Ghislaine Kaes (Stuttgart), Ernst Henne (Munich), Paul Pietsch (Stuttgart), Hanns Geier (Stuttgart), Dr Ferry Porsche (Zuffenhausen), Elly Beinhorn Rosemeyer (Munich), Rudolf Uhlenhaut (Stuttgart), Günther Molter (Stuttgart), the late Professor Robert Eberan-Eberhorst (Vienna), Erica Schwab—formerly Erica Seaman—(Sarasota, Florida), Hermann Lang (Bad Cannstatt) and Schorsch Meier (Munich). Thanks also to Frau Brigitte Geier, Ernst Henne jun., and Schorsch Meier jun.

The majority of the photographs in this book has never been published before. The bulk of them is from the Daimler-Benz Archiv, but many of the people mentioned above loaned me pictures from their private collections. Other sources include Porsche AG, Ludwig Sebastian (Mannheim), Dieter Jockisch (Korbach), Martin Schroder and Hans-Joachim Weise (Hannover), Halwart Schrader (Munich), Rupert Stuhlemmer (Berlin), Jochen and Barbara Essers (Stuttgart). Christoph Eberan-Eberhorst and Hans-Joachim Stuck were kind enough to give me access to their fathers' collections. Finally, in England, Cyril Posthumus and Louis Klemantaski made their collections available.

Matthew Carter and Howard Walker (respectively Editors of *Autocar* and *Motor*) kindly allowed me to reproduce certain pre-war race reports from the pages of *The Autocar* and *The Motor*. The Haynes Publishing Group gave permission for me to quote from Raymond Mays' autobiography, *Split Seconds*, originally published by Foulis; and the Editor of *La Meuse* in Liège allowed me to copy some photographs from the paper's 1939 Belgian Grand Prix report.

Thanks also to Porsche AG Press Department and Archiv, Frank Stroud of The Transport Bookman, René Dreyfus, Eoin Young, Neil Eason Gibson, Tony Cliff, Pedro Barja, Quentin Spurring, Tony Lewin, Hugh Edgley, David Moncur and Elaine Jones of the Quadrant Picture Library, also to Bill Kaye of Blowup and Lofty Rice of Pinewood Studios Stills Department.

Finally, my thanks to Tim Parker for committing Osprey to the book and to Lydia Greeves for keeping up the good work after Tim left for America.

To anyone I have inadvertently omitted, my apologies.

CN

Introduction

Racing the Silver Arrows tells in full—for the first time—the remarkable story of the period from 1934-9 when Grand Prix racing was dominated by the silver cars from Germany.

It came as something of a surprise to realize that such a book had not been written before: the men and machines of Mercedes-Benz and Auto Union provided such stirring racing in the 1930s that the period became recognized as 'A (if not The) Golden Age of Motor Racing' and, as such, surely deserves a book of its own. Although, since the war, much has been written about the individuals, cars and races involved, no-one has ever attempted to cover the whole story in one book, until now. *Racing the Silver Arrows* is that book, and although I am not so daft as to claim that it is the definitive work on the subject (dangerous word, that: 'definitive') it will, I believe, throw some new light on the whole spectrum of a remarkable era.

When I first discussed the project with Tim Parker (then Editorial Director of Osprey—now Editorial and Production Director of Motorbooks International, USA) we quickly agreed that what we did not want was a book comprising a string of race reports and a wodge of technical jargon. (For those who seek proper, detailed technical information, Karl Ludvigsen's excellent *Mercedes-Benz Racing Cars* is the standard reference work on the Stuttgart machines, but to my knowledge no similar book on Auto Union exists, at least not in the English language.)

What Tim and I *did* want was the human interest allied to the racing history of the period, which must include the completely overlooked record-breaking and mountain-climbing exploits of the two teams and—even more important—the role played by the Nazi Party in German racing at that time. We weren't seeking to point any fingers or unearth any horror stories here—we were just keen to find out what went on, as this fascinating aspect of The Golden Age has never been explored before. All these areas are now covered in detail in *Racing the Silver Arrows*.

But, most of all, this book is about the personalities in the Mercedes and Auto Union camps and their lives in the Grand Prix circus of the thirties. Occasionally, it is about their loves, too, for although this is no Harold Robbins saga, I take the view that, as the careers of certain drivers were demonstrably affected—for good or ill—by the

woman (or women) in their lives, to ignore this on the grounds that some might regard it as gossip and having no place in a book about motor racing, would be ridiculous and unprofessional. The saying, 'Behind every great man is a woman' applies to racing drivers as much as anyone else, and there can be no question that the lives of men such as Rudolf Caracciola, Achille Varzi and Dick Seaman, for example, would have been very different without their womenfolk, who bring a very human dimension to my story.

For my previous books, *Racing With The David Brown Aston Martins* (Transport Bookman Publications, 1980) I went directly to the people concerned with the team, starting with John Wyer and going on to the principal drivers, designers, mechanics and their colleagues. The success of this exercise led me to try the same approach with *Racing the Silver Arrows*, although, as some 50 years have passed since they were racing, the survivors from the period were obviously going to be thinner on the ground than their Aston Martin counterparts. During several trips to Germany, where I was greatly helped by various people at Daimler-Benz and Porsche, I found a dozen individuals who had been actively involved with Mercedes-Benz and/or Auto Union, and were happy to reminisce about their racing days.

Once I had typed out the Memoirs, I sent each back to the person concerned for approval. One who is no longer with us, alas, is Professor Robert Eberan-Eberhorst, who died in 1982. I had interviewed him for my Aston Martin books in 1979, and while visiting him in Vienna I asked him for a few memories about Auto Union, although at that time I had no idea how I might use them. Not long before his death, Professor Eberan was interviewed in England by Tony Lewin of *What Car?* and, as Tony was unable to use his piece, he very kindly gave the tape to me. So Professor Eberan's Memoir was made up of those two interviews and later approved by his son, Christoph Eberan-Eberhorst.

Writing about the people no longer with us involved a tremendous amount of research, and the more books and magazines I read the more obvious it became that I was in an historical minefield, as time and again I found conflicting reports and details. As my interest in Mercedes-

Benz and Auto Union only goes back some five years, my enthusiasm was clearly not enough—I needed an expert to guide me through the period. Cyril Posthumus immediately came to mind, for he is acknowledged as the finest motoring historian around, so I asked him to read the book as I wrote it. Happily, the 1930s turned out to be his favourite period of racing and he accepted the task at once. It has to be admitted that even he was stumped for the truth on occasion, but with his considerable help (for which many thanks) I believe that *Racing the Silver Arrows* is as accurate as possible. Any mistakes remaining are mine and I shall be grateful to readers who may be able to correct them.

Racing the Silver Arrows offers a new and complete look at a fascinating era, highlighting the personal, political, financial and racing dramas and revealing the curious system by which the driver with the *least* points at the end of the year became European Champion! It was a time for heroes, when men like Caracciola, Fagioli, Rosemeyer, Stuck, Nuvolari, Varzi, Lang, von Brauchitsch and Seaman were highly visible both in and out of the cockpit, unlike their modern counterparts, who are virtually invisible by comparison.

The book is illustrated with over 250 photographs, the majority of which has never been seen before, and I hope that they, together with the text and contemporary race reports, will enable readers to relive a bygone, but still Golden Age.

CHRIS NIXON
Richmond, Surrey
1986

What's in a name?

Strictly speaking, the name Silver Arrows applies only to the cars of Mercedes-Benz, but as the Auto Unions were also covered in an aluminium paint giving them, too, a silvery appearance, it is perfectly reasonable to use the name for both makes in this book.

Although Germany's national racing colour was white, only Mercedes-Benz produced white racing cars in 1934, the Auto Unions being silver from the outset. The first race for both teams was due to be the Avus GP on 27 May, but Mercedes withdrew at the last minute, making their debut a week later at the Nürburgring in the Eifel GP, and it was there that the name Silver Arrows had its origins.

When the cars were weighed, Team Manager Alfred Neubauer was shocked to find that they were just one kilo over the 750 kg (14.75 cwt) limit. Naturally, the cars had been built with the greatest care to ensure that they would be under the limit, and now that they were not under it, he could think of nothing that could be removed in order to save that wretched kilo. In the English version of his autobiography, *Speed Was My Life*, Neubauer wrote, . . . 'there was nothing on the car that could be dispensed with. But a chance remark by von Brauchitsch gave me my inspiration.' Curiously, his translators could not be bothered to tell readers what that chance remark was, which is a shame, as it is the key to the whole issue.

In his original German version, however, *Männer, Frauen und Motoren*, Neubauer is quite specific about what von Brauchitsch said. '*Schönes Pech*', knurrt Manfred von Brauchitsch mich an. '*Lassen Sie sich doch einen Ihrer berühmten Tricks einfallen. Sonst sind wir die Lackierten* . . .' ('You had better come up with one of your famous tricks,' said von Brauchitsch, 'otherwise we will be the painted ones . . .'). To be 'the painted ones' is a German expression meaning to have bad luck, but it was *der Lack* (the paint) which gave Neubauer the idea that got Mercedes out of trouble. He ordered the cars to be stripped of their white paint overnight, and when weighed again the next morning they were under the 750 kg limit.

That's Neubauer's version and it certainly makes a good story. It also makes sense, but it has to be said that in *his* autobiography, '*Kampf um Meter und Sekunden*', von Brauchitsch makes no mention of the incident. If he was, indeed, the man who—albeit unwittingly—gave the Mercedes racing cars their silver appearance which in turn led to the name, Silver Arrows, it seems unlikely that he would have forgotten to mention it!

Some doubt is also thrown on Neubauer's story by Hermann Lang, who was present at the time in his capacity as Chief Mechanic to Luigi Fagioli. He well remembers the fuss about the cars being too heavy, but cannot recall that the idea for removing the paint came from any one person.

'It could well have come from some of the mechanics, because we were all standing around discussing what was to be done about the extra kilo. Anyway, the decision was taken to remove the paint and we set to work. The cars had been painted white very carefully in order to get an excellent finish, but you must remember that the bodies were of hand-beaten aluminium and so were very uneven. This meant that there was quite a lot of filler applied before the paint was sprayed on and it was probably this filler, rather than the paint, which pushed the cars over the limit. Once all this was removed the cars were covered in a very thin coat of aluminium paint and when they were weighed the next day they were just under the limit. From that point on they were always silver and shortly after the phrase *Silberpfeile*, or Silver Arrows, was coined by the Press.'

Prelude to a Golden Age

At the beginning of the 1930s, Grand Prix racing was in complete disarray. The rot had really set in when the sport's governing body, the AIACR (*Association Internationales des Automobile Clubs Reconnus*) threw out the two-year-old 1500 cc Formula and replaced it in 1928 with a Free Formula, in which engine capacity was unlimited, but the cars had to weigh between 546 kg (10.75 cwt) and 750 kg (14.75 cwt). Races were to be run over a minimum distance of 600 km (375 miles). This did not at all suit Delage and Fiat, and these firms withdrew from racing, leaving the field to Bugatti, with the occasional foray from Alfa Romeo.

For the next two years the AIACR made token changes to their Formula, but these only succeeded in making it more and more unpopular, until their regulations for 1931 were rejected out of hand. That year races were run again to a Free Formula and had to last at least ten hours, which upset all concerned, as it meant two drivers per car, so for 1932 the minimum duration became five hours, with ten the maximum. This was not popular either, so for 1933 races were restricted to 500 km (310 miles).

Doubtless chastened by their failure to come up with a formula that pleased anybody, the AIACR did some serious thinking during 1932 and in October that year announced their new regulations, which would come into force in 1934 and continue until the end of 1936. These retained the minimum distance of 500 km (310 miles) and stipulated that although there would still be no limit on engine size there would now be a limit on the cars' weight, the maximum being 750 kg. Curiously, instead of insisting that the cars be ready to race at this weight, the AIACR excluded such little items as the driver, tyres, fuel, oil and water from the limit!

Then, as now, the men who ran motor racing were worried about the ever-increasing speeds of the cars, and they felt that by keeping the maximum weight low they would preclude the designers from developing larger and more powerful engines. The then current Alfa Romeos and Bugattis all weighed around 750 kg and used engines of around 2.5 litres—figures that were regarded as just about right for Grand Prix racing. The general feeling was that engine size might be increased to as much as 3 litres, but that the power would not rise much above 200 bhp and so speeds would not get out of hand. This was a reasonable

assumption based on the factors known at the time. What nobody could have foreseen was the quantum leap in racing car design and the use of new, lightweight metals about to be made by the old firm of Daimler-Benz and the new one of Auto Union.

Although, of course, both German cars were designed entirely independently, some intriguing cross-references were revealed when they appeared for the first time in 1934. Daimler-Benz—under the direction of Dr Hans Nibel and Max Wagner—opted for a conventional, front-engined design, but with the then novel all-independent suspension and with the gearbox mated not to the engine, but to the differential unit. The car was, in fact, very similar to a design drawn up by Professor Porsche shortly before he had left Daimler-Benz in 1928.

However, for *his* new car Porsche adopted the mid-engined layout that Benz had used in their famous *Tropfenwagen* of 1923. One of the men who had raced that car was Adolf Rosenberger who, in 1932, was Porsche's backer and Business Manager. His enthusiasm for this layout unquestionably influenced Professor Porsche's design, which became the Auto Union. So, eventually, Mercedes-Benz produced a racing car influenced by Porsche and Porsche produced a racing car influenced by Benz!

Word of the new car's existence did not take long to reach the Press. As early as April 1933, *The Motor* announced that an interesting new GP car would be seen 'this season'. It went on, 'Designed by Dr Porsche . . . this remarkable racing job is likely to cause some sensation when it appears. . . . The engine is a 16-cylinder Vee type, with a capacity slightly under 4 litres. Two blowers will be installed, one for each block, and the engine is expected to develop about 300 bhp. Independent suspension is employed for all four wheels and the car has a five-speed gearbox. The chassis is said to be nearing completion and it is hoped that it will be ready for trials within the next week or so.' Apart from the fact that there was no mention of the mid-engined layout and that the car wasn't nearly ready for testing (it made its first running appearance on 13 November), this report was pretty accurate and the revelation of a near 4-litre engine and 300 bhp must have given the men at the AIACR some sleepless nights.

In May, *The Autocar* had a go, stating that there were

rumours of new Mercedes racing cars 'with their engines at the back and the tanks at the front, although this sounds unbelievable'. The writer correctly attributed the car to Professor Porsche, adding that 'it doesn't follow that it will be built by Mercedes'.

While the German teams were busy designing cars that would take Grand Prix racing into a new era, their unknowing opponents were merely updating their existing machines, blissfully unaware of the revolution to come. Alfa Romeo, Bugatti and the relative newcomer, Maserati, made no attempt to build new racers, doubtless being of the opinion that their proven designs would be able to handle the new German opposition.

The Mercedes-Benz W25 was shown to Adolf Hitler in January 1934, and in February was sent to Monza for tests, where it crashed quite heavily when Manfred von Brauchitsch was driving. Even then, without any competition development, its straight-eight, 3.4-litre supercharged engine produced 314 bhp, far more than any of its rivals. Aesthetically, too, it was way ahead of the opposition, with a beautifully streamlined body that made all other GP cars—even the glorious P3 Alfa Romeo—look out of date.

Auto Union also went to Italy, before revealing their cre-ation to the public gaze for the first time at Avus, in March, when Hans Stuck set three new World Records. The thousands of Berliners who lined the track that day must have been stunned by both the odd appearance and the immense speed of the new silver car.

Slowly, details of this astonishing machine came to light. The rumours had been correct—it did indeed have a rear-mounted V-16 engine of 4.4 litres, producing 295 bhp. Like the Mercedes, it was independently sprung all round, but Professor Porsche used torsion bars and trailing links at the front, whereas Mercedes employed enclosed horizontal coil springs and bell-cranks. At the rear, both cars had swing axles with transverse leaf springs.

To drive these very powerful cars the German teams assembled seven drivers of varying talents, Mercedes signing Rudolf Caracciola, Luigi Fagioli, Manfred von Brauchitsch and Ernst Henne, while Auto Union took on Hans Stuck, Prince Hermann zu Leiningen and August Momberger. The two teams were supposed to compete for the first time at Avus, on 27 May 1934, but Mercedes withdrew after practice. A week later they both turned up at the Nürburgring for the Eifel GP and this time, battle was joined!

1934

Let Battle Commence!

Understandably, the two German teams elected to make their debuts on home ground. Victory first time out was a tall order, but the legendary Teutonic efficiency suggested that it was far from being out of the question and with the first big German event—the Avus GP—scheduled for the end of May, Mercedes-Benz and Auto Union appeared to have plenty of time in which to prepare their cars. Scuderia Ferrari, however, had its Alfa Romeos off and running early in April and had won four GPs (not to mention the Mille Miglia and the Targa Florio) before either German team had turned a wheel in anger.

In the event there was no fairytale beginning for the Germans. Although their cars were very fast in practice for the Avus GP, Mercedes were not satisfied with their performance and withdrew them before the race, leaving Auto Union to deal with the Ferrari Alfas. Hans Stuck led by miles for some time, but all the Zwickau cars were soon in trouble and Guy Moll followed up his sensational Monaco victory with another win for Scuderia Ferrari, this time in an especially streamlined Alfa.

Overall, it turned out to be Scuderia Ferrari's year, the Alfas starting in 26 races and winning no less than 13 of

PREVIOUS PAGE **The birth of the Silver Arrows was at the 1934 Eifel GP at the Nürburgring, where the Mercedes' original white paint was scraped off to bring the cars under the 750 kg weight limit. Here the paintless W25 of Manfred von Brauchitsch is pushed up the tunnel to the track before the start of the race, which von Brauchitsch won**

The map opposite shows the locations of the circuits used for European Grand Prix racing and the roads used for record-breaking during the period 1934–39. In the 1930s motor racing was conducted, for the most part, on public roads—but not in England. Despite the existence of some very fine home-grown racing cars and drivers, the English authorities steadfastly refused to allow racing on the streets.

England's loss was Europe's gain. There, racing through the streets was regarded as normal procedure which brought tourists and their money to the town or city. Side roads would be blocked off, numerous straw-bales and/or sandbags would be placed in strategic positions around the course, temporary bridges would be erected over the road for pedestrians and spectator protection would be taken care of by straw-bales or a piece of rope strung between trees or lamp posts and even, on occasion, proper barricades! Some circuits—such as Bern, Reims, Spa and Tripoli—had permanent grandstands, but elsewhere these would be put up for the race and dismantled afterwards.

There was also a handful of purpose-built circuits: Avus, Montlhéry, Monza, Donington and the Nürburgring. The latter was, of course, *the* road circuit to end all road circuits, but although it was open to the public it was, in effect, a private road with one-way traffic, built specifically for racing and testing. It was never part of the German road system.

The character of these circuits varied enormously, from the heart-stopping Nürburgring, Spa-Francorchamps and Monaco to the blindingly fast Avus and Tripoli, the blandness of Milan and Belgrade and the downright silliness of the narrow and twisty Montenero.

The longest circuit used was the Masaryk Ring at Brno, which was 29.14 km (18.10 miles) round and the shortest was Milan at 2.4 km (1.5 miles). The fastest circuit of all was Avus, where Bernd Rosemeyer set the fastest-ever race lap with his Auto Union in 1937 at a staggering 276.32 km/h (171·74 mph); the fastest road circuit proper was Tripoli, where Hermann Lang set fastest race lap in his Mercedes in 1937 at 229.22 km/h (142.44 mph). The slowest circuit of all was Montenero—winning speed: Achille Varzi (Alfa Romeo) 1934—84.77 km/h (52.67 mph). The longest fastest lap time was recorded by Brno in 1934 by Luigi Fagioli (Mercedes-Benz) with 13 mins 16.2 sec. and the shortest fastest lap time was set in the very last race of the era—the Yugoslav GP—when Manfred von Brauchitsch (Mercedes-Benz) and Tazio Nuvolari (Auto Union) both recorded 1 min 14.0 sec.

Although in 1934 and 1935 Mercedes and Auto Union

went to Hungary and Italy for record attempts, it soon became German Government policy that all such attempts should be made on German soil. This ultimately led to the death of the great Bernd Rosemeyer at which point attempts on normal *autobahnen* were forbidden. A special stretch of *autobahn* near Dessau was selected for future record-breaking, including Hans Stuck's attempt on the Land Speed Record with the fantastic, Porsche-designed, Mercedes-Benz T80. Although Rudolf Caracciola set some new records there early in 1939 with specially modified Mercedes-Benz racing cars, Stuck's plans came to nought due to the outbreak of war.

European and North African Circuit and Record-breaking locations

them! The German teams, of course, were only interested in the major Grands Prix and their two important home races, the Avus and Eifel GPs, but Mercedes won four out of seven races entered and Auto Union three out of eight. For a first season with brand-new cars that was a pretty good result.

Of the drivers, the year belonged to Achille Varzi. While his great rival, Nuvolari, had one of the worst seasons of his career, Varzi excelled with five wins, although none was in any of the major races. He also had four seconds and two thirds. Louis Chiron was in great form, too, with three wins, including a sensational one at Montlhéry, where he led the Germans a merry dance until they all fell out and he won one of the greatest victories of his career.

The European Championship had not yet begun, but if it had it would surely have been won by Hans Stuck, who brought the Auto Union home victorious in three major Grands Prix: the German, the Swiss and the Masaryk, and finished second in two others.

Financially, Varzi was an easy winner, taking home 975,000 lire in prize money. The value of the Italian lire went up and down like a yo-yo in the 1930s, but according to the Bank of England, in 1934 there were 93.75 lire to the pound and £1 then was equal to £17.2 in 1985. Here are the top five money winners for 1934:

Achille Varzi— 975,000 lire (£10,400) (£178,880 in 1985)
Louis Chiron— 657,000 lire (£7,080) (£121,776 in 1985)
Guy Moll— 587,500 lire (£6,266) (£107,775 in 1985)
Hans Stuck— 455,000 lire (£4,853) (£83,471 in 1985)
Luigi Fagioli— 287,500 lire (£3,066) (£52,735 in 1985)

(Prize money as reported in *Gazzetta dello Sport*)

Four people very much involved with that first season were Ghislaine Kaes, Ernst Henne, Hans Stuck and Luigi Fagioli. Kaes was Professor Ferdinand Porsche's nephew and also his Private Secretary. He remembers the very early days of the Porsche company, when there was very little money (and sometimes none at all!) and how Porsche persuaded Adolf Hitler to back Auto Union as well as Mercedes-Benz in 1933.

Ernst Henne was the holder of many motorcycle speed records when he was asked to join Mercedes for 1934. He recalls his brief and none-too-happy season with the Three-Pointed Star. By contrast Hans Stuck had a very good first year with Auto Union, but his career with the team was occasionally troubled by the Nazi persecution of his wife, who was supposedly half-Jewish. Stuck, however, found he had an ally at the very highest level of the Nazi Party! Although chiefly remembered as 'King of the Mountains', Hans raced the difficult, mid-engined Auto Unions with considerable skill. His main opponent in the Mercedes team in 1934 was the volatile Italian, Luigi Fagioli, the first of Mercedes' foreign drivers of the thirties. Brilliant but fiery-tempered, Fagioli clearly thought he was the German team's Number One, but was often ordered to give way to Rudolf Caracciola and Manfred von Brauchitsch, for whom he developed a real hatred.

The most important race of the year at this time was the French Grand Prix, and *The Autocar* duly covered it in style. The report is reproduced in full. Four of the principal GPs of 1934 were held on the Lasarte, Montlhéry, Brno and Montenero circuits, all of which are detailed with maps and information.

════ MEMOIR ════

Ghislaine Kaes

Private Secretary to Professor Ferdinand Porsche

Professor Porsche was my uncle, having married my father's sister, Aloisia. My parents were Austrian and my father, Otto Kaes, was Porsche's 'Man-in-the-field' in England and I was born in London on 4 July 1910. I am a British subject and have retained my nationality all my life, in spite of Hitler!

My uncle joined the Steyr company on 1 January 1929, as Technical Director and he got me a job there as soon as I had passed my General Certificate of Education in England. I started in July that year and spent 18 months working as an apprentice, going through most departments. The Wall Street Crash, in October, brought about the end of

Porsche's relationship with Steyr in 1930, when he was given notice.

He was now out of work, but he had a company car which Steyr wanted back, so he told me to go to the Personnel Manager and ask if he could keep the car for another two weeks. I did this and kept on doing it for the next two or three months! Meanwhile the Professor was looking for a job and I became his secretary. I had just finished a course in typing and shorthand and I was also fluent in English, German and French, so I was well equipped to handle all his correspondence.

One day I ventured to ask why he did not accept one of several offers that had come in and he said, 'At my age I shouldn't take a step backwards!' By this he meant that he would only join a company that would have him on the Board of Directors, but he was regarded as too expensive and too close to the workmen. Many companies would have been happy to have him work for them, but they would not give him a say in the running of the company and this he wouldn't accept.

Unable to find a job, in the summer of 1930 he decided to set up a company of his own, but he had no money. He went to see Adolf Rosenberger, a racing driver who had been driving for Mercedes when Porsche was working for Daimler-Benz in the mid-1920s—1923–8. Rosenberger was a wealthy Jew who lived in Pforzheim, about 20 miles outside Stuttgart, and he agreed to back Porsche. He wanted us to move to Pforzheim and open an office there, but Porsche insisted on moving to Stuttgart—not only was it in the centre of the German motor industry, but he owned a house there!

Having found an office, at 24 Kronenstrasse, Porsche now needed technicians to work in it. The first person he approached was his former Chief Designer Karl Rabe, whom he had employed in 1913 when in Wiener Neustadt with Austro-Daimler and who had taken his place as Chief Engineer at Steyr. While we were setting up the new com-pany Rabe was still with Steyr, of course, so it was my job to drive from Professor Porsche's house (which still belonged to Steyr) in Professor Porsche's car (which also still belonged to Steyr!) to Herr Rabe's house and then deliver him to Porsche's home, where they would talk until the early hours. Then I would have to drive Herr Rabe home—without lights—go to bed and get up at 5 am so I could be in the factory at 6.50 am.

We moved to Stuttgart in December 1930. Rabe joined us and he was followed by Karl Frohlich (in charge of gearbox design), Josef Kales (engines), Josef Zahradnik (front and rear axles), Fraulein Junkers (book-keeping), Franz Sieberer (copying and photography) and Josef Goldinger, who was Porsche's driver. I now left Steyr and became the Professor's official secretary and archivist. I did a good many other jobs, too.

For example: I was in charge of the parts list and the copying machine and I had to go to the bank each week to get the money for the wages. Of course, in the early days the money was often not there, as we had very little work. I also had the very important job of sending—by registered mail—the complete detail drawings and parts list of, say, a gearbox, to a customer. The parcel had to be handed in to the Post Office before midnight and usually the last drawing would not be finished until about 6 pm. Then Professor Porsche would direct operations: Herr Rabe would be cutting the drawings and I would type out all their numbers. At about 10 pm Porsche would say to Rabe. 'Alright, now we can leave it to Ghislaine', and they would leave me and Franz Sieberer to work the copying machine and complete the job. We would then take the parcel to the Post Office just before midnight. The following day Herr Rosenberger (who was our Finance Director) would ask me for the receipt and he would then phone the company to which the drawings had been sent and ask for payment.

For a long time I had no salary. I lived with my uncle and aunt, so I had board and food, but no wages. It was

RIGHT **Professor Porsche (in homburg) watches as the very first Auto Union is prepared for its first test run at the Nürburgring in January 1934. On the left are Wilhelm Sebastian and the tall figure of Hans Stuck. Stuck did not drive the car on this occasion**

23

Prof. Porsche in the pits at Brno, 1934

about this time that I had a girlfriend, Johnnie (now my wife), and although she was well-to-do I wanted to be able to take her out at my own expense. One day I asked Herr Rosenberger for five Deutschmarks.

'What for?' he said. 'You know we don't have any money.'

'I want to go out with my girlfriend.'

We talked for half an hour and eventually he gave me the money, insisting, 'Remember, it's top secret. Nobody must know about it and it's only this once—never again!'

It was even more difficult for the others, who were often in trouble having no money to pay the rent. I remember Frau Rabe having a real go at Herr Rosenberger one day. She got some money, too, but then her voice shook the whole building!

Sometimes, when the money ran out completely, Herr Rosenberger would give me the keys to his car (a Porsche-designed, 8-cylinder, supercharged Mercedes Cabriolet) and tell me to go to a certain address in Pforzheim and collect 10,000 DM, which was a lot of money.

In 1932, even this source of money dried up and the company had none at all. Worse, we had no orders, so Porsche chose this moment to design a new, high-powered racing engine. To do this, he and Rosenberger formed a new company financed by a friend of Rosenberger's—a man called Hoffmann. This company was at the same address, but on the third floor, not the second, and was called *Hochleistungs Motor GmbH* (High Efficiency Engines, Ltd).

One day we were visited by a delegation from Russia and they suggested that Professor Porsche become the Chief Designer for all Russian motor vehicles. They invited him to visit their country to see exactly what they had to offer. He accepted the invitation and went on his own. He was shown all over Russia—even some of the most secret places—and he was most impressed. But he decided not to accept the offer, not because he didn't like the Russians or their politics, but because he couldn't speak the language, and felt that at the age of 57 he was too old to learn it.

'I tried talking to some workers in a foundry,' he told me, 'and I couldn't understand them. If I can't talk to the workmen, I can't work.'

Nowadays it is said that he turned the Russians down because he was all for Germany and wanted to stay there because he loved his country. This is nonsense—he was not a German in those days, but an Austrian. No, he didn't go to Russia for the simple reason that he couldn't speak the language.

The Auto Union firm had been formed in 1932, comprising the companies Audi, DKW, Horch and Wanderer. The Chairman of the Board of Directors was Baron Klaus von Oertzen and he arranged for Porsche and himself to meet with the new Chancellor, Adolf Hitler. The meeting was in May 1933 and because they didn't consider themselves to be particularly Germanic in appearance, they took with them a blond, blue-eyed fellow named Hans Stuck. He and Porsche knew each other from the late 1920s, when he had raced the Porsche-designed Austro-Daimler ADM.

Hitler was expecting to see only von Oertzen and appeared rather annoyed to meet three people, but on shaking hands with Porsche, said, 'We know each other.' Porsche didn't know what he was talking about, but Hitler was right. They had met at Solitude in 1926, when Porsche's Mercedes racing car was competing there and Hitler had been present with his close friend, Jakob Werlin, who at that time was District Manager for Daimler-Benz in Bavaria. He was one of the first members of the Nazi Party and often provided cars for Hitler.

After a cold beginning the atmosphere soon got better when Porsche spoke to Hitler, who suddenly took him away from the others to a table by a window. They talked for 20 minutes. I think the reason for this was that Porsche was an elderly man who had met many of the great men of the world and was not at all nervous in Hitler's presence. Also, they were both from Austria and spoke the same language—I think Hitler took a liking to him.

Porsche later told me that Hitler had asked him what he wanted. Porsche showed him drawings of the new engine he had designed with Karl Rabe and Josef Kales —a V-16. He reminded Hitler of his speech at the Berlin Motor Show a few weeks before, in which he had promised to boost the German car industry, and pointed out that the engine was designed for a racing car that would do great things for Germany in the new 750 Kg Formula races in 1934.

Hitler said that just a fortnight previously he had given 500,000 Reichsmarks (RM) to Mercedes-Benz for their racing programme—Porsche was too late. The Professor replied that it would surely be better to have two irons in the fire, as the German cars would be up against Alfa Romeo, Bugatti, etc. Hitler pointed out that Porsche didn't

have a factory, but Porsche countered by saying that Auto Union did.

'But Auto Union have never built a racing car,' said Hitler.

'No, but I have,' said Porsche.

And so it went on, until Hitler finally agreed to divide the 500,000 RM between Mercedes and Auto Union. In March the next year the racing car made its debut at Avus, breaking several world records.

Once Hitler had made his decision we were never again short of money, just short of time. Porsche and Rabe worked very closely together at the Kronenstrasse offices. Rabe, too, was a genius in his way, and very vague about little details like signing and dating his drawings, which were rather necessary when submitting them to the Patents Office! I had to force him to put his name and the date on all his drawings.

He and Porsche would spend some time discussing an idea, then Porsche would leave it to him for a number of hours, and Herr Rabe was not to be disturbed. Later,

On their way to New York and the 1937 Vanderbilt Cup are (*left to right*) **Frau Werlin, Jakob Werlin, Dr Bodo Lafferentz, Bernd Rosemeyer, Ernst von Delius, unknown and Ferry Porsche**

Porsche would go back and they would discuss what Rabe had done, make some changes and then, when the first draft was ready, it would be copied and passed on to Karl Frohlich, Josef Kales and Josef Zahradnik. Every day, from morning to lunchtime, Porsche and Rabe would move from one drawing board to the next, making suggestions and overseeing the whole project. So the design was done in Stuttgart, but the racing cars were built at the Auto Union works in Zwickau, under the supervision of Professor Robert Eberan-Eberhorst.

I went to very few races myself. I didn't enjoy motor racing much, and anyway, I was far too busy most of the time. Everything to do with Professor Porsche came across my desk and one of my jobs was to read all his correspondence and mark the really important lines or paragraphs, as he wasn't interested in reading anything else.

In 1937 I travelled with the Auto Union team to New York for the Vanderbilt Cup. We sailed on the *Bremen* and as I had a British passport Professor Porsche told me to board the ship on my own and let nobody see me! I had no trouble, but then I saw that our entire party was not being allowed to board. The reason was that young Ferry Porsche should have applied for permission to travel from the Military. In fact, this was something I should have done, as I had been in charge of all the passport applications, but no-one had told me about Ferry and not being German myself I did not know about such things. But, of course, Professor Porsche was very well known and we had some high-ranking Nazi Party members with us—Jakob Werlin, for instance, and *Reichsamtsleiter* Dr Bodo Lafferentz, who was Second-in-Command of the Nazi Trade Union and also in charge of the *Kraft Durch Freude* programme (Strength Through Joy), so everything was sorted out and they all came aboard.

The Vanderbilt Cup was a big success for us as Bernd Rosemeyer won, beating the Mercedes and Nuvolari's Alfa Romeo. Rosemeyer had joined us in 1935 and in 1936 won the European Championship. Those were very good years for Auto Union—particularly 1936—but Professor Porsche was never satisfied, he would always ask for more. Most times he would find fault with you, so when he said nothing you could take it for praise!

At the end of 1937 Porsche's contract with Auto Union came to an end and he was now heavily involved in Hitler's Volkswagen programme. In spite of all the work this entailed he still maintained an interest in the racing car, although no longer working directly for the company.

MEMOIR

Ernst Henne

Team Driver, Mercedes-Benz 1934

By the time Mercedes-Benz came back into Grand Prix racing in 1934 I had established quite a reputation with BMW in motorcycle racing, although my main career was speed records. I set 76 World Records on motorcycles and four or five still stand, mainly because they were ice records I set in Sweden and nobody has tried to break them since!

When Alfred Neubauer (Mercedes' Team Manager) asked me if I would like to try a racing car I of course agreed, so in March 1934 I went to the Nürburgring with my great friend, Rudolf Caracciola. Mercedes had brought along two cars—a brand new W25 and the two-seater Monza Alfa Romeo that Rudi had crashed at Monaco the previous year. Mercedes had rebuilt it, but not before they had taken a very good look at it!

I drove the 2.3-litre Alfa first and, of course, it was a beautiful car which handled superbly, but once I got into the Mercedes I found things were very different. To begin with, the 3.3-litre engine was producing about 335 bhp, in contrast to the Alfa's 215 and the supercharger brought the power in very suddenly indeed. Also, there was a fault in the differential which affected the handling badly and this, combined with a sudden surge of power, sent me right off the road and into a field at Bergwerk! The car flew through the air down a steep bank, throwing me out in the process. I landed a short distance from the car with my head in a small stream. I was knocked unconscious and might have drowned, but an old woman who was working in the field saw the crash and ran to pull me from the water. I was taken to hospital where I remained unconscious for four or five hours, but I was not seriously hurt. Alfred Neubauer was not at all upset about the crash, saying it was not the first they had had and it certainly wouldn't be the last!

Later, when I had explained about the problems with the differential, Mercedes corrected the fault and when I next drove the car in practice for the French Grand Prix at Montlhéry (where I was reserve driver) it was much better. I was also reserve for the German GP at the Nürburgring and when von Brauchitsch crashed and broke his arm in practice I was brought into the team. But then I fell ill, so Hanns Geier took my place in the race.

We then went to Pescara for the Coppa Acerbo, where finally I had my first race for Mercedes. I enjoyed the circuit, which was a mixture of very fast, long straights and very twisty bits up in the hills. By now the W25 was handling

very well and it was also extremely quick in a straight line—I set the fastest speed through the timed kilometre at exactly 300 km/h (187.5 mph).

For some time I was second behind Caracciola, with Varzi behind me, but then he overtook. Guy Moll (who was having a marvellous season for Alfa Romeo) had to make a pit stop and then began to drive very fast indeed to make up for lost time. He was really driving too fast and caught up with me at a point where the road was very narrow—maybe three to five metres wide only. I could see that he wanted to pass, but he had only to wait for two or three kilometres and the road was very wide, wide enough for three or four cars to run side-by-side.

But Moll would not wait. We were doing about 270–280 km/h (168–174 mph) down this very narrow road. In those days the Prancing Horse badge of the Scuderia Ferrari was positioned right at the front of the Alfa's bonnet and I could see it out of the corner of my eye. I was just waiting for the terrible moment when Moll's front wheel would collide with my rear, but then he seemed to change his mind and the Alfa fell back. I looked in my mirror and suddenly saw the car swerve violently and go out of control before crash-

The badly bent prototype Mercedes W25 after Henne's crash at the 'Ring in March 1934

ABOVE Henne cornering at Pescara during the Coppa Acerbo. Spectator protection was unheard of in those days!

RIGHT Spectators lean forward to watch the drama as the cockpit cover comes loose during Henne's record attempt at Gyon

ing into some trees. When I came round again I saw that it had finished up against a farmhouse. Although he had been very close to me just before the crash, our cars had never touched and I'm sure he was blown off-course by the *Scirocco*, the desert wind which was very strong at that time of year. After the race I was very shocked to learn of his death.

My next race was the Italian GP at Monza where I had no luck at all. On the first or second lap a car blew up in the Lesmo Curve and spun, dropping a lot of oil on the track. Then my engine started losing oil and overheated, so I had to retire a few laps later. Finally, I practised for the Spanish GP at San Sebastian, but was reserve driver for the race.

I was very disappointed with my motor racing season so I decided to try and set new class C (3–5 litres) World Records for the Flying Kilometre and the Flying Mile. I had already set the Flying Kilometre record for motorcycles, doing 246 km/h (153.75 mph) on my BMW, so I asked Mercedes to let me have two cars for the attempt—one open and one closed—the first closed record car Mercedes had ever built at this time. I had already done 300 km/h (186.5 mph) with an open car at Pescara and I felt sure that I could beat that speed with the closed version.

We went to a new road that had just been built at Gyon, near Budapest, and I did the first run with the open car, but after only four or five kilometres the supercharger exploded. I then went out with the closed car and found that the aerodynamics were so bad that the car was drifting from one side of the road to the other as I approached 300 km/h (186.5 mph) and the streamlined cover over the cockpit came loose and started shuddering violently!

I was quite shaken by this and decided to wait for a little bit before having another attempt, but Neubauer now decided that Caracciola, who was reserve driver, should have a go. Instead of trying to make the cockpit cover fit properly they took it off altogether, which obviously made the car much more stable, as Rudi covered the Flying Kilometre at 317.5 km/h (198.4 mph), the Flying Mile at 316.6 km/h (197.8 mph) and the Standing Start Mile at 188.6 km/h (116.6 mph)!

That was the end of my racing association with Mercedes-Benz, which had been very pleasant on a personal level, but very disappointing in terms of results.

Hans Stuck

Team Driver, Auto Union 1934–39

Whenever the subject of Auto Union comes up, sooner or later someone is bound to say, 'Of course, there were only two men capable of handling them properly—Bernd Rosemeyer and Tazio Nuvolari.' There is, indeed, an element of truth in this claim, for those two charismatic drivers were kissed with genius and brought off some of Auto Union's most memorable wins, but it ignores the undoubted talents of Achille Varzi (before his tragic decline) and completely overlooks the sterling services of Hans Stuck.

No-one (and certainly not Stuck himself) has ever claimed that he was in quite the same league as the likes of Nuvolari, Rosemeyer, Varzi, Caracciola or Lang, but he has all too often been dismissed as *Bergmeister* (King of the Mountains)—a title which he properly earned, but which tends to obscure his talent and success as a racing driver. Of all the men who drove for Auto Union from 1934 to 1939 (and there were 16!), only Stuck remained constant throughout the entire period. He handled the very difficult, swing-axle V-16s of the early years and the much more responsive V-12s with de Dion rear axles of 1938–9, taking both versions in his stride where many others failed. Stuck may not have been one of the all-time greats, but he put up many fine drives and deserves to be remembered as more than just a journeyman racing driver and mountainclimb expert.

There was always an element of doubt about Hans Stuck's true age. At various times he was alleged to have been born in 1895 and even 1890, but he maintained that his birthday was 27 December 1900. What is certain is that he was born in Warsaw, while his parents were there on a business trip.

Stuck's grandfather was Swiss, and the family name was originally Stucki, but by the time Hans was born his parents were living in Germany, where his father owned an estate near Freiburg. Frau Stuck did not enjoy the best of health and so the family moved back to Switzerland for a while so that she could stay in a sanatorium. Her maiden name was Villiez and in the fashion of those days Hans later called himself Hans Stuck von Villiez. This caused immediate confusion in the British motoring press once his career got under way and he was constantly referred to as Hans *von* Stuck. In the same way the British invariably added a 't' to Bernd Rosemeyer's first name—they were wrong on both counts.

In the autumn of 1917, the 16-year-old Stuck was called up and he returned to Freiburg to join Field Artillery Regiment 76. His elder brother, Walter, was already on the Western Front and in 1918 he and his Commanding Officer, Oberleutnant Hahndorff, were killed in an artillery attack.

Hans was sent home to give the sad news to his family—and Hahndorff's, who lived in Garmisch. There he met the officer's sister, Ellen, and although he was five years younger than she, the relationship prospered until it was accepted by both families that they would marry, which they did in 1922. They set up home on a farm, south of Munich.

About this time Stuck bought his first car, a 4-cylinder Dürkopp. Realizing that he could make more money by delivering the farm's milk personally to Munich, rather than putting it on the train, he started transporting it daily in the Dürkopp. Stuck enjoyed driving the milk to Munich in the early hours of each morning and bought himself a stopwatch so he could make a note of his time for every journey. He joined the Bayerischen Automobilclub and soon his milk runs were famous among his friends there. One day they suggested that as he could drive so fast he should enter a local hillclimb. Stuck blithely replied that he would love to—what's more, he would climb the hill faster backwards than they could forwards! He immediately regretted his boast, for his friends gleefully bet him 50 bottles of champagne that he could do no such thing.

However, Stuck was never slow to see a way round a given obstacle. He went home and set about the Dürkopp, fitting it with large rear wheels and reversing the gearbox! He duly won the champagne, whereupon his friends insisted that he now enter a proper hillclimb, at Baden-Baden, and in the summer of 1923 Hans Stuck scored his first official victory, winning his class there. The die was cast.

He went on winning and became quite a celebrity on the German hillclimb circuit and in its social life. Hans was now a handsome young man of 23, six foot two and blond, possessed of considerable charm and winning ways, both on and off the race track. His busy competition programme played havoc with his marriage and he and Ellen drifted further and further apart and finally were divorced, but his good looks and successful career meant that he was never short of female company.

His racing success brought him to the attention of the directors at Austro-Daimler, who made him an offer he couldn't refuse—they would let him have one of their sports cars for four hillclimbs and, if he was successful in those, he could have a proper racing car. Stuck grabbed this opportunity with both hands—and to begin with was an utter failure! His first event was at the Klausenpass in 1926 and, halfway up, the car caught fire and burnt out.

At Freiburg Hans had a brand-new machine. Going up the hill he hit a little dip and the Austro-Daimler did a back-somersault, landing on Stuck and breaking his leg. He was fit in time for the Zugerberg climb in Switzerland. Frustrated by a delay in the programme, he over-revved the engine and blew it up! Amazingly Austro-Daimler were unperturbed. Stuck had made fastest time in practice and the company was convinced that he had the makings of a racing driver. They had promised him four drives and four drives he would have—they would see him shortly at Tauern, in Austria. This time Hans came through with flying colours, beating the works Austro-Daimler drivers in their racing cars!

After his brilliant victory in the 1934 German GP, a jubilant Hans Stuck is carried shoulder-high by his mechanics, Ludwig and Wilhelm Sebastian. *Korpsführer* Adolf Hühnlein looks *very* po-faced about the whole thing . . .

Austro-Daimler were as good as their word and Hans became a works driver in 1927. He repaid their extraordinary faith in him by winning no less than nine major hillclimbs in Germany, Austria and Switzerland that year. He also made his racing debut, taking part in the opening meeting at the Nürburgring and in the German GP a month later.

Now fully embarked on a racing career Hans had the good fortune (or the good sense) to sell his farm for Swiss francs, so when the money markets went wild after the Wall Street Crash in 1929 he was secure in the knowledge that his cash would retain its value. In order to keep it safe he decided to smuggle it into Switzerland and to this end welded the money into two metal boxes shortly before competing in the Freiburg hillclimb, because from Freiburg he was due to drive straight to another event in Switzerland. With the boxes hidden in the racing car he should have no trouble getting through customs.

The first night in Freiburg he kept the money in his hotel room, but he worried about it so much that the next day he deposited the two boxes in a personal safe at the local bank. He won the hillclimb and next morning went to retrieve his money and then get on his way to Switzerland. To his horror he found the bank surrounded by police and angry citizens—during the night the manager had raided all the deposit boxes and done a bunk! Now all Hans owned were the clothes he stood up in and the money in his pocket.

He decided to tell the directors of Austro-Daimler of his misfortune. They might well have regarded it as Stuck's come-uppance for trying to smuggle money out of the country, but once again they stood by their driver, giving him a new contract with all expenses paid. In return, Stuck won the 1929 Mountain Championships of Germany, Austria, Switzerland, Italy, France and Hungary!

That same year he also joined forces with Ernst Udet, the famous World War I flying ace, and together they went barnstorming and ice racing, Stuck on his Austro-Daimler and Udet flying a Pelican. Their friendship prospered and a few years later, when Stuck needed a still-secret aero engine for his proposed Land Speed Record attempt, Udet was in a position to see that he got it. Stuck had a happy knack of making friends with the right people. . . .

Another particular friend by now was a beautiful English girl who, in an unlikely blend of the exotic and the mundane, was called Xenia and hailed from Birmingham. Stuck had first met her in Budapest in 1924 and was immediately attracted to her, although their meeting was very brief and inconclusive. She was, alas, married to the Hungarian Count Szichy.

Two years later Stuck caught up with her again in Austria, where he was entered in the Semmering hillclimb. So, too, was Count Szichy, a handsome playboy who had recently inherited a great deal of money and was in the process of spending it on wine, women and racing cars. He had bought a Bugatti and was out to have some fun.

After practice Stuck found himself having a drink with the young Count in the hotel bar. Szichy was somewhat 'tired and emotional' and rashly bet Stuck that his Bugatti would beat Hans' Austro-Daimler on the morrow. Earlier in the day Hans had noticed that the relationship between the Count and Countess was distinctly strained and confirmation of this was forthcoming when Szichy added that if Stuck beat him in the hillclimb he could take Xenia to the next race! The following morning—at the startline—Hans had the briefest of exchanges with the Countess, but it was enough. 'I know about the bet,' she said, 'and I hope you win!' Stuck won.

The affair was great while it lasted and it lasted for four years, Hans and Xenia going everywhere together as he pursued his career around Europe. Then, in the summer of 1930, Xenia suddenly announced that she had to go home to Birmingham to see her parents. She was no more forthcoming than that, other than to promise that she would catch up with Hans sooner or later at one of his next race meetings. As a bemused Stuck put her on a train for London she kissed him and said, 'Thank you for the loveliest summer of my life. You must never forget me!'

A few months later he was in Montreux, Switzerland. Reading his paper one morning he noticed that it published a list of the town's sanatoria and their principal 'guests'. Staying at the Sanatorium Leysin was Xenia, Countess Szichy, and the Leysin specialized in lung diseases.

Stuck rushed round there, but Xenia refused to see him. Instead she sent a note telling him that she was very ill, so much so that he would not recognize her. 'Forget the girl in the sanatorium—remember only the Xenia you once knew.' Just a few months later she was dead.

Personally and professionally then, 1931 started very badly for Hans Stuck, for not only had he lost Xenia, but Austro-Daimler pulled out of competitions, leaving him with nothing to drive. His knack of making friends in the right places, however, produced results once more.

Back in the days when he was delivering milk to Munich, Hans used to park his Dürkopp under the Liebig Garage where he would often talk to the chauffeur of the car in the next space. Julius Schreck was a keen hunter and, learning of Stuck's estate, asked if he might join him in the chase at some time. Stuck agreed and the two men occasionally went shooting together. A couple of years later, in May 1925, Schreck arrived at Stuck's farm one day, as arranged, and asked if his boss (who was outside in the car) might join them in the hunt. Happy to oblige, Stuck agreed, and was introduced to a slight figure wrapped in a trenchcoat—Adolf Hitler.

Over the years Stuck and Schreck remained friends and when, early in 1931, Hans was bemoaning his lack of a car to race, Schreck suggested he talk to Hitler. Since Hitler was by now very busy trying to gain control of Germany, Stuck could not for the life of him see why he should be interested in the problems of a racing driver. But Schreck insisted, saying that Hitler hadn't forgotten his day's hunting back in 1925 and that he had good connections with German industry. He promised to arrange a meeting.

He was as good as his word and Stuck duly found himself in Hitler's presence at the Brown House—the National Socialist Party's HQ in Munich. The Party leader listened carefully as Hans told him how and why he had no car to drive: both Austro-Daimler and Mercedes-Benz had withdrawn from racing, leaving Alfa Romeo or Bugatti as his only alternative, and he didn't want to drive a foreign car.

Hitler was sympathetic, but pointed out that the Party couldn't, at the moment, afford to give Stuck any financial help. 'But you're an excellent driver, Herr Stuck. If you can avoid driving for a foreign firm I promise you that when I come to power the Reich will place a racing car at your disposal.' Stuck could hardly believe his ears, but Hitler was to keep his word.

Although most encouraging, that meeting did not resolve Stuck's immediate problem of finding a car for the new season, but help was at hand from another old friend. In 1923 Hans had met Crown Prince Wilhelm (one of the Kaiser's sons) when he found himself taking him to be reunited with his wife and children in exile in Holland. They formed a lasting friendship and now—eight years later—the Crown Prince was able to make use of his very good connections with Mercedes-Benz to enable Hans to buy a rare, super-light SSKL at a special price, and he raced this car with great success over the next three years.

He made his debut with the Mercedes on 31 May 1931, at the Zbraslav-Jiloviste hillclimb in Czechoslovakia. Rudolf Caracciola was also there in a similar car but he was in the Sports Car Class, while Stuck competed with the racing cars. Each won his class, Caracciola being 0.1 second faster than Stuck. (Although Stuck always enjoyed the title, 'King of the Mountains', it is worth remembering that Caracciola also won the Sports Car Mountain Championship in 1930 and 1931.) In June Stuck won his first major race, the Lemberg Grand Prix in Poland, and had a rather lean time thereafter until coming second in the Masaryk GP in September. Then, two days after Christmas, he sailed for South America with his Mercedes, and also with the new lady in his life.

Paula von Reznicek was one of Europe's finest woman tennis players who also wrote about the game for the German Press. She was married to the sportswriter Burkhard von Reznicek and it was while they were in Nice for the Riviera Tennis Championships that Stuck (also in Nice for the La Turbie hillclimb) first met them. There was an immediate rapport between the racing driver and the tennis player, so much so that although she had no interest in motor sport Paula started obtaining Press passes for races and Hans, who had no interest in tennis, took up the game!

Their meetings became more and more frequent until Paula began acting as Hans' manager, and it was she who decided that he should compete in the Grand Prix of Argentina, which was to take place in February 1932. She organized the whole trip and made it clear (to Stuck's delight) that she was coming, too. They sailed on the *Andalusia* on his birthday, 27 December 1931.

When they arrived Hans found that the road conditions were so bad that even his big Mercedes didn't have enough ground clearance, so he withdrew from the race. He and Paula moved on to Brazil, where he won the Brazilian Hillclimb Championship (run over 40 km [25 miles] between

Rio and Petropolis!) and then set two new Brazilian speed records with the SSKL, covering the Standing Start Kilometre at 126 km/h (78.75 mph) and the Flying Kilometre at 206 km/h (128.75 mph).

Returning to Germany, Stuck continued his winning way with victories in the Kesselberg, Gaisberg, Klausenpass, Freiburg, Stelvio and Mont Ventoux mountainclimbs, all of which made him Alpine Champion for 1932. In October that year he and Paula were married in Berlin, with Ernst Udet and Crown Prince Wilhelm as witnesses.

On 30 January 1933, Adolf Hitler became Chancellor of Germany and the Third Reich was born. Not long after this momentous day, Stuck got a phone call from the new *Reichskanzler*, who reminded him of the promise he had made two years previously. 'Now I am in control,' said Hitler, 'you shall have your racing car. Make a list of your requirements, then come and see me.'

Stuck was stunned, but not for long. He quickly got in touch with Professor Porsche, who had designed both the Austro-Daimler and the SSKL Mercedes which Hans had raced with such success, and Porsche hurried to Berlin. The next day the two of them, together with Baron Klaus von Oertzen of Auto Union, had an audience with Hitler and Porsche outlined his plans for a mid-engined Grand Prix car, which would be built by the newly formed Auto Union

concern. As a direct result of this meeting, Hitler decided to divide his recently announced State subsidy for a German racing team between Mercedes-Benz and Auto Union, and a new era in motor racing began.

Incredibly, Porsche's new car was ready for its first run in November and Stuck drove it for the first time on the *Sudschleife* (short circuit) at the Nürburgring. The whole area was patrolled by the SA (Stormtroopers), who chased away any would-be spectators. A few months later, on 6 March 1934, Auto Union took their new P-Wagen to Avus and Hans drove it to three new World Records.

Having stolen a march on the new Mercedes (which hadn't even appeared yet), Auto Union must have felt fairly smug when their cars lined up for their very first race—the Avus GP—on 27 May, because the Mercedes team had withdrawn after practice. The Zwickau concern entered three cars for Stuck, Prince zu Leiningen and August Momberger, the latter two being great enthusiasts but simply not in the same league as Stuck as racing drivers. Stuck

Stuck is congratulated by Prof. Porsche after setting three new World Records at Avus in March 1934. On the extreme right is Auto Union Team Manager Willy Walb

put his record-breaking experience at Avus to good use and at the end of the first 19 km (12 mile) lap was *one minute* ahead of the next man, Louis Chiron! Hans continued to pile up a huge lead until he had to stop for fuel and tyres on lap 10. He was in again one lap later and stopped for good the next time round with clutch trouble.

A week later Mercedes made their début at the Nürburgring in the Eifel GP and although Stuck led von Brauchitsch by over a minute at one point, Mercedes' superior pit-work put their man in front for good. Hans finished second. He then won the Feldberg and Kesselberg mountainclimbs on successive weekends before going to Montlhéry for the French GP. He drove splendidly and led the race for some laps, having a tremendous battle with the French idol, Louis Chiron, in the Ferrari Alfa. But then the P-Wagen began to overheat and, after a number of pit stops, Stuck had to retire.

Everything came right, though, in the German Grand Prix a fortnight later. Stuck led all the way, except for a brief moment when Caracciola got by on lap 13, only to have his engine blow up moments later. This superb win turned Hans into a national hero and he was lauded to the skies by Hitler, Göring and Goebbels, among others. He had to drive his winning car from Berlin to Zwickau, where all the schools were closed and thousands lined the route to cheer him as he drove by. At the Horch factory he was welcomed by all the workers and had to make a speech in reply. Heady stuff!

He was brought down to earth somewhat at his next event, though. At the Klausenpass mountainclimb he was beaten by Caracciola in a Mercedes and since Rudi was not yet fully recovered from his Monaco crash the year before, Stuck can't have been very pleased with himself. In the Coppa Acerbo he retired with a blown piston, but then won the German Mountain Championship at Freiburg and a week later covered himself with glory again by winning the Swiss GP by a whole lap and leading from start to finish.

He was leading the Italian GP at Monza, too, but was forced to stop and hand over his car to Prince zu Leiningen. In that first season Auto Union used the chassis tubes as water carriers between the radiator in front of the driver and the engine behind him. It was a very hot day and the water being pumped from the engine transferred much of its heat to the pedals, so much so that Stuck's feet were burnt and he had to stop. In the pits his feet were covered in cream and bandaged, but then his shoes wouldn't fit. Eventually, a pair was borrowed from a big-footed Italian policeman, Prince zu Leiningen was called in and Hans rejoined the race. In ten laps zu Leiningen had dropped to fourth place, but in spite of his blistered feet Stuck drove brilliantly and managed to finish a fine second, behind the Caracciola/Fagioli Mercedes.

Stuck won the Mont Ventoux mountainclimb a week later and then went to San Sebastian for the Spanish GP, on the Lasarte circuit. During practice, Auto Union showed their intention of strengthening their driver line-up for 1935 by inviting Tazio Nuvolari to do a few laps in one of their cars. In the race, Stuck retired early and then took over zu Leiningen's car, which was in tenth position. Perhaps

A fast and furious pit stop for Stuck on his way to victory in the 1934 German GP

spurred on by Nuvolari's trial run a couple of days earlier, Hans drove superbly and fought his way through the field to finish fourth, setting a new lap record in the process.

The next weekend he was in Brno, Czechoslovakia, for the Masaryk Grand Prix, where once again, Nuvolari tried an Auto Union. On the second day of practice Stuck recorded a time of 13 min. 45 sec. for the 29 km (18 mile) circuit, then Nuvolari went out in an Auto Union and did 14 min. 15 sec. Hans was not satisfied with his car's performance (the next day he did 13 min. 39 sec. in the race) and while his mechanics were checking it Alfred Neubauer waved him over to the Mercedes pit and offered him a drive in the team's spare W25! Hans jumped at the chance of beating Nuvolari's Auto Union time and put in four swift laps with the Mercedes, getting down to a very satisfying 14 min. 5 sec.

In the race, Stuck had a terrific battle with Luigi Fagioli for the lead, until the Mercedes driver had to make an unscheduled pit stop at about two-thirds distance, leaving Hans to win easily. Afterwards, Neubauer offered him a contract for 1935, reportedly at twice the fee Auto Union were paying him. Stuck talked the idea over with Caracciola, who succeeded in persuading Hans to stay where he was, saying that two 'aces' in the same team would make life difficult for both of them. Rudi knew whereof he spoke, as he already had enough trouble with Fagioli, who clearly regarded the German driver as his Number Two! The last thing Caracciola wanted was a driver of Stuck's calibre to add to his problems at Mercedes.

For Hans Stuck 1934 had been a marvellous year in which he had established himself as one of the fastest drivers in the world, with three major GP victories and two excellent seconds, a record which should have made him European Champion, but for some reason the AIACR had not instigated a Drivers' Championship to adorn the new Formula. There was, however, a Mountain Championship and Stuck made that his own with four fine wins. To round things off nicely, he finished the season as he had begun—at Avus—where he set five new World Records for Auto Union.

Hans' first race of 1935 was at Tripoli. His new team mate, Achille Varzi, had won this race twice and was looking for a hat-trick. At one point he and Stuck were running first and second, with only two seconds between them on this terrifically fast circuit. Hans was driving one of two Auto Unions with an enclosed cockpit and he had an extremely frightening experience when the car caught fire at high speed. The blaze started behind him in the engine compartment, so he didn't notice it immediately. When he did notice it he braked hard, only to find that he had no brakes as the flames had burnt through the hydraulic pipes! He managed to slow the car by going down through the gears and when he finally came to a halt the blaze had reached the cockpit. Luckily he stopped close to an official with a fire extinguisher, who doused the flames and helped a very shaken Stuck out of the car.

Not surprisingly, he elected to drive an open racer at Avus two weeks later, leaving Rosemeyer and zu Leiningen to handle the streamliners. On the second day of practice Hans stunned everyone with a *standing* lap at 254 km/h (158 mph)—faster than any previous flying lap! The next day, going for his grid position, he was even faster, lapping in 4 min. 31.3 sec.—260 km/h (162 mph)—and no-one else got near this time. Next up were Varzi and von Brauchitsch in 4 min. 47 sec. and then Rosemeyer in 4 min. 49 sec. Hans won his heat easily, leading Fagioli (Mercedes) home by 45 seconds. He was well in the lead in the final, too, when a rear tyre disintegrated at around 290 km/h (180 mph) giving him some exciting moments before he regained control. He finally finished fourth. After the race he reckoned he had touched 326 km/h (203 mph) on the 10 km (6 mile) straights and felt that the Auto Union was capable of an out-and-out maximum of 350 km/h (218 mph)!

Persistent plug trouble put him out of the Eifel GP, and at the French it was brakes that caused his retirement. He won the Kesselberg hillclimb a week later, though, and then finished a very fine second in the German GP, a performance that was largely (and understandably) overlooked, due to the remarkable victory of one Signor Nuvolari. Stuck was a non-starter in the Coppa Acerbo (which team mate Varzi won) due to a cracked cylinder head in the final practice session.

At Bern, Stuck held second place behind Caracciola in the early laps of the Swiss GP until a tyre burst as he passed the pits, forcing him to do a whole lap very slowly. Later the engine began to misbehave and, after a longish pit stop, zu Leiningen took over. Stuck then won the Freiburg hillclimb and followed this with a superb win in the Italian GP at Monza. He retired in the Spanish GP after losing all his gears but top.

The last race of the year was the Czech GP at Brno and here Stuck had the misfortune to be hit in the face by a bird when travelling at high speed. He drove on in great pain, but after five laps had had enough, so he stopped and handed over to Paul Pietsch. After medical attention Hans took his car back, although still suffering from a headache, and then the engine became very rough so he decided to call it a day. Instead of returning to the pits he drove off the circuit and down a side road to the home of the friends he was staying with!

His badly bruised eye could not keep him from the final mountainclimb of the year, however, and a week later he was at Feldberg, where he won.

He began 1936 nicely with another mountain win, this time at La Turbie. Four days later he finished third in the rain-lashed Monaco GP, behind Caracciola and Varzi. After finishing second in the politically rigged Tripoli GP, he took his special, short-chassis Auto Union to Shelsley Walsh, where he equalled Raymond Mays' course record in practice. He was optimistic about breaking the record on race day, but a typically British summer downpour put paid to that!

The year, of course, belonged to Stuck's young team mate, Bernd Rosemeyer, who, from June onward, won practically everything in sight, finishing up as both European Racing and Mountain Champion in only his second season of motor racing. Since jealousy was rife in Grand Prix circles in the 1930s (Fagioli and Caracciola; Varzi and Nuvolari; von Brauchitsch, Caracciola and Lang) many people no doubt expected Stuck to resent Rosemeyer's sudden and astonishing success. To his credit, Stuck did no such thing. He and Paula became close friends with Bernd and Elly and he seems to have accepted Rosemeyer's undoubted genius without rancour.

His own season was a poor one, with only one victory (La Turbie), two seconds and two thirds. The one bright spot in the year was his successful attack on some records in March. With a specially streamlined car he set five new World and three International records, from 5 km to 100 miles. It was his last fling as a record-breaker, as Rosemeyer was to take over the role for Auto Union in 1937.

Stuck had two serious crashes in 1936, from which he was lucky to get away with minor injuries. The first happened during practice for the Coppa Acerbo in Pescara—he was going very fast down one of the long straights when a front wheel came off. The Auto Union slowed somewhat before smashing through one of the artificial chicanes and then Stuck took off the steering wheel and baled out, finishing up in a cornfield. Miraculously, apart from damaging an elbow on the chicane, he was unhurt and when reserve driver Rudi Hasse stopped to help, Hans insisted on taking over his car and doing a couple more laps. After that, though, shock set in and this, coupled with his injured arm, meant that he did not take part in the race.

His second crash came a month later during the Italian GP. In the pits, Elly Rosemeyer was surprised to find that the normally calm and serene Paula Stuck was extremely nervous. She was even more surprised when Paula admitted her disquiet, saying that she had a horror of chicanes after Hans' Pescara crash. Sure enough, Stuck crashed at one of the Monza chicanes and was thrown out of the car, which then smashed into a tree before somersaulting through the air and landing on its wheels right beside its stricken driver. Once again Stuck was shaken but unhurt. Not surprisingly, however, he did not partake in the last event of the year—the Feldberg mountainclimb.

Luigi Fagioli joined Auto Union for 1937, although he was by now a spent force. Rosemeyer and his friend Ernst von Delius took two cars to South Africa at the beginning of the year and then in May Auto Union sent five cars to Tripoli. They could do nothing about Hermann Lang's Mercedes, however, finishing behind it in the order Rosemeyer, von Delius, Stuck and Fagioli. In practice Stuck put in an amazing lap at 235.4 km/h (146.33 mph) but due to constant tyre troubles his fastest race lap was a mere 229.13 km/h (142.41 mph).

Two weeks later the rest of the team made for another very fast circuit—Avus—now made even faster by the addition of the banked North Turn. Stuck, however, took a car to South America and Rio, a city he loved, for the Rio GP. He was apparently surprised to find that Scuderia Ferrari had sent two Alfas there for Carlo Pintacuda and Antonio Brivio, and although it was expected that the more powerful Auto Union would win, the twisty circuit (with more than 50 corners in its seven miles) proved more suitable to Pintacuda's Alfa, and he led Stuck home by just four seconds. To make up for not winning, Stuck went out again in the Auto Union next day and set two new World Speed Records, the Standing Kilometre and the Standing Mile.

He was back in Europe in time for the Belgian GP, in which he and Rudolf Hasse took on the Mercedes of Lang and von Brauchitsch, both teams having divided their forces between Spa and New York's Vanderbilt Cup. Hasse scored his one and only GP victory and Stuck finished a fine second after a sensationally fast dice with Lang in the early laps, but he twice had to make an unscheduled pit stop for new tyres.

He was an early retirement in the German GP, but then scored his only victories of the year and, needless to say, they were in mountainclimbs. First of all, at Freiburg, he won the German Mountain Championship in fine style, beating team mate Rosemeyer and the Mercedes of Lang and Caracciola. Then he went to Nice and set a new record at La Turbie.

The rest of Stuck's year was uneventful—apart from the fact that he was fired by Auto Union! His last race for the team was the Italian GP at Livorno, where he finished seventh with Hasse. There are at least two sides to every argument and Auto Union's version of why Stuck left the team is given in Chapter 4, *Racing and the Nazis*. Briefly, the company claimed that Stuck had twice broken his contract (in 1936 and 1937); that he was no longer capable of winning races and that there was no mutual confidence between the two parties any more.

For his part, Stuck claimed that he was fired for showing his contract to Bernd Rosemeyer. Young Bernd was not the greatest of businessmen and he knew it, but he felt that perhaps he deserved more money than he was getting from Auto Union and asked Stuck for some advice. Hans reminded him that there was a clause in his contract forbidding him from discussing its financial details with other drivers. Nonetheless, he was sympathetic to his young friend's feelings, so he told him where he kept the contract and went for a walk. What he wouldn't see, he wouldn't know about. . . .

A few days later, Stuck got an angry phone call from Auto Union's Finance Director, Dr Richard Bruhn— Rosemeyer had asked for more money and Bruhn knew why. It was clear that Stuck had broken his contract by divulging its details to Rosemeyer and he was out of the team. Although Stuck would indeed appear to have been in breach of his contract, it does seem extraordinary that a driver who had given Auto Union such sterling service for four seasons should be dismissed for such a petty reason without, apparently, being given a chance to defend his action. Also, it was highly unjust that Rosemeyer, who was just as much a party to the 'crime', should get off scot-free! Surely, there was more to it than that . . . ?

In January 1938, the racing world received a body-blow when Bernd Rosemeyer was killed. In spite of the gaping hole this left in their driver line-up, Auto Union did not approach Stuck. They were trying very hard to get Nuvolari to join them, but in the meantime announced their team for the new season as Rudolf Hasse, H. P. Müller and Christian Kautz. Three cars were entered for these drivers in the French GP at Reims, which proved to be a disaster for Auto Union. In practice both Hasse and Müller crashed, Müller putting himself in hospital. Then on the very first lap of the race Kautz and Hasse crashed in separate incidents and had to retire. Two days later Hans Stuck got a phone call.

In his autobiography he records that it was Team Manager Dr Karl Feuereissen on the line—Auto Union were in terrible trouble as the new 3-litre V-12 cars were proving very difficult for the new drivers to handle. Would Herr Stuck be so kind as to do a couple of laps of the Nürburgring and say what he thought was wrong? Herr Stuck said he thought he might, providing his old contract was renewed. Feuereissen was not amused, but Stuck had him over a barrel and he knew it. Finally, he agreed that if Stuck could break the lap record with the new car he could have his old contract back.

Stuck broke the record.

It has to be said that this was so unlikely as to be virtually impossible. In 1938 the lap record for the Nürburgring stood to Bernd Rosemeyer, who had recorded 9 min. 53.4 sec. in his 6-litre V-16 Auto Union during the 1937

German GP. With the best will in the world, the chances of Hans Stuck breaking that record with one of the new *3-litre* Auto Unions were non-existent—doubly so, as the very reason he claims to have been asked to drive the car was that it was not handling well!

As with his firing, so with his re-hiring: Auto Union's version is different (see Chapter 4, *Racing and the Nazis*), but Stuck was back in the team for the German Grand Prix in which he finished third, although in practice he was the slowest of all the four Auto Union drivers with a fastest time of 10 min. 23 sec.—over half a minute away from Rosemeyer's lap record. His third place, however, meant that he won the German Drivers' Championship for 1938. This rather curious victory was explained by the fact that although there were normally three qualifying events for the title—the Avus, the Eifel and the German GPs—only the latter was held that year and although Lang finished ahead of Stuck in that race, he did so in Caracciola's car, so Hans became *Strassenmeister*.

The German Mountain Championship was also decided by one event that year and at a new venue—the Grossglockner Pass in Austria. Stuck first won at La Turbie yet again and then opted out of the Coppa Acerbo in order to reconnoitre the 12.6 km (7.8 mile) climb. He finished fourth in the Swiss GP and then returned to Austria, where he beat the Mercedes of Lang and von Brauchitsch comprehensively to win the Grossglockner and take the title of *Bergmeister* once more.

He was lying second to team mate Nuvolari in the Italian GP, only to be forced out with engine trouble at two-thirds distance. He then won three mountainclimbs—one in Switzerland and two in Rumania—in quick succession, making himself European Mountain Champion again. He did not make it to Donington, probably because the second Rumanian event was only the weekend before and he couldn't get to England in time for practice.

Stuck began 1939 by winning at La Turbie (of course!) but then managed to sprain an ankle while playing skittles

King of the Mountains! Stuck slides his Auto Union exuberantly out of a corner on his way to victory over the Mercedes at Grossglockner in 1938

after a practice session for the Eifel GP and couldn't take part in the race. Surprisingly, he could only manage fourth place in the Vienna hillclimb, where he was beaten by Lang, Müller and von Brauchitsch. Instead of going to Spa for the Belgian GP with the rest of the team, Stuck raced and won in Bucharest, against minimal opposition. Afterwards, he and Paula were entertained by King Carol of Rumania and then flew to Breslau, where Paula's family lived. They stayed there a few days and Hans met the woman who was to become his third wife. Her name was Christa Maria Thielmann and she was then engaged to Paula's youngest brother, Hans Heimann.

The rest of the season just petered out for Stuck. He finished sixth at Reims, retired in the German GP and was tenth in the Swiss. At the Grossglockner mountainclimb he was again unable to do anything about Hermann Lang and saw the great Mercedes driver win the European Mountain Championship, to add to his drivers' title.

After the war German drivers were not allowed to race again until 1950, but Hans had somehow managed to obtain Austrian citizenship and was back on the track almost immediately, driving an 1100 cc Cisitalia. Then he joined forces with Alex von Falkenhausen, who designed the AFM Formula 2 car which was built in Hans' garage. It was very fast but also very brittle and Stuck used it mostly for mountainclimbs.

The early post-war years saw the break-up of Stuck's marriage and in 1948 he and Paula were divorced. (Paula died in 1976, at the age of 81). That same year he married Christa Maria and in 1951 their son, Hans-Joachim, was born. In 1953 he renewed his association with Professor Porsche and drove the new Porsche Spyder, but without any real success. In 1957, just when everyone thought he had retired, he joined BMW, taking their beautiful but heavy Type 507 to several class wins in hillclimbs. When BMW decided to campaign their little Sports Coupé, Hans adapted himself to the tiny, 700 cc power unit as easily as he had to the huge 6-litre Auto Unions before the war and, at the age of 60, he won the German Mountain Championship! On that winning note he did, finally, retire.

Hans Stuck's remarkable career ran through four decades and although he was not quite as gifted or successful as some of his contemporaries he nevertheless could look back on a very full and exciting life. A natural athlete, in addition to his driving skills he had a flair for virtually any sport and became a pretty efficient tennis player and a very fine skier and golfer. But it was for his racing with Auto Union that he will always be remembered, his large frame sitting rather awkwardly in the silver car which invariably bore his name on the side.

He died in February 1978, having lived to see his son succeed him as a Grand Prix driver, in the March and Shadow teams. By then, motor racing had changed almost out of all recognition from that of the 1930s when Hans Stuck proudly took his place among the Titans.

NOTE: In October 1985, Hans-Joachim Stuck—with his team mate, Derek Bell—was declared World Endurance Champion, racing for the Porsche team. And so, 50 years on, the names of Stuck and Porsche were reunited in victory.

Luigi Fagioli

Team Driver, Mercedes-Benz 1934–36

If ever a racing driver thought he saw a golden opportunity it must have been Luigi Fagioli when Mercedes-Benz invited him to join their team for 1934.

Consider the prospect: Mercedes had been racing almost without a break since 1901 and their competition experience was without parallel; the company had vast financial and technical resources at its disposal and the German government was clearly encouraging both Mercedes and the new firm of Auto Union to go racing, as German victories in international competition would be marvellous propaganda for the Third Reich. On top of this, Germany was short of first class racing drivers.

Rudolf Caracciola had been considered by many to be the finest driver in the world, but his crash at Monaco in 1933 had crushed his upper right thigh and hip joint so badly that there were serious doubts that he would ever race again. In addition to his physical damage, early in 1934 he was mentally shattered by the death of his wife, a tragedy which made a successful return to racing even more unlikely. He had done great things for Mercedes in the past, however, and the company's Team Manager Alfred Neubauer (who was also his close friend) insisted on signing him up for the 1934 season, rightly reasoning that what Caracciola sorely needed at this point was a goal to reach for and the active support of his friends in the attempt.

Neubauer's second choice was another German, the young Manfred von Brauchitsch, but with his very limited experience he was a hope for the future, not the proven winner that Mercedes badly needed. So Neubauer had to take a close look at the foreign talent available (see Chapter 5, *Alfred Neubauer*) and he decided upon Luigi Fagioli, a winner, but also a man noted for his unpredictable temperament.

In 1934 Fagioli was already 36 years old. According to Enzo Ferrari he took up racing as a hobby, while making his living producing pastas. Another source claims he was a chartered accountant, but whichever is true he would seem to have been aptly named—*fagioli* translates into English as beans, a product he might well have sold alongside his spaghetti and fettuccini. As for accountancy—how many beans make five?

Built like a middleweight boxer with brawny arms, wide, wide shoulders and no neck to speak of, Fagioli had an aggressive stance which matched his personality. True, he liked to joke and had a winning smile, but he had a fiery temper allied to a colossal belief in his own ability and he regarded racing as a very serious business. He was quick—almost certainly too quick—to see anyone getting in his way or baulking him and sometimes would react with a fury that was frightening.

He began his career with an 1100 cc Salmson. For four years victory eluded him, but all the time he was gaining experience and honing his skills. In 1930 he switched to Maserati and almost immediately started winning, first the Coppa Principe di Piemonte, then the Coppa Ciano and the Coppa Castelli Romani. Things got even better in 1931 and Fagioli got some impressive results. He was second to Chiron at Monaco, second again in the Tunis GP and then, at the season's end, he won the Monza GP against formidable opposition: Nuvolari, Minoia and Borzacchini on Alfas; Varzi, Chiron and Lehoux on Bugattis and Dreyfus who, like Fagioli, was on a Maserati.

There was one more race that year—the Czech GP on the 29 km (18 mile) circuit at Brno—and Fagioli was leading that until he unwittingly put out not only himself but two of the three cars which were chasing him. Several temporary pedestrian bridges had been erected over this very long circuit and on the second lap Fagioli struck a supporting stanchion on one of them and it promptly collapsed behind him! First on the scene was Varzi, who ploughed through the whole mess before grinding to a halt—miraculously unhurt—in time to see Nuvolari clattering over the timbers and breaking his rear axle. He then drove his friend and rival back to the pits where they were joined in retirement by Fagioli a lap later. Chiron went on to win the race.

In 1932 Fagioli again had only one win, but some fine seconds, finishing (with Ernesto Maserati) behind Nuvolari and Campari in the five-hour Italian GP; behind Chiron in the Czech GP and behind Caracciola in the Monza GP. This latter was run in three heats and a final, a final which very nearly started without the Alfa Romeos in protest against Fagioli's driving methods when winning his heat! Shades of things to come. . . . All was smoothed out, however, and Caracciola (now in the works Alfa team) won from Fagioli.

Alfa Romeo were forced to withdraw from racing in 1933, leaving Enzo Ferrari to carry the flag with the 8C Monzas, as to begin with the factory refused to let him have the works P3s. Ferrari recognized Fagioli's talent and brought him into the Scuderia. 'The Abruzzi Robber' as he was now known rewarded his new boss with wins in the Italian and Comminges GPs and the Coppa Acerbo. He also finished second in the Spanish, Marseilles and Czech GPs. At the season's end he was declared Champion of Italy. He was also approached by Alfred Neubauer who asked him to join the new Mercedes-Benz team for 1934. It was an offer Fagioli could hardly refuse. With Caracciola still a semi-invalid and likely to remain so for some time and von Brauchitsch known only as a gifted amateur, here was his chance to lead the most famous and successful racing team in the world. Unfortunately, Neubauer didn't see it quite like that. . . .

In February 1934, Mercedes took their new W25 cars to Monza for testing in the hands of Manfred von Brauchitsch. He proved not to be ideal as a test driver and, indeed, crashed one car rather badly, so Luigi Fagioli was called in to finish the job.

In the interests of patriotism, both Mercedes and Auto Union decided to make their racing debuts on home

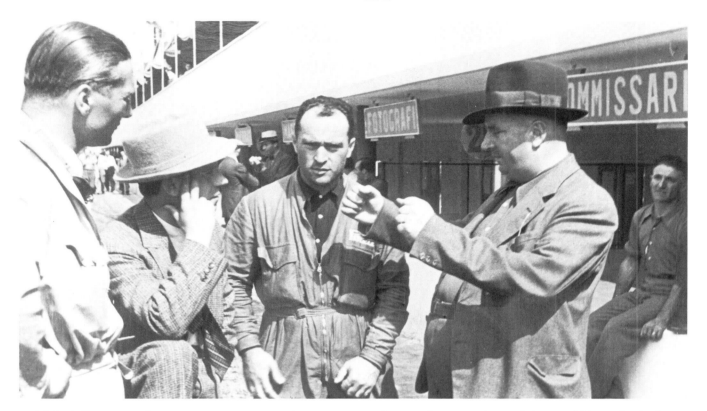

Luigi Fagioli (*centre*) **adopts a pugnacious stance during a break in practice for the 1934 Coppa Acerbo at Pescara, while Alfred Neubauer** (*right*) **demonstrates his driving technique to Fritz Nallinger and Hanns Geier** (*left*)

ground, which meant missing the early events at Monaco and Tripoli and appearing for the first time at Avus at the end of May. Rudolf Caracciola bravely turned up for practice with Fagioli and von Brauchitsch, putting in a few fast laps, although obviously in considerable pain. He did not compete in the race, but then neither did Mercedes, disappointing the German crowds by withdrawing after practice due to carburettor problems.

A week later the team made its debut proper in the Eifel GP at the Nürburgring and here Fagioli received what was to be the first of several blows to his considerable Italian pride. When leading the race he was signalled by Neubauer to let von Brauchitsch through, as Mercedes not unnaturally wanted their German driver to win this German race. Fagioli complied with the order, but when he stopped for new tyres he made it clear to Neubauer (though neither spoke the other's language!) that he was not happy with the situation. Back in the race, he proceeded to harry von Brauchitsch mercilessly, so Neubauer called him into the pits again and another bilingual row ensued. The result was that Fagioli drove off in high dudgeon and simply abandoned his car out on the circuit, leaving von Brauchitsch to win from Hans Stuck's Auto Union. It was

a fine win for Mercedes, and they could have finished one-two, but for their temperamental Italian.

Caracciola finally returned to racing at the French GP in July. Mercedes went to Montlhéry two weeks beforehand for testing on the road circuit and were eventually allowed to use the whole track, including the banked oval. The lap record stood to Nuvolari at 5 min. 19 sec. and Caracciola very soon was down to 5 min. 20 sec. Von Brauchitsch then did 5 min. 16 sec. before Fagioli decided to show who was boss, breaking the record on three successive laps with 5 min. 15 sec., 5 min. 13 sec. and finally 5 min. 11.8 sec., an average speed of 145.1 km/h (90.2 mph). Well satisfied with this, Mercedes went home to Stuttgart.

If they thought—as well they might—that they had frightened the opposition with these impressive times they were wrong. Once official practice had got going Hans Stuck very soon knocked no less than five seconds off Fagioli's time! Then Louis Chiron beat that with his Ferrari Alfa, so Fagioli went out determined to set a new record, but he could only equal Chiron's time. He can't have been pleased when von Brauchitsch managed to beat them both with a time of 5 min. 5.6 sec. just before practice ended.

Grid positions were still decided by ballot, and Fagioli found himself starting the race all alone on the back row! This injustice brought out his true, fighting spirit and at the end of the first lap he was third, behind Chiron and Caracciola. For the next ten laps there was a battle royal between Chiron, Fagioli, Caracciola and Stuck, which had the huge and very partisan French crowd on its feet. It may have been an Italian car that was leading, but it had a French driver!

Fagioli passed Caracciola and began to close in on Chiron. On lap 13 they both equalled Nuvolari's old lap record, then, just as the Mercedes seemed to be about to pass the Alfa, it slowed dramatically and finally came to rest at Les Biscornes corner with a broken brake fluid pipe. A lap later Caracciola retired at the same place and all the Mercedes were out, as von Brauchitsch had retired on lap 12. Chiron won a great victory, but from now on the Germans were to dominate Grand Prix racing.

In the German GP Fagioli finished second, behind Hans Stuck, but he must have been considerably discomfited by Caracciola's tremendous performance. On a circuit that tested his shattered hip to the utmost, Rudi put up a sensational performance for 14 laps, chasing the leader all the way and actually passing him on lap 13, only to retire minutes later with a blown engine. Nevertheless, his astonishing return to his old form must have given Fagioli pause.

Caracciola continued his splendid comeback in the Coppa Acerbo at Pescara, leading the race for 11 laps until he made a rare mistake and crashed badly. Fagioli won the race, but only after a hard fight with Achille Varzi and Guy Moll in Alfa Romeos, Varzi retiring and poor Moll crashing to his death.

After this victory, Mercedes suffered a complete débâcle at Bern in the Swiss GP, Fagioli's lowly sixth place being the best they could do. The team rapidly pulled itself together, though, and Fagioli won the next two races, the Italian GP at Monza and the Spanish at San Sebastian. He was lucky at Monza, where his car retired after a few laps with supercharger trouble. But Caracciola, who lay second to Hans Stuck for 40 laps and then briefly took the lead,

ABOVE **Fagioli leads Hans Stuck (Auto Union) and Achille Varzi (Alfa Romeo) at Pescara in 1934**

LEFT **As the Mercedes team signs on for the 1934 French GP at Montlhéry, the aristocratic Manfred von Brauchitsch (***right***) seems to be regarding the unshaven Fagioli (***left***) with some contempt. In between are (***left to right***) Ernst Henne, Alfred Neubauer and Rudolf Caracciola**

found the relentless braking and gear-changing demanded by the chicane-infested circuit too much for him and when he came into the pits for new tyres he was practically unconscious. He was lifted from the car and Fagioli took over, holding the lead for the remaining half of the race.

In Spain, Hans Stuck led initially, but retired after four laps, leaving Caracciola ahead of Fagioli. When Rudi had a comfortable lead, Neubauer signalled him to ease up. He should have known better, for Fagioli went faster and faster and passed him! Still not 100 per cent fit, Caracciola could not put up a fight and resigned himself to second place.

The last GP of the year was at Brno. After a terrific race with Hans Stuck, Fagioli established a good lead, only to see it disappear when he had to make an unscheduled pit stop which allowed Stuck to beat him to the flag.

So Fagioli was able to look back on his first season with Mercedes with some satisfaction, having scored two wins, one shared victory with Caracciola and two seconds. But he was by now well aware that he was *not* Mercedes' Number One driver and that, for all his skill, German nationalism decreed that he should only win if an all-German victory was out of the question. He signed again for Mercedes for 1935, but clearly it was going to be a bumpy ride.

He began the year brilliantly, with a start-to-finish win at Monaco (the first man to do this), although the Auto Unions were absent. At Tripoli he finished third, behind Caracciola and Varzi, who was now with Auto Union, and then won at record speed at Avus. Long races at this *autobahn*-type circuit in Berlin had proved pretty boring to spectators, so now the Avus GP was split into two heats and a final. Fagioli finished second behind Stuck in the first heat and Caracciola won the second. The Italian then won the ten-lap final after Stuck led initially until forced into the pits for new tyres. He finished fourth in the Eifel GP a couple of weeks later and fourth again in the French GP at Montlhéry.

Here Caracciola proved that he was now very much back to his pre-crash form, having a huge battle for the lead with Nuvolari's Alfa for the early laps with Fagioli some way back in third place. The French had taken a leaf out of Monza's book and infested the Montlhéry circuit with three chicanes in an attempt to slow the German cars. They certainly succeeded in this, but only Nuvolari was able to take advantage of the obstacles and when he retired after 14 laps the three Mercedes of Caracciola, Fagioli and von Brauchitsch were well in the lead. Caracciola slowed, the other two closed up and sure enough, Fagioli went past him into the lead! As *The Motor* gleefully reported, 'They shot past the Tribunes wheel to wheel, apparently exchanging light after-luncheon conversation and then Caracciola went ahead again . . .'. Rudi had obviously learnt his lesson from Spain the previous year and he wasn't going to be caught out again by 'The Abruzzi Robber'! His problems were solved a few laps later when Fagioli slowed with plug trouble.

The Italian got his revenge and his third victory of the year at Barcelona in the Penya Rhin GP, but the two men clashed again at Spa. Caracciola led from the start, with Fagioli and von Brauchitsch giving Mercedes a comfortable one-two-three (Auto Union had not entered this race). Then von Brauchitsch retired and, after their scheduled pit stops, Fagioli went faster and faster, breaking the lap record and closing right up on Caracciola who, it seems, refused to let him through. There followed a great deal of shouting and fist-shaking from Fagioli at the Stavelot and La Source hairpins and as they rushed downhill past the pits. Neubauer had by now had enough of this and he signalled the furious Italian to come in. Another shouting match followed in two languages, with the result that Fagioli jumped out of his car and stalked off, leaving Neubauer to replace him with von Brauchitsch, who was having a nice snooze behind the pits!

He finished a dispirited sixth in the German GP, but was back on song again in time for the Swiss, at Bern. It rained heavily—Caracciola weather—and Fagioli had to be content with a good second place behind *Der Regenmeister*. Once Rudi had established a good lead, Neubauer told him to ease up and, true to form, Fagioli put on a spurt and closed the gap. This time, however, the two Germans were ready for him and Neubauer kept Caracciola well informed of the Italian's progress, allowing him to come home a comfortable winner.

In the Italian GP at Monza (without chicanes this time) all the Mercedes retired, but they came back to win their last race of the season, the Spanish GP at San Sebastian—Caracciola leading Fagioli home ahead of von Brauchitsch.

By the end of the year Luigi Fagioli was nursing a very real hatred of Rudolf Caracciola and a deep mistrust of Alfred Neubauer who, he was convinced, was giving his German driver preferential treatment. In this he was absolutely right, but Neubauer was, after all, a German running a German team and with Caracciola—a close friend—back in superb form he had to treat him as Number One. Rudi had rewarded him by winning six races (to Fagioli's three) and earning himself the title European Champion of 1935. Fagioli must have understood Neubauer's reasoning, but he just couldn't, or wouldn't, accept it.

For his part, Neubauer would doubtless have been happy to dispense with Fagioli's services after two years of trying to keep the volatile Italian in check, but he simply couldn't

Winning smile. Surrounded by excited fellow Italians, Fagioli is fêted after his 1934 Coppa Acerbo victory

afford to. Largely at Caracciola's insistence he added Louis Chiron to the team for 1936, but for all the Frenchman's polish and skill he still needed Fagioli's proven talent with the very powerful Mercedes, which were going to be even more powerful in the coming season.

German nationalism dictated that Mercedes should find more home-grown drivers, but the only new German talent to have surfaced in the previous year was that of Hermann Lang and Bernd Rosemeyer. Both had been discovered in-house, so to speak, Lang while working as a racing mechanic with Mercedes and Rosemeyer had been racing motorcycles for DKW, a division of Auto Union. Both had shown promise in 1935 and were destined for great things, but they were extremely limited in experience and although they were being groomed for stardom they were not deemed ready to join the aces just yet.

Of the other great Italians, Varzi was staying with Auto Union and Nuvolari remained with Alfa Romeo, but supposing they had been available, it is extremely doubtful that either would have accepted playing second fiddle to Caracciola or, when the occasion arose, von Brauchitsch, any more than Fagioli did. When it came to the crunch, Neubauer decided he had to strengthen his team by adding Chiron to it, rather than replacing Fagioli. Better the devil he knew. . . .

The new season opened at Monaco in April and much of the interest in the race was lost in the multiple pile-up at the chicane on the second lap which involved, among others, the Mercedes of Chiron and von Brauchitsch. Caracciola was leading at the time, so was not involved, and Fagioli managed to get through the mess unscathed. Seven laps later, however, he hit the same patch of oil that had caused the crash and slid into the wall. He was forced to retire on the spot, but his arch-rival Caracciola went on to win the race.

It was a deceptively good beginning to what was to be a sad and sorry year for Mercedes. They only won one more race—at Tunis—and, after complete débâcles in the German and Swiss GPs, the team withdrew from racing to reorganize itself for 1937.

Mercedes' disarray, coupled with Fagioli's ongoing feud with Neubauer and Caracciola, meant that the Italian had a very scrappy season. In addition, he was no longer a youngster, being 38 years old and now suffering from rheumatism. After Monaco he raced at Tripoli, finishing third behind the Auto Unions of Varzi and Stuck. But then Mercedes only sent two cars to Tunis and Barcelona and they were driven by Caracciola and friend Chiron. Fagioli was entered for the Eifel GP, but did not practise or race. He was not entered for the Hungarian GP a week later, where his three team mates all retired. Naturally, Mercedes were out in force for their own Grand Prix in July, entering five cars for Caracciola, von Brauchitsch, Fagioli, Chiron and Lang. Fagioli had a miserable time and eventually stopped to tell Neubauer exactly what he thought of the car! He can't have been at all unhappy when his Team Manager told him to get out and let Caracciola take over. Rudi brought the car home in fifth place, the first Mercedes to finish! In his last race for the team—the Swiss GP—Fagioli managed to get his ill-handling car up to third,

behind Rosemeyer and Varzi, only to suffer a puncture halfway round the circuit. By the time he had reached the pits and changed the wheel, he had lost his place to Hans Stuck, giving Auto Union a triumphant one-two-three.

It was no surprise that when Mercedes-Benz announced their driver line-up for 1937 the name Luigi Fagioli was not included. There had been just too much friction in the past three years and it must have been clear to Neubauer—even allowing for the fact that Mercedes had fielded uncompetitive cars in 1936—that the former Italian Champion was now over the hill.

During the winter there were the usual who-goes-where rumours flying about and in Fagioli's case it was widely held that he was going to retire from racing and take up farming. Then came the news that Enzo Ferrari was hoping to sign Nuvolari, Fagioli and Varzi to his Scuderia for 1937—an 'impossible dream' team if ever there was one! But Fagioli fooled everyone and in April it was announced that he would be driving for Auto Union, first race—Tripoli.

The whys and wherefores of this signing are unclear. For three years Fagioli had felt grievously slighted at having to be Number Three to Caracciola and von Brauchitsch—why should he now go to Auto Union where he would still have to be Number Three—this time to the young phenomenon Rosemeyer and the old master Stuck? One can only assume that Fagioli had come to terms with his increasing years and declining health and decided that Auto Union—after their sensational season in 1936—should enable him to enjoy a good swan-song and score a couple of victories over Mercedes-Benz and Caracciola in particular!

For their part Auto Union probably felt that there was life in the old dog yet. They also needed some driver-security, for although Rosemeyer was the hero of the hour, Stuck had a habit of announcing his retirement after almost every season and might just be as good as his word for 1937, and their other signings, von Delius and Hasse, were very inexperienced. Fagioli therefore, with all his drawbacks, must have seemed like a risk worth the taking.

He duly appeared at Tripoli and, as had happened several times in the past, the event became notorious. The race was a fine victory for Hermann Lang, but further down the field there was quite a battle going on between Caracciola and Fagioli. Rudi held fifth place—just—from the Italian who, try as he might, could not get by. Eventually, right at the end of the race, he forced his Auto Union past the Mercedes. But Fagioli was furious, convinced that Caracciola had deliberately baulked him for lap after lap. As soon as he got out of his car he stormed to the Mercedes pit and flung a heavy wheel-hammer at the hapless German. Luckily it missed, but then Fagioli grabbed a knife and lunged at his unfortunate 'enemy'. Before he could do any damage he was dragged away by Alfred Neubauer and mechanic Wilhelm Sebastian, but it was a shocking display of violence. Fagioli did apologize subsequently—in 1952, to be exact!

His next race was at Avus, where he and Rosemeyer drove *Stromlinienwagen*, based on Auto Union's record-breaking car. With the unpleasantness at Tripoli three weeks previously still fresh in his mind, Neubauer told the Avus organizers that if Fagioli and Caracciola were drawn in the same heat Mercedes would not race. Clearly, he felt that Fagioli's hatred was now so intense that it was not beyond him to try and push Caracciola off the track, but why he thought the Italian should try this in a heat and not in the final is not known! In the event the two men were drawn in different heats and while Caracciola won his, Fagioli had to retire, so only the former made it to the final.

Fagioli was now suffering terribly from rheumatism and, as a result, he missed Auto Union's next six races, eventually joining the team again for the Coppa Acerbo, where he finished fourth. A week later, limping heavily and having to walk with the aid of a stick, he made his last pre-war appearance in a racing car, at Bern, for the Swiss GP. He was way down the field when he was called in to hand over to Nuvolari, who was making his debut for Auto Union and who had himself had to give his car to Rosemeyer. The pair finally finished seventh.

It was a dispiriting end to a career which in 1934 had seemed to promise so much yet which, four years later, just fizzled out. There is no question that Luigi Fagioli was a very gifted driver with a boundless belief in his own ability. It was unfortunate, perhaps, that when his talents finally found a team really worthy of them, that team should be backed by the most ruthlessly nationalistic of regimes. Italian skill was no substitute for German pride and propaganda.

Sadly, Fagioli made a comeback after the war. Sadly because he was now 52 years old and well past his best. He joined the all-conquering Alfa Romeo team for 1950 which enabled him to pick up four second places that season and to finish third in the first World Championship, behind team-mates Farina and Fangio.

The next year he entered only one GP, the French, and shared a victory, but only after Fangio took over his Alfa and won. After Alfa Romeo's withdrawal from racing Lancia signed Fagioli for sports car races in 1952. He finished third in the Mille Miglia and this must have given him much satisfaction, as he beat his old enemy, Caracciola, in a Mercedes-Benz 300SL. It was to be his last success, though, for only a few weeks later he crashed at Monaco, while practising for a saloon car race—a curtain-raiser for the Grand Prix which he had won so handsomely 17 years earlier. Three weeks after the crash, he died in hospital and the explosive career of Luigi Fagioli was finally at an end.

This unscheduled pit stop cost Fagioli the 1934 Czech GP at Brno. As he takes a drink, Auto Union Team Manager Willy Walb can be seen in the background about to signal to Hans Stuck that he is now in the lead

THE FRENCH

Overwhelming Victory of Alfa-

OF all the Grand Prix races, and their number is legion, there is none in the world to compare with the one, only, and original Grand Prix of the Automobile Club of France. Nor, given a thousand years, could we create quite the atmosphere, the enchantment of that race.

Consider the matter. From earliest dawn hundreds upon hundreds of cars made their way cheerily to Montlhéry track, perched on a hill-top just off the road to Orleans, shimmering last Sunday in the sunshine. That famous little café, the Potinière, speedily became crowded with all the nations gathered at round tables sipping coffee or other drinks, discussing the coming fight eagerly with waiters only too anxious to voice opinions, or with Madame Berthot, whose knowledge of racing is extensive and peculiar. She, by the way, held stoutly to the opinion that Alfa would win.

Everybody who is anybody seemed to be there; a gigantic Englishman ploughed a solemn way through the tables towards the café. A Frenchman, versed in these things, said, "*Tiens, c'est Cobb,*" and then, after a good look, "*Formidable.*" Paris-Madrid, all those years ago, was represented by that little dark man who drove a Mors as one inspired, Goux, of the Peugeot team, the one and only Chassagne, Roupier, Wagner, Thomas, Brisson, whom we remember so well at Le Mans, names that brought back memory upon memory, they were all there.

The Nations Give Battle

Moreover, the setting was superb as the racing cars of France, Germany, and Italy, thirteen in all, gathered for one of the greatest battles in history, and voluble teeming thousands settled clamorously in their seats. Montlhéry, it seemed, had grown more, many more, trees, until one noticed that those trees walked Dunsinane fashion as more and more people used whole saplings for shade. A faun-like, rich brown man was startling since his clothes had, apparently, been discarded in the scorching heat, a fire extinguisher "made itself to go off" on the grandstand, creating tremendous joy, while over all, on the great staff above the Press box, the A.C.F. flag flew proudly upside down.

Then the loud-speaker demanded that *Messièurs les Commissaires* should order the *défile*, that procession which comes down the ages from the Roman circus, demanded again, became pathetic, and, at last, the cars moved, moved in a slow line while the achievements of each and its driver were recited, to be greeted with enormous applause, Etancelin and Chiron especially. One Auto-Union, Momberger's, was missing, but Momberger was driving the car allotted to Prince Leiningen. As the line of cars passed slowly Brauchitsch calmly filled his ears with cotton wool, Chiron ceaselessly chewed.

The Alfa team, by the way, had arrived impressively in formation and, incidentally, had been the first to weigh out; all cars were spotlessly clean, the Swastika and the German colours were side by side on the tails of the Auto-Unions, the drivers' names on the scuttles of the Bugattis in silver to match the silver numbers.

For a number of laps at the beginning of the race Von Stuck, with the

At last all were arranged in mass, two cars, Stuck's Auto-Union, Varzi's Alfa in front, then Caracciola's Mercédès, Momberger's Auto-Union, then Chiron's Alfa, Nuvolari's Bugatti, and Benoist's Bugatti, behind which came Dreyfus' Bugatti with Trossi's Alfa, and behind that again Brauchitsch's Mercédès, Zehender's red Maserati, and Etancelin's Maserati in French blue. At the extreme rear came Fagioli with the third Mercédès.

It was a wonderful sight, all those cars lined up, and all their possibilities, of which only one could prove victorious. Generally speaking, Mercédès were the favourites, for their speed in practice had been terrific, but their tyres were said to last but eight laps at most, and there had been wild excitement about the steering trammel measurements after

each lap, almost a panic, during which Neubauer as *chef d'équipe* had practically beseeched Wotan to come and do something personally. Auto-Union, though fast, seemed less reliable. Work had been going on with the 3,300's of the Bugatti team up to the last, the Maseratis appeared hard to hold, and only the Ferrari Alfas were supremely ready, twin-propeller-shaft scarlet 3,300 c.c. machines that looked magnificent.

Two minutes to two. As far as the eye could see the grounds, stands, trees, the landscape generally, were black with people, seething with excitement, concentrated on those thirteen brightly coloured silent cars.

The discipline was magnificent. One and a half minutes to go: Not a sound, not a movement. One minute. Every mechanic swung his car's starting handle.

46

The Autocar, July 6th, 1934.   31

GRAND PRIX

Romeos. No Other Cars Finish

Auto-Union (Number 4), duelled with Chiron, driving the Alfa-Romeo.

In one glorious growl of sound the racing cars woke to life. A high official of the A.C.F., prompted by the timekeeper, raised the club's blue flag. The power of many hundred horses welled up in a fierce scream of noise. Four seconds, two, one. Quite deliberately, it seemed, Chiron's scarlet Alfa moved from the third row, the flag hesitated, dropped. Chiron went straight by as the twelve other cars went off in one scream of sound which died slowly away in the distance.

Minutes passed, the loud-speaker announced that 12 led, and 12 was Chiron, at the "Biscornes." More minutes. Then in a fierce snarl the scarlet Alfa swung round the east banking and howled by the stands, leading Caracciola's silver Mercédès, with Fagioli's Mercédès close astern, then Von Stuck's odd-looking Auto-Union, and then the field going

great guns, except that Nuvolari's Bugatti seemed to falter.

Next round—the leader had covered the standing lap in 5 minutes 29 seconds—Von Stuck was right behind the Alfa. Caracciola had fallen to fourth, Fagioli's Mercédès lay third, and Nuvolari came in to the Bugatti pit for a hurried change of plugs.

A pause. Then there came a great roar from the crowd. Von Stuck's Auto-Union flashed into sight well ahead of the Alfa, close behind which was now Fagioli's Mercédès. The German attack had begun. For four more rounds the Auto-Union did its best, the speed terrific, each round exciting the crowd to furious clamour and appreciation, and ever behind came Chiron, then Fagioli's Mercédès, then Caracciola. And the pace told. On the eighth lap Zehender's

Maserati came in for water, and Nuvolari, whose gear seemed to be slipping out of mesh, on the Bugatti, stopped, shrugged his shoulders expressively, and handed over to Wimille, while Etancelin pulled in, climbed out, and talked volubly what time the mechanics wiped oil from the windscreen, scuttle, and steering wheel before he could restart.

On the ninth lap great excitement heralded the slow arrival of Von Brauchitsch, looking glum. Mechanics lifted the Mercédès bonnet, worked awhile, then got the car away with all its exhaust crackle dulled. And on that sensation followed another, for it was Chiron's Alfa once more which led the tenth lap, and Stuck's Auto-Union was in obvious trouble. In the Mercédès pit the team control got busy with the telephone to their signal station, and promptly Fagioli and Caracciola increased speed, the former breaking the lap record with 5 minutes 8.3 seconds—90.67 m.p.h.

Next lap, the red Alfa had Fagioli's Mercédès close behind, and Caracciola's close behind that. Where was Von Stuck? Varzi's Alfa passed, going well, then came the missing Auto-Union, which pulled in to the pit, was refilled and given two fresh rear wheels, then restarted after a loss of 2 minutes 35 seconds, the crowd cheering the driver's long and obviously satisfactory drink while the mechanics did the work.

The German Cars in Trouble

But the German attack, though terrific, was not without its troubles. Momberger's car trailed in slowly, apparently with steering trouble, for after the mechanics and driver had examined the off-front wheel, number 10 Auto-Union was pushed away to the "cemetery" without further discussion. On the heels of which Von Brauchitsch pulled in disconsolately and, amid great excitement, retired, the Mercédès having obvious engine trouble which had persisted since its last stop.

That Etancelin also retired with the Maserati did not affect the situation, however much one might sympathise with the man, for Chiron's Alfa, Fagioli's Mercédès and Caracciola's Mercédès were fighting a duel that could end only when one or the other could attain to supremacy or fall by the roadside. For 50 kilometres, which was approximately four laps, the speed was 87.77 m.p.h., at 100 kilometres it had risen to 88.39, and at 150 kilometres risen again to 88.25 m.p.h. Lap after lap these three cars, the scarlet Alfa, the two dull silver Mercédès, followed each other round at that great speed, the Alfa's note deep, the Mercédès' with that characteristic high supercharger whine that is recognisable several kilometres away.

It was indeed the devil take the hindermost. Fagioli brought the lap record down to 5 min. 6.3 sec.—it looked as though the Italian car must be caught as years ago a blue Peugeot had been caught by the two sharklike cars astern. But on the fourteenth lap Chiron got round in 5 min. 6 sec., 91.35 m.p.h., and then a crowd that had watched intelligently every move saw the Mercédès onslaught fall to pieces before their eyes. Fagioli failed to appear at all just as Neubauer was supervising the arrangements for a refill and wheel change—the

Fagioli makes an attempt to pass Chiron's Alfa-Romeo with the Mercédès (No. 30), and mounts the steep bank. He damaged a brake cable and withdrew.

tyres had lasted wonderfully, by the way.

Seconds lengthened into minutes as the mechanics stood staring towards the point where the German car was expected to appear. Then a telephone tinkled audibly. Someone gave an order, the jacks and wheels were replaced. Fagioli was out. Yet that was not all. Caracciola's car was weakening, Varzi's Alfa passed to second place and, next round, the remaining Mercédès came in, fuel was forced into the tank through a hose, water put in the radiator, both rear wheels were neatly changed, and the car went away again after 1 min. 20 sec. delay, only to disappear as Fagioli's had disappeared. It was extraordinary; six rounds, from the eleventh to the sixteenth, had seen the entire team, which had put up so magnificent a challenge, completely out of the race.

That altered the entire situation. Chiron could now slow, and did; Varzi was comfortably second, for Von Stuck's Auto-Union, though third, was losing ground and sounded fluffy. The third Alfa was not quite so happy, for Trossi, having come in and had the transmission checked over, had handed over to Moll, but the remaining Maserati, Zehender's, was not over-happy either, while the Bugattis could make no challenge.

First Dreyfus came in, and the Bugatti mechanics tried hard to remedy misfiring and harder still to restart the engine with the very nasty little handle that the Bugattis now have on the left side of the frame, restarting by any other method not being allowed, and on the very next lap the car retired with engine trouble. Nuvolari's Bugatti, now in Wimille's hands, not only misfired but was continually in difficulty with its gears, which left only Benoist, travelling regularly and well, just behind the Auto-Union.

Chiron's Alfa came in for a refill—all four wheels, fuel and water—beautifully done in 1 min. 39 sec., whereby Varzi led for one round, and when, on

the next lap, Varzi came in also the mechanics clipped nine seconds off that time for the same work. Against that, German pit work got Von Stuck's Auto-Union away after a refill and a thorough gargle for the driver, which amused the crowd, in 1 min. 32 sec., a later refill, when two rear wheels were changed as well, taking only 1 min. 40 sec.

Against such efforts the Bugattis were terribly handicapped, because their starting handles were inefficient or, perhaps, their engines difficult to start.

Benoist's car, for example, was fitted with four new wheels, refilled with fuel and water, and provided with new brake shoes in under two minutes, yet it was 2 min. 40 sec. before the engine could be started, though mechanic after mechanic worked until he dropped. Bugattis, by the way, have brake drums which change with the wheel, and so it is a matter of a moment to replace shoes with worn linings by new shoes.

It was most noticeable that nobody adhered to the pit regulations. There were certainly three mechanics—instead of two—in addition to the driver, working on one car at the same time, and, as some indication of the curious things that happened, thirty-seven people were counted in a close crowd round Benoist's Bugatti when the latter stopped for replenishment.

Anyhow, by the twentieth lap the Alfa team had practically disposed of all opposition, for Von Stuck's Auto-Union had been passed by Moll's Alfa, and the Italian cars were first, second, and third. To a certain extent that rendered things less exciting, but the huge crowd had its own methods of passing the time, and greeted the arrival of high Ministers of the French Government, whom some of them considered responsible for the extra taxes, with a stupendous chorus of shrieks, howls, and whistling, while the five or so minutes that elapsed before the cars came round again were almost always enlivened by one gentleman in the grandstand dropping a flaming cigarette lighter down another gentleman's back and the fire brigade rushing to deal with the resultant complication.

As Chiron came round on his twenty-ninth lap the Bugatti mechanics made one more effort to restart Wimille on No. 14, Nuvolari's car, but the machine had moved a bare yard before a horrible scrunching noise showed that the trans-

Before an immense crowd in the grandstand Chiron's Alfa-Romeo (Number 12) takes the lead at the start from Caracciola's Mercédès (Number 8).

July 6th, 1934.

L. Fagioli made several record laps with the beautifully built new Mercédès.

Another German car, the Auto-Union, driven by Hans von Stuck, led the race for a considerable time.

mission was in trouble, and a gallant attempt failed. Shortly afterwards Benoist came in again to have the off-front brake shoes of his Bugatti replaced, but the terrible difficulty of restarting the engine made the delay 3m. 25s. During that time Zehender's Maserati came in for water, while immediately afterwards Von Stuck's Auto-Union fell out of place, came to the pits, and the mechanics worked hard to remedy a bad water leak, refuelling the car at the same time, Von Stuck pouring a bottle of water between his shirt collar and himself. One round later the car came in again, water pouring out on to the track, and fifteen minutes' hard work failing to provide a remedy, the last German car retired.

Chiron came to his pit again, and in 55 sec. the mechanics had changed two rear wheels, the Rudge nuts spinning beautifully, refilled with fuel, restarted the engine, and got the car away, while, soon afterwards, Varzi's car was refilled and provided with two wheels, water, and oil, in 1 min. 42 sec., during which time the driver went for a stroll with a cigarette, afterwards to depart happily still smoking, a stop which allowed Moll temporarily to take second place.

Strong Alfa-Romeo Position

In point of fact the issue was now decided. Nothing could apparently alter the beautifully crisp exhaust of the winning Alfa, and its two sister cars were well ahead of all rivals. The average after the Mercédès had fallen out had come down to 86.9 m.p.h., then to 86.62 at 300 kilometres, still further to 86.36 at 350, and 86.19 at 400 kilometres, the leading machine now holding a steady 85.35. Zehender's Maserati had fallen far behind, its back axle adrift from the spring on one side, and twenty minutes passed while the mechanic made desperate endeavours to straighten the U-shaped clip bolts, a trouble which took so long to remedy that in the end the car was declared to have retired, while Benoist's blue car, the only Bugatti still running, was misfiring badly.

The crowd, few of whom had even left their places throughout that broiling afternoon, greeted with great enthusiasm the loud speaker's announcement that their hero Chiron was now upon his last lap. Then, as healthily as ever, the scarlet car flashed round the eastern banking and dropped on to the straight as Chiron acknowledged the chequered flag.

He was followed, some three minutes later, by Varzi's Alfa, back in second place since Moll went to the pits, and was shoo'ed out again hastily, and after

Varzi came Moll himself to complete the Alfa victory.

The chequered flag was also shown to Benoist, four laps behind at the time, who promptly took a short cut on the circuit, thereby causing some confusion, as seemingly his last lap speed must have been terrific.

It had been a magnificent race, magnificently won, and only three of the thirteen cars managed to complete the course.

The weights are interesting. The Mercédès weighed 737, 739.5 and 739 kilograms; Auto-Union 736.5, 740 and 738 kilograms; Alfas 720.5, 730 and 726.5

Caracciola with his Mercédès leads Fagioli (Mercédès) and Von Stuck (Auto-Union) round the sharp turn near the end of the road circuit.

kilograms; Zehender's Maserati 735, Etancelin's private car 748.5, the Bugattis weighing 747, 747 and 749.5 kilograms.

RESULTS.

Place. Car and driver.	Average. m.p.h.
1. Alfa-Romeo (L. Chiron)	85.05
2. Alfa-Romeo (A. Varzi)	83.80
3. Alfa-Romeo (Ct. Trossi and G. Moll)	83.447

Flagged Off.—Bugatti (R. Benoist), 36 laps.

Retirements.—Maserati (Zehender), 33 laps, spring clip; Auto-Union (H. Von Stuck), 32 laps, engine; Bugatti (T. Nuvolari and J. P. Wimille), 17 laps, engine; Bugatti (R. Dreyfus), 16 laps, engine; Mercédès-Benz (R. Caracciola), 15 laps; Mercédès-Benz (L. Fagioli), 14 laps, brakes; Mercédès-Benz (M. v. Brauchitsch), 11 laps; Maserati (P. Etancelin), 11 laps, engine; Auto-Union (P. Momberger), 10 laps, steering. Race distance, 500 kilometres.

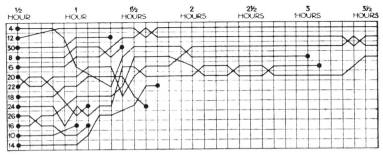

The progress of the race every half-hour. The numbers on the left indicate the competitors: 4 Von Stuck (Auto-Union), 12 Chiron (Alfa-Romeo), 30 Fagioli (Mercédès), 8 Caracciola (Mercédès), 6 Varzi (Alfa-Romeo), 20 Trossi (Alfa-Romeo), 22 Brauchitsch (Mercédès), 18 Dreyfus (Bugatti), 24 Zehender (Maserati), 26 Etancelin (Maserati), 16 Benoist (Bugatti), 10 Momberger (Auto-Union), 14 Nuvolari (Bugatti).

THE YEAR IN PICTURES

CHAMPION

ABOVE LEFT Hans Stuck's Auto Union is prepared for one of its record-breaking runs at Avus in March 1934

BELOW LEFT When the pits really were pits! Neubauer stands guard as Manfred von Brauchitsch, Ernst Henne and Rudolf

Caracciola watch practice for the 1934 French GP at Montlhéry from the Mercedes 'dugout'

ABOVE In May, Auto Unions competed in their first race, the Avus GP. They failed to finish. Here Guy Moll (Alfa Romeo 64),

Hermann zu Leiningen (Auto Union 44) and Peter de Paulo (Miller 66) set off from the start in the rain

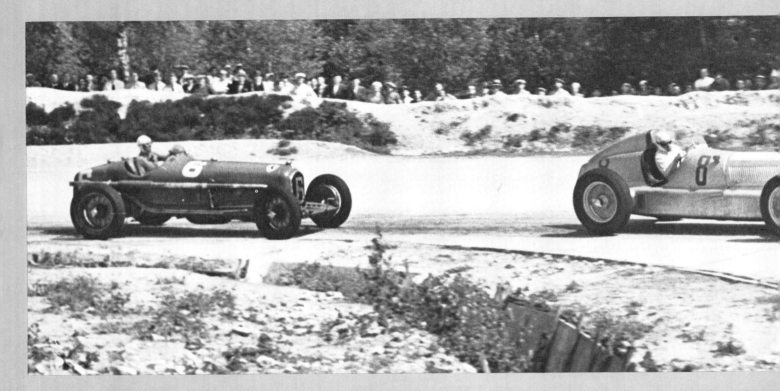

RIGHT **Hero!** The crowds wave enthusiastically to Hans Stuck as he drives on his way to victory in the German GP at the Nürburgring

LEFT Caracciola (Mercedes-Benz) leads Varzi (Alfa Romeo) in the early stages of the French GP

BELOW In August Stuck won the *Deutsche Bergmeisterschaft* at Freiburg with his Auto Union

LEFT Stuck finished off a fine year at Brno with a win in the Czech GP

BELOW In October, Ernst Henne persuaded Mercedes to let him try for some records at Gyon, near Budapest. Here he chats with his friend Caracciola (*left*), who eventually broke three Class C records

Linas-Montlhéry

LENGTH: 12.5 km (7.76 miles)
RACE: French GP (1934 and 1935)

Financed by a French newspaper magnate named Lamblin, the Linas-Montlhéry autodrome was built in 1924 on a huge estate (which included a chateau) at Saint Eutrope, some 25 km (16 miles) south-west of Paris. The banked autodrome was 2.5 km (1.55 miles) round and was built expressly for record-breaking. The road circuit, incorporating the autodrome, was added in 1925 and the two combined to make a lap of 12.5 km (7.76 miles), although the road section could be modified to make three shorter circuits. A huge main grandstand was built opposite the autodrome and was originally covered, but the roof was blown off during a gale in the 1920s and never replaced.

The French GP was first held on this circuit in 1925. It was a tragic debut, for the great Antonio Ascari crashed when in the lead and died on the way to hospital. The Alfa Romeo team immediately withdrew from the race, handing a sad victory to the Delage of Benoist and Divo. Montlhéry hosted the GP again in 1927 and 1931 during a bad period for Grand Prix racing. In 1932 the race went to Reims, only to return to the Paris circuit for the next five years. Although the new German cars were beaten in 1934, the AC de France was very shaken by their tremendous speed and for the 1935 race introduced three chicanes into the circuit, in the hope of reducing the Germans' superiority over the rest! The race was run at a considerably slower pace than in 1934, but this didn't prevent Mercedes from scoring a fine one-two.

To say that the French were miffed by this victory is to be guilty of a serious understatement. Next day the newspapers were full of headlines exclaiming, 'Never again!' and already there was talk of changing the rules or cancelling the race, as the Bugattis were incapable of dealing with the German cars and the much-vaunted Sefac was nowhere to be seen. At the end of the year the AC de France announced that there would be no French GP in 1936. This caused another uproar.

There was, in fact, a race called the French GP at Montlhéry in both 1936 and 1937, although the French ensured that the dreaded *Boche* didn't win by

ABOVE **Round the back of Montlhéry, Caracciola leads von Brauchitsch through Les Lacets des Canards on their way to victory in the 1935 French GP**

RIGHT **Down the tunnel to the Montlhéry pits go the Mercedes of von Brauchitsch (22) and Fagioli before the 1934 French GP**

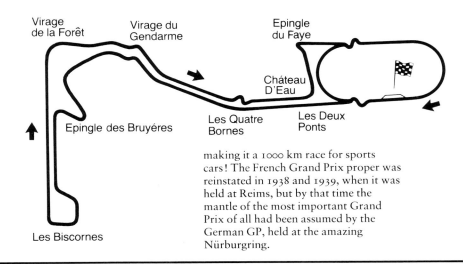

making it a 1000 km race for sports cars! The French Grand Prix proper was reinstated in 1938 and 1939, when it was held at Reims, but by that time the mantle of the most important Grand Prix of all had been assumed by the German GP, held at the amazing Nürburgring.

Montenero

LENGTH: 20.1 km (12.5 miles)
RACE: Coppa Ciano (1934–5)

The Montenero Cup was held on this long and very twisty circuit until 1930, when the race became known as the Coppa Ciano, the cup in question being donated by Count Galeazzo Ciano, who that same year became Benito Mussolini's son-in-law and not long after (surprise, surprise!) was made Italy's Foreign Minister!

The circuit ran clockwise from the start on the outskirts of Livorno, through the very narrow, twisty mountain roads to Montenero and then down to the corniche section which followed the coast through Calafuria, Antignano and back to the start. Montenero was extremely slow (Nuvolari won the last race there in 1935 at only 88.78 km/h (55.18 mph) and very unpopular with the drivers. In 1936 the Coppa Ciano was moved to the shorter Livorno circuit, which used some of the coast road from the old circuit.

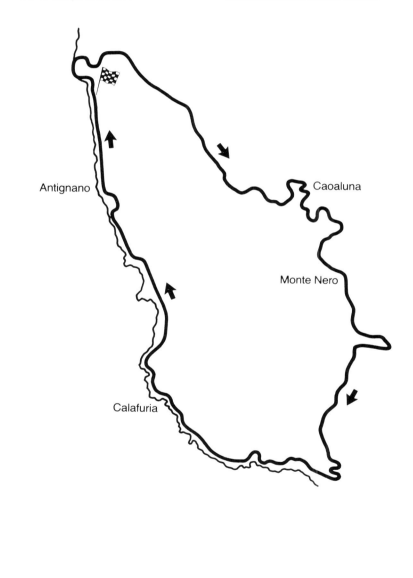

Lasarte

LENGTH: 17.32 km (10.76 miles)
RACE: Spanish GP (1934 and 1935)

Just a few miles south of the seaside resort of San Sebastian, the Lasarte circuit was one of the rare ones which ran anti-clockwise. It was opened in 1923 and the San Sebastian GP was held there annually until 1928. There was no race in 1929 and the last in the series was held in 1930.

The Spanish Grand Prix first appeared at Lasarte in 1925 and was run there again in 1927. In 1928 it was a sports car race, but was held for Grand Prix cars once more in 1929. After a four-year gap, it was brought back in 1934, only to be cancelled due to the political troubles in Spain at the time. Three weeks before race-date it was reinstated and Fagioli won for Mercedes at very nearly 160 km/h (100 mph). The highlight of practice was the sight of Nuvolari having his first drive in an Auto Union. Lasarte hosted the Spanish GP again in 1935, but it was the last time the race was run before World War II.

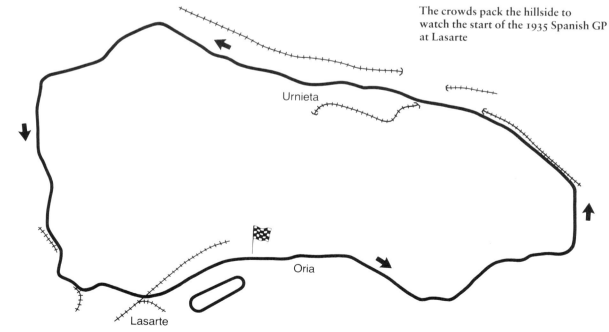

The crowds pack the hillside to watch the start of the 1935 Spanish GP at Lasarte

Masaryk Ring (Brno)

LENGTH: 29.14 km (18.10 miles)
RACE: Czech GP (1934, 1935 and 1937)

The longest circuit used in Grand Prix racing in the 1930s, the Masaryk Ring, was named after the Czech President, Jan Masaryk. The Czech GP was held there every year from 1930 until 1937, with the exception of 1936, when there was no race.

About half the circuit was on the national highway and the other half on local district routes. On the latter the surface was very rough, bumpy and hilly. Due to the extreme length of the circuit, practice was limited and so a thorough knowledge of it was hard to come by and this, coupled with its difficult nature, made crashes frequent. Crowd control was poor, too, and Hermann Lang was unlucky enough to skid off the road in 1937 due to the very rough surface and crash into some spectators who had got into a prohibited area.

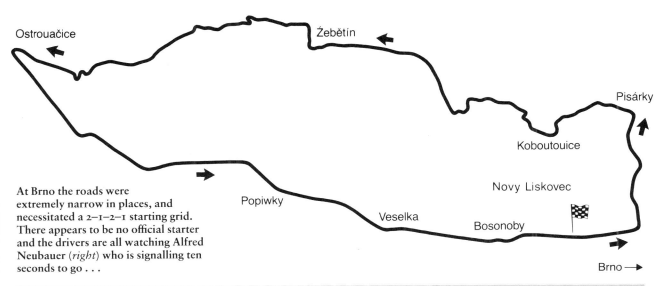

Ostrouačice · Žebětín · Pisárky · Koboutouice · Novy Liskovec · Popiwky · Veselka · Bosonoby · Brno →

At Brno the roads were extremely narrow in places, and necessitated a 2–1–2–1 starting grid. There appears to be no official starter and the drivers are all watching Alfred Neubauer (*right*) who is signalling ten seconds to go . . .

TWO

1935

1935

Caracciola's Renaissance

There was consternation in Italian racing circles when Achille Varzi joined Auto Union for 1935. In Varzi, Fagioli and Nuvolari Italy had three of the finest drivers in the world, and now two of them were driving for German teams! Nuvolari, too, tried to join Auto Union, but was thwarted in the attempt and eventually was persuaded to sign with Scuderia Ferrari.

With Caracciola's return to health and form following his 1933 Monaco crash, Mercedes-Benz were in good shape. They retained the services of Fagioli and von Brauchitsch, but dispensed with those of Ernst Henne, who had not made the grade in Grand Prix racing. Among their mechanics, however, the Stuttgart concern found a young driver of great promise named Hermann Lang, and he joined the team as a cadet.

Auto Union also found a young man of promise on their doorstep—Bernd Rosemeyer. He had been racing DKW motorcycles with some success in 1934 and made an impressive showing in tests on the Nürburgring, as did another young German, Paul Pietsch. They were both signed for the coming season, but Auto Union's real coup was getting Achille Varzi who, with Hans Stuck, virtually put them on an equal footing with Mercedes.

During the previous season, the Stuttgart firm had increased the size of the W25's engine from 3.4 to 3.7 litres, pushing the power up to 398 bhp. Auto Union retaliated for 1935 with a 4.9-litre engine producing 375 bhp, but Mercedes again enlarged their unit to 4.3 litres, which gave 445 bhp. In an effort to improve the Auto Union's handling, Professor Porsche abandoned the transverse leaf spring at the rear and used torsion bars instead.

Lacking anything like the financial resources of the German teams, Alfa Romeo, Maserati and Bugatti simply could not afford to design and build the new cars they so desperately needed. Designer Vittorio Jano had plans for a new 4-litre V-12 Alfa with all-independent suspension, but as the engine would not be ready for some time he concentrated on the new chassis with a 3.8-litre version of the P3's power unit. Meanwhile, Scuderia Ferrari had to make do with the aging P3s in Grands Prix, but with an ever-ready eye to the lucrative non-Formula events, such as Tripoli and Avus, Enzo Ferrari gave his blessing to a project thought up by his great friend, Luigi Bazzi—a twin-engined Alfa Romeo. Dubbed the Bimotore, this had nothing to do with the Alfa factory and was arguably the very first Ferrari and, indeed, it carried the Ferrari's Prancing Horse badge over the radiator intake. The Bimotores proved to be extremely fast, but their very speed was their undoing, as the tyres were just not capable of handling the enormous power of the twin engines.

At the beginning of the year there were rumours of a mid-engined, 4-litre Maserati, but this never materialized and the Bolognese concern persevered with its 1934 chassis powered by the 6-cylinder, 3.7-litre engine. Later in the year Maserati came up with a 4.4-litre V-8, in an independently sprung chassis.

It turned out to be a truly magnificent season for Rudolf Caracciola and Mercedes-Benz. Having been virtually written off by many, following his Monaco crash in 1933, Caracciola made a sensational come-back and scored no less than six major wins in 1935—the GPs of France, Belgium, Switzerland, Spain, Tripoli and Eifel—more than enough to ensure that he was the first European Champion.

The European Championship came into being in 1935. Five international races—each the première race of the year in its country—were chosen as qualifying events for the title and these *Grandes Epreuves* (*épreuve* meaning test, or trial) were the GPs of Belgium, Germany, Switzerland, Italy and Spain. There is one glaring omission here and that is the French GP which, at that time, was still regarded as *the* Grand Prix of the year. The reason for its exclusion from the Championship is as simple as it is sad: when the idea was circulated to the organizing clubs concerned, it was accepted by all—with the exception of the AC de France. The reason? The European Championship was the brainchild of the AC von Deutschland. . . .

Unlike the modern World Championship, in which the more successful a driver is in a race the more points he gets, the European Championship involved what was virtu-

PREVIOUS PAGE **Unlucky Manfred von Brauchitsch comes into the pits on three tyres and a rim, having just had the 1935 German GP snatched from his grasp by Nuvolari**

ally a penalty system—the lower down the order a driver finished, the more points he got, and the Champion was the driver who, at the end of the season, had the *lowest* number of points! It worked like this:

1 point for the winner.

2 points for the second placed man.

3 points for the third placed man.

4 points for the fourth placed man and for all drivers who complete at least three-quarters of the race distance.

5 points for all drivers who complete at least half the race distance.

6 points for all drivers who complete at least one quarter of the race distance.

7 points for all drivers completing less than one quarter of the race distance.

8 points for all non-starters.

There was quite a bit of car-swapping in those days, but a driver could only score points with the car in which he started the race. If Rosemeyer, for example, retired after ten laps of a 70-lap race and took over Pietsch's Auto Union to finish second, he would not get two points for second place, but seven, for completing less than a quarter of the distance in his own car.

†*Department of utter confusion*: It has to be admitted that there does appear to be some sort of mix-up here. The points given above are based on the aforementioned points system as explained in a German book published in 1938, which gave details of the 1937 European Championship. However, the 1935 Championship was reported in both *Speed* and *Motor Sport*, giving Caracciola the title with 16 points and Varzi for example, in seventh place with 40 points. As there were five qualifying races in 1935, Varzi—using the 1937 points system—would have had to score 8 points in each race, yet 8 points were only given to non-starters and the Italian's only non-appearance was in the Belgian GP. Confused?

Using this system, the order of the Championship was as follows: 1) Caracciola—12 points; 2) Fagioli—20 points; 3) Nuvolari—23 points; 4) Stuck—24 points; 5) von Brauchitsch—25 points; 6) Rosemeyer—26 points and 7) Varzi—29 points.†

It may well be that the points system was changed sometime between 1935 and 1937, but there appears to be no evidence of this, so perhaps the published 1935 points were just wrong. Whichever scores are correct, Caracciola emerges as undisputed European Champion for 1935, winning three of the five *Grandes Epreuves*.

*　　　*　　　*

The year is remembered by Paul Pietsch and Hanns Geier, and the careers of Caracciola and Manfred von Brauchitsch are closely examined. Pietsch joined Auto Union for 1935, but wishes he had taken up Alfred Neubauer's offer of a Mercedes drive instead! Hanns Geier suffered one of the most spectacular crashes ever seen when he lost control of his Mercedes during practice for the 1935 Swiss GP. Miraculously, he survived, and although he still has no memory of the accident, he provides some fascinating photos.

Rudolf Caracciola was himself the victim of a terrible crash two years earlier, but made a stunning come-back in 1935. One of racing's all-time greats, his extraordinary career was supported by two remarkable women. His team mate, Manfred von Brauchitsch, was known as *Pechvogel* (the unlucky bird), losing several races he should have won. Among them was the greatest prize, the German GP, which he lost on two occasions, the first in 1935. All the drama of that race, which Nuvolari won in sensational fashion, is reproduced in *The Autocar*'s report. Among the circuits in use in 1935 were Montjuich, Carthage, Monaco and Avus, the latter for the last time before the North Turn was banked.

MEMOIR

Paul Pietsch

Team Driver, Auto Union 1935

I began racing in 1932. I was 20 years old when I went to Molsheim and bought a Type 35 Bugatti which had been raced by a very well-known German driver, H. J. von Morgen. At that time there were a lot of mountainclimbs—in Germany there were about 12 or 15 in the year and people like Caracciola and Stuck began their careers in these events—and von Morgen was very successful with this car. It was a single-camshaft model and when Bugatti brought out his new twin-camshaft car, von Morgen bought one, so I bought his old car from him and I, too, went in for the mountainclimbs. (Poor von Morgen was killed in his new Bugatti that year.)

I was then working in my mother's brewery, but I didn't enjoy it much as I preferred to go racing! At the end of the year I sold the Bugatti and bought a Monza Alfa Romeo. It was a 2.3-litre two-seater and I raced it like that in 1933, but for 1934 I made it into a *monoposto* and increased the capacity to 2.6 litres. It was a very enjoyable car and I had a lot of success with it. In February that year I went ice-racing in Sweden and Norway and won several races. Later, I came sixth in the Avus GP and fourth in the Eifel GP, but by now both Auto Union and Mercedes were racing and you could do nothing about them—they were just too fast! I did a few more mountainclimbs and then had a very bad crash at Gabelbach, breaking my leg in six places. As a result I missed the German GP, but I came back to win the Feldberg mountainclimb and the Swiss Mountain Championship at Montreux Caux.

Auto Union had originally asked me to drive for them in the German Grand Prix, but my crash meant that I couldn't do this. However, in October they held a test session at the Nürburgring with 12 drivers, including myself and two well-known motorcycle racers—Soenius and Rosemeyer. We drove both on the full circuit and the *Sudschleife* and I was the fastest each time. As a result of this test, Rosemeyer and I joined Stuck, zu Leiningen and Varzi for 1935.

I found the Auto Union a very difficult car to drive and I didn't like it very much. To begin with, the driver was sitting right up at the front, between the front wheels, and behind you was almost the whole car, with that long, 16-cylinder engine, so you could never see the position of the car on the road. In 1935 they had swing axles at the rear with a transverse leaf spring, and torsion bars at the front, and when you were cornering fast you never knew when the tail was going to come round. And when it did it was usually too late to do anything about it!

Rosemeyer had never driven a normal, front-engined car, so he had no comparison with the Auto Union and very soon he was able to drive it very, very fast—he was a brilliant driver. He proved this in only his second race, the Eifel GP, when he came second behind Caracciola, who only managed to catch him at the very last moment. That was my first race for Auto Union and I finished sixth.

I'm afraid I did not have a successful time with the team. I finished ninth in the German GP and eleventh in the Swiss. I was reserve driver there and when Stuck's car began to slow he brought it into the pits and handed it over to me! I tried my best, but there was something seriously wrong with it and in spite of several pit stops the mechanics never got it going properly.

The Italian GP at Monza was better, although I had to hand my car over to Rosemeyer after his had transmission failure. We finally finished third and Stuck won. My last race for Auto Union was the Spanish GP, which was a disaster for us and Mercedes finished one-two-three.

After that I left Auto Union and did not race at all in 1936. We all make mistakes in life and two of mine were a) joining Auto Union and b) *not* joining Mercedes-Benz! About the same time that Auto Union approached me in 1934, Mercedes also asked me to join them, but two of my close friends were Hans and Paula Stuck, and Hans insisted that I join him at Auto Union. It seemed a very good idea at the time, but once I was in the team I found that I didn't get on with the car or the Team Manager, Willy Walb. I should have gone to Mercedes. Alfred Neubauer was much better than Walb and the Mercedes was a normal, front-engined machine. I am sure that I would have done much better with it than I did with the Auto Union.

I spent 1936 in Munich doing some business, but I wanted to return to racing so I bought a Maserati for 1937. I bought it from Laszlo Hartmann and it was a terrible car! It was always losing oil, but I had some little successes with it until I had a very bad crash at the Masaryk Ring. The car was destroyed and I was unconscious for two days, but I didn't break anything!

For 1938 I went to Italy and bought a 1500 cc Maserati. At this time the Italians could do nothing against the

Mercedes and Auto Unions, so they held a lot of races for 1500 cc cars to keep the Germans out! I raced my own car and, occasionally, the factory cars, in Italy, France and South Africa—Cape Town, Durban and Port Elizabeth. I had a very good race at the Nürburgring in the German GP, finishing sixth—the first 1500 cc car home. I was to do even better the next year.

Mercedes caught everybody by surprise in 1939, building a special 1500 cc car for the Tripoli race which, of course, they won. I took the Maserati to the 'Ring again for the Eifel GP, but this time all the Auto Unions and Mercedes (except Seaman's) finished and although I was again the first 1500 cc car home the best I could do was ninth overall.

For the German Grand Prix, however, I had the new, supercharged, 3-litre Maserati and with this car I was able to take the lead for some laps, ahead of all the Mercedes and Auto Unions. Unfortunately, I then had plug trouble. It started to rain and got very cold and the plugs oiled up, so I had to stop and change them. In spite of this, I finished third, behind Caracciola and Müller. *Korpsführer*

RIGHT **Paul Pietsch with his Monza Alfa Romeo at the Stelvio mountainclimb in 1933**

BELOW **In the 1935 Italian GP at Monza, Phi-Phi Etancelin (Maserati) leads Pietsch (Auto Union) and Hermann Lang (Mercedes-Benz)**

Pietsch celebrates after his fine third place in his 3-litre Maserati in the 1939 German GP. He was not popular with *Korpsführer* Hühnlein for leading all the German cars for a couple of laps!

Hühnlein, who had shaken me warmly by the hand before the race, was not amused by my success—a German driver in an Italian car leading all the German cars in the German Grand Prix was not his idea of a good thing. What he would have said if I had won . . .

After the race, Neubauer approached me and asked me to join Mercedes-Benz for 1940 but, of course, the war started and that was that, although for a time there was a possibility that the Tripoli race might be run. It would

have been good, for Mercedes still had the 1500 cc cars and I would have come out of the army!

I took up racing again after the war in 1950, competing at various times with Veritas, Maserati and Alfa Romeo. I won the German Sports Car Championship that year and the Racing Car Championship the next, but at the end of the 1952 season I retired, in order to concentrate on my new career—publishing.

In 1946, right after the war, a friend and I started *Das Auto*, the first post-war German automobile journal. It is now known as *Auto Motor und Sport* and has become the biggest magazine of its kind in Europe, selling over half a million copies every fortnight. Our publishing house has grown, too, and we now produce 45 magazines and are involved with publishing houses in Switzerland, France and Spain.

Hanns Geier

Team Driver, Mercedes-Benz 1934–35

I started racing in 1920, when I was 18, first with motorcycles and then with an Amilcar. I won a lot of prizes and in 1927 I joined forces with my friend, Bubi Momberger, and we raced a Bugatti. (Momberger later joined the Auto Union team, in 1934.) We took part in the opening race at the Nürburgring and won our class. The whole circuit was used then, including the *Sudschleife*, so one lap was 28 km (17 miles) and the race was over 500 km (310 miles). I am the only man still alive who drove in that race.

Bubi and I were great friends of Gretel Schwab (whose brother, Kurt, was to marry Dick Seaman's widow, Erica, after the war) and in about 1929 we met her when I was racing at the Solitude circuit. She told me that she could arrange for me to race with Mercedes-Benz, but I'm afraid I didn't believe her, although she was then well acquainted with—or even engaged to—Dr Wilhelm Haspel, one of the Directors at Daimler-Benz. Instead, I went to work in Frankfurt for F. K. Mettenheimer, who sold American cars such as Chrysler and Ford.

Then in 1932 a friend of mine, Hans Hugo Keil, who was also a Director at Daimler-Benz, offered me a job with the company in the Test Department, working on the new, supercharged, 3.8-litre Cabriolet. Later, I had to show the car to all the Mercedes agents in Germany, France, Switzerland and the Netherlands. In 1934 I was doing the same thing with the 500K when I got a call from Untertürkheim, telling me to leave the car where it was (I was in Düsseldorf at the time) and go at once to the Nürburgring to practise for the German Grand Prix, as von Brauchitsch had crashed and broken his arm.

First of all I practised in Caracciola's old Monza Alfa Romeo which Mercedes had bought after his Monaco crash. Then I moved on to the W25 Mercedes which I drove in the race. I finished fifth and although I never got very excited about such things I was quite satisfied with that. I was reserve driver in the Swiss GP and took over Caracciola's car when it developed brake problems, finishing tenth and last. In the final race of the year—the Czech GP at Brno—I took over from Ernst Henne, who was not well, and this time I finished sixth.

My first race of 1935 was at Avus, where I drove the streamlined car with enclosed cockpit which Caracciola had used late in 1934 to set some new World Records, also at Avus. There were two heats and a final and in my heat a tyre burst, so I had to come into the pits for a wheel-change and finished fourth. In the final the carburettor failed and my race was over. The enclosed car was not, as you might imagine, very noisy, but it was rather worrying because it could only be opened from the outside! Although the race was just up and down the two sides of

Geier is wearing the tweed cap Dick Seaman asked him to look after shortly before the 1939 Belgian GP . . .

the *autobahn*, you still had to concentrate very hard for 500 km and there was a special trick involved in getting round the corner at each end without losing too much time or even sliding off the road altogether!

Mercedes never used the enclosed racing cars again. For the German GP my fellow reserve driver Hermann Lang and I both had normal, open cars. Lang retired and I could only finish seventh in a race that gave Nuvolari one of his most famous victories.

My next race was my last and I don't remember a thing about it! It was the Swiss Grand Prix at Bern and Lang and I were again given drives, but I crashed in practice and was so badly hurt that it was the end of my racing career. I lost control at about 240 km/h (150 mph) in the curve by the timekeepers' box, just before the pits and the main grandstand. The road surface was not flat at this point but curved, falling away from the centre at both sides, which made it very dangerous. (As a result of my crash, they changed it before the 1936 race.) My car demolished a wooden fence and some of the timing boxes. It also demolished itself in the process, as you can see from the photographs. The engine was lying on one side of the track, the supercharger was stuck in a tree and the rest of it was scattered over a wide area, but to everyone's concern I was nowhere to be found! I was eventually discovered lying under a parked car some way from the wreckage.

For some reason there was no ambulance available, but Dr Gläser (who was the doctor for both Mercedes and Auto Union teams) commandeered a motorcycle combination, put me in the sidecar and rode with me to the hospital on the pillion, behind the driver, holding my

ABOVE **Geier in the streamlined Mercedes at Avus in 1935**

LEFT **In at the deep end. Geier's first GP was the German in 1934**

tongue to prevent me from swallowing it and choking myself to death. He saved my life, there's no doubt about that.

I had terrible injuries: my face was badly battered, both legs and one ankle were broken, as was my shoulder; the base of my skull was fractured and my spine was damaged. I was unconscious for eight days and in hospital for four months, but they let me out in time to spend Christmas with my mother in Garmisch. When I was able to go back to work in 1936 I returned to my old job in the Test Department and I also became Herr Neubauer's assistant, going with him to all the races. Neubauer was a remarkable man—a very nice, very excitable man. He was both a mother and father to all the drivers and seemed to be able to make himself understood in almost every language.

Geier's Crash

by Raymond Mays

The ERAs having so far performed well, we decided to take things easily on the last day of practice and watch the Auto Unions, Mercedes, Alfas and Maseratis do their stuff. A great deal could be learned by watching these ultra-fast machines, whose drivers knew the course inside out. From the grass patch it was a fantastic sight to see the big GP cars coming over the cobbles at 170 mph (274 km/h). A few of the drivers, such as Caracciola, Rosemeyer, Stuck and Nuvolari, never eased their throttles when taking the banked curve between the pits and the grandstands, but had they misplaced by a hand's-breadth it would have spelled disaster. This was soon proved only too true when a new member of the Mercedes-Benz team—Geier—crashed at that very spot. Standing in the pits as he approached, I could see he was slightly misplaced and knew that a crash was inevitable.

Although such a catastrophe is all over in a flash, the incident seems to last for ages. Geier took the corner too wide and so could not bring the Mercedes near enough to the apex. The tail described an almighty sweep to the left and hit the wooden protection barrier, in front of the grandstands, when doing at least 150 mph (240 km/h). The car then skidded and lurched in all directions and shot across the road into a big tree, just past the pits, where it disintegrated into four distinct parts. The nose and front axle shot across to the far side, the cockpit and middle part lay in the centre of the road, the engine was deposited on the grass verge, just as if it had been lifted out of the chassis, while the rear part of the car came to rest near the engine. Geier was thrown onto the running board of a car which was standing by the edge of the woods. I think almost every bone in his body was broken, but the amazing thing is that he lived and recovered, after nearly a year in hospital.* Practice was immediately stopped while the wreckage was cleared away.

A crash of this sort, on a curve which requires the utmost skill to negotiate flat out, has an extraordinary effect on other drivers. This was particularly noticeable as soon as practice recommenced. Even Caracciola and Nuvolari, who, prior to Geier's crash, had taken this corner brilliantly on full bore, began to ease their throttles a considerable distance before reaching it. It takes quite a number of laps for drivers to regain confidence and in some cases they never do get back their original form on such a hazardous spot as this.

From *Split Seconds* (Foulis)

* Note: Geier says he spent some four months in hospital.

Geier's Bern crash. These dramatic pictures show the aftermath of the accident which destroyed the Mercedes and nearly killed Geier. TOP The engine and front wheels lie on the inside of the track, while the rest of the car can just be seen on the other. CENTRE Spectators take a good look at the remains of the Mercedes. ABOVE A spectator took this photo the moment Geier was found lying under a car

Rudolf Caracciola

Team Driver, Mercedes-Benz 1934–39
European Champion 1935, 1937 and 1938

Rudolf Caracciola smiled and waved to the cheering thousands who lined the circuit as he drove round in his Mercedes. Although this was something he was well accustomed to—a lap of honour—the standing ovation he was now being accorded was a particularly emotional experience for him. For this was not the usual, post-race acclaim for the victor—he was doing this lap *before* the race, and a race that would start without him: the sixth Monaco Grand Prix. Few people present—and certainly not Caracciola himself—could have imagined that this man would dominate Grand Prix racing for the rest of the decade. For in April 1934, Rudolf Caracciola's career—indeed his life—lay in ruins.

Only 12 months before, on that very circuit, he had crashed heavily in practice, shattering his upper right thigh and hip so badly that doctors told him he would never race again. Then, just two months before that lap of honour, on 2 February, his wife, Charly, had been swept away by an avalanche and killed while skiing near their Swiss home in Arosa. His crash had caused him terrible physical pain, but it was nothing to the agonies he suffered on losing his beloved Charly. Caracciola was devastated.

For months he was in a state of shock and his friends were in despair, fearing that he might not return to normal life, let alone racing. Yet 18 months later Rudolf Caracciola was declared European Champion, a title he was to win on two more occasions. His extraordinary career is the story of a remarkable man—and two remarkable women.

He was born on 30 January 1901, in the Hotel Caracciola in Remagen-on-Rhine. The hotel was owned by his father, Georg Caracciola, who was also a wine dealer. In spite of their Italian-sounding name, the Caracciolas had lived in Germany for some generations, having originally come from Sicily.

After schooling and one year's military service, his parents sent him as an apprentice to the Fafnir car factory in Aachen, on the German-Belgian border. Caracciola enjoyed the work, but one evening, while drinking with some friends in a nightclub, he got involved in a fight with a Belgian army officer, knocking him down. Caracciola's friends warned him that staying in Aachen could be very unhealthy, for although it was by now 1922, the Belgians still occupied that part of Germany and held bitter memories of the Great War. Recently, several Germans had been beaten up by Belgian soldiers. Rudi returned to Remagen, but his home town was also in occupied territory and his family, worried that repercussions from his fight might affect them, suggested that he move on. His mother had recently been introduced to a man who was very interested in cars—Rudi could ask him for a job. The man's name

was Theodor Rathmann, and he lived in faraway Dresden.

Herr Rathmann turned out to be a pleasant young man who was, for that week anyway, making wooden dolls, but in the uncertain financial climate of post-war Germany he was prepared to turn his hand to anything. He and his friends were all mad about motor racing and, learning of Rudi's ambition in that direction, they rallied round the newcomer. With their help he got a job with Fafnir again, this time as their Dresden sales representative.

Rudi managed to persuade Fafnir to let him race one of their 1.5-litre cars at the Avus track on 1 June 1922. He finished fourth and, flushed with success, entered the car for the Opelbahn race at Rüsselsheim a month later, which he won. He had to wait until the following April for his next race. His new-found friends in Dresden had other friends, one of whom had a delightfully named Ego car and Rudi was allowed to borrow this for a small-car race in the Berlin Stadium, which he duly won.

The Ego's owner was a man named Wüsthof who, no doubt impressed by young Caracciola's victory, later introduced him to Herr Herzing, a Director of the Daimler company. Caracciola told Herzing that his great ambition was to become a racing driver and to drive for Daimler. As a result, he was summoned to Untertürkheim and sent for a test drive on a bare chassis with a Herr Werner, after which he was told that he had a job. Rudi's elation lasted only a moment as, much to his chagrin, he was informed that he was not going to be a racing driver, but a salesman, back in Dresden! Although he was naturally disappointed he took the job, and just as well, for it was to change his life, both professionally and personally.

In spite of the fact that he proved to be no great shakes as a salesman, Rudi did manage to persuade the company to lend him a Mercedes for competition and notched up no less than 13 wins in races, speed trials and hillclimbs in 1923. This success led to a supercharged, 1500 cc Mercedes for 1924 and Caracciola almost doubled his number of wins the previous year, scoring 25 victories. He also won two motorcycle races on a 350 cc Garelli.

The following year Rudi could only manage a mere dozen victories, the greatest of which took place not on the racetrack, but on the dance floor! Opposite the Daimler showroom was the fashionable *Europäisher Hof* Hotel and one very pretty girl who was staying there caught Rudi's eye. With the help of the senior salesman, who was much better versed in these matters than young Caracciola, he managed to meet the girl at one of the tea dances which were held every afternoon at the hotel.

During the dance Rudi learned that her name was Charly, which pleased him greatly, and that the man she was with was her husband, which did not! He was Chief Buyer for her father, Herr Liemann, who owned three restaurants in Berlin. However, Charly admitted that the marriage was not a success and that she was contemplating a separation, which made Rudi feel better. When she agreed

Caracciola is seen here surrounded by young admirers at Tripoli, 1935

to see him again he felt very good indeed! By the time the dance was over, Caracciola was in love.

Over the next few weeks the young couple met constantly, until Charly had to return to Berlin. For a while Rudi heard nothing, then one day she phoned to say that she was back in Dresden and wanted to see him. They met that evening and walked through the old town to the Bruhl terraces, where Charly told him that while she was away she had obtained a divorce and was now free to marry. Rudi was stunned and delighted, but he was not going to rush into marriage for, after all, he was still earning only 100 DM a week as a salesman. He promised Charly that they would marry, but only when he was able to afford the lifestyle she deserved. First he must make some real money, and to do that he had to win a major race. . . .

In 1926 the German Grand Prix was held at the Avus track in Berlin for the first time and with many victories to his name over the past three years Rudi felt he had a real chance of being in the Mercedes team. But then came the bombshell—Mercedes were not going to enter their own Grand Prix, being more concerned with improving their exports by competing in Spain instead. Disheartened by this news Rudi, together with Adolf Rosenberger, went to see Mercedes Director Max Sailer and persuaded him to put two cars at their disposal for Avus. They would be private entrants, with no official backing, but they were in the race!

The first prize for the Grand Prix was no less than 17,000 DM and though none of the experts gave Rudi a chance of winning, he had other ideas, and so did Charly, for victory at Avus would enable them to marry. But if they thought they could hear wedding bells, that happy sound was banished at the start of the race, when Rudi stalled his engine and had to watch the field stream away from him down the 10 km (6 mile) straight as his hapless riding mechanic tried to give him a push-start.

When they finally got going they were over a minute behind but then, after a few laps, it began to rain. In spite of the very unsettling sight of Rosenberger's Mercedes embedded in the Timekeepers' Box and a body being carried away on a stretcher, Caracciola drove superbly in the appalling conditions, giving a foretaste of his amazing wet-weather skills as he caught everyone in front of him and won the race. It was a sensational victory and that night Rudi was the talk of Berlin, but most of all it meant that he and Charly could now marry, which they did. At about the same time, using his new-found wealth, Rudi went into partnership with his old friend, Theodor Rathmann, opening a Mercedes showroom on Berlin's fashionable Kurfürstendamm. Life was good, indeed.

In 1927 Caracciola won the Sports Car Class in the inaugural race at the Nürburgring, driving the big, 7-litre Model S Mercedes and he also won six mountainclimbs with this car during the season. The next year he had the new SS and with it he won the German Grand Prix, his co-driver on this occasion being none other than Mercedes' former star driver, Christian Werner—the same Herr Werner who had accompanied him on his test drive at Untertürkheim in 1923! Rudi again excelled on the mountains, winning no less than eight climbs.

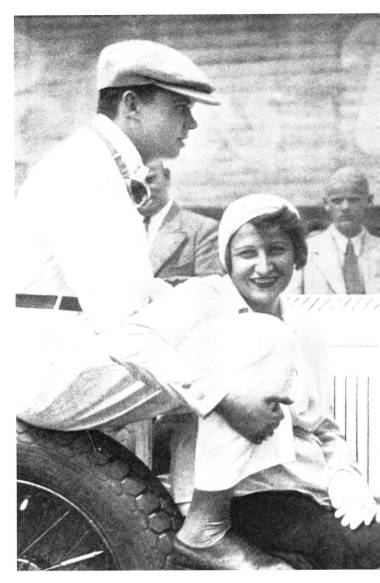

A charming photo of Rudi and Charly, taken at Monaco in 1932

In 1929 he drove the huge Mercedes SSK in the first Monaco Grand Prix, leading the race for a while, until a lengthy pit stop dropped him back to third at the finish. In August he flew to Ireland (a novel departure in those days) for the Tourist Trophy. It poured with rain and Caracciola—already something of a legend for his wet-weather skills—won the race.

Rudi and Charly were naturally elated by all this success, which consolidated his position as one of the finest drivers in the world. But success couldn't protect them from the Wall Street Crash in October 1929, and Rudi was forced to close down his Berlin showroom. He and Charly left Germany and moved to Arosa, in Switzerland, where they had already enjoyed some skiing holidays.

In 1930 Rudi entered the Mille Miglia for the first time. Not knowing the roads (unlike his Italian competitors) he used the race as a recce for 1931 and finished an excellent sixth, partnered once again by Christian Werner. In July he took the big Mercedes to England for the Shelsley Walsh hillclimb, which was included in the European Mountain Championship. He won the Sports Car Class in the record time of 46.8 sec. The bulk of his competition that year was in mountainclimbs, nine in all, of which six counted towards the Championship. He won them all, with either outright or class victories, and at the end of the year was proclaimed European Sports Car Mountain Champion for the first time. A week after Shelsley he went to Dublin, where he won the Irish GP. It had been another great season, but a shock was on its way—late in 1930, Mercedes pulled out of racing!

It was understandable, due to the Depression, but Alfred Neubauer managed to arrange a deal with the company whereby Rudi would buy a special SSK (which became the SSKL) and Mercedes would provide Neubauer (as Team Manager), mechanics and transport. By way of celebrating this new partnership, Caracciola won the 1931 Mille Miglia in record time, becoming the first non-Italian ever to win this race. It was another great year, as Rudi notched up 11 wins, including the Eifel, Avus and German GPs, and seven mountainclimbs, the latter clinching the Sports Car Championship for him yet again.

While 1931 had been a very successful year for Rudi, things had gone badly for Daimler-Benz commercially, so much so that they reluctantly announced that they could no longer afford to support him. So for 1932 Caracciola did the unthinkable and signed for a foreign team—Alfa Romeo.

In December of 1931 the Alfa Team Manager, Aldo Giovannini, visited Rudi in Arosa, bringing with him a contract for the next season. It was a good contract, but Caracciola was puzzled to find a clause stipulating that although he would be driving works Alfa Romeos, he would not actually be a part of the Alfa Romeo team. Giovannini reluctantly explained that the other drivers—Nuvolari, Borzacchini and Campari—had objected strongly to the idea of Caracciola joining them, using the lame excuse that he would find the Alfa too light after the ultra-heavy Mercedes and wouldn't be able to justify sharing the winnings, as was the Alfa Romeo custom. The main objector, apparently, was Campari, and it is far more likely that he simply didn't want a driver of Caracciola's calibre in the team. In spite of all this, Alfa Romeo insisted on approaching Rudi, who duly signed the contract.

His first race for his new team was the Mille Miglia, and he nearly won again, but a dropped valve forced him to a halt at Verona. Nuvolari and Campari also retired, but Borzacchini won and Alfas filled the first seven places.

So upset were the three Italian drivers at the inclusion of Caracciola in their team that they childishly insisted that in Grand Prix races only their cars should be painted red, which is how Rudi found himself driving a white Alfa at Monaco. He very nearly won this race, too, and the manner of his performance changed the whole atmosphere in the Alfa Romeo team.

Clutching his winner's medal, Rudi tells a delighted Charly all about it after his sensational victory in the 1931 Mille Miglia

Nuvolari won, but only just, as Rudi found himself catching the little Italian in the closing laps. With Caracciola drawing ever closer, Nuvolari was making frantic signs to his pit every time he passed, and his car was clearly slowing. On the final lap Caracciola was almost beside him and Rudi found himself faced with a dilemma—as he was not a member of the team there was no reason why he shouldn't pass Nuvolari and win, but for reasons he could never fully explain, he stayed behind him and the Italian won by a few metres as Rudi toured over the line.

As he pulled into the pits, a dejected Caracciola was jeered by the spectators, who clearly thought he had made some sort of deal with Nuvolari. The Little Man himself, however, was delighted and very grateful, insisting that Rudi join him on the winner's rostrum.

For the next few races, however, Caracciola's car (an 8C Monza) remained white. He came second, behind new-comer Manfred von Brauchitsch's streamlined Mercedes SSKL, at Avus and five days later was at the Nürburgring, where he won the Eifel GP. A week later Nuvolari won the Italian GP at Monza in the sensational new single-seater, P3 Alfa, Caracciola finishing third in his Monza, at last painted red. In July, Alfas had three P3s ready for the French GP at Reims and Caracciola finished third behind Nuvolari and Borzacchini, running to team orders. He then won the German GP (to team orders again) for the fourth time and in September he won the Monza GP on his own account. He also won five mountainclimbs, becoming European Mountain Champion proper for the first time. But at the end of the season it was Alfa Romeo's turn to withdraw from racing due to financial troubles and Caracciola was once again without a drive. Enter Louis Chiron.

The embodiment of Gallic charm and grace, Chiron was already a star when he first met Caracciola, which would have been around 1926. In that year he also met Alfred Hoffmann and his wife, Alice, whom everyone called Baby. Being heir to the Swiss Hoffmann–La Roche drug empire, Hoffmann was extremely rich and he was also very keen on fast cars and racing. He owned the Nerka spark plug company and, in order to get publicity for the firm, invited Chiron to race a Bugatti for him. They were very successful,

so much so that Louis was invited to join the official Bugatti team for 1928, with the condition that he could continue to drive for Hoffmann when the works team wasn't com-peting. Thus Chiron continued his successful relationship with his boss—and the boss's wife!

By all accounts Baby Hoffmann-Trobeck was a remark-able woman. Stunningly good-looking, she was also extremely intelligent, quick-witted and fluent in several languages. She was born in America to a Swedish father and German mother and had spent many years living in Europe by the time she met Chiron. She attended all the races with the Hoffman team, and her command of languages and flair for organization made her presence of great value. When Chiron joined Bugatti, Baby continued to go to the races, officially as the team's timekeeper, but by 1932 her relationship with Chiron was known to be more than just a matter of a stopwatch and at the end of the year her marriage to Freddie Hoffmann was dissolved. Now, of course, she was free to marry Chiron, but he, with an uncharacteristic lack of gallantry, made it clear that if he ever did marry, his bride would be somewhat younger than Baby, who was his own age, or thereabouts. In spite of this, the relationship flourished and Chiron and Baby were openly and without fuss accepted as a couple through-out the racing world. They also formed a close friendship with Rudi and Charly Caracciola.

At the end of the 1932 season, Chiron was fired by Bugatti. He was not surprised, as he had frequently been a law unto himself, ignoring Team Manager Meo Costan-

LEFT In 1933, Rudi crashed badly during practice for the Monaco GP. Here, he is carried away from the scene of the accident. It was to be over a year before he raced again

RIGHT Caracciola bravely made his comeback in the 1934 French GP. Here he corrects a slide in his W25 Mercedes

tini's instructions, and was already in the process of planning his own team. That winter he and Baby spent a lot of time in Arosa with the Caracciolas and one day he broached the idea of joining forces with Rudi for 1933. Their team would be called Scuderia CC and they would split all expenses and profits fifty-fifty. They'd been winning for other people for far too long—now they would be racing for themselves.

Caracciola jumped at the idea. In March 1933 it was announced that the new Scuderia CC had bought three Alfa Romeos and two 2.3 Bugattis. As well as competing in all forthcoming Grands Prix, Chiron and Caracciola would be sharing an Alfa at Le Mans. They signed on a couple of Italian mechanics, Mercedes lent them a diesel truck for transportation and they were in business.

The team's debut was at Monaco in April, where each had a gleaming new Monza Alfa, Chiron's in French racing blue with a white stripe and Caracciola's in German white with a blue stripe. The team's insignia—two Cs back-to-back—was prominent on each. But the partnership was destroyed before it ever started a race. After sharing fastest lap with Chiron, 2 min. 3 sec.—93.05 km/h (57.83 mph), on the first day of practice, Caracciola crashed badly on the second. He maintained that, on the downhill run from the tunnel to the chicane, a front brake locked and, rather than go to the left and risk falling into the harbour, he stayed on the right and hit the stone wall, very hard, at almost exactly the spot where Chiron had crashed his Bugatti the year before. It must be said, however, that

various observers were of the opinion that the great man made a rare mistake and misjudged his braking distance.

In his autobiography, Rudi wrote of the moments immediately following the crash: 'Nothing had happened. Only the body of the car was smashed, especially around my seat. Carefully I drew my leg out of the steel trap. Bracing myself against the frame of the body I slowly extricated myself from the seat. Behind me an ear-splitting screech . . . the brakes of Chiron's car. I looked around. He stopped just behind me and jumped out of the car. Other people came running down the stone steps.

'I tried to hurry out of the car. I wanted to show that nothing had happened to me, that I was absolutely unhurt. I stepped to the ground. At that instant the pain flashed through my leg. It was a ferocious pain, as if my leg were being slashed with hot, glowing knives. I collapsed, Chiron catching me in his arms.'

Someone fetched a chair from a nearby tobacco shop and Caracciola was then carried on it to the shop, where he waited in great pain for an ambulance. Meanwhile, in the pits an anxious Charly was waiting for news with Baby, who later recalled, 'Chiron came in and said, "Nothing serious—just a wound on the nose." But to me he pointed to his hip and I understood that it was bad.'

It was worse than bad, it was terrible. Caracciola's right thigh was shattered at the point where it joined the hip. After X-rays at Monte Carlo Hospital, doctors told Charly that her husband would never be able to race again and a day or so later Caracciola—his lower body encased in

plaster—was told that an operation was considered necessary. He refused this, convinced that it would mean the end of his racing career, unaware that the doctors had already come to this conclusion, operation or no operation.

One of his first visitors was Aldo Giovannini, the Alfa Romeo Team Manager. He, too, was horrified at the thought of an operation and insisted that Caracciola see an Italian specialist, Professor Putti. The Professor had Rudi transferred to his own clinic—the Rizzoli Orthopaedic Institute—in Bologna where he stayed for months, still in plaster, but without the dreaded operation.

Eventually, Rudi was allowed to leave the clinic. He and Charly went to stay with some friends at Lugano where, in mid-November, he was visited by Alfred Neubauer. His old friend brought the exciting news that Mercedes-Benz were going racing once more and that their new single-seater—built to the new 750 kg Formula—was well under way. Would Rudi be ready to race for his old team in the new season? Caracciola had only one answer—of course! But Neubauer wasn't convinced. He could see that Rudi was still very much an invalid and that it was highly unlikely that he could be of much use to Mercedes the following year. Nevertheless, Caracciola went to Stuttgart in January and signed a contract with Mercedes for 1934. Then he and Charly went to their chalet in Arosa.

Now that they were back home Rudi urged Charly to go skiing, which she loved to do, but she refused, insisting on staying with him all the time and helping him to walk properly again. His progress was painfully slow, but steady, and as he became fitter and more self-reliant he tried again to persuade her to get out on the slopes. Finally she relented and agreed to go with some friends, spurred on by Rudi's promise to meet her at the station on her return in the afternoon. But Charly never did return.

Caracciola duly met the train, but neither Charly nor any of her friends was on it. He went home to wait, knowing that he could see the trains arrive from his chalet, but as the evening went by there was still no Charly. At 7 pm the phone rang and someone told him that the skiing party would be returning from Lenzerheide on the last train, 'after the accident'. The last train duly arrived at 9.30 pm and an anxious Rudi saw a lone skiier trudging up to the chalet. He brought terrible news—an avalanche had buried the entire group and everyone had got out alive save Charly, who had apparently died of a heart attack.

At that time Louis Chiron and Baby Hoffmann were themselves skiing at Zurs, in Austria. It was Caracciola's doctor who telephoned them with the news of the tragedy and asked them to go to their friend as he was in a state of complete shock. On hearing this, Baby remembered how, a few hours after Caracciola's crash at Monaco, Charly had told her of the horoscope she had had prepared just previously for herself and Rudi. For him it had forecast a bad accident followed by a long convalescence, after which he would leave Charly. Early in 1934 the influence of his wife would cease. . . . Chiron and Baby stayed with Caracciola for some time and slowly he came back to life. It was Louis who suggested that he should do a lap of honour at Monaco and, after some persuasion, he agreed.

It must have seemed to most people that the great man's

career was over. Certainly Neubauer had his doubts about his friend's future as a racing driver—doubts that were reflected in the official Mercedes-Benz entries for the Avus and Eifel races, where the team's three drivers were listed as von Brauchitsch, Fagioli and 'X'. Caracciola, however, had no such doubts, insisting on trying one of the new cars at Avus late in May. He drove very well, but was obviously in considerable pain after only a few laps, and this was on a circuit comprising two very long straights and a slow corner at each end—kid's stuff compared to the Nürburgring. How could he possibly drive there?

He didn't. Wisely he refrained from entering the Eifel GP, opting instead to make his comeback at the French GP at Montlhéry, where he showed all his old mastery in an exciting battle for the lead with Louis Chiron's Alfa and Luigi Fagioli's Mercedes. The battle ended with Chiron victorious after all the Mercedes and Auto Unions had retired—a humiliating defeat for the Germans. Nonetheless, before his engine expired Caracciola had driven brilliantly for nearly 1½ hours—he was back in business.

Two weeks later came the acid test—the German GP at the Nürburgring—and Caracciola passed it brilliantly. For 12 laps of that tortuous circuit he harried Hans Stuck in the Auto Union, both drivers breaking the lap record several times. On lap 13 he actually passed Stuck into the lead, to the huge delight of the packed grandstands. But it was all too much for the Mercedes' engine and Rudi failed to complete the next lap. Stuck went on to win, but Caracciola got his revenge the next month, beating the *Bergmeister* at the Klausenpass mountainclimb.

Rudi's impressive return to form continued in the opening laps of the Coppa Acerbo at Pescara, where he led for the first seven rounds, ahead of a terrific battle between Stuck (Auto Union), Varzi (Alfa Romeo) and Fagioli (Mercedes), who were constantly swapping places behind him. Then, on lap 8, Caracciola had a very big accident on the Pescara-Cappelle sul Tavo leg. It had been raining until shortly before the start of the race and it seems likely that he came suddenly upon a corner in the hills where it was raining again. Whatever the reason, the Mercedes went off the road and into a field, where it crashed heavily. By all accounts Rudi was very lucky to limp away with only cuts and bruises, but that right hip was given a severe bashing, too. Despite this, he was back in action only four days later, at Freiburg, although clearly not at his best. He finished second, nearly 26 seconds slower than Hans Stuck in this German Mountain Championship decider.

The rest of Caracciola's season was none too bright—he finished tenth and last in the Swiss GP (sharing the driving with Hanns Geier) and had to hand his car over to Fagioli at Monza. After the triple tragedy of the 1933 Italian GP (when Campari, Borzacchini and Czaikowski were killed), the Italian authorities over-reacted by reducing the circuit length drastically and littering it with chicanes, giving the drivers 1600 corners to navigate in 116 laps! All this was too much for Rudi's battered leg and he had to retire at half-distance when in second place. Fagioli took over his car and went on to win. Fagioli won again in Spain, with Rudi second, and in the last race of the year at Brno Caracciola retired after breaking a wheel on the very rough

Czechoslovakian roads.

Throughout the year he had been supported and encouraged by his friends Chiron and Baby and they seemed to spend as much time together as they had when Charly was alive. This friendship was of paramount importance where Rudi's mental recovery was concerned, for the two of them cajoled and harried him at the appropriate times, convincing him that life must go on. Another useful, if unintentional, therapy was undoubtedly Neubauer's choice of Luigi Fagioli for the Mercedes team. The volatile Italian was a brilliant driver who clearly regarded the limping Caracciola as his Number Two, and this was a great spur to Caracciola's ambition!

But the greatest spur was Baby. Over the winter of 1934–5 Caracciola spent a lot of time in Paris, where Baby kept an apartment. Sometimes they were with Chiron, sometimes not. Over the next two years their relationship blossomed, as did Caracciola's resurgent career. It has often been said that 1935 was Caracciola's *annus mirabilis*— it certainly was, and how! He won six of the 11 races he entered that year, in spite of (and no doubt because of) the spirited and often furious opposition from Fagioli.

Rudi had no luck at Monaco, retiring with a broken valve. Fagioli won. It was Caracciola's turn at Tripoli, then Fagioli's again at Avus. Caracciola then won the Eifel GP at the 'Ring, but only by the skin of his teeth, from the amazing Rosemeyer. In the French GP he won again, after a fairly long battle with Fagioli, until the latter was slowed with engine trouble and von Brauchitsch closed up to within a couple of cars' lengths. But von Brauchitsch behaved himself, unlike the Italian, and did not attempt to pass his team leader. Fagioli won the next event, however, the Penya Rhin GP at Barcelona, and Caracciola had to be content with second place.

It was his turn to win again at Spa, but only just, as Fagioli again went against Neubauer's orders and tried to take the lead. He eventually abandoned his car at the pits in disgust with Neubauer's 'favouritism' and was promptly replaced by von Brauchitsch, who had retired his own car earlier. He was feeling unwell in the German GP and could only finish third, but it is doubtful if even a fully fit Caracciola could have done much about the amazing Nuvolari on that particular day. He then won the Swiss GP, but at Monza finished nowhere, although he may have got some perverse satisfaction out of handing over his failing car to Fagioli! Finally, he won the Spanish GP at San Sebastian, from Fagioli and von Brauchitsch. He had won six races to Fagioli's three and was declared the first European Champion. For a man who, less than two years before, had been told he would never drive again, it was a truly remarkable comeback.

In spite of Rudi's unconcealed interest in Baby Hoffmann, his friendship with Louis Chiron continued to thrive. Indeed, Caracciola urged Alfred Neubauer to sign Chiron for 1936, which he did, making him the first Frenchman to drive for Mercedes since Louis Wagner in 1914. But it was a disastrous year for the team, whose new, short-chassis cars were completely outclassed by Auto Union and the amazing Rosemeyer. Chiron got off to an encouraging start, making fastest lap in practice at Monaco, but in the

Rudi was back to his old, dazzling form in 1935, winning six GPs. Here he rounds the hairpin of L'Ancienne Douanne at Spa, on his way to victory in the Belgian GP

race—in what was an uncanny repeat of the disasters that had befallen him in 1932 and Caracciola in 1933—Louis crashed at the chicane, part of a famous pile-up.

Moments after the start an oil pipe broke on Tadini's Alfa, and instead of stopping Tadini continued, laying an oil slick right round the circuit, which was already awash with rain. On lap 2 Chiron hit the oil at the chicane and slid helplessly into the wall, followed at once by Farina's Alfa, von Brauchitsch's Mercedes, Trossi's Maserati and Tadini's Alfa—the culprit having done *another* lap! Seven laps later Fagioli slid into the wall right next to Chiron's abandoned car, so three Mercedes were out and the race was hardly begun! After a marvellous early scrap with Nuvolari's Alfa, Caracciola 'the Rainmaster' saved the day and won, with a truly brilliant drive in the most atrocious conditions.

Rudi won at Tunis, too, but that was the end of the line for Mercedes in 1936. Poor Chiron crashed at high speed in the German GP and, although he wasn't badly hurt, he never drove for Mercedes again. After a humiliating year, the company pulled out of racing before the end of the season, reorganized its Racing Department and set about designing new cars for 1937.

Much to Caracciola's relief, no doubt, Fagioli left Mercedes at the end of the year, to join Auto Union. Chiron's career with Mercedes was also over, so Alfred Neubauer was looking for some new faces for 1937 and he found them in Hermann Lang (who had been a cadet driver with the team for the past two seasons) and Dick Seaman.

Like Mercedes, Caracciola decided to put things right for 1937—he asked Baby Hoffmann to marry him. At first she demurred, her affections torn between Rudi and Chiron. On several occasions she had asked Louis to marry her, but he had always refused. Now, with Rudi pleading for her hand, she asked one more time, and again he declined. So, she packed her bags, left her Paris apartment and took the train for Lugano, where Rudi was waiting. When Chiron found out he was furious, and his anger was directed at Caracciola for stealing 'his' woman. It was pointed out to him that Baby was not his woman at all, although he had been given ample opportunity to make her so, and that Rudi had not taken her from her husband, as Chiron himself had done a few years previously. Chiron couldn't—or wouldn't—see the logic of this at all!

Nonetheless, the die was cast and Baby and Rudi were married on 19 June 1937, in Lugano, with Dr Wilhelm Haspel of Daimler-Benz and his wife as witnesses. Ten years before Caracciola had bought a plot of land in nearby Ruvigliana, overlooking the beautiful lake. He promised Baby a house there as a wedding present and within a year, *Casa Scania* was ready. They were to live there for the rest of their lives.

Three days after their marriage, the newly-weds joined the Mercedes and Auto Union teams on the *Bremen* and sailed for New York and the Vanderbilt Cup. It would be nice to record that the honeymooner won the race, but he didn't even finish. So far the season had gone badly (apart from a second place in the Eifel GP) with a lowly sixth at Tripoli and retirements at Avus and in New York. But none of these events counted towards the European Championship and although he missed the first *Grande Epreuve* in Belgium (it clashed with the Vanderbilt Cup), Rudi won three of the remaining four championship races—the German, Swiss and Italian GPs—thus regaining the title he had lost to Bernd Rosemeyer the year before. And that wasn't all—he won the Masaryk GP at the end of September and a week later came third at Donington.

It had been a marvellous comeback by Mercedes after their disastrous 1936 season. The new 5.6-litre W125 was

ABOVE **Rudi and Baby Hoffmann after their wedding in Lugano, 1937**

ABOVE RIGHT **There was a Concours d'Elegance before the 1937 Czech GP at Brno and Rudi and Baby are seen here in a 540K Mercedes. Next day Caracciola won the race**

a superb racing machine which won seven of the 12 races the team entered, and with four of those victories to his credit, Caracciola showed yet again that he was one of the all-time greats.

Mercedes took two of their new 3-litre cars to Pau for a shakedown before the 1938 season proper got under way. One car was damaged in practice, so Caracciola and Lang shared the other in the race, Lang taking over when the W154's voracious appetite for fuel necessitated a pit stop. The 4.5-litre Delahaye of René Dreyfus was not so thirsty, however, and the Frenchman ran non-stop to record a sensational victory over the mighty German team. Rudi finished third at Tripoli, second at Reims and then retired in the German GP with an upset stomach.

He retired again in the Coppa Ciano, but won the Coppa

Acerbo a fortnight later in fine style. Then came the Swiss GP and here Rudi put up one of the finest performances of his remarkable career. The race was run in pouring rain and although Dick Seaman led initially, he was unable to match Caracciola's almost unbelievable wet-weather skills. Rudi led Seaman home to win by 26 seconds. After all their recent success Mercedes came badly unstuck at Monza, where Caracciola's was the only one of their four cars to finish the Italian GP, and was lucky to do so! After an early and uncharacteristic spin, Rudi's car began to overheat, burning his feet. When he stopped for fuel he handed over to von Brauchitsch, who found the cockpit far too hot for comfort and soon handed it back! Rudi finished third, thus clinching the European Championship for 1938. His burnt foot meant that he missed Donington, although 'those in the know' claimed that the poor man was actually suffering from piles!

In February 1939, Mercedes went record-breaking on a specially prepared stretch of *autobahn* at Dessau, where Rudi recorded nearly 400 km/h (250 mph) over the Flying Mile—and this in a 3-litre car! These new records were almost the last taste of success Caracciola was to experience in his great career. Although he was still the Mercedes team leader, the young lions, Hermann Lang and Dick Seaman,

were making their bid for the top and whereas Lang was to succeed in his attempt, poor Seaman was not. Lang won virtually every race he entered that year, leaving Caracciola trailing in his wake. Rudi retired at Pau, was second behind Lang at Tripoli, third in the Eifel GP and, almost unbelievably, went off the road at Spa. This tragic race (in which Dick Seaman was killed) was run in real Caracciola weather—pouring rain—yet *Der Regenmeister* made an extraordinary mistake and accelerated too hard as he left the hairpin at La Source. The Mercedes spun onto the grass and stalled, facing the wrong way, so Rudi was out of the race. Incredibly, he made another mistake just two weeks later, on the very first lap of the French GP at Reims. On a dry road he crashed into a house at Gueux village and had to retire on the spot. Caracciola was now 38 years old and it was clear to most that his phenomenal skills were beginning to desert him, and many people attributed these most un-Caracciola-like lapses to the pressure he was feeling from young Hermann Lang.

Rudi redeemed himself at the Nürburgring, however, winning the German Grand Prix for the sixth time. It was his last victory, though, for Lang beat him again at Bern and he didn't go to Belgrade for what was to be the last Grand Prix for many years.

Caracciola had lived in Switzerland since 1929, and that is where he and Baby stayed throughout the war. Although still a German citizen he was too old for military service and anyway, he had no love for the Nazi Party. He had next to no money, either, for since 1933 it had been illegal to take money out of Germany without special permission, and that permission was seldom given. However, Dr Wilhelm Kissel made him a Director of Daimler-Benz and ensured that his salary was sent to Switzerland, but in 1942 the payments were stopped on the orders of the NSKK (*Nationalsozialistisches Kraftfahrer Korps*). He and Baby had to live on their savings from then on.

For all the love and care Baby lavished on Rudi, she was not able to dissuade him from making a comeback after the war and, indeed, there is no evidence to suggest that she even tried. Racing was his life, even if he was well past his prime.

In 1946 Caracciola went to America and was offered a drive at Indianapolis. He was 45 years old. During his quali-

fying laps—just after he had passed his rookie drivers' test—his car inexplicably went out of control at high speed and crashed terribly. Rudi was thrown out and suffered severe head injuries. After a lengthy stay in hospital he was allowed home to Lugano and early in 1947 Rodney Walkerley met him and Baby in London one day. Within the limitations of their different languages, Rodney had known Rudi quite well before the war and had always found him to be bright and pleasant. 'Now he was a different man,' wrote Walkerley, after their meeting. 'Shaky, uncertain of speech, he needed his sad wife's arm as well as a stick.'

Caracciola took many months to recover, but he did, with tremendous help and encouragement in constant supply from Baby. How she must have longed for him to announce his retirement but, in spite of the advancing years and his terrible injuries, he was determined to race again. When Mercedes decided to take their pre-war cars to Argentina in February 1951, Neubauer invited Caracciola to drive one of them, but he refused, saying the cars were too old. The same, alas, could and should have been said of Caracciola, but he insisted on competing in the Mille Miglia the next year with the exciting new 300SL. He finished fourth in the race he'd won 21 years before. He was going to drive at Le Mans, but a few weeks before the race Mercedes entered a sports car event at Bern, the scene of three of his Grand Prix triumphs. On lap 13 a brake apparently locked up and the 300SL hit a tree at high speed. This time it was his left thigh that was smashed. Finally, Rudolf Caracciola's extraordinary career was over.

He died in 1959, at the relatively early age of 58, his death unquestionably hastened by his two, terrible, post-war crashes. Baby lived with her memories in *Casa Scania*, until she, too, passed away, in the mid-seventies.

Rudolf Caracciola was, quite simply, one of the greatest racing drivers of all time and he had already established himself as such when he crashed at Monaco. What makes him all the more remarkable is that with a handicap that would have wrecked a lesser man's career, he returned to the fray and won no less than 15 Grands Prix and three European Championships. This has to be one of the most astonishing comebacks in sporting history and there is no doubt that a lot of the credit must go to his wife, Baby.

Caracciola was extremely fortunate that in Charly and Baby he found two women whose ambition for him matched his own and who had the strength and intelligence to support and encourage the dangerous career of a great racing driver. Rudi could hardly have made such a success of his life without them and while Charly's death was a crippling blow, his partnership with Baby seems almost to have been pre-ordained. A few years before Charly died Baby gave the Caracciolas a photograph of herself which they kept in their chalet in Arosa. Charly was very fond of Baby and would happily show the photo to friends, saying, 'This is Baby Hoffmann, Rudi's silent love.'

Little did any of them know. . . .

LEFT **After spinning into a wall at Gueux on the very first lap of the 1939 French GP, Caracciola pushes his Mercedes off the course, leaving a trail of fuel from a split petrol tank**

BELOW **Final victory. Caracciola joins *Korpsführer* Hühnlein in a Nazi salute after his victory in the 1939 German GP—the last win of his extraordinary career**

Manfred von Brauchitsch

Team Driver, Mercedes-Benz 1934–39

He was known as *Pechvogel*, the unlucky bird. Not for many racing drivers can you make out a career scorecard of races won and lost, but you can for Manfred von Brauchitsch: won—three; lost—five. His three victories were the 1934 Eifel GP; the 1937 Monaco GP and the 1938 French GP. His five losses (and they really were races the winner lost!) were the 1935 German GP; the 1938 German GP; the 1938 Coppa Ciano; the 1939 Pau GP and the 1939 Belgrade GP. Unlucky Manfred!

Although he was an extremely fast and courageous driver, von Brauchitsch was destined always to race in the shadow of one of his Mercedes team mates—first Rudolf Caracciola, then Hermann Lang—but if he never quite made it to the very top of the Grand Prix drivers' tree, he had a damned good try and in a most spectacular fashion.

He was born in Hamburg on 15 August 1905, into a military family. His father had been a Major in the German Army and his uncle, Walther von Brauchitsch, rose to be a General by 1938. (In February of that year Hitler, by typically devious means, got rid of his Army Commander in Chief, General Werner von Blomberg, and gave the post to von Brauchitsch. In July 1940 he made him a Field Marshal along with 11 other Generals, thus debasing the rank while putting the Generals in his pocket. Once again, the ex-Corporal outsmarted his senior officers!)

In January 1924, when he was 18, Manfred's father entered him as an officer-cadet in the 5th Infantry Regiment, garrisoned at Greifswald, on Germany's north coast, about 200 km (125 miles) from Berlin. A small inheritance enabled von Brauchitsch to buy a motorcycle which, in turn, enabled him to leave the army. In the autumn of 1928 he had a serious accident which put him into the garrison hospital with a fractured skull, four broken ribs and a broken arm and leg. He spent three months in hospital and then went to stay with a cousin in Nischwitz, near Leipzig. His army career was over.

The cousin lived in a 40-room castle. His hobby was motor cars and he owned three, one of which was a supercharged Mercedes. Manfred was fascinated and persuaded his cousin to teach him to drive, but it was a visit to a cinema in the nearby town of Wurzen that was to change his life. There one night he saw the weekly newsreel, the *Wochenshau*, part of which was devoted to a motor race. Manfred was transfixed by the speeding cars, so much so that he went again the next night. And that was it—he had to become a racing driver.

He outlined his ambition to his cousin, who thought it a good idea, but pointed out that first he really ought to get a driving licence! That done, Manfred made his competition debut on 8 September 1929, in the Gaisberg mountainclimb, near Salzburg. Driving his generous cousin's Mercedes SS he won the Sports Car Class at record speed. Impressed, the cousin agreed that Manfred could have the SS modified to SSK specification for 1930, but unfortunately, the combination had no luck that year, although Manfred was learning all the time.

For 1931 the ever-supportive cousin was persuaded to have the SSK turned into an SSKL and with it von Brauchitsch came third at Avus, behind Caracciola (also in an SSKL) and H. J. von Morgen (Bugatti). Then he went to the Nürburgring for the first time. The Eifel GP was still being run on the 7.8 km (4.8 mile) *Sudschleife*—not the full circuit—and once again Manfred finished third behind Caracciola and von Morgen. Later in the year he won the Sports Car Class at Gaisberg once more, but then luck deserted him and he crashed heavily in another mountainclimb and wound up in hospital with his jaw and several ribs broken and concussion.

The crash didn't dull his ambition for a moment and as soon as he was back on his feet he was trying to get some support from Mercedes-Benz for the 1932 season. The Stuttgart concern was not interested (even Caracciola had had to join Alfa Romeo that year) but Manfred did get some help from an accessory firm, which enabled him to enter the SSKL for the Avus GP in May. His entry was to have far-reaching effects on motor racing.

Von Brauchitsch had a friend named Reinhard von Koenig-Fachsenfeld, who was one of the pioneers of automobile aerodynamics. Learning of Manfred's entry in this very fast race, he suggested that he had no chance of winning unless he fitted a special, streamlined body to the SSKL which would enable him to go much faster down the long, long straights of Avus. Von Brauchitsch was interested in the idea, but had no money for what would clearly be an expensive modification. Even so, he and von Koenig-Fachsenfeld made enquiries and found that the Vetter company in Bad Cannstatt could do the job for 500 DM. It was Manfred's mechanic, Willi Zimmer, who came to the rescue by lending him the money for the new body.

The big, streamlined car caused a sensation when it appeared. It also caused problems in practice when the tyres started to throw bits of tread at high speed. New tyres with a much thinner tread were hurriedly produced and von Brauchitsch was able to start the race. His principal adversary turned out to be Rudolf Caracciola in the works Alfa and for a while Rudi led the race. But the new tyres on von Brauchitsch's big white Mercedes held together and, gaining confidence every lap, Manfred increased his speed and eventually took the lead, which he held to the end. His time of 1 hr 30 min. 53.4 sec. for the 20 laps was over four minutes faster than Caracciola's winning time in the 'normal' SSKL the previous year—ample proof that streamlining could pay big dividends. Mercedes-Benz paid von Koenig-Fachsenfeld the compliment of producing a virtually identical car at Avus the following year, and its influence was there for all to see when the W25 appeared in 1934.

This victory by the practically unknown von Brauchitsch in the revolutionary-looking Mercedes was truly sensational and Manfred was the hero of the hour. If this were

Unlucky Manfred von Brauchitsch is seen here after winning the 1938 Coppa Ciano from his team mate Hermann Lang (*right*). Minutes later he was disqualified for receiving outside assistance. Hanns Geier is in the background

a 1930s Hollywood film script, our handsome young hero would now be offered a starring role in a movie. And that's exactly what happened! Manfred was approached by the Majestic Film Company of Berlin, and asked to star in a film based loosely on his life story. It sounded like fun and the money was good, so he agreed. The film, *Kampf* (Battle), was made that same year, directed by Eric Schonfelder. It was quite well received by the public, but von Brauchitsch was not thrilled with movie-making and decided to stick to motor racing.

After its Avus victory the Mercedes SSKL was stripped of its streamlined skin and returned to its old shape. Naturally, Manfred used it as his racing car in the film before going back to proper competition work. He was not able to add to his Avus win, but he did finish third again in the Eifel GP. For the first time this race was run on the 22.8 km (14.2 mile) *Nordschleife* at the Nürburgring and, in order to learn it properly, Manfred put in ten laps a day for several days before the race. Caracciola won on his works Alfa Romeo, with René Dreyfus (Bugatti) second

and von Brauchitsch third.

In 1933 he received some assistance from Daimler-Benz, who were clearly keeping an eye on him for future reference. He came second in the Eifel GP, behind Nuvolari's Alfa, and scored class wins in such mountainclimbs as Kesselberg, Gabelbach and Freiburg. The SSKL was again fitted with streamlined bodywork for the Avus GP, but this time Manfred was plagued with tyre trouble which could not be cured. After no less than seven blow-outs, he could only finish sixth.

He had not had a brilliant year, but nonetheless, that winter Mercedes-Benz approached him and invited him to join them for 1934. This was the ultimate prize—he was now *Fabrikfahrer*—a works driver! Mercedes decided to withdraw from the Avus GP and so their first race was the Eifel GP at the Nürburgring. As his shattered thigh was not yet properly healed, Caracciola wisely gave this demanding race a miss, so von Brauchitsch was entered with Mercedes' third driver, Luigi Fagioli.

Von Brauchitsch's race almost ended at the first corner. A bunch of cars arrived there together and the Bugatti of the Austrian driver, Emil Frankl, touched another car and spun wildly in front of the two Mercedes before flying off the road and killing its driver. Von Brauchitsch missed the Bugatti by a whisker and went on to win the race in fine style. He could hardly have got off to a better start as a Grand Prix driver, winning his very first race for Mercedes in front of their home crowd. It was to be the first of many such victories for the team, but unlucky Manfred was not to win another race for three years.

A few days after the Eifel GP von Brauchitsch took part in the Kesselberg mountainclimb, but he was no match for Hans Stuck on the Auto Union. His next race was the French GP at Montlhéry, which turned out to be a complete débâcle for both German teams. Manfred was very fast in practice, setting a new lap record with a time of 5 min. 05.6 sec.—148.0 km/h (92.04 mph). The opening laps produced a stunning battle between the Mercedes of Caracciola, von Brauchitsch and Fagioli, the Alfa Romeos of Chiron and Varzi and the Auto Union of Stuck, the shrill scream of the Mercedes' superchargers sending shivers down the spines of the spectators as the cars hurtled round the banking and then flashed past the grandstand at around 265 km/h (165 mph). In spite of his superb practice time, von Brauchitsch was never in the hunt and retired with supercharger problems on lap 12.

The next race was the German Grand Prix and naturally, having won at the 'Ring in June, Manfred was determined to repeat his victory in July. Too determined, perhaps, for in practice he crashed heavily, putting himself in hospital with four broken ribs, a broken arm, shoulder-blade and collarbone.

Von Brauchitsch decided that he had to be back in action in time for the Swiss Grand Prix, just six weeks away. After a month in the Nürburgring *Krankenhaus* he had himself taken to Munich and then south to the little town of Urfeld, on the Walchensee. Here the owner of the Jager am See, a little *Gasthaus* Manfred had discovered on his first trip to Kesselberg in 1930, brought him back to health with the aid of mountain air, good food and beer! Manfred duly turned up in Bern for the Swiss GP, but getting there was one thing—driving a racing car was another. His injuries prevented him from getting in and out of his Mercedes unaided and he had to borrow a pillow from his hotel bed to support his back. Nonetheless, he started the race and ran for some time until forced out with engine trouble. It was no reward for all his effort, but the fact that he had achieved his objective of racing at Bern was a great morale-booster, and he flew to Stuttgart already making plans for the Italian GP.

It was not to be. Manfred was bothered by a pain in his left eye and a thorough medical revealed that he was suffering from a fractured skull! This was causing internal bleeding and pressure on the optic nerve, so he was sent immediately to an eye hospital in Davos, Switzerland. For the next ten weeks he was allowed to do nothing—no reading, no writing and no excitement. He wasn't even allowed to listen to the radio broadcasts of the races he was missing.

Von Brauchitsch did not race again in 1934, but he was fully fit in time for the opening race of the 1935 season, at Monaco. He'd never been there before, but was immediately very fast in practice, although apparently driving on the ragged edge much of the time. He got himself on the front row of the grid with team mates Fagioli and Caracciola, only to retire after one lap with a broken gearbox. Unlucky Manfred! At Tripoli the grid positions were still allotted by ballot, and this time von Brauchitsch found himself on the sixth row (of seven). He lasted six laps before retiring with engine trouble. Unlucky Manfred! At Avus he fared a little better, but not much, finishing third in his

heat and a lowly fifth in the final after a stop for new tyres.

Back at the Nürburgring in June, for the first time since his crash, Manfred set about the Eifel GP in a very determined fashion. He was fastest by far in the first day's practice, recording a sensational 10 min. 45 sec., whereas Caracciola could only do 10 min. 59 sec. and Stuck 11 min. 04 sec. It rained the next day, so those remained the fastest times and from the sound of the 'Ring's cannon on the Sunday von Brauchitsch went straight into the lead. At the end of the first lap he was 22 seconds ahead of Caracciola and after three laps had extended this to 55 seconds. The weather was varying from heavy rain to bright sunlight and the changes in temperature around the course were causing a lot of ignition problems. Fagioli stopped for new plugs and suddenly von Brauchitsch's lead was seen to be diminishing rapidly. He, too, was in plug trouble, but he compounded this problem by over-revving disastrously when passing Balestrero's Alfa Romeo, blowing his engine. He toured in to the pits to retire, getting a tremendous reception from the packed grandstands. This time, however, it was not so much 'Unlucky Manfred' as 'Careless Manfred' for with his large lead he had no need to over-stress his engine.

At Montlhéry he at last got a good result, finishing second behind Caracciola in the French GP and dutifully obeying Neubauer's orders not to fight for the lead. Mercedes only sent Caracciola and Fagioli to Barcelona for the Penya Rhin GP, so Manfred's next race was the Belgian GP at Spa. For many laps he held a secure second place behind Caracciola with Fagioli third, but on lap 15 his Mercedes suddenly slowed as it climbed the hill after the Ancienne Douane hairpin. Von Brauchitsch made it back to the pits, where all the plugs were changed, but to no avail and he retired the next lap. Now Fagioli began to challenge Caracciola, which was strictly against team orders. Angrily, Neubauer flagged him in and an equally angry Fagioli got out of his car and refused to continue. Von Brauchitsch was quickly summoned from behind the pits, where he was having a nice siesta and a cool drink, and told to get back in the race. While all this was going on, Chiron and Dreyfus on the Ferrari Alfas had taken second and third places, much to Neubauer's disgust. It was therefore up to von Brauchitsch to drive as fast as he knew how and restore the Mercedes' one-two.

Manfred set about his task with gusto, providing the spectators with a marvellous sight. As Harold Nockolds wrote in *Motor Sport*, 'von Brauchitsch does not possess the genius of a Caracciola, a Fagioli or a Chiron, but he gets amazingly good results all the same. His approach to a corner is always rather ragged, and involves a great deal of vigorous work with the steering wheel and some violent use of the brakes. Now he had his opportunity to show us what he could do.'

What he could do was to catch Dreyfus on lap 27 (of 34) and set off after Chiron. Two laps later he was right on the Alfa's tail as they swept downhill past the pits. Both drivers slid wildly on the left-hander at Eau Rouge and for a moment it looked as though they would crash, but they held the slides and drove on, von Brauchitsch finally passing Chiron at the very top of the hill. He continued to drive flat out, setting a new lap record of 5 min. 23 sec. (165.66 km/h—102.94 mph) in the process.

Sadly, Manfred's marvellous press-on style of driving which served him so well at Spa was to be his downfall in the very next event, the German Grand Prix. This race has passed into legend as Nuvolari's victory, but in truth it was 'the race the winner lost', the losing winner being von Brauchitsch. At half distance Caracciola, von Brauchitsch, Nuvolari and Rosemeyer were virtually wheel-to-wheel all the way round and then all four came into the pits for tyres and fuel. Amid scenes of huge excitement, Manfred got away first, but Nuvolari was badly delayed by sloppy work in the Alfa pit. Furious, the Italian maestro embarked on one of the greatest drives of even his extraordinary career, passing Caracciola into second place and going after von Brauchitsch. But the Mercedes always had the legs of the Alfa Romeo and Manfred started the last lap 35 seconds ahead of Nuvolari. However, his furious driving style—while tremendously thrilling for the spectators—was ruinous for his tyres on the twisty Nürburgring. Two or three laps from the end Neubauer knew he ought to call Manfred in for new rubber, but to have done so would have handed the race to Nuvolari. He just had to hope and pray that the tyres would last under von Brauchitsch's furious assault as he strove to keep Nuvolari at bay. They didn't. As the Mercedes approached the Karussell for the last time, the left rear tyre blew and the race was Nuvolari's. Von Brauchitsch eventually crossed the line in fifth place, his tyre completely stripped from the rim.

Not surprisingly he received a hero's welcome from the grandstand and the crowded pits and, also not surprisingly, he was in tears. His mechanics helped him from the car and made a way for him through the crowds to the pit, where he sat forlornly in a corner looking at the stacks of new tyres that lay all around him. Back at the Eifeler Hof Hotel in Adenau, Louis Chiron stopped by his room for a few minutes to massage his aching limbs and Nuvolari brought him an armful of flowers from his victory bouquet. Unlucky Manfred. . . .

Mercedes did not compete in the next two races, the Coppas Ciano and Acerbo, needing time to recover, perhaps, from their defeat at the 'Ring. In the Swiss GP von Brauchitsch became involved in a fierce duel with Louis Chiron on an Alfa in the rain. Chiron crashed badly, luckily without serious hurt, and very shortly afterwards the Mercedes went off song and retired. At Monza, Manfred was lying fifth in the Italian GP when failing brakes sent him through one of the chicanes and off the road. He had better luck in the Spanish GP, finishing third behind Caracciola and Fagioli. And that was the end of his season.

Like many of his contemporaries—Caracciola, Chiron, Wimille and Seaman, for example—Manfred was very fond of skiing and in the first days of each January he would go to his friendly *gasthaus* on the Walchensee. There he could go for long walks in the mountains and ski to his heart's content. For all that the 1936 season brought him he might as well have stayed there that year.

At Monaco he was involved in the celebrated second-lap pile-up at the chicane and his race was over on the spot. At Tripoli he retired with engine trouble after 16 laps. In the Eifel GP he retired and Mercedes could only finish in fifth and sixth positions. Things got worse a week later in Hungary, when the three Mercedes of Caracciola, von Brauchitsch and Chiron all failed! The problem was traced to a weakness in the cylinder design and a great deal of work was done at Untertürkheim before the all-important German GP on 26 July, but to no avail. Mercedes entered five cars, and only two finished, in fifth and seventh places, von Brauchitsch sharing the latter with Hermann Lang.

Mercedes were now in such deep trouble that they gave the next two races (the Coppas Ciano and Acerbo) a miss, giving themselves a month to get ready for the Swiss GP. Again they failed, and Rosemeyer led Auto Union home to a spectacular one-two-three. Now thoroughly depressed, Mercedes withdrew from racing altogether and set about a complete rethink for 1937.

A fair amount of haggling seems to have gone on over the winter months, before von Brauchitsch signed with Daimler-Benz for the new season. However, he turned up

Manfred's car finished up in the woods following his crash during practice for the 1937 Belgian GP

at Monza for the annual Spring Training and was one of the four-man team which went to Tripoli for the first race of the year. Hermann Lang scored a magnificent victory for Mercedes in the brilliant new W125 and von Brauchitsch was the only member of the team to retire. Unlucky Manfred!

At Avus two weeks later he drove one of the three streamlined Mercedes, his car having the 5.6-litre V-12 DAB engine that had proved too heavy for Formula races. Manfred won his heat at a staggering 258 km/h (160.4 mph), but was forced out of the final with a broken oil line. In the Eifel GP both Caracciola and von Brauchitsch strove mightily, but there was simply nothing they could do about the incredible Bernd Rosemeyer, who won his third consecutive race at the 'Ring. The two Mercedes were second and third.

Both German teams now had to split their forces, in order to compete in the Vanderbilt Cup in New York and the Belgian GP at Spa, the races being run on consecutive weekends. Von Brauchitsch was detailed to go to Belgium with Hermann Lang. He had a very lucky escape during practice when he left his braking too late for the hairpin after the Eau Rouge bend. The car hit an embankment, somersaulted through the air and landed on its wheels in the woods. Apart from a few cuts, Manfred was unhurt. In the race he had a great battle with Hans Stuck in the opening laps, setting a new lap record at nearly 170 km/h (105 mph) in the process, but it was too much for his engine and he had to retire.

Two weeks later von Brauchitsch got his first decent result for a long time, finishing second behind Caracciola in the German GP. Almost unbelievably, it was the first time Mercedes had won their own Grand Prix for six years!

Then came Monaco. Although he had had no success here in the past two years, Manfred enjoyed the little round-the-houses circuit, which might have been made to order for his flamboyant driving style. With its short straights between tight corners running up and down the hills of the Principality, Monaco enabled von Brauchitsch to have fun, throwing the big Mercedes around in a series of ear-splitting powerslides. And have fun he did. He lay second to Caracciola in the early laps, with Bernd Rosemeyer snapping at his heels in the Auto Union until his steering failed and he charged the sandbanks at the Gasometer hairpin.

Instead of easing up after Rosemeyer's departure, Manfred went faster and faster, setting a new lap record at 1 min. 49.1 sec. on lap 21. He now closed right up on Caracciola and started to harry his team leader, much to the annoyance of Alfred Neubauer, who waved his flag at him furiously in an attempt to slow him down. Manfred just stuck out his tongue at Don Alfredo and drove even faster! So hard did he push Caracciola that on lap 32 Rudi set a new record with 1 min. 48 sec., but it was too much for his engine, and he was forced into a long pit stop for new plugs. By the time he got going again, von Brauchitsch was a lap ahead.

Rudi began a glorious charge and slowly regained his lost ground. On lap 69 von Brauchitsch stopped for fuel and rear wheels and as he rejoined the race Caracciola

swooped on him. 'There began', wrote Rodney Walkerley, 'as fine a piece of motor racing as I have ever seen.' They screamed past the pits side by side, with Neubauer and the mechanics shouting and waving at von Brauchitsch to let Caracciola by (at least, Caracciola's mechanics were—Manfred's were doubtless urging him to stay in front!) Von Brauchitsch continued to stick his tongue out at them and continued to keep Caracciola behind him, even though he set another (and final) lap record on lap 74, with the staggering time of 1 min. 46.5 sec. (107.49 km/h—66.79 mph). This beat the old record by 11.9 sec. and was itself to remain unbeaten for 18 years! Finally, after ten laps of this glorious dog-fight, Manfred let Rudi through, knowing that Caracciola would have to stop for new tyres, which he did almost immediately. Von Brauchitsch ran out a most worthy winner, the first man to average over 100 km/h for the race, that average being nearly 5 km/h (3 mph) faster than the previous lap record.

Although Manfred had blatantly disobeyed Neubauer's instructions, there were no recriminations afterwards. Caracciola, too, had no complaints and in the early hours of the next morning, after Mercedes' victory dinner, the two men did one more lap of the Monaco circuit—in a horsedrawn cab!

Von Brauchitsch was unable to repeat that epic victory during the remainder of the season. A week after Monaco Mercedes were in Pescara for the Coppa Acerbo, where Manfred was second to Bernd Rosemeyer, and the following weekend he was third in the Swiss GP behind his two team mates. He retired in the Italian GP at Livorno and finished the season with two second places, at Brno and Donington. He drove brilliantly in England, leading the race for many laps until Rosemeyer passed him during a pit stop. Then, just when the race appeared to be getting very interesting, with Rosemeyer due in for new tyres, von Brauchitsch had a tyre burst at around 275 km/h (170 mph). He held the ensuing heart-stopping slide brilliantly, but his subsequent pit stop meant that he could no longer challenge Rosemeyer and he had to settle for a fine second place.

Amid scenes of great secrecy, with barricades raised and sentries posted, Mercedes-Benz tested their new supercharged, 3-litre V-12 cars at Monza in March 1938. In May, von Brauchitsch had his first race with the new machine at Tripoli, but both he and Caracciola suffered engine problems during the race and Manfred had to visit the pits three times. Nonetheless, the cars were so much faster than the opposition (the new Auto Unions were not present) that he and Rudi were still able to finish second and third behind Lang.

The next race was the French GP at Reims, which became something of a farce. Auto Union entered their new 3-litre cars for the first time and were in such disorder after practice that they threatened to withdraw. They were per-

Side by side past the pits go the Mercedes of von Brauchitsch and Caracciola during their fantastic duel at Monaco in 1937

LEFT Lucky Manfred! Von Brauchitsch with Alfred Neubauer (*left*) and Max Sailer afer his victory in the 1938 French GP at Reims

RIGHT Unlucky Manfred! Watched by Rudolf Caracciola (in raincoat, foreground), Alfred Neubauer has pulled von Brauchitsch out of his burning car during his dramatic pit stop in the 1938 German GP, which he was leading. Dick Seaman, in car number 16, went on to win the race

suaded to stay, only to have both cars crash on the opening lap! In order to give the spectators something to watch, Neubauer allowed Caracciola, Lang and von Brauchitsch to play among themselves, as they were already a minute ahead of the next car after only two laps! Eventually, both Caracciola and Lang were delayed at the pits when their engines proved reluctant to start again after refuelling and von Brauchitsch—lapping very fast and with great regularity—won the race with ease. It was hardly a great victory, but a victory, nonetheless. It is to be hoped that Manfred made the most of his champagne and congratulations, for he was to have almost certain victory in his next two races snatched from his grasp.

Von Brauchitsch loved the Nürburgring and as there was no Eifel GP that year, the German Grand Prix was his one chance to show his home crowd what he could do. At the end of practice he was the talk of the whole Eifel district, having put in a stunning lap of 9 min. 48.4 sec., only two seconds slower than Rosemeyer's magnificent record which he had set with a 6-litre Auto Union. Manfred was now, of course, driving a *3-litre* Mercedes. . . . Only one other driver—Hermann Lang—got below ten minutes, and none was to do so in the race.

At the end of the first lap von Brauchitsch was fourth, behind his team mates Lang, Seaman and Caracciola. On the second lap he overtook them all and held his lead with ease until his first pit stop, when he changed rear wheels and took on fuel in 43 seconds. On lap 15 he was leading Dick Seaman by 13 seconds when he made his second stop for fuel and tyres. While his car was being attended to, Sea-

man, who being a much smoother driver than von Brauchitsch needed only fuel this time, also pulled in. Then, drama! The mechanic refuelling Manfred's car overdid it and gallons of the stuff spurted high into the air and over the back of the Mercedes. Some spilt onto the hot exhaust pipe and in a moment the car was aflame. To their credit, the Mercedes mechanics were equal to the emergency and had extinguishers in action within moments. Alfred Neubauer bravely dragged von Brauchitsch from the car and in just over a minute everything was under control.

With all the excitement it was hardly noticed that Seaman had smartly driven off and into the lead. Once the foam had been wiped off his car and Rudolf Uhlenhaut had checked the controls, von Brauchitsch bravely went back into the race, only to go off the road at Quiddelbacher-Höhe. Unhurt, he walked back to the pits carrying his steering wheel which, to this day, he swears came off in his hand because it hadn't been fitted on properly after the fire. The mechanics—and Uhlenhaut—have always denied this, saying the wheel was properly locked into position and that Manfred's crash was a simple driver-error following the shock of the fire.

Whatever the reason, von Brauchitsch must have been bitterly disappointed to have lost the German GP yet again, when clearly it had been his for the taking. To his great credit, he hid his disappointment very well, and his congratulations to Dick Seaman after his victory were warm and sincere.

Just one week later he was robbed of victory again! He was having a fair old dice with Lang during the Coppa

Ciano at Livorno and tried to go through a right-hander with him side-by-side. Lang had the proper line and refused to give way, so von Brauchitsch found himself sliding gently into the straw bales that lined the road. Immediately his car was set upon by a number of excited Italian spectators, who pushed him back into the race. Lang thus had a secure lead when, with two laps to go, a rear tyre blew and he had to stop for a new one, letting von Brauchitsch into the lead, which he held to the end. Lang was not at all happy with his 'team mate', who had blatantly disobeyed team orders in trying to pass him, but then came the news that Manfred had been disqualified for receiving outside assistance when he had spun into the straw bales.

This was grossly unfair, as in an earlier, small-car race, two Italians had spun at the same corner and they had been pushed back into the race by spectators. Neither was disqualified and, indeed, the organizers didn't want to disqualify von Brauchitsch, but were over-ruled, apparently, by Giuseppe Furmanik personally, he being the President of the Sporting Council of the RACI. So much for the Rome-Berlin pact!

At Pescara von Brauchitsch led at the end of the first lap and retired on the second. At Bern he finished third in the Swiss GP behind Caracciola and Seaman and a few days later at the Grossglockner mountainclimb he could only finish third in both heats and the final. He retired after 20 laps of the Italian GP at Monza and later took over Caracciola's overheating car for a spell, only to hand it back gladly to enable Rudi to finish the race and clinch the European Championship.

After the drama of the Munich Crisis, the teams finally assembled at Donington for the last race of the year on 22 October. It was totally dominated by Nuvolari's fantastic drive in the Auto Union and von Brauchitsch could only manage fifth place. In common with all the German cars save Müller's Auto Union, Manfred's Mercedes was caught out by the oil dropped by Hanson's Alta. It spun twice, but Manfred picked it up superbly and continued. Seaman also spun and finished up stalled on the grass. He was push-started by some marshals and went on to finish third, which must have made von Brauchitsch's disqualification in the Coppa Ciano all the harder to bear!

For Daimler-Benz, the 1939 season began at Pau once more, and three cars were sent for Caracciola, von Brauchitsch and Lang. After the previous year's débâcle, the new, sleeker W154s were well equipped to cover the 280 km (174 miles) without refuelling, but in spite of this von Brauchitsch was caught out. For the first third of the race he lay a close second to Caracciola, taking the lead when Rudi had to stop at the pits with some broken oil pipes. Manfred maintained his lead of some 30 seconds over Lang when, on lap 82, his engine missed a few beats while he was rounding a hairpin. He had been bothered by high fuel consumption during practice and so, fearing the worst, he stopped for a top-up. This let Lang into the lead, which he held to the end. However, some spirited driving by von Brauchitsch forced him to drive harder than he would have liked in order to defend his position. Lang hadn't forgotten last year's Coppa Ciano!

Manfred did not race at Tripoli, as Mercedes had only

ABOVE **Carrying his steering wheel (which he claims was not fixed correctly after the fire), von Brauchitsch returns to the pits having gone off the road during the 1938 German GP. He is accompanied by Max Sailer of Daimler-Benz and *Korpsführer* Hühnlein**

RIGHT **Manfred and Rudi Caracciola take Alice Caracciola for a boat ride on Lake Lugano in 1938**

two of their fabulous 1.5-litre cars for this race. He was back in action at the Eifel GP, where he finished fourth, and he was third overall in the Kahlenberg hillclimb, near Vienna. He was third again in the tragic Belgian GP when Seaman was killed and forced to retire with a blown piston in the French GP at Reims. He had a wretched time at the Nürburgring, too, stopping for new plugs at the end of the second lap and retiring four laps later. He and Lang went to the Grossglockner again in August for the second and final round in the Mountain Championship. Lang won, but Manfred could only finish fourth. He was third in a Mercedes one-two-three at Bern and then he and Lang went to Belgrade for the last Grand Prix for many years.

Race day was 3 September, and that morning—following Germany's invasion of Poland—England declared war on Germany. According to Alfred Neubauer, when he heard the news on the radio, von Brauchitsch phoned the airport and booked himself on a flight out of Belgrade, asking Hermann Lang to tell Neubauer that he had gone home, Lang ruined Don Alfredo's breakfast in doing so for the latter abandoned his meal and took a taxi to the airport. Von Brauchitsch was sitting in the plane, waiting for take-off, when a furious Neubauer stormed aboard and demanded to know what the hell he thought he was doing! Without waiting for an answer, Don Alfredo grabbed Manfred's baggage and virtually marched him off the plane. Mercedes were in Belgrade to race and race they would—and that meant von Brauchitsch. Only when they were back in the airport did Neubauer notice that Manfred's plane was bound not for Germany, but Switzerland!

Von Brauchitsch led the race in the early laps, but his driving was so wild that he was constantly throwing up dirt and stones from the sides of the road, and one stone smashed a lens in Lang's goggles, forcing him to retire. Inevitably, Manfred spun and found that in order to get back on the track he had to drive a little way against the oncoming traffic. In doing this he came within an ace of being collected by Nuvolari, who just managed to squeeze his Auto Union by without hitting the Mercedes. Nuvolari won the race and von Brauchitsch was second, but if he hadn't driven so wildly he could undoubtedly have won. Doubtless he had his mind on other things and other places—like Switzerland!

Manfred von Brauchitsch was 33 years old at the outbreak of war but, due to all the injuries he had received during his career he—like Hans Stuck—was rejected for military service. He spent the war years in Berlin, working as a private secretary to a General. It was during this time that he met his first wife, Gisela.

With the cessation of hostilities, von Brauchitsch set about organizing motorcycle races in 1946 (car racing was banned in Germany until 1950), but got into serious trouble with the authorities for ignoring their regulations. In 1949 he sent a plea for help to Rudolf and Baby Caracciola in Switzerland and Baby was able to arrange for him to go to South America for two months at the expense of the Argentine Automobile Club, on the understanding that he would find a job there. He failed to do so and returned to Germany under a sizeable cloud, having upset many people in Argentina.

In 1951 he made the first of several trips to East Germany and his continuing contacts with the Communists led eventually to his being arrested and charged with high treason! He spent six months in jail and was then released, pending an investigation. When the case came to court in June 1955, Manfred von Brauchitsch was nowhere to be found. He had fled to East Germany, leaving behind his distraught wife and a large unpaid tax demand. Just over a year later, Gisela von Brauchitsch committed suicide.

Von Brauchitsch has lived in East Germany ever since. He is now retired, but as a former official of the Ministry of Sport he and his second wife, Lieselotte, are allowed to visit West Germany once or twice a year. They were guests of Daimler-Benz at the opening of the 'new' Nürburgring in 1984 when, fittingly, he drove some demonstration laps in one of the fabulous W125s—the car with which he had won his greatest race, the 1937 Monaco Grand Prix.

DRAMA AT NÜRBURG!

Nuvolari's Alfa-Romeo Startles Germany by Winning Her Grand Prix : Mercedes Lose the Race Five Miles from the Finish : Tremendous Excitement

Start of a desperate race—in the front row Italy (Alfa-Romeo) is sandwiched by Germany (two Mercedes), with England (E.R.A.) immediately behind.

Nürburg Ring, Eifel, Germany,
July 28th.

THE German Grand Prix has just finished. It has been the most exciting race . . . but words fail to describe the unparalleled excitement, the thrills from start to dramatic finish. Nuvolari has driven the greatest race of his career and has won the event for Alfa-Romeo. Intensely moving was the last-minute defeat of von Brauchitsch's Mercedes, leading till five miles from the finish. He burst a tyre at the Karussell hairpin, and finished on the rim. The crowds disperse, but the memory of such a race will remain always with them.

* * *

The Grosser Preis von Deutschland ! The great day for which hundreds of thousands of enthusiasts of all nations have been waiting has arrived. Even yesterday morning the roads around the wonderful Nürburg Ring, the finest road-racing circuit in the world, were thick with would-be spectators. To-day has dawned with a slow drizzle, attempting vainly to quell the inimitable grandeur of the scene. Mist cloaks the pine-clad mountains amid which the course lies, but from the stands a full view is possible looking down the valley which the cars will traverse. Patches of light fall

upon the distant hill-tops, but the track is wet and glistening. Innumerable flags add brilliant spots of colour to the scene as they float above the pits and grandstands.

Opposite the pits twenty cars are lined up; nine silver-coloured German machines—five Mercedes and four Auto-Unions—three scarlet Ferrari Alfa-

Romeos, three scarlet "official" Maseratis, two other Maseratis, an unofficial Alfa-Romeo, a blue Bugatti, and—a green car at last! England has a champion in the German Grand Prix, and a worthy champion, Raymond Mays with his 2-litre E.R.A. There are many English spectators amongst the crowd, and all wish him luck. Nor are they alone, for the sporting Germans, too, are enormously pleased to have an English car in their race. Mays has won all hearts by his plucky driving with a car far smaller in capacity than its rivals.

The cars are pushed up to the start as files of Nazi troopers parade and impressive anthems blare from the loud speakers. They are arrayed upon the grid, while the usual murmur of excitement from the serried crowds grows louder and louder. But soon, as 11 a.m., the hour of the start, approaches, all other sounds are drowned by the roar of exhausts as engines are started. In a few seconds even these give place to the shrill sound of the Mercedes superchargers, and then an electric signal—similar to a traffic light—releases the champing cars. It is a tremendous sight as white, red, and green—yes, green—cars fight for the lead before the sweeping hairpin after the stands. Caracciola's Mercedes just shoots clear of the pack, and Nuvolari with his Alfa is so close to Fagioli's Mercedes that the scarlet and silver wheels almost touch. Spray is flung high, and car after car hurtles past, while the crowds in the stands leap to their feet amid cries of "*Hinsitzen!*" ("Sit down!").

Now the cars scream past again, this time behind the pits, for the course makes a loop and returns in full view of the grandstands. Then we see them again, dropping with incredible rapidity down the winding valley that leads into the Eifel mountains, where as far as the eye can see the pine trees, with specta-

Things of beauty! The lithe silver Mercedes docile beside their pits before the start.

tors clustered many ranks deep at their feet, line the road.

Behind Caracciola and Nuvolari, Fagioli is off third with his Mercedes, then von Brauchitsch's Mercedes, then, fifth, the green E.R.A.! The acceleration of the English car has given Mays a good start. But a cry goes up "Stuck!" The German favourite Auto-Union driver is delayed at the start for a few seconds, and Pietsch's Auto-Union, too, loses precious distance.

There is never a dull moment at the

Beyond the stands, in the shadow of Nürburg Castle, comes a sharp left bend leading the course down into the woods for the 13-mile country section—Geier's Mercedes.

Nürburg Ring, for though the lap measures 14.1 miles there are announcing stations at several points round the course, notably at the famous Karussell hairpin, where after a steep rise the track doubles back sharply upon itself, with a kind of ditch on the inside of the corner, steeply banked up so that the cars hurtle round the acute hairpin at over 60 m.p.h.

Nor are the loud speakers the only source of information, for an ingenious score board with changing numbers indicates to the people at the grandstand the order in which cars pass a point about two miles distant, before they come into sight. A shrill scream is heard in the distance, and Caracciola's silver car flashes into sight, already leading from Nuvolari by 12 sec. Fagioli comes third, then Rosemeyer, the rising young star who, with his Auto-Union, is coming into the front rank of drivers. Mays has dropped back, but comes by going well, hard on the heels of Etancelin's Maserati. A few seconds pass, and then we get a tremendous thrill as on the return road Raymond Mays passes the red Italian car and leads it round the next corner, down the valley, and out of sight!

The speakers give out that Rosemeyer has taken second place at the Karussell hairpin and is pressing Caracciola! At the stands Caracciola still leads by 12 sec., with Rosemeyer second, but von Brauchitsch and Fagioli have passed Nuvolari. Shortly after this Brivio gives up with differential trouble on one of the Ferrari Alfas, which are again demonstrating their speed, though the German

The Autocar

(Right). A vital pit stop for von Stuck's Auto-Union. The mechanics are changing wheels and filling up with oil and water.

(Above). Changing wheels on Zehender's Maserati while the driver has refreshment in the pits.

(Right). Ruesch's red and while Maserati being refilled at the pit from four-gallon cans.

cars are travelling so fast that at present they hold the supremacy.

Chiron takes up the battle, as Nuvolari falls back for the time, and snatches fourth place behind Caracciola, Rosemeyer, and Fagioli. Then after five laps another disaster befalls the Italian hopes. Chiron still fourth, travels slowly past the back of the pits on the return road, and the scarlet Alfa comes to a stop at the next corner. Chiron climbs sadly from his car and walks back to his pit, while the crowd cheer him, for he is a popular favourite. He gesticulates excitedly as his mechanics question him, but the battle is over for another Italian car.

Next lap there is another thrill. Caracciola comes by, but a much longer pause than usual ensues before Rosemeyer comes in sight. The latter stops at his pit! A wheel is not running true, and in an amazingly short space of time it is changed. Mechanics advance a green battery box to the rear of the car and engage a portable electric starter motor, mounted on a framework of tubes, with the crankshaft. The sixteen cylinders fire, and the Auto-Union shoots off. It has dropped to fifth place, however. Pietsch also stops next lap, and a wheel is changed.

Raymond Mays pursues his course steadily. Obviously, as had been inevitable, his car is outmatched, but he is gaining valuable experience, and the knowledgeable Continental spectators cheer him for they appreciate the wonderful show his 2-litre car is putting up. After eight laps the leaders catch him, but he drives on at a pace that would win many a race.

Nuvolari is increasing speed! On the ninth lap he is up to second place, with von Brauchitsch pressing him hard. As they come back behind the pits the Mercedes gets by again, but the an-

nouncer at the Karussell, almost incoherent with excitement, tells us that at that point the Italian has retaken second place and is close on Caracciola's heels.

The excitement at the grandstands is indescribable. People stand up and none has time to cry "Sit down!" now. Here they are! Nuvolari leads! Rosemeyer is second! Rosemeyer—he has passed Caracciola. "Caratsch" is on his tail, and von Brauchitsch wheel to wheel behind. There they go down the valley. It is tremendous. Now von Brauchitsch is past Caracciola, and Rosemeyer worries Nuvolari's rear wheels. Gone! It is a relief to sit back for a while after those crowded moments of excitement

But even those thrilling events are surpassed when the eleventh lap arrives. Nuvolari's mechanics get ready spare wheels and jacks. He is going to stop! In the Mercedes pit, too, there is orderly activity, in readiness for the half-distance stop. Here comes Nuvolari. Frantic excitement! He stops. Rosemeyer, second—he stops, too. Now here are the third and fourth cars, the Mercedes of von Brauchitsch and Caracciola. By heaven! all four of the leaders are in at the same time. It is a sight for the gods as mechanics leap to the wheels, and others insert the gigantic funnels for the refills. Nuvolari leaps from his car and walks up and down sucking a lemon. The Germans are busy with their cars, like ants. Jacks go under, wheels are spun off, churns of fuel emptied in, while hubbub arises from the packed stands.

German pit work wins! Off goes the first Mercedes—von Brauchitsch's car. Then Rosemeyer with the Auto-Union, and almost at the same time, the other Mercedes—Caracciola's—gets away with supercharger screaming. Nuvolari's car is still at its pit! Fuel is still being emptied in as the jack is let down. At last he leaps in, and away he goes, but he has lost nearly a minute from the leading Mercedes. The Mercedes' mechanics laugh and give the Italian a good-natured cheer as he flashes past their pits.

Meanwhile, Fagioli has passed without stopping in the third Mercedes, and thus leads the race, but next lap he, too, stops, and more lightning pitwork is seen, under the eagle eye of the Mercedes chief, Neubauer. The four protagonists are due! Von Brauchitsch has a big lead at the Karussell, we are told. He comes by at a thrilling pace. The others follow in the order in which they left after the pit stops.

Other cars arrive and stop for their refuel, the E.R.A., still going well, amongst them, Delius now taking over the wheel from Mays. But even our interest in the English car is eclipsed by the stupendous battle for the lead. We await von Brauchitsch, who duly establishes a lead of 1 min. 9 sec. before anyone appears, with a record lap for

(Please turn to page 205.)

Italian victory on Germany's home ground: Nuvolari—visored against rain showers—flashes past the crowds after his win

THE SPORT BY CASQUE (CONTINUED)

under the International formula Caracciola, Fagioli and von Brauchitsch will drive Mercedes, Balestrero and Barbieri Maseratis, Lord Howe and Brian Lewis Bugattis, and Sommer probably an Alfa.

*   *   *

Liége-Rome-Liége

AS to trials, the regulations for the Liége-Rome-Liége are out, the classes being 1½-litres and over 1½-litres, with a general classification as well, and each class with its own prizes. There is a team prize into the bargain, and all sorts of queer regulations appear. If there's a tie, for example, the smaller engine wins, the overhead-valve engine against the supercharged, the two-stroke against the four-stroke, and even the experience of the driver counts. Entries must be sent to the Motor Union of Liége, Place Marechal Foch, 4, Liége, at 900 francs, before August 13th.

*   *   *

Brooklands Changes

QUITE considerable alterations will take place at Brooklands track this winter after the season is over. A ramp has already been formed in the public enclosure alongside the finishing straight, so that rows of people can see cars in mountain races quite easily. The fork grandstand seats are to be rearranged so as to give a wider angle of view and much more accommodation; that chicken-house thing, Chronograph Villa, which blocks up the view and is very little use, is to disappear altogether, and thank heaven!—there's a prospect that the pits will at last have wooden floors to deal with the sand nuisance. Then it is possible that an electrical signalling board will be tried to show plainly the number of a car leading in a race, the number changing as soon as the leader for the moment is overtaken, and that will be worth having because the loud speakers are so often drowned by exhaust noise.

*   *   *

Entries for the next Donington meeting, which is on August 17th, should be in by the 10th, and vary according to the race, being £1 for a ten-mile handicap or any one of the three five-lap races, and £3 for each of the two 25-mile handicaps.

*   *   *

Ten guineas is the entry fee for the South African Grand Prix, the list closing on November 1st.

R. F. Turner is progressing much better. He has a fractured skull, which, fortunately, is not very serious, and slight injuries to the spine.

At 9 a.m to-morrow the Mid-Surrey's Barnstaple Trial starts from Minehead, and tackles Doverhay, Station, Lyn and Beggar's Roost, finishing at Barnstaple itself. No non-skid devices of a special character

will be allowed, and axles normally with a differential must not be converted to solid axles. The number of competitors is over seventy.

A speed hill-climb is being run on the 17th in the grounds of Backwell House, near Bristol, under the auspices of the British Motor Cycle and Light Car Club.

The new Grossglockner mountain pass will be used next Sunday for a hill-climb, in which Seaman is driving an E.R.A., Zanelli a Nacional Pescara, and one of the Mercedes and an Auto-Union are expected to compete, as well as at least one special Alfa.

*   *   *

George Eyston and Denly had to stop their attempt on the 48-hour record with the Hotchkiss owing to trouble with the streamlined tail of the body, due possibly to the fact that there are several new and nasty bumps on Montlhéry. They succeeded in

taking the 500 kilometres two-litre class record at 112.37, the 500 miles at 112.25, the 1,000 kilometres at 112.26, 1,000 miles at 109.50, three hours at 112.42, and the six hours at 110.91 m.p.h.

*   *   *

Drewitt Trophy Trial

FOURTEEN cars started in the Brighton Club's Drewitt Trophy Trial, some of the test hills being made much easier by the fine weather. Richards' M.G. put up a fine performance on the restart, Cable's M.G., Ward's Morris, Stafford's Magnette, and Jones' Morris failed on South Street, Harrington's Magnette was best in the brake test, and Gardner's Frazer Nash was the most successful at Coldharbour; Seely, Miss Blathwayt and Richards obtained first-class awards with M.G.s, Chappell with a Ford, Gardner with a Frazer Nash, Stephens with a Morris, and Johnson with a Hudson also being successful.

DRAMA AT NÜRBURG (*Continued from page* 202)

(*Continued from page* 202)

the course at 80.73 m.p.h Wait, two cars arrive together, the Auto-Union and the Alfa. Rosemeyer stops at his pit again, while Nuvolari takes second place amid tremendous shouting once more. Somehow he has managed to pass Caracciola during this lap, and the two fight a furious duel.

Rosemeyer loses a lot of time with engine adjustments, and a new figure appears in the limelight—the famous Stuck, who with his Auto-Union has been steadily retrieving that bad start. Seventh at seven laps, he has held sixth place up to this point (14th lap); he now takes fourth position, but is some distance behind Caracciola. Rosemeyer is fifth, and Fagioli sixth.

The E.R.A. makes another stop. This time the trouble is more serious. The bonnet is opened, and adjustments are made, but after a short time Delius climbs back into his pit and the car is pushed away. Never mind, the English car has put up a brave show, and goes out with colours flying.

Never for a moment does the excitement of the titanic struggle relax. Nuvolari, driving the race of his exciting career, is striving hard to reduce von Brauchitsch's lead. The gap lessens every lap. At seventeen laps he is 1 min. 4 sec. behind. At eighteen laps he has reduced the gap to 34 sec.! The Mercedes' control are not relieved by the fact that Caracciola—third—is dropping back also, so we have Nuvolari catching von Brauchitsch and Stuck catching Caracciola. Neubauer now exhibits faster signals. There are only four laps to go.

Von Brauchitsch responds nobly. At nineteen laps he has increased his lead over Nuvolari to 45 sec., and at the same time a light drizzle begins again. However, Stuck still continues to catch Caracciola, and at the Karussell is close behind him. Fever point once more! On the twentieth lap Nuvolari's scarlet Alfa is only 32 sec. behind the leading Mercedes. The Italian, too, has speed

in reserve. Now for Caracciola and Stuck. Who will appear first? Here they are! Stuck has got by the Mercedes, and leads by a few yards only. It is a sign of a crisis when Neubauer begins to walk up and down in front of his pit.

Now for the last lap. Von Brauchitsch! A pause. Here is Nuvolari, driving like a demon; but the Mercedes has gone faster still, and is now 35 sec. ahead. A minute and a half later Stuck comes by third, and then Caracciola as he passes his pit shakes his head and gestures that he can go no faster.

The Karussell anouncer is on the air! "Von Brauchitsch is followed close by Nuvolari!" "Von Brauchitsch has burst a tyre!" "Nuvolari has passed him." There is a silence in the stands. Every man is on his feet. The suspense cannot be borne. "Von Brauchitsch is trying to catch up on a flat tyre!" "Caracciola has passed the Karussell driving all out!"

Now we turn our eyes to the changing numbers on the indicator board. "Nuvolari!" Now the little Italian appears, and such a shout goes up as never before was heard. Alfa-Romeo wins the Grosser Preis von Deutschland! A magnificent ending to a race in which thrill has followed thrill; but it is cruel luck for Mercedes, cruel luck for von Brauchitsch.

Stuck arrives and is cheered to the echo. Caracciola now! Second place for Auto-Union, third place for Mercedes. What a reversal of fortunes. Rosemeyer is fourth, after a good race.

But one more scene is to be played in this finest of all races. Von Brauchitsch is signalled on the indicator board. All hats go off, every man begins to cheer and clap, long before he comes into sight! Von Brauchitsch, leader till five miles from the finish, brings his gallant Mercedes over the line *on the rim!* Von Brauchitsch climbs from his car. He is crying like a child. So ends a drama.

THE YEAR IN PICTURES

RIGHT Waiting for the start at Monaco are (*left to right*) *Korpsführer* Hühnlein (out of uniform for once), Luigi Fagioli (on pit counter), Rudolf Caracciola, Manfred von Brauchitsch and mechanic Hermann Lang

LEFT Hans Stuck's specially streamlined Auto Union is readied for his attempt on the Flying Mile record on 2 February. He achieved 320.27 km/h (199.01 mph)

RIGHT The Mercedes of Caracciola and Fagioli (the eventual winner) before the start of the Monaco GP

RIGHT Two of the Mercedes at scrutineering for the Avus GP. Car no. 6 is that of von Brauchitsch and the streamliner, no. 8, was driven by Hanns Geier

BELOW Neubauer waits as Caracciola comes in after winning Heat 2 of the Avus GP. He is followed by von Brauchitsch, Louis Chiron on the Bimotore Alfa and Achille Varzi (Auto Union)

BELOW **Italians in German cars. Achille Varzi (Auto Union) leads Luigi Fagioli (Mercedes-Benz) during the French GP at Montlhéry**

ABOVE The Germans give the Nazi salute in honour of Caracciola's victory in the Belgian GP at Spa

RIGHT Hans Stuck on his way to a fine second place behind Nuvolari in the German GP

BELOW Hans Stuck won the *Deutsche Bergmeisterschaft* again at Freiburg for Auto Union

Montjuich

LENGTH: 3.79 km (2.35 miles)
RACE: Penya Rhin GP (1934–6)

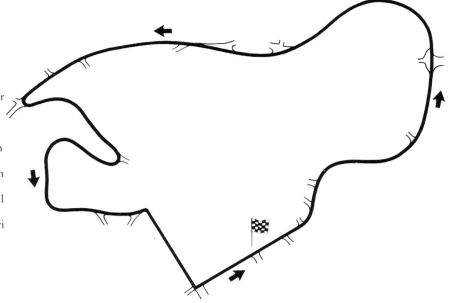

In 1921 a Barcelona businessmen's club, the Club Penya Rhin, decided to sponsor a race for voiturettes. The race was run until 1923 on a 14.79 km (9.19 mile) circuit just outside the city, the Circuito Villafranca del Panades. There was then a ten-year gap until the event was revived (this time for Grand Prix cars) in 1933 and moved to a new location in Montjuich Park, where it remained until 1936. The Penya Rhin GP was run for the last time in that year, when Nuvolari administered a sound thrashing to both the Mercedes and Auto Union teams with his Ferrari Alfa.

Carthage (Tunis)

LENGTH: 12.6 km (7.8 miles) (1935)
12.714 km (7.90 miles) (1936)
RACE: Tunis GP (1935–6)

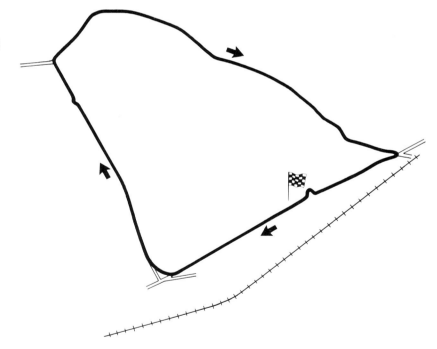

Racing began in Tunis in 1928, when the first Grand Prix was held on the 8.023 km (4.98 mile) Bardo circuit. In 1931 the race was moved to the longer, triangular circuit just outside Carthage. Very flat, the course comprised a 3.5 km (2.25 mile) pit straight and two other very fast legs, the second of which led back to the only slow corner on the circuit, a virtual hairpin which directed the cars onto the main straight.

Originally, there was a large chicane just before the grandstand, but for the 1935 race this was removed, an action which was not approved by the drivers, as it meant that they were now flat out all the way down this long straight, which was subject to very dangerous crosswinds virtually all the time.

The chicane was replaced for the 1936 Grand Prix and a second was erected on another straight, so it was Sod's law that someone should be blown off the road that year. That someone was the 1935 winner, Achille Varzi, whose Auto Union crashed at very high speed, although miraculously without injuring the driver.

Tunisia was a French colony and in 1936 the French abandoned their own GP in favour of a sports car race, so it was hardly surprising that the same thing happened to the Tunis GP in 1937, the last year in which the race was held.

Avus

LENGTH: 19.57 km (12.16 miles) (1921–35)
19.29 km (11.98 miles) (1937)
RACE: Avus GP

Strictly speaking, Avus is AVUS—yet another set of initials to reduce a long-winded German title to manageable proportions. These initials stand for *Automobil Verkehrs und Ubungs Strasse*, which translates rather clumsily into 'Automobile Traffic and Practice Street'. Such a road was proposed for Berlin as far back as 1907, one source attributing the idea to the Kaiser, who first suggested a national highway right across Germany, another to a group of enthusiasts who wanted a national racetrack. Whatever its origins, the plan was held up for lack of finance until 1913 and a year later the project was effectively stopped by the advent of World War I. Work on the foundations of the track was continued later in the war, however, to employ thousands of Russian prisoners from the Eastern Front.

The half-finished motorway lay derelict until 1921, when an entrepreneur named Hugo Stinnes managed to raise the necessary two million DM and had the job completed. The track comprised two two-lane roads each 8 m (26 ft) wide and separated by a grass strip of the same width running for 9.78 km (6.08 miles) in each direction between the Kaiserdamm, in the Charlottenburg district of Berlin, and the railway station at Nikolasee. The two tracks were joined by a wide-radius loop at one end (the North Turn) and a virtual hairpin at the other (the South Turn). The circuit was opened with a series of races (the *Avusrennen*) on 24 and 25 September 1921. The opening was not a

great success and in order to make the track pay it was soon made into a public toll road from Berlin to Wansee and Potsdam.

For the next three years the Avus races were very minor ones but then, in 1926, the German Grand Prix was held there. This event is chiefly remembered as Rudolf Caracciola's first major victory, but it was also a sad chapter of disasters. First, an Italian driver was killed in practice and then, in the race, Adolf Rosenberger's Mercedes crashed into the telephone hut behind one the scoreboards and killed the three men (two of them students) who were manning the scoreboard. There were three more big accidents during the race, fortunately without serious injury, but the day's tragic events very nearly had racing banned in Germany.

Avus really became known internationally from 1934 onwards. In that year Hans Stuck set the first of many new speed records in his Auto Union and later Caracciola and Mercedes used it for the same purpose, but with two German teams now involved in GP racing the Avus GP took on a new importance. Naturally, the circuit was extremely fast—in 1935 Luigi Fagioli won the race at almost 240 km/h (149 mph) in his Mercedes, but Hans Stuck made the fastest time at a staggering 260.65 km/h (162 mph) in his Auto Union. The race was not held in 1936, but that winter the North Turn was completely rebuilt with a banking,

making the circuit even faster.

The immediate reason for the rebuild was that the Berlin Motor Show was held nearby and a new access road was needed to take traffic to it. This road encroached slightly on the North Turn, so the Berlin Corporation agreed to pay for a new one, complete with steep banking. Originally, the North Turn was banked only at an angle of 1 in 10 and the South (which was not altered) at 1 in 9. The new North Turn was banked at nearly 1 in 1—43 degrees—over a width of 12 m (39 ft), with an almost vertical retaining wall at the very top. The new construction meant that the circuit was shortened by a few hundred metres but, as always, the start was to one side of the North Turn, so that the first lap was always 545 m (596 yds) longer than the others.

The new banking meant that the fastest cars were taking the North Turn at around 200 km/h (125 mph) and in 1937 Lang's Mercedes won the race at 261 km/h (162 mph)—the same speed as Stuck's fastest lap in 1935! The fastest lap this time went to Rosemeyer's Auto Union at 276.32 km/h (171.74 mph).

Although the 1937 Avusrennen were very successful and a splendid example of German technology triumphant, they were never held again, probably as a direct result of Bernd Rosemeyer's death on the Frankfurt-Darmstadt *Reichsautobahn*.

BELOW RIGHT **For the 1937 race the North Turn was banked. Here Caracciola (Mercedes) leads the Auto Unions of Rosemeyer and von Delius and the Mercedes of Seaman**

Achille Varzi (Auto Union) leads Luigi Fagioli (Mercedes-Benz) into the North Turn during the 1935 Avus GP Final

Monaco

LENGTH: 3.18 km (1.98 miles)
RACE: Monaco GP (1929–37)

'For days on end I went over the avenues of the Principality until I hit on the only possible circuit. This skirted the port, passing along the quay and the Boulevard Albert Premier, climbed the hill of Monte Carlo, then passed round the Place du Casino, took the downhill zig-zag near Monte Carlo Station to get back approximately to sea level and from there, along the Boulevard Louis II and the Tir aux Pigeons tunnel, the course came back to the port quayside. Today, the roads comprising this circuit look as though they were made for the purpose. But then!'

That is how Antony Noghes, Founder-President of the Automobile Club de Monaco, described the beginnings of what was the very first 'round-the-houses' circuit. All that walking of the avenues took place in 1928 and in 1929 the first Monaco GP was held. It was an audacious idea and Noghes had to fight to get it off the ground, but once the race had been agreed and publicized, 23 entries were received. In the event, only 16 cars turned up and half of them were Bugattis. The race was an unqualified success, but 100 laps of the tight little circuit proved to be a very tough assignment and so from 1930 on, entries were by invitation only. At that time, starting grid positions were decided by ballot, but for the 1934 race the AC de Monaco became the first organizing club to set grid positions according to practice times.

Over the years the Monaco circuit changed hardly at all. The pavements on some of the corners were eased a bit; the tramlines which ran along the Boulevard Albert Première and up the steep Avenue de Monte Carlo were removed in 1932 and for 1935 the chicane was moved 183 m (200 yds) further down the Quai de Plaisance, as close as was possible to the Tabac corner.

In the 1930s Monaco was one of the loveliest towns on the Mediterranean coast and it formed a stunning backdrop for the Grand Prix, which became hugely popular and provided some truly great racing, notably in the 1933 and 1937 events. It came as a terrible shock to the motor racing world when, early in 1938, it was announced that the Monaco GP would not be run that year. Lack of money was given as the reason, but politics had a hand in it, too, and there was to be no more racing there for 11 years.

BELOW RIGHT **Early morning practice photo shows Caracciola's Mercedes leading Dreyfus' Alfa Romeo round the Station Hairpin in 1935**

BELOW **This spectacular shot of the opening lap of the 1937 Monaco GP shows the Principality as it was in the 1930s. Few, if any, of the buildings remain today**

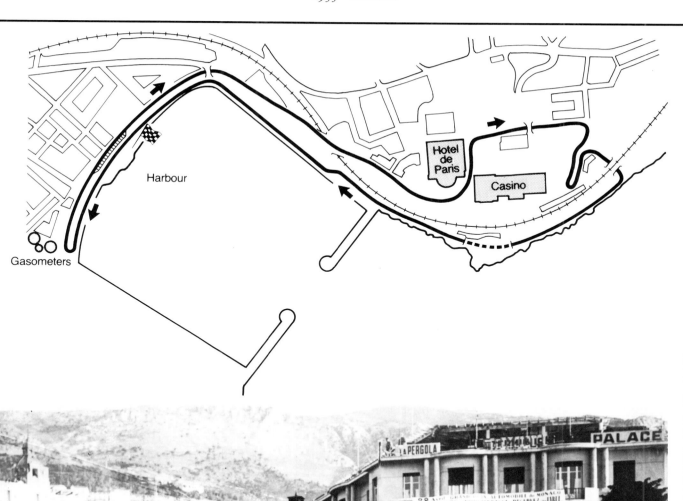

THREE

1936

The Irresistible Rosemeyer!

This was supposed to be the final season of the 750 Kg Formula, but nobody—least of all the AIACR—could agree upon what the new Formula should be. In December 1935, the Association called a meeting in Zurich, which was attended by Ettore Bugatti; Vittorio Jano (Alfa Romeo); Dr Karl Feuereissen and Hans Stuck (Auto Union); Dr Schippert, Alfred Neubauer and Max Sailer (Daimler-Benz); Signor Dacco (Scuderia Ferrari) and Raymond Mays (ERA). A number of ideas was promoted but, basically, all they could agree upon was to disagree about the new Formula. A majority did agree, however, that the present Formula should stay until 1938, as it was felt that manufacturers needed at least two years in which to design and build new cars.

That said, it was something of a surprise to many when, in February 1936, the AIACR announced its new Formula for 1937-8-9. Briefly, this stated that unsupercharged cars could have a maximum engine capacity of 4.5 litres with a minimum weight of 850 kg (16.72 cwt). Supercharged engines were considered to be one-third more powerful than those that were not, so their maximum capacity was to be 3460 cc with the same weight—850 kg. This time the weight was to include tyres and oil in the gearbox and rear axle, but not fuel, water, engine oil or the spare wheel!

Although they had enjoyed a marvellously successful season in 1935, Daimler-Benz had not been resting on their laurels. In August that year they had produced a new, slimmer and lower version of the W25 during practice for the Swiss GP and two of these cars duly made their racing debut at Monaco. The wheelbase was 25 cm (10 in.) shorter than before, the engine was now a 4.7-litre unit giving 490 bhp and a new transaxle allowed a lower prop-shaft. All this was clothed in a beautiful, streamlined body and Mercedes looked set to repeat their 1935 success, but it didn't work out that way.

They had not been sleeping at Auto Union, either. Professor Porsche made no radical changes to his car, but the capacity was increased to 6 litres and the power output was now an astonishing 520 bhp. No wonder the AIACR wanted to change the Formula—and fast! The only real opposition to the German teams was likely to come from the Scuderia Ferrari Alfas, with their new V-12 engine in an all-independently sprung chassis.

There were few driver changes among the teams. At Mercedes, Louis Chiron joined his friend Caracciola, with Fagioli, von Brauchitsch and Lang, while at Auto Union Ernst von Delius joined *his* friend Rosemeyer, with Stuck and Varzi and—occasionally—Rudolf Hasse. Nuvolari stayed with Scuderia Ferrari.

The year was a total triumph for Auto Union and the phenomenal Bernd Rosemeyer. In only his second season of motor racing, the young German won no less than five of the 11 Grands Prix he started, three of these victories being *Grandes Epreuves*. He also won the *Deutsche Bergmeisterschaft*.

There were only four Championship *Grandes Epreuves* that year, as both the Belgian and Spanish GPs dropped from the calendar. This left the German, Swiss and Italian GPs, to which was added that of Monaco. Rosemeyer retired early in the latter, but won the other three, scoring only ten points for his Championship victory. Team-mate Hans Stuck was second, with 13 points, with Nuvolari and Varzi tying for third place with 17. A distant fifth was Caracciola, with 20 points, his new Mercedes hopelessly outclassed.

Rosemeyer may have won the Championship, but he didn't win the most money, by a long way, as these figures show. In 1936 the value of the Italian lira was still fluctuating madly, but its average rate of exchange that year was L70.56/£.

1) Tazio Nuvolari—690,000 lire (£9,779) (£168,198 in 1985)
2) Achille Varzi—380,000 lire (£5,385) (£92,622 in 1985)
3) J-P Wimille—350,000 lire (£4,960) (£85,312 in 1985)
4) Bernd Rosemeyer—336,000 lire (£4,761) (£81,899 in 1985)

At first sight these figures seem unlikely, for Rosemeyer won five GPs and took one second place, whereas Varzi had only one win and three seconds. But that one victory

PREVIOUS PAGE **Bernd Rosemeyer gets a tumultuous reception after his victory in the 1936 German Grand Prix**

was at Tripoli, where the rewards were very great and included a percentage of the lottery profits. Nuvolari, on the other hand, won three of the major European Grands Prix (but none of the *Grandes Epreuves*) and the Vanderbilt Cup which, like Tripoli, brought a large bag of gold to the winner, all of which doubtless accounts for the fact that Tazio won almost twice as much money as his great rival that year.

Just as interesting is the money won by the three leading teams of 1936:

1) Scuderia Ferrari—1,227,000 lire (£17,389) (£299,090 in 1985)
2) Auto Union—1,084,000 lire (£15,363)(£264,244 in 1985)
3) Mercedes-Benz—372,000 lire (£5,272) (£90,678 in 1985)

The differentials here are easily explained: Scuderia Ferrari won no less than 11 of the 22 races they entered; Auto Union won six out of 12 and Mercedes-Benz a miserable two out of eight. The Alfa Romeos may not have been a match for the Auto Unions most of the time, but Enzo Ferrari certainly knew where the money was, and much of it was in Italy, as figures for the forthcoming 1937 season revealed. The Italians scheduled 38 races for the year with a total of over two million lire in prize money, with such relatively small events as the circuits of Turin, Naples, Florence, Milan and Modena each putting up 100,000 lire (£1400)! The Coppas Ciano and Acerbo were worth 135,000 lire each, the Italian GP 165,000 lire and the Tripoli GP 175,000 lire. Motor racing in Italy could be a very profitable business, but in England the rewards were not so gratifying. The total prize money for the first five places in the 1936 Donington GP was a paltry £520 (or 36,690 lire) and this was British motor racing's main event of the year!

In September, the AIACR announced that the new GP

Formula would not now start in 1937 as, clearly, nobody was ready for it. It would come into force in 1938 and while unsupercharged engines would still have a maximum capacity of 4.5 litres and a minimum weight of 850 kg, supercharged cars would now be restricted to 3 litres, but with the same minimum weight.

* * *

The year 1936 was the high point in Auto Union's racing history, and for four people involved with the Zwickau concern, life would never be quite the same. Dr Ferry Porsche is the son of Professor Porsche, and he recalls being caught up in the exciting days of the development of the Auto Union which climaxed with that sensational season. Already world famous for her flying exploits, Elly Beinhorn was swept off her feet by a younger man who just knew that they were meant for each other. She remembers her all-too-brief marriage to the mercurial Bernd Rosemeyer, whose career is one of the most extraordinary in all motor racing—European Champion with just 20 car races to his name. But tragedy lay ahead for Bernd and Elly, and he was to be killed in a record attempt, for 'the greater glory of the Third Reich'.

If 1936 was the pinnacle of Rosemeyer's career, it was the beginning of the end of his team mate, Achille Varzi's. The Italian fell in love with another driver's wife and she, with the best of intentions, introduced him to the drug, morphia. It wrecked his career and nearly killed him.

The crowning triumph of Rosemeyer's year was his victory in the German Grand Prix, as recorded in the pages of *The Autocar*. Hungary held its one and only GP in 1936 and other races were run on the Milan, Livorno and Tripoli circuits, which are detailed with maps and facts.

======= MEMOIR =======

Dr Ferry Porsche

When Adolf Hitler opened the 1933 Berlin Motor Show he announced, among other things, that Germany should have a successful Grand Prix racing team. Later, he decreed that the Government would give 500,000 Reichsmarks to subsidize any firm which would design and build such a car. One of Hitler's closest friends was Jakob Werlin, who now held a position of importance at Daimler-Benz, and they were quick to claim the subsidy for themselves.

Meanwhile, my father had already made drawings for his V-16, mid-engined machine and when the new company of Auto Union expressed an interest in building a racing car he showed them his plans. Before committing themselves, however, Auto Union wanted to be sure of getting the subsidy, so my father went to see Hitler, knowing that he had virtually agreed to give all the money to Daimler-Benz.

He persuaded the Chancellor that two German Grand Prix cars—not one—would do wonders for German prestige and Hitler agreed to split the subsidy between Mercedes and Auto Union. Mercedes were not very happy about this, pointing out to Hitler that their racing car was also a Porsche design, and indeed it was. In 1928, shortly before he had left the Daimler-Benz company, my father had designed a new racing car for them and I remember seeing it on the drawing board. It was a supercharged, 8-cylinder in-line with independent suspension and a rear-mounted gearbox—basically the car that Mercedes produced in 1934.

We had started our own design office in Stuttgart in April 1931, beginning with two designs for the Wanderer. The next year my father laid out his first drawings for his racing car, which was to become the Auto Union.

The new 750 Kg Formula set no restriction on power, so my father decided on a large-capacity, low revving engine—a supercharged V-16. The Formula was originally to run for three years and our plan was to design a car that could be developed over that period so the engine, for example, was designed as a 6-litre, but we started with a 4.3-litre because, to begin with, we didn't want too much horsepower. Mercedes, on the other hand, made three different engines during this time, but my father knew that most production engines were designed to grow in size and power during their life and he used that principle for his racing engine.

At that time our Business Manager was Adolf Rosenberger who had been a successful racing driver in the twenties. He had driven the mid-engined Benz *Tropfenwagen* and he told my father that it was an extraordinary car—he had been very impressed with it. After listening to Rosenberger's experiences we came to the conclusion that, as our new engine was going to produce a great many horsepower, we must have most of the weight over the rear axle, which is why the Auto Union was mid-engined. We also decided to put the fuel tank in the middle, so that no matter if it was full or empty there was always the same weight distribution front and rear. All other racing cars had enough weight at the rear at the beginning of the race,

but by the end there was not enough for good traction.

The cars were designed at the Porsche office in Stuttgart but built at the Horch works in Zwickau, where I spent a lot of time. I was present when the first engine was run on the test bed and later I drove the car on its first run—on the road outside the factory. Of course, I had never driven anything nearly as powerful and the acceleration was astonishing! With the narrow tyres we used then it was terribly easy to get wheelspin and the car would snake all down the road, but by using the throttle carefully you could accelerate like a rocket. Afterwards I got into my car (the prototype, 8-cylinder Wanderer) and I thought the throttle had broken—nothing seemed to happen!

It wasn't very safe on the road, of course, as there was quite a lot of traffic about, so we took the car to the Nürburgring. We had no lorry to transport the car, so a Horch 830 was equipped with a towbar and trailer to do the job. At the 'Ring the car was driven by Willy Walb (our first Team Manager) and Chief Mechanic Wilhelm Sebastian. Hans Stuck was also there with his wife, but he did not drive on that occasion.

For our first season we built five cars—one each for our three drivers, Stuck, zu Leiningen and Momberger, and two

FAR LEFT **Dr Ferry Porsche with a portrait of his father, Professor Ferdinand Porsche, designer of the Auto Union**

BELOW **Professor Porsche** (*extreme left*) **watches as the first Auto Union completes its first test run on the Nürburgring in January 1934**

for practice. We found that the first car weighed a little over the 750 kg limit, so one of our engineers was instructed to go through the entire machine and see what he could do to make it lighter. This action saved us around 30 kg.

I remember that on one occasion at the Nürburgring both Mercedes and Auto Union had to put their cars on the weighbridge and all of them were too heavy! We couldn't believe this, so we asked the racing commission if we could weigh our cars—in their presence—on our own weighing machine. The commission agreed, providing we weighed the Mercedes, too, and if the cars were under the limit this time we could race. They were and we did.

Naturally, we had our share of development problems and these began with the crankshaft which, on our 16-cylinder engine, was very long and made of steel, whereas the crankcase was made of alloy. I suggested that as these two metals expanded at a different rate we should build larger tolerances into the bearings. At first, this was thought to be too simple an explanation, but heat tests proved me right and the problem was corrected. Later we adopted a Hirth crankshaft and roller bearings.

Next we found that our Roots supercharger was not as efficient as it should be. Tests showed that it was heating up the mixture too much, so by the time that mixture reached the cylinder it had lost a lot of its ability to expand. This was because the blades of the supercharger were building up air pressure which, in turn, built up heat. Having discovered that, we simply drilled a groove in the supercharger casing so the heat could expand.

To begin with we used the chassis tubes as water-carriers from the radiator to the engine. This was a very good idea, but we found that the chassis was too flexible and that water was escaping through tiny cracks in the welds. We tried bracing the tubes and changing from round to oval, but eventually we moved the water through normal pipes which were not affected by the flexing of the chassis.

Late in 1935 we made a change to the car which provided a dramatic improvement in its handling. One day I went with my father to the Nürburgring for some testing and took a good look at the car's behaviour during cornering. When accelerating out of the corner, the inside rear wheel would spin furiously, trailing a stream of rubber smoke. We already had experience of this problem on some of our touring cars which had a locked differential and we had cured it by fitting a limited-slip unit. I pointed this out to my father and suggested the same cure for the Auto Union. He immediately agreed and we went back to the pits straightaway and put in a call to ZF in Stuttgart. They built up a limited-slip differential for us very quickly and the difference was quite extraordinary.

Throughout 1936 all the Mercedes drivers noticed how much better the Auto Unions accelerated out of the corners, but they didn't know why. At the end of the season Rudolf Caracciola came to visit us in Stuttgart and by then he knew the reason. Although he had lost the European Championship to Bernd Rosemeyer he was very good about it and admitted that for many months he had no idea why the Auto Union was suddenly so superior!

Bernd Rosemeyer was a remarkable man and like another son to my father. He was the best driver we ever had and very competitive—if someone beat his time during practice he would take his car out again and go faster still! His death in 1938 was a terrible shock. My father's contract with Auto Union had terminated at the end of 1937, so when Rosemeyer made his fatal record attempt in January 1938, it was the first time he had done such a thing without my father being present. The previous fall he had set new records for the Flying Mile and the Flying Kilometre, but just before the 1938 Berlin Motor Show Mercedes went to the Frankfurt-Darmstadt *autobahn* and Caracciola broke our records. Rosemeyer tried to regain them in a car which had a very good drag coefficient, but which was easily affected by side-winds and he crashed on his second run. Afterwards Frau Rosemeyer—who was not present for the attempt—said that she felt sure that if my father had been there he would not have allowed Bernd to run because the wind was too strong.

In 1938 and 1939 we had contracts with Daimler-Benz and Professor Eberan-Eberhorst took over at Auto Union, building a new 3-litre V-12 car to my father's design for the new Formula. We, on the other hand, were now working for the opposition! Our engineers produced a two-stage supercharger which Mercedes used on their W163 cars throughout the 1939 season. They had decided to build a 3-litre supercharged engine for this Formula instead of the alternative 4.5-litre unsupercharged unit but, just in case, we did some design studies for the latter, drawing up a V-12. It was never built and further studies were stopped by the war.

The one great advantage Mercedes-Benz always had over Auto Union was Alfred Neubauer. We had two Team Managers—first Willy Walb and then Dr Karl Feuereissen —and while Feuereissen was very good there was only one Neubauer! I had known him for a very long time because during World War I he was an Austrian officer in charge of testing military vehicles built by Austro-Daimler, and my father was then General Manager of that company. After the war Neubauer became head of Quality Control and Testing for the entire production and when my father left Austro-Daimler and went to Mercedes he took Neubauer with him. He had a tremendous talent for organization and a unique temperament!

Mercedes also had two groups of drivers—the mechanics and the gentlemen! Over the years they had a stock of good mechanics who became good racing drivers, men like Christian Werner, Otto Salzer, Otto Merz and Hermann Lang. They also had Caracciola, von Brauchitsch and Seaman, the gentlemen drivers. At Auto Union we only had gentlemen drivers, as none of our mechanics became racing drivers.

BELOW LEFT **Early Auto Union featured a streamlined windscreen, but this was never used in competition. Note also slats in the air intake, later replaced with a scoop**

BOTTOM **Professor Porsche drives his own creation in 1934**

BELOW **Bernd Rosemeyer enjoyed a very close relationship with Professor Porsche. Here he prepares for a practice run before the 1937 Vanderbilt Cup, watched by the Professor (*centre*), Ernst von Delius and Professor Robert Eberan-Eberhorst (*right*)**

Although Hitler had given both Auto Union and Mercedes a subsidy for racing we had no interference from the government—even when we lost! Hitler's decision to back both teams turned out to be a wise one, for if one team failed the other usually won. Usually, but not always, as Nuvolari and Scuderia Ferrari proved on more than one occasion!

All German motor sport came under the ruling of the NSKK—*Nationalsozialistisches Kraftfahrer Korps*—and this was run by *Obergruppenführer* (later *Korpsführer*) Adolf Hühnlein. He was quite a humourless man who seemed to have absolutely no qualification for his job apart from a genuine interest in racing. He was a career soldier who had fought in World War I and clearly loved being in uniform and ordering people about. He was not a nice man and always seemed to be angry with someone or something. Although he turned up everywhere—for racing, practice, record breaking and sometimes even at Monza for pre-season testing—he didn't try to tell us how to do our job. As he had no mechanical knowledge at all, that could have made things very difficult!

Although we went racing with a mid-engined Grand Prix car, Auto Union never produced such a car for the public. Some people could not understand why this was—surely the company should race cars that bore a reasonable resemblance to those it made for sale? But Auto Union was after the publicity that racing could bring and was not interested in building production cars based on the racing machines, although we did design a three-seater sports car based on the GP car and also a limousine. Neither car was built.

Racing certainly was good for Auto Union. I remember that when we raced in South Africa in 1937 the sales of DKW and Wanderer increased three or four times afterwards. It is interesting to recall that in our original contract with Auto Union there was a clause stating that we should call the car the P-Wagen—P, of course, for Porsche. But very soon after our first races the management came to us and asked if we could now call it the Auto Union, as everyone was talking about the new Porsche car and not the Auto Union!

We designed the Mercedes Land Speed Record car, but it was ready at the moment war began. It was a very interesting design for us because Hühnlein insisted that the record be achieved in Germany, not on the Bonneville Salt Lake in America. This presented many problems, not least being—where do we make the attempt? To beat John Cobb's record of 369.7 mph (594.8 km/h) we needed at least six miles of road. A special section of *autobahn* without any central divide was built at Dessau, but although it was used for record-breaking our LSR car never ran there.

Dessau bore no comparison with the Salt Lake at Bonneville, which was both immensely wide and long. And it had another advantage: it was 1100 m (3600 ft) above sea level, so the air pressure was much lower, offering far less resistance. In spite of this, we were told that we had to make the attempt at Dessau, but it was not to be.

========= MEMOIR =========

Elly Beinhorn Rosemeyer

I met Bernd for the first time in September 1935, when the Brno Aero Club invited me to Czechoslovakia to give a lecture on my flying exploits. It was the weekend of the Czech Grand Prix at the Masaryk Ring and they took me to the race, which Bernd won. It was his first GP victory.

I had started flying in 1928, when I was 21. My father was a successful merchant who had no thoughts of a flying daughter, as flying was absolutely *not* done by women at that time! Once I had my licence I thought that I would, in some way, make a living out of flying—get a factory to employ me, perhaps—but none did. To get my career started I took up aerobatics and spent the summer of 1929 giving exhibitions at flying meets every Sunday.

From the moment I became interested in flying my dream was to fly to Africa, which I did for the first time on 7 January 1931. Later that year I set off on my first round-the-world flight, during which I became only the second woman to fly solo to Australia, the first being Amy Johnson. In 1933 I flew round Africa and in 1934–5 all round Central America and the USA. I financed my flights by writing articles and giving lectures, which is why I was in Brno when Bernd won his first race, and, of course, I went to congratulate him afterwards. Then, in the evening, I was giving my lecture at the Flying Club and they invited Bernd and Hans Stuck. After the lecture there was a dance and, as the winner of the Grand Prix, Bernd had to ask me for the first dance so we could lead the others onto the floor.

Later he told me that he decided immediately that he would have to keep in touch with me, so after the dance he asked if he could come and get a photo of me with my signature—in Berlin!

So he came to Berlin—and again, and again! Then in the autumn he accompanied me on my lecture tour through Czechoslovakia, Switzerland, Poland, the Netherlands and so on. It was during this time that I had first-hand experience of his extraordinary eyesight. I owned a huge Mercedes which would hardly start in the winter, but nonetheless I was terribly proud of it. Bernd laughed at me, saying it was just the sort of car one could only sell to a young girl who knew nothing about cars!

On this occasion he decided that we would leave it behind and he would drive me to the lecture in his Horch. It was very foggy—you really couldn't see more than about 20 metres ahead—yet he was driving at 80 km/h! I said, 'Bernd, you are crazy—you're risking our lives in this fog!'

'What do you mean?' he replied. 'I can see very well.'

'Nonsense! You can't tell me that you can see anything in this!'

'Alright,' he said, 'I'll show you. Do you see the cyclist in front?'

Of course, I couldn't see a thing, but a few seconds later, sure enough, there was a man on a bicycle! I had very good, better-than-average eyesight, yet I couldn't see the cyclist until he was right in front of us, so Bernd must have had a special gift—a kind of infra-red vision. I had more examples of this later on and, of course, it helped him win the Eifel GP in the fog in 1936.

We never became officially engaged—it was impossible in our situation at that time, but after a while we decided that we would marry. I was not sure that it would be a success, but Bernd just told me not to worry. He was always very definite in everything he did and he was so sure of himself, but in a good way, not selfishly. We met on 29 September 1935 and were married on 13 July 1936 (we both felt that the number 13 was lucky for us). Not long after our first meeting he had told me that he was going to marry me, but he was two years younger than me and I was at the height of my flying career, which I did not want to give up. Marriage seemed a rather foolish thing at that time, from my point of view.

But from the moment we were married I became a part of his life, because I realized that he was more successful at racing than I was at flying. He was one of the top five racing drivers in the world, whereas there were quite a number of pilots of my quality. However, just three weeks after our marriage I had to do my flight to three continents in one day. I should have done this a long time before, but the papers and the visas didn't arrive in time and I thought of cancelling it. However, Bernd insisted that I should see it through, as the people at Messerschmitt, and others, had worked very hard for me.

I flew down to Damascus and made the flight on 6 August, which meant that I missed being with Bernd for the Coppa Ciano at Livorno. He found that he couldn't concentrate properly while I was far away in the air, so a few laps after the race started he came into the pits and retired! Dr Feuereissen, the Team Manager, was very understanding and when Stuck retired he gave him Bernd's car. Two weeks later, when I was back with him again, he won the Coppa Acerbo at Pescara and the rest of the year he won everything he entered.

After my flight he insisted that I went to all the races with him in future. Before we were married I'd hardly ever been to a race, except to one at Avus (and, of course, the one at Brno where we met) and even when we were engaged I didn't go. I moved in a completely different circle then, but once we were married I tried to make everything as comfortable as possible for my husband, who had a very demanding job.

I gave up long-distance flying, but kept my plane for my lecture tours where possible and I flew Bernd to all the races. In the meantime he learned to fly and bought his own machine, so we had three cars—Bernd's 6-cylinder Horch

FAR LEFT **Elly Beinhorn Rosemeyer (Bernd Rosemeyer's widow)**

BELOW **A hug for Bernd after a victory—one of many in 1936**

(which he called Manuela), a Wanderer and a DKW—and two aeroplanes—he had a Klemm KL 35 and I had my Messerschmitt.

Although I found motor racing fascinating I didn't really enjoy it. I thought that nothing could ever happen to Bernd because I believed absolutely in his superior driving and his good luck. It was not as bad as some people thought—that I was always worrying that something dreadful might happen.

With both Auto Union and Mercedes racing together there was a great deal of national interest and enthusiasm and, of course, the Mercedes people were our friends as well as rivals. Our particular friends at Auto Union were Ernst von Delius and Hans and Paula Stuck. In those days Hans was known as King of the Mountains, but in 1936 Bernd beat him at both Freiburg and Feldberg, winning the European Mountain Championship and becoming *Deutsche Bergmeister*. He enjoyed mountainclimbs very much. He used to practise first of all on a motorcycle and he had an extremely good memory for climbs and circuits—once he had been over the course he seemed to know it straightaway and was able to go very fast very quickly. Although Bernd 'stole' his title from him, Hans took it very well. They were good friends and he was a very sympathetic colleague to have around the racing business. Paula had been a German tennis champion and the four of us became very friendly. We used to play silly tricks on each other and we had a lot of fun.

During practice for the 1936 Italian GP at Monza I was allowed to drive an Auto Union for a lap. It was the 6-litre V-16 and if you just looked at the accelerator it took off like lightning! Bernd was very keen to see how I handled the car, but on the other hand he was a bit frightened for me. I was very, very careful—I didn't go much over 250 km/h (155 mph), but when I came in he said, 'That was alright, but you might have gone a *little* bit faster!'

On another occasion he took me for a lap of the Nürburgring in his Auto Union—I squeezed in beside him and off we went! At each corner I thought my last moment had come! I knew he wouldn't take any risks with me, but I couldn't believe that we would get round. Of course, we did, but then came the next bend and I thought the same. I suppose we must have taken 12 or 13 minutes and it was the most dreadful time of my life!

Very early in 1937 we flew to South Africa for some races there with Auto Union. We used the trip as our honeymoon and Bernd also used it to put in a lot of flying hours and qualify for his B-licence.

Later, Auto Union entered two cars for the Vanderbilt Cup in America and, as they considered me to be Bernd's lucky star, they asked me to go with him, at their expense. At first I was not sure that I wanted to go, as little Bernd was then on his way and I thought I might be a burden for my husband, but I didn't take much persuading! Bernd won the race, so the Auto Union management felt fully justified in sending me with him.

I had met Bernd at the Czech GP in Brno and by coincidence, the last race I went to with him was the Czech GP, in 1937. I was very pregnant at the time and we drove there in our Horch, which we then entered in a Concours

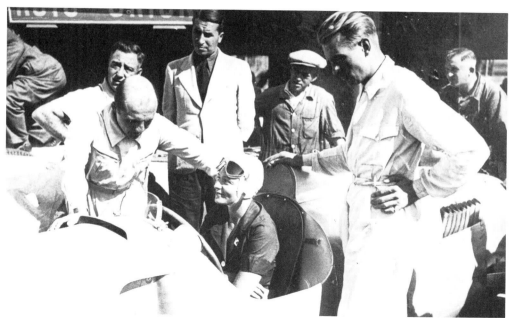

ABOVE **Watched by Bernd and Ernst von Delius (left), Elly prepares for her run in the Auto Union at Monza in 1936**

LEFT **He may have his back to the camera, but the Tyrolean hat is the give-away. It could only be Bernd Rosemeyer, surrounded by the Press as he talks to _Korpsführer_ Hühnlein before the 1937 German GP**

d'Elegance. Luckily I did not have to get out of the car, so my condition was hidden from the public! We won the Concours and Bernd came third in the race.

After Brno Bernd went to Donington for the last race of the year and I stayed at home. It wasn't broadcast on the radio, so I had to wait until he phoned me afterwards to find out that he had won. I asked him if he had met Kay Petre, as we had become good friends in South Africa and he told me that she had had a bad accident at Brooklands. He had gone to see her in hospital, but she was still unconscious. In spite of his victory, he was very depressed about Kay.

Bernd jun. was born on 12 November and a few weeks later we learned that Mercedes had been given special permission to try for some new speed records on the Frankfurt-Darmstadt _Reichsautobahn_ at the end of January. Auto Union asked to be allowed to go, too, in order to defend the records Bernd had set the previous October, and they were also given permission. Bernd had done a lot of record-breaking in 1937 and he had enjoyed it, but by the time of the attempt in January 1938, he knew that the limits had been reached where setting records on _autobahnen_ was concerned.

(On 28 January 1938 Bernd Rosemeyer was killed during an attempt to regain his International Class B records for the Flying Kilometre and Flying Mile, which Rudolf Caracciola and Mercedes-Benz had broken earlier that morning.)

During the war I married again and had a daughter, Stephanie, but the marriage ended after some five years. Naturally, I wanted to put my flying ability to good use—perhaps as a ferry pilot, as many women did in many countries—but I was told that I could only do this if I joined the Air Force full time. This was impossible, as I had two small children to look after, and it was not until 1948 that I went flying again.

Bernd Rosemeyer

Team Driver, Auto Union 1935–38,
European Champion 1936

'*Will Rosemeyer race at Avus?*'

The question was scrawled on a page of the calendar which stood on Willy Walb's desk and he noticed it as soon as he arrived in his office. The Auto Union Team Manager shook his head and went about his morning's work. Young Rosemeyer would have to learn patience, for after all, he had never driven in any kind of car race and yet, here he was, demanding to be let loose in one of the most powerful racing cars the world had ever seen and at Avus—one of the fastest circuits in the world! Ah, youth!

The next morning, Walb tore off the previous day's page from his calendar, to find the same question in the same handwriting. 'Will Rosemeyer race at Avus?' This went on for days, until eventually Walb gave in. The next time Rosemeyer sneaked into the office to write his question, he found that Walb had beaten him to it. On the calendar was the one, all-important word.

'*Yes!*'

Has there ever been a motor racing phenomenon to match Bernd Rosemeyer? Most assuredly there has not. In the astonishingly brief span of two and a half seasons the young German driver shot from obscurity to immortality, so that today—nearly 50 years after his tragically early death—he is spoken of in the same breath as Nuvolari, Caracciola, Fangio, Ascari, Moss, Clark and Stewart. Perhaps even more extraordinary is the fact that his name is still magic to countless enthusiasts who weren't even born until long after his demise.

Bernhard (Bernd) Rosemeyer was born on 14 October 1909 in Lingen, Germany, close to the Dutch border. His father, Wilhelm, owned a garage and Bernd developed a fascination with cars and motorbikes at a very early age. He began his racing career on grass tracks in 1930, graduating to road racing two years later on a Sports BMW bike. This gave way to a 500 cc NSU racing machine and in his first race of 1933, in Hannover, he was spotted by Walter Moore, formerly with Norton and now Team Manager for NSU, who signed him up. He won six races that year and was then promptly signed by DKW for 1934!

By this time DKW was a part of Auto Union and the bikes carried the new insignia of four linked circles on the sides of the fuel tank. That year their big brothers—the Auto Union racing cars—had a successful first season in Grand Prix racing, but were, with the honourable exception of Hans Stuck, woefully short of Grand Prix drivers. At the end of the season, therefore, they decided to look for some new talent among Germany's car and motorcycle racers and 12 men were invited to present themselves at

the Nürburgring on 24 October 1934. One of them was Bernd Rosemeyer, who was already 'in-house' so to speak and had won three races for DKW that year and also collected three Gold Medals in endurance trials.

On that first day the hopeful dozen were restricted to driving the formidable 16-cylinder Auto Union on the 6 km *Sudschleife*. The next morning the best five were let loose on the full 22.8 km circuit and those five were Paul Pietsch (who already had a fair amount of racing experience on four wheels), Simons, Steinweg, Soenius and Rosemeyer. Not surprisingly, Pietsch was fastest on both circuits, recording 3 min. 05.4 sec. and 11 min. 14.6 sec. respectively. On the short circuit Rosemeyer was second fastest with 3 min. 07 sec., then came Simons (3 min. 09.4 sec.), Steinweg (3 min. 18.6 sec.) and Soenius (3 min. 25 sec.). On the full circuit Simons was second fastest to Pietsch with 11 min. 46 sec., then came Rosemeyer with 12 min. dead, Soenius almost exactly as fast with 12 min. 0.8 sec. and finally Steinweg with 12 min. 57 sec. To put all this in perspective, in the German GP a few months previously, Hans Stuck had set fastest lap with a time of 10 min. 44.2 sec.

After some deliberation, Willy Walb decided to sign Pietsch and Rosemeyer to the team for 1935, but as junior drivers. Varzi and Stuck would form the front line of attack, with Pietsch, Rosemeyer and zu Leiningen trying to back them up while learning their craft.

As promised, Rosemeyer duly got his chance at Avus. Although the track was very fast (in practice for the 1934 event Stuck had lapped at 243 km/h [152 mph], there were no fast and dangerous corners, as at Tripoli, and Walb doubtless felt that Rosemeyer could be trusted not to do anything silly on the 9 km (6 mile) straights. Auto Union entered four cars for the event, which was run in two heats and a final in an attempt to combat spectator boredom, which was almost inevitable in one long race at Avus.

So Bernd Rosemeyer made his motor racing debut on 26 May 1935. He was given one of the semi-streamlined cars with enclosed cockpit and fairings behind the wheels. The starting positions were decided by ballot and, as if it were pre-ordained, Bernd found himself on the front row for his heat, with Hans Stuck. His team mate immediately went into the lead, which he never lost, and Rosemeyer lay second, some way behind, until he was passed by Fagioli's Mercedes. On the fourth lap he had to retire after a tyre shed its tread at high speed on the North Turn. Among the spectators who watched him bring his car under control with apparent ease was a young lady named Elly Beinhorn.

If Rosemeyer had no chance to make an impact in his first race, he put things right in the second! In a truly astonishing drive in the Eifel GP at the Nürburgring, he had the nerve to pass the great Caracciola into the lead right in front of the main grandstand! He held the Mercedes driver at bay for the next two laps, but the very experienced Rudi was quick to see a chink in the young man's armour.

On those two laps he noticed that, coming out of the corner that led onto the three-kilometre straight, Rosemeyer changed up into top gear very early on the low-revving Auto Union. So, on the 11th and final lap he closed

Bernd and what the well-dressed racing driver was wearing in the 1930s . . .

right up on Bernd, held the Mercedes in fourth as they accelerated out of that final bend and went by into the lead as his young rival changed gear too early yet again. Rudi held his advantage down the straight and crossed the line 1.8 seconds ahead, to roars of approval for both men from the hugely excited crowd. The old master had won, but the young tyro had served notice that he was going to play a large part in Grand Prix racing from now on.

Bernd had no luck in the French GP at Montlhéry a week later, retiring his own car and taking over Varzi's after it had developed a water leak. He finished fifth, after numerous pit stops. He was fourth in the German GP, which was dominated by Nuvolari's bravura performance in the Alfa.

His next race was the Coppa Acerbo at Pescara, where there occurred one of the many incidents that were to fuel the Rosemeyer legend. Troubled by locking brakes, he went off the road at some speed, flew over a ditch and hurtled between a bridge parapet and a telegraph pole

before managing to regain the road. Later, Professor Porsche went to have a look at the scene of this excursion and found that the distance between the telegraph pole and the bridge was just two inches more than the width of the Auto Union. . . . In spite of this and an earlier detour into the scenery when trying to pass Nuvolari, Rosemeyer finished second.

He held second place, too, in the Swiss GP for some time before being passed by Fagioli. He was third again at Monza and then went to Czechoslovakia for the last race of the year, at Brno. It turned out to be an event of great significance on two counts. First he scored his first victory (and it is not given to many drivers to score their *first-ever* race win in a Grand Prix!). Secondly he met the girl who had watched him spin at Avus and who would shortly become his wife, Elly Beinhorn.

In Brno to give a lecture on her flying exploits, Elly was invited to the Grand Prix and, as a visiting celebrity, was asked to congratulate the winner. Herr Rosemeyer seemed

LEFT Stunning is the word for Rosemeyer's performance in only his second race, the 1935 Eifel GP. Here he leads Caracciola through the last left-hander before the Nürburgring's main straight on the final lap. Caracciola got past to win by 1.8 sec.

RIGHT Victory in the 1936 German GP. (*Left to right*) Professor Porsche, Bernd, Elly (in headscarf) and Hans Stuck

to be a pleasant young man and she was happy for his success, but for her, their meeting was of no great significance. Herr Rosemeyer, however, had other ideas and was soon calling at Elly's Berlin apartment. He also had the nerve to address her—without her permission—with the familiar '*du*'. Elly, at least, had been properly brought up and she insisted upon using the formal '*Sie*'.

Her formality did not last long. Try as she might (and she did) she could not resist Bernd's boyish charm, *joie de vivre* and the sheer force of his personality which, she was reluctant to admit, was even stronger than her own. By the end of the year they were seeing each other constantly.

The first race of 1936 was the Monaco GP and due to her lecture commitments Elly was unable to be there. Before leaving Berlin for the South of France Bernd told her that he was going to marry her. It was not a proposal—just a statement of intent. They were optimistic about the race, as it was being run on 13 April and both regarded 13 as their lucky number. But not this time. Bernd managed to avoid the second-lap mêlée at the chicane, but then he spun in the rain at Casino Square and crashed tail-first into a parapet. It was no consolation to him that he was on lap 13!

Elly's busy itinerary meant that she couldn't accompany Bernd to Tripoli and Tunis. She didn't miss much, as his car caught fire on both occasions.

In practice for the Penya Rhin GP at Barcelona Bernd crashed heavily when his steering failed and he banged his nose and knee quite badly. In the race he could only finish fifth. It had been a pretty disastrous start to the season thus far, but that was about to change as Bernd was on the threshold of a truly sensational string of victories, beginning with one that would become a legend on its own.

He can have had no inkling of this when he turned up at the Nürburgring for the Eifel GP on 14 June. His lucky 13th had passed and the circuit was covered in fog and drizzle on race morning. When the cars left the start the fog had lifted, but it was raining steadily. Caracciola—*Der Regenmeister*—led for the first two laps, but was then passed by Nuvolari in the Alfa, with Rosemeyer in hot pursuit. Caracciola retired and Rosemeyer closed relentlessly on Nuvolari, passing him behind the pits to the delirious joy of the packed stands. Then the fog returned and everyone slowed dramatically—everyone except the astonishing Rosemeyer, who scarcely slowed at all. His extraordinary eyesight enabled him to lap more than 30 seconds faster than Nuvolari and when he took the chequered flag he was no less than 2 min. 12.8 sec. ahead of the Italian. Immediately after this quite extraordinary drive, Rosemeyer was dubbed *Der Nebelmeister*—the Fogmaster.

Due to her lecture commitments, Elly missed this great excitement, although she listened to the race on the radio. She missed the next race, too, in Hungary, where Bernd was beaten by Nuvolari. As soon as he returned home, Bernd was due to go to hospital for a few days to check a liver condition, but before he went he informed Elly that he would not be going to any more races without her. He also took her to the Registry Office to give notice of their forthcoming marriage.

They deliberately chose 13 July as their wedding day, and 13 days later Bernd won the German Grand Prix! He led his team-mate, Hans Stuck, home by nearly four minutes and set a new lap record in the quite phenomenal time of 9 min. 56.4 sec. On this occasion Elly was there to see him do it and was very relieved to find herself welcomed into the Grand Prix fold by all the other drivers, their wives and girlfriends. Having for some years been celebrated in her own right as Fräulein Beinhorn, she did take time to

become accustomed to being Frau Rosemeyer!

Although Bernd was determined that Elly should accompany him to all the races from now on, she had to miss the next one! For some time she had been planning to fly across three continents in one day and this flight had originally been scheduled for June, but due to the German rearmament programme, work on her plane had been delayed. Now it was ready. To cover three continents in 24 hours meant starting from Damascus and flying to Cairo, Athens and on to Berlin. Elly determined to leave Berlin on 2 August, the same day that Bernd would be racing in the Coppa Ciano at Livorno. Due to appalling weather conditions it took her two days to reach Damascus, where she was greeted by a telegram from Bernd: 'Retired after six laps. Come home soon. You must never leave me again.'

Elly began her flight back at 2 am on 6 August, landing at Tempelhof after covering 3750 km (2343 miles) across three continents in one day. She was welcomed by a huge crowd and a joyous Bernd.

It was only later that Elly learned the reason for Bernd's 'retirement' in Livorno, when Dr Karl Feuereissen (now Auto Union's Team Manager) told her that her husband was so nervous about her flight that he was not in a fit state to race. After six laps he'd had enough! Once he was reunited with Elly though, all was well again, so much so that Bernd won the remaining five events of the year! In a hectic 15 days he won the Coppa Acerbo, the Swiss GP and the mountainclimb at Freiburg.

The Swiss race was not without incident, as Caracciola went straight into the lead and proceeded to baulk Rosemeyer for all of eight laps on the very fast Bern circuit. After much waving of blue flags and shaking of fists Bernd got by and led until the end, but when he got out of his car he was steaming with anger at the way Caracciola had refused to let him past. Later, back at the hotel, Bernd and Elly stepped into the lift to go down to the prize-giving ceremony and found it occupied by Caracciola and Baby Hoffmann. In a rather condescending fashion Rudi congratulated his opponent and Bernd replied by telling him exactly what he thought of his blocking tactics! Very embarrassed, Elly couldn't wait to get away once the lift had reached the lobby, but Bernd continued to berate the European Champion for some time. Indeed, he held his grudge for six months, before deciding to bury the hatchet after a dinner given by Dr Goebbels in Berlin.

The last race of the year was the Italian GP at Monza and, as it took place on 13 September, Bernd felt pretty certain that he would win. Sure enough, he did.

In order to try and boost the sales of DKWs, Auto Union decided to send two cars to South Africa for the South African and Grosvenor GPs, to be held on 1 and 16 January 1937. In the face of considerable opposition, Bernd persuaded the powers-that-be that he should be allowed to fly to Cape Town with Elly in her Messerschmitt Taifun. Very nervous about the whole thing, Auto Union baulked, however, at the idea of Ernst von Delius going with them. Determined that at least one of their drivers should arrive safe and sound, they insisted that he travel with Wilhelm Sebastian (standing in as Team Manager for the trip) on a scheduled air service.

Both parties left Tempelhof on 4 December 1936. Bernd and Elly had decided that this South African adventure should be their honeymoon, so they took their time, stopping at Cairo to look at the pyramids, then overtaking von Delius and 'Bastl' Sebastian while their Hannibal aircraft refuelled at Luxor and going on to Nairobi, where they spent a few delightful days. Elly, of course, had made this trip before, on her own, so now she was able to show Bernd the sights and sounds of Africa, as they drove for miles in the game reserves and marvelled at the wildlife.

All too soon they had to move on and landed in Johannesburg on 12 December where they were met by Sebastian and von Delius. As the first race was on New Year's Day, Sebastian insisted they spend Christmas in East London (the venue of the South African GP), so while he, von Delius and the mechanics took the racing cars overland—a journey of several days—Bernd and Elly flew there in four hours.

Although overwhelmed by the South African hospitality, the team was very disappointed to find that its cars were severely over-handicapped for the race. They had known from the start, of course, that both races were handicap affairs, but they were not prepared for the fact that while Rosemeyer would start last, on scratch, Hans Ruesch on his 3.8-litre Alfa would set off 6 min. 30 sec. ahead of him and the eventual winner—Pat Fairfield on an 1100 cc ERA—no less than 28 min. 13 sec. ahead!

Nonetheless, Bernd was determined to give the spectators a run for their money and began with a standing lap that was 4.83 km/h (3 mph) faster than the previous lap record, set by Jean-Pierre Wimille the year before! He then proceeded to give an electrifying demonstration of his genius, lapping at around 177 km/h (110 mph) and sliding the big Auto Union about on the rough surface with apparent abandon. This surface played havoc with the tyres, however, and not long after Bernd had brought the packed stands to their feet with a new lap record of 185 km/h (115 mph) (old record—164.15 km/h [102 mph!]) his near-side rear tyre exploded with a bang that was heard in the grandstands, nearly half a mile away! Rosemeyer was going very fast indeed at the time and the ensuing skid was heart-stopping, but he controlled it brilliantly and

Elly and Bernd at the Grosvenor circuit, scene of the Cape Town GP, in January 1937

Bernd with a streamlined Auto Union at the Avus test day in April 1937, when cars were allowed on the new banking for the first time

made for the pits and some new rubber. He was eventually classified fifth, at 174 km/h (108.16 mph), Pat Fairfield winning at 143.5 km/h (89.17 mph). That evening, Bernd Rosemeyer was the talk of the town.

The man himself, however, was none too pleased to learn that all his efforts had only resulted in fifth place, and said so, forcibly, but in spite of the ridiculous handicapping Auto Union were still committed to race in Cape Town two weeks later.

Once again, Bernd was giving away nearly 40 minutes to the smallest car, but this time the handicapping proved to be much more sensible and made for a very exciting race, as von Delius and Rosemeyer fought their way through the field, both finally overtaking the leader—Earl Howe in his ERA—on the very last lap. Delius was delighted with his first victory, which more than made up for his retirement in East London.

The first race of the Grand Prix season proper was the Tripoli GP in May and it was a scorcher. First Caracciola led, then Rosemeyer, but he had to come in for new tyres after five laps. Stuck set up a new lap record at over 228.5 km/h (142 mph) but then he, too, suffered tyre trouble. In all, Auto Union mechanics changed 35 wheels during the race, which was finally won by Hermann Lang, with Bernd only ten seconds behind.

The next race was at Avus and was even faster. For the first time the new, steeply banked North Turn was being used. In practice Rosemeyer lapped at a staggering 283 km/h (176 mph), which put him on the front row with

Caracciola. They were both driving fully streamlined cars and in the first heat had the huge crowd on its feet as they screamed up and down the *autobahn* only inches apart. Bernd led initially, but then Rudi got by and—going right round the very edge of the North Turn on the last lap—managed to beat Rosemeyer to the line by seven-tenths of a second! In the final Bernd had to stop for new tyres and could only finish fourth.

Things had to go better at the Eifel GP—it was to be run on 13 June. Sure enough, Bernd won, but not until he'd had a tremendous battle with Caracciola again. He also unofficially broke his own lap record with a time of 9 min. 54 sec. in practice, but could 'only' do 9 min. 58.8 sec. in the race.

Three days later Bernd had his first taste of the super-high speed of record attempts. Driving a streamlined Auto Union on the *Reichsautobahn* between Frankfurt and Darmstadt he set five new International Records and one World Record. He very much wanted to be the first man to exceed 400 km/h (250 mph) on a road, but on this occasion could only do 393 km/h (245.6 mph).

Rosemeyer and von Delius had been chosen to race in America for the Vanderbilt Cup in New York, while Stuck, Hasse and Müller would represent Auto Union at Spa the following weekend.

Bernd did not like the circuit, with its short straights and tight bends, but nevertheless he was second fastest in practice, behind Caracciola. The race was set for Saturday, 3 July, but with the cars on the grid it began to rain heavily, so it was rescheduled for Monday—the Americans weren't in the habit of racing in the rain or on a Sunday.

Rosemeyer had a great dice with Caracciola in the early laps, until the Mercedes retired and he was then threatened by Dick Seaman, who took the lead when he had to stop for fuel. Bernd regained the lead when Seaman, in turn, stopped, but in the final laps the Englishman was closing on him rapidly until, with two laps to go, he had to refuel once more. Rosemeyer won, 50 seconds ahead of Seaman, with the American Rex Mays third in an Alfa Romeo.

Bernd had won the last three races on the Nürburgring, and so, with his confidence sky-high after his Vanderbilt Cup victory, he approached the German Grand Prix on 25 July with keen anticipation. That he was in a winning mood was amply demonstrated in practice, when he made fastest lap with the astonishing time of 9 min. 46.2 sec., beating his old lap record by no less than 17 seconds.

He made a less than brilliant start and was passed by both Lang and Caracciola. He made two electrifying attempts to pass the latter, at Fuchsröhre and on the run down to Adenau Bridge, and then got by on the climb to Bergwerk. On lap 2 he passed Lang into the lead, breaking his own lap record with a time of 9 min. 56 sec. On the fourth lap an NSKK man appeared in the Auto Union pit clutching a wheel nut from one of their cars. At the end of the lap four Mercedes went by, with no sign of Rosemeyer. He eventually arrived with a rear tyre trailing rubber. It took 2 min. 26 sec. to replace the wheel and the wheel nut, before Bernd could rejoin the race, now down in tenth place.

On that fifth lap Hans Stuck retired and von Delius, who

had seen Rosemeyer delayed at his pit, was now fifth, behind the Mercedes of Caracciola, von Brauchitsch, Lang and Seaman. The previous Friday, von Delius had been involved in a collision with a lorry, while driving to the circuit. Although he wasn't hurt, he was badly shaken and told Rosemeyer that he was going to take things easy in the race, his 13th for the team. 'Auto Union will have to be in a very bad way before I take any risks on Sunday.' Seeing Bernd's car in the pits and knowing that his was the only Auto Union in a position to do anything about the Mercedes, it would seem that Ernst von Delius decided to take some risks. On lap 7 he made a bid to pass Dick Seaman, as Rodney Walkerley wrote in *The Motor*:

'Delius made a terrific effort to pass Seaman and came up close as the cars entered the two-mile straight. The crowd rose in horror—just over the brow of a hump-back bridge the two collided and in a flash were gone, Delius off the road on one side end-over-end; Seaman crammed on his brakes and slid broadside down the road, then spun round and round and shot backwards into the hedge. The smash occurred at 150 mph.'

News of the crash reached the pits almost immediately, and Elly rushed over to the hospital tent to see if she could do anything for her friend. The news was reassuring—Delius had a broken leg and concussion, but was conscious and telling everyone not to worry. Seaman apparently had only a broken nose and cuts and bruises. Elly returned to the pits to find that Bernd was putting up an extraordinary fight. Rodney Walkerley again:

'All this time Rosemeyer was driving on the brink of disaster with complete indifference and was gradually coming back into the picture, running fifth on lap 11. Then he went a bit too far, his car went clean off the road and another tyre stripped, costing him 35 seconds in the pits.'

In spite of this, he proceeded to catch Nuvolari in the Alfa and had an electrifying duel with him until he was forced to stop again for tyres, letting the Italian by into third place. Once again Rosemeyer drove like a man inspired and managed to catch Nuvolari, finally finishing a brilliant third behind Caracciola and von Brauchitsch. In spite of all his pit stops, he was only one minute and one second behind the winner. It was a truly remarkable drive and he got as big a reception from the crowd as did Caracciola.

While frustrated by all his tyre problems, Bernd was nonetheless elated by his performance, but his elation was short-lived as he learned of his friend's crash, and by now the news of von Delius' condition was becoming alarming. He was in a bad way and had been transferred to a hospital in Bonn.

Next morning Elly was awakened by Bernd's father—Ernst von Delius had died during the night. She, in turn, woke Bernd and broke the news to him. Later, sick at heart, they drove to Adenau to visit Dick Seaman, who they were relieved to find was in fine spirits and unaware that Delius was dead. They could not bring themselves to tell him. From Adenau they drove to Bonn, where Bernd said farewell to his friend.

The Monaco Grand Prix was completely dominated by the extraordinary battle between the two Mercedes 'team

ABOVE **Rosemeyer with his great friend, Ernst von Delius, on their way to America for the Vanderbilt Cup**

RIGHT **Bernd celebrates his fine victory in that race**

mates', Caracciola and von Brauchitsch, with victory going finally to the latter. Bernd held third place behind this battling duo until lap 19, when his steering failed at the Gasworks Hairpin, putting him into the sandbags. Later, he took over Stuck's car, which was suffering from failing brakes, handed it back at around half-distance and then took it over again for the rest of the race on lap 68. The two of them finally finished fourth, three laps behind the winner.

Elly now had to return to Berlin and could not go with Bernd to Pescara for the Coppa Acerbo which, in spite of their separation, he won. During this race there occurred another incident which has become part of the Rosemeyer legend: he clipped a paving stone, breaking a wheel nut which fell off on one of the twisty bits at the back of the long circuit where Auto Union had an emergency tyre and fuel depot. The right rear wheel came off, overtook Bernd and proceeded to roll and bounce down the hill where it landed at the feet of the astonished mechanics. Seconds later Bernd arrived on three wheels, to depart about a minute later on four again!

In the Swiss GP Bernd suffered locking brakes on lap 2 and shot off the road and into a field. The car was undamaged but several spectators helped him back onto the track, so Bernd very correctly drove to the pits and retired. The sensation of practice had been the appearance of Tazio Nuvolari in the Auto Union team, but even 'the great little man' had been unable to get to grips with the car in the short time available to him, so when he was called in to hand over to Rosemeyer he did so at once. Bernd finally finished fifth.

The Italians moved their Grand Prix to the town circuit

of Livorno, in the hope that it would give the Alfas a better chance against the German cars. It didn't and not even Rosemeyer could do anything about the Mercedes of Caracciola and Lang, who finished one-two nearly 1½ minutes ahead of him. Two weeks later he again finished behind two Mercedes in the Czech GP at Brno. As in Switzerland, locking brakes sent him off the road, damaging a wheel so badly that he had to get a lift back to the pits. H. P. Müller was duly flagged in and Bernd took over, driving to such effect that he caught a very surprised Dick Seaman on the last lap, depriving Mercedes of a nice one-two-three.

With only four wins in the year, Auto Union had definitely been second-best to Mercedes-Benz throughout 1937 and the Zwickau concern was not at all happy at the prospect of another beating in the last race of the year at Donington Park, in England. Even Rosemeyer, great fighter that he was, did not think he had a chance and would have been very happy to stay at home with Elly, who was expecting their baby in mid-November. Having entered for the race, however, Auto Union decided they should honour their agreement, so the team went to Donington. It was Bernd's thirteenth race of the year and he won a famous victory, but tragically, it was to be his last.

Ten days later he was back in the cockpit for more record attempts on the *Reichsautobahn* during the official Speed Week. This time he achieved his great ambition and became the first man to break the 400 km/h (250 mph) barrier on the road. Using a streamlined, 6-litre car he achieved 406.32 km/h (253.95 mph) over the Flying Kilometre and 406.29 km/h (253.93 mph) over the Flying Mile. Altogether that year he set three new World Records and 15 Class Records. Although 1937 had been a disappointment compared to 1936, Bernd had finished it on a high note.

But the best was yet to come: on 12 November, Bernd jun. was born and not long afterwards a delighted father gently chided his son—for not waiting another day and arriving on the thirteenth!

Early in January Bernd learned that Mercedes-Benz had applied for permission to make some more record attempts, as they had had no luck during the Record Week. Obviously, if permission were granted, Auto Union would want to be there, too, to defend their records. Permission was granted and both companies made plans for 27 January.

Elly had already agreed to give some lectures in Czechoslovakia around the end of January and Bernd was not at all happy at the thought that she might not be able to be with him at the *Reichsautobahn*, but he grudgingly agreed that she must honour her commitments. On the morning of 25 January a photographer called at their home in Berlin and took a number of pictures of the family. Shortly afterwards Bernd flew to Frankfurt and Elly set off for Czechoslovakia. On the evening of the 27th Bernd phoned to say that the weather was not too good so, with luck, the record attempts might be postponed for a couple of days, allowing Elly to finish her lectures and join him in Frankfurt. He added that the new Auto Union 'should be damned fast'.

But the weather improved and on the following morning

both Auto Union and Mercedes were ready to go. As the latter had instigated the attempts, Caracciola was the first off and he was immediately very fast, breaking Rosemeyer's record with a speed of 432.6 km/h (270.4 mph). Mercedes seemed well satisfied with this, so now it was Rosemeyer's turn. His first run was really only to get the car warmed up on that cold morning—even so his average was 429.92 km/h (268.7 mph). The car was turned round and Rosemeyer set off once more. He was never to return.

Just after the 9-kilometre mark the big Auto Union went out of control at around 430 km/h (270 mph) and crashed, spreading itself over a large area of the *autobahn*. Rosemeyer was found lying among some trees by the roadside.

Germany was stunned by his death. He and Elly were enormously popular—a delightful, gifted couple who had achieved much in a very short time. Now Elly was inundated with letters from people all over the world who admired Bernd and felt they knew him, such was the strength of his personality. Officialdom, too, was equally moved—Adolf Hitler sent a personal note to Elly:

'I was deeply moved by the news of the tragic fate of your husband. I offer you my sincerest condolences. May the thought that he fell in his devotion to the honour of his country mitigate your profound grief.'

There were similar notes from Hermann Göring, Dr Goebbels, Rudolf Hess, Heinrich Himmler and von Rib-

Rosemeyer slides out of a corner on his way to victory in the 1937 Donington GP. It was to be his last race

bentrop, but the vast majority was from thousands of ordinary people to whom Bernd's death was a personal loss. He was buried, with full military honours, close to his friend Ernst von Delius in Berlin's Dahlem Cemetery and a memorial was set up on the spot where he was found, beside the *Reichsautobahn* between Frankfurt and Darmstadt.

*　　*　　*

So what sort of a man was Bernd Rosemeyer, that he could have such an appeal for people from all walks of life? He was young, blond and undeniably handsome and was obviously charismatic to a degree. The English racing driver, Earl Howe, knew him well and wrote of him: 'A more delightful, charming and attractive character I have never met in my racing career; gay, carefree, with a most delightful sense of humour and a most charming personality. He combined in my judgement all the finest attributes of a sportsman. He, apparently, had never known how to spell fear, and his technique at the wheel was absolutely brilliant.'

In his three short seasons with Auto Union that technique, allied to considerable courage and phenomenal natural skill, won him ten races from just 33 starts, and 12 fastest laps. He also won two mountainclimbs. This would be an extraordinary set of results for an experienced racing driver, but Rosemeyer drove his first race in 1935

never having competed in any kind of car before! And in only his second race he gave the great Caracciola a considerable run for his money, in itself an extraordinary achievement and made almost unbelievably so by the fact that it was on the Nürburgring!

For a brief, foolish moment this fosters the thought that perhaps the Auto Unions weren't all that difficult to drive after all. Surely, if Rosemeyer could handle the mid-engined, 16-cylinder car with such ease after absolutely zero racing experience, what was all the fuss about? Then sanity prevails and one realizes that in their six years of racing Auto Union tried no fewer than 16 drivers in competition and almost the same number again in private testing. Only five or six showed any real promise and only four—Stuck, Varzi, Rosemeyer and Nuvolari—proved to have the necessary talent.

No, in an era of some very great drivers Bernd Rosemeyer was a true phenomenon—a racing driver of genius. He was also blessed with a rare personality which caught the public's imagination in such a way that it produced a legend. Fifty years on, the legend thrives.

Achille Varzi

Team Driver, Scuderia Ferrari 1934; Auto Union 1935–37

'Story running about in Italy that Achille
Varzi, who was missing from the Auto Union
team in the German Grand Prix, is neither
unhappy with the team nor disappointed with
the car but simply in love. A German lady,
moreover. Whole thing very complicated. All
Italy hopes that the course will run smooth.'

The Motor, 4 August 1936

Regular followers of the Grand Prix scene who read that
paragraph in Rodney Walkerley's *Grande Vitesse* column
will no doubt have shrugged off the item as a bit of chit-chat
that had little, if anything, to do with motor racing. This
would have been a reasonable reaction because, on the face
of it, the story was simply about a love-sick racing driver.
Good for the gossip columns, perhaps, or the plot of a B-
movie, but of no importance to the real world of racing.
Had they but known, however, they were reading one of
the very few published references to the tragic decline of
one of the great drivers of the era.

The whole thing was indeed very complicated, for
Achille Varzi had not just fallen in love with a German
lady, but a *married* German lady. To make things even
worse, she was married to one of his Auto Union team
mates and the final, tragic ingredient was that, with the
best of intentions, she had introduced him to the drug,
morphia. By the time Walkerley's seemingly innocent
paragraph appeared in print, a great racing driver was
already on the path to oblivion.

Life had begun pretty well for Achille Varzi. He was born
on 8 August 1904 in Galliate, near Milan, the son of a well-
to-do textile manufacturer. Like most racing drivers of his
era, Varzi began his career on motorcycles. He had two
brothers, Angelo and Anacleto, and in the early 1920s
he and Angelo went racing. By 1923 he was beginning to
make a name for himself, as was a certain Tazio Nuvolari
and although they seldom raced against each other, they
were both so gifted and so different that a definite rivalry
was built up between them by their supporters. Whereas
Varzi was tall, elegant and always immaculately dressed—
whether on or off a motorcycle—Nuvolari was a very
slightly built 1.6 m (5 ft 3 in) who looked distinctly scruffy
in his racing outfit of knee-breeches, puttees and thick jer-
sey with leather elbow pads. It was the same with their
racing, whether on a motorcycle or in a car—Varzi stylish
and smooth as silk; Nuvolari all arms and elbows and
apparently on the very edge of disaster all the time. Apart
from their Italian blood, about the only thing they had in
common was a quite dazzling skill on wheels. Although
12 years apart in age, they were seemingly born to be rivals.

Varzi began racing with a 500 cc Sunbeam, then switched
to a 350 cc Garelli. In 1924 he became only the third Italian
to compete in the fabled Isle of Man TT, where he rode
a Dot. It was not the most competitive of machines, but
Varzi was doing quite well when he had to take to the grass
to avoid another rider who fell in front of him. For this
sporting gesture he was awarded the Nisbet Trophy. In
spite of a slightly damaged knee, Varzi hastened back to
Italy for what was known as the Italian TT, in which
Nuvolari was competing on a new 350 cc Bianchi. Tazio
had to retire and so did Varzi, who was riding his 500 cc
Sunbeam, but the family honour was saved by brother
Angelo, who won the 350 cc class on his Sunbeam. Varzi
returned to the Isle of Man for the next three years, and
again in 1930, but never enjoyed any success on the demanding TT course.

In spite of their budding rivalry on the race track, Achille
and Tazio became good friends off it and used to meet
socially quite often. Nuvolari had already enjoyed some
small success in cars and in 1926 Varzi took the plunge
into motor racing, buying a Type 37 Bugatti. He achieved
very little, but when, in 1927, Nuvolari decided to form
his own motor racing team, Varzi was immediately interested. With the help of some mutual friends they put the
project together and, deciding that it would be foolish to
buy Alfa Romeos and race against the factory team, bought
two Type 35 Bugattis.

By the time they were ready to race the season was over,
so the new team made its debut at Tripoli in 1928. The
race provided the first of numerous fierce battles between
the two Italians that were to delight and enthral thousands
of spectators over the next few years. Varzi led initially,
only to suffer ignition problems which forced him into the
pits. Tazio won and Achille finished third and this set the
pattern, for Nuvolari won the next three races at Pozzo,
Alessandria and Messina, much to Varzi's disgust. He
could hardly complain, as the team was Nuvolari's idea
and he had really set it up, but Varzi willingly took second
place to no-one, so in mid-1928 he left and bought a P2
Alfa Romeo from the great Giuseppe Campari. This car
was already four years old, reputedly the one in which
Campari had won the GP d'Europe at Lyons in 1924.
Campari later bought it from the works and won the Coppa
Acerbo with it in 1927 and 1928, before selling it to Varzi
and co-driving it with him to second place in the Italian
GP.

In 1929, driving this same car, Varzi came into his own,
winning the Coppa Montenero at Livorno, the Circuit of
Alessandria and the Monza and Rome GPs, all of which
made him Champion of Italy. As a result, he was invited
to join the Alfa Romeo team for 1930, which he did, in
spite of the fact that Nuvolari had joined, too. After the
Mille Miglia in April he probably wished he hadn't, for
Nuvolari beat him in a way that immediately passed into
legend (see Chapter 6, *Tazio Nuvolari*), catching his rival
apparently by driving through the early hours of the morning without lights. One up to Nuvolari.

Within the month, Varzi got his revenge, and with a drive
that also passed into legend. When he joined Alfa Romeo,
the factory asked him to sell back his very successful P2,

which Vittorio Jano planned to up-date (with two others) for the new season. Varzi agreed, providing he could have the car for the Targa Florio. This was agreed and after a trial run in the Circuit of Alessandria—which he won easily—Varzi scored an epic victory in the Targa. He won in the record time of a shade under seven hours and set a new lap record, in spite of the fact that the revised P2 was regarded as a bitch to drive, its handling not up to its horsepower. Because of this, Nuvolari and Campari preferred the new 1750 cc supercharged cars, but they could only finish fourth and fifth and Varzi became the hero of the hour.

His main rival in the race turned out to be Louis Chiron in a Bugatti, who was definitely catching Varzi until his riding mechanic became violently ill. Momentarily distracted by this, Chiron went off the road and damaged a wheel. He changed it and continued, but had lost valuable time. Varzi, meanwhile, had troubles of his own. His mechanic had picked up a spare can of fuel at their last pit stop as the Alfa's petrol tank had sprung a leak. He tried to refuel while on the move during the last lap and, inevitably, some petrol was spilt onto the hot exhaust pipe and caught fire. Varzi wasn't about to stop on account of a little conflagration—on the contrary, he drove faster than ever while the hapless mechanic tried to smother the flames with his seat cushion. And so the fiery trio crossed the finish line, beating Chiron by just under two minutes. This remarkable win established Achille Varzi as one of the greatest drivers in the world.

So Alfa Romeo had won the Mille Miglia and the Targa Florio, but in Grand Prix racing a new name was making a big impact—Maserati. This new Italian make beat the Alfas and Bugattis at Rome and in the Coppa Montenero, now renamed the Coppa Ciano. Varzi didn't hesitate—he left his rival at Alfa Romeo and bought a Maserati! Driving it for the first time in the Coppa Acerbo at Pescara he won easily, while poor Nuvolari could only finish fifth in the P2. A week later Tazio got his revenge, leading Campari and Varzi—all of them on 1750 cc supercharged Alfas—to victory in the Tourist Trophy in Belfast. But Varzi had the last laugh that year. He went on to win the Monza and Spanish GPs in his Maserati and was once again declared Champion of Italy.

In spite of this success Varzi joined Bugatti for 1931. Quite why he should leave a winning team is not clear—it can't have been for money, as *Le Patron* was not overfond of paying people to drive his cars, that was reward enough in itself! Whatever the reason, Varzi decided to throw in his lot with Molsheim, just as René Dreyfus left to join Maserati!

He began by winning at Tunis with Bugatti's new Type 51. He retired in the Mille Miglia (driving a 4.9-litre car) and could only finish third in the Targa Florio, having persuaded Team Manager Costantini to let him have a twin-cam machine after Bugatti had decided not to race. Varzi lightened the Bugatti as much as possible, removing—among other things—the mudguards. As luck would have it he took the lead, only to see the heavens open and turn

Elegant as ever, the young Varzi sits in his Bugatti before the 1931 French GP at Monthléry, which he won, driving with Louis Chiron

129

the road into a mudbath. Unlike Varzi, Enzo Ferrari was ready for this as, sensing rain, he had lightened the Alfas of Nuvolari and Borzacchini by removing only the rear mudguards, retaining those on the front. As a result, his drivers could see where they were going, whereas Varzi was practically blinded by mud thrown up by his front wheels. He made a frantic stop for clean goggles, a peaked cloth cap and a cigarette, but it was no use—Nuvolari and Borzacchini passed him to win. Varzi's performance, however, was regarded as just as brilliant as his winning drive the previous year.

He joined forces with his Bugatti team mate Louis Chiron for the ten-hour French GP at Montlhéry and they won by miles. They were paired again at Spa for the Belgian GP and in the opening laps Varzi and Nuvolari had a marvellous duel. After the first driver change Chiron easily got away from Borzacchini until magneto trouble forced the Bugatti out. Varzi then came third in the German GP and third again in the Monza GP.

Tazio Nuvolari dominated 1932, winning six races and the Italian Championship. Varzi won once, at Tunis, and he finished third in the Targa Florio. In spite of this bad year he stayed with Bugatti for 1933 and began the European season in truly brilliant style by scoring an epic victory over Nuvolari at Monaco.

It was one of the classic races of all time, Varzi on the Bugatti and Nuvolari on the Monza Alfa Romeo. For three and a half hours over 100 laps the two Italians fought a duel which can seldom, if ever, have been equalled. The cars were never more than a few feet apart, Nuvolari leading for 66 laps and Varzi for 34. Then, going up the hill

to the Casino on the last lap, Varzi held the Bugatti in third and, engine screaming, passed Nuvolari. Tazio, too, took his revs sky-high, but the effort was too much for the Alfa's engine and an oil pipe broke, spraying hot lubricant on the exhaust. With smoke pouring from under the bonnet, Nuvolari drove on until the engine stopped, then pushed the stricken Alfa to—but sadly not over—the finishing line. Varzi won and poor Nuvolari was not even classified as a finisher!

They next met at Tripoli in May and again Varzi won, but this time with the full co-operation of Nuvolari! The force that brought these two great rivals together was, of course, money. That year, for the first time, the Tripoli GP was run in conjunction with a state lottery, the state in question being Italy, which held Libya as a protectorate. Tickets were sold for months before the race and then, three days before it, 30 tickets were drawn to correspond with the 30 starters. An Italian lumber merchant named Enrico Rivio learned that he had drawn Achille Varzi. If Varzi were to win the race, Signor Rivio would win nearly eight million lire! (That was worth approximately £50,000 in 1933—virtually £1 million in 1985.) Rivio flew at once to Tripoli and went to see Varzi. He had a *wonderful* idea! Varzi listened very carefully, accepted the man's written offer and wished him good-day. He had a few phone calls to make. . . .

The race was, to put it mildly, extraordinary. First Campari in a works Maserati led from Sir Henry Birkin on his own Maserati and Nuvolari on a Monza Alfa. Then Campari fell out and Nuvolari took the lead, from Borzacchini and Birkin. Varzi was seemingly miles behind, but

pulled up to third before his Bugatti started making some very nasty noises. He pressed on and managed to catch up with Borzacchini, whose Alfa was clearly slowing drastically, although it sounded perfectly healthy. It slowed even more drastically when Borzacchini drove it into an oil drum marking the side of the road, before hobbling to the pits with a burst tyre, where he promptly retired!

So Nuvolari led from his arch rival Varzi, led on the last lap until a few hundred yards from the finish, when his Alfa came to a halt. Nuvolari leapt out, cursing his luck and bemoaning the fact that he had run out of petrol. But was this not the man who had pushed his car so gallantly to the finish at Monaco? Surely he would do the same now? It was and he wouldn't, for Tazio just stood there as his mechanics rushed from the pits with petrol cans and Varzi's Bugatti appeared spluttering its way to the line. As he passed Nuvolari, the Alfa burst into life once more and Tazio took the chequered flag just one-tenth of a second behind Varzi. What a finish! What a fix!

So Signor Rivio won his eight million lire, half of which—as arranged—he gave to Varzi who, in turn, shared his half with 'certain other drivers'. They got away with it, too, for although the whole thing stank to high heaven and people were asking some very awkward questions almost before the chequered flag had fallen, an official enquiry decided that it was best to sweep the whole thing under the carpet and to see that such a fix should not happen again. From 1934 on, the draw for the lottery was made just before the race.

Varzi won again—legally this time—at the Avus GP a few weeks later, but it was to be his last victory of the season, so perhaps it was just as well that he had made a financial killing at Tripoli. The Bugattis had become quite outclassed by the middle of the year and the promised 2.8-litre car didn't appear until the very last race of the season—the Spanish GP at San Sebastian. Varzi finished fourth. First and second were the two Scuderia Ferrari Alfas of Chiron and Fagioli, who between them had won almost everything in the last half of the year. Varzi was allowed to try one of the cars during the practice for the Coppa Acerbo in August and—lo and behold—for 1934 he signed with Scuderia Ferrari. And Nuvolari? He went independent.

The arrival of Mercedes-Benz and Auto Union on the Grand Prix scene altered the face of racing forever, but the German teams didn't make the impact they hoped for straight away. Scuderia Ferrari won at Monaco (where no German cars were entered) and then again at Avus and Montlhéry, the Germans suffering humiliating defeats, first at the hands of Guy Moll and then Louis Chiron. From that point on, though, it was *Deutschland über Alles*, and the Silver Arrows won every race.

Varzi finished second at both Avus and Montlhéry and scored a marvellous win in the Mille Miglia on a 2.6-litre Monza Alfa, but he was lucky. At the Imola control Enzo Ferrari told him that as it was raining in the North, he should change to micro-tread rain tyres. Varzi wasted precious time arguing against this advice while Nuvolari—in second place, driving a privately entered 2.3-litre Monza—was catching him rapidly. Finally, Ferrari prevailed and Varzi set off on the new tyres (which were not available to his rival) just as the rain began to fall. He won the race, beating Nuvolari by nine minutes.

That year he also won the Targa Florio (for the second time, but against very limited opposition) and notched up other wins at Tripoli (no nonsense on this occasion, although he only beat Moll by a car's length), the Circuit of Alessandria and in the GPs of Penya Rhin and Nice.

Although Hans Stuck was performing nobly for them, it must have been clear to Auto Union midway through that first season, that their policy of employing only German drivers was misguided, for the others in the team were simply not good enough. This can hardly have gone unnoticed, either, by Varzi and Nuvolari, who were both having a fairly unhappy time in Grand Prix racing. Always one to look ahead, Varzi doubtless had the same thoughts as Nuvolari when he saw the tremendous speed and efficiency of the German teams and, once again, he proved quicker off the mark than Tazio.

Towards the end of August, Auto Union went to Monza for a test session prior to the Italian Grand Prix, and Varzi was there. Almost certainly he had made his interest in the team known through its Italian representative, Ugo Ricordi, and Auto Union were only too happy to give him a run in Hans Stuck's car. His inclusion in the team for 1935 was quite possibly settled—if not signed—there and then, for although Nuvolari was later twice to have brief

Varzi testing Hans Stuck's Auto Union at Monza in August 1934

tests in the German car it was Varzi who was given an official reception by Auto Union at the DKW works in Chemnitz in November. A few weeks later, Nuvolari received a letter from Auto Union, telling him that the firm would not be seeking his services for 1935 . . . (see Chapter 6, *Tazio Nuvolari*).

Auto Union did, however, sign two other drivers for the coming season. The first was Bernd Rosemeyer, who had made quite a name for himself on NSU and DKW motorcycles, and the second was another young man who had also caught people's attention, first with a Bugatti and then with an Alfa Romeo. Paul Pietsch was 22 years old and, like Varzi, came from a wealthy family. In 1934 he had married Ilse Engel, a beautiful divorcée from Wiesbaden.

Fifty years on, Pietsch looked back on his brief first marriage without pain or rancour. 'We were married much against the wishes of my mother and to begin with we had a very good time, but I was too young and Ilse was too nice! It was while I was driving for Auto Union that she and Achille Varzi fell in love.'

Nearly 30 years old at that time, Varzi was still unmarried, although never short of female company. Regarded by many as cold and aloof he nevertheless had a very forceful personality which, allied to his good looks, an impeccable taste in clothes and good living, made him very attractive to women, who flocked around him. Initially, only one seemed to make any real impact, a beautiful Italian girl named Norma, who was just 20 when Varzi first set eyes on her in Milan. So taken with her was he that he immediately introduced himself to her on the street, which was hardly acceptable behaviour to a well brought up young Italian girl in those days. Cold and aloof he may have been, but Varzi could turn on the charm to tremendous effect and Norma had no chance. He swept her off her feet and she was soon his companion at the race tracks. Eventually they would marry, but not before Varzi had essayed a love affair with Ilse Pietsch that would ruin his career and nearly kill him.

In the spring of 1935 Varzi did some pre-season testing at Avus, where he drove both Stuck's streamlined record-breaking car and a regular racer. He found the Auto Union much faster than anything he had ever driven before and very much to his liking. Auto Union didn't enter for Monaco, but Varzi insisted on having a car for the Tunis GP, for he was well aware of the good money available there, having won the race twice before. There was virtually no opposition and he won by nearly four minutes from Jean-Pierre Wimille's Bugatti. Afterwards he remarked that he thought the Carthage circuit magnificent, 'but I should have liked it a great deal better if there had been no wind.' That same wind was nearly to take his life just one year later.

In Tripoli he was brilliant, holding off the Mercedes of Caracciola and Fagioli and the blindingly fast Bimotore Alfa of his old rival, Nuvolari. The Alfa went through tyres at an alarming rate and pit stops dropped Tazio to fourth place at three-quarter distance, but by driving absolutely flat out he caught and passed the two Mercedes and was soon wheel to wheel with Varzi! At around 220 km/h (135 mph) Achille held him off, knowing Nuvolari was

ABOVE **Varzi gets off to a good start in the 1935 French GP at Montlhéry, wheel-to-wheel with Caracciola (Mercedes-Benz)**

RIGHT **Ilse Pietsch has eyes only for Varzi in the pits during the 1935 Coppa Acerbo. Also in the picture are** (*left to right*) **Hans Stuck, Varzi's brother, Angelo, and Paul Pietsch**

ruining his tyres. Indeed he was, and another pit stop let the Auto Union into a secure lead, now from Caracciola's Mercedes. But then, with five laps to go a piece of tread flew off one of his rear tyres as he screamed past the pits. Varzi slowed, but by the time he completed the lap and stopped at the pit the tyre was in shreds and the wheel buckled. Caracciola roared by into the lead, but with new tyres Varzi went after him 'in an ice-cold fury'. He had held off Nuvolari—now he would catch Caracciola. He did, too, crossing the line at the end of the 39th and penultimate lap only two seconds behind the Mercedes and gaining visibly. But then another tyre blew and Caracciola disappeared into the distance to win an electrifying race by 67 seconds.

Varzi was again troubled by burst tyres at Avus, where he finished third in the final after a very fast race. Trouble of another kind now beset him—appendicitis—and he was too ill to attend the first day's practice for the Eifel GP.

He started the race, but eventually had to hand over to zu Leiningen. In the French GP at Montlhéry he handed over to Rosemeyer after several pit stops for new plugs and in the German GP he was never in the picture, giving his car to zu Leiningen once again. He was back on form for the Coppa Acerbo, however, leading from start to finish, but the rest of the year was a washout, as he could only finish fourth in the Swiss GP and retired in Italy, Spain and Czechoslovakia.

At the end of the season Paul Pietsch left Auto Union and separated from Ilse—who joined Achille Varzi. There had been an almost instant attraction between the suave Italian and the beautiful German blonde and, as the year went on, they saw more and more of each other, clandestinely at first, but then quite openly, until by the end of the season their affair was well known to the Grand Prix circus.

Although he had won two races, Varzi was not altogether happy at Auto Union. The language barrier was one problem and money was another, and in August he tested the new V-8 Maserati at Monza. Whether this was a ploy to get him a better deal with Auto Union is not known, but he did eventually sign with the German concern for 1936.

Early in the New Year he went into hospital for a minor operation on his throat before going to Monza for a winter testing session with Auto Union. He then departed for Garmisch-Partenkirchen and the Winter Olympics, where he captained one of Italy's two bob-sleigh teams, Varzi's consisting entirely of racing drivers—Trossi, Taruffi and

Cortese being his team mates. Unfortunately, it is not known what success, if any, they enjoyed. In March he was back in hospital, this time to have his troublesome appendix removed.

In May Auto Union paid their first visit to Monaco and Varzi finished a very fine second in the rain behind *Regenmeister* Caracciola, after a race-long duel with team mate Stuck. Next came Tripoli and his third victory in this event although, as in 1933, it was a contrived win. This time, however, the drivers concerned—Varzi and Stuck— didn't know about the fix until the race was over. Politics, not money, was the cause on this occasion and the whole affair left both men feeling very angry. It was also the trigger that fired Varzi into the world of drugs.

Run at close to 210 km/h (130 mph), the race was largely a battle between the two Auto Union drivers, with Stuck gaining the upper hand towards the end. But then the new Team Manager, Dr Karl Feuereissen, began giving him 'slow down' signals, at the same time telling Varzi to speed up. The result was that Varzi put in a last lap at a staggering 227 km/h (141 mph) and passed a very surprised Stuck almost on the finish line. Stuck was not only surprised, he was very angry and complained bitterly to Feuereissen, who then admitted his part in the proceedings. He was, he said, acting on orders from very high up—the Fascist governments of Germany and Italy were now very close and it had been decided that, where possible, Italian drivers should win Italian races. Libya was part of the Italian Empire, and so. . . . Stuck was stunned and, when he heard how he had won the race, Varzi was furious.

His fury increased that night at the victory dinner given by the Governor of Libya and founder of the race, Marshal Italo Balbo, who proposed a toast to the winner, 'the *real* winner', and raised his glass to Hans Stuck! Varzi stormed from the room. Later, back at his hotel, he brooded about the day's events long into the night and it was at this point, apparently, that Ilse offered him morphia for the first time.

'When Ilse was with me she never had anything to do with morphia,' recalls Paul Pietsch, 'but it is true that once, when she was in hospital, she was given the drug as a painkiller, which was common practice then. We were divorced in 1936 and it was only afterwards that I heard that she and Varzi were using it. I was told that she gave some to Varzi when he was feeling very depressed and that eventually he became addicted to it. It certainly had a terrible effect on him and ruined his career—he became very ill and was in a sanatorium for some time.'

Varzi's first reaction to Ilse's suggestion was one of horror. He was unquestionably addicted to nicotine and was seldom seen without a cigarette, often smoking during a race. Cigarettes, however, were not then regarded as dangerous, but morphia! At first he refused to touch it, but later that night—still unable to sleep—he succumbed.

The following weekend, at Tunis, Varzi was leading the race (determined to win without any help from officialdom this time) when the wind that had bothered him the previous year swept his car off the road. Depending upon which report you read, he was travelling at anything between 195–290 km/h (120–180 mph), but anyway, it was a very high-speed shunt which horrified those who saw it,

one of whom was Raymond Mays. He later recalled that it was one of the two most terrifying crashes he had had the misfortune to witness (the other being Hanns Geier's at Bern the year before) and that he and some other spectators approached the stricken Auto Union in the awful certainty of finding Varzi dead. They were amazed to find that he was not only very much alive, but completely unhurt! Not only unhurt, but apparently unmoved, for his first concern as he was helped to his feet was to brush the dirt and dust off his neatly pressed overalls. Signor Varzi wished to appear immaculate at all times!

In spite of his apparent unconcern, Varzi was considerably shaken by the crash, which was the first of his career. (It was also to be the only one until his final, fatal accident at Bern 12 years later.) That night he took another dose of morphia from Ilse. She was right—it banished the pain and calmed the nerves. He started using it regularly, and now things began to go wrong.

The next race was the Penya Rhin GP in Barcelona. At Varzi's suggestion Auto Union had built a short-chassis car for him to drive in this race, but in practice both he and Rosemeyer agreed that it was no good. Varzi then asked if he could swap it for Rosemeyer's normal, long-chassis car (Rosemeyer still being the junior driver at that time), but Bernd had badly banged his knee in a practice shunt and couldn't drive with his knees bent, as he would have to in the short-chassis car. Varzi then refused to take part in the race, although, of course, he was well aware of Rosemeyer's problem and that he had asked for the short-chassis car in the first place! Auto Union told Varzi that if he didn't drive he would be in breach of his contract, whereupon the Italian announced that he was ill! He was examined by Dr Peter Gläser, who declared that he was perfectly fit, but nevertheless Varzi did not start and Ernst von Delius took his place, as Hans Stuck was hillclimbing at Shelsley Walsh that weekend.

A week later Rosemeyer scored the first of his many victories that year with a sensational drive in the fog in the Eifel GP. Varzi could only finish seventh. He was third in Budapest behind Nuvolari and the flying Rosemeyer and then persuaded Auto Union to enter a car for him in the Milan GP, but again he was beaten by his old rival on the Alfa.

He did not turn up for the German GP, which prompted Rodney Walkerley's item in *The Motor* the following week, but he was back in action at the Coppa Ciano at Livorno, where he led the race until troubled by failing brakes, allowing Nuvolari (again!) to pass him into the lead before he retired. Two weeks later Auto Union were in Pescara for the Coppa Acerbo and, once again, of Varzi there was no sign.

By now it was clear that there was something seriously wrong—Varzi seemed to have undergone a complete personality change. The man who previously had little to say for himself became quite garrulous, but his chatter had no sense to it; the fellow whose dress sense and elegance had been the envy of his friends was now untidy and unkempt; the man who always kept appointments went missing without a word of warning.

At the beginning of the season Varzi could clearly have

looked upon himself as Auto Union's team leader, in spite of Hans Stuck's unquestioned seniority. He was definitely faster than both Stuck and the newcomer Rosemeyer, who was still regarded as a learner, in spite of his fine win in the last race of 1935. But by the time of the Coppa Acerbo, Rosemeyer was the golden boy, the new German hero who, in only his second season of motor racing, had already won the Eifel and German GPs. To a man already unbalanced by morphia, this may well have had a very unsettling effect, depressing him still further. The cure was more and more morphia.

Unable to find Varzi, Dr Feuereissen asked Dr Peter Gläser to go and look for him and try and uncover his problem. This was easier said than done, for Dr Gläser learned that not even Varzi's parents knew where he was. But the doctor had many contacts throughout the motoring world and eventually he was directed to a villa in Rome. There he found Varzi surrounded by a strange group of hangers-on.

Peter Gläser expressed Auto Union's concern for their driver's well-being and asked him to submit to a medical. Varzi readily agreed and Dr Gläser was happy to report that he could find nothing physically wrong with him, but he couldn't explain the man's personality change. He asked Varzi to report to Dr Feuereissen in Pescara for the Coppa Acerbo and Varzi complied. He duly took part in the race and, despite four stops for tyres, finished third, behind team mates Rosemeyer and von Delius. He also set fastest lap and was timed at 295.47 km/h (183.64 mph) over the Flying Kilometre. Nothing much wrong with that performance.

A week later he and Ilse arrived in Bern for the Swiss Grand Prix, but his attitude was so distant and he seemed so uninvolved that this time Dr Feuereissen himself went in search of an answer. While Varzi was practising, he went to his hotel and confronted Ilse, demanding to know what had happened to change Varzi's personality so. Ilse prevaricated and made feeble excuses, but then Feuereissen saw a hypodermic syringe, half-hidden on a table. Beside it lay a small bottle of morphia. Now he understood.

Varzi finished a good second in the race in what was a marvellous one-two-three for Auto Union. He turned up again at Monza for the Italian GP but was forced to retire with engine trouble.

By now there were the usual rumours about driver changes for the next year. In September it was suggested that Varzi would rejoin Scuderia Ferrari and that Louis Chiron was to retire, following his high-speed crash in the Mercedes at the Nürburgring. In November, Rodney Walkerley reported in *The Motor* that, 'Achille Varzi the taciturn has gone hunting and shooting. When asked whether he is leaving Auto Union next year he smole a smile and said nothing.'

In December it was reported that Varzi had stated categorically that he would only drive an Italian car in 1937, although by now Nuvolari had already signed for Ferrari. Also in December, Walkerley wrote, 'Varzi the inscrutable is many miles from his native land. Speculation mentions two possible reasons—a love affair or merely winter sports.' It was almost certainly the former, for the Italian authorities had become so alarmed by their great driver's

Varzi shields his head from flying rubber, having thrown a tread in the 1936 Coppa Acerbo. He finished third

condition that they refused to allow Ilse into the country—reportedly on the personal instructions of Mussolini, no less! The couple did meet, of course, because Varzi was not prevented from leaving Italy.

As for the new season, Auto Union did not renew their contract with Varzi for 1937. Instead they replaced him with another Italian—Luigi Fagioli—who had finally had enough of being forced to play third fiddle to Caracciola and von Brauchitsch. To be fair, Mercedes had had enough of Fagioli's tantrums, too!

Varzi simply disappeared from view. Motor racing heard nothing of him until July 1937, when he turned up at San Remo with a 1.5-litre Maserati, winning his heat and the final. Two months later he appeared at Livorno and asked a startled Karl Feuereissen for a drive in the Italian Grand Prix. Not surprisingly, Feuereissen demurred, reminding Varzi of his behaviour the previous year, but Varzi managed to convince him that he had given up drugs and was now separated from Ilse—he was his old self again. Spurred on by a sympathetic Bernd Rosemeyer, Feuereissen not only gave him a drive at Livorno, but also signed him up for the last two races of the year, at Brno and Donington.

For a while it looked as though Varzi was telling the truth. He was brilliant in practice, setting second-fastest time to Caracciola, but in the race he could only finish sixth, and almost in a state of collapse. Two weeks later he turned up at Brno with two fingers of his right hand bandaged. During practice he was very slow and seemed distinctly nervous, claiming that the wounds on his fingers were very painful.

On the second day's practice he asked for some changes to be made to his car and then, when they had been carried out, refused to drive any more. That evening he told Dr Feuereissen that he wasn't going to race, maintaining that it was very good of him to withdraw instead of just driving round slowly for a few laps and then giving up. He asked permission to leave Brno at once as he wanted to catch a train to Vienna. Feuereissen conferred with Dr Gläser, who told him that the wounds on Varzi's fingers were so minor that no German driver would have considered withdrawing from the race because of them. Varzi's problems, however, were clearly not confined to his fingers, so Feuereissen gave him permission to leave. He did not turn up at Donington.

Again, nothing was heard of him throughout the winter, but when the teams turned out at Tripoli in May 1938, there was Achille Varzi on a brand-new, 3-litre Maserati. He ran well in practice, too, but was forced to retire from the race with back axle trouble. Both he and Count Trossi were down to drive Maseratis in the French GP at Reims in July, but neither turned up. Varzi disappeared once more and didn't race again until 1946.

In March 1939 Hans Stuck came across a wretched Ilse in Munich. She begged him for money to enable her to buy a forged passport so she could get into Italy, but Hans refused, fearful that she would just spend it on morphia. He did, however, promise to pay her hotel bill. Next morning, while Hans and Paula were having breakfast in the Hotel Continental, the waiter told them of a tragic suicide attempt during the night—a young girl had been found

unconscious in the street, wearing only a pink nightdress. There was no way of identifying her, but she had been heard to murmur a strange, Greek-sounding name—Achille. . . . Hans and Paula drove immediately to the hospital, where they were told that Ilse was too ill to receive visitors. As he had promised he would, Stuck paid her hotel bill before leaving for Berlin that evening.

Somehow Ilse made a recovery from her addiction and during the war she married a German opera singer. She died in the early seventies. Varzi, too, got married—in 1941—to Norma, the woman who had waited so patiently for him during all his troubles. With her help he, too, beat his addiction and during the war he was able to run the family business, being too old (and presumably unfit) for military service.

As soon as hostilities were over he set about reviving his career and the immediate post-war years were initially kind, but ultimately fatal. In 1946 he was 42 years old, but apparently restored to full health once more, so Alfa Romeo were delighted to have their former star back in the team when they resumed racing that year. He joined Jean-Pierre Wimille, Count Felice Trossi and Giuseppe Farina to drive the beautiful 158 Alfas. It was immediately clear that while the passing years might have slowed his reactions a shade, he was driving with all his old skill. He won at Turin and then won his heat and finished second to Trossi in the final of the Milan GP.

He began the 1947 season in Argentina with a pre-war Type 308 Alfa, winning at Rosario and Interlagos and coming second in the Buenos Aires GP, before returning to Europe to compete in the four races that Alfa Romeo had entered that year. He won his heat in the Swiss GP and finished second to Wimille in the final. He was second to the Frenchman again at Spa, but then won at Bari. Finally, he was second to Trossi in the Italian GP.

Varzi had enjoyed himself in Argentina and went back at the beginning of 1948, taking with him a 4.6-litre version of the 1939 Alfa 312. He won again at Interlagos and came second at Mar del Plata. Back in Europe, before joining Alfa Romeo, he drove a Cisitalia at Bari and Mantua, coming third in both races. Then it was on to Bern for the Swiss GP.

On the evening of the first day's practice, Varzi lost control in the rain and, just when it seemed that the Alfa would come to rest with no harm to the driver, it hit a curb and rolled over. His head protected by nothing more than his familiar white linen wind helmet, Achille Varzi was killed instantly. Stunned, Alfa Romeo immediately withdrew from the race, but Norma bravely persuaded them to change their minds. Fittingly, Varzi's team mates, Trossi and Wimille, finished first and second. A few days later, amid huge and emotional crowds, Achille Varzi was buried at his birthplace, Galliate.

The subject of drugs is a very emotive one, but it is hard to believe that Ilse had anything but the best of intentions when she introduced Varzi to morphia. Like so many people before (and since), she found that it could relieve her from stress and loneliness, both of which can be very much part of the life of a racing driver's wife or mistress. There's no doubt that she loved Varzi very much, and

simply wanted to help him when she saw that he was troubled. But drugs are a false friend, and instead of helping him she almost destroyed him.

From 1936 Achille Varzi's life was in direct contrast to that of Rudolf Caracciola. After his terrible Monaco crash and the death of his first wife, Charly, Rudi was undoubtedly saved from some kind of oblivion by Baby Hoffmann who, older and wiser than Ilse, was able to give him the proper support he so badly needed. As a result, Caracciola went from the depths of despair to the height of achievement. Varzi, alas, went in exactly the opposite direction.

Caracciola and Varzi, the triumph and the tragedy.

Cherchez la femme.

Varzi being congratulated by Marshal Balbo following his controversial win in the 1936 Tripoli GP. It was after this race that he first took to drugs

196   *The Autocar, July 31st, 1936.*

Germany's

350,000 Spectators Watch Smashing Suc

(Below) Zanelli's and Seaman's Maseratis have retired, while Chiron (Mercedes) screams by.

A vast crowd watches the triumphant

NÜRBURG RING, EIFEL, GERMANY,
July 26th.

IT is half an hour before the start of the Grand Prix of Germany. The scene is impressive beyond words, but let us attempt to convey it. Only at a classic horserace, the Derby, or the St. Leger, is such excitement known in England; 350,000 people have been arriving all night—the roads have been thick with a ceaseless stream of traffic. The weather is bright but cloudy. It may rain, but we hope it will hold off.

Flags in brilliant colours deck the pits, sharply outlined against the dark green of the pine trees. All around is an excited multitude. The stand is packed. Below on the *promenadenplatz*, to the right, looking towards the start, and to the left looking towards the South Turn, are thousands of heads close together. Then in the near foreground, where the track returns past the back of the pits, and beyond, as far as the eye can see, the people are packed close, right down the winding valley road which leads into the mountains.

The race is over twenty-two laps of the 14.1 mile circuit, making 316 miles in all. A desperate struggle is anticipated in this, the big race of the year, for last year Italy won the Grosser Preis of Germany in a spectacular finish, and the Germans are burning for revenge. The new Alfa-Romeos are even faster than last year's cars. Two of these are twelve-cylinder cars, the other two eight-cylinders. Against them are five Mercedes and four Auto-Unions for Germany, while Italy has also two "official" Maseratis, one to be handled by Seaman, the English driver. Then there are two other Maseratis—one driven by Cholmondeley-Tapper, the Englishman—another Alfa, and two Bugattis.

Twenty cars are wheeled up to the starting grid, and as the hour of the start (11 a.m.) approaches, files of uniformed Nazis parade, and the great crowd salutes. An excited murmur grows louder and louder, and the cars, which have been swathed in dust-sheets, are uncovered. Soon all other sounds are drowned in the stirring music of the exhausts as the engines are started. The ride of the Valkyries is about to begin!

Bang goes the maroon! A tremendous thunder of sound arises. Germany's white cars shoot ahead. Von Brauchitsch takes the lead for Mercedes! His acceleration is terrific. Stuck's Auto-Union is second off, favoured by a good position on the starting grid. Brivio leads the Alfa-Romeos, with Severi close behind. But as the cars scream back behind the pits four white cars lead, von Brauchitsch, Stuck, Lang (Mercedes) and Rosemeyer (Auto-Union). The excitement leaves one breathless. One can count no more, but merely watch the red and white dots streaking down the valley out of sight. Germany is off well, at all events.

Following the Cars Round

Now the announcers at different points take up the tale, at Adenau, at the Karussell, at the Swallow Tail (two hairpin corners where the cars scream round at amazing speed on the steep banking), at Döttinger-Hohe, a bridge on the long straight—the only straight on this amazing course—where cars leap into the air, so great is their speed. Von Brauchitsch leads! Eagerly the crowd follows their excited accents. Finally, a signalboard gives the order about two miles away as the cars approach.

Von Brauchitsch is signalled first!

Then Rosemeyer! Then Lang! Lang is the youngest driver in the race, and the "baby" of the Mercedes team. He gets a rousing cheer, drowned by a shrill scream as Caracciola, the Mercedes champion, follows close behind. Then comes Stuck, and, 20 sec. behind von Brauchitsch, follows the leading Italian —Nuvolari, of course! Two more Mercedes hurtle by behind him, with Fagioli and Chiron up.

Again we await the announcers, and the shrill note of speeding cars is relayed from the distant mountains. At the Karussell, most spectacular of all the corners at the Ring, there is a sensation. The announcer, his concern mingling with his excitement, gives out that von Brauchitsch has stopped down in the valley below his hut! Alas! it was at the Karussell last year that von Brauchitsch's great drive came to an end.

So next lap Rosemeyer leads Lang by 18 sec., with Caracciola third, and Stuck and Nuvolari battling for fourth place. Stuck passes the Italian on the return road behind the pits, and a cheer goes up from the fiercely enthusiastic crowd.

The Autocar, July 31st, 1936   197

Revenge

cess of Auto-Unions at the Nürburg Ring

Auto-Unions returning to the paddock.

(Below) Germany ahead after the start! Von Brauchitsch (Mercedes), Lang (Mercedes), and Stuck (Auto-Union).

Long after the others von Brauchitsch arrives, and pulls in to his pit. It is not a long stop, and off he goes again, cheered to the echo. He is a great favourite with the crowd. Severi, too, makes a quick stop at his.pit.

On the third lap the order is not changed, but Rosemeyer is going ahead! Yes! He has made a record lap at 85.45 m.p.h. Now he leads by 23 sec., while Nuvolari has got by Stuck again. Already two cars have retired, Zanelli's Maserati, with fuel feed trouble, and, alas! Seaman's Maserati, too, with faulty brakes. The English driver has had but a short drive in the Grosser Preis. Wimille's Bugatti also appears no more. His gear box has given out.

The fourth lap brings fresh excitement, for Caracciola, arriving in third place as before, pulls in to his pit! Lightning adjustments are made by deft mechanics, and he gets away in tenth position. This leaves Nuvolari third, a growing danger to the two German cars which still lead at a thrilling pace. Lang is being tried hard indeed! The Mercedes hopes now rest on him, with von Brauchitsch and Caracciola in trouble, and Fagioli and Chiron no better than sixth and eighth.

Von Brauchitsch, a lap behind, comes by, going well again, not far ahead of the leader, Rosemeyer, on the fifth lap, but Rosemeyer is catching him once more; on the sixth lap he is but 4 sec. behind. Will he pass him on the seventh? No! Von Brauchitsch is signalled first. Here he comes! Here's Rosemeyer! He's going in to his pit! Both rear tyres are worn out already! Like ants mechanics swarm round the tail of the long silver Auto-Union. Lang tears through— Mercedes lead again! But Rosemeyer stops for only just over half a minute, and gets away still in second place. Nuvolari comes through. As he disappears down the valley road, he is 31 sec. behind Rosemeyer. Stuck is still fourth, Chiron fifth, and Brivio (Alfa) sixth.

Caracciola Retires

Meanwhile Caracciola has not come round again, and at last he walks in to his pit. A defective fuel pump has caused his retirement. But one has no time to watch those who retire—even Caracciola. With the eighth lap tyres begin to play further part in the great battle, which is developing lap by lap. Lang flashes through with a 21 sec. lead over Rosemeyer, but Nuvolari pulls in! Out jumps the Italian. He wipes the screen, then paces nervously backward and forward as mechanics change his rear wheels. A minute drags by before he starts again, but he is still fourth, for only Stuck has passed. But Chiron's Mercedes is now only 5 sec. behind Nuvolari.

The air is full of the shrill note of passing Mercedes, the deep roar of the Alfa-Romeos, the staccato, high-pitched bark of the Auto-Unions. One looks round the stand. Faces are white and tense with excitement. No make has the advantage so far, but Germany holds her lead! The sun is now shining bravely.

At the ninth lap von Brauchitsch maintains his position, ahead of the leading cars, though he is a lap behind on distance. Lang is slowing for his pit! Rosemeyer goes by to lead again, while tyres are changed on the Mercedes. Lang is getting out! Caracciola takes his place! The young Mercedes driver has damaged a finger, after his splendid drive. Stuck is now second, and leads Nuvolari by 34 sec. Caracciola gets away in Lang's car in fifth place. Next lap another change over takes place in the Mercedes team, for von Brauchitsch stops at his pit. Tyres are changed, the car is refuelled, and Lang, who has had his hand bandaged, takes over amid terrific cheers. But the car is a long way behind. Meanwhile Dreyfus has retired with one of the twelve-cylinder Alfas, while Brivio has stopped for tyres. Seaman has taken Trossi's place in the Maserati —a 1½-litre chassis with a four-cylinder 2½-litre engine.

HALF DISTANCE ORDER
1. Rosemeyer (Auto-Union), 82.78 m.p.h.
2. Stuck (Auto-Union), 2m. 13s. behind.
3. Nuvolari (Alfa-Romeo), 2m. 23s. behind.

At half-distance (eleven laps) Stuck, in second place, makes a stop for tyres, and the change is made very quickly; but meanwhile Nuvolari annexes the second position. Then Chiron stops, so that Caracciola, returned to the area, goes up to third place, while Stuck and Nuvolari are stationary. Severi stops, too, with his Alfa, Hasse with the Auto-Union Varzi was to have driven, Fagioli with his Mercedes!

Rosemeyer has such a commanding lead at this stage that the tension is eased. But the thirteenth lap is unlucky for Caracciola, for he comes in again, in third place, and makes a long stop while mechanics attempt to mend a leaking water connection. The job is done! Caracciola climbs back into the seat. But no! the mechanics wave him back. Caracciola gets out and lights a cigarette.

Feverish activity ; changing wheels on Rosemeyer's Auto-Union.

Nuvolari at the Bergwerk turn with his Alfa-Romeo.

Then at last a mechanic gets into the car, and drives it round the pits back to the tunnel leading to the paddock.

Is Rosemeyer going on to the finish without challenge? Hardly have the words been written than an excited murmur heralds the leader making for his pit, having covered fifteen laps. All four wheels are changed and the car refuelled. The pit personnel cast anxious glances up the track, but no Nuvolari appears. Away goes Rosemeyer. Now, how much has Nuvolari gained? The watch ticks on. Two minutes, three minutes! Something must have happened to the Italian. Stuck comes by amid cheers, but there is a sympathetic murmur when news is given out that Nuvolari has retired, it is thought with ignition trouble.

Surely Chiron, as well, has not appeared for some time. Yes, a glance at the board shows him a lap short. The announcer at the Swallow Tail, too, asks where he is. Cholmondeley-Tapper is reported from the same point to be going slowly, but comes by the stands all right. He has held on gallantly with his Maserati.

Chiron has Crashed !

Now news comes through of Chiron. He has crashed badly, striving to regain the lost Mercedes' fortunes. At the Antoniusbuche bridge, at the end of the long straight, where cars are travelling at 160 m.p.h., Chiron has left the road ! The car has gone down a steep embankment, much as Hartmann did last year with his Bugatti. Miraculously, Chiron is not badly hurt, and a sigh of relief goes up. He has only bruises on the head and shoulder.

After these sensational occurrences, Rosemeyer is left with a big lead, amounting to over 3 min., in front of Stuck, while Stuck is 5 min. 24 sec. ahead of Brivio, whose Alfa has come up to third place. In the lull, the announcer comments on the extraordinary absence of rain in a race at the Nürburg Ring ! Certainly it is strange to see the sun still shining on the brilliant scene, and no umbrellas amongst the serried crowds.

There are big gaps now between the leading cars, and, barring misfortune, the Auto-Union position seems secure. After seventeen laps the order is : Rosemeyer, Stuck, Brivio, Hasse (Auto-Union), and then the remaining two Mercedes, for

Brivio's Alfa-Romeo dives through the Swallow Tail corner.

behind Fagioli Lang has continued his gallant efforts and is now sixth with von Brauchitsch's car. Von Delius is

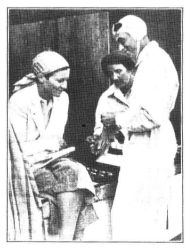

Rosemeyer—winner at a record speed, with his wife and Frau Stuck.

seventh with his Auto-Union, and eighth comes the next Italian, Severi. Thus Brivio alone maintains the Italian challenge. Seaman and Trossi struggle on, their small Maserati not equal to the others.

After nineteen laps the three leaders appear to be secure, but Fagioli's Mercedes has a chance of catching Hasse's Auto-Union for fourth place. At all events, Fagioli comes in and Caracciola takes his place at the wheel, this being the third car he has driven to-day ! But it is not to be, and the race runs its course without further incident.

Rosemeyer finishes with an enormous lead, while Stuck, the second man, has an even longer lead over Brivio, third. Hasse's Auto-Union is fourth, and the last two Mercedes fifth and seventh, their shrill supercharger whines dying defiantly away as they finish. It has been a race of great excitement up to half-distance, but dominated by the speed and daring of Rosemeyer in the closing stages.

RESULT.

1. Rosemeyer (Auto-Union), 81.75 m.p.h.
2. Stuck (Auto-Union), 3m. 57s. behind.
3. Brivio (Alfa-Romeo), 8m. 26s. behind.
4. Hasse (Auto-Union), 10m. 34s. behind.
5. Fagioli (Mercedes-Benz). 6. von Delius (Auto-Union). 7. von Brauchitsch and Lang (Mercedes-Benz). 8. Trossi and Seaman (Maserati).

THE YEAR IN PICTURES

In March Hans Stuck set eight new speed records on the Frankfurt-Heidelberg *autobahn* including the 10 Miles, at the astonishing speed of 267.21 km/h (166.0 mph)

ABOVE **At Monaco, the great pile-up started when Chiron's Mercedes slid into the chicane. Rosemeyer (Auto Union) got through unscathed, but spun next time round**

RIGHT **Moments later there was chaos, as other cars hit the oil laid by Tadini's Alfa.** (*Left to right*) **Sienna (36), Tadini (28), Trossi (32), Williams (18), Chiron (10), von Brauchitsch (14) and Farina (30)**

BELOW This extraordinary shot taken from the Tripoli timing tower shows an Auto Union passing the pits at speed, leaving a wake of swirling sand

LEFT Bernd gets a victory kiss from his mother, Louise, while his equally proud father, Wilhelm, (behind cup) looks on

ABOVE It was the year of the fog at the Eifel GP. Nuvolari managed to stay this close to Rosemeyer until the fog rolled in and Bernd's phenomenal eyesight enabled him to win by a mile

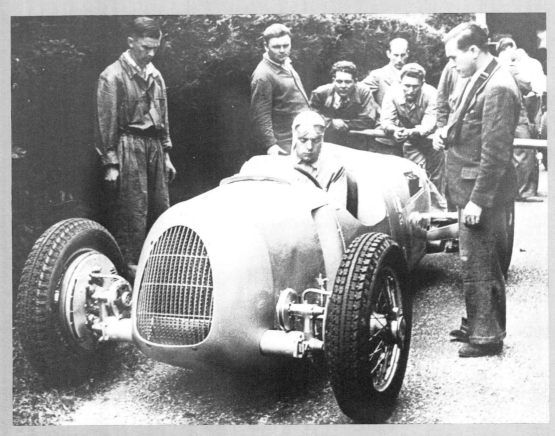

LEFT Rosemeyer won his
first mountainclimb for
Auto Union at Freiburg.
Ludwig Sebastian stands on
the right

ABOVE Rosemeyer
continued his sensational
season with a win in the
Coppa Acerbo at Pescara

BELOW The four Auto Unions are wheeled out for the start of the Swiss GP at Bern. (*Left to right*) Hasse (2), Rosemeyer (4), Stuck (6) and Varzi (8)

After their disastrous
racing season, Mercedes
went record-breaking in
October and November.
Here is Caracciola after
setting a new world record
for the F/S 10 Miles at
333.48 km/h (207.24 mph)

Budapest

LENGTH: 5.0 km (3.1 miles)
RACE: Hungarian GP (1936)

Held just the once, the Hungarian GP
was run in the Budapest Public Gardens
and was remarkable on three counts: it
was one of the few races Bernd
Rosemeyer did *not* win in 1936; it
provided a rare and thoroughly well-
deserved victory over the German teams
by Tazio Nuvolari and Alfa Romeo and
it saw the complete débâcle of
Mercedes-Benz, whose three cars all
retired.

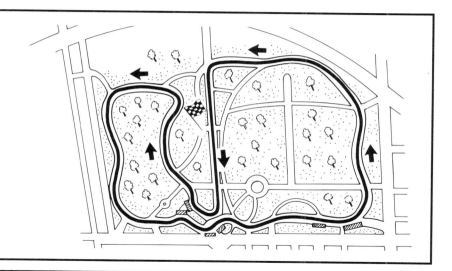

Livorno

LENGTH: 7.22 km (4.48 miles)
    (1936, 1937)
    5.80 km (3.6 miles) (1938)
RACE: Coppa Ciano (1936, 1938)
    Italian GP (1937)

The British called it Leghorn, for some
reason, but the town's Italian name is
Livorno, and it's on Italy's west coast,
just a few miles south of Pisa. The
circuit wasn't really in Livorno, but ran
south from nearby Ardenza to
Antignano and Miramare along the
coast and then returned inland to
Ardenza. The Coppa Ciano was moved
to Livorno from the Montenero circuit
in 1936 and the following year the
Italian GP was also held there, in the
vain hope of giving the Italian cars a
better chance against the Germans. The
GP returned to Monza in 1938 and the
Coppa Ciano was held again at Livorno,
but on a shorter version of the circuit
which cut off the Miramare loop. In
both its forms, Livorno was very narrow
and bumpy, making it difficult to pass
and not very popular with the drivers.

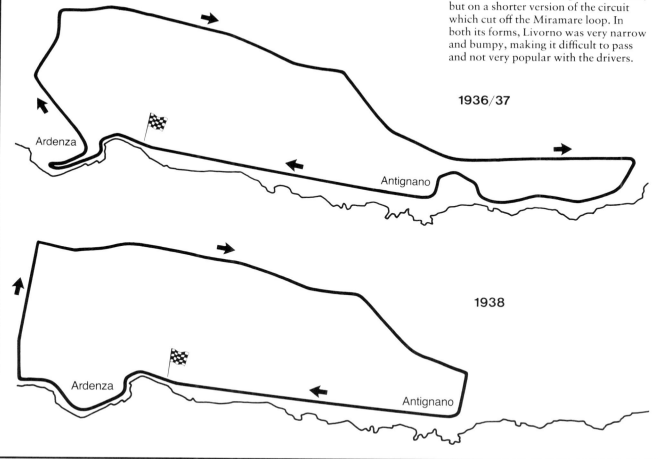

Milan

LENGTH: 2.6 km (1.6 miles) (1936)
        2.4 km (1.5 miles) (1937)
RACE: Circuit of Milan

One of the many street circuits that sprang up in Italy during the 1930s, this one was laid out in Sempione Park, right in the centre of Milan, and comprised eight corners, two of which were hairpins. It was shortened slightly for the 1937 race and the modifications made it quite a bit faster than the previous year. Auto Union understandably entered a car for Achille Varzi in 1936, but why they sent one for Rudolf Hasse in 1937 remains a puzzle.

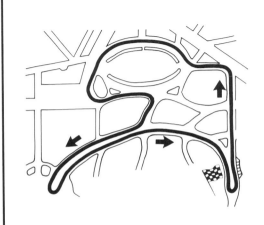

Mellaha (Tripoli)

LENGTH: 13.14 km (8.14 miles)
RACE: Tripoli GP (1934–9)

The Mellaha circuit was one of the finest and fastest in the world. Situated between Tripoli and the small town of Tagiura, on the North African coast, it surrounded the Mellaha salt lake which gave it its name. It was opened in 1925 and the Grand Prix was held every year until 1931, there being no race then or in 1932. Libya was an Italian Protectorate and in 1933 the Italian air ace and former Minister of Aviation, Marshal Italo Balbo, was made Governor.

Not long after his arrival in Tripoli, Balbo was approached by a dentist, who suggested reviving the Grand Prix, this time in conjunction with a state lottery. Balbo jumped at the idea and the 1933 event became the first of the great Tripoli lottery Grands Prix. Some four million tickets were sold throughout Italy and her colonies, which brought a great deal of money to Libya and to the winner of the lottery, who received about £50,000 that year. Unfortunately, the driver of the winning car only received about £700, and this led to one of the very few fixes (if not the only one) in Grand Prix history (see Chapter 3, *Achille Varzi*).

For 1934 the rules were altered to prevent such a fix from ever happening again and Balbo ploughed some of the lottery money back into the circuit. The road was widened in many places and a truly magnificent grandstand was built which, at that time, was probably the finest in the world. It was surrounded by lush green lawns and beds of brightly coloured flowering shrubs and its huge, cantilevered roof provided shade for more than 10,000 spectators.

The pits were equally splendid, built—like the grandstand—in dazzling white concrete and dominated by a huge, white timing tower. Dick Seaman described Mellaha as 'The Ascot of motor racing circuits', and there it was, in the North African desert.

Right from the start, Tripoli was very fast, but once Balbo had made his modifications it became the fastest of all road circuits used in the thirties. The Grand Prix was very popular with all the teams, and not just because of the vast sums of money to be won. Marshal Balbo was, by all accounts, a delightful man and a superb host who entertained everyone royally at his palace before and after the race, and the Hotel Uaddan—with its casino and theatre—was generally considered to be the best of all that the drivers stayed in during the racing season, and they stayed in some pretty good ones!

RIGHT Tickets for the Tripoli lottery were on sale for months before the race

BELOW The magnificent pits/grandstand complex at Tripoli is well illustrated in this photograph, which was taken by Nuvolari in 1937. Hans Stuck is in the foreground

FOUR

Deutschland Über Alles

Deutschland Über Alles

By the end of 1936 Germany completely dominated Grand Prix racing. Her cars and drivers were almost unbeatable; the German Grand Prix had become the most important race of the year; the Nürburgring was the most celebrated circuit in Europe and the whole German racing programme was designed to extol the virtues of Nazi Germany.

Just how much influence did the Nazi Party have on Mercedes-Benz and Auto Union? *Racing and the Nazis* takes an in-depth look at the origins of the German racing programme, the money involved and how the Nazis used racing, record-breaking and mountainclimbing for propaganda purposes. How the racing was supervised by *Korpsführer* Adolf Hühnlein; how Hans Stuck tried to protect his wife from Nazi claims that she was a Jew and how

those claims were later revived to try and thwart his attempt on the Land Speed Record; how the kissing had to stop, on Hühnlein's orders; how Caracciola's livelihood was disrupted and how Neubauer dealt with a very officious Nazi during the German Grand Prix.

The fantastic Nürburgring became the greatest and most important of all circuits in the 1930s, but the man who was the driving force behind it was driven to suicide. The history of the 'Ring is examined in detail.

Writing under the name *Grande Vitesse*, Rodney Walkerley was Sports Editor of *The Motor*, and unquestionably the finest motor racing journalist of the period. In March 1937, he lucidly described *Motor Racing German Fashion* for his avid readers, and the feature is reproduced here.

LEFT Adolf Hitler set the German GP racing programme in motion with his offer of 500,000 Reichsmarks to the manufacturer which would build a racing car to the new, 750 Kg Formula

PREVIOUS PAGE The shape of things to come: Germany's superiority in Grand Prix racing began at Mercedes-Benz' very first race—the 1934 Eifel GP. The next day the team was welcomed back to the factory with the now obligatory Nazi panoply. The winner, Manfred von Brauchitsch (in car number 20), and Team Manager Alfred Neubauer can just be seen in the background, amid the delighted throng of workers

Racing and the Nazis

Since the war a considerable myth has grown up around the Mercedes-Benz and Auto Union teams regarding the extent to which their racing programmes were financed by Adolf Hitler's Nazi government. In numerous books and articles it has been written that they were 'heavily subsidized', 'government-financed' and 'Nazi-backed', claims that, without any qualification or explanation, might well lead the gullible reader to believe that the German racing effort from 1933 onwards was paid for and orchestrated entirely by the Nazi Party. This was not so.

All the time Hitler was plotting to take control of Germany and to regain her 'lost' territories, he was also on the lookout for ways of presenting the 'acceptable face' of his Nazi Party to the world. International motor racing offered one such way and it would seem that Hitler had this in mind quite early on in his quest for power. Back in 1925 he had met Hans Stuck—then a mountainclimb expert, but not yet a racing driver—and although their relationship never got past the acquaintance stage, Hitler took a continuing interest in the young man's career, some years later going so far as to promise Stuck a racing car once he had won control of Germany (see Chapter 1, *Hans Stuck*).

Hitler came to power in January 1933, and in March, at the Berlin Motor Show, he let it be known that he wanted a German car manufacturer to go motor racing. He had no doubts about the propaganda value of German success in any sport, but success in motor racing could also reap huge benefits for German industry. The new 750 Kg Grand Prix Formula had not long been announced and Hitler decided that Germany should be involved.

'The *Führer* has spoken. The 1934 Grand Prix Formula shall and must be a measuring stick for German knowledge and German ability. So one thing leads to another: first the *Führer's* overpowering energy, then the formula, a great international problem to which Europe's best devote themselves and, finally, action in the design and construction of new racing cars.' (*Mannschaft und Meisterschaft.*)

But in spite of 'the *Führer's* overpowering energy', the Depression was having its effect on motor racing, as on everything else, and car manufacturers were not keen to spend money on a racing programme. Well aware of this, Hitler offered some bait—500,000 Reichsmarks a year to the company that would build a German Grand Prix team, 450,000 RM as a subsidy and the remainder as prize money. In making this offer he was clearly looking to Daimler-Benz, for that company was not only the oldest and (*pace* Rolls-Royce) most illustrious motor car manufacturer in the world, but it had a long and successful racing history. Having put the money on the table, Hitler naturally expec-

ted the Stuttgart concern to be the one to pick it up—and fast. The subsidy was not so much an offer, as an order to go racing!

Daimler-Benz did indeed take up the offer, only to get a shock when they learned that another company was also bidding for the subsidy. The upstart was the new firm of Auto Union, formed by the merger of Horch, Audi, Wanderer and DKW, and it already had plans for a Grand Prix car designed by the remarkable Professor Ferdinand Porsche. On 10 May Porsche, Hans Stuck and Klaus von Oertzen (one of the Directors of Auto Union) had an audience with Hitler in the *Reichskanzlerei*, with the result that the *Führer* was persuaded that two teams racing for Germany would be better than one. Unfortunately, instead of giving 450,000 RM to each, he divided that sum between the two, which must have put everyone's nose out of joint, as 225,000 RM was hardly a great deal of money in terms of a racing budget.

It is virtually impossible to ascertain the true amount of money spent annually on racing by Mercedes-Benz and Auto Union, because almost everywhere you look you will find a different sum given. Professor Eberan-Eberhorst reckoned that Auto Union spent around five million RM a year and that Mercedes spent at least twice that. In 1947, however, the British Intelligence Objectives Sub-committee published a report by Cameron C. Earl entitled, *Investigation into the Development of German Grand Prix Racing Cars Between 1934 and 1939*, for which Earl interviewed—among others—William Werner, who had been Technical Director of Auto Union. He claimed that the company's racing programme cost two and a half million RM per annum, not five million.

Whichever sum is correct (if either), it is worth looking at this money at today's values: according to the Bank of England, in 1935 the £ was worth 12 RM, so the 225,000 RM given to each team was then worth £18,750. The Bank of England also states that what you could buy for £1 in 1935 would cost you £17.2 fifty years later, in 1985—the time of writing. So, in today's money, the two German teams each received an annual subsidy of £322,500, which still left an awful lot of cash to be found, whatever the teams' real budgets were.

The subsidy was indeed Hitler's idea, and although he announced it himself it would appear that he made the offer known to the German car industry, but not to the public at large. It seems to have been a closely guarded secret until after the war, when Cameron Earl revealed it in his report. In the 1930s, however, its existence was strongly denied.

Rodney Walkerley was Sports Editor of *The Motor* at the time. Always very well informed, he was not one to be fobbed off with an old wives' tale, but in December 1936, he was sufficiently convinced to write: 'Ever since the fabulously expensive Grand Prix Mercedes and Auto Unions appeared in 1934, it has been generally accepted in this country that the cars were heavily subsidized by the German Government, and many a letter has been published in *The Motor* using this to explain why a British Grand Prix car is economically impossible.

'It was recently explained to me by one whose authority is reliable that he had received a first-hand denial of this

story, and that neither Mercedes nor Auto Union has ever received a penny from the German Government. Naturally, the Government has been keenly interested in anything appertaining to German prestige, and the Nazi Government has a way of ordering things to be done.

'This story seemed to have a ring of truth about it, particularly from such an authority. I don't know what evidence there is to the contrary.'

There's no telling just who this 'one whose authority is reliable' was, but clearly Walkerley was taken in by a clever piece of German 'disinformation'. However, the rumours of Government subsidy refused to go away so, almost a year later, when the German teams were in England for the Donington Grand Prix, Walkerley made further enquiries.

'Delicately approached on that thorny subject of whether the German teams are Government subsidized, Auto Unions snorted loudly and said that any money the German Government had ever given them was like a spot of oil on a hot plate—gone with a bang. They race a) because the Government was anxious to see German cars beat the world; b) because they felt patriotically bound to do so; c) because they are grateful to the Government for the fillips it has given to the motor industry by reducing taxes, building motor roads and generally encouraging the movement; d) because racing definitely sells touring cars and e) to establish prestige for themselves and Germany.'

So there!

Just who was responsible for the German teams' racing programmes and choice of foreign drivers also came under Walkerley's scrutiny in December 1936.

'I am informed that whether the Mercedes' team races or not is purely a matter for the Board of Directors (some of whom are a bit sniffy about the economics of it) and

January 1934, and the new Mercedes-Benz is shown to Adolf Hitler in Berlin. Dr Hans Nibel of Daimler-Benz describes the car to the *Führer*. On his right is Dr Joseph Goebbels and on Hitler's left is Alfred Neubauer

that they engage in racing primarily as a business proposition. Indeed, the racing programme is passed only after very careful consideration before each season, and there has been some question as to whether they will go ahead next year.' (The latter point was hardly surprising in view of the team's disastrous performance in 1936. Happily for all concerned, however, Mercedes decided to continue.)

Walkerley went on to state that, contrary to many reports, 'Dick Seaman has *not* signed up with the Mercedes team. He is perfectly willing to do so, and Neubauer is perfectly willing to sign him up. The whole thing is under the final decision of Major Hühnlein, Nazi Sports Leader, who alone can give permission for a foreigner to drive in the German team—not only because this is regarded as a national matter, but because there are all sorts of side issues. For one, no-one can earn money and take it out of Germany without very special permission.'

(After his first test drive at Monza, in November 1936, Seaman signed a provisional contract with Mercedes-Benz, but was told that no official announcement could be made yet, as the German teams could not sign a foreign driver without Hitler's personal permission. Presumably Hühnlein had to recommend the foreign driver concerned to the *Führer*, and official confirmation of Seaman's signing didn't come through until February 1937.)

Major Adolf Hühnlein was a professional soldier who

156

was given the title *Korpsführer* and put in charge of all German motor sport, the governing body of which was the ONS (*Oberste Nationale Sportbehorde für die Deutsche Kraftfahrt*). As far as Mercedes and Auto Union were concerned, Hühnlein was responsible for overseeing all the races and record attempts on German soil and for reporting back to Hitler the success (or otherwise) of the German teams abroad during the season. He did not interfere with their racing policy which, as Walkerley correctly stated, was decided in the boardrooms, but when Avus needed to be closed for the Avusrennen, for example, or an *autobahn* was required for a record attempt, Hühnlein gave the orders.

The building of the *autobahnen* was the responsibility of Dr Felix Todt, whom Hitler had appointed as the Inspector General of all German roads. The programme called for 15 main highways and 41 secondary roads, a total of 6900 km (4300 miles) to be built at the rate of 1000 km (620 miles) per year by a workforce of 250,000 men. The total cost was estimated at around 430 million RM (£36 million).

The main highways were to be known as *Reichs-autobahnen* and the first long stretch to be completed was between Berlin and Munich. Todt was very keen to see how quickly a really long journey could be covered on one of his new roads and so was Hitler—so much so that in 1936 they made a bet. Hitler doubted that the run from Berlin to Munich could be done in under three hours and Todt bet him that it could. To settle the matter they called upon Hans Stuck. One whole side of the *autobahn* was closed off by NSKK (*Nationalsozialistisches Kraftfahrer Korps* or National Socialist Motor Corps, a subsidiary of the ONS) troops and a fuel and tyre depot was set up some 250 km (155 miles) south of Berlin. Accompanied by Hermann Göring flying above in a Junkers Ju 52, Stuck covered the 420 km (260 miles) in 2 hr 17 min. at an average speed of 184 km/h (115 mph), thus winning the bet for Todt and earning himself a telegram of congratulations from a delighted Hitler.

Stuck made the run in an Auto Union—hardly the sort of machine the German workers would be using as their everyday transport, but never mind. Just how many troops were needed to close off the *autobahn* for the run is not recorded, but some idea of the numbers available for marshalling record attempts can be gained from the fact that the NSKK reportedly turned out 10,000 men for another run by Stuck—an official one, this time.

In March 1936, Hans and Auto Union set out to improve upon some of the records they had set at Avus in October 1934, including those for the Standing Start 100 Kilometres and 100 Miles. In order to avoid the constant turnarounds that had been necessary on the 10 km (6 mile) stretch at Avus, they sought a length of *autobahn* that would give them, as near as dammit, the full 100 miles (160 km) in one go. In the event the longest piece of road they could find without any serious bends was a 112 km (70 mile) stretch between Frankfurt and Heidelberg, allowing Stuck to do 113 km (70 miles) before slowing, turning round and driving back the remaining 48 km (30 miles) in the opposite direction.

Naturally, this record attempt—together with the closing of the *autobahn*—received a great deal of publicity and thousands turned out to watch—hence the 10,000 troops to keep control. Quite how many must have been dispersed for Stuck's Berlin-Munich run is mind-boggling, but clearly, for a military dictatorship bent on enhancing German prestige, it was no problem.

It is a curious fact that Hitler, although he initiated the German Grand Prix programme with his subsidy, never once saw Mercedes-Benz or Auto Union race. He is known to have attended a few events and the odd hillclimb in the 1920s, but from the time he took control of Germany until the outbreak of World War II, he was only once seen at a circuit. In May 1933, barely four months after he came to power, Hitler went to the Avusrennen in Berlin. For the previous two years the Avus GP had been won by a Mercedes-Benz, although the company had officially withdrawn from racing due to the Depression. On this occasion, however, Hitler was faced with the humiliating sight of foreign cars and drivers filling the first three places, Achille Varzi winning on a 4.9-litre Bugatti from Count Czaikowski on another Bugatti and Nuvolari/Borzacchini on an Alfa Romeo.

This can only have convinced him that his decision to promote a German racing team was the right one, and that the sooner it got going, the better! As things turned out, the two German teams dominated Grand Prix racing over the next six years in a way that must have given him great satisfaction, but although he certainly took an interest in their activities he never went to see them in action, not even in the German Grand Prix, which by 1936 had replaced the French GP as the most important race in the calendar. Nor did he visit either of the two Racing Departments, confining his physical contact with the teams to the Berlin Motor Show where, each year, the drivers were presented to him.

Although each team had to be led by a German, Hitler was clearly not averse to having foreign drivers on the strength, for not only did Daimler-Benz and Auto Union have to sell their products abroad, but if leading drivers from Italy (Fagioli, Varzi and Nuvolari), England (Dick Seaman) and France (Louis Chiron) drove for the German teams, it was obviously because their own countries had no proper GP cars to offer—yet another demonstration of German superiority! Although utterly dogmatic in his Nazi ideals, Hitler could be quite pragmatic when it came to achieving them!

Having joined a German team, a foreign driver then had the problem of getting his retainer and prize monies out of the country, as Hitler had forbidden the movement of all private money from Germany. What arrangement Luigi Fagioli made in this direction is not known, but the old 'Abruzzi Robber' certainly knew his worth, so you can bet your boots that he made a very good deal with Neubauer when he signed with Mercedes and you may be equally sure that he wasn't about to leave his money in Germany!

Another very shrewd Italian was Achille Varzi, who joined Auto Union in 1935. Naturally, he knew that there was a lot of money to be made in Italian races and had a clause in his contract which insisted that Auto Union

enter a car for him in certain of these events. He also insisted on being paid in *lire* and when Auto Union first sought official permission to do this the ONS refused. A temporary way round the problem was found by letting Varzi enter his first races with the team as a private entrant. These races were at Tunis (a French Protectorate, where Varzi had won the race the previous two years—he was keen to score a hat-trick, which he did) and Tripoli (an Italian Protectorate whose Grand Prix—run in conjunction with an Italian national lottery—was worth a *lot* of money!).

Varzi was delighted with the idea of being a private entrant, as not only would start and prize monies be paid directly to him, but if he won the success would be his and not Auto Union's. Unfortunately for him, the ONS woke up to this fact before the Tunis GP and agreed that Varzi could be paid in Italy by Auto Union's Italian subsidiary company. Varzi was furious at being deprived of his private entry in the two races, but nevertheless, while he was driving for Auto Union he had no trouble in getting his money out of Germany.

Dick Seaman, it appears, was not so lucky. Before he joined Mercedes-Benz he—in common with many other foreign drivers when racing in Germany—would take any start and prize monies home by the simple expedient of stuffing the *Reichsmarks* up the exhaust pipe of his racing car. Although the cars were usually checked at the German frontier on the way back, this ruse was never rumbled and Seaman was able to change the money into sterling when he got back to England. Once he joined Mercedes, however, his situation changed. Just how much he earned during his two and a half years with the team is not known,

but in his German memoirs, '*Männer, Frauen und Motoren*' Alfred Neubauer gives Seaman's retainer as 12,000 RM (£1000) in 1937. Rudolf Caracciola's retainer for the same year, on the other hand, was said to be around 150,000 RM (£12,500), and this discrepancy between payments made to the former European Champion who had been racing with great success for 15 years and the young Englishman starting only his fourth season would seem to be about right. So in today's money Seaman's retainer would be £17,200 and Caracciola's £215,000, with prize money still to come. As a rule, Mercedes let their drivers keep the prize money they won, less ten per cent which went to the mechanics, but in the very rich races, such as Tripoli, Avus and the Vanderbilt Cup, the rewards were divided equally between the team. This would have benefited Seaman, the junior driver, considerably.

Be that as it may, Seaman's great friend, Tony Cliff, is convinced that Dick was unable to get his money out of Germany—why else would he have taken up residence there by renting a chalet on the Starnbergersee, near Munich? Although he had given up flying in 1935, he was a qualified pilot and could have flown in and out of Germany as he pleased. But the only way he could spend his German income was by living in Germany and even then his outgoings must have been very small.

It is worth remembering that Mercedes' drivers had all their travelling expenses paid by the company (and they went everywhere first class) and were each given a company car. Dick rented his chalet until he married, whereupon he and his bride, Erica, were given one of their own by Erica's father. While he was living on the Starnbergersee, Seaman often invited his friends out from England to stay with him,

ABOVE Dr Goebbels and his wife (*right*) attended the Avus GP in 1937. Here the *Reichsminister* congratulates winner Hermann Lang as *Korpsführer* Hühnlein (*left*) looks on

ABOVE LEFT Each year at the Berlin Motor Show, the German teams were presented to the *Führer*. Here he greets the Mercedes drivers in February, 1937. (*Left to right*) Hermann Lang, Manfred von Brauchitsch (shaking hands with Hitler) and Rudolf Caracciola. The new W125s clearly weren't ready, so Mercedes presented the unsuccessful 1936 cars

BELOW Hitler summoned Caracciola and von Brauchitsch to see him in Bayreuth after their 1937 German GP success

and this was one way of 'transferring' some of his money back home, as he could pay for his friends' holidays in Germany and could be repaid the same way when he visited England, but this was not often.

Over the years, then, it seems certain that Dick earned a fair sum from Mercedes and had very little to spend it on. It is equally certain that, despite the fact that Adolf Hitler was supposed to admire the English and that Mercedes had a British distribution company through which they could have paid Seaman in England, permission to do so was not forthcoming from the ONS. Dick was due to inherit a considerable sum from his father's estate when he reached the age of 27, but he never lived to celebrate his 27th birthday. After his death in June 1939, his will revealed that he left just under £1500 so, clearly, his English estate never saw his German income, and neither did Erica.

It wasn't just foreigners who had difficulty in getting money out of Germany. When Rudi Caracciola married Baby Hoffmann in Lugano in 1937 he tried to withdraw some of his money in order to buy her a fur coat as a wedding present. The ONS refused his request, the fact that he was one of Germany's leading sportsmen and a hero throughout Europe cutting no ice with the authorities. No doubt they were mindful of the fact that Rudi had left the Fatherland to live in Switzerland as long ago as 1929, a move that was to cause more problems for Caracciola once Germany was at war. The fact that he was living abroad, making no contribution to the Nazi war effort *and* still drawing a salary from Mercedes-Benz did not go down well with the Third Reich and in 1942 his payments were stopped.

Nazi propaganda—of which the German Grand Prix programme was very much a part—was not just to impress the rest of the world, it was for home consumption, too. Paul Joseph Goebbels, Hitler's brilliant but evil Minister for Propaganda, had a positive genius for theatrical display and made sure—through Hühnlein—that events such as the German Grand Prix and the Eifel and Avusrennen were not just motor races, but demonstrations of German power, panoply and efficiency. Nazi flags and banners flew everywhere; thousands of jack-booted soldiers lined the course and others goose-stepped up and down before the packed grandstands while the racing cars were lined up in front of the pits. Then a fleet of Mercedes would arrive, bringing *Korpsführer* Hühnlein and other dignitaries. (Dr Goebbels himself attended the Avusrennen in 1937.) After a great deal of Nazi saluting Hühnlein would move to a microphone and address the multitude. Not for the Germans was there anything so un-Aryan as a display of good manners, such as a welcoming 'Ladies and Gentlemen . . .'. Hühnlein simply scowled and shouted at them: 'Men and women of Germany!' Only when he had finished haranguing his captive (and doubtless, for the most part, enthusiastic) audience, could the race begin, the start being signalled (appropriately enough, in the highly militaristic atmosphere) by the firing of a cannon. . . .

It was not only the simple courtesies of life that were frowned upon by the Nazi regime. Public displays of affection – even between husbands and wives—were regarded

as distinctly non-Aryan and were therefore not to be tolerated. This reached the height of absurdity at the 1937 German GP when, at the drivers' pre-race briefing, Hühnlein made it clear that drivers and their wives and girlfriends should not wander around the starting grid arm-in-arm before the race and that German men and women in particular should not kiss in public! This nonsense brought a marvellous response from all the drivers who, no sooner was Hühnlein seated in the grandstand minutes before the start, leapt from their cars and ran to their pits, where they gleefully kissed their ladies long and hard, to the roars of delight from the thousands of spectators opposite!

Having made one speech before a race, Hühnlein then naturally had to make another after it, invariably praising to the skies yet another German victory. Occasionally, however, things went badly awry, as when Nuvolari won the German GP for Scuderia Ferrari in 1935 (after the thoroughly German Manfred von Brauchitsch ruined his tyres) and—to a lesser degree—in 1938, when Dick Seaman won, after von Brauchitsch again seemed to have the race in the bag until his second pit stop. At least Seaman was driving a German car, but while his victory was undoubtedly a good thing for Anglo-German relations, it was not the wholly German win that had been expected. Although he manfully congratulated Seaman with a rather forced smile, Hühnlein was visibly embarrassed about the whole thing and this was probably the reason why he began his speech before all the stragglers had finished the race. This meant that he had to go on talking until the last one was

LEFT The 1937 German GP and *Korpsführer* Adolf Hühnlein (marching beside the lead motorcycle) is about to get into his Mercedes and open the circuit

RIGHT *Korpsführer* Hühnlein was very embarrassed by Dick Seaman's victory in the 1938 German GP, which von Brauchitsch was expected to win

back at his pit, which made for a very long, boring speech. Apparently he ended up more or less talking to himself!

But even when he did finish, his problems were still not over. He had yet to send his regular telegram to Hitler in Berlin, telling the *Führer* of Germany's latest brilliant success. The telegram became quite famous afterwards, for Hühnlein almost (but not quite) managed to avoid mentioning Dick Seaman at all! The telegram read as follows:

'My *Führer*. I report: the 11th Grand Prix of Germany for racing cars ended with a decisive German victory. From the start the new German racing construction of Mercedes-Benz and Auto Union dominated the field. NSKK *Sturmführer* Manfred von Brauchitsch, leading from the beginning and giving admirable proof of his courage and ability, was deprived of victory by his car catching fire while refuelling. The winner and consequently gainer of your proud prize, my *Führer*, was Richard Seaman on a Mercedes, followed by NSKK *Obersturmführer* Lang, also on a Mercedes, Hans Stuck and Tazio Nuvolari on Auto Union cars. Heil, my *Führer*.'

This is really rather funny in a pathetic way—a classic example of a lackey desperately trying to give his boss the good news in such a way that he won't notice the bad!

All this flag-waving and drum-banging was not confined to the race track—the workers in the factories were not forgotten, either. On several occasions the victorious Auto Unions were driven through the streets of Zwickau to the Horch factory, and thousands turned out to cheer and give the Nazi salute. Likewise, the winning Mercedes would be driven on trucks through Stuttgart and on to Untertürkheim, with the cheers of thousands ringing in the ears of those who had brought success to Germany. Then the drivers—Stuck, Rosemeyer, von Delius and Hasse for Auto Union; Fagioli, von Brauchitsch, Caracciola and Lang for Mercedes-Benz—would be presented to the crowd and would thank all the workers who had made their vic-

tory possible. On each occasion the streets and buildings were decked out with Nazi flags and swastikas, making the whole affair into a political rally, but that aside, it was a brilliant example of public relations to let the workers share in their teams' success.

Goebbels also turned the Berlin Motor Show into a vast display of Nazi prowess. Both Mercedes and Auto Union were ordered to bring their racing cars and drivers to the capital and the two teams would then drive down Unten den Linden to the Kaiserdamm, where the show was held. The entire route was lined with thousands of cheering Germans, held back by Stormtroopers. At the show, the drivers would be presented to Hitler once he had made his opening speech. He would then make a tour of the stands with Dr Goebbels.

In February 1938, Dick Seaman was on hand to meet the *Führer* and was suitably impressed by the way the show was presented. He later wrote to his friend, George Monkhouse, 'Unable as I was to understand most of it (Hitler's speech) I found him a most electrifying orator. At the end of his 17-minute speech, plush curtains at his back swept aside disclosing with a fanfare of brass instruments the main exhibition hall beyond. In fact, I doubt if Cecil B. de Mille could have done it better himself.'

As a matter of course all German racing drivers and motorcyclists had to join the NSKK, the Drivers' Corps, which, in common with the ONS, was run by Adolf Hühnlein. None of those who drove for Mercedes-Benz or Auto Union seems to have had any real interest in politics, any more than today's drivers (or sportsmen in general) have. Although the NSKK was a political organization it didn't really make any political demands of them—they simply had to wear a badge on their overalls occasionally and say the right things from time to time to Hühnlein and others. Otherwise they were allowed to get on with the job of driving racing cars.

RIGHT After winning their very first race—the 1934 Eifel GP—the victorious Mercedes were transported through the streets of Stuttgart in triumph

BELOW The Auto Union team—led by Bernd Rosemeyer—is welcomed into Zwickau after Bernd's victory in the 1936 German GP

ABOVE Winner Manfred von Brauchitsch and teammate Luigi Fagioli (at base of flag-pole) are greeted by a forest of Nazi salutes from the workers at Untertürkheim after the Eifel GP

LEFT After their one-two victory in the 1937 German GP, Caracciola and von Brauchitsch were welcomed back to Untertürkheim by a brass band and thousands of delighted Mercedes workers. Hitler's prize—*Der Siegerpreis*—is in the foreground

If any one driver was 'used' more than the others it was probably Bernd Rosemeyer, but even he was never called upon to make any great political statements or endorsements of Nazi policy. He was, however, blond, handsome, charming and enormously successful, added to which he was married to the equally attractive and successful German airwoman, Elly Beinhorn. Willy-nilly this young couple were regarded as a perfect example of the Aryan breed that would make Germans into the Master Race. Alone among Germany's racing drivers, Rosemeyer was singled out by Heinrich Himmler and made a member not of the NSKK, but of the SS, or *Schutzstaffel*, in which he became an *SS-Obersturmführer* following his epic victory in the fog in the 1936 Eifel GP. The next year, after his great win in the Vanderbilt Cup, Himmler promoted Rosemeyer to *Hauptsturmführer*. Also in 1937 he was appointed racing adviser to the ONS, following his European Championship, succeeding Rudolf Caracciola in the post.

Bernd and Elly Rosemeyer were enormously popular throughout Germany and although they didn't embrace the Nazi regime they couldn't avoid having their success manipulated to some extent by the government. Just how popular they were with the German public can be gauged to some degree by the fact that Elly's biography of Bernd — published a year after his death — sold over 300,000 copies, an astonishing number for the time.

The Nazi persecution of the Jews affected the lives of at least three people who were involved with Professor Porsche and Auto Union: Adolf Rosenberger, Baron Klaus von Oertzen and Hans Stuck. Rosenberger was a Jew who had been a successful racing driver in the twenties. He was also a very successful businessman and when Professor Porsche was trying to fund his own design company in Stuttgart it was Rosenberger who provided most of the backing and became the infant firm's Business Manager. However, he was quick to see the Nazi writing on the wall and left Germany for America just as Hitler came to power in 1933.

Klaus von Oertzen was a Director (and one of the founders) of Auto Union and his wife was of Jewish descent, so the company quietly arranged for them to go to South Africa, where he took charge of the DKW concern.

Hans Stuck fell foul of the Nazi-inspired, anti-Jewish feeling late in 1935, when he competed in the Feldberg mountainclimb. He was astonished to find posters stuck on trees and banners being waved, claiming that his wife, Paula, was a Jew. 'Spit on him—Hans Stuck, the husband of a Jewess' was one sentiment expressed with some force. 'Stuck—traitor to Hitler' was another. Even worse was the fact that similar slogans appeared on the walls of the Auto Union HQ at Zwickau. All this gave rise to numerous rumours in the European motoring press and it was widely held that Stuck would retire from racing. He certainly considered the notion and thought seriously of moving to Switzerland and running a farm there which belonged to some relatives.

In truth Paula Stuck was not a Jew, but she did have a grandfather who was. This, of course, was enough, if not too much, for the Nazis, who were already giving Germany's Jews a hard time. But Stuck was assured from very high up that there were no 'official' complaints against his wife and he was persuaded to stay with Auto Union for 1936. Incidentally, he won the Feldberg mountainclimb and his prize was a framed portrait of Adolf Hitler. . . .

Early in the next season, Stuck found himself under the scrutiny of the Gestapo. He was not a gambler, but he was very much a celebrity and it was as such that the Director of the Monte Carlo Casino invited him to throw some dice one evening before the race. Stuck, of course, was not allowed to take money out of Germany, so he had no cash for gambling, even if he'd felt inclined. The Director, René Leon, knew this and he also knew that having a famous racing driver at his gaming tables would encourage other people to gamble, so he invited Stuck to play with the Casino's money. Stuck was happy to oblige and duly drew the crowds.

Later that night he was fast asleep in his hotel when he was awakened by a knock on the door. Two men walked in, announced themselves as members of the Gestapo and demanded to know where Stuck had got the money for his evening's gambling. An angry Stuck ushered them out of the room, saying he would talk to them in the morning. When he awoke, he found one man sitting on a chair outside his door, the other under his balcony. . . . Stuck took them to the Casino, where René Leon confirmed that he had provided the money. Appalled by this harassment, Stuck couldn't resist telling Leon that the two men were members of the Gestapo spying on German citizens, so Leon had them expelled from the Principality.

Stuck's problems with the Jew-baiters would not go away. In August 1936, *Speed* reported: 'Late Night Final sensation—Hans Stuck will be "independent" next season . . . with what has not yet been decided . . . still annoyed over Nazi jibes at wife, who is a very charming Jewess . . . agreed, after accepting abject apologies, to drive German till end of year, but not after.' This prompted a letter from Stuck himself, which was published the following month:

'Your August number contains a paragraph in which you refer to my wife as a Jewess and say that I have decided not to race for Germany after this year because of trouble with the Nazis. I should be obliged if you would publish the real facts, which are as follows:

'My wife is not a Jewess, but a Christian, as are both her parents. She has, however, one Jewish grandfather. Under the new laws she is recognized as a person of mixed blood, and as such she retains her membership of the Authors' Club and is ranked third among German women lawn tennis players. Before these laws were passed, certain people attacked my wife and myself, but such attacks never had the approval of the Government. This being so, I have neither reason nor desire to leave Germany, or to sever my connection with the Auto Union firm.'

That is a sad, terrible letter and it must have pained an intelligent, worldly man like Stuck to have to write it. But in the political climate prevalent in Germany at the time he obviously felt it necessary to exonerate Paula publicly

ABOVE LEFT The Mercedes and Auto Union record-breakers were given pride of place at the 1938 Berlin Motor Show. The Auto Union carried a wreath in memory of Bernd Rosemeyer, who had been killed only days before

RIGHT Hans Stuck tells the workers how he won for Germany

from the 'crime' of having some Jewish blood.

The Jewish 'problem' arose again when Mercedes-Benz and Auto Union went to New York for the 1937 Vanderbilt Cup race. Several Nazi officials went with the teams, among them Hitler's great friend, Jakob Werlin, and Dr Bodo Lafferentz, who was Second-in-Command of the Nazi Trade Union and in charge of the *Kraft Durch Freude* (Work Through Joy) programme. Also on the trip was Ghislaine Kaes, Professor Porsche's nephew and Private Secretary.

He remembers the racing party sitting at the Captain's table for dinner one evening aboard the *Bremen*. At an adjoining table sat what was clearly a Jewish family and, seeing them, Lafferentz said in a loud voice, 'Jews must not be allowed on any German ship in future.'

The Captain of the *Bremen*, however, was a tough old sailor who wasn't about to be cowed by the officious Nazi and replied, 'That is a family of ten, from Hungary. They travel on my ship at least twice a year and they are most welcome.'

Kaes was convinced that the Captain's brave talk would get him into trouble, for apart from Werlin and Lafferentz there were several Nazi officials travelling with the party to ensure that the Mercedes and Auto Union personnel behaved themselves. This meant, among other things, that they did not socialize with any of the many Jewish passengers. Young Ferry Porsche was also on the trip and he made the mistake of taking a shine to one of the pretty daughters of the Hungarian family. He was rash enough to dance with her a few times, only to be warned off with the chilling rebuke, 'You have no business to be dancing with a Jewish girl.'

These Nazi officials were clearly on board to report any 'anti-German' behaviour or remarks back to Berlin, so while the trip was pleasant and—for Auto Union at least—succcessful, it had distinctly unpleasant undertones.

It must be said, however, that the Nazis did not interfere with the German teams' racing programmes and there were no dire threats made to either company or individuals on the rare, but inevitable, occasions when a German car didn't win. Failure meant pressure on the Racing Department from the Board of Directors, not the Nazi Party.

The one recorded occasion when a Nazi turned nasty was at the Nürburgring, when Dick Seaman won his famous victory in the 1938 German Grand Prix. On the very first lap Nuvolari went off the road in his Auto Union, apparently while trying to wipe some oil from his goggles. Soon after, NSKK *Obergruppenführer* Krauss appeared at the Mercedes pits and ordered Neubauer to call in all his cars and check them for oil leaks! Neubauer bravely refused and when Krauss persisted with his ridiculous demands Don Alfredo accused him of favouring Auto Union! This didn't go down at all well and a furious Krauss stormed off, but he hadn't finished with Neubauer.

Later in the race von Brauchitsch came in to make his second pit stop for fuel and tyres while holding a slender lead over Dick Seaman. His car caught fire during refuelling and Seaman inherited the lead and won the race. The fire was quickly extinguished and von Brauchitsch rejoined the fray, only to crash a few kilometres from the pits. He was unhurt and it was generally considered that his crash was

simply due to nerves, following the fire, although Manfred insisted that his steering wheel came off in his hands, not having been put back properly after the fire.

Shortly after the race, Neubauer was summoned to a meeting with *Obergruppenführer* Krauss, Prince Max von Schaumburg-Lippe and *Korpsführer* Hühnlein, the three senior men in the NSKK Sporting Commission. Krauss did the talking, accusing Neubauer of sending von Brauchitsch out in a defective car after the fire. Neubauer replied that it was Hühnlein himself who had 'suggested' that von Brauchitsch rejoin the race, and Hühnlein agreed that this was so. Krauss was not beaten yet, however, and suggested that the crash was due to the fact that the brake lines had been burnt. Had Herr Neubauer checked them before von Brauchitsch set out again? Herr Neubauer had not, although Rudolf Uhlenhaut had personally checked all the controls before allowing the driver to get back into the car. However, this was not absolute proof that the brakes had *not* been damaged by the fire, and Neubauer had an anxious half-hour or so until the car could be checked. The brake lines proved to be quite undamaged and the brakes in proper working order. That was the end of the matter, but Neubauer knew that he had had a close call.

When Hans Stuck was planning his attacks on the Land and Water World Speed Records he found that he had both allies and enemies in the Nazi Party. His plan for an LSR car was met with enthusiasm by Professor Porsche, who agreed to design it, but not by Auto Union, who simply hadn't the resources for such an expensive project. Mercedes-Benz, however, agreed to build the car to Porsche's design (see Chapter 5, *Record-breaking*), but were unable to release the still-secret aero engine they were developing for the *Luftwaffe* to power it, so Stuck went to see his old friend, Ernst Udet, who was the Nazi official in charge of Aircraft Procurement.

LEFT **The Auto Union team at Bern in 1938.** (*Left to right*) **Ulli Bigalke, Tazio Nuvolari, Rudolf Hasse, Christian Kautz, Hans Stuck, H. P. Müller and Paula Stuck. Paula's Jewish background caused considerable problems for Stuck with the Nazis**

BELOW LEFT **The German domination of Grand Prix racing was the theme of the 1939 Berlin Motor Show**

He found Udet in his Berlin home, practising quick-draw target shooting with a Wild West-type revolver. He was using real bullets, too, having placed his target on a large, lead screen which covered one wall of his living room! Stuck outlined his plans and told Udet of his problems in getting hold of the new engine. Without pausing from his target practice, Udet promised Hans an engine.

In January 1937, Stuck received a letter from Dr Wilhelm Kissel of Daimler-Benz, announcing that he had heard from Udet who had authorized not one, but two of the new engines for Stuck's use. A delighted Stuck immediately got in touch with his boatbuilder—now he could go for the World Record on water as well as land! He promised the startled designer an engine delivering nearly 3000 bhp.

Just to make sure that his projects got official blessing at the highest level, Stuck now sought an audience with Hitler, who immediately recognized the propaganda value of both records to the Third Reich. He promised Stuck his full support, adding that he would make sure that everyone who mattered would be made aware of his personal interest. So far, so good, but later in the year Stuck began to realize that certain people were apparently working against him. There were rumours that it was felt that the Land Speed Record car ought to be driven by one of the Mercedes drivers, as it was being built by Daimler-Benz. But he soon learned that the real reason was more sinister, and that once again he was being linked with the unfortunate Paula's grandfather. Germany, it was said, could not allow the Land Speed Record to be held by a man whose wife was half-Jewish. . . .

But Stuck had Hitler's personal promise on the matter. Alarmed by the continuing references to Paula's supposed Jewishness, he tried to see Hitler again, only to find his way blocked at every turn. Eventually he learned from *Korpsführer* Hühnlein that people close to Hitler had been

17. FEBRUAR BIS 5. MÄRZ

INTERNATIONALE AUTOMOBIL- UND MOTORRAD-AUSSTELLUNG BERLIN 1939

instructed—by whom he was not told—not to allow any of Stuck's messages to reach him. Stuck was very shaken by this, but he had come too far to be stopped now. He bided his time until the 1939 Berlin Motor Show and when Hitler made his customary visit to the Mercedes and Auto Union racing cars and their drivers he was relieved to find that the *Führer* greeted him warmly, shaking him by the hand. Stuck grabbed his chance and asked to be allowed to bring Hitler up to date on the progress of the record attempts. Hitler, who had heard nothing on the subject for some time, quickly grasped what Stuck was getting at and, speaking in a loud voice so that all his staff could hear, said, 'I want no misunderstanding about this—Stuck will drive the World Record car!' Alas, it was not to be, for Hitler had much bigger prizes on his mind than a couple of speed records. . . .

Stuck's nodding acquaintance with the *Führer* had also proved its worth a year earlier, when Auto Union decided that they would not offer him a contract for 1938. In fact Stuck had announced his retirement in October the previous year, later claiming that he had been fired by Auto Union for showing his contract to Bernd Rosemeyer (see Chapter 1, *Hans Stuck*). Auto Union's side of the story, however, is somewhat different, as Peter Kirchberg revealed in his book, *Grand Prix Report*.

When, in the spring of 1938, it became clear that Auto Union were not going to sign Stuck for the new season, the management suddenly found that it had aroused the displeasure of the SS. To try and discover the reasons behind this, Public Relations Director Dr Richard Voelter went to see SS *Gruppenführer* Wolff—*Reichsführer* Himmler's personal Adjutant—early in May 1938. Voelter wanted to know why the SS favoured Stuck so, particularly in view of the fact that he had a non-Aryan wife. Wolff told him that following the anti-Jewish attacks on Frau Stuck a few years previously, Stuck had written to Himmler to complain. The matter went to both the SS and the Gestapo, before finally being passed to Hitler himself. Although far from being a close friend of the *Führer*, Stuck had clearly established a rapport with him, and Hitler had personally ordered that the whole matter of Paula Stuck's Jewishness should be forgotten and not allowed to hinder Stuck's career. Wolff concluded by saying that while the SS had no intention of forcing Auto Union's hand regarding Stuck's signing, the *Reichsführer* would think it was a great pity if a man of his ability was left out of the team!

Voelter pointed out that Stuck had not enjoyed much success in recent years, for although he had won several mountainclimbs, he hadn't won a race since the 1935 Italian GP. To make matters worse, he had not got on well with his team mates in the past season and they particularly resented the interference of Frau Stuck in team matters! This cut no ice with Wolff, who asked that Stuck be given another chance. If Stuck was unsuccessful, then Auto Union would have proved their point, but they would not

have to face adverse public opinion for not giving the very popular driver the chance he deserved. Voelter got the message.

Shortly after this meeting, Auto Union issued a Press Release announcing that they had signed Hans Stuck for 1938, but that he would not be an official team driver. Instead he would race as a private entrant and drive a 1937 car, concentrating on Free Formula events and mountainclimbs. This brought an immediate and angry response from *Gruppenführer* Wolff, who telephoned Dr Richard Bruhn, Auto Union's Finance Director, on a direct order from Himmler. The *Reichsführer* was very surprised and upset that Stuck should be treated in this way and, as a personal favour, asked that Stuck be included in the team and given a proper contract. If this was not done, Wolff added, Himmler would see to it personally that the SS and the entire German police force would never again order any cars made by the Auto Union concern, and that, if necessary, he would give his reasons to the top Auto Union management.

Faced with this ultimatum, there was nothing Auto Union could do but include Stuck in the team proper, and he duly made his return to the fold in the German GP on 24 July. Although he was slower than his three team mates (Nuvolari, Hasse and Müller) in practice, his was the first Auto Union to finish, a fine third behind the Mercedes of Seaman and Lang. He went on to win five mountainclimbs that season, and the European Mountain Championship, which must have gone some way to answering Auto Union's doubts about his ability, although, to be fair, they were primarily interested in Grand Prix racing.

While Hans Stuck undoubtedly had an ally in Adolf Hitler, the same could certainly not be said for Dick Seaman. Although he loved Germany and had a German bride, by the beginning of 1939 his position as an Englishman working for a German firm was becoming untenable. He liked the people at Daimler-Benz very much and they, in turn, thought highly of him, but he was still the junior driver and didn't get to drive in the early races of the year. More important was the fact that, in the larger scale of events, Hitler's troops were on the march in Europe.

Shortly after the Pau GP (where he had been reserve driver) Seaman had a stormy meeting with Alfred Neubauer in the latter's Stuttgart office, during which he loudly called Hitler a liar. Well aware that their conversation might be overheard and reported to the authorities, Neubauer quietly asked him to keep such opinions to himself. Seaman pointedly replied that, as an Englishman, he was used to free speech. By then, however, free speech had long been dead in Nazi Germany.

Tragically, Seaman was killed a few weeks after that meeting, but Grand Prix racing went on until Germany invaded Poland in September 1939. Racing was over, but 'only for a while'—the Nazis really believed that the war would be won in two or three months. . . .

MOTOR RACING-GERMAN FASHION

How German Enthusiasm at the Nürburg Ring Produces Crowds of a Size only Associated with Derby Day in this Country

IT is probably true to say that if 100,000 people arrived at Brooklands or any other motor racing event in this country, the organizers would have three fits, each more convulsive than the last, although their delight would know no bounds. Yet if such a number turned up at the Nürburg Ring for a German Grand Prix the authorities would weep tears of blood and wonder what on earth was keeping the people away.

To many enthusiasts in this country, and to the normal motorist who visits Brooklands and Donington once or twice a year just to see what is going on, it must seem incredible that nearly half a million Germans trooped out to Nürburg for the German Grand Prix last year, and that over 300,000 paid for admission to the Eifelrennen earlier in the season at that same circuit.

People in this country have a sort of idea that on the Continent the common people take far more interest in motor racing than we do over here. To say that this is true, is a kind of understatement. If you can imagine Hyde Park being closed for a motor race, including the bodily removal of all central islands and obstructions, or the policing with constabulary and military of the road from London to Edinburgh and back through the Lake District and Wales (as they do in the Mille Miglia), or even a motor race through the streets of Brighton (as you have at Monte Carlo), you would get some idea of the kind of enthusiastic things they do abroad. But you would still not grasp the fever surrounding the German G.P.

It may be that the Germans are not interested as we are in horse-racing or football, it may be that they attach a real International importance to the race, it may even be that they simply want to see their own cars beat the rest of Europe, but whatever it is, they flock to the 14-miles of mountain road which is the Nürburg Ring twice a year, no matter what the weather, in such numbers that Derby Day would seem a choir outing in comparison.

Of course, it is admitted that the Continentals have a natural flair for the spectacular staging of their races. The very sites of the circuits are spectacular. Nürburg is breathtaking. But the German way of doing these things, to my mind, outstrips for sheer drama, spectacle and enthusiasm anything to be seen at any other meeting in Europe.

First of all, the circuit itself is about as spectacular as a circuit very well can be. It starts on a plateau of concrete 2,000 ft. above sea level, where a full-blown hotel is combined with the gigantic covered grandstand, and the pits opposite are concrete rooms with a promenade on top. Away in every direction stretch the rolling Eifel mountains, clad in dark pine forests. Dominating the whole circuit is the ruin of the ancient Nürburg castle, and to the north looms the Hohe Acht.

The road goes turning and twisting through the mountains, cleaving the forest with a swathe of black highway, now climbing, now plunging dizzily down, twisting as it goes, never straight for more than a few hundred yards, with corner after corner, first this way, then that, for over 14 miles. Lastly, within the last three miles, comes a straight run back to the start, and even here all is by no means plain sailing—for the road leaps hump-back bridges as it goes.

On such a Homeric circuit, it is scant wonder that things are done on the Homeric scale. And it extends to enthusiasm as well.

Things start happening a week before the race, when the teams arrive for training, and almost to a man they invade the little village of Adenau, huddling its quaint roofs under the very shadow of the Ring.

Every day the teams are out on the circuit, and siting sipping one's beer on the veranda of a café the thin wail of superchargers can be heard drifting down the wind, and the good people of Adenau stop and listen, smiling. In the village colossal stocks of beer are laid in. Every shop breaks out into flags and badges and photographs of the Germans cars and their drivers. You can buy pictures of the Ring wrought in wondrous colours on anything from a beer mug to a slice of tree with the bark still upon it.

Every night the villagers forgather on the pavement opposite the

By Grande Vitesse

MOTOR RACING—GERMAN FASHION . . . . . Contd.

A small section of the vast crowds thronging the grandstand at the 1936 German Grand Prix, when over 400,000 attended. Note the motorcycle corps lining the road.

Eifelerhof to watch the drivers come and go, and to observe how, after a day's practising with lap speeds of over 80 m.p.h., a man may still stroll out of his hotel after a good dinner and walk very like an ordinary man up the street to buy a packet of cigarettes.

Outside the hotel is a blue-clad policeman, very pleased at being on duty to superintend parking the great drivers cars and to wave the through traffic past. There is Caracciola's huge black and chromium Mercedes coupé, Stuck's impressive black Horch coupé, Chiron's blue Mercedes, Nuvolari's modest Pescara Alfa-Romeo saloon with his travelling trunk streamlined on the roof, Trossi's fine Packard two-seater. . . .

The atmosphere inside the hotel is more like a school treat. The teams sit at long tables, and talk at the top of their voices. Auto-Union aces come in and slap Mercedists on the back, pulling their legs and swapping lies about lap speeds, and the air is full of motor racing . . . motor racing . . . motor racing. . . .

As race day draws nearer there is terrific activity in the village. Flags appear in even greater profusion, the crowd watching the front door of the Eifelerhof increases. The military arrive in light lorries and start building pedestrian bridges over the narrow Hans Andersen streets, barricades spring up, and a squad of sappers goes down the street lifting one stone really from the cobbles every few yards and setting up a stake, then roping them all together to keep the crowd off the road.

On the day before the race the spectators begin to arrive on bicycles, motorcycles, and whole families in cars, all wearing the white linen helmets so typical of German motoring and all fluttering the Nazi flag. They are going to the Ring 24 hrs. in advance to camp out all night in the forest. At night the forest is alive with little twinkling points of fire the whole way round the circuit.

As the day wears on the stream of arrivals swells, and all night the street echoes with the hooting of horns, the ringing of bicycle bells and the staccato beat of motorcycle engines. There is little sleep in the Eifelerhot that night. When dawn breaks, the main stream is just beginning, and by seven o'clock the solid jam of vehicles is moving a few yards at a time, all heading to the Ring.

There are 127 car parks on the Nürburg Ring and they are full hours before the race is due to start. Motor coaches come in droves, and long before break-fast lorries go lumbering past filled with police and soldiers, all singing like the B.B.C. male-voice choir, lorry after lorry. I counted 15 as I watched from a balcony this scene which takes an English motor racing enthusiast's breath away.

Everybody sings or shouts or waves flags. Everyone is full of smiles or subdued excitement. There is an atmosphere of Hampstead Heath on Bank Holiday, except that there are far more people.

Up at the Ring the crowds are in position early in

(Continued on page 279.)

The crowd seen above are cheering their heroes, Rosemeyer (on right) and Stuck, the white-clad drivers arm in arm walking up to receive their laurels after finishing first and second.

MOTOR RACING—GERMAN FASHION . . . . . Contd.

the morning, thousand upon thousand of them crowded on the slopes overlooking every part of the course. There are usually 20,000 on the Karussel corner alone. They sit munching sausage and bread and argue over the merits of the drivers, studying the pictures in their programmes. They bring notebooks and stop watches and follow the race as eagerly and as accurately as the official timekeepers, and they drink a staggering quantity of beer.

Up at the Startplatz the concrete seethes with uniforms—police, army, and Nazi Party uniforms. The air is full of flags and brass bands and excitement. The terrace in front of the grandstand is a solid mass of people through which it is almost impossible to move.

Away in the distance there is a deep roar of exhausts and up through a tunnel the cars shoot, one by one, coming from the subterranean passage out of the paddock into the sunlight rather with the effect of a jack-in-the-box. Soon the cars are drawn up before their pits. The German cars are nearly always the first to arrive and are drawn up in a precise echelon with military smartness and despatch, at which the crowd goes a little mad.

As the starting hour draws near a company of Storm Troopers of the N.S.K.K., with black crash helmets, lending them a peculiarly Robot-like appearance, forms up behind the pits, and with its band blaring a martial air and the Nazi flag carried in front, they march round the row of pits and up the concrete in front of the stands, where they form up facing the special building which houses the timekeepers, on the roof of which stand the great men of the day, with Major Huhnlein, leader of German Sport, stiffly at attention in the front.

The flag drops, the band crashes out into the German National Anthem, everyone stands at attention, and slowly a huge Nazi flag is hoisted to the masthead dominating the scene.

Then Major Huhnlein addresses the gathering of 400,000 over the loudspeakers, and everyone cheers. Then the troopers march away, and as they move off they reveal the cars all ready drawn up on the starting grid with engines running, and a great hush falls on the huge assembly. A maroon bangs, a flag falls, thousands of throats shout with excitement and their roar is drowned by the nazal screech of the cars streaking forward on the concrete. The race has begun.

* * *

After the race the scenes are no less amazing. When 400,000-odd people want to leave a place at the same time there is liable to be a little confusion. At the Eifelrenen last year, I was five hours driving back the six miles to Adenau. At the German Grand Prix I was more cunning and got back round the circuit itself in half an hour.

Back in the village the crowds pour slowly homewards through the narrow streets lined with police and soldiers. Unending strings of motor coaches, solid jams of cars and bicycles and motorbicycles. The pavements are impassable with people streaming on foot to the station, where special trains are waiting. The cafés are crammed. Vast quantities of beer disappear down vast numbers of throats. You fight your way into the hotel and find the place in an uproar. Literally hundreds of people are clamouring for food or drink, tired waiters dash about with loaded trays. Tired drivers are surrounded by excited friends, the drivers with faces still blackened from the race; some waving their arms, shrugging their shoulders, explaining, excusing or triumphing. Nuvolari sits on a table with that quiet smile of his whether he has won or lost, gently sipping his drink. No one can hear what anybody is saying because everyone is shouting. And all the time the human tide rolls by outside.

Hours go by and the stream is thinning now. A few more hours and then, when it is quite dark and the stream has ceased, the laggards assemble outside the hotel, and there is no more room for passing traffic and no use trying to get through. The road becomes choked with people, all staring up at the hotel to catch a glimpse of their idols. The pressure is so great that those in front are carried into the hotel itself, whence they have to be ejected with a great deal of good-humoured force and a great deal of laughter and shouting (this is usually while I am trying to make London hear what I am saying in a telephone box made of three-ply.)

The traffic arrangements for dealing with the thousands of cars are planned with characteristic efficiency. Hours before the race certain of the main roads for miles around are scheduled as one-way arteries leading to the Ring. Afterwards they are again restricted to one-way traffic, away from the Ring. Every available forest track is pressed into use and these narrow avenues present a picturesque sight as the sun glints through the trees on the endless lines of cars. Armies of workmen have been driving still more approach roads through the forest and several of them, wider than our own by-passes, were roughly surfaced in time to take some of the Grand Prix traffic last July.

Then the crowd tries another game. They start shouting for the drivers by name, and succeed in sounding to those at the back of the hotel rather like the crowd burning down the Bastille in the worst excesses of the French Revolution. "We want Caracciola . . . we want Car . . . ac . . . ciola. . . . Nuv . . . ol . . . ar . . . i . . . Nuv . . . ol . . . ar . . . i." They are still blocking the street and shouting (with short spells of community singing) past one o'clock in the morning.

And 20,000 people is a good crowd at Brooklands.

Military sappers building a pedestrian bridge in Adenau a few days before the German Grand Prix, when the narrow streets are chock-a-block with thousands of cars and pedestrians go to the wall.

The Nürburg-Ring

LENGTH: 28.27 km (17.56 miles) (1927–29)
28.27 km (14.17 miles) (1931–39)
RACE: German GP (1934–9)
Eifel GP (1934–7 and 1939)

'When the Nürburgring was planned, an intoxicated giant must have been sent out to trace the road.' So wrote the celebrated motoring writer, W. F. Bradley, about what quickly became recognized as the most demanding road circuit in the world. The man largely responsible for it was not an intoxicated giant, but a Councillor for the Eifel District, Dr Otto Creutz, and his creation—the Nürburg-Ring (as it was originally called)—is central to this book as it became the most important circuit in European racing in the thirties.

Traditionally, the French Grand Prix had always been the dominant race in the European calendar, as Grand Prix racing had begun in France in 1906, and this dominance continued for the next 30 years. After the sweeping success of Mercedes-Benz in the 1935 GP at Montlhéry, however, the French decided that, as they didn't have the Grand Prix cars with which to beat the Germans on their home ground, the French GP would, in future, be for sports cars. From that moment, the French GP lost for ever its pre-eminence and so, for the rest of the decade, the German Grand Prix became *the* race of the year, held on the fabulous Nürburg-Ring.

The idea of a permanent racetrack in the Eifel Mountains was proposed as long ago as 1907. Four years earlier, Camille Jenatzy had won the Gordon Bennett Cup in Ireland, driving a Mercedes, which meant that Germany had the honour of staging the next race in 1904. This was run over a closed circuit at Bad Homburg, just north of Frankfurt, under the patronage of Kaiser Wilhelm II, no less. In 1907 the Kaiser instigated his own race, the *Kaiserpreis*, and this was run over a 120 km (75 mile) circuit which incorporated part of that used in 1904.

The race was only held the once, but the Kaiser—very much an enthusiast and one who recognized the importance of racing to the fledgling German motor industry—decided that Germany ought to have its own permanent circuit. The *Kaiserpreis* had been run in the Taunus area, but new sites were now sought on Luneburg Heath, just south of Hamburg, and in the Eifel Mountains.

Luneburg was considered too small and too flat, but in the Eifel district—close to the small town of Adenau and the twelfth-century castle of Nürburg—was a large, mountainous area of forest that would be ideal.

The project got no further until after World War I when, in the early 1920s the ADAC (*Allgemeinen Deutschen Automobil Club*) revived the idea of a permanent circuit. There was no Kaiser to help them now, but instead they had the active support of the Mayor of Cologne, Konrad Adenauer, who—in later years—would become Chancellor of the Federal Republic of West Germany. Adenauer proposed a 4.5 km (2.8 mile) track on the outskirts of Cologne, but this idea foundered due to a lack of money.

In the 1920s the small town of Nideggen, situated between Aachen and Bonn, was host to an annual race meeting known as the *Eifelrennen*. In 1924 the old Eifel project was revived when three influential men—Franz Xaver Weber from Adenau, Hans Pauly from Nürburg and Hans Weiderbruck from Bonn—went to the race meeting at Nideggen and were so appalled by the dusty, pot-holed road and the way that the racing inconvenienced both the

spectators and the townsfolk that they decided an entirely new circuit was called for. They found an ally in Dr Creutz, who was desperately seeking something that would bring prosperity to the Eifel District, for which he was responsible. Creutz jumped at the idea of a racing circuit in the mountains and he, in turn, found an ally in Dr Erich Klausener, a State Secretary in Berlin. Together these five men were able to convince the German government that the building of the circuit they had in mind would not only be of great use to the German motor industry and a boost to tourism, but that it would also go some way to alleviate the country's terrible unemployment problem.

Dr Creutz was a man of great vision and drive and his plan for the circuit was stunningly ambitious. It called for a total length of 28.27 km (17.56 miles), to be made up of two loops, the *Nordschleife* being 22.8 km (14.17 miles) long and the *Sudschleife* 7.75 km (4.81 miles). The drawings were ready by the end of April 1925, and Creutz celebrated the official birthday of the Nürburg-Ring on 27 September, when Dr Fuchs, President of the Rhineland Province, laid the foundation stone of the start and finish area.

Some 25,000 men worked on the circuit, which comprised no less than 172 corners—88 left-handers and 84 right-handers—and rose from 310 m (1017 ft) above sea level at Breidscheid to 616 m (2020 ft) at the start and finish point. To complement his magnificent circuit Creutz designed an equally

Nürburg-Ring: Start und Ziel mit Nordkehre Original-Fliegeraufnahme

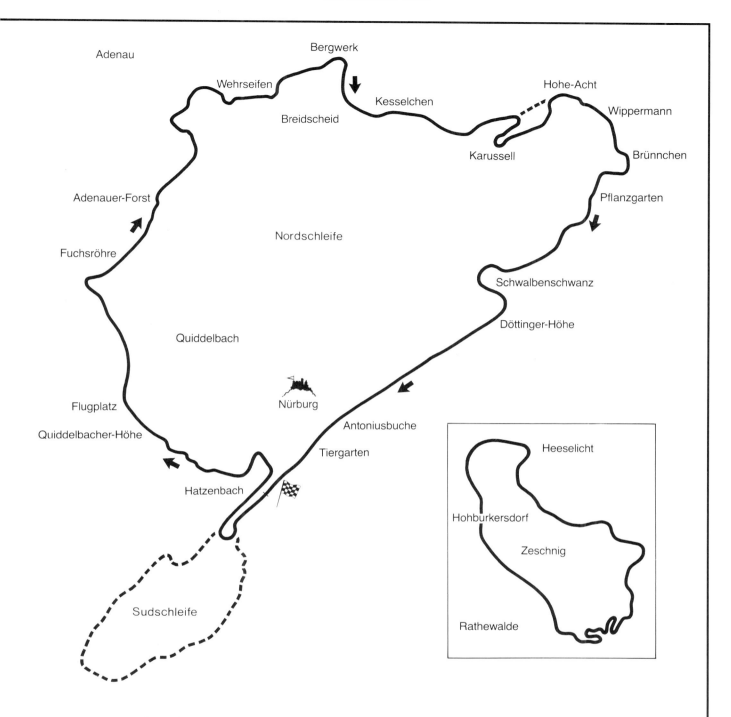

Adenau

Bergwerk

Wehrseifen

Hohe-Acht

Kesselchen

Wippermann

Breidscheid

Karussell

Brünnchen

Adenauer-Forst

Pflanzgarten

Nordschleife

Fuchsröhre

Schwalbenschwanz

Döttinger-Höhe

Quiddelbach

Nürburg

Flugplatz

Antoniusbuche

Quiddelbacher-Höhe

Tiergarten

Hatzenbach

Sudschleife

Heeselicht

Hohburkersdorf

Zeschnig

Rathewalde

ABOVE RIGHT **The 10-km Deutschland Ring, near Dresden, was planned for the 1940 German GP . . .**

LEFT **A very early photo of the pits/ grandstand/garage complex**

magnificent pits/grandstand/paddock complex, the grandstand (incorporating an hotel) seating 2500 people and overlooking 50 pits and Continental Tyres' superb tower, built for time-keepers and officials. Beside the grandstand was a vast, square paddock with 70 lock-up garages and a tunnel leading under the track to the pits. The entire circuit was 6.7 m (22 ft) wide,

broadening out to 20 m (66 ft) at the start and finish area, and was linked by 16 main telephone posts and 72 smaller ones, so accidents and incidents could be reported and dealt with immediately. The total cost of this colossal undertaking was 14.1 million RM.

On 18 June 1927, 150,000 spectators turned up for the opening race and began to learn the names of the corners

Nürburg-Ring continued

which, like the circuit itself, would soon become legend—Fuchsröhre and Adenauer-Forst, Bergwerk and the Karussell, Pflanzgarten and Döttinger-Höhe. They saw the inaugural race won, fittingly, by young Rudolf Caracciola in an S-type Mercedes-Benz at an average speed of 101.1 km/h (62.82 mph) over 12 laps of the full circuit, the first of ten victories Caracciola would score at the 'Ring in the next 12 years. The following month the German Grand Prix was held at the Nürburg-Ring for the first time and this, too, was won by a Mercedes, driven by Otto Merz. The Grand Prix continued to be run on the full circuit for the next two years, but due to the Depression the race was not held in 1930. It returned in 1931, but was restricted to the *Nordschleife*, where it stayed. In 1928 the *Eifelrennen* moved to the 'Ring, but was run on the short *Sudschleife*. There was no race in 1929, but the event was back again in 1930 and 1931, moving to the *Nordschleife* in company with the Grand Prix in 1932.

The circuit was an immediate success and Dr Otto Creutz was rightly

acclaimed for what was a brilliant feat of engineering and hailed as 'The Father of the Nürburg-Ring'. Naturally, it didn't solve all the district's problems, but it brought hundreds of thousands of people into the area and they all brought money, which they spent in the local hotels, shops and restaurants. The unfortunate Dr Creutz was not to enjoy his success for long. In 1933 the Nazis came to power and Creutz soon found that he had enemies within the Party. Rumours began to circulate that the Nürburg-Ring hadn't really cost 14.1 million RM, so what had Dr Creutz done with the money that was left over? Creutz was innocent, but the Nazis wanted him out of the way and so he had to go. A few years later his business fell on hard times and all the old accusations were brought up again. This time Creutz had had enough. He shot himself.

His creation quickly became the yardstick by which racing drivers were judged, so difficult and demanding was it, so it is not surprising that the skills of such men as Caracciola, Nuvolari, Rosemeyer, von Brauchitsch, Lang and Seaman shone like a beacon there. (It

has to be said that Dick Seaman was *slightly* dismissive of the circuit, describing it in 1937 as 'too slow for modern Grand Prix cars'!) The 'Ring had every conceivable type of corner and plunged up, down and around the Eifel mountains like a switchback. The steepest gradient uphill was 1 in 6 and the steepest downhill 1 in 9, the sharpest corner being the Karussell, which had a radius of only 32 m (105 ft).

This bend was unique and began life as an ordinary corner surrounding a ditch. To begin with the cars stayed on the road and drove around the ditch at a speed of about 50 km/h (30 mph), but one evening before the 1931 German GP, Caracciola's mechanic, Wilhelm Sebastian, took his fellow-mechanic Willi Zimmer out in the racing Mercedes and, very carefully and daringly, drove round the Karussell *on the banked side of the ditch*! While Sebastian drove, Zimmer checked the ground clearance and they found that by taking the corner like that they could go much faster, centrifugal force holding the car on the road. Sebastian duly reported his findings to Caracciola, who used this new-found technique during

ABOVE **The garage square, filled with Mercedes and Auto Unions before the 1939 Eifel GP**

LEFT **The opening race was held on 18 June 1927 and was won by Caracciola in car no. 1. Clearly, the grandstand had not been finished in time for the race**

the race, which he won. Other drivers soon caught on to this device and it was not long before the ditch was properly surfaced and Sebastian's brainwave became the accepted way of taking the Karussell.

The Nürburg-Ring proved to be a magnet for racing fans, a quarter of a million regularly turning up for the German Grand Prix and sometimes more than 300,000. In 1935 Adrian Conan Doyle (the son of the famous novelist, Sir Arthur Conan Doyle) attended the race and wrote about it for *Motor Sport*:

'From far and wide, throughout the last two days and nights, the people of Germany have been streaming to the Nürburg-Ring. Charabancs of elderly people (can you imagine that at

Brooklands!), droves of men, women and children on cycles singing their way through the darkness as they pedal along. Line upon line of cars jostling and accelerating with glare of lights and continual blowing of horns, their mud-stained number plates showing that they come from every part of Germany and even beyond the borders from France and Switzerland. Every hotel, large and small, within a radius of 35 miles is completely filled and, in Adenau, whole families are sleeping on the pavements. Near Altenahr a regiment of Nazis are resting and eating around their cookers. They have marched 350 miles to see the race! As I scribble I am sitting in the pine woods on the edge of the Karussell curve and dawn is just breaking through the sky to the east. The Nürburg-Ring lies deserted, but all around is the glimmer of camp fires and lines of huddled sleeping forms are grouped around the boles of trees. All honour to the Germans for their whole-hearted support of a great sport in direct contrast to the apathy of England in matters motor racing.'

In 1938, as Hitler pushed Europe closer and closer to war, it was reported that the Nürburg-Ring was going to be

taken over by the army and used as a military camp, just as Brooklands had been in 1914 and Donington was to be in 1939. At about the same time the Germans built a new circuit just outside Dresden not, it was claimed, because the 'Ring was to be taken over, but because it was more centrally placed and more easily accessible via the *Reichsautobahnen*. The Deutschland Ring, as it was called, was 10 km (6.21 miles) long and no less than three-quarters of its length was reportedly visible from the main grandstands! It was designed to cater for *one million* spectators and 350,000 cars! Apart from its better location it was also felt that the spectators would appreciate seeing the cars go by more frequently than once every ten minutes or so, as was the case at the Nürburg-Ring, although this time lag never seemed to bother the hundreds of thousands who camped out in the Eifel Mountains twice a year. Be that as it may, it was intended that the Deutschland Ring should be the venue for the 1940 German Grand Prix. . . . Losing the Nürburg-Ring would have been sad, indeed, but what began in September 1939 was sadder beyond compare.

FIVE

1937

1937

The Year of the Titans

Instead of simply refining their highly successful 1935 car, Mercedes had made considerable alterations to it and, as a result, came badly unstuck in 1936. The lesson was not lost on Auto Union, who made only token changes to their all-conquering 1936 car for the coming season. Mercedes, however, had to do something drastic and the result was—until quite recently—the most powerful racing car the Grand Prix world had ever seen.

The W125 had a straight-eight engine based on the original unit, but enlarged to 5.6 litres, giving a staggering 580 bhp! The old, box-section chassis was dispensed with and an oval tubular frame employed which was 35.5 cm (14 in.) longer than that of the ill-handling 1936 car. Front suspension was now by wishbones and coil springs, with de Dion at the rear. This formidable machine combined with the almost as formidable 6-litre Auto Union to produce the most awe-inspiring season of Grand Prix racing ever seen.

Sadly, after some sterling performances in the hands of Nuvolari during 1936, Alfa Romeo were totally eclipsed by the Germans in 1937. They built a new, lower version of their V-12 car, but it turned out to be inferior to the previous model. Also, the company signalled its intention to return to racing itself by employing the former Bugatti driver and Team Manager, Meo Costantini. In the meantime, however, Scuderia Ferrari continued to run the cars.

There was a number of driver changes among the German teams. Luigi Fagioli left Mercedes to retire (or so it was thought), but to everyone's surprise he joined Auto Union. In his place Mercedes signed Dick Seaman, which was a tremendous break for the young Englishman, although he was very much the junior driver, after Caracciola, von Brauchitsch and Lang.

Auto Union dispensed with the failing services of Achille Varzi, but retained the meteoric Rosemeyer. Hans Stuck and von Delius were once again on the team, although the latter was not really able to cope with the big, mid-engined cars. Two promising newcomers, H. P. Müller and Rudolf Hasse, were also signed up.

PREVIOUS PAGE **Bernd Rosemeyer on the banking at Avus in 1937**

Of the 12 major races in which both teams competed, Mercedes-Benz won seven and Auto Union five. The Belgian GP was held once more, and joined the GPs of Germany, Monaco, Switzerland and Italy to make up the five *Grandes Epreuves* counting towards the European Championship. Although Caracciola and Rosemeyer won four races each, none of Rosemeyer's victories was in a *Grande Epreuve*, whereas Caracciola won three of the Championship races and took the title for the second time, with 13 points to von Brauchitsch's 15. Lang and Kautz were third equal with 19 points each.

And that was the end of the 750 Kg Formula. Conceived (some would say ill-conceived) by the AIACR in an attempt to curb the speed of Grand Prix cars, as such it proved to be a glorious failure, providing some of the fastest, most powerful and exciting racing cars the world has ever seen. The new Formula for 1938–39 was also designed to reduce speeds, but already there were those who foresaw even faster cars.

* * *

At the end of their disastrous 1936 season, Mercedes-Benz brought in a gifted young engineer named Rudolf Uhlenhaut to try and solve their problems for 1937. He succeeded brilliantly, and the new W125 Mercedes—together with the 6-litre Auto Unions—provided a stunning finale to the 750 Kg Formula. Uhlenhaut recalls his fascinating years as Technical Director of the Mercedes *Rennabteilung*. An enthralled spectator throughout this season was 17-year-old Günther Molter, who used to cycle from his home to the Nürburgring. He remembers the spectacular Grand Prix cars and the charisma of the men who drove them.

One of the most charismatic of all GP personalities was Alfred Neubauer. His ambition to be a racing driver was quickly dashed, but he went on to become the most famous and successful Team Manager the sport has ever seen.

Record-breaking became properly organized in Germany in 1937 when *Korpsführer* Hühnlein announced a Record Week, to be held each October on the Frankfurt/Darmstadt *Reichsautobahn*. Following the tragic death of Bernd Rosemeyer in January 1938, the Record Week was abandoned, but the Third Reich continued to encourage record-breaking for its propaganda value.

The 1937 Monaco Grand Prix was one of the most electrifying races in history—a battle royal between team mates Caracciola and von Brauchitsch. This was one race that 'Unlucky Manfred' won, and a breathless Rodney Walkerley managed to recapture the atmosphere in *The Motor*.

Faraway places were the locations for four of the circuits in 1937, The Germans travelling to Rio de Janeiro, New York and South Africa in search of victory.

=== MEMOIR ===

Rudolf Uhlenhaut

Technical Director, Daimler-Benz Racing, 1936–39

I graduated from Munich University in 1931 with a Diploma in Engineering and joined Daimler-Benz in Stuttgart that same year. At that time I had no interest in motor racing at all—I was working on passenger cars and had nothing to do with the racing programme when it began in 1933.

In the 1920s the Benz company had built a mid-engined racing car—the *Tropfenwagen*—which wasn't a great success. So when the Auto Union appeared in 1934 it wasn't quite so new as many people imagined. It had a swing axle at the rear, which made it very difficult to drive and there were really only three people who could manage it properly—Rosemeyer, Varzi and Stuck. Stuck wasn't of quite the same calibre as the others, but he managed the car comparatively well.

Like the Auto Union our W25 Mercedes of 1934 also had a swing axle and it, too, was quite difficult to drive, but it was successful. It started with a 3.4-litre engine, going up to 3.9 litres in 1935 and 4.7 in 1936. The Auto Unions always had bigger engines, but they couldn't rev as fast as ours, which was to their disadvantage. We could always pass them at the last moment because we could over-rev our engines and they couldn't. There was a good example of this at the Eifel GP in 1935, when Caracciola was able to pass Rosemeyer at the very last gasp and win the race by just over one second. The Auto Union V-16 was a very nice engine—very smooth, naturally, and good at low revs, but it didn't have that last bit of 'pep' at the top end.

Late in 1934 Mercedes began work on a 5.6-litre V-12, to go into a new short chassis, but this engine turned out to be too heavy. It was quite good for setting records on a straight road, but quite unsuitable for the Nürburgring, for example. Although the new car was within the 750 kg limit, it had too much weight at the front end.

After two good years in 1934–35, Mercedes were not so successful in 1936, so much so that the company pulled out of racing before the season ended and reorganized the entire racing department. It was not so much the design of the car that was wrong, it was more the fault of the workshop, which was not very well organized. So in August 1936 I was appointed Technical Director of the *Rennabteilung*, a new department that came between Alfred Neubauer, the Team Manager, and the Design Department.

Naturally, we had a good Design Office, but the people there were cautious and our opinions often differed. However, if I wanted something I said so and they would generally let me have it, for I was now responsible for building, running and developing the racing cars. Racing is a risky job and not only for the drivers. Every Sunday it is proved whether you are right or wrong and many men don't like that, especially when they get a bit older. I didn't care, but I was just 30, which was very young for such a job and I was very surprised to get it. The technical management seemed to be glad that I had taken over, so I could do more or less what I thought was right.

The main problem in 1935 and 1936 was that there was no-one in the racing department who could drive the cars, so they had to rely on what the racing drivers said and they had very little technical knowledge. When I started my new job I took two cars to the Nürburgring and began to learn how to drive a racing car, which is not difficult until you want to go fast, which you have to do if you're going to find out what's wrong with it. During the four or five years I had been working on passenger cars we often drove them on the Nürburgring and we always drove them as fast as we could! I found out that driving a racing car was not much different from driving a passenger car at high speed. Gradually, I developed my skills until I could lap the 'Ring (and Monza and Hockenheim) almost as fast as our Grand Prix drivers! I loved driving the racing cars, but I never raced so I can't say if I'd have been a good racing driver or not. I had the technique, but I also had the track to myself, which made things a lot easier.

I went to the 'Ring with just a handful of mechanics and

no Neubauer, so I could start slowly and get used to things. I took a late 1936 car with the de Dion rear axle and a 1935 car with the swing axle and my first impressions were of quite simple faults that any engineer could have found. First of all, the frame on both cars was much too weak—it bent and vibrated on rough roads. Also, at that time our design department had the idea that the damping of the axle had to be very stiff, so they incorporated both hydraulic *and* friction dampers! This meant that there was very little movement of the axle against the frame—much of the springing was done in the frame itself. That was completely wrong and the car jumped all over the place because the wheels couldn't follow the road surface.

The swing axle caused the 1935 car to oversteer very easily and although the car with the de Dion axle was better it was not perfect. Mr Wagner (who was responsible for the chassis design) had wanted a good-looking car and so he designed a simple-looking rear axle where the wheel forces were taken by the actual casing in the middle. As this was built quite lightly it bent—some three or four inches! Naturally, it would have been much better to have had a strut from the outside of the axle, bringing the forces into the frame. Also, the friction damping was very stiff and the front axle transmitted a terrific amount of vibration to the steering wheel. It was a very good-looking axle with no spring to be seen (there was a cross-strut with the spring inside it) but it had very little movement, very little jounce and bounce. On one occasion during this testing period I lost a rear wheel at top speed on the straight. The chassis was so stiff that nothing happened—it was just like driving a motorcycle with a sidecar!

The gearbox was bad too—the gears tended to slip out of mesh and when that happened the revs went sky-high and the valves got bent by hitting the pistons. Sometimes the drivers didn't have time to rev the engine when changing down—they'd just pull the lever through, which often broke the cog-wheels. So we changed to dog-clutches with constant-mesh engagement of the gears and they were so strong you couldn't break them.

Once we had sorted all these things out we were able to build our new car for 1937—the W125. It had hydraulic damping only, and was very easy to drive, but what sort of reaction did we get from our drivers? Practically none! To begin with they thought it was wrong to leave off the friction dampers, so I let them drive a car which had both, but oiled up the friction dampers without telling them! After the test run they declared that the car was now alright, so I said, 'Good—now come and look at this.' I took off the linkage and moved the oily dampers to and fro with my hand. From then on we had no friction damping!

We went to Monza in March 1937 to test the new car. Only one was ready, so we took a 1936 car, too, and Dick Seaman crashed this one badly. He said the crash was entirely his fault and that was quite remarkable—he would always tell you exactly what happened and blame himself if necessary. Other drivers had a tendency to blame the car, but he was very honest in this way. We didn't take his crash too seriously, although it was not the best way to start his career with us. . . .

Our first race of the year was at Tripoli, which was a very fast circuit. I drove round it and liked it very much, but the engines used to wear out quite quickly as there was so much sand about, and the long straights meant that they were at full revs for quite some time. Our new car won first time out, Lang scoring the first of his three consecutive victories there. Seaman ran second until he had supercharger trouble—the mechanics had put a rag into the intake to prevent sand being blown in while the car was at the pits and then they forgot to take it out. It got sucked into the supercharger and, of course, blocked it. Seaman was not pleased!

Then came the Avus GP, which was a non-Formula event. Lang won again, but Caracciola and von Brauchitsch retired. All three were driving streamlined cars—the first time we'd used them—and we'd had no opportunity to try them out beforehand. In the race the gearboxes got too hot as the streamlined bodies kept any cooling air away from them. One of the oil pipes to the gearbox was soldered on and it got so hot that the solder melted and the oil escaped. Lang was lucky, though. He had the newest car in which the oil pipe wasn't soldered on but made as one part with the flange which attached it to the gearbox, so there was no oil loss and he won the race.

I drove one of the cars in practice and although we were doing around 385 km/h (240 mph) on the straights there were no problems at that speed. The main problem on the circuit was the newly banked North Turn, which didn't have a curve in the banking, so if you went too fast you just slid over the top. It was very dangerous and you had to treat it exactly as if you were driving on a normal road. Had the banking itself curved up to the perpendicular, then you could have cornered just as fast as your body could stand.

Having won our first two races we then lost the next three! Rosemeyer beat us at the Eifel GP—Caracciola and von Brauchitsch coming second and third—and he beat us again in the Vanderbilt Cup. I went with Neubauer, Caracciola and Seaman to New York for this race, while von Brauchitsch and Lang went to Spa for the Belgian GP the following weekend. We went on the *Bremen*—one of the fastest liners in the world—and you could get anything you wanted. We travelled first class, of course, and I ate much too much! I tried to combat this by swimming two or three times a day and running round the deck, but it was no use!

When we got to the race track we found that the cars weren't accelerating out of the corners fast enough. At that time the supercharger compressed air through a carburettor into the engine, which gave the Mercedes a very distinctive, shrill scream. At medium revs the pressure wasn't very high, for the rotors of the Roots compressor had to have a clearance between them and the casing and when they turned relatively slowly a lot of the air passed through that gap. We had an alternative design whereby the Roots compressor *sucked* the air through the carburettor and into the engine. We were using alcohol then and we had to use considerable quantities as its thermal heat is about half that of gasoline. Putting alcohol through the supercharger made it function as a seal between the rotor and the casing, so the air didn't pass through the gap and we got far greater

Uhlenhaut (with flag, *top right*) watches as Rudolf Caracciola makes a pit stop during his winning drive in the 1937 German GP. The fabulous W125 was virtually all-conquering that year

supercharger pressure at low and middle revs. That increased our acceleration considerably and so we changed the system on all our cars in New York and I remember that I didn't go to bed for three nights—it was a tremendous amount of work!

Dick Seaman very nearly won that race. He was catching Rosemeyer easily, only to run out of fuel with a couple of laps to go—very frustrating after all the hard work we'd put in. One curious thing I remember is that the Americans made us paint swastikas on our cars, for some reason.

We travelled home on the *Europa* and I got off at Cherbourg and continued by air to Stuttgart. I had to start preparing for the next race—the German GP. In the meantime, however, Lang and von Brauchitsch were beaten at Spa by the Auto Unions of Hasse and Stuck. I don't know what went wrong there! Obviously, they didn't have the different supercharger arrangement that we had effected in America. Lang led for a while, but then had to stop for new tyres and never regained the lead.

Altogether it was a bad month for Mercedes. Losing three races in succession made things rather uncomfortable for those responsible for the cars, which were definitely

faster than the Auto Unions, yet were being beaten by them. There was a lot of pressure from above and it got worse with every race we lost! However, we managed to get things right in time for the German GP, Caracciola and von Brauchitsch finishing one-two and Kautz and Lang sixth and seventh.

We then scored a one-two-three at Monaco, lost the Coppa Acerbo to Rosemeyer, scored another one-two-three at Bern and a one-two at Livorno, where they held the Italian GP that year. We came first and second at Brno, but lost the Donington GP to Rosemeyer, once more. It was his last victory and had he lived I'm sure we would have seen some marvellous races between him and Lang in 1938 and 1939, as Lang was getting better all the time.

That was the end of the 750 Kg Formula. For 1938 we had a choice of using a 4.5-litre unsupercharged engine or a 3-litre supercharged unit and, having by now considerable experience with supercharging, we decided to go for the latter. Our 3-litre V-12 was, in detail, the same as the previous straight-eight, with cylinders, crankshaft and conrods built in the same way, but smaller, naturally.

The chassis was also very similar, but shorter, and

LEFT Uhlenhaut was a brilliant test driver and very nearly as fast as the men paid to do the racing! Here he puts the new, 3-litre, W154 through its paces at Monza early in 1938

RIGHT Fire! A split-second after this photo was taken, von Brauchitsch's Mercedes (12) caught fire during the 1938 German GP. Neubauer (*bottom right*) pulled Manfred clear and Dick Seaman (16) went on to win the race

because of the increased fuel consumption of the 3-litre engine we had to have two fuel tanks—one behind the driver and one in front of him. The W125 had carried 250 litres (55 gall.), but the new W154 had to carry 400 (88 gall.)! I remember that at the Nürburgring the fuel consumption of the 485 bhp 3-litre car was 140 litres per 100 km (30.8 gall. per 60 miles) and the 580 bhp 5.6-litre car used only 100 litres (22 gall.) over the same distance. Stepping up the power of the W154 meant that we had to cool the pistons with fuel, which is why the consumption was so high, and it was difficult to get it all into the car.

After testing the cars at Monza early in the year we took two to Pau for the first race of the season. Lang's car was withdrawn during practice and only Caracciola started the race. Pau is a very slow circuit and we couldn't use our power to proper advantage. René Dreyfus was there with a 4.5-litre unblown Delahaye which was nearly as fast as we were on this slow course, but his fuel consumption was about half! Caracciola had to stop for fuel (when Lang took over) but Dreyfus didn't, so he won the race.

From Pau we went to Tripoli, where Lang won again, and then to Reims, where von Brauchitsch scored one of his rare victories. Seaman then won the German GP, which was his first race of the year as we didn't have enough cars for four drivers in the early races.

For a time Seaman ran second behind von Brauchitsch, who complained bitterly about him at his first pit stop: 'I can't stand having Seaman following so close behind me!' This was silly, because he was in a race, but it was a team rule that if one man was leading, well ahead of our competitors, none of his team mates should try and harass or pass him. Seaman was obeying this rule, but running fairly

close behind. They came in for their second pit stop almost together and von Brauchitsch's car caught fire. After refueling the mechanic had turned off the fuel tap too late and the tank had overflowed. Instead of waiting to have water poured over the spilt fuel, they started the engine and the fuel caught fire.

Seaman was refuelling just behind von Brauchitsch, but when he was ready he stayed where he was. Neubauer couldn't believe it! 'What are you waiting for?' he shouted. 'Last time you told me I've got to wait behind von Brauchitsch,' said Seaman. Neubauer sent him off with a flea in his ear and, of course, he won the race. He had become a faster driver than von Brauchitsch and better—he could have passed him any time, but he was very honest and stuck to the rules. He was a very fine chap in that way—if he said something about his car you could always rely on him. The other drivers usually said nothing so if they put up a bad performance they could blame the car but I can't remember a single time when Seaman made an excuse.

In spite of scoring the greatest victory of his career, he didn't get a drive in the next two races. This was simply because von Brauchitsch had damaged his car when he had crashed after rejoining the race, leaving us only three cars for the Coppa Ciano and the Coppa Acerbo. Seaman was the junior driver of the team so he was out of luck. Von Brauchitsch actually won the Coppa Ciano, but was then disqualified for receiving outside assistance after a spin, so the race went to Lang. Caracciola then won the Coppa Acerbo at Pescara.

We had four cars ready for the Swiss GP at Bern and Caracciola won again, from Seaman. It poured with rain for most of the race and although Seaman set fastest time in practice—in the dry—and led the race for some laps, he couldn't beat Caracciola in the wet. Somehow Caracciola could see through the blinding rain—incredibly, he used to take his goggles off and drive without them! Seaman did very well to be only half a minute behind him at the finish. He was a good rain driver, whereas in 1938 Lang was not, although by 1939 he had learned how.

The Italian GP was back at Monza which in those days was very hard on engines—they wouldn't stand for top revs and top power for very long because the pistons overheated, and there was a very long straight at Monza. It was a disastrous race for us owing to a malfunction in some new carburettors. That evening I remember Neubauer—who was very fed up—saying that he was going out to dinner with his wife and that nobody was allowed to accompany them, but it ended up with a tremendous party in a restaurant where Dick Seaman announced his engagement to Erica Popp.

When we got to Donington the political situation had become very tense due to the Munich Crisis. The RAC gave a lunch in Seaman's honour to celebrate his German GP win and during the meal the gentleman sitting opposite me said, 'If things go on like this we're going to have a war and you'll have all the rest of the world against you!' I didn't forget that. Things then got very bad and we were called back to Germany. We were prepared to destroy the

cars—burn them—if we couldn't get them out of England, but when we got to Harwich we learned that Chamberlain had met with Hitler at Munich and everything was all right. In the race, which was postponed for a month, Lang led until his windscreen was shattered by a stone. The wind pressure on his face forced him to slow and Nuvolari passed him to win. Seaman was third.

During the winter we were terribly busy, improving the cars for the 1939 season. The roller bearings on our 1938 V-12 engine had not been completely reliable, as the cages which guided the rollers had a tendency to crack. The stronger cages for the 1939 engine were broader, demanding a longer crankshaft and therefore a new engine. Also in 1939 we used two-stage supercharging, which increased torque in the lower and middle rev ranges by 12–15 per cent.

All this, of course, was to do with the 3-litre cars, but not only were we preparing them—we were designing and building the new 1.5-litre cars for the Tripoli race. The Italians were fed up with being beaten by our cars all the time, so they decided to run all their 1939 races with a 1.5-litre limit. We only heard about this at the Italian GP, so once the decision had been taken to build a car for this race we had to work very hard.

Lang and von Brauchitsch finished first and second at Pau with the 3-litre cars and then we took the new 1.5-litre cars to Tripoli. We only just got them ready in time for the race, but we were able to do so because the design was similar to our 3-litre machines. The engine was a 1.5-litre V-8, of course, but the valve gear, pistons and chassis were the same, only smaller. We only made three engines—two for the race and one spare for testing. We managed to get one car ready for a test run at Hockenheim, but we tested all the parts of the engine first on separate test beds—valve gear, con-rod bearings, etc—so when we assembled the engine every part had been tested and it worked properly straightaway. We had no breakages and the cars finished first and second, driven by Lang and Caracciola. We also planned to run in the 1940 Tripoli race and we built a streamlined car with a two-stage supercharger, but the race was cancelled at the last minute and the car has disappeared.

In 1939 Lang won any race his car finished. After Pau and Tripoli he won again at the Eifel GP, setting a new lap record in the process, and then he won the Belgian GP at Spa where, of course, Dick Seaman was killed. All I remember about the Spa race is that it was very rainy and we were quite sure we would beat the Auto Unions. When Seaman crashed we didn't know it was so serious at first. Later, Lang came in to refuel and his engine wouldn't restart—there was some evaporation in the fuel lines. We weren't allowed to use the electric starter motor so we told him to try and start it himself on the run downhill to Eau Rouge. The engine refused to fire all the way down, but just as he reached the uphill gradient it caught, and he was able to finish the race and win it.

Afterwards I went to see Seaman in hospital. He was terribly badly burnt but fully conscious and told me that he was probably trying too hard and that the crash was entirely his own fault. The doctor told me he was going

to die, it was just a matter of how long his heart could keep going. He died just after midnight and we were all terribly depressed—everybody liked Dick Seaman. Curiously, before the race he had said to me that if they continued to race on tree-lined circuits such as Spa, some drivers were going to be killed. And, of course, he hit a tree and his car caught fire. He wasn't seriously injured—I believe his right arm was broken—but he was obviously knocked unconscious on impact and so was unable to get out. He died as a result of his burns.

Seaman was a very good driver, but I believe he tried to get to the top too quickly. He should have taken things a bit easier, but he wanted to be as fast as the others straightaway and if you're always on the limit you're going to have accidents. After his crash at Spa, Lang—who had not been far behind him—told me that Seaman had been taking considerable risks on the wet road, putting his inside front wheel just over the edge of the track on the corners, driving on the limit. This was not really necessary as he was in the lead and Lang would not have tried to overtake him. If Seaman had taken a bit more time, allowed himself to develop gradually—as Lang did—he would have been in the same class as Lang. The big difference between them was that Lang started his career with us, whereas when Seaman joined Mercedes he was already used to winning races. He always liked to go very fast, but I believe he didn't have quite enough experience with our very powerful cars, which is why he had several crashes. Lang held back and learned carefully. He only had one crash while I was in the Racing Department—at Brno in 1937—and that wasn't his fault.

From Spa we went to Reims for the French GP, which Lang led easily for three-quarters of the race, but then his

engine blew up. None of our three cars finished, which was an appalling result. Von Brauchitsch retired and Caracciola hit a house in Gueux village on the first lap! Almost certainly he was trying too hard in his efforts to beat Lang, who was now clearly the fastest driver in the world. Caracciola was used to being Number One and although he was still not yet 40 he was past his prime and I'm sure he found this hard to accept.

He did, however, win the German Grand Prix—for the sixth time. Lang led at the end of lap 1—by nearly half a minute, which was almost unbelievable—but at the end of lap 2 he had to come in for new plugs and after one more lap he came in to retire. He continued his winning way in the Swiss GP, however—his fifth victory of the season, which made him European Champion for 1939.

There was one more race—the Yugoslav GP in Belgrade, which was held on the day war broke out—3 September. Nuvolari won that for Auto Union, from von Brauchitsch.

Lang also won the Mountain Championship that year. There were two events, at Kahlenberg in Austria and at the Grossglockner, and we built special cars for them, using steam cooling. We wanted as much weight as possible on the rear axle for good traction, so we took the radiator from the front and put it in a water-filled tank behind the driver. For cooling fluid we used glycol, an alcohol which boils at about 140 degrees, and we ran the engine at around 120 degrees Centigrade and pumped the hot fluid back to the radiator in the water tank where we had a difference of 20 degrees, so we boiled the water away, using about 20 litres (4.4 gall.) at the Grossglockner.

We used twin rear tyres at Kahlenberg because the road there was very broad and flat, but not at the Grossglockner, which was narrow and bumpy. The width of the car at

LEFT Glum faces tell the story. (*Left to right*) Uhlenhaut, Caracciola and Max Sailer look distinctly unhappy during Mercedes' unsuccessful record attempts in October 1937. The car is a W125 modified for standing start record attempts

RIGHT With his fluent English, Uhlenhaut established a good relationship with Dick Seaman (they are seen here at Monza before the 1938 Italian GP) whom he found to be refreshingly honest when it came to admitting mistakes!

the rear was considerably increased and we thought that the drivers might forget that and bang the rear end against the side of the road.

We never thought of twin rear tyres for racing, but you must remember that the roads on which we raced in those days were very uneven and the four tyres would seldom have been in contact with the surface at the same time. It was not possible then to make high-speed tyres of small diameter and great width, such as you see today. We had two types—one for wet weather and one for dry—and there were no special soft tyres for making a fast practice time. We did have three different sizes for the rear wheels: 19 in. (48.2 cm) for normal races, such as at the Nürburgring; 22 in. (55.9 cm) for fast circuits such as Tripoli and 24 in. (61 cm) for the ultra-fast Avus.

I'm surprised to recall that in those days the cars were set up at the beginning of the season and given to the drivers, who were told, 'Here they are—now get on with it!' We really regarded pre-race practice as a period for drivers to get to know the circuit and to get used to the cars as they were—there were hardly any alterations made. We had a rolling road at the factory for testing the cars up to full speed in all the gears and so on, so all the testing was done by the time we reached the circuit and we knew that they were going to work. This way the drivers had time to practise and get used to the track—we felt it was a bad thing if they had to come in continuously to make changes to the car, changing the plugs or the carburation or the gears.

Today, racing drivers seem to have a better grasp of the technical side of things, but then they knew very little. The one exception in my experience was Dick Seaman, who was very knowledgeable. When he first joined us in 1937 he

spoke hardly any German so, as I had been born and partly brought up in England, I had the most contact with him. (Neubauer spoke very little English, but nevertheless he and Dick got on very well together. I don't know how they managed it, but they did!) I developed a very good understanding with him and we used to talk a lot about technical details. I listened to his ideas and they were often quite useful.

We did our main testing at Monza at the beginning of the year, spending about three weeks there. The cars we built for the races were replicas of the Monza cars and they were changed very little during the season. Each driver had his own seat made to measure and the cars were very comfortable. For some reason they all liked to sit very close to the steering wheel—none liked to sit back at arm's length, as they did after the war. It has been claimed that the pre-war cars were physically hard to drive and needed a lot of shoulder-power, but this is not true. Before we built the 2.5-litre cars for 1954 I took a 1939 3-litre car to the 'Ring, having changed it in keeping with many of the ideas we had for the new car, including independent rear suspension. I also altered the seating position so I could sit at arm's length and I found it very easy to drive.

Over the years, between 1934 and 1939, we won more races than Auto Union, but we technicians never felt quite satisfied. Success was expected of us and when things went wrong we were in trouble. In factory life you're very seldom praised—things are expected to work and if they don't you have to explain yourself. Auto Union were our main rivals, of course, and we hated losing to them, although we were on good terms with all the people there, but if we had to be beaten, we'd rather be beaten by Alfa Romeo!

Günther Molter

Press Director, Daimler-Benz, 1973–86

I first went to the Nürburgring on my bicycle when I was 15 years old. My home town was Landau in Palatina, about 240 km (150 miles) away, and I stayed the night at Oberwesel, in the Youth Club there, going on to the 'Ring the next day in time for practice. As I came closer to the circuit I could hear the scream of the supercharged engines and that gave me a little more power to pedal up the hills.

My first stop was the road on the Döttinger-Höhe. I turned right under a bridge going down to Adenau and shortly after this bridge, on the left side, there was a wooden tower built for the radio reporter. I put my bicycle down and climbed up the ladder. From the tower I could see the cars come through the wood from Brünnchen and then all the way down the Döttinger-Höhe—it was fantastic.

This was 1935—the year when von Brauchitsch took the lead but didn't change tyres at the right time. On the very last lap he had a blow-out and Nuvolari won the race in his Alfa.

At that time the farmers let you have a sleeping place in some of their barns for a few pfennigs a night. You slept on straw and when I arrived on the Wednesday or the Thursday the whole barn was empty, but when I got back on the Saturday night it was so crowded I had a problem to find a space!

The Grand Prix always started at 11 am on the Sunday, so I used to be at the Karussell between 8 and 8.30 am.

This was my favourite place because you could get very close to the cars and you could see them coming from Bergwerk and into the right-hand turn that leads to the Karussell.

Before the race all the drivers—most of whom stayed in the Eifelerhof in Adenau—drove themselves to the pits. They were all great individuals, each with his own car—Caracciola had a red Mercedes 540K with his special Berlin licence plate 1A 4444. Von Brauchitsch had a blue car and you saw all the others, Lang, Dreyfus, Nuvolari, Stuck and so on. They all had their own distinctive overalls—Nuvolari, for instance, with his yellow shirt and brown leather vest—and you could recognize every one of them. They drove with their wives (or lady friends) up to the start and finish line as did Crown Prince Wilhelm, the Kaiser's son, who was a big racing fan and had a big blue Mercedes with compressor. All this was like a big theatrical spectacle, building up the tension.

At 11 am they fired a cannon to start the race and we heard the noise of the cars as they began the first lap. They took about six minutes to reach the Karussell, but we could hear them all the way because the tremendous noise was reflected by the mountains—it was like an animal scream! Then, when the cars at last came into view you saw the driver fighting the machine, not like today, when they are anonymous, hidden in the bodywork and wearing a full-face helmet. Then you could see the faces and the effort they were putting into driving these big machines which had about 500 bhp. The Mercedes and Auto Unions were initially in front, but later on Nuvolari moved up in the P3 Alfa Romeo and won the race.

ABOVE Rudolf Caracciola with his great friend, Louis Chiron. Caracciola's Mercedes bears his own, personal Berlin number plate

LEFT The Mercedes team at their Nürburgring HQ, the Forsthaus St Hubertus. The cars are setting out for the 1937 Eifel GP

The next year Rosemeyer won. He was outstanding—like an artist—and the only one who was really able to get on with the 16-cylinder Auto Union. When he came down Wehrseifen, crossing the bridge at Adenau and going up through the right-hand turn to Bergwerk, he was sideways all the way—it was fantastic!

The last race I went to before the war was the 1939 German Grand Prix. There was a tremendous crowd, perhaps the biggest ever, because everyone had the feeling that something terrible was about to happen—the future was in the dark. Two Zeppelins flew over the Nürburgring—the LZ 127 and the larger LZ 130, which was the sister ship of the *Hindenburg*, which had crashed in May 1937 at Lakehurst. This was the last time the two ships appeared in public. In the race Hermann Lang took the lead and finished the first lap way ahead of the others, only to retire at the end of lap 2. Then it began to rain and on lap 3 Paul Pietsch took the lead in his 3-litre Maserati, but he had plug problems due to the change in temperature when it rained and he had to stop at the pits several times for new plugs and to have part of the radiator covered up. In those days engines were very sensitive to weather conditions and at the Nürburgring the temperature could change dramatically as you went down from the hills.

This was the first time Pietsch drove the new Maserati, which had two 4-cylinder engines joined together to make a straight-eight, and this was the type of car which won the 1939 and 1940 Indianapolis 500, driven by Wilbur

187

Shaw. In spite of his troubles Pietsch finished third in the German GP, which was tremendous.

I think over 300,000 people watched that race, which was Caracciola's last great victory. He was our greatest hero and we boys used to pretend we were him and the other drivers as we raced each other on our bicycles. We all wanted to be Caracciola—he was Number One. In those days Mercedes always stayed at the Forsthaus St Hubertus—it was on the way to Nürburg and it was the team Headquarters. I used to spend hours leaning over the fence looking at the cars as the mechanics worked on them. And the smell! They used Castrol R, which had that sweet, exotic smell. It was a fascinating atmosphere and it was my dream to sit in one of those cars one day. I had to wait until 1952 but I did it—not as a successor to Caracciola, but as a member of the team, for I was then assistant to Alfred Neubauer, for the Carrera Panamericana.

For me Neubauer was one of the biggest actors I have ever met! He was always acting—always selling Neubauer. But, on the other hand, he was a very smart man who prepared for each race very carefully and always studied the regulations very closely to find a way of using them to his advantage. Being his assistant was a wonderful experience. He was a fascinating person, a modern-day Falstaff who really knew how to enjoy life. To dine with him was quite something; to drink with him was quite something and when he was around there was nothing else—just Neubauer!

When he was chasing the photographers away from the pit with his flag, that was a show—he was acting then, just as he was when he was giving signals to the drivers. It was all part of the Neubauer act, making sure everybody knew that he was Number One! He was a great personality and he sold his team in the best possible way.

Neubauer considered Caracciola the greatest driver ever, but personally I'm against declaring one driver as the best of all time—you can only be the best of your particular time. Before World War I there was Christian Lautenschlager, who won the 1914 French Grand Prix. He drove the 750 km (466 miles) in seven hours, and had to change his own tyres. Up to 1939 Caracciola had his time, Rosemeyer had his time and, in 1939 itself, Lang was Number One.

I met Caracciola after the war and he was quite a personality, very good-looking but something of an introvert. After his crash at Monaco in 1933 his hip never mended properly and Uhlenhaut told me that he was always in tremendous pain, especially on a dry road as the brakes in those days required a lot of pressure from the right leg, and it was this leg that was shattered at Monaco. This also explains why his driving was so sensitive on wet roads, when he didn't need to press the pedal so hard.

By 1939 Lang was faster than Caracciola, but as far as continuity of success is concerned, Rudi was Number One. He was successful all through his career: he won the Mille Miglia, he won the Tourist Trophy, he won the German Grand Prix six times, he won nearly everything. I think Nuvolari was probably as good as Caracciola. He, too, won practically everything and was able to drive the 3-litre Auto Union just as well as he had driven the P3 Alfa Romeo.

ABOVE **Alfred Neubauer considered his friend Caracciola the greatest driver ever. They are seen here at Montlhéry in 1934**

ABOVE RIGHT **Caracciola and Lang. By 1939 they had become keen rivals—and Lang was definitely the faster of the two**

Rosemeyer was a very bright personality, a sunny boy! He was great in every respect: he was charming, he was good looking and a brilliant driver. He married Elly Beinhorn, the famous flyer, and in a short time he, too, learned to fly, because he wasn't the man to let others do things and not be involved himself. He took risks, but he was so talented that he was sure that nothing could happen to him. Then, on 28 January 1938, he didn't calculate the risks as he should have done on the *autobahn* during his record attempt, and the wind—blowing through a gap in the woods beside the road—blew him off course when he was doing over 430 km/h (270 mph).

He was a fantastic personality who was also a winner and the newspapers loved him. They loved him even more

Alfred Neubauer

Team Manager, Daimler-Benz, 1934–39

Alfred Neubauer virtually invented the job of Team Manager. It seems hard to believe today, but there was a time when drivers raced without being given any information as to their progress—they just drove for hours on end and only learned the results of their endeavours at the finish, if they finished. This ridiculous state of affairs was brought home to Neubauer during Germany's first Grand Prix, which was held at Avus in 1926. The race was won by his young friend, Rudolf Caracciola, who knew nothing about his sensational victory until he was surrounded by jubilant Mercedes personnel. Afterwards, Neubauer decided that it was high time that drivers were allowed to know what was going on during a race—how many laps they had completed, how far they were ahead or behind other competitors and just when they should make a pit stop.

This was a very novel idea in European racing, although in America they had been passing such information to the drivers for some years. Indeed, when Mercedes had entered three cars for the 1923 Indianapolis 500 they were surprised to find that many American drivers raced to a prearranged plan and were brought into the pits by signals, rather than stopping when they felt like it. The efficiency of this system was not lost on the Germans, but surprisingly, they did nothing about it.

So it was left to Alfred Neubauer—three years later—to devise a system of signals that could be easily understood by a driver speeding past the pits, a system that made its debut at Solitude in September 1926. For the first time Neubauer's imposing figure was seen in front of the Mercedes-Benz pits (Daimler and Benz had merged in June that year), waving his black and red flag at his drivers and giving them information with the aid of chalk and a board. That day—12 September—changed the face of motor racing forever, taking the sport into a new realm of efficiency and setting in motion the legend of Alfred Neubauer and Mercedes-Benz.

It was Professor Ferdinand Porsche who really started Neubauer on the road to immortality by inviting him to join the Austro-Daimler works properly at the end of World War I. Properly because, during the war, when serving in the Imperial Austro-Hungarian Army as an officer-cadet, Neubauer had been attached to the works on 'special duty', whatever that meant. When the war ended in 1918, Professor Porsche (who was then Managing Director of Austro-Daimler) offered him the job of running the Road Test Department. The 27-year-old from Northern Bohemia (now part of Czechoslovakia) grabbed this opportunity with both hands, as not only was he mad about cars, but he also nurtured an ambition to be a racing driver.

when he married Elly Beinhorn—the blond German youth and the beautiful aviatrice. They made stories everywhere, and his style of driving made him very attractive. Whereas Caracciola's driving appeared almost effortless, Rosemeyer took risks and showed the public that he was taking risks.

Von Brauchitsch was always very fast but, as Uhlenhaut said, he always needed a strong machine. Caracciola, Rosemeyer and Lang all had a feeling for their machines, but von Brauchitsch was always very hard, very demanding on the car. In 1935 it was absolutely unnecessary for him to lose the German GP, but he drove too hard and destroyed his tyres when he had a big lead.

Seaman, like Caracciola, had a feeling for machinery and was a very intelligent man. He was very popular in Germany—the British gentleman who drove for Mercedes and married a German girl.

The 1930s was the time of the great personalities—they were all individuals and you couldn't mix up one with another. Each had his own driving style, his own way of dressing and you could see them at work and recognize them instantly. Today's racing drivers are like men from space—anonymous—hidden away in their machines. Then they were recognizable personalities.

He was able to realize that ambition when Porsche nominated him as one of four drivers for the Austro-Daimler entry in the 1922 Targa Florio. Until then, the firm had been building very large cars for very rich customers, but a close friend of Porsche's—Count Sascha Kolowrat—was certain that there was a good market for a small, nimble machine and in order to impress the Professor with this idea he took him to Italy early in September 1921. That year the Italian GP was held on a circuit near Brescia and four days later, on the same circuit, there was the GP di Vetturetti and among the 1.5-litre cars competing were Bugatti, OM, Chiribiri, SB and Restelli.

Porsche got the message and, the following year, produced the Sascha Austro-Daimler, a 4-cylinder, 1100 cc car, four of which were entered for the Targa Florio. Count Kolowrat was, naturally, one of the drivers and Alfred Neubauer another and his car was fitted with a slightly larger engine, although whether this was because he was a slightly larger fellow than the others is not known! In the event, poor Kolowrat was the only one of the team not to finish, Neubauer coming 19th in his very first race and his other team mates, Kuhn and Peecher, 22nd and 23rd.

At the end of the year, Professor Porsche decided to leave Austro-Daimler and in the spring of 1923 joined Daimler Motoren in Untertürkheim, Stuttgart, taking Neubauer with him. There, the would-be racing driver found himself in illustrious company, rubbing shoulders with the likes of Otto Salzer, Max Sailer and the two Christians—Lautenschlager and Werner. He also met for the first time another aspiring racer, one Rudolf Caracciola.

Neubauer joined Lautenschlager and Werner in the Mercedes team for the 1924 Targa Florio, which Werner won. Lautenschlager finished 10th and Neubauer 15th and together they won the Team Prize. Later in the year, Mercedes entered the Semmering mountainclimb and Neubauer—who by now was really beginning to fancy himself—was shattered to find that he could do no better than fifth, nearly 40 seconds slower than Werner. To cap it all, his fiancée, Hansi—clearly not a girl to be blinded by love in this instance—suggested that his poor result was due to the fact that he had driven 'like a night watchman'.

His racing career finally came to an ignominious halt in

The unmistakeable figure of Alfred Neubauer steps forward to watch as one of his cars flashes past the pits during the 1935 French GP at Montlhéry. Mercedes finished one-two

October that year, when he joined the Mercedes team of Christian Werner and the Counts Giulio Masetti and Louis Zborowski for the Italian Grand Prix at Monza. Caracciola went along as a reserve driver, although by now he had notched up a very impressive list of wins in races and mountainclimbs and was far more experienced than Neubauer! Rudi wasn't sorry to be left out of the team, however, as the 2-litre, straight-eight Mercedes experienced all sorts of problems.

In the race the cars were hampered by plug trouble and did not run at all well. Neubauer stopped for new plugs after 17 laps and his place at the wheel was taken by Otto Merz, but these problems paled into insignificance when

Count Zborowski crashed on the Lesmo curve and was killed. It was a disastrous day for Daimler-Benz and marked the end of Alfred Neubauer's career as a racing driver.

For some time he had been aware that he had a flair for organization and this had not gone unnoticed at Daimler. He quickly came to terms with the fact that he was never going to make the grade as a racing driver and, since racing was still his grand passion, he was delighted when the company made him Team Manager.

From 1926 until the end of 1930, Neubauer worked hard at learning the art of team management. The new company of Daimler-Benz eschewed Grand Prix racing and concentrated on sports car events, competing first with the SS (Super Sport), which led to the SSK (K for *Kurz*—short), which in turn led to the legendary SSKL (L for *Leicht*— light). With this series of formidable machines, Mercedes scored dozens of victories throughout Europe and the British Isles, victories which included the German Grand Prix (run for sports cars), the Ulster TT, the Irish GP and the Mille Miglia.

The Wall Street Crash in 1929 and the subsequent Depression, however, meant that Mercedes could no longer continue with their racing programme and at the end of 1930 the company signed off all its drivers. The one most affected by this was Rudolf Caracciola, who had by this time established himself as Mercedes' Number One and was regarded by many as the finest racing driver in the world and when news of Mercedes' withdrawal broke, Alfa Romeo were quick to offer him a contract for 1931. Urged on by his wife, Charly, who had become his unofficial business manager, Caracciola was ready to sign it, but Neubauer was horrified by the idea.

Although still employed by Daimler-Benz, he was not at all happy at the prospect of having no racing team to manage, and the thought of his great friend and Germany's finest driver going over to the Italians filled him with gloom. He fully understood, however, that as a professional racing driver Rudi had to find employment elsewhere now that Mercedes were no longer in a position to offer him a job. Knowing that Caracciola had not yet signed with Alfa Romeo, Neubauer desperately sought a way of keeping him at Mercedes and came up with a plan that would, he felt, be acceptable to both parties: Daimler-Benz would sell him a new SSKL at a very reasonable price and provide mechanics and a transporter. They would also provide Alfred Neubauer, for Rudi would need a Team Manager and Neubauer's distaste of his upcoming desk job was as great as, if not greater than, his distaste of Rudi joining Alfa Romeo! Caracciola, for his part, would have to share all starting and prize money with the company. Not surprisingly, this was not such a good deal as was on offer from Alfa Romeo, but it provided a way of staying with Mercedes, so Rudi took it. Neubauer had little difficulty in persuading Mercedes to accept it also, and afterwards must have felt pretty pleased with himself, for not only had he kept Mercedes and Caracciola together on the race tracks, but he had kept himself in the job he loved best.

It was a very good year. In 1931 the 'private entry' of Caracciola and the SSKL Mercedes won no less than 11 events, including the Mille Miglia and the Eifel, Avus and German GPs, but it was not to last. At the end of the season Mercedes decided that they could not afford the partnership any longer and once again, Rudi was without a drive. This time Neubauer had no way of solving the problem and for 1932 Caracciola signed with Alfa Romeo.

Late that same year, the AIACR announced its new 750 Kg Formula for Grand Prix racing, to run from 1934 to the end of 1936, and in March 1933, Daimler-Benz decided that, Depression or no Depression, the company would return to the circuits. This they did, and very nearly without Alfred Neubauer.

By the end of 1932 he was desperate to get back into racing and one of the people he confided in was the former Daimler-Benz Sales Director in Dresden, Herr Herzing, the same man who had given Caracciola a job in the Daimler showroom nearly ten years before. Herzing had recently left Daimler-Benz to join the new Auto Union concern and he suggested that Neubauer follow him.

Intrigued by the idea, but not at all sure that he wanted to leave Daimler-Benz, having virtually grown up with the company, Neubauer went to see Auto Union's Managing Director, Baron Klaus Detlof von Oertzen. It was now November 1932, and Auto Union had already undertaken to produce a Grand Prix car to the design of Professor Porsche, who had himself left Daimler-Benz in 1928. If Neubauer were to join the new concern, not only would he find himself managing a racing team once again in 1934, but he would be reunited with his former mentor. It was a very tempting offer and Neubauer signed the contract von Oertzen offered him.

A couple of days later he had another meeting with another Managing Director, this time Dr Wilhelm Kissel of Daimler-Benz. Kissel had received Neubauer's letter of resignation and was astonished that he should even think of leaving the company. The decision to go racing again in 1934 had not yet been taken, but Kissel knew just which way the wind was blowing and assured Neubauer that Mercedes-Benz *would* be back. He promised to better Auto Union's terms if Neubauer would stay and once the slightly chastened Team Manager had agreed, Kissel set about disengaging him from the contract he had signed with von Oertzen.

It was just as well, for in the coming years Alfred Neubauer would prove himself without peer in the role of Team Manager and his contribution to the success of Daimler-Benz was to prove incalculable. Von Oertzen released him from his contract with good grace and then set about finding another Team Manager. He found him, too, at Daimler-Benz, for Willy Walb had been with the company for almost 20 years, having joined the Benz works in 1914, in the aero engine division. He had moved over to the Experimental and Racing Department in the early 1920s and had been actively involved with the Benz *Tropfenwagen*, the mid-engined car which the company raced in 1923, driving it in several events. He had stayed in competitions when the companies merged in 1926 and had obviously worked closely with Neubauer so he brought to Auto Union experience as an experimental engineer, racing driver and assistant Team Manager which, together with his practical knowledge of the mid-engined Benz racer, must have made him seem like a useful acquisition to Auto Union. Unfortunately, Walb did not prove to be a success running the team. He clearly didn't get on well with the drivers and for the 1935 season he was replaced by Dr Karl Feuereissen of the German Automobile Club who, while lacking the experience—not to say the charisma—of Alfred Neubauer, nonetheless did a very good job.

Once Daimler-Benz had taken the decision to build racing cars for the new Formula, Neubauer's first task was to take a look at the available talent and hire some drivers for 1934. Obviously, his first choice fell upon Rudolf Caracciola who, following Alfa Romeo's withdrawal from racing, had formed an independent team with his friend Louis Chiron for 1933. But then, within weeks of Mercedes' decision to return to Grand Prix racing, Rudi crashed disastrously at Monaco and rumours were rife that his hip was so badly damaged that he would never race again.

Neubauer knew his friend extremely well, so he refused to believe the rumours, although he had to accept that they might, in the end, prove to be correct. Meanwhile, he could only hope that Caracciola's wounds would heal in the year that lay ahead of Mercedes' first race and start looking for some other drivers to make up the team. Giving Rudi the benefit of the doubt, he now sought two team mates for him.

German nationalism demanded that, where possible, the Mercedes and Auto Unions should be driven by German drivers, but with the enforced absence of Caracciola these were few and far between. Probably the first name that came to Neubauer's mind was that of young Manfred von Brauchitsch, whose sensational win at Avus the year before in his specially streamlined SSKL had made him a hero overnight. But while he clearly showed promise, von Brauchitsch had very little experience.

Then there was Hans Stuck. The tall, handsome Hans had firmly established himself as a star, but in mountain-climbs, and although he had achieved some success in races, he was not yet regarded as a racing driver. Stuck, however, was never really in Neubauer's sights, as he was already closely allied to the Auto Union concern, due to his friendship with Professor Porsche. So Neubauer signed von Brauchitsch. He still needed a third driver and so, facing the inevitable truth that Caracciola, Stuck and von Brauchitsch were the only Germans remotely capable of handling a Grand Prix car properly, he was forced to look abroad, which meant France and Italy.

There were some fine French drivers around in the mid-1930s: Chiron, Wimille, Dreyfus, Etancelin, Lehoux and Sommer, for example, and doubtless Neubauer considered their potential, but there were at least two constraints upon him here. In the first place, for all their Gallic talent, those drivers were not the equal of the three top Italians, Nuvolari, Varzi and Fagioli; and in the second, Italy was a Fascist country run by Benito Mussolini, a dictator whom Germany's new leader, Adolf Hitler, admired and with which his National Socialist Party was already beginning to align itself. On top of this, of course, was the fact that the French had not forgotten World War I and it is doubtful whether public opinion would have allowed a French

A fairly slim-line Neubauer is seen here at Monza during his first year as Manager of the Mercedes GP team—1934

driver to join either Mercedes-Benz or Auto Union, for 1934, had one been asked.

So Neubauer looked to Italy, signing Luigi Fagioli, and it is really hard to see why, when both Nuvolari and Varzi were also available. Neubauer must have known that the former was unsettled, having broken with Scuderia Ferrari midway through the previous season, and that the latter, after a good beginning, had had a miserable year with Bugatti. Fagioli was brilliant, it's true, but he was also erratic and known to have a very short fuse, on top of which he would—in 1934—be 36 years old. Nuvolari, to be sure, was even older—by six years—but he had proved that he could win in almost anything he laid hands on and although he was regarded in some circles as a car-breaker, there was no doubt that he could get more out of a car than virtually anyone else. Varzi, on the other hand, was in his prime,

being just 30, and although regarded as something of a cold fish he was unquestionably a racing driver of genius, as yet untouched by the drugs that would eventually destroy his career. Why, then, did Neubauer prefer Fagioli to Nuvolari and Varzi? In his memoirs he gives no clue at all. . . .

By the end of 1933 Rudolf Caracciola seemed to be making a good recovery, but Neubauer was by no means convinced that he would ever be a great racing driver again. He had promised him a place in the team, though, and in January the following year Rudi once more signed a contract with Daimler-Benz. Less than a month later, however, he was dealt another shattering blow when his wife, Charly, was killed by an avalanche while skiing.

For some time, Rudi lost all interest in everything. While sympathizing fully with his friend's tragic situation, Neubauer still had his job to do and because it now looked even less likely that Caracciola would be back he had to find at least one more driver. He found two. Ernst Henne was well known as a motorcycle racer who had also broken a number of speed records on two wheels. Neubauer gave him a test drive at the Nürburgring and the poor man crashed heavily, although he was not seriously hurt. In spite of the accident, which was in some way due to a fault in the car (see Chapter 1 *Ernst Henne*), Neubauer offered him a contract as a reserve driver.

Then, in the middle of the season, Neubauer had to find yet another driver, and at very short notice. To his great relief Caracciola had begun his comeback, but in practice for the German GP von Brauchitsch crashed badly and Henne was unable to replace him, as he was ill. Neubauer called in a very surprised Hanns Geier, a Mercedes employee who had done a fair amount of racing but who had no expectation of driving a GP Mercedes. Geier handled himself and the car extremely well, finished a very creditable fifth in the race and so immediately became a reserve driver, with Henne.

Caracciola's return to form was astonishing and he won the 1935 European Championship with ease. Fagioli was second and von Brauchitsch third, so Neubauer's choice of drivers was fully vindicated that year. But although it had been a successful team, it hadn't been a particularly happy one, due to Fagioli's reluctance—and at times, blank refusal—to accept team discipline and the fact that whatever he might think to the contrary, Caracciola was the Number One driver.

In spite of the problems he caused, Fagioli was still extremely quick and capable of winning races, so Neubauer could not seriously think of letting him go at the end of 1935. To try and keep Caracciola happy, though, he agreed to sign his great friend, Louis Chiron, a very gifted driver who would, he hoped, afford Rudi some protection from the wilfulness of Fagioli. Not surprisingly, Chiron's signing received a very mixed reaction in France and the fact that it was announced that his contract with Mercedes had been given the personal approval of Adolf Hitler (who regarded it as a gesture of Franco-German friendship) did not make the news any better received. Chiron and his supporters, of course, took the view that he was much better off driving a good German car than a not very good Italian or French one. When he first tested the 1936 Mercedes at Monza in December 1935, Chiron was delighted with it, describing it as '*une veritable bicyclette!*', but the machine turned out to be a disaster and his career as a Mercedes driver was over almost before it had begun, following his high-speed crash at the Nürburgring in the German GP.

Before the 1936 season was over, Mercedes withdrew from racing to lick their wounds, reorganize their racing department and set about designing a new car for 1937. Alfred Neubauer set about finding some new drivers, as Chiron and Fagioli both left the team.

Over the years a constant stream of letters arrived on Neubauer's desk, all from young men ambitious to become Grand Prix drivers. Some actually had racing experience— usually on motorcycles, as car racing was very expensive— but others just *knew* that they had what it takes. All they needed was a chance to show their talent in a racing car. Neubauer sifted through many of these letters, looking for people with some experience, whom he then invited to the Nürburgring for a test session in late 1936. He also invited drivers and riders who had recently scored some successes in Germany and elsewhere.

ABOVE **Alfred Neubauer 'chats' to Luigi Fagioli, but in what language? The fiery Italian proved to be a tricky customer**

RIGHT **Watched by an anxious Neubauer, Rudolf Caracciola sets out on his first drive in a racing car since his 1933 Monaco crash—a practice run at Avus in May 1934. Mercedes withdrew from Avus and made their debut at the Eifel GP, by which time the handbrake had been moved in-board. The scoop on the scuttle fed cooling air to the clutch**

On 8 November, 30 hopefuls assembled at the Nürburgring and Neubauer sent them off three at a time in 2.3-litre Mercedes sports cars, with instructions to take things easily and not to lap in *less* than 22 minutes. The result was chaos, with one driver killed, another seriously injured and several very bent motor cars. But of the original 30 drivers, Neubauer decided that ten were promising enough to be allowed to try a Grand Prix car and from these, two emerged with real promise—Dick Seaman and Christian Kautz. Both were invited to undergo further tests at Monza, later in the year.

In his memoirs, Neubauer implies that Dick Seaman had been brought along by Kautz, on the off-chance of getting a trial, adding the astonishing claim that 'Only then did I learn something of his (Seaman's) past history.' This has to be nonsense, for not only was Seaman invited to the tests by a telegram from Daimler-Benz (and surely from Neubauer himself), but he had been winning races up and down Europe throughout 1935 and 1936 to such effect that *everybody* knew about him, and Auto Union had also invited him to test their cars.

Dick Seaman was subsequently signed by Daimler-Benz for 1937, becoming the first Englishman to join the legendary team. He was, of course, Number Four in the pecking order, behind the German trio of Caracciola, von Brauchitsch and Lang.

If, by chance, Neubauer thought his problems were over with the departure of Luigi Fagioli, he was wrong, for 1937 saw the emergence of Hermann Lang as a very real talent and this did not go down at all well with Herr Caracciola, who was very jealous of his position as Team Leader. When Lang first joined the racing team he naturally offered no threat to Caracciola who, although never the most outgoing of men, Lang found to be pleasant and friendly. 'But he expected me to be like the "helpers" in the *Tour de France* bicycle race—those people who support the star rider,' recalls Lang. 'So long as I did that he liked me and always called me "du"—very friendly and informal. Once we were staying at the Hotel Astoria in Paris and in our room we found a beautiful leather case—a gift for my wife, Lydia, from Baby Caracciola. However, when I became successful and a real competitor for him, all that sort of thing stopped and he no longer referred to me as "du". It was always the formal "Sie".'

While Lang had been the junior driver, Caracciola had not been very friendly towards von Brauchitsch, who considered himself to be something of an aristocrat but who never posed a threat to Caracciola's position in the team. Once Lang's ability started to assert itself, however, they became friends out of necessity and joined forces against Lang who, after all, was only an ex-mechanic! One who did not share this attitude was Dick Seaman. Although he was very much the upper-class Englishman, he was no snob and he and Lang—the two junior drivers—formed a friendship despite their inability to communicate, although by 1938 Seaman had acquired a smattering of German. Unlike Caracciola and von Brauchitsch, Seaman had a pretty fair grasp of the technicalities of motor racing and respected Lang's mechanic's background, instead of despising it.

As the advancing years slowly chipped away at Caracciola's skills, so Lang's increasing experience enhanced his and in 1939 Neubauer was constantly having to handle the older man's tantrums as he complained that Lang (and occasionally Seaman) was being given preferential treatment. By this time the 'youngsters' were clearly faster than their Team Leader and Neubauer had to balance his long-standing friendship with Rudi against the first requirement of his job, which was to ensure that Daimler-Benz had the best possible chance of winning races, and by 1939 that best chance lay with Lang rather than Caracciola.

Dick Seaman's inclusion in the team must have caused Neubauer some headaches, just as it did for Seaman himself. It was a very good propaganda coup to have England's finest racing driver on the strength, but Neubauer was not really able to make the best use of his talent, simply because he was not German. Seaman was a proven winner, but he had never driven anything remotely as powerful as the formidable W125 Mercedes he was given in 1937. His first crash—during testing at Monza—was, by his own admission, his fault, but his subsequent accidents at the Nürburgring and Pescara most certainly were not and his results in his first season (including a second and two fourths) were by no means bad. He took part in nine races that year and it is fair to say that by the season's end he was definitely faster than von Brauchitsch (and much easier on his car) and probably as quick as Lang.

In spite of his good progress, however, Neubauer only entered him in four of Mercedes' nine races in 1938, which was a gross misuse of his talent. The team's first race was at Pau in April and, as only two cars were ready they were driven by Caracciola and Lang. The next race was at Tripoli and although Mercedes took four cars and four drivers, Seaman went as a reserve and did not take part in the race. This seems distinctly odd, as Mercedes had raced four cars in 1936 and 1937 and Tripoli always had a field of 30, all tied in with the lottery!

The situation was equally ridiculous (but in reverse, so to speak) in the French GP, at Reims, where only nine cars started, yet the organizers insisted that no team could enter more than three! Madness! Once again, Seaman went as reserve and didn't get to drive. Finally, in the German GP, he did race and, much to everyone's surprise, he won. Not

that he wasn't good enough to win a Grand Prix—he just wasn't supposed to win this one, which was Germany's showcase. It was a lucky victory, without a doubt, but nonetheless it was a very fine drive by a man who hadn't raced a car for ten months!

In spite of his success, Mercedes made him sit out their next two races, the Coppas Ciano and Acerbo. Von Brauchitsch's pit fire and subsequent crash meant that his German GP car was too damaged to take part in the Italian races and so Mercedes only took three cars to them, leaving the other four in Stuttgart to be prepared for the Swiss GP. Although Seaman had caused a sensation throughout Europe by winning at the Nürburgring *and* in the past had won twice in the Pescara races, Neubauer could not give him a drive in either of the Italian events. There can be no doubt that the Italian fans would much rather have seen Seaman race than von Brauchitsch, but German nationalism demanded that German drivers took precedence. So, while his team mates went to Italy, Dick stayed at home and went about the more exciting business of getting engaged to Erica Popp!

Mercedes fielded four cars for the remaining three races of the season, at Bern, Monza and Donington, and Seaman drove in them all, but the 1939 season began in the same

ABOVE **Manfred von Brauchitsch and Rudolf Caracciola joined forces to keep the young lions—Hermann Lang and Dick Seaman—at bay!**

LEFT **A word in your ear. Neubauer whispers encouragement to Caracciola at Avus in 1935, while Hermann Lang tries to find out what's going on**

way as the previous one had, with not enough cars ready to enable Seaman to have a drive. In spite of only sending three cars to Pau, Neubauer asked Dick to go along as reserve and he did, but with bad grace. He was eventually allowed a few practice laps and showed just how he felt about the whole situation by setting fastest lap. There was no place for him in the race, though. He got his first drive of the year in the Eifel GP, only to have his clutch fail at the start and then all the problems of an Englishman driving for a German team were tragically resolved at Spa.

Caracciola's animosity towards Lang blew up in Neubauer's face at the Eifel meeting. There had been an unpleasant scene at Tripoli, when both drivers had wanted to race the same 1.5-litre car (see Chapter 7, *Hermann Lang*) and now, at the Nürburgring, Caracciola claimed that—among other things—Neubauer had favoured Lang during the race by ordering 300 litres (66 gall.) of fuel to be put in his car instead of only the 100 that were necessary, thus lengthening Caracciola's pit stop and, by virtue of the added weight, slowing his car for the remaining laps. Rudi seemed convinced that Neubauer was actively siding with Lang against him and refused to be placated after the Grand Prix. Instead, he demanded a meeting next day with Mercedes Director, Dr Wilhelm Kissel, at which Neubauer and Uhlenhaut were also present and, once again, he repeated his accusations. Having listened to what all three had to say Kiesel was unimpressed with Caracciola's arguments and went about his business, telling them to sort it out among themselves. Eventually, they shook hands and dispersed, but Neubauer—who had regarded himself as a close friend of Caracciola for over a decade—was sadly aware that their friendship would never be the same again.

Managing a team of four and sometimes five drivers must often have taxed even Neubauer's remarkable reserves of energy and tact. Apart from the problem of

appeasing the very considerable egos involved there was the matter of communication. In 1934 and 1935 Neubauer had to handle the volatile Fagioli, who spoke no German. In 1936 his troubles increased with the inclusion of Chiron in the team, so he had to add a little French to his minimal Italian, although as Chiron was a good friend of Caracciola—who spoke only German—it is reasonable to assume that the worldly and urbane Louis had a fair command of German, too. Certainly Baby Hoffmann, who was at that time still Chiron's 'constant companion', was fluent in several languages, and must have been a useful source of help to Neubauer in this department. That source remained even when Chiron left the team, following his big accident halfway through the 1936 season, for early in 1937 Baby Hoffmann married Rudi Caracciola and so was able to put her linguistic talents to further use for the team upon the arrival of Dick Seaman, who found her both charming and helpful. Rudolf Uhlenhaut, too, spoke fluent English, having an English mother and an early English education. Such was the force of Neubauer's personality, however, that he seems to have had little difficulty in making himself understood in any language, when necessary!

The success of the Daimler-Benz Grand Prix team in the 1930s has often been put down to money, and it's quite true that their racing budget was far in excess of anything that had gone before. But money alone does not guarantee success, and it fell to Alfred Neubauer to ensure that the right results were achieved. The Daimler-Benz *Rennabteilung* was impressive, to say the least. Where possible, the team had two sets of cars which were raced in rotation, so while one set was away at one event, the other was back at Stuttgart being prepared for the next. Each car had its own group of mechanics and its own transporter and all the drivers had their own Mercedes touring cars. In all, up to 100 mechanics accompanied the cars to the circuits, depending on how many cars were being raced. In most Grands Prix, only three men were allowed to work on a car during a race (curiously, this number was reduced to two at Avus) and Neubauer detailed two of them to change the wheels and the third to refuel the car and then start the engine. Many a race has been won or lost in the pits, and Neubauer drilled his mechanics until they were able to replace all four wheels and refuel the Mercedes in well under 40 seconds, so much so that their pit stops became legendary for their brevity and set such a yardstick for efficiency that, even today—when, seemingly, any number of mechanics are allowed to work on a car—pit stops are measured against the speed of three Mercedes mechanics 50 years ago.

Neubauer was a strict disciplinarian, but this never impaired his very good relationship with his mechanics, for whom discipline and efficiency were a part of the German way of life. The same cannot be said of Neubauer's drivers—even the German ones! Caracciola generally behaved himself, but then he was the leader of the band and he expected the team to revolve around him. Unfortunately, Luigi Fagioli expected the same and his Italian temperament was not at all receptive to German discipline, which meant that he disobeyed Neubauer on several occasions, the classic one occurring during his very first race

Happy family. At Tripoli in 1939 the team presented a united front for this photo, but relations between Caracciola and Lang were very strained. (*Left to right*) Rudolf Uhlenhaut, Alfred Neubauer, Rudolf Caracciola, Max Sailer, Max Wagner (above Sailer), Hermann Lang and Herr Dietrich of Continental Tyres

for Mercedes when, after twice having been told to let von Brauchitsch win the Eifel GP, he simply abandoned his car out on the circuit, giving Neubauer a very early taste of things to come. . . .

Von Brauchitsch, too, caused a few headaches, the most notable being the 1937 Monaco GP, which Neubauer wanted Caracciola to win. On that particular August day, however, von Brauchitsch was not in the mood to obey orders. He knew he could win the race and answered Neubauer's frantic signals to allow Caracciola to pass by sticking his tongue out at his Team Manager and roaring with laughter, to the delight of all who saw it, including Rodney Walkerley, who later wrote: 'There were some very amusing things at Monte Carlo in the Grand Prix, not least of which was dear Herr Neubauer trying to keep calm when the wicked Manfred von Brauchitsch didn't seem to be worrying about the pit signals. Neubauer keeping calm is always a splendid spectacle.'

Spectacle is the right word, for Alfred Neubauer was very much an actor and his stage was Grand Prix racing. A very large man, invariably dressed in a double-breasted suit and a homburg, he dominated the pits at every race, shouting orders at drivers and mechanics and often chasing photo-

graphers away from pit stops by brandishing his red and black flag. All this was part of his larger-than-life image, however, and nothing could detract from the fact that he was a delightful man whose *bonhomie* touched all those around him. He was a gourmet who knew all the best hotels and restaurants in Europe and who liked nothing better than to eat and drink good food and wine with a large group of friends. Mercedes' victory dinners were always memorable, but Don Alfredo—as he was known to most—didn't need a victory as a reason for a party, and after a good meal and a few cognacs he would need little persuading to get up and do some of his splendid impersonations.

George Monkhouse was one who enjoyed Neubauer's theatrical talent on several occasions during the 1937 season, as he later recalled in his book, *Grand Prix Racing*: 'His first character generally used to be Caruso, and believe me, Neubauer had a very good operatic voice. After much applause, several more cognacs and a lot of persuasion, he would impersonate *Korpsführer* Hühnlein, delivering an oration to the assembled multitude at the Nürburgring and, finally, let it be whispered now, but this only after a great deal more cognac and patting on the back by Rudi, Manfred and Dick—the *Führer* himself !'

While Neubauer was held in great esteem by all the German drivers, this didn't stop him from becoming the object of some of their practical jokes. One night, after a rather alcoholic reception given by Marshal Italo Balbo before the Tripoli Grand Prix, Neubauer got into his car, started it and found that it wouldn't move. He was in no condition to investigate this problem so he walked, unsteadily, back to the Hotel Uaddan. Returning to the car next morning he found that its rear wheels were a couple of inches off the ground, due to some bricks under the rear axle— courtesy of Hans Stuck. One night at the Eifeler Hof at the Nürburgring his bed collapsed under him—courtesy, this time, of Manfred von Brauchitsch. After the 1938 Coppa Ciano in Livorno, many of the drivers—and Neubauer—made their way to a fairground in the town, where they virtually took over the dodgem cars. There followed a no-holds-barred contest to see who could up-end Don Alfredo's racer, but the heavyweight Team Manager gleefully repelled their efforts!

All this off-duty fun and games was welcomed by Neubauer, who had a great sense of humour and could not abide pomposity. But when there was work to be done, he was not to be taken lightly, as Mercedes cadet driver, Heinz Brendel, found out in the 1939 German Grand Prix. After a sensational first lap, when he led the field by a staggering 28 seconds, Hermann Lang was forced to retire and so Neubauer decided to put him in Brendel's car. He sent a mechanic up the track to signal Brendel to come in immediately, thus avoiding keeping Lang standing idle for another lap. Brendel, however, missed the signal—either by accident or design—and continued on another round, only to have Paul Pietsch spin his Maserati right in front of him at Wehrseifen, just before the Adenau Bridge. In trying to avoid Pietsch, Brendel went into the ditch and out of the race.

His plight was duly announced over the loudspeakers, much to the displeasure of Neubauer and Lang. Brendel then capped his indiscretion by phoning through to the pits and blithely asking for a car to be sent out to pick him up. Neubauer seized the phone and told the hapless cadet in no uncertain terms that he could bloody well walk back!

For the first two years of the war Alfred Neubauer stayed with Daimler-Benz in Stuttgart, but early in 1942 he was sent to occupied Holland on a training course, prior to being put in charge of the workshops that were repairing the aircraft from the *Afrika Korps*. He never got the job because the African campaign collapsed, so he was sent to Berlin to look after the administrative side of more repair workshops, this time dealing with the Army's heavy transport. At the war's end he was imprisoned for two weeks, then released and allowed to return to Stuttgart, where he found the Daimler-Benz works at Untertürkheim had been flattened by Allied bombing.

Although motor racing got going again seemingly within weeks of the end of the war, Germany was not allowed to take part for some years. By 1950, Daimler-Benz was back on its feet again and the company decided to revive its *Rennabteilung*, the Racing Department. Miraculously, many of the company's racing cars of the past 50 years had survived the war and Mercedes were able to prepare three 1939, 3-litre machines for the Argentine races that year. Naturally, Neubauer was once again Team Manager, but not even he was able to make the 11-year-old cars win.

With a new Formula for Grand Prix racing due in 1954, Mercedes saw no point in trying to design and build new cars to the then current, 1.5-litre supercharged/4.5-litre unsupercharged Formula so, in the meantime, they decided to move into sports car racing, for which they designed the legendary 300SL. At last his team was once again equipped with modern—even futuristic—racing cars, and Neubauer was back in his element. Driven by the old firm of Caracciola and Lang, with the addition of Karl Kling, the Mercedes very nearly won their first race, the 1952 Mille Miglia. They went on to score two brilliant one-two victories at Le Mans and in the Carrera Panamericana.

In 1954 Neubauer's greatest wish came true—Mercedes were back in Grand Prix racing! Once again, the familiar figure in the suit and hat strode up and down the pits, running his team in his inimitable way. Mercedes-Benz swept all before them—almost—in 1954 and again in 1955, when they also returned to sports car racing, this time with the formidable 300SLR. But their success was blighted with tragedy, when one of the Silver Arrows scythed into the crowd at Le Mans, causing the biggest disaster in the history of motor racing. The crash could in no way be laid at the door of Daimler-Benz, but it was the beginning of the end of the company's racing programme.

Mercedes continued until the end of the season, but on the very evening of what Alfred Neubauer considered to be one of his greatest victories—the Targa Florio—he was informed by the Daimler-Benz Directors that his racing days were over. Mercedes had won the 1955 Drivers' World Championship (with Fangio), the Sports Car World Championship and the European Touring Car Championship. It was time to shut up shop.

Neubauer was now 64 years of age and although he was undoubtedly shaken by the decision, he conceded that it was probably for the best. Racing had changed considerably in the 30 years of his involvement as Team Manager and, much as he admired Juan Fangio and Stirling Moss, he considered that his drivers of the 1930s were the greatest he had known. In addition, doubtless the ever-increasing pace of life on the Grand Prix circuits of the world made him realize that his beloved job as Team Manager was better suited to a younger man, rather than one who was on the verge of retirement.

He remained with Mercedes, of course, acting as racing adviser to their magnificent new museum at Untertürkheim, until he eventually retired to his home at Aldigen, near Stuttgart. He died in 1980, aged 89, but his name lives on—a legend from a legendary era.

Record-breaking

If you take *Autobahn* 5 from Frankfurt, heading south towards Darmstadt, not long after you pass the airport you will come to the Morfelden-Langen crossing. Go under that bridge and you will very soon come to a lay-by where you will find a sign pointing to the woods. The sign says simply 'Bernd Rosemeyer Denkmal' and it points to the spot where that great racing driver was found, barely alive, shortly before midday on 28 January 1938, following a high-speed crash in his streamlined Auto Union.

Earlier that morning Rudolf Caracciola, driving a Mercedes-Benz, had handsomely broken Rosemeyer's road-records for the Flying Kilometre and Mile. In an attempt to regain those records almost at once Rosemeyer had crashed at around 430 km/h, (270 mph) when his car was struck by a fierce gust of wind. As befitted one of Germany's great sporting heroes he was given a state funeral in Berlin and, not long after, a memorial was set up at the spot beside the *autobahn* where he was found. Today, nearly 50 years later, the memorial is still there and still cared for, the encroaching foliage cut away regularly and fresh flowers appearing all the time. It is nice to know that the great man is so well remembered and that people still make the effort to visit his memorial, but the memorial is not just to Bernd Rosemeyer. It is also, unwittingly, a memorial to folly—the folly of national pride taken to lunatic extremes.

When Adolf Hitler came to power he immediately set about a comprehensive road-building programme throughout Germany. At the same time he planned a massive increase in Germany's car production and, in particular, the creation of a cheap 'people's car'. He proudly claimed that the new network of super-roads would enable Germans to move about freely in their new cars. He did not say that these same roads would also be very handy for his rapidly growing German war machine.

One of the first stretches of such road to be completed was that between Frankfurt and Darmstadt, and it was named the *Reichsautobahn*. Today it is a superb highway with four lanes in each direction, but in 1938 it was only four lanes in all. Next time you're travelling on a three- or four-lane motorway that's straight and fairly traffic-free, move into the centre and try and imagine doing 400 km/h (250 mph). Then remind yourself that Rosemeyer and Caracciola were doing that speed on a *two-lane* road not much more than 8 m (25 ft) wide, and that on those same roads they also set records for distances as great as 10 km and 10 miles at speeds of around 360 km/h (233 mph)! The mind boggles!

The quest for speed began innocently enough in January 1934, when the recently formed Auto Union firm sent its still-secret, mid-engined racing car (then called the P-Wagen) to Monza for testing. That completed satisfactorily, it was taken to the Milan-Varese *autostrada* where, driven by Hans Stuck, it was timed at over 252 km/h (157 mph). This was not a record, nor was it an attempt at one, but it showed that the new breed of Grand Prix car, built to the 750 Kg Formula, was going to be very quick indeed.

When Adolf Hitler agreed to split his Government's subsidy of 500,000 RM between Mercedes and the newcomer, Auto Union, he did so secure in the knowledge that the competition between the two companies would bring much better results than just the one firm racing on its own. The rivalry that developed between them on the racing circuits spilled over onto the *autobahnen*, where it was actively encouraged by the governing body of German motor sport, the ONS (*Oberste Nationale Sportbehörde für die Deutsche Kraftfahrt*).

It is doubtful that either firm learned anything from record-breaking that it didn't already know from racing, but this was still very much the age of records on land, sea and air and the prestige value was enormous. This didn't go unnoticed by the Nazi government, which was always on the lookout for ways of proving Aryan superiority to the world, even peacefully, if necessary. So, record-breaking was actively encouraged as a means of showing the German flag in this period of extreme nationalistic fervour.

The ONS was run by *Korpsführer* Adolf Hühnlein, who was also in charge of the NSKK (*National Sozialistisches Kraftfahrer Korps*, or Drivers' Corps), and it was he who instigated the *Rekordwoche*, or Record Week, on the Frankfurt–Darmstadt *Reichsautobahn* in October 1937. This was intended to be an annual affair, conveniently set just a couple of months before the Berlin Motor Show in order to give the two companies a chance to set new records and then brag about them in a blaze of Nazi publicity. And by the time the first (and, as it turned out, the only) *Rekordwoche* was held, Germany was already planning an attack on the ultimate prestige-booster, the World Land Speed Record, which had been firmly in the hands of the British since 1929.

In the meantime, Class Records would have to suffice. However, it was surely begging disaster to involve Mercedes and Auto Union in what was virtually a one-by-one race to see who could go the fastest on a two-lane highway in the middle of the German winter. The disaster duly occurred, although not during the *Rekordwoche* itself, but as a direct result of Mercedes' failure to break any records that October. The company sought, and won, permission to try again the following January, only days before the opening of the Berlin Motor Show. Auto Union demanded equal time and Bernd Rosemeyer was killed, thus needlessly depriving motor racing of one of its greatest drivers and Germany of one of her greatest heroes. And all in the name of pride.

But the passion for record-breaking really began with Hans Stuck and Auto Union. The high-speed run on the Italian *autostrada* in January 1934 had been no more than that—a test to see how fast the car could go in a straight

Rudolf Caracciola was undoubtedly King of the Recordbreakers in the 1930s, setting new records on no less than eight occasions between 1934 and 1939. He is seen here in a successful 1936 attempt on the Frankfurt/ Heidelburg *autobahn*

750 Kg Grand Prix Formula but in October, with racing behind them for a few months, they both went after new speed records. Auto Union returned to Avus, where Hans Stuck set five new World Records, again in Class C, beating the old records by huge margins. For the Standing Start Kilometre he averaged 163.451 km/h (101.56 mph) (old record: 144.375 km/h [89.73 mph]—Raymond Mays); for the Standing Start Mile 187.86 km/h (116.73 mph) (old record: 164.95 km/h [102.52 mph]—John Cobb). Stuck then did the 50-Kilometre Standing Start at 241.77 km/h (150.23 mph); the 50-Mile Standing Start at 243.89 km/h (151.54 mph) (old records: 219.712 km/h [136.52 mph] and 224.68 km/h [139.61 mph]—Fred Frame) and finally the 100-Kilometre Standing Start at 244.898 km/h (152.18 mph) (old record: 216.78 km/h [134.73 mph]—George Eyston).

A week later Mercedes were in Budapest with two cars to be driven by Ernst Henne, holder of many motorcycle speed records who had been brought into the Mercedes GP team for 1934. He had not had a very successful time and so had asked Neubauer if he could try for some four-wheeled records for a change. Neubauer agreed and two cars were sent, W25 models, neither of which was fitted with front brakes and one of which had a special, enclosed cockpit, in an effort to reduce wind resistance. Henne's great friend, Rudolf Caracciola—having made a marvellous recovery from his 1933 Monaco crash—went along, too.

Mercedes eschewed Avus, preferring instead the 6 m (20 ft) wide concrete road at Gyon, between Budapest and Apatfalva. Henne began with the open car, which promptly blew its supercharger, so he switched to the streamlined W25. Unfortunately, the cockpit canopy wasn't fitted properly and broke loose from its side mountings at very high speed, giving Henne a severe fright. The canopy was removed and Henne was then quite happy to let Caracciola have a go. Rudi had no problems, setting a new World Record for the Standing Mile at 188.65 km/h (117.23 mph) breaking Stuck's week-old mark. He also set new International Class C Records for the Flying Kilometre: 317.46 km/h (197.26 mph) and the Flying Mile: 316.59 km/h (196.72 mph).

Caracciola had come very close to breaking the magic 200 mph barrier, and with a car of only 4 litres. Before the year was out—on 10 December—Mercedes tried again, this time at Avus, where Caracciola once more had two cars available, one open and one closed and both fitted with brakes all round. It was not a really successful day, Rudi only managing one International Record in Class C— the 5-Kilometre Flying Start at 311.96 km/h (193.85 mph). But although he had yet to exceed 200 mph, he was still the fastest man in the world—on the road.

But not for long. In February 1935 Auto Union sent a car to Gyon for Hans Stuck to make further record attempts on the same stretch of road that Mercedes had used in October. Stuck made two trial runs, but the weather was bad and the countryside covered in snow so the team took the train to Milan and went to inspect the Milan-Varese *autostrada*. That, too, was covered in snow, so they moved on down to Florence and there, on a 15 km (9.3

line. Two months later, however, Auto Union took their car (still called the P-Wagen) to the Avus track with the specific intention of breaking records and on 6 March Hans Stuck did just that. He set three new Class C World Records: the One Hour at 217.11 km/h (134.91 mph); the 100 Miles at 216.88 km/h (134.76 mph) and the 200 Kilometres at 217.02 km/h (134.85 mph). Not only was this considerable achievement a tremendous boost for German prestige, but it was one in the eye for Mercedes-Benz, whose new racing car hadn't even been shown to the public.

For the rest of the season both teams were preoccupied with the problems attending the first year of the new,

mile) stretch of *autostrada* between Altopascio and Lucca, they were able to go to work in chilly but fine weather. Here Stuck became the first man to exceed 320 km/h (200 mph) on a road, although he couldn't manage it in both directions, so it wasn't a record. During his attack on the Flying Kilometre record he covered the distance in 11.01 sec., a speed of 326.975 km/h (203.182 mph). He just failed to beat Caracciola's Flying Kilometre record with a speed of 316.90 km/h (196.92 mph), but he did beat his Flying Mile record at 320.27 km/h (199.01 mph).

Stuck's car (which now had a 4.9-litre engine) took Mercedes' streamlining attempts one stage further, having an enclosed cockpit, discs over the front wheels and fairings over the rear ones. Both teams raced streamlined cars almost identical to their record-breaking machines at Avus, in May.

Mercedes took no part in record attempts during 1935, devoting all their energies to racing, but in Italy two men heard of Stuck's new speeds with considerable interest. Enzo Ferrari was at that time in the process of building the first of his Bimotore Alfa Romeos. These remarkable machines were the brainchild of Luigi Bazzi, then Technical Director of the Scuderia and one of Ferrari's closest friends. Well aware that the 3-litre Alfas could never compete with the 4- and 5-litre Mercedes and Auto Unions, Bazzi suggested putting two 3-litre engines at either end of a lengthened P3 chassis. The car would be far too heavy for the Formula races, but ideal for Tunis, Tripoli and Avus. Ferrari agreed to the project and design work began in December 1934.

With a little help from *Il Duce*, Benito Mussolini, Ferrari had persuaded Tazio Nuvolari to return to the Scuderia for 1935. He had also promised the little Mantuan that he could try for some records and the news in February that Stuck had had the nerve to set some new times on Italian roads spurred them into action. The first Bimotore to be completed was tested by Attilio Marinoni on 4 April, blasting down the road to Maranello where it apparently reached over 280 km/h (175 mph). Six days later Nuvolari had his first go in it, this time on the Brescia-Bergamo *autostrada*, and just how seriously Scuderia Ferrari and Alfa Romeo were taking this project can be gauged by the presence of Ferrari himself, Vittorio Jano and Signor Carioni of Alfa Romeo and Cavalieri Perego of Pirelli.

Marinoni had a trial run to make sure everything was well and then Nuvolari took over. After dawdling along at around 280 km/h (175 mph) and finding the new car to his liking, he put his foot down and recorded a shattering 341 km/h (212 mph). Although rather nervous about the tyres at such high speeds, Tazio was otherwise delighted with the Bimotore and felt sure it was capable of its projected maximum of 362 km/h (225 mph).

Nuvolari's fears about tyre problems proved to be well-founded and, as a result, the Bimotore didn't go to Tunis. Two cars were sent to Tripoli, however, a twin 3-litre machine for Chiron and a twin 3.2-litre for Nuvolari. Both cars positively devoured tyres although they were very fast while they lasted. It was the same story at Avus, where Chiron just managed to finish second.

Enzo Ferrari had decided upon 16 June for the

ABOVE **Having set three World Records at Avus in March 1934, Auto Union returned there in October and set five more. Hans Stuck watches his car being readied for a run**

ABOVE RIGHT **The streamlined Mercedes at Gyon in October 1934. The cockpit cover came loose while Ernst Henne was driving it . . .**

RIGHT **16 June 1935, and Tazio Nuvolari sets off on a run in the Bimotore Alfa on the Florence/Lucca *autostrada*. He became the first man to exceed 200 mph (323 km/h) in both directions on the road**

Bimotore's record attempts, as on that day Mercedes-Benz and Auto Union would be fighting it out in the Eifel GP at the Nürburgring. But after the tyre débâcles in the Bimotore's two races, Ferrari—at Nuvolari's insistence—went over to Dunlop for the record attempt. The car was fitted with two 3.2-litre engines, giving around 540 bhp, and Tazio covered the Flying Kilometre at 321.41 km/h (199.76 mph) and the Flying Mile at 323.06 km/h (200.79 mph). His best one-way run was at a speed of 336.25 km/h (208.94 mph).

These successful attempts were made on the same stretch of *autostrada* that Stuck had used in February but, unlike Stuck, Nuvolari found himself bothered by side-winds, one of which struck the Alfa while it was travelling at a good 320 km/h (200 mph), sending the car into a heart-stopping

skid for some 180 m (200 yds). Nuvolari held the slide somehow, but when the same thing happened at the same spot on the return run he decided, wisely, to call it a day. No doubt news of the new records reached the Nürburgring later that same day, but one wonders whether Caracciola and young Bernd Rosemeyer (who had yet to make a record attempt) were informed of the near-catastrophe caused by the side-wind.

Nuvolari was out again the next morning, as Ferrari were still after the Standing Start Kilometre and Mile records, as well as those for the 5 km and 5 miles, all of which were in German hands. Weather conditions were not favourable, however, and after a few runs at well below maximum speed the attempt was called off.

Although the Bimotore had not achieved the speeds it had reached in the April test run, Scuderia Ferrari had still won a very satisfactory result, with two Class B (5-8 litres) Records that made the Nuvolari/Alfa Romeo combination the fastest ever on the road. Indeed, only three men—Ray Keech, Sir Henry Segrave and Sir Malcolm Campbell—had been officially timed at a higher speed, and all in huge, aero-engined machines driven on the wide-open spaces of Daytona Beach.

None of the three teams made any more record attempts that year, but in September Sir Malcolm Campbell was back in America with his huge, Rolls-Royce Schneider Trophy-engined *Blue Bird* to try and break his own Land Speed Record of 445.39 km/h (276.816 mph), which he had set at Daytona in March. After that successful run he had come to the conclusion that the beach was no longer suitable for the speeds he was now achieving and so when the Utah Chamber of Commerce invited him to run on their salt lake he readily accepted. He made his new attempt on 3 September, determined to break the 482.8 km/h (300 mph) barrier and, in spite of being troubled by fumes getting into the cockpit, he succeeded, although at first the official time keepers insisted that his mean average was only 482.5 km/h (299.9 mph). Campbell didn't believe them, but made provision to have another go the next day. Later that evening, however, the time keepers admitted their mistake—his average had been 484.5 km/h (301.13 mph). Campbell was furious with them for ruining what should have been his moment of crowning glory, but nonetheless, the record was his.

He returned to England and promptly announced his retirement from record-breaking, but with the proviso that he and *Blue Bird* would return to the fray if his record was broken by a foreigner and there was no other British car available to try and regain it!

Among the many people who took a keen interest in Sir Malcolm's exploits were an Englishman and a German—Dick Seaman and Hans Stuck. Shortly after Campbell had set his earlier record at Daytona in March 1935, Rodney Walkerley reported in *The Motor*:

'Rumour hath it that Hans Stuck contemplates having a stab at the World's Land Speed Record—with some form of Auto Union, one supposes.'

Six months later, *Speed* announced:

'According to reliable information, Auto Union will make a determined attempt to capture Sir Malcolm Campbell's world speed record.

'For this purpose a special car will be built with two of the existing 16-cylinder supercharged engines set tandem-wise, the driver sitting in the centre. The exact size of these engines is still a secret, but they are believed to be between 5000 cc and 6000 cc. The new car will definitely not be completed before 1936.'

Walkerley was almost on target, but *Speed*'s item was nonsense. Stuck was indeed thinking of going for the Land Speed Record, but Auto Union most certainly was not, having none of the resources needed for such an undertaking. The company did, however, have Professor Porsche, who was an old friend of Stuck's and also an old friend of Daimler-Benz. . . .

Meanwhile, in England, Dick Seaman had heard that the Daytona Town Council, somewhat piqued that Campbell had forsaken their beach for the salt flats at Bonneville, was now offering no less than £20,000 to anyone who could beat Campbell's record at Daytona! Such a large sum of money was of great interest to Seaman and he immediately started thinking seriously of a record attempt. Since he was also thinking seriously of trying to buy an Auto Union for his 1936 racing season, what more natural than he should approach Professor Porsche about designing a Land Speed Record car?

In January 1936, Tony Birch—Seaman's Team Manager—went to Germany to see Porsche. Birch had spent some time there as an MG Agent and spoke the language fluently, so he was ideally suited to the task. It was Seaman's intention to use two Napier Dagger aero engines in a chassis of Porsche's design for his LSR car, which he hoped would do 565 km/h (350 mph). Initially, he had apparently suggested that Porsche design both a chassis and an engine, but Birch wired to say that he had talked with the Professor who had indicated that the cost of doing both would be prohibitive for a private individual, so he proposed to begin by making a one-tenth scale model of a car to take the two Dagger engines, lying flat.

The project got no further than that, for Seaman was shortly informed by Napier that their engines would have to be considerably redesigned if they were to be run on their sides and that this could not be attempted for some time, due to important Government work. The whole thing was an intriguing idea, but one has to ask just how far it would have got had the engines been available. An Englishman already held the Land Speed Record and the very idea of Germany's top designer producing a car for yet another Englishman to have a go at it would surely not have gone down very well with the Third Reich! It is extremely doubtful whether Professor Porsche would have been allowed to design such a car for Dick Seaman, especially as Hans Stuck's own plans were now slowly getting under way, and Stuck had a certain amount of access to Adolf Hitler, no less.

If Auto Union weren't interested in the LSR, they were interested in other records and in March 1936, Hans Stuck spent two days on the Frankfurt-Heidelberg *autobahn* where he set no fewer than five new World Records and three in the International Class B. The car was the latest 16-cylinder model, now enlarged to 6005 cc and producing

520 bhp. It had an open cockpit, but with a curved wind-screen and streamlining discs on both sides of all four wheels.

On this occasion Auto Union were after some really long-distance records up to 100 miles, so they chose a stretch of the *autobahn* where Stuck could run for 70 miles (113 km) in one direction, turn round and run back for 30 miles (48 km)! All the attempts were made with flying starts and by the evening of 24 March had established the following new World Records:

10 Miles: 3 min. 22.25 sec.—286.451 km/h (177.99 mph)
50 Km: 11 min. 17 sec.—265.879 km/h (165.21 mph)
50 Miles: 17 min. 55.4 sec.—269.371 km/h (167.38 mph)
100 Km: 22 min. 49 sec.—262.966 km/h (163.40 mph)
100 Miles: 36 min. 8.20 sec.—267.209 km/h (166.04 mph)
Class B records:
5 Km: 57.61 sec.—312.419 km/h (194.13 mph)
5 Miles: 1 min. 39.53 sec.—291.035 km/h (180.84 mph)
10 Km: 2 min. 4.73 sec.—288.612 km/h (179.33 mph)

Considering Stuck had to slow right down and do a virtual hairpin turn, the 100 Mile and 100 Kilometre records are remarkable.

In August the normally accurate Rodney Walkerley got it wrong for once, writing: 'Mercedes alleged to have built a car with an engine in front and an engine behind. If true (I think it is) does this mean an attack on the 300 mph record?' The 'engines-in-front-and-behind' story had already appeared in *Speed* almost a year earlier, but attributing the car to Auto Union! Now, in September 1936, *Speed* had another go.

'According to a reliable source (!) Auto Union is to construct a car for an attack on Sir Malcolm Campbell's land speed record of 301.13 mph. Hans Stuck will be the driver. He states that the new car will not be a four ton monster on the lines of *Blue Bird*. Stuck added "The limiting factor in this record is tyres, and it is madness to expect rubber to carry four or five tons in excess of 300 mph. The car will not weigh more than a ton, and with such a low weight tyres should have a comparatively easy task."'

In truth, Stuck was by now working hard to get his LSR project off the ground. He had approached Professor Porsche and Auto Union, but where the good Professor was highly excited by the idea and offered to design the car for nothing, Auto Union were not interested. The company was finding it terribly expensive keeping up with (and, in 1936, ahead of) Mercedes-Benz on the race tracks and to

Rudolf Caracciola tells a radio commentator how he did it after one of his successful runs on the Frankfurt/ Darmstadt *Reichsautobahn* in October 1936

build a special, ultra-fast machine for the LSR was out of the question.

Undismayed, Stuck continued to talk about the car with Porsche who, contrary to some of the stories being bandied about, wanted to use only one engine, not two (or even three, as Ray Keech had done). Campbell's *Blue Bird* used one Rolls-Royce 24-litre aero engine giving 2500 bhp, a figure then unheard of in German flying circles. But Daimler-Benz was developing a high-power aero engine of its own, for the German Government, which meant that ordinarily Hans Stuck would have no chance of getting hold of one. But the man in charge of aircraft procurement for the Reich was Ernst Udet and, like Professor Porsche, Udet was an old friend of Stuck's.

Like Porsche, Udet took to Stuck's project immediately, fully aware of the immense prestige awaiting Germany's successful attack on the Land Speed Record. He promised Stuck two engines and with this promise—and Porsche's—Stuck went to see Mercedes-Benz.

That summer of 1936 was not, perhaps, the best time to approach the company, as in Grand Prix racing it was taking a terrible beating from Auto Union. Nonetheless, Stuck went straight to the head man, Wilhelm Kissel, who quickly came to the conclusion that if Mercedes refused to build the car, Stuck could no doubt get Udet's permission to take their engines elsewhere for a chassis. If the attempt failed, it would still reflect badly on Daimler-Benz. Better by far to build the car to Porsche's design and retain control of the project. In October 1936, the Daimler-Benz Board of Directors gave its approval.

In that same month the company went record-breaking again, in an attempt to make up for its appalling racing season and to boost morale. This time Rudi Caracciola was given a brand new machine comprising a 1936 chassis and the V-12 5.6-litre DAB engine that had proved too heavy for racing in the 750 Kg Formula. All this was enclosed under a fully streamlined body that was very advanced for its time and Mercedes had hopes of a maximum speed of around 385 km/h (240 mph) for the car.

On 26 October the team went to the Frankfurt-Darmstadt *Reichsautobahn* and set three new Class B Flying Start records: 1 Km at 364.4 km/h (226.4 mph); 1 Mile at 366.9 km/h (227.99 mph) and the 5 Km at 340.5 km/h (211.58 mph). Bad weather prevented any further attempts until 11 November, when Caracciola set one World Record and two more in Class B. The World Record was the 10 Mile Flying Start at 333.48 km/h (207.24 mph), and for the 5 Miles he recorded 336.84 km/h (209.28 mph) and for the 10 Km 331.89 km/h (206.24 mph). It was a satisfying conclusion to a poor year for Mercedes-Benz, but they were not going to set any more records for 15 months—Auto Union and Bernd Rosemeyer would see to that!

Over the winter of 1936–37 Professor Porsche continued to work with Daimler-Benz on the outlines of the Land Speed Record car, now designated the T80 by the Porsche design team. In March 1937 he presented detailed plans to the Mercedes Board of Directors—a mid-engined, six-wheeled vehicle, the back four wheels to be driven by the new DB 600 series engine of 33.9 litres. With Campbell's record standing at 481 km/h (301 mph), Porsche was aim-

ing for a huge leap to 550 km/h (340 mph) and for this, he told Daimler-Benz, he would need at least 2200 bhp and preferably 2500.

The Mercedes-Porsche project was now very much an open secret, with snippets of news—still almost entirely guesswork—appearing in the press quite regularly. Just a couple of weeks after Professor Porsche's meeting with the DB board, the April edition of *Speed* carried the following:

'Dr Porsche, the designer of those wonderful 16-cylinder rear-engined racing cars, is also working on a design with which to attack the world's land speed record. The car is expected to be ready at the end of this season and will, according to him, be taken to America for the actual records. The type of car is naturally being kept a secret but it is certain that, in the words of Dr Porsche, it will not be a "lorry" like Sir Malcolm Campbell's *Blue Bird*.'

On 30 May, both Mercedes and Auto Union appeared with fully streamlined cars at the Avus where the North Turn of the circuit had been given a spectacular new banking which considerably increased the lap speeds. Mercedes had learned a lot from their 1936 streamlined record-breaker and their entry included three cars with all-enclosed bodywork for the race. Auto Union appeared with two streamliners and on the long, 10-kilometre straights both makes were running close to 385 km/h (240 mph)! Avus was a non-Formula race, so the two teams were able to experiment with their super-fast models, clearly with an eye to future record attempts.

A notable absentee at Avus was Hans Stuck. He had taken an Auto Union to South America for the Rio GP on 6 June and the day after the race (he finished second) he set two new World Records, raising his own Standing Start Kilometre record of 163.4 km/h (101.56 mph) to 170.95 km/h (106.25 mph) and Caracciola's Standing Start Mile record of 188.62 km/h (117.23 mph) to 201.07 km/h (124.97 mph). This was to be Stuck's last fling at record-breaking, for a new hero was about to enter the arena.

Bernd Rosemeyer was in love with speed. Almost from the moment he joined Auto Union he had been badgering the company to let him try for some World Records. Just two weeks after the streamlined Auto Unions' debut at Avus (where he had briefly enjoyed a *very* high-speed dice with Caracciola), Bernd won the Eifel GP at the Nürburgring (on his lucky 13th). It was while standing on the victory rostrum with Bernd and *Korpsführer* Hühnlein that Team Manager Karl Feuereissen suddenly had a brainwave. The Englishman, Major Goldie Gardner, had been given permission to attempt some records with his new MG on the *Reichsautobahn* during the coming week. Everything necessary for record-breaking was in hand, so why not take advantage of this and let Rosemeyer have a go?

Feuereissen immediately put his idea to Hühnlein and Rosemeyer, both of whom agreed to it at once. The only problem was one of time, for Bernd and Ernst von Delius were due to leave—with two cars and all their equipment—for America and the Vanderbilt Cup in a matter of days. Nonetheless, Feuereissen further decided that it would make good publicity even better if Bernd could set new records with the engine from his Eifel-winning car so, under the supervision of *Obergruppenführer* Krauss, Manager of

the NSKK Technical Department, the engine was removed, sealed and taken to the Auto Union works at Zwickau, where it was installed in one of the Avus streamlined cars.

On the morning of 16 June, Bernd made his first attempt at record-breaking, beginning with the Flying Start Kilometre and Mile. Only the southbound side of the *autobahn* was closed off, traffic heading to Darmstadt from Frankfurt being diverted on to the northbound lanes. This caused a few heart-stopping moments for the Auto Union team when, on his warm-up run, Bernd misjudged his speed and went sailing past the barrier (which was snatched away *just* in time) and found himself in amongst the traffic headed for Darmstadt! He thought this highly amusing, but it could have had very serious consequences.

Having established the amount of road he had to play with he then set off on a series of four runs and by 8.30 am had set two new Class B Records—the Flying Kilometre at 389.2 km/h (241.84 mph) and the Flying Mile at 389.6 km/h (242.09 mph). The roadblocks were then altered to allow runs of up to ten miles (16 km) and Rosemeyer immediately established one new World Record and three Class Records. The World Record was for the 10 Miles, which he covered at an average speed of 360.3 km/h (223.89 mph). At the same time he set Class Records for 10 Km—357.2 km/h (221.96 mph) and 5 Miles —368.49 km/h (228.98 mph).

Hans Stuck about to take over his Auto Union from a mechanic prior to a record run in Rio on 6 June 1937. The road looks *awfully* narrow . . .

After the runs Rosemeyer was clearly overwhelmed by the experience and also a little shaken, although he didn't admit it at the time. Twice on the return journey the Auto Union had been flung off line as it went under bridges at almost maximum speed, putting two wheels on the grass centre strip on each occasion.

After the runs it was learned that the timing mechanism at the 5-kilometre mark had failed so, in spite of his unpleasant experience, Bernd took the car out again and set a new record for that distance at 376.3 km/h (233.83 mph). In one morning he had set one World Record and six Class Records—not bad for a first attempt!

In September the ONS announced that an official Record Week would be held on the *Reichsautobahn* between Frankfurt and Darmstadt, beginning on 25 October. The 'official' status meant that both Mercedes and Auto Union would have to appear and, clearly, both would be determined to be the first to break the magic 400 km/h (250 mph) barrier. The worldwide prestige for the winner would be enormous.

ABOVE **Bernd Rosemeyer sets off on a run during the _Rekordwoche_ in October 1937. As the car has no wheel covers, this was presumably a Standing Start attempt**

RIGHT **With all wheels covered, Rosemeyer drives away for a Flying Start run**

Auto Union took three cars to the _Reichsautobahn_—two streamliners and an open, short-chassis mountainclimb car for the Standing Start Kilometre and Mile. The streamliners looked identical, but were fitted with different engines—an old 4.3-litre unit for Class C records and a new 6.3-litre for Class B.

Mercedes stuck to their V-12 5.6-litre DAB engine, but installed it in a 1937 GP chassis and covered it with a new body, based on that of the 1936 record car, but narrower and lower. They also prepared a normal W125 GP car for attempts on Standing Start records.

On the Monday Rosemeyer began with the big-engined car and before long had achieved his ambition, becoming the first man to exceed 400 km/h (250 mph) on the road. His average time over the Flying Kilometre was 8.86 seconds, a speed of 406.3 km/h (252.48 mph) and over the Flying Mile 14.2 seconds—406.28 km/h (252.46 mph).

From then on Rosemeyer and Auto Union could do no wrong. Over the three days of 25, 26 and 27 October they established two World Records and 13 International Class Records. On the Tuesday he had another very unpleasant experience when he nearly lost consciousness towards the end of a flying 5 Kilometre run in the 6-litre car. He managed to bring it to a halt, but had to be lifted from the cockpit and Dr Peter Gläser found that his pulse was racing. That evening Bernd told his wife about it over the phone, saying it must have been due to fumes gathering in the cockpit, but he was not concerned as he had still averaged 404.58 km/h (251.39 mph).

Having set 10 Kilometre and 10 Mile records with the 6-litre car in June he now went after the same distance

records with the smaller-engined Auto Union, averaging 341.6 km/h (212.27 mph) for the former distance and 340.9 km/h (211.83 mph) for the latter.

Obviously, enormous powers of concentration were required for these record attempts and the 10 Mile run must have been a mind-bending experience. Rosemeyer was driving on a two-lane concrete highway no more than 7.6 m (25 ft) wide which took him under a good number of bridges—all at around 360 km/h (225 mph) in the larger Auto Union! It must have been the motoring equivalent of crossing the Niagara Falls on a tightrope. He described it thus:

'The most intense concentration is required to hold the car in the middle of the road. The sideblasts of air felt when going through bridges demand instant reactions and after a few minutes the driver's nervous energy is exhausted. The strain of a Ten Mile attempt is, therefore, greater than that of a Grand Prix, even though it only lasts about two minutes and forty seconds.'

If the _Rekordwoche_ was one success after another for Bernd Rosemeyer and Auto Union, it was a total disaster for Rudi Caracciola and Mercedes-Benz. After his first

did not have the extended front wheel covers, as it did not have to turn corners (it was turned round at the end of each run by means of a small-wheeled trolley which fitted under the back of the car, lifting the rear wheels off the ground) but it did have a larger ground-clearance and a nose that turned up, allowing a great deal of air to get under the car. As Lang approached 400 km/h (250 mph), he, too, felt the front lift off the ground and only seconds after he had backed off and felt all four wheels on the road once more he had the added excitement of a huge explosion as the engine cover blew off! The air pressure in the engine bay had been so great that the cover's anchor bolts were ripped out too. Lang was not the only one to be given a severe fright by this as, standing on a bridge over the *autobahn* watching the run was Mercedes Director, Max Sailer, and the flying engine cover went right over his head!

Back at the starting point a very shaken Lang was able to confirm Caracciola's story to Neubauer, who ordered the car to be taken back to Stuttgart, where the front bodywork was completely revamped. Mercedes returned to the fray on the Thursday, the car now having its nose much closer to the ground. It had also been fitted with a full-length, flat undertray. Although this cured the lifting problem, Caracciola could only do 399.8 km/h (248.5 mph) — still some way off Rosemeyer's new record. So the streamliner was abandoned and Rudi made some attempts at Standing Start runs with the W125 GP car, but when these, too, were unsuccessful, Mercedes packed up and went home. They had been soundly beaten by Auto Union, who would doubtless make a meal of their new records at the Berlin Motor Show in February. Mercedes had to do something dramatic — and quickly — in order to regain their lost prestige.

Just three weeks later Mercedes — and Professor Porsche — received another jolt when Captain George Eyston broke Sir Malcolm Campbell's Land Speed Record at Bonneville. Eyston's car was a seven-ton monster called *Thunderbolt*. Powered by two Rolls-Royce aero engines giving nearly 5000 bhp, it ran on eight wheels — two pairs (both steering) at the front and twin rears on the driven axle at the back. With this extraordinary device Eyston covered the Flying Kilometre in an average of 7.17 sec., a speed of 502.32 km/h (312.2 mph) and the Flying Mile in 11.56 sec. — 501.07 km/h (311.42 mph). In spite of this spur to their own LSR ambitions, Mercedes had to slow down work on the T80 as they were now building and preparing their Grand Prix cars for the new 1938–40 3-litre Formula, and Professor Porsche was considerably occupied with the *Führer's* pet motoring project, the Volkswagen. Also, they had to do something about all those Auto Union records.

Mercedes had a very useful ally in Jakob Werlin. An old friend of Hitler's, Werlin had been the District Manager for Mercedes in Munich, but was now quite high in the Nazi Party, so when Mercedes decided to ask permission to make some new record attempts in January 1938, Werlin spoke to the right people and permission was granted. Auto Union learned of this shortly after the *Rekordwoche* and, naturally, asked to be allowed to defend their records. This, too, was granted and the date was set for 27 January.

high-speed run Rudi stopped to report a frightening and potentially disastrous problem — at around 395 km/h (245 mph) the nose on the new Mercedes streamliner began to lift as the air pressure built up under the front of the car. It lifted so much that Caracciola found that he had practically no steering and could hardly see where he was going! In spite of this he had still averaged 379 km/h (235 mph) one way, but he told Neubauer that he wasn't prepared to try and go any faster and to make the point he went back to Frankfurt!

Also on hand to watch the record attempts were Manfred von Brauchitsch and Hermann Lang, so Neubauer asked von Brauchitsch for a second opinion of the car. Manfred declined to drive it, very possibly because Caracciola had told him not to bother! So Neubauer now turned to his Number Three, saying, '*Los Lang, fahren Sie!*' This was not so much a request as an order, so Lang got in the car and set off.

He was none too happy about this run, having had a virtually identical experience to Caracciola's at Avus, five months previously. (See Chapter 7 – Hermann Lang). Although very similar to the Avus cars, the record machine

For this attempt Mercedes considerably revised their record machine. After more wind tunnel tests the body was lengthened and lowered and the radiator was placed in a tank where it was cooled with water and ice, instead of by cold air. The inlets at the front of the car were only to deliver air to the carburettors of the DAB engine. All this was of considerable benefit to the car's streamlining.

Professor Porsche's contract with Auto Union expired at the end of 1937, so responsibility for the development of the company's racing and record cars fell to Professor Eberan-Eberhorst. For the new record attempt he revised the car's bodywork dramatically, raising the sides to the top of the wheel arches and adding fairings in front of, between and behind the wheels. These fairings almost touched the ground and channelled the air right under the car without allowing it to spill out between the wheels, thus creating a vacuum effect which sucked it down onto the road, giving a tremendous increase in roadholding. Professor Eberan was way ahead of his time here—it would be 40 years before Grand Prix racing—and Colin Chapman in particular—obtained the same effect with 'skirts'.

After wind tunnel experiments with the new body, Rosemeyer tested the car on the Halle-Leipzig *autobahn*. In spite of bad weather the new Auto Union was clearly faster than its predecessor and everyone was satisfied that it would successfully defend the company's records.

Rosemeyer flew from Berlin on 26 January, very nearly got lost in foul weather and had to make an emergency

landing at a military airfield. The next day there was a lot of rain and while the Auto Union personnel were waiting for it to clear Rosemeyer called from Frankfurt airport, asking to be picked up. The weather did not improve, so after checking the turning points on the *autobahn*, the team went back to Frankfurt.

They reassembled at 8 am the following morning, to find the Mercedes-Benz team already there and ready to go. The weather was cold but dry and shortly before 9 am Caracciola set off. It was immediately apparent to him that this 'new' car was a completely different beast to the previous one. 'The gears worked wonderfully easily and the car hugged the road beautifully. It handled altogether differently from the car they had given me in October.'

At the end of the first, outward, run, the car was turned round and the radiator box refilled with ice and water. As Caracciola waited, his time came through: he had covered the Flying Kilometre in 8.40 sec., a speed of 428.5 km/h (266.26 mph) and the Flying Mile in 13.42 sec.—431.7 km/h (268.25 mph). He was well on the way to a new record.

On the return run he drove even harder, noticing that a slight wind was pushing the car to the right as he hurtled in the direction of Frankfurt. 'Again the road constricted to a narrow, white band with overpasses that seemed like small, black holes and at the speed I was going I had to

Rudolf Caracciola gets a push-start in the 1938 Mercedes, with which he beat Rosemeyer's October 1937 speeds

steer accurately to pass through them. But even before the brain quite grasped what was to be done the car had already streaked on. I couldn't understand why my brain should be slower than the speed of my car. Again and again I had that strange impression that I had to aim in order to get through, and there was still the struggle against the resisting air currents. Then the starting line once more—the flag.'

This time he had been even faster, covering the Kilometre in 8.24 sec.—436.69 km/h (271.35 mph) and the Mile in 13.38 sec.—433.0 km/h (269.06 mph). His average speed for the two runs was 432.69 km/h (268.87 mph) for the Kilometre and 432.42 km/h (268.7 mph) for the Mile. He had beaten Rosemeyer's record handsomely and, for the moment, he would leave it at that, although he was convinced that with a higher axle ratio he could go even faster. His wife embraced him warmly and together they drove back to the Park Hotel in Frankfurt for breakfast with Manfred von Brauchitsch. The meal was interrupted by a phone call from Neubauer—Auto Union had arrived with their new car and Rosemeyer was going to try and break Rudi's new records almost before the Mercedes' dust had settled. Neubauer urged Caracciola to return to the *auto-bahn* at once, but Rudi suddenly felt very apprehensive about the whole affair.

'Who ever heard of records being run like races? It was murder.... And besides, it was too late in the day now; the air wasn't calm enough any more. Even during the morning I had felt the breeze coming through the trees. At that speed the tyres barely touched the ground and you could feel the faintest whiff of air.'

Rudi stayed in the hotel, but after breakfast he and von Brauchitsch decided they ought to go and watch the Auto Union attempt. They arrived back at the starting point shortly before 11 am, to find Rosemeyer in the car, surrounded by people. Rudi pushed his way through and shook hands with Bernd, who grinned happily and congratulated him on his new record. Suddenly Caracciola wanted desperately to warn his rival about the windy conditions that now prevailed and to suggest that he should wait until the calm of the early hours of the following morning, but someone else then spoke to Rosemeyer and Caracciola walked away. How could he tell another brave, experienced driver not to go after his own, newly minted record?

Auto Union's Team Manager shared Caracciola's concern about the conditions. In fact Hanns Geier (present as Neubauer's assistant) recalls that he decided to call off the attempt until the next morning. 'But Rosemeyer was determined to beat Caracciola's new record there and then and said, 'No, I'll try now. I know where the wind comes through the gap in the woods and I can handle it.' (He had already made a thorough inspection of the road in his own car.) Dr Feuereissen still refused to allow the run to go ahead, but Rosemeyer was quite determined to have his own way and he could be very persuasive! Finally, Dr Feuereissen gave in and Rosemeyer got into the car and set off.'

A few minutes later he was back, complaining that the engine hadn't reached the right temperature, due to the cold air. In spite of this he had achieved a speed of 429.9 km/h (267.1 mph) on the return run! While the radiator was being closed off a bit more Wilhelm Sebastian—Feuereissen's assistant—got into his car and drove towards the turnaround point, knowing that Rosemeyer would overtake him before he got there. The Auto Union never appeared.

When he reached the end of the run he was met by an NSKK man who told him that Rosemeyer had crashed just past the 9-kilometre post. Sebastian knew at once that at that point the car would be well into the measured mile and doing around 430 km/h (270 mph).... He turned round and raced back. Just past the Langen-Morfelden bridge he found the scattered wreckage of the Auto Union's bodywork and, close by the bridge itself, the chassis.

Back at the starting point, Dr Feuereissen had been on the phone, listening to the officials reporting Rosemeyer's progress along the road. As soon as he heard of the crash he leapt into his car which chose that, of all moments, not to start! Alfred Neubauer, who was standing nearby, immediately offered him his and Feuereissen, Dr Peter Gläser and Ludwig Sebastian (Rosemeyer's mechanic) were driven to the scene of the crash by Hanns Geier, who recalls:

'Of course, we ignored the wreckage and went looking for Rosemeyer. We found him lying among some trees, apparently unharmed—he looked as though he was asleep. Dr Gläser examined him very carefully and found that his heart was still beating, but a few minutes later it stopped. We stayed with him until some members of the NSKK came and took him away.'

Rosemeyer's body was taken to Frankfurt and thence to Berlin, where he was buried a few days later with full military honours. Then the recriminations began. A photograph published widely in the German press appeared to show dents in the side of the Auto Union's bodywork. It was claimed that the picture was taken moments after Rosemeyer set off on his fatal journey and that therefore the dents must have been inflicted by the enormous wind pressure during his earlier trial run. Once he had reached maximum speed again, the damaged bodywork caused the car to go out of control, crashing Rosemeyer to his death.

In their efforts to create a scandal the newspapers carefully refrained from pointing out that at least one of the several hundred people at the starting point would have noticed these 'dents' after the trial run and if, indeed, they had occurred on that run why did they not cause Rosemeyer to crash then or, at the very least, give him a severe fright?

Professor Eberan-Eberhorst was so angered by these accusations that he had another car built to the exact specification of the crashed vehicle and then photographed by the Press at a similar angle to the original, sensational photo, and under the same cloudy conditions. The new photographs showed similar 'dents' in what everyone knew was the perfectly flat side of the new car. The 'dents' were, in fact, reflections in the aluminium!

Alfred Neubauer claimed that Professor Porsche himself (who had not been present at the fateful record attempt) had shown him the original photograph in Stuttgart only

days after the crash and had been convinced by it, as was Neubauer. It seems odd that two such brilliant men should accept the idea of dented bodywork at face value and not even think of the reflective properties of polished aluminium. . . .

The true reason for the crash was, of course, never properly resolved. In his autobiography, published after the war, Alfred Neubauer launched a new theory. Right after the crash, Wilhelm Sebastian had obtained detailed weather reports from the nearby aerodrome which showed that a sudden gust of wind had blown across the *Reichsautobahn*, through the clearing at the Morfelden crossing, just as Rosemeyer reached the spot. Neubauer's theory was that this gust of wind —travelling at between 110–130 km/h (70–80 mph) had struck the Auto Union when it was just about at maximum speed, say 430 km/h (270 mph), and that the combined forces had simply shattered the thin aluminium bodywork, destroying the car almost before it subsequently left the road.

Professor Eberan-Eberhorst rejected the latter part of this claim absolutely. It was his belief that the Auto Union was indeed hit by a very strong gust of wind which moved it across the road to the left. Examination of the road showed that the car's two left wheels had been on the central grass strip before Rosemeyer's instantaneous correction had brought them back onto the track. The correc-

tion, however, had clearly been too much, for tyre marks on the concrete showed where the car had skidded as Rosemeyer lost control and the Auto Union had launched itself into the wooded banking beside the *autobahn*.

Bearing in mind Caracciola's reaction to the 'breeze' he had felt during his early morning run, it is easy to understand that no driver in the world would have a chance against a really strong side-wind such as clearly hit Rosemeyer when he was doing around 430 km/h (270 mph). Whether or not the destruction of the Auto Union's bodywork was a cause of the crash, as Neubauer suggested, or an effect of it, as Professor Eberan-Eberhorst claimed, is merely academic. A remarkable and much-loved man was dead and no accusations or explanations would bring him back.

As a result of this national tragedy the *Reichsautobahn* was declared unsafe for record-breaking and any thoughts of a 1938 *Rekordwoche* the following October were abandoned. However, *Korpsführer* Hühnlein, well aware of the ongoing Porsche/Mercedes LSR project, declared that the car—when ready—must be run in Germany. There was no question of it going to Bonneville.

A new location was sought and found just 80 km (50 miles) south-west of Berlin, near the town of Dessau. Here the Berlin-Munich *autobahn* ran dead straight for nearly 10 km (6 miles), with a gentle curve at either end. The

central grass strip was filled in with concrete for a distance
of some 14.5 km (9 miles) and three black guide lines were
painted on the concrete. The total width of this road was
now some 27 m (88 ft) and the official measurements for
the Flying Mile, the Flying Kilometre and the Flying Five
Miles and Five Kilometres were marked out. It was still
clearly far from ideal for a Land Speed Record attempt,
but it was the best site that could be found in Germany.

Although the T80 was still supposed to be top secret,
it continued to make news in the motoring press. In March
1938, *Speed* reported, 'There seems little doubt that Germany has designs on the world's land speed record, and
that before the end of the year a car, under the Auto Union
or Mercedes banner, will enter the lists. At present the German ambition is to capture the record with a German car
driven by a German on a German highway and using tyres
and fuel produced in the country. As a result of Bernd
Rosemeyer's death, however, this ambition may have to be
modified, for there now seems a doubt that the *autobahnen* are not (sic) wide enough for such a venture. The
new record-breaker will be constructed on similar lines, as
regards streamlining, to the Auto Union and Mercedes, but
will have double the horsepower and scale between
25–30 cwt.'

The same issue of *Speed* noted details of two new contenders for the LSR, John Cobb's twin-engined, 2700 bhp,
four-wheel-drive machine, with which Cobb was aiming
for 560 km/h (350 mph), and Captain Eyston's latest version of his *Thunderbolt*, which was said to be being
redesigned as an eight-wheeler. In fact the car had eight
wheels to start with, the four at the rear being 'twinned'.

In April, Alfred Neubauer was reported as saying that
neither Mercedes nor (so far as he knew) Auto Union were
contemplating any attack on the LSR. He did admit, however, that Dr Porsche ('a freelance, not directly connected
with either firm') had a design for a record car on the drawing board, of which more might be heard later!

Just one month later, *Speed* reported, 'The much-talked-
about German car to make an attempt on the world's land
speed record is under construction in the Mercedes-Benz
works. Designed by Dr Porsche, of Auto Union fame, the
car is perfectly streamlined with all wheels enclosed, and
the driver almost entirely enclosed. The car is a six-
wheeled, twin-engine vehicle weighing only 30 cwt, or
slightly less than half John Cobb's 2500 hp Railton. The
Germans plan to make the attempt on one of the new motor
roads, but if this is not found possible the attempt will be
made on the Bonneville Salt Flats.'

The two British contenders made a concerted attack on
the record in the autumn. First, on 27 August, Captain
Eyston raised his own record considerably, covering the
Flying Mile at an average speed of 555.89 km/h
(345.49 mph) and the Flying Kilometre at 555.4 km/h
(345.21 mph) in the 73-litre *Thunderbolt*. Three weeks
later, John Cobb increased these speeds to 563.5 km/h
(350.2 mph) and 563.3 km/h (350.1 mph) respectively, in
his 47.8-litre *Railton Mobil Special*. That lasted for all of
24 hours, for next day Eyston went out again and clocked
574.9 km/h (357.3 mph) for the Kilometre and 575.2 km/h
(357.5 mph) for the Mile. All this made Porsche's original
objective of 555 km/h (345 mph) look pretty silly, so he
now aimed for 600 km/h (373 mph). For this, he told
Mercedes, he would need 3000 bhp.

Early in 1939 Mercedes went record-breaking again with
no less than three cars. As they were aiming for Class D
records, all had 3-litre engines, but whereas one car was

ABOVE LEFT **After
Rosemeyer's fatal crash,
Professor Eberan-Eberhorst
had one side of another
Auto Union built up to
refute the claims that the
aluminium had buckled.
He proved that the
'buckling' was in fact, just
reflections on the metal**

RIGHT **Caracciola about to
go for a Standing Start
record at Dessau in 1939
with the new, 3-litre car.
Korpsführer Hühnlein is on
the right**

fitted with the familiar envelope-style body and was intended for the high-speed, flying start records, the other two had a new shape that retained the basic, tubular form of the Grand Prix cars and covered the wheels in streamlined fairings that were blended into the main bodywork. These were for the standing start attempts. Like the previous year's Frankfurt-Darmstadt record-breaker, all three machines were cooled by putting the radiator in an ice-tank, the GP-style cars having the tank in the tail.

Hermann Lang tested these cars on the Stuttgart-Ulm *autobahn* and Alfred Neubauer told him that he would be making the record attempts, but when Caracciola heard about it he made his feelings very clear—he was still Mercedes' Number One driver and he would be doing the driving!

The three cars were taken to Dessau on 8 February and when Caracciola made his first trial run he found the new track to be very disappointing. He took a flying start through the timed section, using the centre of the ultra-wide road, but the surface was covered in dirt, causing the wheels to spin and the car to slide about a lot. This was simply because the traffic, sweeping by on either side, had deposited a mass of dirt in the middle, which Caracciola was now using and which had not been cleaned.

Rudi moved the Mercedes over to the right-hand lanes, where he immediately found some grip, but on the 27 m (88 ft) wide road he had no impression of speed. When he returned to the start line he complained that the car appeared to be slow, and felt sure that he hadn't managed to better 300 km/h (187 mph). Neubauer, Uhlenhaut and the mechanics laughed at him—he had very nearly hit 400 km/h (250 mph)!

Reassured, and now knowing better than to use the centre strip, Rudi went after some records. On that first day Mercedes confined themselves to standing start runs and Caracciola set new records at 175.09 km/h (108.8 mph) for the Kilometre and 204.57 km/h (127.12 mph) for the Mile. The next day—in the envelope-bodied car—he covered the Flying Kilometre at 398.23 km/h (247.46 mph) and the Flying Mile at 399.56 km/h (248.29 mph) just breaking the 400 km/h (250 mph) mark on the return run over the latter distance. And all this with a 3-litre car! But Mercedes weren't quite satisfied and returned on 14 February, when Caracciola had another go at the SS Kilometre, setting a new record at 177.4 km/h (110.23 mph).

No doubt those three days at Dessau gave Mercedes some very useful information about the stretch of road that had been especially modified to cater for the T80 LSR car, but while it was perfectly adequate for 400 km/h (250 mph), they must have had their doubts about its length and width for speeds of 600 km/h (375 mph).

Certainly Professor Porsche wanted to go to Utah. The Bonneville Salt Lake was 1200 m (3600 ft) above sea level, with more space than any record car could possibly need. Porsche was confident that in such favourable conditions his T80 could easily exceed 645 km/h (400 mph), but for his most recent estimate of 600 km/h (375 mph) he had calculated that the car would need a run-in of 5.9 km (3.7 miles) before the measured kilometre and then a further 2.25 km (1.4 miles) for braking, with perhaps another

1.6 km (1 mile) for the Flying Mile. This meant a total distance of just over 9.6 km (6 miles). Dessau just about offered a straight stretch of this length, but there was a curve at each end and Porsche felt that this was not good enough.

Nonetheless, work progressed on the T80 back at Stuttgart and in answer to Porsche's request for 3000 bhp, Mercedes produced a new, larger version of their V-12 33.9-litre DB 601 aero engine. The DB 603 was a 44.5-litre unit and Mercedes confidently expected it to produce the magic 3000 bhp in due course. One of these engines was fitted into the T80's chassis late in 1939 and the ONS decided to revive the *Rekordwoche* in 1940—this time at Dessau—when Hans Stuck was expected to do his stuff and set a new Land Speed Record for the Third Reich.

This dream was pushed further out of reach in August, when John Cobb returned to Utah with his Railton Mobil Special and upped Eyston's year-old record by ten mph to 594.91 km/h (369.74 mph). Three weeks later, Great Britain declared war on Germany and the T80's career was over before it had begun.

Mercedes managed to preserve a great many of their racing and record cars throughout the war, including the T80. In 1947 Cameron C. Earl spent a month in Germany com-

piling his *Investigation Into The Development of German Grand Prix Racing Cars Between 1934 and 1939 (Including a Description of the Mercedes World's Land Speed Record Contender)*. This description was very brief, but revealed the car's principal dimensions and projected maximum speed.

The T80 was not exactly the lightweight vehicle of 'less than one ton' that Hans Stuck had predicted in 1936. It weighed nearly 2½ tons (with driver) and its smooth, all-enveloping body was 26 ft 8 in. long and 5 ft 9 in. wide. Earl remarked upon 'the unusual ratio of track to wheelbase. The track at both front and rear was 4 ft 3 in. (this is 6 in. less than the 1939 3-litre GP machine), and the wheelbase, if taken from the centre of the rear four-wheel driving bogie, was 14 ft.'

Of the engine he wrote, 'The power unit was a modified, inverted V-12 44.5-litre DB603 aircraft engine with direct fuel injection. This unit was expected to develop 2850 bhp at 3000 rpm on alcohol fuel.' He was also told that the car was expected to achieve 750 km/h (466 mph)—considerably more than Professor Porsche had aimed for—but he wasn't able to talk to the Professor himself.

That same year, 1947, John Cobb went back to Bonneville, where he became the first man to exceed 640 km/h

The extraordinary Porsche-designed Mercedes T80, in which Hans Stuck hoped to set a new Land Speed Record

(400 mph). His two-way speeds were 620.5 km/h (385.645 mph) and 648.6 km/h (403.135 mph)—an average of 634.26 km/h (394.196 mph). This was comfortably in excess of Professor Porsche's last projection for the T80. No doubt Mercedes gave some thought to the idea of giving the T80 a chance to see what it could do, now that they were no longer restricted to German soil for their attempt. But wise counsel prevailed and the car was never run. It might well have been an intriguing battle between the two giant machines, but in truth, if the German car had broken the record it would certainly have been greeted with contempt. It was too soon after the war for such a German success.

So the T80 became a museum piece and can be seen today in the splendid Mercedes Museum in Stuttgart. With its dull, somewhat battered aluminium body it cannot help but look rather shabby, but it remains one of the most fascinating might-have-beens in motoring history.

Date	Driver	Car	Class	Location	Distance	Speed km/h (mph)	
1933 LAND SPEED RECORD							
22 February	**Sir Malcolm Campbell**	**Blue Bird**		**Daytona**	**F/Km**	**437.83 (272.11)**	
1934 6 March	Hans Stuck	Auto Union	C	Avus	One Hour 100 Miles 200 Km	217.11 (134.91) 216.88 (134.76) 217.02 (134.85)	+ + +
20 October	Hans Stuck	Auto Union	C	Avus	SS Km SS Mile SS 50 Km SS 50 Miles SS 100 Km	163.45 (101.56) 187.86 (116.73) 241.77 (150.23) 243.89 (151.54) 244.89 (152.18)	+ + + + +
28 October	Rudolf Caracciola	Mercedes-Benz	C	Gyon	SS Mile F/Km F/Mile	188.65 (117.23) 317.46 (197.26) 316.59 (196.72)	+
10 December	Rudolf Caracciola	Mercedes-Benz	C	Avus	F/5 Km	311.96 (193.85)	
1935 LAND SPEED RECORD							
7 March	**Sir Malcolm Campbell**	**Blue Bird**		**Daytona**	**F/Km**	**445.49 (276.88)**	
3 September	**Sir Malcolm Campbell**	**Blue Bird**		**Utah**	**F/Km**	**484.52 (301.13)**	
15 February	Hans Stuck	Auto Union	C	Florence-Lucca	F/Mile	320.27 (199.01)	
16 June	Tazio Nuvolari	Alfa Romeo	B	Florence-Lucca	F/Km F/Mile	321.41 (199.76) 323.06 (200.79)	
1936 23/24 March	Hans Stuck	Auto Union	B	Frankfurt/Heidelberg	10 Miles 50 Km 50 Miles 100 Km 100 Miles F/5 Km F/5 Miles F/10 Km	286.45 (177.99) 265.88 (165.21) 269.37 (167.38) 262.97 (163.40) 267.21 (166.04) 312.42 (194.13) 291.04 (180.84) 288.61 (179.33)	+ + + + +
26 October	Rudolf Caracciola	Mercedes-Benz	B	Frankfurt/Heidelberg	F/Km F/Mile F/5 Km	364.40 (226.40) 366.90 (227.99) 340.50 (211.58)	
11 November	Rudolf Caracciola	Mercedes-Benz	B	Frankfurt/Heidelberg	F/10 Miles F/5 Miles F/10 Km	333.48 (207.24) 336.84 (209.28) 331.89 (206.24)	+

Class A—Over 8000 cc
Class B—5000–8000 cc
Class C—3000–5000 cc
Class D—2000–3000 cc

World Class Records marked +

Date	Driver	Car	Class	Location	Distance	Speed Km/h (mph)	

1937 LAND SPEED RECORD

Date	Driver	Car	Class	Location	Distance	Speed Km/h (mph)	
19 November	George Eyston	Thunderbolt		Utah	F/Km	502.97 (312.60)	
7 June	Hans Stuck	Auto Union	B	Rio de Janeiro	SS Km	170.95 (106.25)	+
					SS Mile	201.07 (124.79)	+
16 June	Bernd Rosemeyer	Auto Union	B	Frankfurt/ Darmstadt	F/10 Miles	360.30 (233.89)	+
					F/Km	389.20 (241.84)	
					F/Mile	389.60 (242.09)	
					F/5 Km	376.30 (233.83)	
					F/5 Miles	368.49 (228.98)	
					F/10 Km	357.20 (221.96)	
25 October	Bernd Rosemeyer	Auto Union	B	Frankfurt/ Darmstadt	F/Km	406.30 (252.48)	
					F/Mile	406.28 (252.46)	
			C		F/Km	351.90 (218.67)	
					F/Mile	353.30 (219.54)	
					F/5 Km	346.20 (215.13)	
					F/10 Km	334.51 (206.86)	
26 October	Bernd Rosemeyer	Auto Union	B	Frankfurt/ Darmstadt	SS Km	188.70 (117.25)	+
					SS Mile	217.63 (135.23)	+
					F/5 Km	404.60 (251.41)	
27 October	Bernd Rosemeyer	Auto Union	B	Frankfurt/ Darmstadt	SS Mile	224.45 (139.50)	
			C		SS Km	169.80 (105.51)	
					SS Mile	199.50 (123.96)	
					F/5 Km	346.15 (215.09)	
					F/5 Miles	345.10 (214.45)	
					F/10 Km	341.60 (212.27)	
					F/10 Miles	340.90 (211.84)	

1938 LAND SPEED RECORD

Date	Driver	Car	Class	Location	Distance	Speed Km/h (mph)
27 August	George Eyston	Thunderbolt		Utah	F/Km	555.89 (345.49)
15 September	John Cobb	Railton Mobil Special		Utah	F/Km	563.47 (350.20)
16 September	George Eyston	Thunderbolt		Utah	F/Km	575.22 (357.50)
28 January	Rudolf Caracciola	Mercedes-Benz	B	Frankfurt/ Darmstadt	F/Km	432.69 (268.87)
					F/Mile	432.42 (268.70)

Bernd Rosemeyer was killed later on this day, trying to break Caracciola's records.

1939 LAND SPEED RECORD

Date	Driver	Car	Class	Location	Distance	Speed Km/h (mph)
22 August	John Cobb	Railton Mobil Special		Utah	F/Km	594.91 (369.74)
8 February	Rudolf Caracciola	Mercedes-Benz	D	Dessau	SS Km	175.09 (108.80)
					SS Mile	204.57 (127.12)
9 February	Rudolf Caracciola	Mercedes-Benz	D	Dessau	F/Km	398.23 (247.46)
					F/Mile	399.56 (248.29)
14 February	Rudolf Caracciola	Mercedes-Benz	D	Dessau	SS Km	177.40 (110.23)

August 10, 1937.   75   The**Motor**

MONACO GRAND PRIX

The Greatest Race Ever: Furious Duel between two Mercedes drivers, won by Brauchitsch at 63.27 m.p.h., faster than previous lap-record figure. Caracciola's record lap at 66.79 m.p.h.

THE ninth Grand Prix of Monaco, forerunner of all round-the-houses races, and run last Sunday on the 1.98-mile circuit through the streets of Monte Carlo, was crowded with sensation from start to finish. The speeds were fabulously high for a course which has no straight at all and two things unusual in motor racing lifted the event straight out of the ordinary.

The record lap of the race was faster than the fastest lap in practice and, secondly, the third man home was two laps behind the leader.

Manfred von Brauchitsch drove a wonderful race and won at 63.27 m.p.h. by 1 min. 24 secs. from Caracciola with a race average faster than the record lap in any race at Monte Carlo before. Although he did not win, Caracciola motored magnificently with a car which was not always behaving as it should, but in his brilliant hands it went with astonishing vigour and set up the lap record at 66.79 m.p.h.

Auto Unions had no luck at all. Two cars were crashed, the third, driven alternatively by Stuck and Rosemeyer, lacked brakes, but just before the end Rosemeyer snatched fourth place, thus spoiling what would have been a 1, 2, 3, 4 finish for Mercedes. The duel between the leaders made motor-racing history.

RESULTS

1. Brauchitsch (Mercedes), 3 hrs. 7 mins. 23.9 secs. (63.27 m.p.h.).
2. Caracciola (Mercedes), 3 hrs. 8 mins. 48.2 secs.
3. Kautz (Mercedes), two laps behind leader.
4. Rosemeyer, driving Stuck's Auto Union, three laps behind leader.
5. Zehender (Mercedes), three laps behind leader.
6. Farina (Alfa-Romeo), three laps behind leader.
7. Sommer (Alfa-Romeo), five laps behind leader.
8. Ruesch (Alfa-Romeo), eight laps behind leader.
9. Pintacuda (Alfa-Romeo), 13 laps behind leader.

FASTEST LAPS

Caracciola: 1 min. 49.6 secs. (64.9 m.p.h.) on the 13th lap.
Brauchitsch: 1 min. 49.1 secs. on the 21st lap.
Caracciola: 1 min. 48 secs. (65.86 m.p.h.) on the 32nd lap; then 1 min. 47.9 secs. (65.93 m.p.h.) on the 64th lap; and, finally, **THE RECORD LAP** in 1 min. 46.5 secs. (66.79 m.p.h.) on the 74th lap.

RETIREMENTS

Hasse (Auto Union) crashed on first lap. **Soffietti** (Maserati), petrol feed. **Rosemeyer's** Auto Union withdrawn with steering trouble. **Brivio** (Alfa-Romeo), split radiator. **Biondetti** (Maserati), engine trouble. **Hartmann** (Maserati), engine trouble.

The start was terrific: Caracciola, Brauchitsch and Rosemeyer lead the howling pack into the Sainte Devoté corner, striving furiously to take the first place. (Telegraphed picture from Monte Carlo).

From Grand Vitesse. Monte Carlo. Sunday.

THIS afternoon I saw the most breath-taking exhibition of motor racing that it has ever been my fortune to witness in many years devoted to watching the sport. Here we have a gathering of the fastest road-racing cars the world has ever seen, racing on a most dangerous circuit and driven by men whose sheer brilliance, daring and perfect control leave a mere Englishman gasping for breath. The duel between Caracciola and Brauchitsch on Mercedes will go down to history as one of the greatest spectacles of racing under the present Grand Prix formula.

Before detailing the events of the afternoon, let me remind you that this circuit measures only 1.98 miles and runs round the harbour and through the streets of Monte Carlo, uphill and down, with corners of every type and severity following each other every few seconds. On this circuit modern Grand Prix cars achieve well over 100 m.p.h. on stretches of a few hundreds yards, and throughout the 100 laps (just under 200 miles) the cars are subjected to

MONACO G.P. . Contd.

ambulance, which is a motor boat, and taken away with injuries reported to be slight.

Behind Caracciola, Brauchitsch sat grimly at the wheel, then came Rosemeyer and Stuck, then Kautz driving like a master. Next came Zehender and the first of the Alfas, Farina. For several laps Brauchitsch was only a matter of a length behind Caracciola, and Rosemeyer was 15 secs. behind the leader and closing in. Pintacuda was early in trouble with his brakes and fell to last place. Farina nicked past Zehender at the most unlikely spot when both were flat out on the long curve past the grandstand.

Rosemeyer went round like a demon and closed up still more. Then on the 13th lap Caracciola lapped in 1 min. 49.6 secs. (64.9 m.p.h.), the

(Above) A final look-over for the Auto Unions. Observe the box of plugs—a few spares, indeed.

Clipping the corners in practice, during which a highest speed of 66.17 m.p.h. was made by Caracciola.

the terrific strains of braking and acceleration every few seconds; the drivers finish exhausted.

Thanks to their terrific speeds set up in practice, the three men in the front row were Rosemeyer (Auto Union), Brauchitsch and Caracciola (Mercedes). Each had done record times; the fastest was Caracciola's in 1 min. 47.5 secs. (66.17 m.p.h.). Lord Howe, looking marvellously fit after his recovery from his Brooklands crash, did a tour of honour, to open the circuit, in a beautiful green 4½-litre open 4-seater Lagonda and was greeted everywhere with tumultuous applause.

A Few Seconds to Zero!

Then the air was rent with the deafening din of the 15 roaring exhausts, in which the Mercedes, without their high-pitched scream these days when they are using an altered induction system, drowned even the discharges of the 16-cylinder 6-litre 560 b.h.p. Auto Unions. The Alfas, as is well-known, were outclassed and have come to be looked upon as slow racing cars. Nuvolari was not driving.

Mercedes had four cars, driven by Caracciola, Brauchitsch, Kautz and Zehender (his first race this year). Auto Union had Rosemeyer, Stuck and Hasse. The Ferrari Alfas were handled by Farina, Brivio, Pintacuda on 12-cylinder models and Sommer on an 8-cylinder. Ruesch, as an independent, had his well-worn 3.8 8-cylinder Alfa; Soffietti and Biondetti

drove Maseratis. Hungary was represented by the independent Lazlo Hartmann with a 3-litre Maserati in a short chassis.

M. Farous dropped the monagasque flag, and with an ear-splitting roar the cars were off.

For 100 yds. Rosemeyer, Caracciola and Brauchitsch raced side by side. Then Caracciola shot ahead, with Brauchitsch half a length behind, and Rosemeyer and Stuck howling in their wake.

The thunder of the cars as they screamed past baffles description, and we were all a little deaf when they disappeared up the slope towards the Casino, sending the echoes flying.

Caracciola Leads

Right from the start Caracciola was in the lead, hurling his car through the bends, sliding and snaking at every curve. Each driver was handling his car with the utmost zeal and goodwill. On the first lap Hasse was over-zealous through the tunnel, and touched the cliff wall just beyond. He spun round and round, crashed violently and was thrown out. He was lowered into the famous Monte Carlo

fastest lap ever seen in a Monte Carlo race, and already the tail-enders, Pintacuda and Hartmann, had been lapped twice! Hartmann on a slow car was driving the race of his life, quite unperturbed by the fact that his tennis shirt was rapidly coming adrift up his back.

Rosemeyer was catching Brauchitsch until he was only a length behind. He was taking the corners with a front wheel rubbing the kerb and the back wheels 2 ft. out of line across the road, sliding viciously but perfectly held.

It is difficult to convey in words the terrific spectacle of these cars racing . . . the deafening noise, the tyres smoking under acceleration, the cars shuddering and jerking under the brakes, whilst the tyres sent up a howl of protest on the corners.

On the 18th lap Rosemeyer leapt along catching Brauchitsch going into the corners, with his car dancing madly, but he lacked speed up the long hill to the Casino and seemed under-geared.

(Continued after the Photogravure Section.)

August 10, 1937.   77   The **Motor**

MONACO G.P. . Contd.

On the 19th lap his steering refused to work at the Gaswork's hairpin, Rosemeyer twirled the wheel but he ran straight ahead into the sand bags and his car was out of the race.

The Auto Union team was thus reduced to one car—Stuck's—running fifth behind a line of four Mercedes. On the 21st lap Stuck's car made horrible screeching noises and he stopped to tighten brakes, thus falling to eighth place. Brauchitsch went round in 1 min. 49.1 secs., the fastest lap so far, while Brivio split his radiator.

Brauchitsch Ignores Pit Signals

On the 30th lap the Mercedes pit waved the flag at Brauchitsch, who was pressing Caracciola hard, but Brauchitsch took not the slightest notice. The next lap, when they flagged him again, he even made rather rude gestures and continued with unabated enthusiasm. Caracciola replied with a lap in 1 min. **48** secs. (65.86 m.p.h.), while Stuck was waving his arms and shaking his fist trying to lap Pintacuda, the last man in the race. Three laps later they were still frantically waving to Brauchitsch, and still he put his tongue out, so they gave it up and signalled him no more. On the 36th lap Kautz had plugs, and on the 37th Stuck stopped for plugs, when Rosemeyer took over his car, and all the while Hartmann, driving as he had never driven before, way back at the end of the race, was having more and more of his shirt coming out in the wind. On the 44th lap Caracciola's Mercedes suddenly made the most disturbing exhaust noises whenever he cut out for a bend, and the next lap he stopped for rather a long time, changed the plugs and restarted, sounding a little better.

Brauchitsch leapt into the lead and poor old Hartmann went on revealing more and more of his shirtless torso. Rosemeyer was going like a crazy man with failing brakes and soon caught Sommer, then went ahead after Kautz.

Mercedes Four Leading Places

On the 51st lap Farina tightened brakes and Kautz passed him in the fourth place—four Mercedes leading the race. On the 52nd lap Rosemeyer stopped and Stuck took over again

Mercedes v. Auto Union—the early phases of the race were punctuated by a terrific scrap between the two master drivers, Brauchitsch and Rosemeyer. (Telegraphed picture.)

behind Farina. On the 55th Brauchitsch signalled Caracciola by on the Promenade, so that they were both on the same lap, although Brauchitsch was nearly a lap ahead of his team mate.

For the next 10 laps Caracciola steadily gained on Brauchitsch and Stuck was picking up two seconds per lap from Farina, who was looking tired. On the 64th Caracciola went round like a flash in 1 min. **47.9** secs. (65.93 m.p.h.) and the crowd shouted with delight. Already Zehender, third man, was two laps behind the leaders.

The Greatest Duel Ever

On the 68th Stuck handed the Auto Union back to Rosemeyer and, on the 69th, Brauchitsch changed wheels and refuelled. Caracciola roared down the Promenade as Brauchitsch restarted, and now they were only a few lengths apart and there began as fine a piece of motor racing as I have ever seen.

Caracciola closed up to within one second on Brauchitsch, which means that the two cars were howling round a length apart. The crowd was on tiptoe with excitement. On the 75th lap Brauchitsch was flagged again from the pit and again made rude gestures.

Then Caracciola did the record lap of the day in 1 min. **46.5** secs. (66.79 m.p.h.) and drew level with Brauchitsch as they flew along the curve past the start. Caracciola slid sideways, held

the car and then had to fall back as they swung through Sante Devoté corner, and Brauchitsch drew away again up the hill. The next lap exactly the same happened.

This was the only bit of circuit where two such fast and evenly matched cars could hope to pass. The third time Caracciola slid more wildly than ever, and falling in behind again waved his hands in despair. Two laps later he tried again. Brauchitsch drew right over into the camber and Caracciola was past, leader once more.

Two laps later he had to stop at the pits for fuel and tyres, so that Brauchitsch, smiling, led again. Caracciola lost nearly a lap at rest and could no longer hope to catch Brauchitsch. During all this, Rosemeyer was closing up on Farina. On the 86th lap they were half a length apart, and on the next time round Rosemeyer shot past on the climb up to the Casino going like a streak of lightning after Zehender, the fourth of the leading Mercedes, whom he finally displaced. For the remaining few laps Brauchitsch motored steadily over half a lap ahead of Caracciola. Whew, what a race. . . .

THE YEAR IN PICTURES

Two of the Mercedes streamliners are towed back to the garage after practice for the Avus GP. The tow car is carrying eight people too!

BELOW **Caracciola's streamliner is pushed up to the start at Avus**

ABOVE AND ABOVE RIGHT **Hermann Lang entering and leaving La Source hairpin during practice for the Belgian GP at Spa**

RIGHT **Rudolf Caracciola gets away from the start at Freiburg, watched by Bernd Rosemeyer (*left*) and Alfred Neubauer. He and Bernd were both beaten by Hans Stuck**

YLINDRES MONDIALE

atford V8

15 RECORDS INTERNATIONAUX
(CLASSE C)

RIGHT Von Brauchitsch
(Mercedes) leads
Rosemeyer (Auto Union)
through a tight right-
hander during the Swiss GP
at Bern

LEFT During their tremendous battle at Monaco, Caracciola leads von Brauchitsch down towards the Station Hairpin

RIGHT Caracciola thunders through one of the Pescara villages in the W125 during practice for the Coppa Acerbo

LEFT Caracciola rumbles over the cobbles and under a temporary bridge on his way to victory in the Czech GP

BELOW Bernd Rosemeyer receives the victor's laurels at Donington. Tragically, it was to be his last race

Gavea

LENGTH: 11.6 km (6.93 miles)
RACE: Rio de Janeiro GP (1936, 1937)

Known locally as *Trampolin Do Diablo* (The Devil's Springboard), the Gavea circuit was inaugurated in 1933 by the Brazil Automobile Club. By 1936 the race had grown in stature sufficiently to persuade Scuderia Ferrari to send Carlo Pintacuda and Attilio Marinoni over, although the latter retired on the first lap and the former just after the halfway mark, when well in the lead.

The circuit began in the centre of Gavea town and headed out to the sea front, where it turned along the very edge of a 30 m (100 ft) cliff, with only a little wall between the road and the sea below. This was the springboard. Then the road turned inland and up to the mountains where there were many tight corners, again with long drops beneath them.

For 1937 the whole circuit was resurfaced, making it much faster, Pintacuda (driving with Antonio Brivio on the Ferrari Alfas this time) taking nearly a minute off his 1936 lap record. Hans Stuck was very fond of South America and he persuaded Auto Union to send a car for him to drive, but although he was very fast, he couldn't match Pintacuda's nimbler 8-cylinder Alfa Romeo, and had to be content with second place.

BELOW **Led by Hans Stuck in the Auto Union, the field gets away at the start of the 1937 Rio GP at Gavea. It's raining and the spectators have no protection whatsoever . . .**

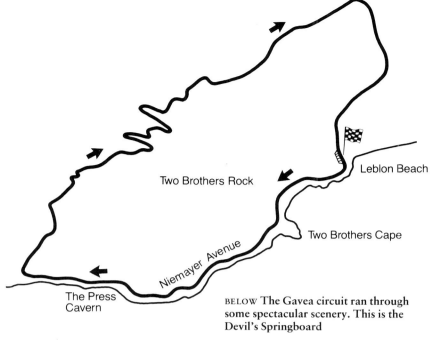

Two Brothers Rock

Leblon Beach

Two Brothers Cape

Niemayer Avenue

The Press Cavern

BELOW **The Gavea circuit ran through some spectacular scenery. This is the Devil's Springboard**

Roosevelt Raceway

LENGTH: 6.4 km (3.97 miles) (1936)
5.63 km (3.32 miles) (1937)
RACE: Vanderbilt Cup (1936, 1937)

The Vanderbilt Cup was originally presented to the American Automobile Association in 1904 by Willy K. Vanderbilt jun., who wanted America to have a race similar to the Gordon Bennett Cup. The event was held almost every year until 1916, when Dario Resta won the last one.

In 1936 it was announced that the race was to be revived on a new circuit at Mineola, Long Island, New York. This time, however, the cup was presented by George Vanderbilt, a distant relative of Willy K.

Great claims were made for the track which, in many ways, was the forerunner of modern FI circuits. It was to have run-off areas on the corners, an escape road at the end of the main straight and steel guard rails right round on each side. (In the event these turned out to be made of wood.) Also, there were to be red, yellow and green warning lights at various points on the circuit, so cars could be slowed down or stopped altogether if necessary. In common with Indianapolis, the cars were to run anti-clockwise.

Billed as 'The World's Richest Race', the Vanderbilt Cup carried prize money totalling $75,000 (£15,000) of which $20,000 went to the winner, so it was no surprise that Enzo Ferrari sent three Alfas for Nuvolari, Farina and Brivio. Although the Americans fielded some of their best cars and drivers, they were completely outclassed. But then so was everyone else, for Nuvolari won by over 11 minutes from Wimille and Brivio.

The European drivers were loud in their praise of the Americans' hospitality, but condemned the race as the worst-run they had ever attended. To their credit, the organizers set about altering the circuit considerably, reducing the number of curves (which had kept the speeds very low) and promising a really professional set-up for 1937. They were as good as their word and managed to attract not only the Ferrari Alfas, but also two cars each from Mercedes-Benz and Auto Union.

This time there was a very exciting race. Rosemeyer won, averaging almost 35 km/h (20 mph) faster than Nuvolari had, and the speed of the German cars

staggered the Americans. There was no Vanderbilt Cup in 1938 and in 1939 it was announced that the Roosevelt Raceway was to be the venue of the American Midget Racing Championship.

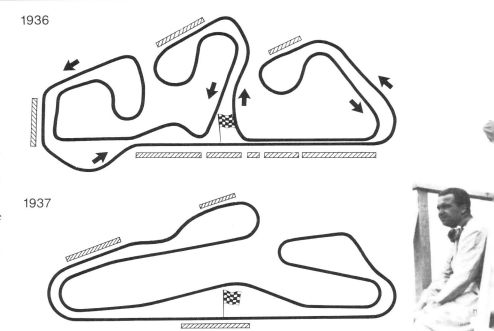

1936

1937

BELOW **Rosemeyer and Caracciola battle for the lead moments after the start of the 1937 Vanderbilt Cup at Roosevelt Raceway**

ABOVE Timing facilities appear to have been somewhat primitive at the Vanderbilt Cup. Here Neubauer clicks a stopwatch while Alice Caracciola (*right*) notes the times. Rudi sits unhappily on the steps

Prince George

LENGTH: 18.90 km (11.74 miles)
RACE: South African GP (1937)

Motor racing began in South Africa in 1934 and Whitney Straight won the first Grand Prix there, on a 24.45 km (15.4 mile) circuit at East London. For the 1936 race this Prince George circuit was shortened to 18.9 km (11.7 miles) and the GP was run in conjunction with races at Cape Town and Johannesburg. The next year an excellent number of entries from Europe was received, including two Auto Unions for Rosemeyer and von Delius. Dick Seaman, Earl Howe, Pat Fairfield, Hans Ruesch and Piero Taruffi also went and found that, in the Grand Prix at least, they were virtually handicapped out of the race. Seaman was so disgusted that afterwards he packed up and sailed for home, but the others stayed on and von Delius actually won the Cape Town GP for Auto Union.

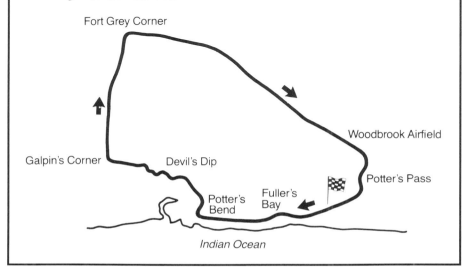

Grosvenor

LENGTH: 7.42 km (4.61 miles)
RACE: Grosvenor GP (1937)

The second in South Africa's series of three races, the Grosvenor GP, was run on a new circuit on the outskirts of Cape Town. Comprising four long straights and several hairpin bends, it had the great advantage of being visible from the grandstands almost in its entirety. This was another handicap race with Rosemeyer—on scratch—giving nine laps to an MG Midget!

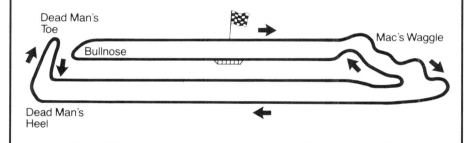

SIX

1938

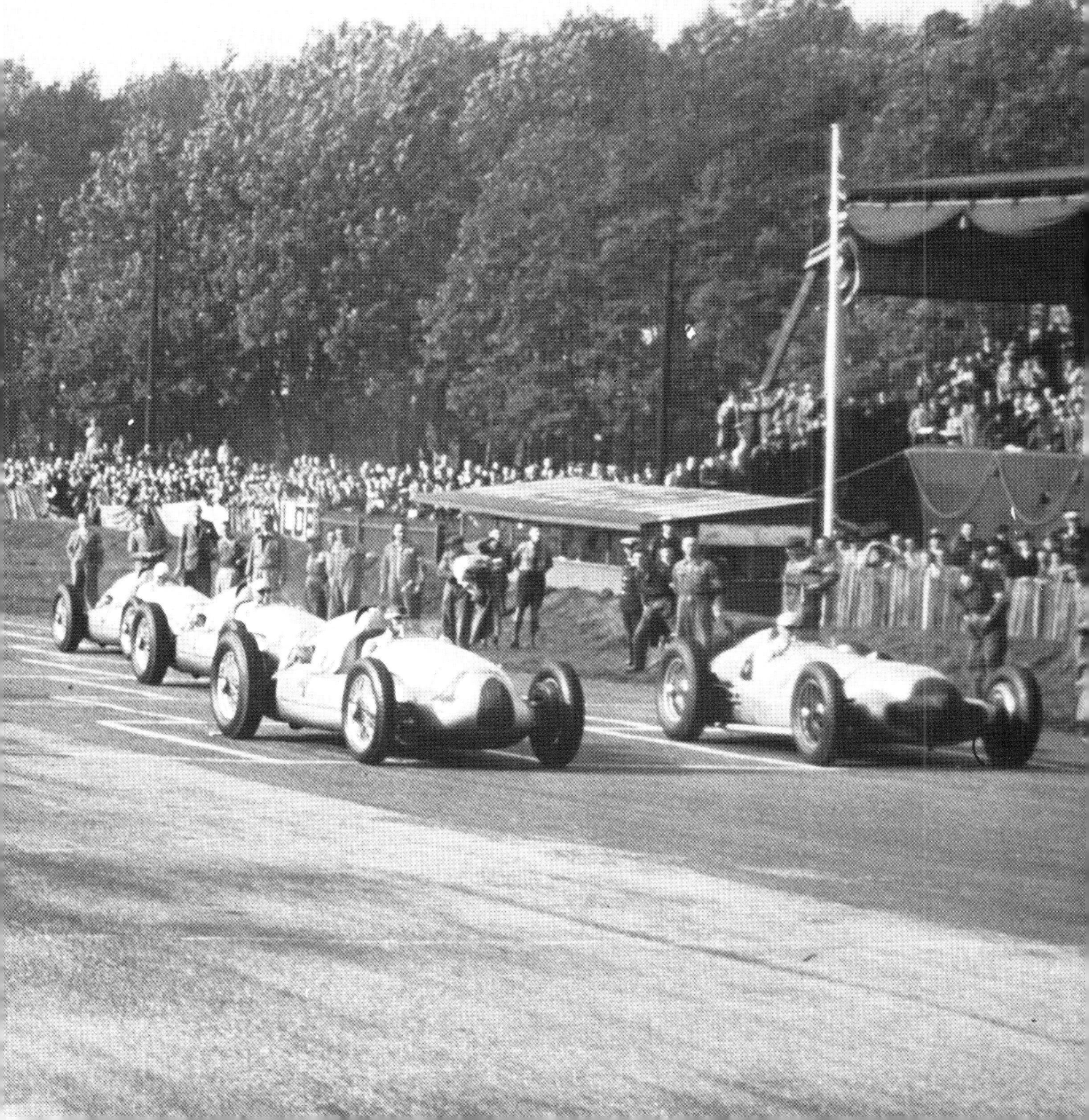

The New Formula

Auto Union were in deep trouble at the beginning of the season. Not only had they lost their star driver, the irrepressible Bernd Rosemeyer—killed in a record attempt—but not long before they had sacked Hans Stuck for breach of contract. On top of that, Professor Porsche's contract with the company had expired at the end of 1937, and he was no longer responsible for the design and development of the racing cars. Luckily, Professor Robert Eberan von Eberhorst had been with the team since its inception and he now took charge in these areas. On the driver front, however, the outlook was initially bleak, for although Rudolf Hasse and H. P. Müller were very capable, they were inexperienced and no match for the formidable Mercedes quartet of Caracciola, von Brauchitsch, Lang and Seaman. The situation changed dramatically in time for the German GP, however, as Auto Union signed the great Tazio Nuvolari and—under pressure from very high up in the Government—reinstated Hans Stuck. Good results were not immediately forthcoming, but Nuvolari eventually won the last two races of the year.

Amid much secrecy, both teams went testing at Monza in March, Auto Union going so far as to fit 16 exhaust pipes to their new 12-cylinder engine in an attempt to confuse any spies who might be around! There were stories of an unblown, 4.5-litre engine and even a front-engined Auto Union, but neither materialized. It was clear, however, that the Zwickau concern had produced a shorter car than the previous C-type, and had moved the driver further back in the chassis by reducing the size of the midships-mounted fuel tank and adding a pannier tank either side of the car. Also, the V-12 engine took up less room than the V-16 and so, by having less of the car behind the driver (and by following Mercedes' example and employing a de Dion rear

axle), Auto Union hoped to make the D-type's handling much more predictable.

Dubbed the W154, the new Mercedes also used a supercharged, 3-litre V-12 engine, which was mounted in a shorter version of the W125 chassis. By setting the engine at an angle to the chassis, the Stuttgart engineers were able to run the propshaft beside the driver, thus making the car considerably lower than its predecessor. Both teams used much higher-revving engines than of yore, the Mercedes producing its 450 bhp at 8000 rpm and the Auto Union 485 at 7000.

In January, Scuderia Ferrari became part of Alfa Corse, the new racing department set up by Alfa Romeo. Still run by Enzo Ferrari, Alfa Corse went racing with no less than three different engines—a straight-eight, a V-12 and a V-16—all 3 litres supercharged. Another Italian challenge came from Maserati in the form of a blown, straight-eight, 3-litre. None achieved any GP success.

The French at last got into the act again, both Delahaye and Talbot producing 4.5-litre, unsupercharged machines, but they were no competition for the German cars. Bugatti made a half-hearted attempt with a blown, 3-litre version of his unsuccessful single-seater of 1936. In England, ERA now had a 2-litre car, but it was still really a voiturette, with no place in Grand Prix racing.

Two *Grandes Epreuves* were lost to the 1938 Championship, the Belgian GP being swapped that year for the Spa 24-Hour race and, much to everyone's consternation, the Monaco GP was cancelled. The French, however, had come to their senses and made the French GP for GP cars once more, but the race was now held on the road circuit at Reims. Of the four *Grandes Epreuves* (the French, German, Swiss and Italian GPs), Caracciola, von Brauchitsch, Seaman and Nuvolari won one each, but Caracciola did better—just—in the other races, to win the European Championship by one point. 1) Caracciola—13 points; 2) von Brauchitsch—14 points; 3) Seaman—17 points; 4) Nuvolari and Stuck—20 points. (The last three were handicapped by being non-starters in the French GP.)

* * *

With the departure of Professor Porsche, the responsibility for the design of the new 3-litre Auto Unions fell to Pro-

PREVIOUS PAGE **In spite of political problems (the Munich Crisis) the German cars returned to Donington in October 1938, Auto Union without Rosemeyer (killed in the previous January) and Mercedes-Benz without Caracciola (who was unwell). The cars are seen here as the flag falls to start the race, on the front row** (*left-right*) **Seaman (Mercedes), von Brauchitsch (Mercedes), Nuvolari—the eventual winner—(Auto Union) and Lang (Mercedes).**

fessor Robert Eberan-Eberhorst. Shortly before his death in 1982, he remembered with affection his time at Zwickau and the genius that was Ferdinand Porsche.

Erica Popp was just 18 when she fell in love with Dick Seaman in 1938. What should have been a fairy-tale romance was blighted by political and family problems and ended in stark tragedy just a year after the young couple met. Seaman himself appeared to have everything—wealth, talent, good looks and a successful career that peaked with his marvellous victory in the 1938 German Grand Prix. But the politics of the time were against a British driver in a German team, added to which his widowed mother was bitterly opposed to his marriage to Erica.

Mountainclimbs were a very prominent feature of the European racing scene in the 1930s and both Mercedes-Benz and Auto Union put considerable effort into them from time to time. Hans Stuck was the acclaimed King of the Mountains, but Bernd Rosemeyer and Hermann Lang each took his crown once.

Donington was the scene of another marvellous Grand Prix and Tazio Nuvolari capped his first season with Auto Union by winning it in brilliant style. An awe-struck Rodney Walkerley reported it for *The Motor*.

Pescara, Bern and Tripoli were three of the most important circuits in Europe, and by now Donington was well on the way to joining them. Maps and details of all four are given.

MEMOIR

Professor Robert Eberan-Eberhorst

Development Engineer, Auto Union, 1933–39

For five years I was Assistant Professor in the Institute of Combustion Engines and Automotive Industries at Dresden University. One day in February 1933, Dr Porsche called me and invited me to join Auto Union and look after the development of the racing car he had designed and sold to the new company. It was a very interesting offer and I agreed to it immediately.

One of the Directors of Auto Union was Baron Klaus von Oertzen and he was the real initiator of the racing car. He was already in contact with Dr Porsche before the four companies in Saxonia—Horch, Wanderer, DKW and Audi—came together in 1932. He was then in charge of Wanderer and they had bought some designs from Porsche—engines of 4 and 6 cylinders with overhead camshafts which were used in their more sporty cars in rallies and so on. When Auto Union was formed it was von Oertzen who suggested that the brand new company should get publicity by producing a successful Grand Prix car, built to the new 750 Kg Formula.

We started the Racing Department from scratch, building test-beds and tooling up for all the equipment we were going to need. The parts for the racing cars were built according to Dr Porsche's design at the Horch factory toolroom.

In the beginning the Racing Department was very small. The Racing Manager was Willy Walb, a former racing driver who had driven the famous Benz *Tropfenwagen* in the mid-1920s—a car which used the mid-engine concept well before Auto Union. There was also a very good friend of mine, Otto Langsteiner (like me, from Vienna), who took over the management of the Racing Department while I took over the technical side—the Research and Development—all done under the supervision of Willy Walb and, of course, Dr Porsche.

The mechanics included Fritz Mathaey who later became Chief Mechanic for Hans Stuck. Then there were the two Sebastian brothers, Wilhelm and Ludwig. Wilhelm was a former co-driver and mechanic for Rudolf Caracciola and he later became our Chief Mechanic overall. His younger brother Ludwig was to become possibly our best mechanic and Chief Mechanic for Bernd Rosemeyer. Heinrich Kellinger was in charge of the bodyshop and Kurt Schubert headed the Engineering Department. It was a very select group and in those days the development of a racing car was done in strict secrecy—no-one was allowed into the Racing Department without a special permit.

Willy Walb was the very first person to drive the car—in the factory grounds—and he conducted the first tests on the south circuit of the Nürburgring in September 1933. In March 1934 Hans Stuck drove it on its first public appearance at Avus, setting a new 1-Hour World Record very easily at 217.11 km/h (134.9 mph), as I remember.

The P-Wagen (as it was then called) had a V-16 engine of 4.3 litres to begin with and this model, the A Type, didn't change much visually throughout its development, except for the rear axle, which was originally on transverse leaf springs, but then we changed to torsion bars fitted inside the frame.

For Stuck's record attempt the car had a very slippery, pointed tail, but for the 750 Kg Formula races this was extra weight, which we couldn't afford. Also, it had very little to offer aerodynamically, so we cut it off. Dr Porsche's design had been studied in a small wind tunnel, using a model. Later, we went into the problem deeper with an actual car at the *Deutsche Versuchsanstalt für Luftfahrt* in Berlin—at that time the best wind tunnel in Germany. The open car was very bad aerodynamically, with a drag co-efficient of about 0.64, which was useless for speed record attempts, so we tried to improve things.

The wind tunnel taught us a lot—for example that the poor drag coefficient of the GP car was caused by the open wheels and suspension. This seems terribly obvious today, but you must remember that in those days we were quite ignorant in this area. We enclosed the wheels, but the car proved undrivable, so we started taking off all the bits which hindered the steering and springing movements. In this way we increased the drag, but we knew afterwards to what extent each component was contributing to it, and we developed the closed body which Stuck used for the record attempt in 1935, with enclosed rear wheels and front suspension, but open front wheels. In a later version we enclosed the wheels totally in an aerodynamic body which, of course, added some 75 kg (143 lb) and so couldn't be used in GP racing. This was used as a record car and in the 1937 Avus race, which was not to the 750 Kg Formula, although it was nearly impossible to change wheels with the streamlined body in place.

Nevertheless, the improvement was such that when Rosemeyer took the World Record for the Standing Start Kilometre and the Mile he used the open GP car for the former because it was so light. But for the Mile, where a higher top speed was needed, he used the streamlined body—it was heavier, but much better aerodynamically.

From a drag coefficient of 0.64 on the open car we eventually got down to 0.22 on the fully streamlined record car which was used when poor Rosemeyer had his fatal crash in 1938. In the light of recent GP racing it is interesting to see that on that car I used skirts, so that we got aero-dynamic downdraft. I don't think anybody did that again until Jim Hall brought out the Chaparral, using skirts and a fan to suck the car down onto the road.

The Auto Union was very difficult to handle, especially in the early days when it had a swing axle and the mass was concentrated at the centre of the car. The mid-engined concept has great advantages, especially in respect of weight, the main one being that the driver sits in front of the fuel tank which is right in the centre of the car, so the weight distribution doesn't change during a race. (On the Auto Union it was about 50–50, perhaps 1 or 2 per cent more on the rear.) Our car had a very low polar moment of inertia, which made it very nervous and the driver did not get the same feeling as did the driver of a front-engined car, which was the traditional configuration in those days.

The Mercedes drivers were sitting virtually on the rear axle, so they immediately felt any side movement or slide, whereas our drivers—sitting in the very front, and later in the middle—got much less sensation, so it was not easy to drive. I don't recall that any circuit favoured Mercedes over Auto Union, but it did come to the public's attention that very few people were able to drive the Auto Union to its limit. Only two drivers ever really handled them properly—Rosemeyer and Nuvolari.

Nuvolari had the easier job because by the time he joined us the cars' roadholding had been improved enormously by the use of the de Dion rear axle. Interestingly, both he and Rosemeyer had started on motorcycles and Rosemeyer, of course, was fortunate enough never to drive any racing car other than an Auto Union, so he had no comparison. Luckily he was very happy with us, but I must confess that if he had driven another racing car he would have found it easier to drive!

In those days there was no theoretical investigation into car behaviour, so roadholding was more or less a question of trial and error, no-one did any serious calculations and all the theory of oversteer and understeer was unknown. There was only one common theory about fast cars: they must have very hard springs.

Mercedes were the first to use soft springs on racing cars—they must get the credit for that. We learned from them and when we changed to the de Dion axle in 1938 and went to the 3-litre, V-12 cars, we lowered the spring rate considerably, at the same time changing from friction-type shock absorbers to telescopic. Actually, during the transformation we used both—a belt and braces operation—as to begin with the hydraulic dampers were not good enough on their own.

Our cars were individually tailored—each driver having his own seat which went into whichever car he was going to use, and the steering column was adjustable. We could make certain changes to the suspension for different circuits, mainly by adjustments to the friction dampers and also by the interchanging of the torsion bars, so we could adjust spring and damper rates. The suspension geometry was not changed individually from race to race—it was set according to experience and the type of tyres we were using.

In those days we had only one type of tyre for the dry and another for the wet. We used the same make as Mercedes—Continental—who supplied us with identical tyres. There was never the competition you see today because it was in the national interest that a German team won, so there was really no urge to compete with other tyres.

Dr Porsche believed in a large, lazy engine. The V-16 weighed 248 kg, about a third of the car's dry weight. We always had trouble keeping to the 750 kg limit, especially when increasing the power. When Porsche originally delivered his design to Auto Union it was 4.3 litres giving 295 bhp. In 1935 it was enlarged to 4.9 litres, giving 375 bhp

ABOVE LEFT **With Hans Stuck's winning car after the 1934 Czech GP** (*left to right*) **Wilhelm Sebastian (in car), mechanic Frenzel, Professor Eberan, Fritz Mathaey (Stuck's mechanic) and Kurt Schubert (Foreman, Racing Dept)**

RIGHT **Professor Eberan (*right*) supervises the refuelling of Bernd Rosemeyer's streamlined Auto Union between heats at Avus in 1937. Professor Porsche and Rosemeyer are on the left. Note air hose for compressed air jacks**

and finally in 1936 it went up to 6 litres and 520 bhp. All that meant some weight increase! We needed a bigger blower, bigger carbs and so forth. To begin with we used a double carburettor, later on we used three and finally, on the 3-litre, we developed our own, together with SU in Berlin.

We never used fuel injection—all our improvements came through the carburettor, the mixture distribution in the engine itself and in the blower. The carburettor fed the blower and it was important that the feeding was along the whole height of the blower, so the correct mixture was distributed to all 16 cylinders. This was always a great problem and the only way to check it was by measuring exhaust gas emissions.

On the C-type we were using boost of about 0.7 bar, and later, on our big record-breaker, about 0.9 bar. On the 3-litre D-type it was finally as high as 1.6 bar. We had some blow-ups, but not because the boost was too high. As soon as those engines got a lean mixture in one cylinder, the piston was gone.

The engines were driven hard for over 500 km, but we developed them in such a way that they would stand up to it for three or four hours. We tested our engines on the dynamometer, running them at full speed for at least 30 seconds. On the V-16, peak power was developed at about 4800 rpm—you could take it higher, but the engine didn't like being run at above 5500. The drivers didn't use high revs very often—they didn't need to because the engine developed so much power at low revs. It had an enormously wide power band—the peak was about 4.8, but the real power started at 1000 revs! One day Rosemeyer showed us that he could do a whole lap of the 'Ring in top gear, he didn't need to change at all—even for the Karussell! That was fantastic because the Karussell was very slow and in top gear the engine would only have been pulling about 800 rpm. It was not quite the same with the 3-litre V-12, which developed its peak power at about 7000 rpm. The span an engine can cover is at best 1:5, or thereabouts, and so the lowest speed of the 3-litre was about 1500 to 1800 rpm—the whole range was further up the scale.

For our first season we signed Hans Stuck, Prince Hermann zu Leiningen and August Momberger. Of course, none had any experience of such fast and powerful cars and it was soon apparent that Stuck was the only one really capable of handling them properly, so we had to look for more competent drivers. At the end of 1934 we were approached by Tazio Nuvolari and, would you believe it, we turned him down! This was because our drivers were opposed to him being signed for 1935, and our PR man, Dr Richard Voelter, had to write and tell him so!

Several young drivers were tried out at the 'Ring and also Monza, where one of the Horch experimental drivers, Rudolf Heydel, was killed. Rudolf Hasse joined us (he won the Belgian GP in 1937) and Georg Meier. Others included Ulli Bigalke, who was tremendously talented. Unfortunately, he only drove one race for us and never had a chance to prove himself. And I must not forget H. P. Müller. He was very successful with our 3-litre car, winning the French GP in 1939 and getting several good placings. He was always in strong competition with Nuvolari.

ABOVE **H. P. Müller proved to be a very competent development driver**

RIGHT **Professor Eberan gives Rosemeyer some information after a record attempt during the *Rekordwoche* in October 1937**

Müller was also extremely helpful with our development work. At Auto Union we were handicapped in comparison with Mercedes-Benz as we had no-one like Rudolf Uhlenhaut, who was a brilliant development engineer who could also drive the cars at racing speeds. Rosemeyer was a great driver but he had not the faintest idea of technicalities, so Müller was, in a sense, our Uhlenhaut. He was a good, fast driver and full of technical understanding.

(Although I was never a racing driver I drove our cars frequently during testing. On one occasion at Monza I didn't fit the steering wheel lock properly and the wheel came off in my hands as I came out of the corner before the pits! In those days there was a rather wide strip of grass beside the track in front of the grandstand and although I was doing about 180 km/h (112 mph) I managed to brake to a stop on the grass without mishap, but it was a nasty experience.)

Hans Stuck was the senior driver on the team. He was the first we had and won some splendid victories for us

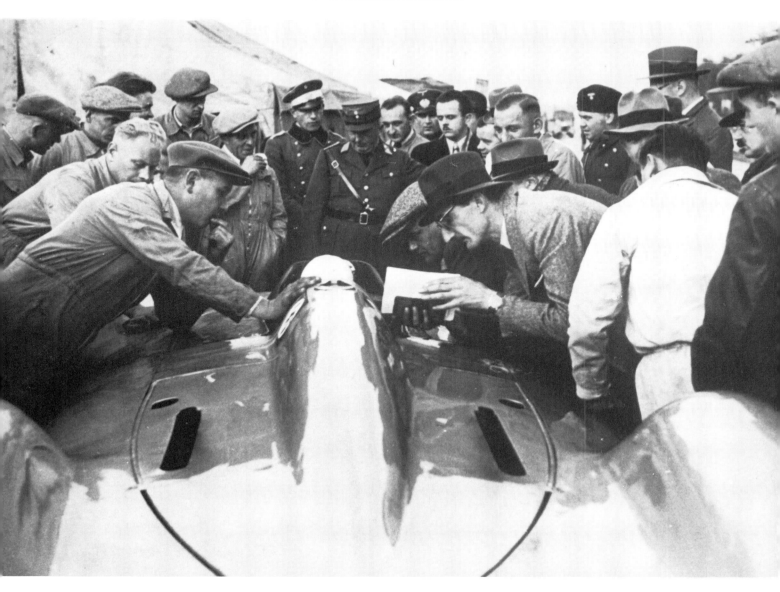

in the early days, so he was always given certain privileges. He was also the only driver to stay with us through the whole period—1934–39. He was a mountain specialist, but once Rosemeyer arrived he was faster than Stuck—even on the mountains.

Rosemeyer was an absolute maestro at the wheel and away from the track he was a young man full of enthusiasm and life and courage, so gay and optimistic—a really great personality. Caracciola was a very different character to Rosemeyer. He was, of course, a maestro too, and while I don't want to say anything unkind about him he was not a very good sportsman. He was never a good loser and he was rather cynical. He and Rosemeyer were never really friends, but I suppose friendship rarely exists between great rivals, although Rosemeyer was friendly even to his competitors—he was very sporting. I wouldn't make the same judgement about Caracciola—as a driver he was a great, great man, but as a character I wouldn't allow comparison with Rosemeyer.

After poor Rosemeyer was killed in 1938 we signed Nuvolari. He was a marvellous man—a genius—tiny, but enormously tough. Although we had no genuine understanding—he couldn't speak German, English or French and I couldn't speak Italian—I liked him very much. He was very friendly and a great comrade. He could just drive incredibly fast and he never complained about his car. (One who always had to complain was Stuck, who also was always trying to impress journalists with his performance.) Because Nuvolari never complained he was not very helpful in development—he never made any criticism and still drove very fast! What could we do? We couldn't do anything, so we just let him get on with it! We could have put him in a car that was a piece of junk and he would still have made record laps.

Achille Varzi was a great figure in racing and a great driver when he was mentally OK, which was not always the case as he became addicted to drugs, although he put up some splendid performances for us. Ernst von Delius

237

ABOVE **Professor Ferdinand Porsche talks with Max Sailer of Daimler-Benz at Bern in 1937**

TOP **Tazio Novolari is carried shoulder-high by Ludwig and Wilhelm Sebastian after his victory for Auto Union in the 1938 Italian GP at Monza**

was very fast and very daring, but he had several bad crashes in his career and was ultimately killed at the 'Ring in 1937.

I am sure that all today's top Grand Prix drivers would have been able to handle the Auto Union. Can you imagine our 3-litre car with today's tyres . . . ? I don't think there are any lessons to be learned today from Dr Porsche's designs because, in my opinion, the present GP formula is wrong—it has turned Grand Prix racing into show-business—it has nothing to do with technical development any more.

In the 1930s our cars were looked upon as the forerunner of the fast car of tomorrow. The development of aero-dynamics in racing cars showed the way for production cars, but look at the Grand Prix cars of today—they are so ugly and so inefficient aerodynamically that they need enormous power to be fast. If they had ordinary-sized tyres, similar to the ones on normal cars, it would give much more realistic results, in my opinion. I would suggest that people who are presently designing GP cars should go to a school to learn how to design useful cars, not extremely fast cars that are otherwise utterly useless. Also—and I have been arguing this for centuries—there should be a limitation on fuel consumption to force people to design and develop cars which are fast, safe and economical. Today they are doing just the opposite, but the technicians are not to blame—it's the people who make the regulations. (NOTE: Professor Eberan's wishes have now come true. Fuel consumption limits have been imposed on both Formula One and Endurance Racing.)

Ferdinand Porsche was a technical genius. He had tre-mendous experience, a prodigious memory and he always managed to produce the right ideas at the right moment. In my view he was not so much a designer as a perfect experimental engineer and developer—I always make a very clear distinction between the two. If you have a very good development man on the job you might be able to get good results from a bad design, but if you have a good designer and a bad development engineer you can ruin the best design. The development side is so important and in this respect I had the highest possible esteem for Dr Porsche, who was a genius in developing things. And he had the perfect team, with collaborators like Karl Rabe, Josef Mickl and Erwin Komenda.

So design and development were perfectly matched and the result was, in my view, outstanding because the success was in sound relation to the expenditure. Auto Union's Racing Department was always poor in comparison with that of Mercedes—we used half the money they did. Half a million RM from the Government was divided between us each year, but our annual racing budget was about five million RM, whereas Mercedes spent about ten million! That is why in a certain way I'm really proud of having been with Auto Union—it was not only a good engineering job that was done, but also it was good engineering in the economic sense. Porsche must take the credit for this—he was the presiding genius. He seemed to have a sixth sense—he could smell success and knew how to avoid mistakes.

=== MEMOIR ===

Erica Seaman

I met Dick through Aldy and Ivy Aldington and Tony Fane. They were great friends of my father, Franz-Joseph Popp, as he was co-Founder and President of BMW and Aldy and Tony were partners in Frazer-Nash-BMW in England and they used to visit Germany a lot. In June 1938 they organized a rally in Germany for members of the Frazer-Nash-BMW Car Club and the highlight was a party given by my father at a very chic restaurant in Munich, the Preysing Palais, which was right next door to the famous Buergerbraukeller, where Hitler had staged his abortive *putsch* in 1923.

When he joined Mercedes, Dick rented a chalet at Ambach, on the Starnbergersee, and when he arrived there from Munich on the evening of 15 June he found a telegram from Aldy or Tony, inviting him to the party that night. He turned right round and drove back to Munich and the Preysing Palais where he found us, all in evening dress. He was wearing a tweed suit. . . . Although somewhat embarrassed by this he joined the party and naturally ended up at the big table where the Aldingtons, the Fanes, my mother, my sister Eva and I were all sitting. (Unfortunately, my father couldn't attend his own party, being away on business.)

Dick sat next to me and we started to chat and I thought he was rather cute and very shy. I guess he thought that I was rather cute, too! There was a big orchestra with all the trimmings and Dick and I danced a lot and there's no doubt that we did make a very attractive couple, so much so that other couples seemed to stop dancing themselves and watch us, although the fact that I was in a full-length evening gown and Dick was in tweeds could have had something to do with this! I couldn't help noticing that his nose—which he had damaged at the 'Ring the year before—was a little off-colour after plastic surgery, but that was his fault as he had gone skiing shortly after the operation and the cold had affected the new skin! However, he was so handsome it didn't matter.

The next day my family was due to go with the Fanes and the Aldingtons to the home of Ernst Henne and his wife. He was the world champion motorcycle rider who held many speed records and as he rode BMWs we were all good friends. He had a charming house across the lake from Dick's chalet, so I invited Dick to come and join us at some stage and he did come over in his speedboat.

I had, of course, heard of Dick before I met him, as he was very well known in Germany by then. About two months before we met I was with my sister in her studio at the top of our house—she was a photographer and had a darkroom up there—when some mail arrived which included a brochure from Mercedes about their racing drivers, with their pictures and brief biographies. I read it and said, 'Eva, do you know what Dick Seaman's full name is? Richard John Beattie-Seaman, how about that!' I thought it was hilarious, but a little over six months later I was married to this long name.

I was not wild about racing at that time—I had only been to a few small races and hillclimbs and to one of Ernst Henne's world record attempts. But I was taken to the 1938 German Grand Prix by Hans Friederich Wessels and his wife and Dr Wilhelm (Helmi) Haspel and his wife, Bimbo. (Her real name was Gretel Ruth, but nobody ever called her that!) Bimbo was some years older than me, very attractive and quite a woman. In spite of our age difference we became great friends. Helmi was one of the top Directors at Mercedes and our two families were very close.

So we went to the Nürburgring and we stayed at the Eifeler Hof Hotel, which was not very fancy, but very nice. Then Dick won the race, which was madly exciting, and we watched from the best seats in the grandstand opposite the pits (after all, we were with one of the heads of Mercedes-Benz!), so we had a first-class view of von Brauchitsch's fire and Dick driving away from the pits to take the lead.

That night there was the victory dinner at the Eifeler Hof and I sat on Dick's right, which caused a few eyebrows to be raised as he was known to be too involved with racing to have any time for girls! I told him that I really shouldn't be there, as I had the Aldingtons and their three children as my house guests in Grainau and would be going back there in the morning. He was delighted to hear this as Grainau is not far south of the Starnbergersee and as he was not due to race again for nearly a month he decided we would have to visit each other a lot, which we did!

ABOVE LEFT **Erica Schwab (formerly Mrs Erica Seaman) at her home in Florida**

We went swimming and he taught me to water-ski and we had some wonderful times. Then, a couple of weeks before the Swiss Grand Prix in August he told me that Neubauer had asked him if he was interested in the Grossglockner mountainclimb, so he had decided to take a look at it and invited me to go along. He picked me up bright and early one morning in his Mercedes and pointed to a big hamper in the back—he'd brought a picnic lunch.

We drove happily to the beautiful Grossglockner Pass, right up to the top of the mountain where there is a big hotel, and who should we bump into but Hans Stuck and his wife, Paula. They were delighted to see Dick and they knew me through my father. Hans was always trying to persuade him to give him a BMW aeroplane engine so he could put it in a boat and try for some water speed records.

He and Paula invited us to join them for lunch in the hotel, which I thought was a lovely idea, but Dick would have none of it. I thought this was rather strange, but he took me back to the car and we drove off to find a really lovely secluded spot for our picnic. We spread out everything from the hamper and I noticed that Dick was hardly eating anything. This was *very* strange, because boy—did he like to eat! He was very nervous and I thought, 'What is the matter with you?', but he said nothing so I chattered away gaily and then suddenly he gave me a big kiss and said, 'Do you love me?'

'Yes!' I said.

'Seriously, or only for a flirt?' (I was a flirt in those days, I must admit.)

'Seriously!' I said.

'Enough to marry me?'

'Yes!!!'

I surprised myself at this, really, because I was still only 18 and had—until that moment—absolutely no intention of marrying anybody, but Dick changed all that. When he appeared all my good intentions of staying single went out of the window and there I was—madly in love and engaged to a man I'd known for only nine or ten weeks. And that was really the first time we had been truly alone, as we had always been surrounded by people before.

So, newly engaged but not telling a soul, I went to stay with the Haspels and, of course, Bimbo knew all about Dick and me anyway, so I told her. My father didn't know a thing about it, but I was the apple of his eye and I wondered how he would accept my getting engaged to a racing driver. He loved the English, so that was in Dick's favour, but my sister had just married that June and I had told my father, 'Don't worry, Daddy, *I'm* not getting married!'

He came to visit and, unbeknown to me, Bimbo told him that Dick and I were engaged. Bimbo could charm a snake, so Daddy was putty in her hands. He, of course, didn't tell me that he knew, so I crawled onto his lap and confessed. I thought he'd give me hell, but not a bit of it—he was an angel.

Dick had just left for Monza and the Italian Grand Prix, so the Haspels said, 'Right—now it's official, let's get reservations on the sleeper and go to Milan.' So Bimbo, Helmi and I took the train and Dick met us at the station still in his overalls, having come straight from the circuit

after early morning practice. We went to the Hotel Principe di Savoia and when we went to the dining room for lunch many of the other drivers were there and they all did a double-take—Seaman with a girl! What's this? Some of them had seen us together at the Nürburgring, of course, and now we could tell them of our engagement.

Mercedes didn't do well in the race and I was sitting in the grandstand, missing Dick and getting so bored. Then his car retired and he came up to join me—it was the only time, I think, that he was perfectly happy that his car didn't last. His heart was *not* in that race! That evening we had a wonderful party in a restaurant after a very disappointed Herr Neubauer had gone there for a quiet dinner alone with his wife. It turned into a riotous evening and the crowning glory was our visit to The Ambassador's nightclub afterwards, where Dick and I taught everyone the Lambeth Walk. They all thought it was great and we were 'Oi!'-ing all over the place.

Although we had now been engaged for a couple of weeks, I still had no engagement ring, but Rudi Caracciola told Dick that Zurich was the best place to buy diamonds, so on the way back from Monza we stopped there and bought one. I still have it, of course.

Needless to say, Dick and I were as happy as could be, but there were two large clouds in our otherwise clear blue sky: one was the ever-growing threat of war between Germany and England—the other was Dick's mother, Mrs Lilian Seaman.

She visited Dick for the first time right after he had won the German GP and her initial reaction to me was very nice.

ABOVE Dick with his mother, Mrs Lilian Beattie-Seaman, at his chalet at Ambach. She became violently opposed to his marriage to Erica

LEFT Newly-engaged, Erica has eyes only for Dick as he chats to Max Sailer in the Monza pits during practice for the 1938 Italian GP

Dick's great friend, George Monkhouse, was staying at the chalet with his father and they, of course, were well aware of our growing romance and were all for it, but when they told Mrs Seaman that they felt that I was the ideal wife for Dick her attitude changed completely. A few days earlier she had apparently told her travelling companion that I was the loveliest thing she had ever seen, but once she heard the Monkhouses talk of marriage she warned Dick that such a move would be fatal and would wreck his whole life!

Of course, up till then Dick had been so involved with motor racing that he had never really had time for girls, but now Mrs Seaman could see that he was clearly in love for the first time and it was a terrible shock to her, as previously she had been the only woman in his life. Although we hadn't even talked about getting engaged at that time we were obviously in love and I guess Mrs Seaman could see the writing on the wall. Happily, Dick's friends didn't resent me at all. They were very happy for him and thought I was the cat's whiskers!

I suppose the main thing that Mrs Seaman had against me was that I was German and perhaps, better than most, she could see that Hitler was leading Europe towards war.

Although, of course, Dick was aware of what was going on in Germany to some extent and disliked the Nazis intensely, he was not a political animal at all. He was a very patriotic Englishman and a fine ambassador for his country, but first and foremost he was a racing driver whose ambition was to become a top-flight Grand Prix driver. He couldn't do this in England and so the invitation to join Mercedes was a golden opportunity for him—they were the best. He was in no way compromised by driving for a German team and there were no political pressures on him from Mercedes or the German government.

Before she returned to England, Mrs Seaman gave a dinner party at the Alpen Hof Hotel in Garmisch. My family used to go there a lot because we knew the owner, Hans Killian, very well— he was great fun. After dinner we went downstairs to the Casino bar to dance. At that time there was a very popular dance called 'The Catch', in which the bandleader threw coloured ping-pong balls over the dancers and any couple who failed to catch one had to leave the floor until there was only one couple left. Of course, Dick was 6 ft 3 in. so he always caught one and we were the winners. There were quite a few cadet soldiers of 18 or 19 also in the bar and Mrs Seaman surprised us all by sweeping several of them onto the dance floor during the evening.

I didn't see her again until the end of September, when Dick and I flew to England for the Donington GP. We stayed with her at Ennismore Gardens in Kensington and a lot of Fleet Street reporters came round to take pictures of the famous English racing driver and his German bride-to-be. Mrs Seaman was *not* pleased and spent a long time trying to persuade Dick to break off our engagement. Of course, he refused.

In honour of his victory in the German GP the Royal Automobile Club gave a lunch for Dick in Pall Mall and most people seemed to be wondering if the Mercedes team—who were there—would stay in England or return home, as the political situation was getting very bad. But we did go to Donington. We stayed at the Black Boy and the mood was so depressing! Dick and I were not depressed, of course—we were about to get married, but the others on the team who were also anti-Nazi knew what was coming and they were very, very sad characters. They all advised me to stay in England with Dick, but we had already made that decision. War or no war, Dick wasn't going to let me out of his sight!

Then Chamberlain went to Munich to see Hitler and suddenly everything was great! The race was postponed for three weeks, so Dick and I returned to London and went to dinner at Luigi's to celebrate. Saved by the bell!

Things went from bad to worse with Dick and his mother, though. We had found a very nice flat just off Belgrave Square which we wanted to rent. Dick had given up his chalet at Ambach and my father was going to give us a brand new one in Grainau for a wedding present, but we needed a London home and this flat seemed just right. However, although Dick's father had left him a considerable sum when he died, he had put it in a Trust Fund to be administered by Mrs Seaman until Dick reached the age of 27. When Dick asked her to sign the lease on the flat she refused. She was still determined to stop our marriage and wasn't going to let Dick have a home of his own. There was a very big row and Mrs Seaman left London for her house in the country, telling Dick she never wanted to see me at Ennismore Gardens again! All this did not leave him in a very happy frame of mind for the Donington GP, which was held on 22 October, but he finished third.

He made one final attempt to patch things up with his mother, but it was no good—she threatened to disinherit him unless he broke off the engagement. She told him that she would rather see him lying dead in his coffin than agree to his marriage. What a thing for a mother to say! Dick was naturally furious at this and walked out—he never saw her again. He told me he was quite proud of himself because he wanted to slam the door behind him as he left, 'But I resisted the temptation and closed it quietly.' He had tried very hard to heal the rift that had come between them, but she didn't want to know. It was upsetting, naturally, but he didn't regret leaving her, it did not break his little old heart. He had a whole new life to start with me.

We had always planned a small wedding in London with no fuss. (We couldn't have had a quiet affair in Munich—we would have had to invite everybody!) So we were married at Caxton Hall on 7 December and the only witnesses were Dick's great friend from his school days, Tony Cliff, and my sister, Eva. Dick had ordered a limousine to take Eva and me to the wedding and as we settled happily in the back the driver said, 'Where to, Madam?'

I said, 'What do you mean—"Where to?" Didn't Mr Seaman tell you?'

'No, Madam.'

I couldn't believe it! 'He must have done—it's the famous place where everyone gets married.'

'It's probably Caxton Hall, then,' he said, and off we went. We were late, of course, and when we got to Caxton Hall there was a crowd of photographers so I said, 'That's it!'

Afterwards the Aldingtons gave a reception for us at the Rembrandt Hotel and Dick Shuttleworth gave us two little cocker spaniel puppies—Whisky and Soda—as a wedding present.

We had planned to spend our honeymoon skiing in Davos, but there was no snow, so we went to our new chalet in Garmisch, where we spent some very happy weeks until Christmas, when we went to Munich to stay with my parents. From there we went to Davos (where the snow had now arrived) and we met up with two of Dick's closest friends, Charlie and Marjorie Martin.

We stayed at the Passen Hotel which was owned by Hans Fopp, a very famous skier who went to America with Christian Kautz when war broke out and later became the US skiing champion. The Martins arrived the day after us in their Lancia with Dickie Shuttleworth almost hidden under all their luggage—apparently before leaving London they had called in on Dickie to say goodbye and he had decided that it was a wonderful idea to go skiing, so they

LEFT **Dick and Erica photographed by the Press in London on the announcement of their engagement**

BELOW **Seaman at Pau in April 1939. He was fastest in practice, but didn't drive in the race**

said, 'Come with us.' Dickie threw some clothes into a case, grabbed his skis and jumped into the Lancia. Of course he had no reservation and the only room available at the Passen was one which Hans Fopp admitted was so tiny that a German visitor had turned it down for his chauffeur! Dickie, however, thought it would do very nicely.

In the New Year we moved on to St Anton and St Moritz, always dragging the puppy-dogs along, and then in February we went to Berlin for the Motor Show, where all the Mercedes drivers had to appear in racing overalls to shake the hand of *Der Führer*. I remember the night before Dick saying, 'Here I am—about to shake hands with Hitler! What I should do now is phone the Home Office and say "If I kill him, will you give a million pounds to my widow?"' Knowing him I was a little worried and I was glad when the day was over!

The team's annual Spring Training took place in March, so we all went to Monza for about ten days, the testing taking place between great eating binges led by Don Alfredo and his Little Black Book, in which he kept full details of all his favourite restaurants.

Neubauer was divine—a great guy with a tremendous sense of humour. He liked Dick so much because he was easy-going and didn't snap and snarl and complain, which the others were inclined to do. They could be a little difficult—von Brauchitsch extremely so and always had been. He hated Fagioli (that was before my time)—he couldn't stand him. Caracciola was nice, rather phlegmatic, which may have had something to do with the fact that he had been badly injured in that crash at Monaco. His wife, Alice, was a dream—a fantastic person. Hermann Lang and his wife, Lydia, were very nice—he wasn't flashy or madly amusing, but a damned nice guy and von Brauchitsch and Caracciola were so nasty to him!

Then we went to Pau, where Dick was reserve driver because Mercedes had only built three cars and he was still the junior on the team. He was very angry about that and showed how he felt by making fastest time in practice! From Pau we went to Paris and stayed at the Plaza Athenae, where he recovered somewhat. He loved his food and we went regularly to La Tour d'Argent and L'Escargot. He was still smarting about Pau when we went to La Tour one night and who should be there but Neubauer! Things were a bit frosty to start with, but it all ended up quite well.

It was about this time that Dick wrote to Earl Howe again, asking whether or not he should continue to drive for a German team, in view of the political situation. He was now thinking very seriously about giving up racing, but I never tried to influence him in any way—it had to be his decision. He loved racing so much—what if he had given up at my request and then had been unhappy? He would have blamed me and that would have been terrible.

Had he given up he would have gone into the motor business in one way or another and I've no doubt that he would have been a great success—he had a fine business brain as well as great personality and charm. And we were certainly planning to have a family. Dick loved children and would have been a marvellous father. When he was in the London Clinic having his nose patched up he spent a lot of time in the Maternity Ward—he just adored looking at all those new-born babies.

Anyhow, Earl Howe advised him to stay put as long as he could, so we remained in Germany. Dick was on very good terms with everybody at Mercedes, most of whom were anti-Nazi. They loved their racing drivers and were extremely generous to them. Right after our wedding we went to Stuttgart on our way to Munich and the Directors, led by Dr Kissel, held a reception for us and gave us a lovely silver salver as a wedding present. The Mercedes Directors were not all that young, but boy—did they like parties! And you couldn't say 'no'. Dick used to be exhausted afterwards and I would drive home at around 2 am. At 8 am, they would be at their desks again!

Dick's first race that year was the Eifel GP, but he only completed one lap. We stayed on at Adenau afterwards as the Mercedes and Auto Union teams were involved in a film about racing. Mercedes fitted a special seat on the back of one of the 1937 GP cars so a cameraman could film the 1939 cars running round the 'Ring. The drivers were allowed to take their wives around on this car and it was most exciting—the highlight of my year. Everybody had a go and then Caracciola took Neubauer for a lap. Don Alfredo had been a racing driver in his youth, but it was a long time since he had been round a circuit at speed and he was pretty impressed!

Then we went to Vienna for a little hillclimb, although Dick didn't take part. Neubauer had so many friends there that we were wined and dined and pampered all the time.

At Spa we had the most fantastic luncheon at the home of the President of the Belgian Automobile Club and that was the last really lovely thing that happened to me for a long time. Dick and I were so happy—he was always saying, 'Marriage is so wonderful—why didn't I know about it earlier?' Before the race Dr Gläser told him to be careful as it was very wet and conditions were absolutely awful.

'Are you kidding?' said Dick. 'I'm a family man now— I'm more careful than ever before. I've got so much more to live for.'

After the crash I spent the night with Rudi and Alice Caracciola. Of course, I went to the funeral in London, but I was in such a daze I hardly remember anything about it. Then I stayed with my sister for a while until I decided I had to get out of Germany. My father, knowing how I felt about Germany and the Nazis, understood. You can't live in a country where you hate the regime so much that you want it to lose the war. Daddy felt the same way, but he couldn't get out. I could, although in many ways I could have had a much easier life if I had stayed, but I felt I had to get away. I went to England and stayed with Charlie and Marjorie Martin and then with Robert Fellowes and his mother. Then I spent a lovely summer on my own in Torquay, where I started to live again and—comparatively—to enjoy myself. I was known as 'The beautiful Mrs Seaman with the sad eyes'. You can only cry so much. Either you go on with life or you withdraw from it completely, and Dick wouldn't have liked that.

Eventually I went to America and made a new life for myself there, but my one year with Dick was the most beautiful of all. I was lucky to have it and I still treasure my memories.

After a late breakfast, Dick and Erica enjoy a cigarette before leaving the hotel for the 1939 Belgian Grand Prix . . .

Dick Seaman

Team Driver, Mercedes-Benz, 1937–39

On 24 July 1938 Dick Seaman won the German Grand Prix at the Nürburgring. At that time, such a victory by an Englishman was about as likely as a German scoring a century at Lord's or a Chinaman winning at Wimbledon. It was, in a word, news. At least, it was to the European press which put Seaman into the headlines next day. In England, however, this very considerable achievement went almost completely unremarked by Fleet Street. Of the 14 daily papers then published only one—*The Daily Mail*—saw fit to mention it.

Dick Seaman was unquestionably Britain's greatest racing driver of the 1930s, yet British newspapers, which rightly lavished space and praise on such foreign sporting heroes as Don Bradman, Joe Louis and Helen Wills Moody, ignored Seaman's career almost entirely. Until, that is, he was killed. Then his death made banner headlines in national and provincial papers up and down the country.

* * *

William John Beattie-Seaman was a wealthy widower of 50 when he married Mrs Lilian Pearce, a wealthy widow of 29, on 1 June 1911. On 4 February 1913 their son was born and later christened Richard John, Richard being the name of his father's best friend, who had died at the age of 27.

When he was 13 Dick went to Rugby School, where he soon became firm friends with two other boys, Tony Cliff and Ray Lewthwaite. Cliff recalls that Dick had an obsession with cars from the age of 15, and used to draw pictures of his own Seaman Special. As soon as he was old enough to have a driving licence his parents gave him a Riley sports car and when he went up to Cambridge they gave him an MG Magna.

During his first year at university Dick took part in several reliability trials and even tackled the International Alpine Trial, but without any success. For 1933 he persuaded his parents to exchange the MG for a 2-litre Bugatti, which he occasionally raced (also without success) at Brooklands and Donington. He refused to take his studies seriously and his consuming interest in motor racing was a source of great distress to his father, who was now over 70 and suffering from a weak heart. Mr Beattie-Seaman dearly wished that his son would read for the Bar and possibly stand for Parliament later, and so it was a terrible shock to him when, in March 1934, Dick arrived home from Cambridge and announced that he was not going back. Instead, he was going motor racing with Whitney Straight, a wealthy young American whom he had met at the Cambridge University Automobile Club.

Dick bought Straight's old MG Magnette, or rather, his mother did. He was never short of cash, having a generous allowance, but this was not sufficient to enable him to buy the MG. Owing to his father's ill-health, the family finances were now being handled by Mrs Beattie-Seaman and Dick persuaded her to pay for the car. She realized that the only way to prevent Dick from going racing was to cut off his allowance, but this she was not prepared to do.

Well aware that there was money to be made on the Continent, Seaman planned his first racing season accordingly, making his European debut in the GP de L'Albigeois, where he stalled on the grid and had to be push-started, for which he was subsequently fined 100 francs. He retired not long after.

From Albi he went to Pescara for the Voiturette race that preceded the Coppa Acerbo and which was run over four laps of the 26 km (16 mile) circuit. Hugh Hamilton won in his Whitney Straight MG and Seaman was very content to finish third. He and Hamilton then moved on to Bern for the supporting race to the Swiss GP. Starting from the ninth row of the grid, Dick slowly worked his way up to the front, taking the lead on the 11th of the 14 laps and staying there until the flag. Victory! And in only his third race on the Continent!

Dick was not able to enjoy his success for long, however, for that afternoon Hugh Hamilton crashed his Maserati on the penultimate lap of the Grand Prix and was killed instantly. This in itself was bad enough, for Dick had a high regard for Hamilton, who was a very popular man, but his death had serious repercussions for Seaman back home. His father read of the crash in the newspapers the next day and, being quite unwell, got things muddled up. He was convinced that Hamilton had won the race and that *Dick* had been killed, and as a result he suffered a heart attack that night and had to be taken to a nursing home. On Dick's return, his mother told him only that his father had been taken ill, not that he had suffered a stroke, and why. Eventually, Mr Beattie-Seaman recovered sufficiently to be allowed home and went to Pull Court in Worcestershire, a large house he and his wife had purchased in the forlorn hope that Dick would give up racing and become a country gentleman.

Dick's next race was in Brno, Czechoslovakia, where he finished fifth. Then he returned to England for the last race of the season, at Donington. The Nuffield Trophy was a handicap race and Dick finished second, after a fine drive which was rather overshadowed by Raymond Mays' first win in the new ERA. Dick was impressed by the ERA and decided that perhaps this was what he ought to have for 1935.

So, in mid-October he asked his mother for £2000 with which to buy the car. By now Mrs Beattie-Seaman had promised her ailing husband that she would not help Dick buy any more racing cars and she refused his request at once. Dick, however, had an ace up his sleeve: his father had recently settled a large sum of money into a Trust Fund for him, that money to be held until Dick reached the age of 27. Now he blandly stated that if his mother refused him the money for the ERA he would borrow the £2000 against his Trust Fund. Mrs Beattie-Seaman was powerless in the face of such naked ambition and she signed the cheque. She would sign many more over the next two years.

A month later Dick went to see Peter Berthon at Bourne and came away with an agreement that he would buy the ERA at cost price and, in effect, be a part of the ERA team. It was not to be the happiest of associations. . . .

Late in January 1935 Dick wrote to his mother at Pull Court, telling her of his plans for the ERA. By chance, his father, too, read the letter and was horrified to learn that Dick had bought another racing car, and with the help of his mother. He confronted his wife with the letter, accusing her of jeopardizing their son's life by giving him the money. Mrs Beattie-Seaman gently pointed out that Dick was so determined that he would have got the money from someone, if not from her. Her husband, however, had had enough, and announced that he was going to London in the morning to tell Dick that if he went racing with the ERA he would be cut off from the family without a penny.

Mrs Beattie-Seaman went with him, but they found that Dick had gone shooting in Suffolk with Tony Cliff. A few days later Mr Beattie-Seaman had a bad fall in his room and was taken to a nursing home again. This time he did not recover and in the early hours of 3 February, he died. He was buried at Putney Vale Cemetery, in South London. Mrs Beattie-Seaman never told Dick that his father had found out about the ERA, or that he had planned to disinherit him if he did not give up racing. Just four years later she would again be standing by the same grave. . . .

The ERA was supposed to be ready for the opening meeting at Donington on 13 April but it wasn't, so the works lent Seaman one of their 1934 cars for the 25 mile (40 km) handicap event, in which he finished second. Seaman's car still wasn't ready for the next Donington meeting on 11 May nor for the Isle of Man races at the end of that month. He finally got his hands on it in the first week in June, just in time for the Grand Prix des Frontières, at Chimay. He led the race for two laps, but then a piston burnt out and he had to retire. He led again at the Nürburgring the next weekend in the 1500 cc race of the Eifelrennen, but the oil pressure failed and he could only struggle home in fourth place. Two weeks later at the Kesselberg mountainclimb a front brake locked up during a test run, bending the front axle. Exactly the same thing happened in practice for the Nuffield Trophy at Donington, and he had to withdraw from the race. At Dieppe a week later the supercharger drive sheared. . . .

Seaman had had enough. It was clear to him that the mechanics at Bourne were over-stretched, looking after both the works ERAs and those of their customers, so he decided that from now on he would have his car prepared in London by his own mechanics. He took over a double garage in Ennismore Gardens Mews and assembled a small team around him. As Team Manager he chose Tony Birch, who had been ERA's Business Manager up to that point and who had also looked after Hugh Hamilton's racing affairs until his untimely death. Dick persuaded Harry Rose to let Giulio Ramponi work on the ERA as well as Rose's Maserati and Jock Finlayson and Billy Rockell (the ex-Bentley racing mechanic) also joined in.

Ramponi immediately got to work on the ERA's front suspension. This had basically been copied from Alfa Romeo and Giulio (an old Alfa hand) knew it to be a bad copy. He got Laystall Engineering to alter it to his satisfaction and also had the supercharger modified. All this was done in time for Dick to enter the new Grossglockner mountainclimb in Austria on 4 August. He celebrated his new lease of life with a brilliant climb that was beaten only by the remarkable Italian, Mario Tadini, on his 2.9-litre Alfa Romeo.

Next came Pescara, and Seaman won the 1500 cc race prior to the Coppa Acerbo with ease. Ten days later he was in Switzerland where he won the Prix de Bern, beating all the other ERAs present, including that of Raymond Mays. From Bern he—and Mays—went to Freiburg where once again he was in brilliant form, beating Mays on this very difficult climb by over ten seconds and just failing to beat Hans Stuck, the King of the Mountains, by one!

His last race of the season was the 1500 cc event in the Masaryk GP meeting at Brno. For the first time Ramponi accompanied him abroad, and having sorted the ERA to great effect after Dieppe, he now proved to be an invaluable ally in the pits. Giulio had been to Brno before, with Alfa Romeo, and he knew that at night the trees around the very long circuit perspired, making the road very greasy in the early morning. Practice started at 6 am, so he told Seaman to be very careful, otherwise he would slide off the road. Which is just what he did, on his very first lap!

Seaman struck a curb and badly damaged a front hub,

With the remarkable, ten-year-old Delage, Seaman was virtually unbeatable in 1936. He is seen here with the car in his Kensington Mews Garage

so he sent a telegram to ERA in Bourne, asking for a spare. He was later advised that it would arrive on the Friday before the race. It didn't. Dick was furious, but Ramponi came to the rescue. On one of his previous visits with Scuderia Ferrari he had made friends with the people at Skoda, in Brno, and they allowed him to use their workshop to straighten the axle by heating it gently and bending it back. Dick won the race easily, but the new axle never arrived and he never raced the ERA again.

Although he had been very successful during the latter part of 1935, Seaman determined to find another car for 1936 and, after discussing the matter at length with Giulio Ramponi, made a decision that was to stun the motor racing world. Ramponi suggested that he buy Earl Howe's supercharged, straight-eight, 1500 cc Delage. It was an outrageous idea and Seaman was at first incredulous. Ramponi could only agree, but insisted that 'If you're prepared to

spend some money on the engine we'll beat the Maseratis and everything in the 1500 cc class!' The idea of beating the latest ERAs with a ten-year-old car was irresistible, and as there were rumours that Howe was prepared to sell the Delage, Dick invited him to lunch.

A deal was done, and not long after, in exchange for a cheque for £3000 (signed by Mrs Beattie-Seaman) Dick took delivery of the Delage and virtually one other, which Howe had in pieces in his garage. With everything safely tucked away in Ennismore Gardens Mews, Dick sent Ramponi to Paris to see Monsieur Lory at Delage. He returned with all the drawings for the engine and a spare gearbox, and then set about stripping down the car completely and modifying it extensively, in which he was helped by Billy Rockell.

After a two-week shakedown period at the Nürburgring in April, the rejuvenated Delage made its debut at Donington on 9 May when Dick won two short races. Delighted with the car's performance, he entered it for the RAC's Light Car race at Douglas, Isle of Man, and won at a canter. All the other cars had to refuel during the 200 mile (320 km) event, but the incredible Delage was doing 9 mpg and finished the race with seven gallons still in the tank! It was an immensely satisfying win for Seaman, not least because there were nine ERAs in the race! But the main thing was that he (and, more to the point, Ramponi) had been proved right, for there were many who had felt that he was making a serious mistake when he bought Howe's ten-year-old car. Ramponi, however, had worked his magic and the Delage was to amaze everyone who saw it throughout the year.

Pride, however, does indeed come before a fall, and in Seaman's case it came before two falls. The first was at the Eifelrennen, when he went off the road while leading on the first lap. It was his own fault and the car was not damaged, but a week later he had a really bad crash at Péronne, again he was unhurt, but this time the car was quite badly bent and was out of action for a while. In the meantime, Dick drove an Aston Martin in the French Grand Prix for Sports Cars at Montlhéry and then drove a works Lagonda in the Spa 24-Hour race, finishing fourth with Freddie Clifford.

He took up the offer of a works Maserati drive in the German GP, but retired the V-8 car after four laps. He later took over Trossi's 2.5-litre machine and finished eighth. The Delage was ready again in time for the 1500 cc event of the Coppa Ciano in Livorno, but after being held up at the Italian Customs for three days Dick was only allowed one hour's practice. This was not nearly enough for any proper sorting and although he led the race for three laps, the engine eventually went off-song and he dropped down to sixth place. Dick took the car on to Pescara, where he was joined by Ramponi, who put it right to such good effect that he won the Voiturette Race with ease, beating Trossi by 40 seconds. It was the same in Switzerland the following weekend, where he won the Prix de Bern for the third year running. Then it was on to Donington for the Delage's third race in 14 days. Seaman won by 51 seconds.

He capped his brilliant season by winning the Donington GP with Hans Ruesch, in the latter's Alfa Romeo. It was his sixth win of the year and established him, at the age of 23, as Britain's finest racing driver.

Dick returned home to London after the Donington GP to find a telegram from Daimler-Benz waiting for him. They were about to hold some driver-trials at the Nürburgring and would Herr Seaman like to take part? This was what he had been aiming for all along and why—financial considerations apart—he had done so much racing abroad, to get noticed by the Grand Prix teams. Although Mercedes' offer was one he couldn't refuse, he nevertheless had some doubts: first of all, the Stuttgart concern had had a disastrous season in 1936, whereas Auto Union had won almost everything in sight. Then there was the political aspect—with Germany making so many warlike noises, should he join a German team? For the moment he pushed the problem from his mind and went to the Nürburgring, where he completed his trial without incident, impressing Alfred Neubauer with his calmness and consistency, rather than any exceptional speed. Neubauer made no promises, except that he would be in touch.

In November Dick received another telegram, this time asking him to go to Monza for more tests. He was very excited, but Mrs Beattie-Seaman was deeply worried about the political implications of her English son driving for Ger-

many, and she urged Dick to seek advice as to whether it was the sensible thing to do. He did so, talking to friends at the RAC and also to Earl Howe. They all told him to grab the drive if it was offered—things might indeed become difficult if Germany became more belligerent, but in the meantime it was an opportunity not to be missed. Thus reassured, Dick left for Monza on 20 November, returning to London on 2 December. He told his mother that he had signed a provisional contract with Mercedes for 1937, but that this was subject to Adolf Hitler's approval.

Early in February 1937, he received a draft contract, together with the news that the *Führer* had approved his appointment. Late in March he went again to Monza for Mercedes' annual Spring Training. Only one of the latest W125 cars was ready, so a 1936 W25 had been brought along as well and it was while driving this that Seaman had the first of four crashes he was to experience with Mercedes, each of which was—in quite the most extraordinary way—tied in with the number 13.

At Monza, Dick simply made a mistake, which he immediately admitted to Neubauer. The Mercedes' 450 bhp, or thereabouts, was more than double the power he had been used to in the Delage and he just gave the German car too much throttle as he drove out of a curve. The tail swung very wide and before Dick could do anything about it the car plunged off the road and clobbered a large tree. He was thrown out as—much to his astonishment—was the engine! Apart from some cuts and bruises and wounded pride, his main injury was a broken knee-cap, which required a few days' treatment in a nursing home. During his stay Dick recalled that his Milan hotel room had been number 113; that he had twice been one of 13 people at the same dining table there and that he had once changed for a swim in booth 13. Unlike Bernd and Elly Rosemeyer, Seaman did *not* regard 13 as a lucky number!

To Dick's surprise and relief, Neubauer was not at all bothered by the crash, regarding it as an occupational hazard. Dick soon returned to Germany and to the chalet he had rented in the little village of Ambach, on the Starnbergersee, about 40 km (25 miles) south of Munich. A few weeks later, although his knee was not yet fully mended, he joined the Mercedes team *en route* for Tripoli. He found the very fast circuit much to his liking and made a very impressive debut for Mercedes. At half-distance he lay second behind Lang, but supercharger trouble dropped him to seventh at the end.

The next race was at Avus, an even faster circuit than Tripoli but one that Seaman didn't enjoy at all, as it was just a flat-out blind up and down the *autobahn*. His three team mates were each given streamlined cars but Dick had to make do with an ordinary 'open-wheeler'. He finished fourth in his heat at 247 km/h (154 mph) and was lying a comfortable second behind Lang in the final, but two thrown treads in rapid succession meant that he finally finished fifth.

Run on 13 June, the Eifel GP proved lucky for Bernd Rosemeyer, but unlucky for Seaman, who retired with ignition problems on lap 2. Shortly afterwards, both Mercedes and Auto Union teams sailed on the *Bremen* for New York and the Vanderbilt Cup. Here Dick was unlucky again, because although he finished a fine second to Rosemeyer, he really should have won. On two separate occasions when chasing Rosemeyer he was badly held up by Bernd's team mate, Ernst von Delius, whom he was about to lap. Each time von Delius refused to give way and each time Rosemeyer increased his lead over Seaman. Also, Dick's Mercedes proved to be very thirsty for some reason and he had to make an unscheduled stop for fuel right at the end of the race. Three weeks later he was again involved with von Delius and this time with tragic results.

From the very beginning of his career, Dick had resolutely refused to allow his mother to watch him race. He knew that it would make her very nervous and that, in turn, would make him nervous and unable to concentrate properly. Mrs Beattie-Seaman, therefore, had made it a habit to phone the news desk of *The Sporting Life* on the evening of Dick's races to find out how he had got on. She called as usual on 25 July and was told that the German Grand Prix had been won by Rudolf Caracciola. She was then asked if she wanted to know about the young English driver, Dick Seaman, who had been badly injured in a crash. Mrs Beattie-Seaman was shattered by this news, but shortly afterwards she received another call, this time from a friend of Dick's in Germany, who told her that Dick was not badly hurt, but that the other driver involved, Ernst von Delius, was believed to be dying. Mrs Beattie-Seaman never rang *The Sporting Life* again.

The crash had occurred on lap 7 of the race when von Delius, for some reason, made a desperate attempt to pass Seaman as they hurtled down the long straight towards the pits. The Auto Union apparently brushed the hedge at the side of the road and was thrown across the bows of Seaman's Mercedes. They were doing close to 240 km/h (150 mph) and Dick was powerless to avoid a shunt. The Auto Union then struck the other hedge, which propelled it back across the road, through the left-hand hedge this time, across a field and over the main road to Koblenz which runs parallel to the Nürburgring straight. The car rolled several times and von Delius suffered terrible injuries, to which he succumbed the next morning. Seaman's Mercedes stayed on the road, more or less, until it struck a kilometre post and flung him out. He landed on his nose (which was a considerable one!) and took most of the skin off it. He also broke a thumb but, all things considered, he got off very lightly and after a few days in the local *krankenhaus* he was able to go home to Ambach.

There he had time to ponder the fact that, once again, the number 13 had preceded an accident: he had arrived back from the Vanderbilt Cup on 13 July and his second place in that race meant that he had 13 points towards the British Racing Drivers' Club Gold Star for 1937.

Much to his regret, Dick's injuries meant that he was unable to take part in the Monaco GP. Hermann Lang, too, was ill and had to miss the same race and when he was still too ill to drive in the Coppa Acerbo a week later, Neubauer asked Seaman if he could make it to Pescara. Although he looked terrible (his nose was a mess) Dick's thumb had healed well and he readily agreed, for he was very keen to drive the Mercedes on the circuit where he

Seaman chats with Rudolf Uhlenhaut at Avus, in 1937. Uhlenhaut, who spoke fluent English, proved to be a good friend

had won the 1500 cc race the previous two years.

On the first day's practice (a Thursday) he had a nasty scare when a front brake locked up as he approached a chicane, although he managed to stop without mishap. He should have known better than to go out the next day—it was Friday, 13 August. Sure enough, a front brake locked up again as he was going through Cappelle village at around 160 km/h (100 mph) and he hit a house very hard. He was unhurt, but the car was badly damaged and could not be repaired in time for the race. Seaman cannot have been very surprised to find that his crash occurred close to the 13-kilometre post.

Thirteen hadn't finished with him yet, though. In the race, Caracciola came in after 11 laps complaining of a misfire. Plugs were changed and he went out again, only to return at the end of the lap and hand over to Seaman in disgust. Dick set out on what was now the 13th lap of the race and, sure enough, the engine caught fire! Dick stopped and the flames subsided, so he got going again and managed to finish fifth. It had not been a good weekend, but then what chance did he have? It was, after all, the 13th Coppa Acerbo and, needless to say, Bernd Rosemeyer won. . . .

Probably as a result of all this excitement, Alfred Neubauer decided that Dick should not race in the Swiss GP. He came fourth in the Italian, at Livorno, and fourth again at Brno, where the amazing Rosemeyer caught him napping and passed him into third place just before the finish.

At the end of September Dick returned to England for the Donington Grand Prix and met up with his mother for the first time in nearly seven months. Although his nose had healed somewhat after his Nürburgring crash, Mrs Beattie-Seaman was appalled by what she saw, but Dick was able to assure her that he was going to have plastic surgery carried out very soon.

The appearance of the Mercedes and Auto Union teams at Donington caused a sensation in England, and Dick must have desperately wanted to do well in front of his home crowd. His hopes were dashed on lap 2 of the Grand Prix, when he was punted off the track at Coppice Corner by H. P. Müller's Auto Union! He rejoined the race, but a rear shock absorber had been damaged and eventually broke altogether, forcing him to retire on lap 29. Incredibly, Donington was to be Dick's last race for *ten months*.

In March 1938 Seaman went to Monza for his first run in the new supercharged 3-litre, V-12 W154, which Mercedes-Benz had built for the new Formula. He was greatly impressed with it but, despite their much-vaunted Teutonic efficiency, Mercedes didn't have a car for him to race until the German GP in July.

Dick spent the early summer months 'on holiday' at his chalet at Ambach. He bought a little sailing dinghy and then a speedboat. He made friends with former Mercedes driver Ernst Henne, who lived on the other side of the lake at Garatshausen and they did a lot of water-skiing together, Dick becoming very proficient very quickly. Blessed with a superb physique (he was 6 ft 3 in. (1.9 m) tall and weighed just over 13 stone (82.6 kg)) he was a natural athlete and became an excellent snow-skier, too. He was also extremely good looking and very attractive to the ladies, but in spite of this he had, as yet, shown no real romantic interest in the fair sex. This was put right, however, in June, when there occurred a meeting which was dramatically to alter his life.

At the end of a trip to Germany, members of the Frazer-Nash-BMW Car Club of Great Britain were entertained by the BMW company at a ball in Munich's Preysing Palais. As England's Number One racing driver, Dick was naturally invited and there he met Erica Popp, daughter of the President and co-Founder of BMW—Franz-Josef Popp. Erica was 18, blonde and very beautiful and she and Dick

ABOVE Crossing the Adenau Bridge on his way to an historic victory in the 1938 German Grand Prix

RIGHT Accompanied by Max Sailer of Daimler-Benz, Dick is congratulated by von Brauchitsch after his great victory. Dick was on his way to be presented with Hitler's *Siegerpreis* by *Korpsführer* Hühnlein

took one look at each other and then spent almost the entire evening dancing together. This did not go unnoticed by the other guests, as clearly there was 'something going on'. They met again the next day at Ernst Henne's house and the romance took off, but it was to have a troubled life and a tragic end. . . .

Having pleaded a lack of new cars for the first half of the season, Mercedes produced no less than *seven* W154s during practice for the German GP, so Seaman finally got a drive—his first since Donington the previous October. In spite of this long period of inactivity he was soon back in the groove and was third fastest in practice, putting himself on the front row of the grid with Lang and von Brauchitsch. Watched by an excited Erica and her parents in the grandstand, he held a cool second place until leader von Brauchitsch's car caught fire in the pits. Dick had followed his team mate in about ten seconds later and the two of them were joined almost immediately by reserve driver Walter Baumer, who had taken over Lang's sick car after Lang had replaced a sick Caracciola! Having three cars in the pits was not Neubauer's idea of a good thing and the fire merely compounded his problem, but Seaman

(who had stopped only for fuel) simply drove through the smoke and extinguisher foam and off into the lead, which he held until the end.

A few days later Mrs Lilian Beattie-Seaman arrived in Munich for a pre-arranged visit, her first to her son's Bavarian home. It was not a success. When she first met Erica she could not help but be impressed, for the young German girl was exceptionally beautiful, spoke fluent English and had an impeccable background. Almost any mother would have welcomed her as a future daughter-in-law, but as soon as she heard of the romance Mrs Beattie-Seaman became implacably opposed to the affair. This was the beginning of a deep rift in her relationship with Dick which, before the year was out, would end in acrimony and bitterness, never to be healed.

In spite of his great victory at the 'Ring, Seaman didn't get a drive in either of Mercedes' next two races, the Coppas Ciano and Acerbo, having to wait until the Swiss GP on 21 August. He made good use of his spare time by proposing to Erica, who was delighted to accept.

In the Swiss GP, Seaman drove what was unquestionably the finest race of his career, coming second to Caracciola in the pouring rain. He had thoroughly deserved his German GP win but, to be fair, it had been handed to him on a plate the moment the leading Mercedes had caught fire. Had this not happened he would (as always) have obeyed team orders and stayed behind von Brauchitsch

without challenging him. At Bern, brimful of confidence and wildly happy with his still-secret engagement, he seemed determined to show that he was now a real force to be reckoned with in Grand Prix racing. In practice (run in the dry) he was no less than 3.2 seconds faster than the next man, Lang, and 3.4 seconds faster than Caracciola, the acknowledged master of the Bremgarten circuit. In the race, when it was *very* wet, he led *Regenmeister* Rudi for the first 11 laps, finally finishing only 26 seconds behind him in a masterly drive that really established him as one of the aces.

Dick's happiness was soon to be badly bruised. On 29 August he flew to London and stayed at Ennismore Gardens before going up to Donington for the Tourist Trophy. It was a long night, for he and his mother talked into the early hours about Erica. Mrs Beattie-Seaman was shocked to hear of the engagement and told Dick bluntly that she was firmly opposed to the marriage.

Next morning Seaman went unhappily to Donington, where he was given the fastest of the four BMWs which H. J. 'Aldy' Aldington had entered for the German firm. (The others were driven by Bira, A. P. F. Fane and 'Aldy' himself.) All were soon in trouble and, although Dick finished, he was way down the field. From Donington he returned to Germany and then went on to Monza for the Italian GP. The race was a disaster for Mercedes, only Caracciola managing to finish, struggling home in third place. Seaman retired quite early on and was only too happy to join Erica in the grandstand.

Tazio Nuvolari won the race for Auto Union, so there was to be no victory dinner for Mercedes. Disgusted with the performance of his cars and drivers, Alfred Neubauer went off for a quiet dinner with his wife, Hansi, in one of his favourite Milan restaurants, *La Grocetta*. Their 'quiet dinner' turned into a full-scale party as they were followed into the restaurant—at brief intervals—by Rudi and Baby Caracciola, Hermann and Lydia Lang, Manfred

von Brauchitsch, Dick Seaman and Erica, the Auto Union team and most of the other drivers. Neubauer quickly realized that this was all part of a plot and he was not best pleased, but when Louis Chiron broke the news that Dick and Erica were now officially engaged, Don Alfredo beamed with pleasure and ended up paying the bill for the entire party!

That was on 11 September. By the 14th, Hitler was threatening Czechoslovakia and newspapers across Europe were full of the impending war. The Donington GP was scheduled for 2 October and the Royal Automobile Club decided to give a lunch on 27 September in honour of Seaman's German GP win. Dick and Erica flew to Croydon on the 25th and the next day 3 Ennismore Gardens was besieged by newspaper reporters and photographers. No, they hadn't at last woken up to the fact that Dick had won the German Grand Prix—the story they were after was that here was an Englishman engaged to a German girl at a time when the two countries were on the verge of war.

The Munich Crisis, as it became known, caused the postponement of the Donington GP. In the meantime, Dick's relationship with his mother got worse and worse. Mrs Beattie-Seaman threatened to cut off his allowance and his inheritance and she refused to have Erica in the house. It was a very unhappy Dick Seaman who went to Donington late in October for the rescheduled GP, following the last-minute 'Munich Agreement' between Neville Chamberlain and Adolf Hitler. In the race, Seaman was lying a comfortable second behind Müller's Auto Union when an Alta blew up, dumping most of its oil on the approach to the hairpin. In the high-speed confusion that followed, almost every German car left the road and Hasse crashed his Auto Union quite badly. Seaman spun off and ended up undamaged near Hasse's car, losing quite a lot of time before he was able to rejoin the race. Nuvolari eventually scored another of his classic victories and Dick finished third behind Lang.

In mid-November Dick had a final, bitter meeting with

LEFT Seaman drifts the Mercedes in the rain during his magnificent drive in the 1938 Swiss GP. He finished second to Caracciola

RIGHT Seaman tries to get back into the race after spinning on some oil dumped by an Alta when he was lying second in the 1938 Donington GP. Hasse's Auto Union is in the ditch

his mother in which she again demanded that he break off his engagement. He refused and left the house, never to see her again. Dick and Erica were married at Caxton Hall in London on 7 December. The only witnesses were Dick's great friend, Tony Cliff, and Erica's sister, Eva. Mrs Beattie-Seaman went to a matinée in the West End.

On their return to Germany Dick signed a new contract with Daimler-Benz for 1939, although by now he was becoming increasingly worried about driving for a German team, as the political situation was getting worse and worse. Mercedes only had two of their new cars ready for the season's first race, at Pau, but Seaman had to go along as reserve driver, much to his disgust.

After an abortive Eifel GP, where a slipping clutch put him out of the race within seconds of the start, Dick and Erica went to Spa for the Belgian GP. The race was run in a downpour. Müller went straight into the lead and proceeded to keep everyone in his spray, with Lang, Caracciola, Seaman and Nuvolari all unable to get by. On lap 9, much to everyone's amazement, *Regenmeister* Caracciola spun off at La Source hairpin and was unable to restart. On the next lap Seaman took the lead and, driving brilliantly, proceeded to stay there with apparent ease. But then the rain stopped and the road began to dry in some places, but not in others. Instead of taking things easy, Seaman began to go faster and faster, until on lap 22 he lost control at Club Corner, just before the hairpin, and shot off the road into the trees.

The Mercedes struck one tree violently at the cockpit, the impact breaking Dick's right arm and knocking him unconscious. That in itself was hardly serious, but also broken was the large-diameter fuel pipe connecting the car's fore and aft tanks. Seaman had refuelled only five laps earlier and gallons of fuel poured onto the hot exhaust pipe and ignited. There have been, over the years, several conflicting reports about who tried to pull Dick from the blaze, but next day, the Liège newspaper, *La Meuse*, was quite

specific in naming a Lieutenant Hauman of the 1st Belgian Lancers as the first to reach Seaman. Initially, the courageous Lieutenant was hindered by the terrible heat and his inability to release the Mercedes' detachable steering wheel. Eventually, and with the help of two marshals who had run to the scene from the hairpin, Hauman dragged Seaman free, but by then the Englishman had suffered the most appalling burns.

He was rushed to hospital where he recovered consciousness and told his friend Robert Fellowes and Alfred Neubauer that the crash was his own fault—he had been trying to show Caracciola that he was no longer the *Regenmeister*. Shortly afterwards he lapsed into unconsciousness again and died just before midnight.

He died in Room 39 at the Spa Hospital and it was quite extraordinary how the number 13 and its multiples caught up with Dick again that day. He was 26 years old; he had been driving car number 26 in a race of 13 cars; his stop for fuel had lasted 26 seconds; he crashed close to the 13-kilometre stone on the circuit at the end of his 13th lap in the lead with just 13 laps to go. And the grille over his Mercedes' air intake had 13 upright bars in it. . . .

Dick Seaman was buried in his father's grave at Putney Vale Cemetery, near London, on Friday, 30 June 1939. Both Mrs Beattie-Seaman and Erica were there, of course, but there was no graveside reconciliation. The entire Mercedes-Benz team was present and Adolf Hitler sent a huge wreath, which was *not* taken to the cemetery.

Inevitably, the British press—which had ignored all his achievements—now went to town over his death, with photos of the blazing Mercedes and strident headlines. Ironically, less than a year earlier, when he had been complaining about the total lack of national interest in his German Grand Prix win, Dick had said to his mother, 'It is only when some poor devil kills himself in a racing car that the British press sits up and takes notice.'

Mountainclimbs

'The French course is fairly easy for the first four miles, after which bends and corners rapidly become more and more difficult, the final five miles consisting of one hairpin turn after another.'

The words are those of George Eyston and Barré Lyndon, from their book, *Motor Racing and Record Breaking*, and the course they were writing about was not a circuit, but the mountainclimb at Mont Ventoux, in the South of France. And don't be fooled by 'the first four miles' and 'the final five miles'—Mont Ventoux was not a mere 9 miles ($14\frac{1}{2}$ km) long—Eyston and Lyndon ignored the $4\frac{1}{2}$ miles (7 km) in the middle! The total length was 13.4 miles (21.6 km) and when a Monsieur Chauchard drove his Panhard to victory in the very first event in 1902, the climb took him no less than 27 minutes and 17 seconds. And you thought Shelsley was tough?

People have been racing against the clock up hills and mountains almost as long as they have been racing against other cars—initially from town to town and then round circuits. The first official motor race was from Paris to Bordeaux and back, in 1895, and the first official hillclimb took place two years later, at La Turbie, near Nice. In 1899 two more climbs appeared, at Semmering, south of Vienna, and Gaillon, between Paris and Rouen, and in 1902 the Mont Cenis and Mont Ventoux events began. England's Shelsley Walsh was a relative late-comer, starting in 1905 (along with Kesselberg), but it has out-lasted them all and is still being run as enthusiastically as ever today, 80 years on!

Shelsley Walsh is no mountain, of course, it is a hill which started with a length of 992 yds (907 m) and was increased to 1000 yds (914 m) in 1907. Despite its brevity, it attracted two of the greatest climbers of all time in 1930, when both Hans Stuck and Rudi Caracciola competed there. It was an awfully long way to travel for 40-odd seconds of driving, but the beauty of a short course like Shelsley is that it can be properly learned.

Mountains and hills presented a completely different set of problems to those of circuits, for the obvious reason that you can drive continuously round a circuit, whereas once you reach the top of a mountainclimb you not only have to return to base and start again, but before you can do that you have to wait until everyone else has had a go, and with a hundred and some competitors at Mont Ventoux

or Klausen—or even a 'short' climb, such as Freiburg's 12 km (7.5 miles)—that takes time. No-one could ever hope to learn Klausen during the two or three days of the event, but men like Caracciola and Chiron, who raced there on three or four occasions, would naturally have had a pretty good knowledge of it by 1934, the time of its last run.

The popularity of these events led the AIACR to introduce a European Mountain Championship in 1930, for both Racing and Sports Cars. There were ten events listed that year, at Zbraslav Jiloviste in Czechoslovakia, Cuneo in Italy, Shelsley Walsh in England, Klausen in Switzerland, Freiburg in Germany, Mont Ventoux in France, Tatra in Poland, Semmering in Austria, Svab in Hungary and Feleac in Rumania. Of those ten, only one—Shelsley Walsh—seems to have lasted through the decade to the outbreak of war. The last event at Klausen was held in 1934, at Semmering in 1933, Mont Ventoux in 1936 and Freiburg in 1937 and the fate of the European Championship by the middle of the decade is uncertain. What is certain is that the first Champion was Hans Stuck (1930—Austro-Daimler), then Juan Zanelli (1931—Nacional Pescara) and Rudi Caracciola (1932—Alfa Romeo). After that, further details are sketchy.

The Germans had their own Mountain Championship which centred on Freiburg initially, with qualifying climbs at Felsberg and Kesselberg (1934), Kesselberg and Feldberg (1935), and Feldberg (1936). Freiburg stood alone in 1937, but then the Championship moved to the Grossglockner Pass in 1938 and again in 1939, when it was supported by the Kahlenberg climb in Vienna. Hans Stuck won no less than four of these German Championships, the other two going to Bernd Rosemeyer (1936) and Hermann Lang (1939).

1934

Not surprisingly, it was Hans Stuck—the King of the Mountains—who set the ball rolling for the German teams in mountainclimbs, just as he had in record-breaking. In June he took an Auto Union to two events on successive weekends, at Felsberg and Kessselberg. Near the town of Saarbrücken, Felsberg was the fastest climb in Europe and Stuck—who had no real opposition—stormed up the 8 km (5 mile) course to win at over 147 km/h (91 mph)—Auto Union's very first victory.

A week later Mercedes entered the fray for the first time, sending Manfred von Brauchitsch in his Eifel-winning W25 to compete at Kesselberg, near Munich. It was a tough assignment, for Stuck had virtually made this climb his own, winning the Racing Car class three years running (1928-29-30) in his Austro-Daimler and the Sports Car class in 1932 with his SSKL Mercedes when he just beat von Brauchitsch in a similar car. In 1933, however, Manfred had broken Stuck's Sports Car record and won the class, so Hans was keen to settle the score.

As he had done in the past, von Brauchitsch stayed in his favourite little *Gasthaus*—the Jager am See—at Urfeld, where he did not endear himself to other competitors who

King of the Mountains! Hans Stuck in his Auto Union on the way to victory at Grossglockner in 1938. Stuck won 12 major climbs between 1934 and 1939

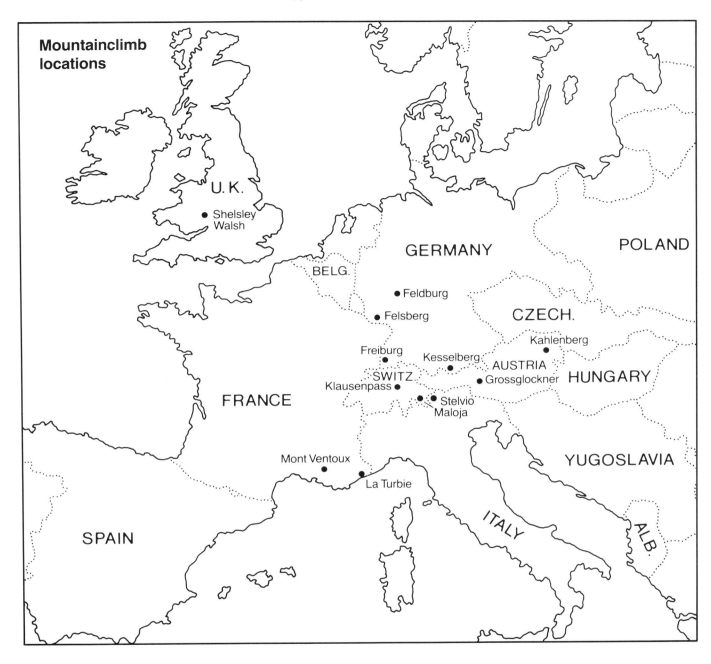

Mountainclimb locations

were also staying there as his mechanics insisted upon warming up his Mercedes every morning—just before dawn! In the event he was beaten again by Stuck, who also broke Caracciola's course record by eight seconds. Paul Pietsch was third in his Alfa Romeo.

Having returned to racing in the French GP in July, Caracciola took to the hills for the first time in two years in August, when he entered the Klausen climb. His shattered hip meant that his right leg was now two inches shorter than his left and although he had made a remarkable recovery from his injuries, the damage would never be properly mended. He was still far from being 100 per cent fit and in spite of his brave comeback, many people were convinced that his great career had ended at Monaco.

As if in a conscious effort to prove them wrong, Rudi made his return on two of the most arduous courses in the world—Montlhéry and the Klausen Pass.

Whereas Kesselberg had been an easy 5 km (3 miles), Klausen shared with Mont Ventoux the distinction of being the longest climb in Europe—21.5 km (13.4 miles)! The course, which included 35 very sharp bends, climbed nearly 1200 m (4000 ft) from the village of Lintal on the road to Altdorf, some 50 km (30 miles) south of Zurich. Caracciola had raced there almost every year since 1924, so he knew the road as well as anyone, having set the current record of 15 min. 50 sec. in 1932. (There was no race in 1933.)

The climb was nearly washed out, as for three days and nights before the event it rained and snowed almost

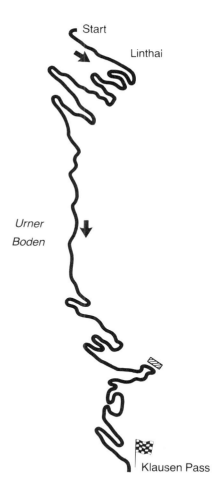

Start

Linthai

Urner
Boden

Klausen Pass

ABOVE **Klausen—21.5 km (13.4 miles)**

LEFT **Caracciola made a
remarkable comeback after
his Monaco crash by
winning the 21 km/13 mile
Klausen climb for
Mercedes in 1934**

without a break. Mountain streams became swollen rivers, an avalanche swept across the relatively straight stretch at Urner Boden and the constant rain loosened boulders and stones on the Kilchenstock Mountain, sending them crashing and bouncing down into the valley. This appalling weather meant that many contestants had no chance of practice, seeing the course for the first time on the day of the race!

Over 50 competitors finally had one run each and from the start the battle for outright victory was between Caracciola and Stuck. It proved to be a sensational win for the Mercedes driver, who broke his own course record with the remarkable time of 15 min. 22.2 sec., just three seconds ahead of Stuck, who made one error which allowed

his Auto Union to slide broadside on the exit to a corner. This quite possibly lost him the contest, but Caracciola never looked like making a mistake and won the day.

Stuck got his revenge a fortnight later in the important *Deutsche Bergmeisterschaft* at Freiburg. The 12 km (7.5 mile) course followed a sinuous road up the Schauinsland Mountains just south of the town of Freiburg, which is itself some 75 km (47 miles) north-west of Zurich.

During a practice run Hans found himself wondering why the spectators were waving at him so enthusiastically as he roared up the road. Suddenly he saw a red flag, so he obediently braked to a halt, whereupon he was immediately surrounded by flames! The engine compartment of his Auto Union was well and truly ablaze and although

ABOVE **Caracciola at Freiburg in August 1934. He finished second behind Hans Stuck**

he leapt out unhurt, the car was quite badly damaged before the fire was extinguished. Hans felt sure that his chances of starting the next day had gone up in smoke, but the mechanics had other ideas. Helped by none other than Professor Porsche himself (who ordered Hans back to his hotel to get some sleep), they worked through the night and next morning Stuck was able to give the car a brief trial run through the back streets of Freiburg before presenting himself at the start-line. The car worked perfectly and Stuck drove brilliantly, repaying the all-night efforts of the mechanics and Professor Porsche by beating Caracciola by 26 seconds and bettering Rudi's course record by 29.

Stuck's last climb of the year was at Mont Ventoux, where he had won the Sports Car class in 1932 with his Mercedes. Some 60 km (35 miles) north-east of Avignon, the course had been in use since 1902. It started in the village of Bedoin at 206 m (676 ft) above sea level and wound its way for 21 km (13.4 miles) up to the finish by the Observatory, at a height of 1689 m (5541 ft).

In 1932 Caracciola had taken his Alfa Romeo up in a new record time of 15 min. 12.4 sec. and Stuck had won the Sports Car class in 15 min. 48.6 sec. in his Mercedes. Whitney Straight had beaten Caracciola's record handsomely in 1933, recording 14 min. 31.6 sec. in his Maserati. Caracciola was not present in 1934, but Stuck demolished

Straight's record by nearly a minute, hurling his Auto Union up the course in 13 min. 38.6 sec. and Straight, too, broke his old record with a splendid climb in 13 min. 58.8 sec.

Also making his mark was young Richard Seaman who, fresh from his superb win in the Voiturette class of the Swiss GP three weeks earlier, put in another brilliant drive with his little MG (which he had bought from Straight) and climbed in the remarkable time of 16 min. 15.8 sec. This was not only a new 1100 cc Racing Car class record, but was faster than the 1500 cc class winner by over a minute and faster than the 2-litre class winner by 1 min. 45 sec! On top of that, he beat Renato Balestrero's 2.3-litre sports Alfa by five seconds! It was an astonishing performance and one wonders how much attention Stuck paid to it, for he was to come up against Mr Seaman himself almost exactly a year later, and the Englishman was to give him a *very* good run for his money.

So the season ended with Stuck as undisputed European Mountain Champion and *Deutsche Bergmeister*, and he was to have it all his own way again in 1935, as Mercedes-Benz stayed away from the mountains altogether.

1935

Stuck had to wait until the end of June for his first climb of the year, which was at Kesselberg. He won easily from Juan Zanelli in his Spanish machine, the Nacional Pescara, just failing to beat his own 1934 record by 0.3 sec. Dick Seaman was now racing an ERA, which he entered for Kesselberg with no success. During a warm-up run a front brake locked solid, bending the front axle and brake rods, forcing him to make his climb with the front brakes disconnected. Naturally, he finished nowhere, but this didn't dampen his enthusiasm for the 5 km (3.1 mile) course and its superb location between two lakes, the *Kochel See* and the *Walchen See*, which he thought was 'the most beautiful venue for a racing event that I know'. The whole area— about an hour's drive south of Munich—clearly delighted him, for when he joined Daimler-Benz two years later he was to rent a chalet at Ambach, on the Starnbergersee, not far from Kesselberg.

The Klausen climb was cancelled in 1935, as the appalling weather the previous year had persuaded many of the expected spectators to stay away, leaving the organizers with a deficit of some £3000. In addition, the road itself was now in a very bad state and the cost of resurfacing its great length would have been enormous. As if that wasn't enough, there were problems with local authorities and farmers, so there was nothing to do but call off the event, but the Swiss (who considered their mountainclimbs to be the finest in the world) were very hopeful of returning there in 1936. Sadly, this they were unable to do and Klausen was never run again.

However, as one great race disappeared, another arrived. On 3 August, President Miklas of Austria officially opened the new Grossglockner Hochalpen Pass, a 34 km (21 mile) road over the mountains connecting Austria with Italy, part of the ceremony including the unveiling of a chapel at Fuscher Törl, from which point no fewer than 37 mountain peaks could be seen! The next day the Austrian Automobile Club organized an International climb to mark the opening of the new pass, using a 19.5 km (12 mile) stretch of the route, which rose 1593 m (5226 ft), finishing at a height of 2428 m (7965 ft). Of all the European mountainclimbs, only Stelvio reached a higher altitude.

Although a strong German entry was hoped for, it did not materialize as the road surface had a loose dressing on it and this was considered too dangerous for really fast cars! The brilliant Italian, Mario Tadini, won the day in his Scuderia Ferrari Alfa, with Dick Seaman coming a fine second in his ERA. Tadini's skill on the mountains was quite extraordinary and for Seaman to lose only a second a mile to him was a terrific achievement on the Englishman's part, but the best was yet to come. One month later, he was at Freiburg for the German Mountain Grand Prix, and he caused a sensation!

Seaman and Raymond Mays arrived in Freiburg straight from Bern, where Dick had once again won the Voiturette class in the Swiss GP, beating all the other ERAs including, of course, Mays' own. There was undoubtedly a certain atmosphere between the two English camps as Seaman had not long before removed his car from the care and preparation of the Bourne concern, feeling that the ERA mechanics could not give it the amount of attention he required.

Arriving in Freiburg on the Monday evening after the Swiss Grand Prix, Dick lost no time in learning the course, driving up and down in his Ford V8 (which he'd had fitted with Leslie Ballamy's LMB independent front suspension). Later, on his second official practice run, he recorded a very satisfactory time of 8 min. 40 sec. which was well inside the class record and only just outside Caracciola's 1932 course record, which he had set with an Alfa Romeo. But Mays then bettered his time and they were both beaten by Hans Stuck in his Auto Union. Then at the very end of practice all three of them were ordered to run again— *Korpsführer* Hühnlein had arrived and he wished to see the three fastest cars in action. What Hühnlein wanted, he got....

That night Mays had the unpleasant experience of being woken by a menacing phone call, as he recalled in his memoirs, *Split Seconds*.

'A voice said: "You are Raymond Mays?" to which I replied, "Yes, and what the hell do you mean by waking me up at this time of night?" The voice continued, "You are now in Germany, not England, and certain of your conversations during the last few days have been overheard. You are advised to leave Germany straightaway . . . I am speaking from the Gestapo HQ at Koblenz and you had better take notice of what I say." I banged the receiver down but, believe me, I felt very uneasy.'

Mays could not recollect saying anything to anybody that could possibly have upset the Gestapo, but he went to the start the next day in a very nervous state of mind, constantly looking over his shoulder to see if he was being followed. Not surprisingly, perhaps, his climb was not one of his best and a spectacular slide on one bend slowed him considerably.

Dick Seaman, however, had not been troubled by any midnight phone calls and went up in fine style, recording 8 min. 25.1 sec., nearly 12 seconds faster than Mays and comfortably inside the class record. The real sensation occurred when Hans Stuck's time was announced. Far from beating his 1934 record of 8 min. 06.6 sec., Stuck could only do 8 min. 24.1 sec.—just one second faster than Seaman! The 40,000 spectators who lined the course were stunned by Seaman's achievement and there were many who felt that Stuck's win was, perhaps, more a matter of German face-saving than driving skill!

On that same day—1 September—the Stelvio mountain-climb was being held in the Italian Alps. Rather unwisely, Achille Varzi persuaded Auto Union to let him have a car for this event and was soundly thrashed by two Alfas and two Maseratis! This was in no small way due to the fact that the Auto Union's considerable length meant that he had to reverse in no less than five hairpins in order to get round them! The sheer straightline speed of the big V-16 made up for some of the lost time, but Varzi could do nothing about the amazing Mario Tadini, who won the event for the third year running. Nor, indeed, could Tazio Nuvolari, who was 12 seconds adrift of his Scuderia Ferrari team mate at the end of the 14 km (8.7 mile) run, which finished at an altitude of 2755 m (9038 ft)! Third and fourth were Piero Dusio and Hans Ruesch on Maseratis, with Varzi a frustrated and weary fifth. To add to his misery the Italian *tifosi* (fans) greeted his arrival with considerable ribaldry and raspberries, for they were delighted to see the German car so soundly beaten. Such was their rudery that the Public Address announcer had to appeal to them to stop!

Six weeks later Hans Stuck finished his mountainclimb-ing year just as he had started it, with a victory. The event was at Feldberg, in the Taunus hills near Frankfurt, and afterwards Stuck probably wished he hadn't bothered, for during the event he was astonished to find himself publicly vilified for being 'the husband of a Jewess' (see Chapter 4, *Racing and the Nazis*). However, this unpleasantness didn't prevent him from taking his special, short-chassis Auto Union up the 12 km (7.5 mile) course in winning style—the only driver to beat seven minutes. Having also won at Kesselberg and Freiburg, Hans was once again *Deutsche Bergmeister* and European Mountain Champion.

1936

Stuck opened his new season on 9 April, at La Turbie, near Nice, just a few days before the Monaco GP. First held in 1897, the 6.3 km (4 mile) climb was the oldest in the world. Stuck had won there in 1929 with his Austro-Daimler, when he set a new record with a time of 4 min. 9.8 sec. In the following years that time had been steadily reduced and the record now stood to Jean-Pierre Wimille, who had recorded 3 min. 43.2 sec. in his 3.3-litre Bugatti in 1935. The Frenchman was on hand to defend his record with the same car, but he failed to beat it by one-fifth of a second. Stuck, however—handling his short-chassis Auto Union in brilliant fashion—took 3 min. 39.8 sec., breaking Wimille's record by nearly four seconds.

In June Stuck took his Auto Union to Shelsley Walsh and, needless to say, created a sensation. He had been there before in 1930, when he set a new record for the hill in his Austro-Daimler. His time of 42.8 seconds remained unbeaten until 1933, when Whitney Straight recorded 41.2 seconds in his Maserati. Two years later Raymond Mays lowered this to 39.6 seconds and that was the record Stuck now hoped to beat. But his Auto Union was a very different proposition from the Austro-Daimler and his main worry was that once over the finishing line he might not have enough room in which to stop, as he estimated that he would be going at least 15–20 mph faster than anyone had gone before!

The presence of the King of the Mountains and one of Germany's amazing Grand Prix cars together in England for the first time brought huge crowds to Shelsley, and the Auto Union and its driver were the centre of attraction in the paddock. Interviewed in *The Autocar*, Stuck revealed that his car had been specially built for mountainclimbs with a chassis 20 cm (8 in.) shorter than the normal GP cars. It also had a smaller fuel tank, 'and a Grand Prix, 5.3-litre engine,' said Stuck. This is a curiosity, as Auto Union don't appear to have built a unit of that capacity. The V-16 started out at 4360 cc, was increased to 4950 cc in 1935 and to 6010 cc in 1936, although there was an interim version of 5.6 litres made in 1935 which first appeared in the French GP of that year.

The situation is further confused by *The Motor*'s report of the meeting, which stated that Stuck's car was giving 350 bhp, but did not mention its capacity. A 5.3-litre, 350 bhp Auto Union is an oddity, indeed (the 4.9-litre engine of 1935 gave 375 bhp), but perhaps some explanation of the low power output can be found in a post-war *Motor* article, which claimed that Stuck had his personal mechanic, Fritz Mathaey, 'reduce the bhp of his 600 bhp car by 200 bhp for hillclimbs where excessive power was an embarrassment, but he never told the management about this'.

The management would doubtless have been intrigued to know how Stuck was getting 600 bhp from one of their engines, for which they were only claiming 520, but whatever the actual size and power of his Shelsley car, Stuck

ABOVE Hans Stuck winning at La Turbie in April 1936. He won here four years running

RIGHT Bernd Rosemeyer hangs out the tail of his Auto Union at Freiburg in August 1936. He and Ernst von Delius finished one-two for Auto Union

still found that he had 'too many horsepowers', and that was in the dry! On race day it poured with rain and although he was unable to break the record, Hans did not disappoint the thousands who had turned out to watch him. In practice he had equalled Raymond Mays' record, but in the rain he could only do 45.2 seconds, which gave him equal fifth place overall. Even so, he gave the spectators an experience they were unlikely to forget in a hurry, as *The Motor* reported, when describing his second run.

'Before the climb opened he had broadcast, "I hope I can show you vat you vant." He made a bad start with tremendous wheelspin, and then, going berserk, gave us a *tour de force* of sheer driving brilliance which will live long in the memory of all those who saw him on the dangerous lower slopes of the hill.

'With gritted teeth and glaring eyes he banged the throttle open where others shut it. The car slid all over the road. Between the high banks it nearly turned sideways, and Stuck had to lift his foot. He heaved the car straight, and then he fought it up the hill with his elbows jerking like a man rowing, wrenching the wheel through half a turn with immense speed. The tail wagged viciously, the engine roared, his arms worked like pumps, and while the trees re-echoed the bellowings of the big engine, he flung the car through the curves, slid the Ess in one long skid, opened out again and rocketed up the final straight with the steering wheel spinning from lock to lock as fast as he could turn it.

'All the way out of sight the tail was never straight, and one rear wheel clouted the bank as he shot across the line. Although the bad start gave him a time of 48.8 sec., he gave the slightly frightened spectators "vat they vanted". There has never been a climb like that at Shelsley since Jean Bugatti's practice run with the four-wheel-drive Bug. years ago.' Magic!

The organization of the Grossglockner climb in 1935 had left quite a lot to be desired, so much so that the event was not held again until 1938. The next climb on the 1936 calendar, therefore, was at Freiburg, and here Bernd Rosemeyer made his debut in company with his friend, Ernst von Delius. Hans Stuck had been lucky to walk away from a considerable accident during practice for the Coppa Acerbo, at Pescara, when he had badly hurt his arm. As a result, he had to miss Freiburg.

Rosemeyer was no stranger to mountainclimbs, having competed in several during his motorcycle days and during practice he shattered Stuck's record with a climb at 94.7 km/h (58.8 mph)! He could not manage this on the day, however, as his practice run had been done at 6 am, and by the time he made his official attempts it was extremely hot and the road surface was very soft. Nonetheless, he became the first man to break eight minutes, recording 7 min. 59.3 sec. By now, this sort of performance was expected of Rosemeyer, but the real surprise was Ernst von Delius, who was only just over 1.5 seconds slower!

The unlucky Stuck had yet another crash during the Italian GP and so was not fit for the final climb of the year, at Feldberg. Rosemeyer and von Delius again took part and Bernd won easily against virtually no opposition. The weather was foul and his only serious competitor was his team mate, but poor von Delius overdid it on a damp corner and slid off the track. In practice Rosemeyer had put in a stunning climb in 5 min. 46 sec., completely demolishing Stuck's record of 6 min. 22.3 sec. Just as the heat had played havoc with the road surface at Freiburg, now it was the turn of the rain to make things difficult at Feldberg, and on the day Bernd could 'only' manage 6 min. 23.2 sec., so he just failed to beat Stuck's record by nine-tenths of a second.

1937

Mountainclimbs were very thin on the ground in 1937. Klausen, Kesselberg, Semmering and Gaisberg (both last used in 1933), Mont Ventoux, Feldberg and Grossglockner—all were missing from the calendar. However, the Germans ensured that Freiburg remained the première event in Europe and to give it added significance this year Mercedes-Benz returned to the mountains.

The climb was held on 1 August, which meant that it fell nicely between the German and Monaco GPs, so Rodney Walkerley was able to cover the three events for *The Motor* during a two-week European trip. In his report,

Walkerley described Freiburg as 'the most dangerous thing I have ever seen', and went on to explain himself:

'To begin with, the hill is a perfectly good zig-zag mountain pass, measuring 7.7 miles (12.4 km) from starting line to finish—that is, about 14 times longer than Shelsley. The road is as narrow for most of the distance as the lower reaches of Shelsley Walsh are and has a similar surface except that it is extremely bumpy all the way up. And on such a narrow road bumps fling the cars clean across the road from one side to the other.

'The edges of the course vary between deep ditches, steep banks, sheer precipices or overhanging cliffs which jut out into the road, where the drivers miss the jagged edges by inches. And the whole pass climbs up through the mountains of the Black Forest, just outside Freiburg, and is known as the Schauinsland, rising from 400–1200 m— about 3900 ft.

'The hairpins, curves and corners are far too numerous to describe, but there are 27 really sharp or complete hairpin bends, and in between there is very little straight—merely a succession of fast Ess bends and gentler curves. Quite near the top, however, the road runs out of the forest, quite straight for about a kilometre, then comes a fast, steeply cambered open bend, good for about 55 mph (88.5 km/h) on the apex, followed by another short straight of about 300 yards, and then the road plunges back into the forest and the series of hideous zig-zag corners. And it is on this open section overlooking the semi-circular bend known as the *Holzschlagermattenkurve* that the permanent grand-

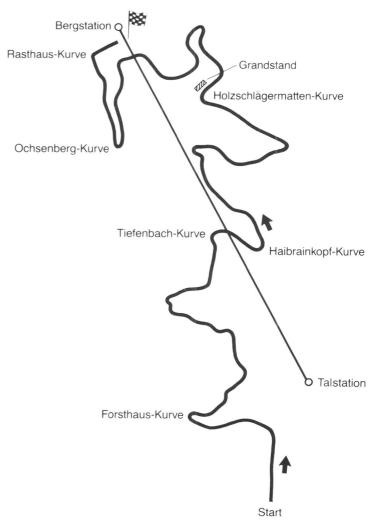

Bergstation

Rasthaus-Kurve

Grandstand

Holzschlägermatten-Kurve

Ochsenberg-Kurve

Tiefenbach-Kurve

Haibrainkopf-Kurve

Talstation

Forsthaus-Kurve

Start

ABOVE **Freiburg—12.4 km (7.7 miles)**

ABOVE LEFT **Watched by Bernd Rosemeyer** (*right*)
Hermann Lang gets off to a wet start at Freiburg in 1937

stand is built. All around stretches the panorama of the Black Forest Mountains.'

The promise of Caracciola, von Brauchitsch, Stuck and Rosemeyer doing battle on this spectacular course guaranteed a huge crowd and the official figure for the day was 140,000! In the event, von Brauchitsch didn't drive, as he was not feeling well. Although Dick Seaman had already demonstrated his considerable skills on the mountains, he was still recovering from his crash with von Delius in the German GP, so was not available for Freiburg. Had he been fit, it is doubtful whether he would have taken precedence over his German team mate, Lang, even though Lang hadn't seen a mountainclimb since his motorcycling days. So Hermann got the drive and, by his own admission, he performed very poorly.

Caracciola had won either the Racing or Sports Car class at Freiburg on five previous occasions and Stuck had done the same on three. Rosemeyer, of course, was the current record-holder, but he was still deeply upset by his friend Ernst von Delius' death the previous weekend and it was Caracciola who set the pace on the first day's practice, beating Rosemeyer's 1936 time by 21 seconds. The next day Bernd improved on this by four seconds, recording 7 min. 34 sec. Stuck then did 7 min. 41 sec., so the prospect for race day was exciting, to say the least.

First came the motorcycles—nearly 200 of them. Then the sports cars—nearly 80 of them. Then the smaller racing cars, so that by the time the Grand Prix machines were on their way the spectators had seen almost 300 vehicles

go up the mountain! Now it was raining and the lower slopes were very wet indeed, which was reflected in the times. Paul Pietsch did 8 min. 44.5 sec. on his 3.7-litre Maserati, then Clemente Biondetti did 8 min. 41.2 sec. in his 12C Ferrari Alfa. (Curiously, Ferrari's acknowledged mountain expert, Mario Tadini, was not driving a GP car, but a 3.2-litre Mille Miglia Alfa, in the Sports Car class.) Hermann Lang—still not at all happy in the wet—managed 8 min. 29.8 sec., but this was put into perspective on the next run by Hans Stuck, who recorded a superb 8 min. 11 sec., his Auto Union running with twin rear wheels, as it had at Shelsley.

Next was Caracciola—*Der Regenmeister*—surely he would beat that? No, he wouldn't. Rudi could only manage 8 min. 17.7 sec. Now it was all down to Rosemeyer. He

263

1938

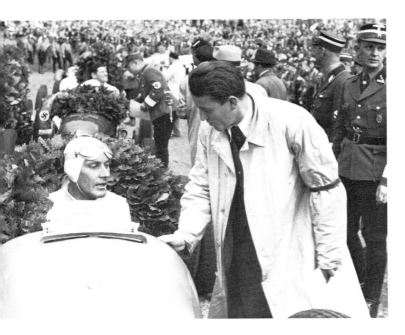

ABOVE **The place is crawling with Nazi troops as Hans Stuck gets his laurels for his magnificent victory at Freiburg in 1937**

Exactly a year later, on 5 August, Stuck was back at La Turbie, where he succeeded in breaking his 1937 record by 1.4 seconds. Then it was on to the Grossglockner at the end of the month for the most important climb of the year, and the *Deutsche Bergmeisterschaft*. At Freiburg the previous year there were rumours that there was to be no race in 1938, but so popular was the 1937 event that Hühnlein agreed that it should continue. Events overtook him, however, and in March Germany appropriated Austria, so it must have seemed a very good idea to hold the *German* Mountain Championship in that country, just to make it clear to other states that Austria was now a part of the German *Reich*.

At first it was intended to use the entire 33.5 km (20.8 mile) length of the Grossglockner Pass, starting at Ferleiten and finishing at Franz Josefs Höhe—the very top. The problem was that at roughly three-quarters distance the road went downhill to the 117 m (383 ft) long Mittertörl-Tunnel. It then climbed again some 200 m (656 ft) to another and even longer tunnel—311 m (1020 ft)—at Hochtor, before plunging 717 m (2352 ft) through a wicked series of hairpin bends to Guttal. It

defended his title brilliantly, driving on—and often over—the limit, as usual, but it wasn't enough. He finished in 8 min. 12.8 sec., almost two seconds slower than the old Mountain King, who thus won the day. It was a dazzling victory for Stuck, who won the title for the third time.

Later, Rodney Walkerley watched the post-race celebrations. 'After the race there was a great presentation of laurel wreaths to the victors in the various classes, presented by Major Hühnlein, with special reference to Hans Stuck, who thus becomes once more *Bergmeister* of Germany. And in the evening down in Freiburg there was a presentation of the actual prizes in the open air, from the steps of the *Rathaus*, in the big square by the wonderful cathedral. After that, it being dark, there was a wine feast, with the whole of Freiburg sitting beneath lanterns at long tables, and the whole of Freiburg grew rapidly inebriated to a greater or lesser degree. And after that there was dancing in the square and the most amazing fireworks, chiefly characterized by deafening detonations to the unstinted admiration of at least 5000 Freiburgers packed in the square.

'Which rather made one think of British races where 20 people have been known to clap the winner, the rest having but a vague idea who actually won, anyway.'

From Freiburg Stuck went straight to Nice and La Turbie, where he used the Auto Union he was to drive in the Monaco GP three days later. Using single rear wheels this time he beat his own record, 'with a terrifying climb, in which he came round all the corners with the rear wheels a yard out of line, and kept his throttle wide open into the corners long after other drivers had thought better of it'. His time of 3 min. 31.6 sec. was eight seconds faster than his 1936 record.

Grossglockner—
Part 1 12.6 km (7.8 miles)
Part 2 7.9 km (4.9 miles)

eventually became clear to the organizers that sending Grand Prix cars through this middle stretch was asking for trouble, so the climb was split into two parts. The first run started at Ferleiten (1152 m/3779 ft) and climbed to Fuscher Törl (2428 m/7965 ft), a distance of 12.6 km (7.8 miles). The cars would then be driven 13 km (8 miles) to the next start at Schobereck, near Guttal (1859 m/6099 ft), the second run being over a distance of 7.9 km (4.9 miles) to Franz Josefs Hohe (2362 m/7749 ft). The times for the two climbs would be added together to find the winner.

Auto Union entered two cars for Hans Stuck and H. P. Müller, but Müller crashed in the Swiss GP the weekend before and so did not turn up for the Grossglockner. Another who was entered but did not start was Dick Seaman. Mercedes proposed to send three cars—two 5.6-litre W125s for Hermann Lang and Manfred von Brauchitsch and a 3-litre W154 for Seaman. These entries appeared in the programme, so Neubauer must have notified the organizers before he bothered to tell his English driver. In the event, he wrote to Dick on 12 August, asking him to go and have a look at the Pass with a view to competing there.

Seaman had raced at the Grossglockner in 1935, so he had a good idea of what it entailed, but a trip to the mountains gave him a splendid opportunity for something that had nothing to do with racing. He went to the Pass, taking Erica Popp with him. He decided that he didn't like the look of the Grossglockner at all, but he very much liked the look of Fraulein Popp, so in that very romantic setting he proposed to her, and his proposal was accepted!

A few days later he wrote back to Neubauer to say that he had found the road in bad repair and considered it very dangerous. He also pointed out that the idea of racing a

450 bhp Mercedes downhill and through two tunnels did not appeal, so thanks, but no thanks! Obviously, at the time of his visit, the decision to split the climb into two parts had not been taken, but Neubauer seems to have made no attempt to change Dick's mind subsequently and he did not take part.

So it was to be the two 5.6-litre Mercedes against the one short-chassis, 6-litre Auto Union. Well aware of the task in front of him, Hermann Lang took himself off to the Mercedes HQ at Zell am See several days before the official practice sessions and spent hours driving up the Grossglockner, trying to familiarize himself with at least some of the landmarks.

On race day the weather was foul and the second climb was found to be under a blanket of cloud! In spite of this, the organizers still wanted to use it, and it took a sit-down strike by the drivers to make them see sense. Eventually the upper climb was abandoned and the event confined to two runs on the lower one—the times being added together. The first heat was run in pouring rain and Hans Stuck mastered the conditions better than the rest with a time of 10 min. 42.1 sec., but Lang was only 2.3 seconds behind. Von Brauchitsch could not break 11 minutes. By the time everyone had driven back to the start, the weather was much better and the road was mostly dry, as the times showed. Stuck took 70 seconds off his previous time, but von Brauchitsch improved by over a minute and a half, beating Lang into second place by 0.3 second! Overall, though, Stuck was the winner, with Lang second and von Brauchitsch third. Once again, the extraordinary Hans Stuck was *Deutsche Bergmeister*. He rounded off the year by winning three minor climbs—the Maloja Pass in Switzerland and the Romanian events at Feleac and Schulerau.

Manfred von Brauchitsch slides his Mercedes exuberantly on the Grossglockner in August 1938. He finished third

1939

In April Stuck won at La Turbie for the fourth year in succession, setting a new record in the process, two seconds faster than his 1938 time. Freiburg was not reinstated, as many must have hoped it would be and indeed, there was again no German mountainclimb as such, but yet another climb was found in Austria. This was at Kahlenberg, just outside Vienna, and it, together with the Grossglockner, would count towards the *Deutsche Bergmeisterschaft*.

Mercedes-Benz and Auto Union entered two cars each for this short, 4 km (2.5 mile) climb, but whereas Stuck and H. P. Müller had to make do with a 6-litre V-16 apiece, Lang and von Brauchitsch had a choice, as Mercedes had put together two very special W125s and two equally special W154s. All four cars had steam cooling (see Chapter 5, *Rudolf Uhlenhaut*) and single or twin rear wheels. Both drivers opted for the latter, but whereas von Brauchitsch raced a W125, Lang found that even with twin wheels at the back, he couldn't get all the 5.6-litre engine's tremendous power onto the road, so he elected to drive the 3-litre car.

Lang won—just. Müller gave him a severe fright by winning the first of the two heats, beating the Mercedes driver by 0.9 sec. But whereas Lang was able to improve his time—by 0.6 sec.—on the second run, Müller was exactly two seconds slower than before, so, on aggregate, Lang won by 0.8 second! Von Brauchitsch was third and, much to everyone's surprise, a very off-form Mountain King Hans Stuck was fourth, and in serious danger of losing the title he had held for so many years.

And lose it he did. Mercedes again took their four special machines to the Grossglockner and this time Lang and von Brauchitsch both chose to use the big cars, but decided to do without the twin rear wheels on this course, which was very narrow in places. The organizers had learned the lessons of 1938 and this year the climb was restricted to two runs on the lower, 12.6 km (7.8 mile) course. Once again it was H. P. Müller who sprang the surprise and won the first heat from Lang, by one second. Stuck was third, just 0.4 sec. behind the Mercedes.

Shortly before the start of the second heat it began to rain, and with the rain came a thick fog. As in 1938, Lang had done a great deal of practising before the event (this time in his new 3.4-litre drophead coupé Mercedes), but all his efforts were for nothing, as the landmarks he had memorized were now hidden in the fog. Just how bad the conditions were is illustrated by his times for the two heats—on the first run he clocked 8 min. 55.3 sec. and on the second, 11 min. 12.6 sec! After what he described as

Hermann Lang practises at Kahlenberg with single rear wheels on his Mercedes. In the event he used twin rears— and won

ABOVE Manfred von Brauchitsch races past the packed rows of spectators at Kahlenberg on his way to third place

RIGHT H. P. Müller won the first heat of the 1939 Grossglockner, but couldn't match Lang's time in the second heat

'the toughest, most uncomfortable drive of my life', Lang had to sit in his car for a few minutes at the finish, in order to pull himself together! One of the first people he met when he did get out was Hans Stuck, who congratulated him on winning the Mountain Championship. Lang couldn't believe it—he had been so slow on that second run! But so had everyone else—except Stuck, who was just 3.2 seconds behind Lang. Müller had ruined his chances with a climb over 20 seconds longer than Lang's and von Brauchitsch was nearly a minute slower than Müller!

So Hermann Lang was *Deutsche Bergmeister* for 1939, bringing the title back to Stuttgart after a gap of several years, during which Hans Stuck (and Bernd Rosemeyer) had reigned supreme.

Mountainclimb Results

1934

June 10—Felsberg 8 km/5 m
1 Hans Stuck (Auto Union) 147.3 km/h (91.53 mph)
2 Paul Pietsch (Alfa Romeo)

June 17—Kesselberg 5 km/3.1 m
1 Hans Stuck (Auto Union) 3 min. 44.0 sec.—80.4 km/h (49.96 mph)
2 M. von Brauchitsch (Mercedes-Benz) 3 min. 49.2 sec.
3 Paul Pietsch (Alfa Romeo) 3 min. 52.2 sec.

August 5—Klausenpass 21.5 km/13.36 m
1 Rudolf Caracciola (Mercedes-Benz) 15 min. 22.2 sec.—83.87 km/h (52.13 mph)
2 Hans Stuck (Auto Union) 15 min. 25.4 sec.
3 Whitney Straight (Maserati) 16 min. 20.6 sec.

August 19—Freiburg 12 km/7.45 m
1 Hans Stuck (Auto Union) 8 min. 06.6 sec.—88.78 km/h (55.17 mph)
2 Rudolf Caracciola (Mercedes-Benz) 8 min. 32.5 sec.
3 Ernst von Delius (Alfa Romeo) 8 min. 45.6 sec.

September 16—Mt Ventoux 21.6 km (13.4 m)
1 Hans Stuck (Auto Union) 13 min. 38.6 sec.—94.38 km/h (58.64 mph)
2 Whitney Straight (Maserati) 13 min. 58.8 sec.
3 Benoit Falchetto (Maserati) 14 min. 14.4 sec.

1935

June 30—Kesselberg 5 km (3.1 m)
1 Hans Stuck (Auto Union) 3 min. 44.3 sec.—79.96 km/h (49.7 mph)
2 Juan Zanelli (Nacional Pescara) 3 min. 48.2 sec.
3 Renato Balestrero (Alfa Romeo)

August 4—Grossglockner 19.5 km (12 m)
1 Mario Tadini (Alfa Romeo) 14 min. 42.7 sec.—79.56 km/h (49.45 mph)
2 Richard Seaman (ERA) 14 min. 54.0 sec.
3 H. Kessler (Maserati) 14 min. 57.0 sec.

Magnificent shot of von Brauchitsch sliding on the cobblestones in Heat 1 of the 1939 Grossglockner

September 1—Freiburg 12 km (7.45 m)
1 Hans Stuck (Auto Union) 8 min. 24.1 sec.—85.6 km/h (53.19 mph)
2 Richard Seaman (ERA) 8 min. 25.1 sec.
3 Raymond Mays (ERA) 8 min. 36.1 sec.

September 1—Stelvio 14 km (8.69 m)
1 Mario Tadini (Alfa Romeo) 14 min. 15.5 sec.—58.88 km/h (36.6 mph)
2 Tazio Nuvolari (Alfa Romeo) 14 min. 32.7 sec.
3 Piero Dusio (Maserati) 14 min. 36.2 sec.
4 Hans Ruesch (Maserati) 14 min. 45.7 sec.
5 Achille Varzi (Auto Union) 14 min. 51.6 sec.

October 6—Feldberg 12 km (7.45 m)
1 Hans Stuck (Auto Union) 6 min. 22.3 sec.—112.9 km/h (70.16 mph)
2 Bobby Kohlrausch (MG) 7 min. 05.3 sec.
3 H. Wimmer (Bugatti) 7 min. 12.1 sec.

1936

April 9—La Turbie 6.3 km (3.9 m)
1 Hans Stuck (Auto Union) 3 min. 39.8 sec.—103.18 km/h (64.11 mph)
2 J.-P. Wimille (Bugatti) 3 min. 43.4 sec.
3 Chambost (Maserati) 3 min. 52.8 sec.

June 6—Shelsley Walsh 0.91 km (0.56 m)
1 Raymond Mays (ERA) 41.6 sec.
2 Walter Baumer (Austin) and A. F. P. Fane (Frazer-Nash) 42.6 sec.
4 C. L. Goodacre (Austin) 43.2 sec.
5 D. G. Evans (MG Midget) and Hans Stuck (Auto Union) 45.2 sec.

August 30—Freiburg 12 km (7.45 m)
1 Bernd Rosemeyer (Auto Union) 7 min. 59.3 sec.—90.1 km/h (55.99 mph)
2 Ernst von Delius (Auto Union) 8 min. 01.9 sec.
3 Antonio Brivio (Alfa Romeo) 8 min. 27.6 sec.

September 27—Feldberg 12 km (7.45 m)
1 Bernd Rosemeyer (Auto Union) 6 min. 23.2 sec.—112.7 km/h (70.3 mph)
2 H. Mehl (Mercedes-Benz)

1937

August 1—Freiburg 12 km (7.45 m)
1 Hans Stuck (Auto Union) 8 min. 11.0 sec.—88.0 km/h (54.68 mph)
2 Bernd Rosemeyer (Auto Union) 8 min. 12.8 sec.
3 Rudolf Caracciola (Mercedes-Benz) 8 min. 17.7 sec.
4 Hermann Lang (Mercedes-Benz) 8 min. 28.9 sec.

August 5—La Turbie 6.3 km (3.9 m)
1 Hans Stuck (Auto Union) 3 min. 31.6 sec.—
 107.18 km/h (66.6 mph)
2 Raymond Sommer (Alfa Romeo) 3 min. 40.0 sec.

1938

August 5—La Turbie 6.3 km (3.9 m)
1 Hans Stuck (Auto Union) 3 min. 30.2 sec.—
 107.89 km/h (67.04 mph)
2 René Dreyfus (Delahaye) 3 min. 40.6 sec.
3 Raymond Sommer (Alfa Romeo) 3 min. 45.2 sec.

August 28—Grossglockner 12.6 km (7.82 m)
Heat 1
1 Hans Stuck (Auto Union) 10 min. 42.1 sec.—
 70.63 km/h (43.88 mph)
2 Hermann Lang (Mercedes-Benz) 10 min. 44.4 sec.
3 M. von Brauchitsch (Mercedes-Benz) 11 min. 07.4 sec.

Heat 2
1 Hans Stuck (Auto Union) 9 min. 32.4 sec.—79.19 km/h
 (49.20 mph)
2 M. von Brauchitsch (Mercedes-Benz) 9 min. 34.0 sec.
3 Hermann Lang (Mercedes-Benz) 9 min. 34.3 sec.

Total Times
1 Hans Stuck (Auto Union) 20 min. 14.5 sec.—
 74.91 km/h (46.50 mph)
2 Hermann Lang (Mercedes-Benz) 20 min. 18.7 sec.
3 M. von Brauchitsch (Mercedes-Benz) 20 min. 41.4 sec.

September 25—Maloja Pass 4.8 km (2.98 m)
1 Hans Stuck (Auto Union) 72.73 km/h (45.19 mph)

October 5—Feleac 7 km (4.34 m)
1 Hans Stuck (Auto Union) 149.18 km/h (92.7 mph)

1939

April 13—La Turbie 6.3 km/3.9 m
1 Hans Stuck (Auto Union) 3 min. 28.2 sec.—
 108.93 km/h (67.69 mph)
2 J.-P. Wimille (Bugatti)
3 Raymond Sommer (Alfa Romeo)

June 11—Kahlenberg 4.12 km/2.56 m
Heat 1
1 H. P. Müller (Auto Union) 2 min. 18.7 sec.—
 106.9 km/h (66.42 mph)
2 Hermann Lang (Mercedes-Benz) 2 min. 19.6 sec.
3 M. von Brauchitsch (Mercedes-Benz) 2 min. 20.5 sec.
4 Hans Stuck (Auto Union) 2 min. 20.7 sec.

Heat 2
1 Hermann Lang (Mercedes-Benz) 2 min. 19.0 sec.
2 M. von Brauchitsch (Mercedes-Benz) 2 min. 19.2 sec.
3 H. P. Müller (Auto Union) 2 min. 20.7 sec.
4 Hans Stuck (Auto Union) 2 min. 22.8 sec.

Total Times
1 Hermann Lang (Mercedes-Benz) 4 min. 38.6 sec.—
 105.3 km/h (65.43 mph)
2 H. P. Müller (Auto Union) 4 min. 39.4 sec.
3 M. von Brauchitsch (Mercedes-Benz) 4 min. 39.7 sec.
4 Hans Stuck (Auto Union) 4 min. 43.5 sec.

August 6—Grossglockner 12.6 km (7.83 m)
Heat 1
1 H. P. Müller (Auto Union) 8 min. 54.3 sec.—84.8 km/h
 (52.69 mph)
2 Hermann Lang (Mercedes-Benz) 8 min. 55.3 sec.
3 Hans Stuck (Auto Union) 8 min. 55.7 sec.
4 M. von Brauchitsch (Mercedes-Benz) 9 min. 13.9 sec.

Heat 2
1 Hermann Lang (Mercedes-Benz) 11 min. 12.6 sec.
2 Hans Stuck (Auto Union) 11 min. 15.8 sec.
3 H. P. Müller (Auto Union) 11 min. 35.7 sec.
4 M. von Brauchitsch (Mercedes-Benz) 12 min. 27.3 sec.

Total Times
1 Hermann Lang (Mercedes-Benz) 20 min. 07.9 sec.—
 75.09 km/h (46.66 mph)
2 Hans Stuck (Auto Union) 20 min. 11.5 sec.
3 H. P. Müller (Auto Union) 20 min. 30.0 sec.
4 M. von Brauchitsch (Mercedes-Benz) 21 min. 41.6 sec.

HONOUR for Donington: H.R.H. The Duke of Kent, who started the race and made a tour of the circuit, seen with Mr. Time-keeper Ebblewhite and on the right, Alfred Neubauer, Mercedes team chief.

The great little man in action: Nuvolari at Coppice.

NUVOLARI: MAESTRO!

Nuvolari (Auto Union) Wins Donington Grand Prix in Brilliant Style After Losing Lead and Regaining It.   Dobson First British Driver

IT is true to say that every Grand Prix in which the Formula cars take part is in its own way sensational. The very progress of these 400 h.p. 1-ton cars round the circuits of Europe is sensational enough. The Donington Grand Prix was no exception. First of all the speed, the noise and the very shape of the cars staggered the largest crowd which has ever watched a motor race in this country—over 60,000 of them, literally awe-struck during the first few laps and bubbling over with enthusiasm throughout the race.

Then sensation piled on sensation. Nuvolari leaped into the lead from the moment H.R.H. the Duke of Kent started the race—a signal honour for the Derby and District Club. The Italian led for 26 laps from Muller and Seaman at over 80 m.p.h. Then he stopped to change a plug and fell to fourth place. Next came the episode of oil on the course, which sent every German car flying off the road, put Hasse out of the race, and delayed Seaman a lap. Thus at 37 laps Muller led from Lang and Nuvolari. At 38 laps Lang stopped for fuel, without losing his place. Then Muller stopped and Lang led, Muller second, Nuvolari third. At 42 laps Nuvolari refilled but was still third. Nuvolari set about catching up, made up the gap of nearly a minute, did the race's fastest lap at over 83 m.p.h., caught Muller at 52 laps, caught Lang at 67 laps, and then ran right away to win by 1 min. 38 secs. at 80.49 m.p.h.

FRUITS OF VICTORY: at the prize-giving in the grandstand. From left to right in front: Lord Austin, Tazio Nuvolari, Mrs. Bemrose, General Huhnlein and Frau Huhnlein. Left of the General is Mr. Shields, owner of Donington Park and between the General and Frau Huhnlein, Dr. Feureissen, Auto Union team manager.

Kautz crashed twice on the third lap and retired; Villoresi (Maserati) and both Delahayes all retired. Hasse crashed and retired. Arthur Dobson led the British cars all through with some ease and finished only six laps late. Cudden-Fletcher ran off the course, Hanson and Maclure blew up.

The Race, by " Grande Vitesse "

NEVER has there been such a race in England. Never has such a crowd watched motor racing. A lovely autumnal morning, streams of traffic from every point of the compass, well over 60,000 people thronging to Donington. A signal honour for the

LAP ONE at the Hairpin: Nuvolari's 3 secs. lead from Muller, Brauchitsch (Mercedes) third man.

RESULTS :

Date: October 22. Circuit: Donington, 3.125 miles to the lap. Distance: 80 laps, 250 miles.
1. Tazio Nuvolari (Auto Union), 3 hrs. 6 mins. 22 secs.; 80.49 m.p.h.
2. Hermann Lang (Mercedes), 3 hrs. 8 mins.; 79.79 m.p.h.
3. Richard Seaman (Mercedes), 79.48 m.p.h.; one lap behind.
4. Hermann Muller (Auto Union), 79.01 m.p.h.; one lap behind leader.
5. Manfred von Brauchitsch (Mercedes); one lap behind.

6. Arthur Dobson (E.R.A.); six laps behind leader.
7. Billy Cotton—Wilkinson (E.R.A.); six laps behind leader.
8. Ian Connell—Monkhouse (E.R.A.); six laps behind leader.
Fastest Lap: Tazio Nuvolari's 63rd lap— 2 mins. 14.4 secs. Speed, 83.71 m.p.h. Receives Craner Trophy and £100.
Leader at Half-distance: Hermann Muller. Receives £50.

race and its organizers, as well as for the foreign drivers; H.R.H. the Duke of Kent there to start the race. General Huhnlein, head of German motor sport and high in Nazi councils, came specially for the race, and with him the president and vice-president of the O.N.S. (German "R.A.C.") and members of the German Embassy from London. The grandstand packed, the military band playing, a crowd several deep right round the entire course, car

And they say motor racing is not popular in England.

NUVOLARI: MAESTRO! . . . Contd.

parks black with cars; there has never been anything like it in this country before.

Just before the start Dick Seaman drove the Duke of Kent round the circuit twice—one quite fast lap—in a fine 12-cylinder Lagonda, and Lionel Martin performed a like service for General Huhnlein in a Bentley.

Then the cars came in slow procession down the course with mechanics at the wheel, a sight which set the crowd buzzing with excitement. The line-up on the grid, engines silent now. The drivers get in, Nuvolari last of all in red helmet, yellow jumper and blue trousers. Seaman in a green helmet, Brauchitsch red, Lang white, Baumer blue.

Thirty seconds to go. The Duke raises the Union Jack. The portable electric starters whirr, the air shakes with the roaring song of the eight German cars, the British cars seem silent in that din. The crowd goes dumb.

Down goes the flag, the crashing exhausts howl to an ear-splitting shriek, and as one the field surges forward wheel-to-wheel.

feeling ill for days, went off the road at Coppice, restarted and went off again at Melbourne, embedding his Auto Union in the earth bank.

On the fourth lap, while the crowd was still recovering, Seaman passed Brauchitsch into third place. Villoresi, 11th on the first lap, began to pass car after car on successive laps, ripping off the revs. with a fine crispness. Raph (Delahaye two-seater) came to the pit after three laps with the engine smoking, stopped again at eight laps and retired at 10 laps.

Muller, 14 secs. behind Nuvolari and with Seaman on his very tail, shot past Hanson (Alta) on the inside at McClean's corner. Dobson, 10th and easily leading the British race, was just behind Dreyfus (single-seater Delahaye) and holding him, but at 13 laps Nuvolari lapped Dobson, and at 16 laps lapped Dreyfus as well!

Maserati Gains and Retires

At 15 laps Villoresi was sixth, in front of Hasse and Baumer. At 16 laps he passed Brauchitsch, and at 18 laps a piston broke. Exit Maserati. Cuddon-Fletcher ran off the road at Melbourne

SLIDE: *Manfred von Brauchitsch enjoying himself.*

roared—Nuvolari shot into the pit and had a plug changed, sitting calmly at the wheel. He lost 53 secs. and fell back to fourth place. So Muller led from Seaman (just behind him), Lang and Nuvolari. Seaman neatly slipped past Billy Cotton as they shot under the Stone Bridge. Wow!

Whenever he wanted to pass a slower car Nuvolari waved one hand to the flag marshals, they gave the signal, the other driver pulled over, and Nuvolari went by. The system worked like a charm—but imagine taking one hand off at over 90 m.p.h. down the bumpy hill to the Hairpin! I ask you!

Slump in Oil

Then, at 30 laps, Hanson broke a con-rod and dropped oil near the Old Paddock. The German cars flashed down the winding hill one after the other, and then everything began to happen at once. Cars flew off the road in all directions. They went broadside, they spun round, they went backwards.

Of course, My Man George (The Most Thrown-out Man in Europe) was on the spot when the Great Oil Crisis happened, and I can do no better than quote him, as I was seated in front of a lap chart and stop-watch at the time:—

"Hanson blew up completely, coming out of Holly Wood, and on the very fast downhill bend towards the Old Paddock dropped very large quantities of oil, likewise on the Hairpin, and then pulled off the course near the Stone Bridge. Nuvolari, following him, sensed something wrong and in avoiding the biggest patch of oil got into a slide and went straight on onto the grass on the right of the road, recovered, went back on the road, and with a lot of dicing got up to the Hairpin and away.

"Brauchitsch was next. He got into a series of wild slides just off the

(Continued after Photogravure Section.)

LANG *in a hurry, trying to get away from Nuvolari, takes the bump at the Hairpin.*

As they shot for Red Gate, Nuvolari left the ruck as if catapulted. He led all round the first lap, Muller (Auto Union) on his tail, then Brauchitsch (Mercedes)—with his injured hand and feeling off form—then Seaman. Lang, Baumer, Hasse, Kautz, Dreyfus, Dobson (going marvellously) and Villoresi, after a sluggish get-away. And Nuvolari led the first lap by 3 secs.

Lap after lap the grand little Italian dropped the pursuit—5 secs., 6 secs., 7 secs., 10 secs.—lapping at 82 m.p.h. On the third lap Kautz, who had been

and retired. Percy Maclure (Riley) broke his back axle. The order in the British field was: Dobson, Connell, Cotton (E.R.A.s) and Hanson (two-seater Alta—which was slow).

At 20 laps Nuvolari had pulled out to 21 secs. lead at 82.07 m.p.h. Muller (next up) was one second ahead of Dick Seaman, who was driving marvellously. Then came Lang, 4 secs. behind Seaman, Brauchitsch (half a minute behind), Hasse, Baumer, Dreyfus, Dobson and the rest.

Three laps later Dreyfus was out. Three more laps and the crowd

October 25, 1938.   611   The **Motor**

NUVOLARI: MAESTRO! . . . . Contd.

road and back, spun round twice on the road, arrived sideways at the Hairpin and got round it all right.

" Next came Hasse. He went off to the right on the grass, then slammed across the road on to the grass on the left, took down some fencing, missed a hut and a tree by inches, slid on and finished astride the safety bank, thrown out of his car. Mrs. Craner (wife of the Clerk of the Course) was in the hut and got a close-up view. Hasse was unhurt and tried hard to impress on the officials that something should be done about the oil as he thought it a bit perilous.

" Seaman came next, travelling fast and apparently not seeing the yellow flag. Went out wide to the right, slammed across the road and ended up on soft ground on the left beyond Hasse's bent car. He shouted to the crowd not to touch the car and tried to manhandle it himself. An official said it was all right for officials to assist, and Dick shouted for them to push. Eventually they arrived and he restarted amidst great cheering."

After all this—which might have been a frightful catastrophe—Seaman was a lap behind and the order was: Muller (5 secs. lead), Lang, Nuvolari, Brauchitsch, Baumer, Seaman, Dobson, Connell, and Cotton's car now driven by Wilkinson.

At 38 laps (119 miles) Lang stopped to refill (no tyres) and was off in 33 secs. still second. At 40 laps (125 miles—mid-distance) leader Muller refilled and changed rear wheels in 40 secs., dropping to second place. At 42 laps Nuvolari made his second stop, refilled, changed all wheels and was off again in 35 secs. Is this pit work or is it?

Baumer and Seaman refilled on their 41st lap, a lap behind the leaders, Seaman in 44 secs. (fuel only), Baumer in 1 min. 19 secs. (fuel and plugs). Connell handed over to Monkhouse. Brauchitsch refilled on his 39th lap in 30 secs.

Sheer Wizardry

After all this Nuvolari was a long way behind, still third, with Lang leading Muller by 23 secs. Nuvolari rolled his sleeves up and, roaring with laughter, set about motor racing in earnest. He came through the bends with his elbows flashing up and down like pistons, the steering wheel jerking quickly from side to side—and yet all the time the car ran as if on rails, the front wheels always pointing dead on the line of travel. Maestro.

There's no doubt little Tazio was on top of his form. He is 49 years of age. He was driving a car, he said, last year was unmanageable. And yet he was driving as he drove 15 years ago, doing things no one else can do, and slowly catching up after his two pit stops to his rivals' one.

At 43 laps Baumer came in with the engine on fire and retired. Dobson, driving better than I have ever seen him, was 2½ mins. ahead of the next E.R.A. and sixth in the race. Magnificent. And then Nuvolari pulled out a fastest lap at 82.72 m.p.h., just to show them. At 50 laps he was 58 secs. behind leader Lang, 17 secs. behind Muller. At 53 laps he passed Muller. At 54 laps he was 39 secs. behind Lang.

Gradually the gap lessened. Lang could do nothing about it. I suspected his brakes weren't too good any more. Neubauer warned him every lap as he fled past the pits. But every lap Nuvolari drew closer and closer, still smiling all over his face, never making a mistake, changing down and braking at exactly the same spots on every corner every lap. At 56 laps he did 82.96 m.p.h.—fastest lap of the day. At 60 laps he was 21 secs. behind, Lang averaging 80.01 m.p.h. At 63 laps Nuvolari went faster still—83.71

BANG! Rudolf Hasse (Auto Union) comes to a full stop against the earth bank down by the Old Paddock, after skidding off the road on the pool of oil dropped during the early stages. All the German cars flew off the road at this point one after the other—an eye-witness sketch by Nevin.

PUSH, you chaps! Arthur Dobson, easily leading the British contingent, restarting in his veteran E.R.A. after a refuelling stop. He drove a magnificent race—which must also be said for the other British drivers as well.

NUVOLARI: MAESTRO! . . . . Contd.

All honour to the little British cars, which went so well and reliably, only 20 miles behind at the end of 250 miles; and, what is more, winning the team prize outright, for both German teams lost a member en route.

What a race! And over 60,000 delighted spectators departed swearing to come back in greater numbers next year. Which reminds me, both Mercedes and Auto Unions intend to visit us again in 1939.

Starting Positions

Giving best practice lap in brackets

First Row (left to right facing up the course): Lang (Mercedes—2 mins. 11 secs.), Nuvolari (Auto Union—2:11.2), Brauchitsch (Mercedes—2:11.4), Seaman (Mercedes—2:12.2).

Second Row: Muller (Auto Union—2:12.6), Baumer (Mercedes—2:13.8), Hasse (Auto Union—2:15.4).

Third Row: Kautz (Auto Union—2:18.6), Villoresi (Maserati—2:21), Dobson (E.R.A.—2:24.6), Dreyfus (Delahaye—2:25.4).

Fourth Row: Connell (E.R.A.—2:27.2), Cotton (E.R.A.—2:28.6), Cuddon-Fletcher (M.G.—2:29.8).

Back Row: Maclure (Riley—2:30.4), Hanson (Alta—2:32.2), Raph (Delahaye—2:36.4).

How the Order Changed

10 laps (31¼ miles)
1, Nuvolari, at 81.57 m.p.h.
2, Muller; 14.6 secs. behind.
3, Seaman; 15.8 secs. behind Nuvolari.
4, Lang; 22 secs. behind Nuvolari.
5, Brauchitsch; 30 secs. behind Nuvolari.

20 laps (62½ miles)
1, Nuvolari; leading at 82.07 m.p.h.
2, Muller; 21.8 secs. behind.
3, Seaman; 22.6 secs. behind Nuvolari.
4, Lang, 26.8 secs. behind Nuvolari.
5, Brauchitsch; 1 min. 6 secs. behind Nuvolari.

30 laps (93¾ miles)
1, Muller; leading at 80.10 m.p.h.
2, Seaman; 2.8 secs. behind Muller.
3, Lang; 4 secs. behind Muller.
4, Nuvolari; 59.4 secs. behind Muller.
5, Brauchitsch; 1:32.8 behind Muller.

m.p.h., and closed to 12 secs. Lap by lap the lead vanished—10 secs., 6 secs., 3 secs.—and at 67 laps the little Italian caught the Mercedes on Starkey Straight, pulled out, slammed his foot down, and shot past on maximum speed—about 160 m.p.h.

After that it was all over bar the very considerable shouting. Nuvolari ran clean away, Lang next, then Muller, then Seaman and Brauchitsch a lap behind. Seaman was actually about 8 secs. behind Nuvolari on the course, gained a yard here, lost it there, driving, in my view, better than any German on the circuit. At 69 laps he caught Muller and left him, running a minute behind Lang.

And so the last enthralling laps ran out with Nuvolari's lead mounting and mounting—41 secs., 1 minute, 1:7, 1:15, 1:20, 1:30—there was nothing Lang could do against this mighty display of sheer wizardry. And then, just after 3 p.m. (the race started at noon), Nuvolari finished amidst such an ova-

tion as I have never heard in this country before.

During the closing stages Cotton took over again from Wilkinson, overtook the Connell—Monkhouse combine, and chased Dobson, but could never get near enough to hurt.

Nuvolari Mobbed

After the race the crowd mobbed Nuvolari, who was very affected. Never, he said, had he had a warmer reception. After the prize-giving in the stand the "Deutschland Uber Alles" for Germany and the "Giovinezza" for Nuvolari, his only thought was some food. He'd had only a cup of coffee and four sandwiches. He spoke little on his way back to his hotel, except to repeat how delighted he was at his ovation. "England is lucky for me," he said, "three times I have raced here, three times I have won." And Auto Unions, in face of strong Mercedes opposition, have twice won the Donington Grand Prix.

STAG-ERING. Maestro Nuvolari started well during practice before the race. First he ran over a stag which wandered on the course (and sent the head home to Italy as a trophy) and next he did a record lap in 2 mins.11.2secs.—faster than the 1937 race lap record. Lang beat this in practice next day in 2 mins. 11 secs. dead.

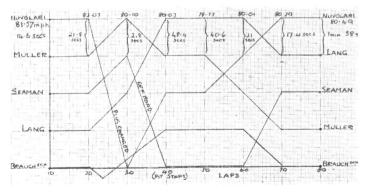

GRAPHIC.—This graph illustrates most clearly the changes in leadership during the course of the race, and the manner in which Nuvolari regained his lost lead.

THE YEAR IN PICTURES

ABOVE 28 January 1938. Rudolf Caracciola sets out on a record-breaking run with the new Mercedes. A few hours later Bernd Rosemeyer crashed to his death trying to win the records back for Auto Union

RIGHT Caracciola chats to his mechanics shortly before the start of the Tripoli GP

RIGHT The Mercedes mechanics are jubilant as Dick Seaman wins the German GP. Caracciola (in raincoat, *centre*) is apparently unmoved, but Rudolf Uhlenhaut (*right*) is clearly delighted

BELOW Alfred Neubauer (with flag) and Rudolf Uhlenhaut wave Caracciola in after his Coppa Acerbo victory

ABOVE **Caracciola is about to devour two Auto Unions (8 is Stuck's) as he comes onto the pit straight at Bern during the Swiss GP**

LEFT **Happy man! Rudi looks well pleased with himself after his brilliant victory in the rain at Bern**

BELOW **Caracciola again—
clinching the 1938
European Championship—
with third place in the
Italian GP**

280

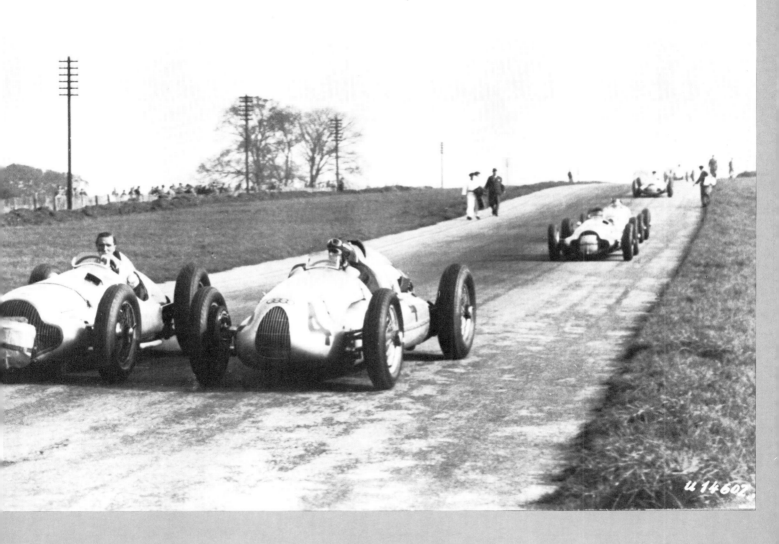

ABOVE **Manfred von
Brauchitsch** (*left*) **and
Tazio Novolari lead the
cars down to the pits before
the start of the Donington
GP. Nuvolari won a great
victory**

Bremgarten (Bern)

LENGTH: 7.28 km (4.52 miles)
RACE: Swiss GP (1934-9)

Throughout its life the Bremgarten circuit was considered to be one of the finest and most demanding in the world. Situated in a huge park which itself was part of a great forest to the north-west of Bern, the circuit was originally used for motorcycle racing in 1931 and the success of that led to the first Swiss Grand Prix being held there in 1934.

The man responsible for organizing the race was a Monsieur Huber, and it was he who had the huge concrete grandstand built with the pits opposite, set well back from the track. Because they were set so far from the road, signalling from them was impossible, so special wooden signalling pits were built on the inside of the track, just beyond the grandstand.

Grand Prix racing got off to a bad start in Switzerland because in the very first race the English driver Hugh Hamilton was killed when he lost control of his Maserati and hit a tree. The next year, during practice, Hanns Geier had one of the most gi-normous accidents of all time when he crashed his Mercedes at very high speed in front of the pits (see Chapter 2, *Hanns Geier*). There was another bad crash during the race, when Louis Chiron went off the road. Fortunately, he was not hurt, but the accidents worried Monsieur Huber and in 1936 he turned up at the Monaco Grand Prix to talk to the drivers about the possibility of putting some chicanes up at Bremgarten. Whereas the French and Italians had been scattering chicanes about their circuits in an attempt to give their cars a better chance against the enormously fast German machines, Monsieur Huber had no such axe to grind—he was simply concerned for the safety of drivers and spectators on his very fast circuit. Clearly, the drivers he spoke to did not see the need for chicanes, so Bremgarten remained free of them and continued to provide some of the most spectacular sights in Grand Prix racing for the rest of the decade.

RIGHT **Hermann Lang blasts through Tenne Corner in the 1937 Swiss GP. The bridge in the background crosses the Wohlensee**

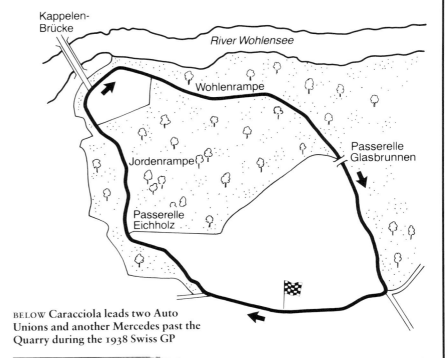

BELOW **Caracciola leads two Auto Unions and another Mercedes past the Quarry during the 1938 Swiss GP**

Donington Park

LENGTH: 5.03 km (3.125 miles)
RACE: Donington GP (1937, 1938)

The races in which the two German teams took part in 1937 and 1938 should, by rights, have been called the British Grands Prix, but since they were entirely the work of Fred Craner and the Derby and District Motor Club, the snooty RAC in London refused to allow the national title to be used, so they were proudly called the Donington Grand Prix.

Craner was the driving force behind Donington. He was a former racing motorcyclist who had taken part in seven Isle of Man TTs, among many other races, so it is hardly surprising that the first races at Donington—in 1931—were for motorcycles. The first circuit was 3.52 km (2.19 miles) long and this was lengthened in 1934 to 4.10 km (2.55 miles). The first two Grands Prix were held in 1935 and 1936 and while Craner was very keen to get the European GP circus to Donington he was well aware that various improvements were needed before a full, international Grand Prix could be held—at one point the road ran between a farmhouse and some cowsheds where no overtaking was allowed, and at another there was a very narrow stone bridge to be navigated!

However, Craner made all the necessary alterations—including the addition of an extra loop from Starkey's Corner down to the new Melbourne Hairpin, lengthening the circuit to 5.03 km (3.12 miles)—in time for the 1937 race. These were enough to bring three cars from Auto Union and four from Mercedes. When the Germans eventually arrived, the sight and sound of their stupendous machines as they positively devoured the Donington circuit boggled the minds of all beholders, as Rodney Walkerley recorded in *The Motor* a week later.

'The British spectators, who had read about these cars and only partly believed what they had read, were struck all of a heap. Even Fleet Street journalists were going about in a daze during the practising, mouthing and gibbering.'

In spite of a few problems, the Germans were generally impressed with Donington and the way it was run, Neubauer going so far as to say that if the bumps were smoothed out and the track made a bit wider he couldn't wish

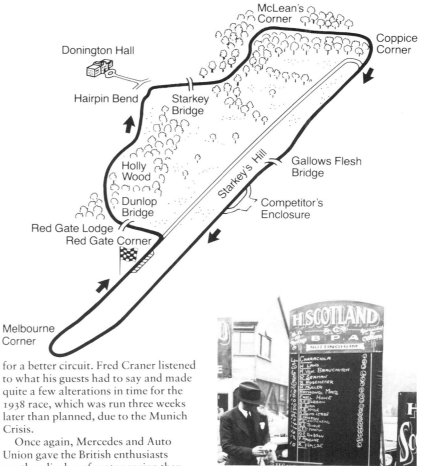

for a better circuit. Fred Craner listened to what his guests had to say and made quite a few alterations in time for the 1938 race, which was run three weeks later than planned, due to the Munich Crisis.

Once again, Mercedes and Auto Union gave the British enthusiasts another display of motor racing they would never forget, even if they were no longer able to watch the Silver Arrows take off as they roared over Melbourne Rise! Naturally, Fred Craner made plans for the 1939 Donington Grand Prix, but by the time it was scheduled to take place, England and Germany were at war.

ABOVE At Donington in 1937 the bookies' odds were as strange as their spelling! Sadly, most of them did a bunk right after the race rather than pay out

BELOW Under the bridge at Donington go H. P. Müller (Auto Union) and Dick Seaman (Mercedes) during the 1938 GP

Pescara

LENGTH: 25.58 km (15.84 miles) (1924–33)
25.80 km (16.03 miles) (1934–39)
RACE: Coppa Acerbo

Pescara was a triangular circuit comprising two ultra-fast 6.4 km (4 mile) straights joined by a very hilly and twisty 13 km (8 mile) stretch. The Start/Finish was three-quarters of the way down the straight which ran along the Adriatic coast from the railway station at Montesilvano to the outskirts of the old fortress town of Pescara. There it turned sharp right and headed inland through a series of bends and hills, past the Villa Raspa, through the village of Spoltore and on to Cappelle sul Tavo. Just outside this village the road curved right round through a hairpin bend which led on to the second straight. This led downhill to Montesilvano Station and was the fastest part of the course, on which the AC di Pescara marked out a timed kilometre.

Racing began at Pescara in 1924 and the event was named by one of Benito Mussolini's Cabinet Ministers,

Under a dramatic Mussolini banner, the fields gets away at the start of the 1937 Coppa Acerbo at Pescara, Caracciola just leading from Rosemeyer (10) and Stuck (4).

Professor Giacomo Acerbo, in memory of his brother, Captain Tito Acerbo, who had been killed in the last year of World War 1. The first Coppa Acerbo was won by Enzo Ferrari, no less, on an Alfa Romeo and with the exception of 1929 the race was held every year until 1940.

The great length of the coastal

Caracciola sweeps through Cappelle village during practice for the 1938 Coppa Acerbo

straight meant that the cars were passing the pits/grandstand area at very high speed, so a large chicane was introduced just before the pits in 1934. This chicane was, in fact, four right-angle corners which formed a detour sufficient to increase the length of the circuit a little.

Over the Flying Kilometre the Mercedes of Caracciola and Henne were timed at very nearly 290 km/h (180 mph) and although the Alfa Romeos put up a brave fight (during which poor Guy Moll was killed) they

were clearly out-paced, so for 1935 the Italians introduced two more chicanes, one halfway down each straight. In spite of the fact that one was positioned shortly before the timed kilometre, Bernd Rosemeyer managed to record 277 km/h (172 mph) that year and in 1936 Achille Varzi went even faster, hitting 295.4 km/h (183.64 mph). The last Coppa Acerbo before World War II was held in 1939 when, like all Italian races that year, it was restricted to cars of up to 1500 cc.

Monza

LENGTH: 10 km (6.214 miles) (1922–33)
4.31 km (2.69 miles) (1934)
6.95 km (4.32 miles) (1935, 1936)
6.99 km (4.35 miles) (1938)

RACE: Italian GP

Situated in an old royal park close to the small town of Monza, just north of Milan, the Monza Autodrome was built by the Milan Automobile Club in 1922. Both Felice Nazzaro and Vincenzo Lancia were present at the ground-breaking ceremony and the circuit itself was reportedly completed in the incredibly short space of 100 days, no less than 3500 labourers being brought in to see that the job was done on time.

The course was unique in that it incorporated a banked speed bowl with a normal road circuit. The road ran under the banking at one point and the two tracks ran side by side in front of 13 grandstands!

The race was a great success until 1928, when Emilio Materassi's Talbot came off the South Curve and onto the finishing straight where it swerved violently and went into the crowd,

killing Materassi and 27 spectators, another 20 being badly injured. Although racing continued at Monza, the Italian GP did not return there until 1931 and tragedy struck again in 1933 when three drivers, Giuseppe Campari, Baconin Borzacchini and Count Stanislas Czaikowski, were all killed when they slid off the track on a patch of oil during a heat.

In something of a panic after this disaster, the Monza authorities drastically altered the circuit for the 1934 race. Well aware of the very high speeds of the new German cars, they put a chicane in each of the slightly banked South Curves and ran the race anti-clockwise over a much shorter circuit of 4.31 km (2.69 miles). The drivers had to cover no less than 116 laps, which

proved to be very tiring indeed. The circuit was altered again the next year, being run clockwise once more and over a longer, 6.95 km (4.32 mile) track, which had four straw-bale chicanes as well as the double chicane which had been employed on the South Turn the previous year. This circuit was used again in 1936, but for 1937 the Italians moved their Grand Prix to Livorno—home of the Coppa Ciano—in the hope that a slower circuit would improve the chances of the Italian cars. It didn't, so the race was returned to Monza for 1938 and 1939. The Germans won the former again, but at least Nuvolari was driving the winning Auto Union. For 1939 the Italians restricted all their races to 1500 cc cars, but by the time of the Italian GP, Germany was at war.

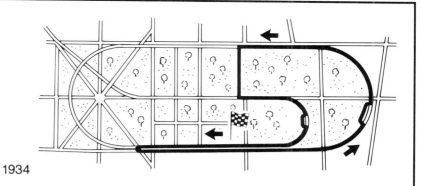

1934

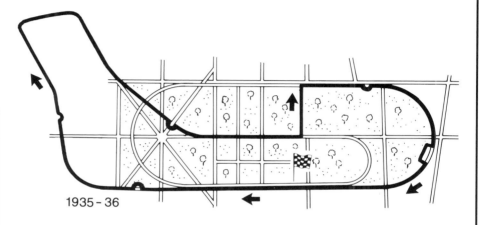

1935 – 36

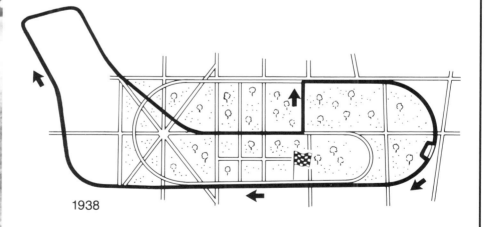

1938

LEFT in 1934 the Monza track was divided to allow cars to run in both directions on the main straight during the Italian GP, as demonstrated here by two Auto Unions

SEVEN

1939

=====1939=====

The End of a Golden Age

After the Munich Crisis (which had caused the postpone-ment of the Donington GP for three weeks) a jittery Europe settled down a bit over the winter. In Stuttgart and Zwickau, Mercedes and Auto Union refined their cars for the new season, both resorting to two-stage supercharging in their successful search for more power. Visually, the 1939 Auto Union looked almost exactly the same as it had the year before, but Daimler-Benz made the lines of the W154 even lower and smoother, designating it the W163.* And that wasn't all they were doing. . . .

Over the past year the Italians had been getting more and more fed up with the German domination of Grand Prix racing and had turned their attention to the 1500 cc class, so much so that after the Italian GP they had announced that in future, *all* Italian races would be for 1500 cc cars. This, of course, included the very rich Tripoli race which, over the years, had contributed a considerable sum to the Mercedes coffers. Also, politically Italy was very cross with France, accusing her of siding with the Spanish government in the Civil War against the Fascists. Mussolini therefore slapped a ban on any Italian competing in any French race. Auto Union had signed Nuvolari again and were now faced with the prospect of being unable to use him at Pau or (and more importantly) in the French GP.

The Germans were not at all happy at this turn of events, and *Korpsführer* Hühnlein did his best to make the Italians change their minds, but they wouldn't, so the Pau GP went ahead without Auto Union and Nuvolari.

Over the winter months Mercedes had been flatly deny-ing that they were building any 1500 cc cars, but that was exactly what they were doing! These little gems—virtually

*There has always been an element of doubt as to whether or not the 1939 car was officially dubbed the W163, some observers claiming that it was still the W154. As the 1938 and 1939 cars looked very different I have retained the W163 prefix to the latter for clarity.

PREVIOUS PAGE **Nuvolari winning the last race of the 1930s—the Yugoslav GP**

scaled-down V-8 versions of their 3-litre V-12 cars—were ready in time for Tripoli and, much to the Italians' fury, Lang and Caracciola won at a canter. Sadly, the little Mercedes never raced again, but Stuttgart was obviously aware that Hühnlein and his Italian opposite number, Giuseppe Furmanik (well known as a record-breaker) were having serious talks about getting a 1500 cc Grand Prix Formula ratified for 1940, 1941 and 1942.

As the Italian GP was now restricted to 1500 cc cars it was no longer a *Grande Epreuve*, but luckily the Belgian GP was back and it became the first of the year's Cham-pionship qualifying events, to be followed by the French, German and Swiss GPs. The race was the first of Hermann Lang's two victories on his way to the title, but the day was ruined by the death of his team mate, Dick Seaman. Although he did not finish in either the French or German GPs, Lang won the final *Grande Epreuve* in Switzerland to become the very last European Champion, with 13 points to Caracciola's 16, von Brauchitsch's 18 and Nuvolari's 19 points.

Lang recalls his remarkable rise from racing mechanic to European Champion, with some fascinating insights on the personality clashes within the Mercedes-Benz team. As an ex-mechanic, he found himself held in some contempt by his German colleagues, but by 1939 he was the fastest driver in the world.

Schorsch Meier was an Auto Union recruit from the motorcycle world and, briefly, looked set to emulate the great Bernd Rosemeyer's career. He recalls finishing second in only his second ever car race—the French Grand Prix! However, a bad crash on a motorcycle and the outbreak of war meant Meier's GP career was over before it had really begun.

After being kept out of the Auto Union team in 1935 by the machinations of 'certain other drivers', Tazio Nuvolari finally joined the Zwickau concern in 1938 and put it back on the map with two great wins at Monza and Donington. He wasn't so lucky in 1939, but he did have the distinction of winning the last Grand Prix of the Golden Age, in Belgrade.

The Motor reported the 1939 German Grand Prix, won fittingly by the great Caracciola, but the war clouds were now gathered over Europe and the end of the era was just weeks away. . . .

The last four circuits examined are Spa, Reims, Pau and Belgrade, the latter the scene of the final GP of the 1930s, the Yugoslav Grand Prix. It was run on 3 September 1939—the very day an exasperated and nervous England finally plucked up the courage to challenge Adolf Hitler. . . .

Complete results of the six years' racing, together with 'who-won-what?' statistics concludes the chapter and Rodney Walkerley has The Last Word.

═══ MEMOIR ═══

Hermann Lang

Team Driver, Mercedes-Benz, 1935–39. European Champion 1939

My racing career began on a motorcycle sidecar combination. This proved very beneficial to me when I started racing for Mercedes because with a sidecar you can't just lean the machine over when you corner, as you do with a bike—you have to slide it and although it was only on three wheels, nevertheless the driving style was similar.

After a period of unemployment in 1932 I looked for a job in the trade I had learned—as a motor mechanic. I applied to Daimler-Benz in Stuttgart and was taken on in the Experimental Department at the very time when the Silver Arrows were being built for the 1934 season. I worked as an engine fitter, never imagining that one day I would drive the cars I was now working on.

I was delighted to have the job, but I so nearly didn't get it! My application had been sent in with notes from some former employers and, naturally, my success on motorcycles (I was German Hillclimb Champion on motorcycle combinations in 1931) was mentioned. Because of this my papers went to Herr Neubauer in the Racing Department, not to the Personnel Department, and Neubauer turned me down because he thought I was trying to become a racing driver! Luckily, some friends got me an interview with Personnel and I got the job, but my career with Mercedes-Benz very nearly ended before it began.

In February 1934, the first car was ready for testing and we went to Monza, where Manfred von Brauchitsch did the driving. One way and another he was not successful as a test driver, so they brought in Luigi Fagioli, who did the job very well.

Because of the bad weather we travelled to Monza by train with the cars and equipment and it was on the return journey that Jakob Krauss (our Foreman in charge of chassis building) asked me if I wasn't the man who had raced motorcycle sidecars. I remember it distinctly—it was as we were approaching the St Gotthard Pass—and I said, 'Yes, that's me.' No more was said and I thought nothing of it, but from that point Krauss began to play my sponsor, so to speak, in the factory. He selected me to drive the racing cars from the garage to the starting grid, so I could get the feel of them and, to give me even more driving experience that winter, he transferred me to the Test Department, where I drove production cars for miles on end.

I was with Luigi Fagioli as Foreman Mechanic from the beginning, working on his car with Erwin Grupp and Max Mäckle. Three mechanics worked on each car, but there were many more in the Racing Department who actually made the parts. Once the season began we racing mechanics had nothing to do with the manufacture, we just concentrated on preparing the cars for the races.

Fagioli spoke not a word of German and I spoke no Italian, so all communications were made through Neubauer, who could get by in several languages. Caracciola and von Brauchitsch didn't speak any foreign language, either, and they never tried. The reason was simple—Neubauer attended to everything like a mother!

After practice for the 1934 Italian Grand Prix at Monza the brakes on Fagioli's car were practically worn out, so we had to fit new linings. By the time we had finished the circuit was closed, but the brakes had to be bedded-in, so Jakob Krauss sent me with the car and two mechanics to the Turin *autostrada* to do the job. It was at this point that I really took to driving a racing car, although my instructions were to use normal spark plugs—not racing ones—and to drive the W25 carefully up and down to bed-

in the brakes. Once I had done this—not exceeding 3000 rpm— I produced a set of racing plugs and announced to Erwin Grupp and Max Mäckle that I was going to use them.

'You can't do that!' said Grupp. 'What if you crash and are thrown out of the car?'

'That's my problem.' I said. 'I'll screw the plugs in myself, but you must give me a push.' I didn't go near the car's maximum, which was around 265 km/h (165 mph) but for the first time in my life I exceeded 190 km/h (120 mph), which was very fast for those days.

When we got back to Monza Herr Krauss asked me how the brakes were. 'Very good,' I said, 'even from high speed.' He gave me a funny look, 'Are you crazy? You'd better watch out!' But he said it in such a way that I realized that he was secretly rather pleased.

Sometime later, back in Stuttgart, Neubauer called me to his office one day and told me that Krauss had suggested that I might make a good racing driver—would I like to try? I could hardly contain my excitement, especially when he told me that I would be taking part in some driver trials at Monza in the spring.

Three of us drove in those trials, Soenius, Kohlrausch and me. Soenius had been very successful on motorcycles

but had never driven a racing car and it showed. Kohlrausch had raced voiturettes and was quite confident, but I was well satisfied when—at the end—Neubauer told me that I had been selected for further training.

The Mercedes team for 1935 was the same as the previous year—Caracciola, von Brauchitsch and Fagioli, with Hanns Geier as reserve. Although still working as Fagioli's Chief Mechanic I joined Geier as a reserve and we were both promised a drive at the Avus—or Eifelrennen. As it turned out, Geier drove first, at Avus, and I then took part in the Eifel race. We both used 1934 cars and at one time I was in third place, but then I spun at the Pflanzgarten and, as a result, finished fifth.

I had three more races that year, the Grands Prix of Germany, Switzerland and Italy, and nobody took much notice of me. This was good, because it allowed me to get used to race driving step by step and nobody expected me to be the winner. There were times—especially during my very first race—when I asked myself if I really should be taking such risks, but my skills and confidence increased all the time until eventually I could tell myself that I was on the same level as Caracciola and von Brauchitsch—I was able to rise gradually to the very highest level. My reserve colleague, Geier, was not so lucky. He crashed very badly at Bern during practice for the Swiss GP and suffered terrible injuries. He recovered in time, but he never raced again.

In the spring we went back to Monza for our annual pre-season testing. In order to save time, we used to have lunch at the circuit, rather than go back to the hotel. One of our trucks was equipped as a workshop and it also had a kitchen, so we used to go shopping for pasta and meat and then have a picnic lunch at the circuit, which was very pleasant. I've always enjoyed cooking and I often prepared these meals, but not without interruption. I'd be boiling a nice piece of beef and Neubauer would come and say, 'Lang, I need you, go and do three laps.' So I would leave my kitchen and—still with my chef's apron on—get into the car and do my laps. By the time I returned the beef was done and we all had a very nice picnic!

That year my practice nearly ended in disaster. I was doing some fast laps one day when I was hit on the arm by a stone. A group of boys watching from one of the corners was having a game to see who was the best shot and one of them had hit me when I was doing around 210 km/h (130 mph). Neubauer and some of the mechanics rounded up these youths and the culprit got a good hiding. No serious damage was done, but my arm was badly swollen and I did no more practising.

I had my first drive of 1936 at Tripoli, but not in the race. I was still a reserve driver and because of the annual lottery only drivers entered for the race were allowed to practise. This didn't stop Neubauer from sending me out for a few laps when he thought the officials weren't looking! They spotted me, of course, but not before I got myself into trouble.

Early in 1936 Mercedes were still using the superchargers to force fuel into the engine via the carburettor and this gave our cars a very high-pitched scream. While watching our drivers—Caracciola, von Brauchitsch, Fagioli and Chiron—from the pits I noticed that they all went past and into the left-hand bend without lifting their foot from the throttle, the supercharger's scream continuing right the way through. So I did the same and put in a couple of very fast laps before the officials spotted me and I was flagged in.

To my astonishment, Neubauer took me to task, but this was due to Caracciola's initiative. Caracciola had told him, 'Lang is crazy—he's taking that corner at full throttle!' I protested that the others were doing it as well, but Caracciola said, 'Never! Do you want to be thrown out of the car? You must back off there!' And then I realized that the others *were* lifting off the throttle, but not enough to change the sound of the supercharger!

In spite of being told off this incident gave me—unconsciously—a certain strength, because I learned that if you have the courage you can take certain risks and overcome them.

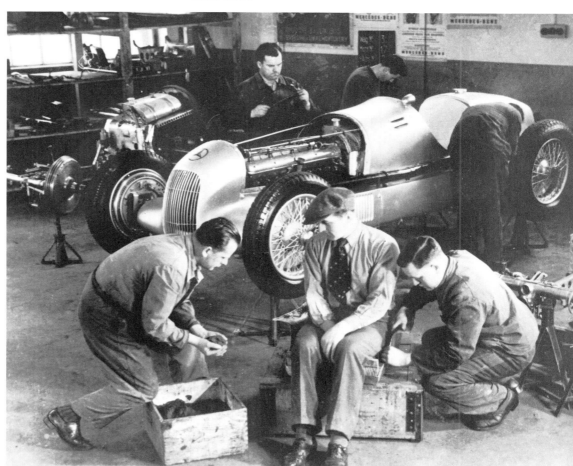

ABOVE LEFT **Luigi Fagioli has a welcome drink after winning the 1934 Spanish GP. His Chief Mechanic, Hermann Lang, is second from left**

RIGHT **Lang is fitted for his seat as his 1935 GP Mercedes is prepared at Untertürkheim. With him are Paul Hägele (*right*) and Otto Müller**

My first race of the year was the Eifel GP, where I came fifth—the first Mercedes to finish. It was not turning out to be a good year for us and we failed in the German GP, too. It was during this race that I broke the little finger on my right hand by catching it on the bodywork while changing gear. It happened at Brünnchen and it hurt terribly, but as I went past the pits I got a signal telling me that I was in the lead! This was the first time I had ever led a race and it was the German Grand Prix! I forgot the pain in my hand and drove on, but when I had to make a pit stop for fuel I found Caracciola waiting to take over my car, as his had stopped with carburettor trouble.

When I arrived at the pits I got a terrific ovation from the spectators in the grandstand and their cheers turned to boos and hisses when they saw Caracciola taking over but, of course, they did not know of my handicap. Caracciola drove off and the doctor put a splint on my finger. Then von Brauchitsch came in and got out of his car and I saw that Zehender was about to take over. I told Neubauer that my finger was no longer hurting and that I wanted to continue the race, so he told me to take von Brauchitsch's car.

But now I found that the splint on my finger banged on the bodywork every time I turned the wheel, never mind when I changed gear. I have never felt such pain in my life! However, I had asked to take over the car so I had to finish the race, which I did, but in a lowly seventh position. Rosemeyer won in his Auto Union and it was a disastrous day for Mercedes-Benz. Because of our poor showing we missed the Coppa Acerbo but were back for the Swiss GP where we failed again. Licking our wounds, we withdrew from the last race of the year, the Italian GP.

In spite of these setbacks the year ended for me, personally, on a high note—Mercedes offered me a contract for 1937! Although they were obviously satisfied with my performance, I think they were perhaps also influenced by the fact that Auto Union were showing interest in me! Professor Ferdinand Porsche was a good friend of mine and he would have liked me to join his team but, as I explained to him, I was 'lost' to the Three-Pointed Star. Mercedes had given me my chance and I was determined to be loyal to them.

After three seasons with the team, my old boss, Luigi Fagioli, was leaving to join Auto Union and Louis Chiron's first year with us had ended after his high-speed crash during the German GP. Fortunately he was not seriously hurt, but he never drove for us again. So Mercedes were down to two drivers: Caracciola and von Brauchitsch. I was then given my first contract (a very good one, but obviously not as good as those of the two senior drivers), and the Englishman, Dick Seaman, was also signed to the team.

We began the new season at Tripoli, where the circuit was very hard on tyres. At the pre-race drivers' conference I was told to take things easy and be prepared to take over if the others dropped out. In spite of following my instructions I still lost a tread but then, suddenly, I got a signal from the pits telling me that I was in the lead! Naturally, this gave me a wonderful feeling, but the same signal told me to hold my speed, which worried me in case they wanted me to let Caracciola and von Brauchitsch catch up—you

have to be very careful in such circumstances! Later it turned out that I had such a lead that Neubauer didn't want me to risk anything by going faster than necessary, but of course I didn't know this at the time.

Worse was to come, however, because in the pits they did not notice that Rosemeyer was on the same lap as me and gaining fast. It was only when Auto Union gave Rosemeyer a signal telling him to go flat out that they realized what was happening and told me to go flat out, too. By this time I could see him in my mirror, so I gave the car full throttle and won by ten seconds, but if the pit hadn't woken up to the situation he would have passed me and won the race for Auto Union!

At Avus we raced the streamlined cars for the first time, and as we had no experience with them Seaman was given an open-wheeled car to be on the safe side. During practice we tried the streamliners with covers over the wheels. Those at the front were fairly wide to allow the wheels to turn in the bends at either end of the circuit and on one run I was doing around 390 km/h (245 mph) when the front of the car began to lift until all I could see was the sky! I immediately thought, 'I must not move the steering, for if the front wheels return to the road in a different position there is bound to be an accident.' Luckily there was no cross wind and I backed off the throttle very carefully, but it was a long time before the front wheels touched the ground again. I must admit that this incident gave me quite a fright and I stopped at the pits, white-faced, and said, 'For Heaven's sake—take those covers off!' The air was getting trapped inside the wheelarches and it was like having two balloons under there! The covers were removed and I had no more problems with front-end lift. Needless to say, the wheels were left uncovered for the race.

There were two heats and a final and I had another moment in my heat when I had a tyre blow out, again at maximum speed. Strangely enough, I hardly noticed it—only when I braked to slow for the pits did I have any problem, but at high speed the car remained level and stable. The wheel was changed very quickly and I finished third.

In the final Caracciola and von Brauchitsch both retired with back axle trouble, but my car ran perfectly and I won at an average of 261 km/h (163 mph). At that time it was the fastest race ever run and, coupled with my win at Tripoli, where I'd averaged 212 km/h (132 mph), it gave me a reputation as a good driver on long, fast circuits, but the 'experts' said I still had to prove myself on the slower, more twisty ones.

So, I started my first full year as a Mercedes driver by winning the first two races and this success was so overwhelming that my wife and I couldn't really grasp it properly! Lydia and I had met when I was 18 and she was 17 and she had accepted my interest in motorcycle racing, but when I started racing cars she raised serious objections. She didn't want me to be a racing driver, but I was already sold on the plan so of course I went ahead. I must say that once I had made the decision she never complained again.

However, when success came my way we were quite unprepared for it, so much so that after my Tripoli victory we at first refused to go to the prize-giving! This was a very glamorous affair hosted by Marshal Balbo, but Lydia and I didn't want to go, so we locked ourselves in our hotel room!

All of a sudden there was a loud knocking on our door— Herr Neubauer! I whispered to Lydia, 'Shhhh—he'll go away!' But he continued knocking and I had to open up. He was furious, but in a nice way! 'Are you crazy?' he said. 'You are the winner! Marshal Balbo is waiting— everybody is waiting in the Palace and the gardens. The party can't start without you!'

'Herr Neubauer,' I said, 'we don't have any evening clothes—you can accept the prize in my place.'

'I can do no such thing,' he said. 'You are the winner and you will accept the prize, even if you have to come in your bathing trunks!'

He planted himself in front of our open door and my wife and I had to get dressed in front of him. Then he took us down to the reception and this was much more embarrassing than if we had gone at the right time, as everybody was waiting and all eyes were upon us! This was exactly what I had wanted to avoid, because I was very shy in those

days and didn't enjoy being the focus of so many people's attention. I hated prize-giving, when you had to walk across a large carpet in front of everybody—sometimes I wished the carpet would open up and swallow me! But Herr Neubauer would have none of it—'You're not going to do this ever again,' he said. 'You must always accept your prizes!'

After Avus came the Eifel GP and I was on a hat-trick, but several stops for plugs meant that I could only finish sixth.

The next two races were on successive weekends, but they were so far apart that our whole team couldn't compete in them both—the Belgian GP at Spa and the Vanderbilt Cup in New York. So Caracciola and I were assigned to the American race and von Brauchitsch and Seaman were to go to Belgium. But then the Belgians complained— they wanted either Caracciola or me in their Grand Prix and Mercedes agreed that one of us should go. However, Caracciola was the senior driver and he insisted on going to America, so von Brauchitsch and I went to Belgium and Seaman went with Caracciola to America.

I led the race for some laps, but then a universal joint broke at the rear axle. Not completely—I was still able to drive—but when I accelerated the car jerked so badly that I was unable to use full throttle and I finished third.

I had no better luck in the German GP. I must tell you

Local hero. After his first victory (at Tripoli in 1937) Lang got a tremendous welcome from his workmates back at Untertürkheim

something: I was always very fast at the Nürburgring and usually on the front row of the grid, but I never won the German Grand Prix. On this occasion I had trouble with tyres and plugs and could only finish seventh. That was the year when Seaman and von Delius crashed. Von Delius was killed, but Seaman was not badly hurt. I didn't go and see him in hospital—racing drivers don't like to visit other drivers in hospital as we don't like to see what might happen to ourselves!

From the Nürburgring I went to Freiburg for the German Mountain Championship but, try as I might, I just could not put up a decent time. There were two reasons for this: a) I was not feeling at all well and b) it rained a lot of the time and I lacked confidence on a wet track. I just managed to finish fourth and went home to bed!

My illness turned out to be influenza and I had to miss the Monaco GP. Listening to it on the radio while I was in bed was no substitute for taking part and I got very angry when, every now and then, they would interrupt the commentary with periods of music! I got over my influenza, only to develop inflammation of the kidneys, so I had to miss the Coppa Acerbo, too.

Then Neubauer came to see me and said, 'Well, what's doing? Are you fit enough for the Swiss GP?'

'Yes,' I said, 'I can make it.' but actually I did not tell the truth—I still felt rather weak.

We went to Bern, my wife and I, and on the way I felt so ill and so weak from lying in bed for so long I wasn't at all sure I could take part in the race. But then a miracle happened—a doctor I knew well once told me that when you are very weak you have to drink lots and lots of cream, so I took to my bed in our hotel and ordered some cream to be sent up.

In the first practice session I did one lap and felt so giddy I came in immediately. Neubauer said, 'Can't you continue?'

'Not today,' I said, 'not any more.'

I went back to the hotel right away and had some more cream. The next day I felt much better and on race day better still—I felt fit and ready to win. But in the race I came up against Mercedes team orders, which were that we were not to race against each other, so when Caracciola took the lead and I was in second place I didn't try to pass him. We finished in that order.

Neubauer was very strict with his team orders, but his rules were designed to win races and they did. He knew that two of his own drivers racing against each other could very easily lose a race for Mercedes, but in spite of the fact that his discipline was supposed to be adhered to by all of us, when I was in front of Caracciola and von Brauchitsch they often tried to get ahead of me! I say this now, but I also said it when Caracciola was alive and von Brauchitsch knows it as well.

Caracciola was the senior driver at Mercedes and Seaman and I were the youngest—at Auto Union it was the same with Stuck and Rosemeyer. We youngsters didn't like having to accept that we should let the older drivers have the victories and it was difficult for Neubauer to keep me and Seaman under control. On the other hand he needed us because of the strength of the opposition, so the older drivers had to reconcile themselves to the fact that we were pretty fast, too.

A classic example of this problem arose at the very next race, the Italian Grand Prix, which was held this time not at Monza but at Livorno, through the streets of the town. Neubauer was not pleased!

Caracciola took the lead but I soon passed him and led until I had to stop with a damaged tyre. Then Caracciola was being threatened by the Auto Unions of Rosemeyer and Varzi, so I was signalled to catch him—even pass him if I could. I caught up with him and we had a great battle, but I couldn't pass—I don't know if he blocked me or if he needed that stretch of road!

I do know that there was no signal from our pit at that time for me to slow down and I would have passed Caracciola if I had been able to. As it was, we finished with him about one wheel-length ahead of me—and then Neubauer was mad! But I was mad, too. First, I had been given instructions to take the lead and then Caracciola wouldn't let me past and finally Neubauer was angry with me. I told him, 'You can't do that to me and you won't do it any more!' If the Auto Unions had been closer I think Caracciola would have let me by . . . I think! But these situations arise now and then and at the time we all got excited, but we just had to digest them. We all got over it, eventually.

Next we went to Brno in Czechoslovakia for the Masaryk Grand Prix and it was there that I had the one bad crash of my career. The circuit was 29 km (18 miles) long and although the roads were properly surfaced there was no hard shoulder, just gravel on either side. I led on the first lap, but many of the drivers behind me ran over the edges of the track and on lap 5, when I got to one particular corner—at the 13-kilometre stone—I found there was a lot of gravel on the road and when the car hit this it started to slide. I was only doing about 120 km/h (75 mph) and could easily have corrected the slide, but the car struck the granite kilometre stone and turned over. I fell out and, apart from a cut on my head, was unhurt, but my car bounced into the forest where it killed two spectators and injured 12 others.

An ambulance came to take the injured to hospital and took me as well. Some of the injured were very abusive and although I could not understand what they were saying it was clear that they were very angry with me. However, the ambulance driver protected me from them. At the hospital I was stitched up—without anaesthetic—and then we learned that a lawsuit was going to be brought against me, as in Czechoslovakia, when there was a road accident with fatal results to pedestrians, the driver of the car was automatically arrested. The organizers told Neubauer to get me out of Brno as quickly as possible and go to Austria. With no more ado we packed our bags and crossed the border to Vienna.

Later it was found that the law concerning accidents did not apply as the road had been closed for the race and so was not a public road at the time. Also, I was a professional racing driver whose job it was to go fast, so there was no negligence on my part. To cap it all it turned out that the spectators I had hit were in a forbidden area—they had ignored the signs telling them to keep out. In spite of this

Lang about to set off for a practice run at Tripoli in 1938.
At this stage the new W154 Mercedes had their exhaust
pipes hidden in the bodywork

were often served venison at mealtime, but they must have
been very old deer as it tasted like the soles of our shoes!

The race was another great victory for Bernd Rosemeyer
and, sadly, it was to be his last. I did not know him well,
but before the end of the year he had a talk with me and
he was not very happy. He felt very much on his own at
Auto Union, having to race against Caracciola, von
Brauchitsch and me at Mercedes, so he asked if I would
think about joining him. I gave him the same answer I had
given Professor Porsche. On 28 January I was doing some
shopping in Stuttgart when a storekeeper who knew me
asked if I'd heard about Rosemeyer. I knew of the record
attempts, of course, and naturally asked how fast he'd gone
now. When the storekeeper told me he had been killed, I
was stunned. Everyone from the Auto Union and Mercedes
teams went to his funeral in Berlin and we buried him next
to his friend von Delius.

For 1938 we had the new 3-litre cars and we took two
of them to Pau for the opening race of the season. In practice I had trouble with the oil scavenge pump and all the
plugs oiled up. We could not solve the problem, so I did
not start. Instead I took over Caracciola's car about halfway through the race when he had to stop for fuel. Dreyfus
on the unsupercharged Delahaye did not have to stop and
he beat us—we could not make up the lost time on that
twisty little circuit.

We had three cars for Tripoli and as the new Auto
Unions weren't ready our opposition consisted of a lot of
Maseratis and some Delahayes and Alfas—there had to be
30 cars in the race for the lottery. Naturally, we dominated
the race, although Count Trossi had a Maserati which was
very fast—he really was a danger for us. I was instructed
to go as fast as possible from the start, even if it meant
damaging my engine, and von Brauchitsch and Caracciola
would stay behind. We were three against one and the
Maserati didn't last long. As I had beaten the Italian I was
given the signal to stay in front, but I was not given the
race on a silver plate—I really had to fight for that victory.

We now went to Reims for the first time. The new Auto
Unions took part, but they both crashed on the first lap,
so it was left to us to have a race amongst ourselves. Caracciola, von Brauchitsch and I swapped the lead many times,
but when I stopped for fuel it took a long time to restart
the engine due to evaporation in the fuel lines, so I finally
finished third behind von Brauchitsch and Caracciola.

I had more bad luck in the German GP—after leading
for the first two laps a plug oiled up and I had to make
a long pit stop which dropped me back to seventh position.
Later Neubauer called me in so that our reserve driver,
Walter Bäumer, could have a drive. Then Caracciola came
in, complaining of severe stomach ache, so I took over his
car. That was the year von Brauchitsch's car caught fire
and Dick Seaman went on to win. I finished second, some
way behind Seaman and even if I had been closer I wouldn't
have challenged him for the lead. He was a very fair man
who always kept to the pre-arranged plan and we were
alike in this, whereas some others were not!

I won the Coppa Ciano at Livorno, but only after von
Brauchitsch was disqualified. There were no Auto Unions
present but once again Trossi and his Maserati were very

the case dragged on until it had to be postponed due to
the war. It was reopened after the war and one day, out
of the blue, I received a pile of files attesting that I had
been acquitted in all 14 cases.

The last race of the season was at Donington. It was
just one week after the Brno event, so our second team of
cars had already been sent to England by the time we were
ready to leave Vienna. Lydia and I flew to London in a
Junkers Ju 52 and on the way the pilot flew round a lap
of the Nürburgring in our honour!

I led the Donington GP for 12 laps until a front shock
absorber broke, otherwise I would have won that race very
easily. We liked Donington—Lydia and I stayed in Castle
Donington where there were deer roaming the park. We

fast, passing Caracciola and me into the lead briefly! But it was too much for the Italian car, and Trossi had to retire. Then von Brauchitsch tried to pass me and ran into some straw bales. He stalled his engine and was pushed back into the race by some spectators, which was forbidden, but in spite of the fact that the organizers threatened to disqualify him, he was allowed to continue. I was instructed by my pit to hold my speed and von Brauchitsch caught and passed me. We were now leading one-two, as Caracciola had retired. So von Brauchitsch won the race, but several competitors protested and he was disqualified, making me the winner.

From Livorno we went across Italy to Pescara for the Coppa Acerbo, and here my car caught fire. It was a very long circuit which goes into the mountains and then comes down to the coast and a very long straight. On this straight the Italians had made a chicane out of straw bales, to reduce the cars' speeds—we were doing about 310 km/h (193 mph) down there!

I was on the straight when a con-rod broke and cut through the fuel line and the ignition cable, starting a fire and leaving me no engine braking. This happened just before the chicane and I had to try and get through it with flames already coming through the fire-wall into the cockpit. I managed to do this, but my overalls were on fire as I undid the steering wheel and leapt out. My Mercedes was almost completely destroyed, except for the parts made of steel—if you have ever seen a camel lying down in the desert you will know what it looked like! After the race they put the remains on a truck with a shovel.

I walked down the road a bit and came to a house where the family had just had lunch. They offered me some food, but all I wanted was a telephone so I could tell the pits I was alright. They said, 'We have no phone, but we have some wine—please have some.' So I had a glass and then started walking down the road again.

Along came René Dreyfus—a very fine chap—and on the same lap that my car caught fire his Delahaye developed transmission trouble, but instead of going straight to his pit to retire he did one more lap so he could pick me up—a fine gesture! I sat on the fuel tank and clung on to him for the ride back to the pits. By this time everyone knew that my car had caught fire, but they didn't know if I was alright, so when we got back to the pits there was a terrific demonstration of sympathy and enjoyment once they saw that nothing had happened to me. That was Pescara!

Then came the Swiss GP at Bern and here I was the biggest slob of my whole career! It was dry throughout practice and I was second fastest, so I started on the front row, between Seaman and Caracciola. But for the race it rained! At the start I accelerated too hard and sat there with wheels spinning as all the others passed me. It rained so hard that it was impossible to pass even the slowest cars. I was really down—almost ashamed of myself—as I found it impossible to catch up with the others in this weather and I resigned. I was getting nowhere when a stone thrown up by another car shattered my goggles and tiny pieces of glass went into my right eye. I stopped at the pits and Dr Gläser found that the eye was not damaged, but it was very painful and what with that and the rain and my poor performance

I was thoroughly fed up. Bäumer took over my car and, although the race was a one-two-three victory for Mercedes, Bäumer and I could only finish tenth. I was thoroughly ashamed of myself and knew that somehow I had to make my peace with the rain.

At Monza I had a great dice for the lead with H. P. Müller in his Auto Union until I had to retire with engine trouble. It was a bad day for Mercedes, as Seaman and von Brauchitsch retired also.

Once again, the last race of the year was at Donington, but it was postponed for three weeks because of the Munich Crisis. When we did turn up for the race, the risk of war had receded and we were very well received in England—everyone seemed glad to see the German teams back after the very successful race in 1937.

As in 1937 I was leading quite easily when I was forced to slow down. This time a stone smashed my windscreen leaving my head exposed to the cold October air. It seemed to affect my circulation—my body was warm but my head was cold—and I found it difficult to breathe in the terrific wind that was now hitting me in the face. At times I could hardly focus my eyes and at the end of the race I got out of my car and fell down flat! The mechanics started massaging me and got my blood circulating again, but it was most unpleasant. All this cost me the race, as Nuvolari had passed me and won, after a brilliant drive.

Because the German cars had won so often in 1938, the Italians decided to change the formula for their races in 1939. They already had lots of 1.5-litre cars, so they announced—very late in the day—that for 1939 all races in Italy would be for cars of this capacity, and no more. They thought that we couldn't possibly build new machines in such a short space of time, but by working day and night the Mercedes engineers built two cars especially for the Tripoli race—Tripoli, of course, being in the Italian Protectorate of Libya.

Before going to Africa, though, we went to Pau, where Dreyfus had beaten us the year before. I had an unhappy moment in practice when a sleeve dropped in the brake master cylinder, leaving me with no brakes! I managed to slow the car by using the gearbox brutally and went into the straw bales, but the car was undamaged and next day I won the race, although von Brauchitsch gave me a hard time, in spite of the fact that we had lapped the entire field by half-distance!

Shortly after we returned home, Caracciola and I were summoned to Hockenheim, where we saw for the first time one of the little Tripoli cars. We both drove it and were delighted with it, but we were not too optimistic about our chances because the cars had had no proper testing—indeed, the second one was only completed on the boat!

As soon as we started to practise, the problems began—problems between me and Caracciola. I would really rather someone else told this story, but . . . Maserati had brought along a new, streamlined car for Gigi Villoresi and it was very fast. After the first day's practice I had fastest lap, with Villoresi second and Caracciola third. We felt sure of having both our cars on the front row of the grid so we decided not to practise on the Saturday, not wishing to work our cars too hard.

Lang storms up the snow-covered Grossglockner in the W125 Mercedes in 1938. He finished second, behind Hans Stuck

But then Villoresi beat my time, so Caracciola went out and also beat my time, but not Villoresi's. Neubauer then told me to have a go and this annoyed Caracciola who, at that moment, was unaware of Villoresi's new time. He wanted to be fastest and didn't want me beating him! Neubauer calmed him down and explained that as he hadn't been able to beat Villoresi, Lang was to have a go. As it turned out I wasn't able to beat Villoresi's time, either—he was still about half a second faster than me—so Neubauer told us not to bother any more. We did no more practising, but by that time there was a considerable 'atmosphere' between Caracciola and me!

Things got worse at our pre-race meeting that evening. The cars had the same final drive, but different intermediate ratios, so one could accelerate faster than the other. In practice Caracciola and I had taken turns in both cars, but now we had to decide who would drive which in the race. Of course, Caracciola wanted the car with the better acceleration—and so did I! But here Director Sailer stepped in, saying that as Caracciola was the senior driver he should have first choice.

I accepted Herr Sailer's decision, but on race day I was really angry. My orders were to try and break the opposition by going really fast and then changing tyres, whereas Caracciola was to take things easier and go through the whole race on one set.

I was in the middle of the front row, with Villoresi on my right and Caracciola on my left. The race was started by Marshal Balbo and there is a photo of the start with me so far ahead that it looks as though I must have left the line before he dropped the flag. But I had noticed that on the pit wall there was a camera to photograph the start and finish and, above the camera, a pair of lights—one red and one green. I called to Neubauer, 'What do I do—watch the lights or Balbo?'

Neubauer made a quick check with an official and then pointed to the lights, so I was watching them while the others all looked at Balbo. The camera was connected to the lights and showed what a super start I made! From that moment I only saw the others in my mirror. I led from the first lap to the last, beating Caracciola by nearly three minutes. Of course, the fact that I was so angry with him helped! Did he speak to me afterwards? Not much!

Two weeks later I won the Eifel GP at the Nürburgring— my first victory there and my third in a row that year. I also set a new lap record of 9 min. 52.2 sec., which easily beat the old record held since 1936 by Rosemeyer in the 6-litre Auto Union.

At Spa it rained and we all had problems at the start. Müller came through from the back in his Auto Union, with Caracciola behind him, then me, von Brauchitsch and Seaman. I must say that Müller was very unfair, blocking us all the way round. There were fountains of water coming up from his tyres and we just couldn't see and although we were clearly able to go faster he wouldn't let us by. Caracciola waved his fist in protest, but nothing was done and in his pursuit he spun at the hairpin and went off the road.

I now moved up behind Müller, who still wouldn't let me pass, so when Seaman moved up behind me I waved him through, but he couldn't pass Müller, either! Finally, Müller went into the pits and when he rejoined the race

he immediately lost ground—it was clear that he had been holding us up.

I was now a little way behind Seaman and it would have remained like that for the rest of the race, but then the rain stopped and the road dried a bit, which is worse than if you have heavy rain, as adhesion becomes poorer. From my position behind Seaman I could see how the rear end of his car was sliding, and I kept my car well under control so I wouldn't run into him if he spun. Suddenly, in the bend before the hairpin, he just slid off the road and hit a tree right at the cockpit. He must have hit his head against the tree and, at the same time, the fuel line broke pouring fuel onto the hot exhaust pipe.

The flames roared high into the air and nobody could get to Seaman. He couldn't help himself as he must have been unconscious after the impact, but then a very courageous soldier managed to pull him out, although by that time he must have suffered burns on about 60 per cent of his body.

I stopped at the pits to tell them that Seaman had crashed and then continued, but I can tell you I could hardly drive after what I had seen. By the end of the race I was getting worried about my fuel and, as I came round the hairpin with one lap to go, my engine stopped—the tank was empty! Luckily, it's downhill from the hairpin to the pits, so I was able to coast in for more, but the fuel lines were now empty, too, and the car wouldn't start. It still wouldn't start even when the mechanics pushed me down the hill to Eau Rouge. We had almost given up when suddenly the engine caught, just as we reached the uphill stretch and at that moment Hasse passed me in his Auto Union! Now I forgot everything I had seen and set off in pursuit, driving so fast that I caught Hasse and won by 16 seconds.

I must say that it was a very sad victory after what had happened to Seaman. When we learned that he had died we were very, very upset. I don't want to flatter him, but I must say that he was a very fine personality—quiet, not

a boastful man, but a very good comrade to have in our team.

The French GP was at Reims again and here I had a terrific battle with Nuvolari in the Auto Union for the first six or seven laps—first he led, then me, but we both ruined our engines, although mine lasted much longer than his! I retired after 35 laps, but I had the consolation of setting a new lap record at nearly 115 mph (185 km/h).

I set another lap record at the Nürburgring—9 min. 43 sec., but that was in practice, so it didn't count! After that I was the favourite for the Grand Prix and at the end of lap 1 I had a lead of 28 seconds! After three laps I was 57 seconds ahead, but at the end of lap 4, when I was on the straight leading to the pits I felt the engine tighten up. I was convinced it was going to burst, so I came straight into the pits and told them, but they would not believe me—they thought I had just given up!

The following morning I woke up in the Eifeler Hof in Adenau and I heard noises. It was 'our' sound and it was coming from the 'Ring. I got dressed and went to the circuit. What did I see? Uhlenhaut, driving my car to try and prove that I had retired without reason, just to be naughty.

Director Sailer was also there and he said, 'If the engine is OK you will have a lot to answer for.'

I then demanded that the cylinder heads be removed and the engine checked, but there at the Nürburgring—not back at Untertürkheim, when I might not be present. Eventually Sailer agreed and I stood there while they removed the heads. Lo and behold—when the second one was taken off it revealed a very beautiful piston seizure!

'So?' I said.

Neubauer was very quiet and said nothing, but Sailer said, 'Well, if you wish to put it that way you could say that you saved the engine.'

'And you want me to forget what you said earlier?' I

asked. 'OK. Now we can go home.'

But if I had not demanded that they take the engine apart then and there they could have said it was something else, or nothing. And I can tell you candidly that Uhlenhaut was very abashed about the whole thing!

In spite of my failure at the 'Ring I was still leading the European Championship and if I could win the Swiss GP I would make sure of the title, but standing between me and victory was—Caracciola. I can only say that Caracciola was a Swiss resident and I could not help feeling that many people wanted him to win, as he had done three times in the past.

The race was a curious affair that year, run in two heats

LEFT Tripoli, 1939 and Lang has a huge lead in the little 1½-litre Mercedes at the end of the first lap. He scored his third successive victory in this race

BELOW Lang on his way to victory at Spa in 1939. He is climbing the new right-hander after Eau Rouge, which cut off the old Ancienne Douanne hairpin

and a final, but one heat was for 1500 cc cars and the other for 3-litre machines, with the best from both going into the final. This was the organizers' way of attracting the Italians as, of course, all Italian races were now restricted to the 1500 cc limit. Farina was amazingly fast in the new Alfa Romeo, winning his heat from Biondetti in a similar car. I then won my heat from Caracciola and von Brauchitsch, with Nuvolari fourth in an Auto Union.

The starting grid for the final was arranged by alternating cars from each heat—the fastest car from the 3-litre heat next to the fastest from the 1500 cc heat, and so on. Caracciola and I were therefore on the front row with Farina between us in his Alfa. Just before the start it began to rain.

I had not forgotten my dismal performance at Bern in 1938, but I had not been sleeping since then, either! In the spring of 1939, when we were testing the new cars at the Nürburgring, it rained all the time and I drove and drove in order to overcome my inferiority in the wet, and I succeeded. However, Caracciola was known as *Der Regenmeister* and naturally people felt that I wouldn't be able to hold him in the final, but I thought, 'I'll show you!'

I went straight into the lead and, much to my surprise,

found a red car behind me—Farina! He stayed with me for six laps and I couldn't get away from him, nor could Caracciola get past. Then the rain stopped and Caracciola was able to get by, but that little Alfa was very fast!

Now I was getting signals from the pit that my team mate was catching me. For some reason my wife, Lydia, was in the pits that day—normally she never watched from there—and she heard Neubauer say, 'Now we have to slow Lang a little bit.' Then I saw a sight I had never seen before—Neubauer standing by the track giving me a 'slow' signal and Lydia standing behind him, urging me to go faster! I knew immediately what was going on, so I speeded up, keeping Caracciola about five seconds behind me until the end.

Afterwards he was quite angry. 'Why were you going so fast?' he said. 'I would never have passed you.'

'Listen Caracciola,' I replied, 'it's better to be on the safe side!'

That was the Swiss Grand Prix.

There was one more race before the war finished it all— the Yugoslav GP. On the second day of practice we heard that Germany was at war with Poland, but nonetheless the Yugoslav organizers demanded that the race go ahead. Von Brauchitsch wanted to go home, but we agreed to stay, although there were only to be five cars in the race—two Mercedes, two Auto Unions for Nuvolari and Müller, and an old Bugatti.

It would have been better for me if von Brauchitsch *had* gone home! The race was run through the town of Belgrade and he got the better start, forcing me to follow. I tried to pass, but he pushed me up onto the pavement, so I had to drop back. Then a stone smashed my goggles and I had to give up, so Bäumer took over my car. Von Brauchitsch now led from Nuvolari, but then he spun, letting the Auto Union into the lead and Nuvolari won the race.

That was the end of my one Championship year. I had started in eight races and won five of them, setting fastest practice lap seven times and fastest race lap four times. The European Championship was mine without question.

On 3 September—the day of the Yugoslav GP—England declared war on Germany and we all went home very depressed. We were told not to travel through Hungary, as our safety could not be guaranteed, so we had to go through Yugoslavia to Austria, and some of the roads were just country lanes in the fields. We eventually arrived home with the war four or five days old. We all had company cars—mine was a lovely 3.4-litre drophead—and we had hardly driven through the factory gates when they were confiscated, as were our trucks! The military had taken over Mercedes and motor racing was over for a long time to come.

=== MEMOIR ===

Schorsch Meier

Team Driver, Auto Union, 1939

I started racing motorcycles—always BMWs—in 1937. I won about 150 races altogether in my career and several championships, including the European Championship of 1938 and seven German Championships. Early in 1938 Bernd Rosemeyer was killed and Auto Union took on Nuvolari to replace him, but at the end of the season they started looking for some new German drivers.

By this time I had won a lot of races and was attracting a great deal of attention in the sporting press. One writer in particular—Wolfgang Hornickel—gave me a very good write-up and even suggested to Dr Feuereissen (Auto Union's Team Manager) that I be given a trial in a racing car. Nothing happened at the time, but at the end of 1938, when I'd just become the 500 cc European Champion, Feuereissen phoned me and asked me to go to the Nürburgring for a test drive.

This took place on 9 November on the short circuit of the 'Ring and I was one of several young men being tested. Another was Ewald Kluge, the 250 cc champion, who rode DKWs. I was the fastest of the lot (we drove an early D-type Auto Union) and Kluge was also very quick. As a result we were both asked to drive for Auto Union in the coming season. This could have proved difficult, as I was already under contract to BMW again for 1939, but fortunately the car and motorcycle Grands Prix were on alternate weekends, so I was able to do both.

Before that test drive I had never driven any kind of racing car, or even a high-powered sports car, just ordinary saloons in which I drove very normally. The D-type Auto Union had nearly 500 bhp, so the difference between that and anything else I had driven was colossal! I found it very heavy to drive, of course, after motorcycles and the rear engine was always trying to slide round in front of me—I spun three or four times!

My first race was supposed to be the Eifel GP, at the Nürburgring, but something went wrong with the car at the last moment and I couldn't start. Then I went to the Isle of Man, where I was determined to try and win the Senior TT. Things got off to a bad start when my team mate, Karl Gall, was killed in a practice crash, but in the race my supercharged BMW was uncatchable and I became the first foreign rider to win the TT. I won at record speed and it was my greatest victory up to that time.

The next weekend I went to Spa-Francorchamps for the Belgian GP with Auto Union. I knew the circuit very well, having raced motorcycles there twice and having won both times! I had, of course, practised at the Nürburgring for the Eifel GP where I found the Auto Union quite a handful on all those twists and turns and ups and downs. All that horsepower and those narrow tyres made it very difficult for me, but even so, I managed to lap in just over 10 min. 16 sec. in practice when Caracciola and Nuvolari did 10 min. 5 sec. For a beginner, that wasn't bad! Spa had its ups and downs, too, but it was very fast and so was I, as I knew the circuit well and the car handled beautifully on those fast curves.

The starting grid was decided by ballot and in spite of my good practice times I found myself on the third row. Farina, however—whose Alfa Romeo was much slower than the Auto Unions and Mercedes—was on the front row and he made a good start and took the lead in the pouring rain. He then proceeded to hold everyone else up for quite some time!

We all got past him eventually, but the rain and spray were terrible and even Caracciola spun off at the hairpin! After 12 laps I was in sixth place, but on lap 14, as I tried to overtake Mandirola's Maserati at Blanchimont, he moved over on me and I went into the ditch. There was no damage, but I couldn't get back onto the road, so I took off my steering wheel and started to walk back to the pits, which were about three or four kilometres away.

As I approached Club Corner, just before the hairpin, Seaman came by well in the lead but lost control and crashed into the trees. I was about 300 metres away and saw the whole thing. It was a very unlucky accident because the car hit a tree at the cockpit and the fuel line running from the rear tank to the engine broke, pouring fuel onto the exhaust pipe. By the time I got to the scene of the accident he was lying on the ground with the Red Cross people looking after him, but he died in hospital that night.

The next weekend I was back on my motorcycle again, winning the Dutch GP at Assen for BMW. Then I went to Reims for the French GP with Auto Union. Lang and Caracciola were fastest in practice, but Nuvolari managed to get his Auto Union onto the front row of the grid with them. Müller was on the second row and I was on the third. Caracciola crashed on the first lap and Nuvolari and Lang had a tremendous battle for the lead, followed by Müller,

New recruit. Schorsch Meier in the Auto Union at Reims, 1939

von Brauchitsch and me. Then von Brauchitsch retired, so by the time I came into the pits for fuel I was fourth, but during the stop my car caught fire! I jumped out, but my arm was quite badly burned—I still have the scars. The mechanics quickly put the fire out and I went back into the race.

My arm was very painful, so I held it out in the wind to cool it, although this made driving very difficult as the Auto Union was very heavy to steer. But it was worth it, because I finished second behind H. P. Müller—a wonderful result for Auto Union. And, of course, to finish second in only my second Grand Prix was marvellous! Things got even better the next weekend because I went back to Spa-Francorchamps for the motorcycle GP and won that, so in the space of two weeks I had won two motorcycle Grands Prix and come second in a car GP. Very satisfying!

My last race for Auto Union was the German GP at the Nürburgring. I went off the road during practice and although there seemed to be no damage at the time I think something must have broken and nobody noticed it. On lap 13 I was driving down the Füchsröhre very fast when the front stub axle broke, so when I came to the next right-hand turn, one wheel turned right but the other didn't! I managed to stop without hitting anything, but my race was over.

And that was the end of my motor racing career until after the war. I had to miss the Swiss GP at Bern as I was contracted to take part in the Swedish motorcycle GP at Malmö two weeks before and there I had a very serious crash. This put me in hospital for the next seven months, which wasn't such a bad thing as it meant I couldn't be a soldier!

Of all the drivers I met during my season with Auto Union I think Nuvolari was the best. He was also a gentleman and a friend, although he couldn't speak German and I couldn't speak Italian! In spite of this he was very helpful to me, which may have had something to do with the fact that we had both started our careers on motorcycles. He would tell me which gear he was using through all the corners and when he said that this was a third-gear corner and that one was flat out in fifth you knew he was telling the truth. Other drivers, however, would say that this corner was flat in fourth and then you would watch them go round and you could hear that they were in third! Nuvolari was always very correct, but the others were always one gear higher than the truth!

Of the Mercedes drivers, only Hermann Lang took me seriously when I began racing cars. Caracciola, von Brauchitsch and Seaman all regarded me as just a motorcycle rider, not a racing driver. But Hermann Lang also started on motorcycles and he believed that I could have been successful on four wheels—he told me he thought it was a pity I hadn't started sooner on cars. The other three were 'gentlemen drivers' who had never driven anything but cars and they looked down their noses at anyone who had started on bikes!

When I started racing motorcycles I never dreamed of moving on to cars. Motor racing was very expensive and you couldn't get rich on bikes! Racing drivers were very well paid and well looked after—when I was racing motorcycles I had a little DKW *Meisterklasse*, but when I joined Auto Union I was asked what would I like, an 8-cylinder Horch? But I chose a 2.7-litre Wanderer.

I enjoyed my time with Auto Union. The Team Manager, Dr Feuereissen, was a superman! He was like a father to me and I had the impression that he felt that if I took it easy to begin with I would soon show the others. Professor Eberan was also a gentleman—always.

Auto Union paid me a monthly salary and a fixed sum for the year of 20,000 RM at a time when the Wanderer car they lent me cost about 7000 RM. Also I kept any prize money I won, so my second place in the French GP was quite profitable, although the money was nothing to what the drivers can get today!

Meier's Auto Union caught fire during the 1939 French GP at Reims. While the mechanics deal with the blaze, Meier (in white, *left*) attends to his burnt arm

Tazio Nuvolari

Team Driver, Scuderia Ferrari 1935–37;
Auto Union 1938–39

On 4 December 1934, Dr Richard Voelter—Press and Public Relations Officer for Auto Union—found himself faced with the unlikely and unhappy task of informing the greatest racing driver in the world that there was no place for him in the Auto Union team for the forthcoming season. The driver was, of course, Tazio Nuvolari, so any suggestion that he was not good enough would have been ridiculous, not to say libellous. No, as Dr Voelter explained, the reasons for his rejection were entirely personal! Writing in French (for he spoke no Italian and Nuvolari no German) the good doctor told Nuvolari that, '. . . *quelques de nos autres conducteurs de véhicles que nous avons pris en égard pour l'année 1935, ont exprimé de certaines doutes au sujet de votre engagement*'. Bluntly, certain other drivers did not want him in the team.

If this rebuttal hurt Nuvolari, he did not let it show, but over the next three years—driving the outclassed Scuderia Ferrari Alfa Romeos—he put up some superb drives and on several memorable occasions defeated the Auto Union and Mercedes teams handsomely. The Great Little Man, as he was known, would, eventually, sign for the Zwickau concern, but not until 1938, by which time the Auto Union was quite a different beast from the one he would have raced in 1935 and 1936. It really was a shame that the man regarded by many as the greatest racing driver of all time never had a chance to get to grips with the awesome, mid-engined V-16. . . .

Tazio Giorgio Nuvolari was born on 18 November 1892, in Casteldario, a small village near Mantua, in northern Italy. His parents were Arturo and Elisa Nuvolari and Tazio was the first of their three children. At the outbreak of the Great War Tazio joined the Italian Army as a driver. Four years later, a civilian once more, he married Carolina Perrina, a beautiful local girl he had met not long before he had been called up. They went to live in Mantua and Nuvolari resumed the job the war had interrupted, as a car salesman. The best thing about this job was that it allowed Tazio to indulge in his great passion—driving. He decided that he would become a racing driver, but although motor racing was under way again in Italy it was very expensive, so his career began on a motorcycle, which was something he could afford. He was no overnight success, being noticed more for his daredevil riding style than any victories to begin with, and it was not until 1922 that he won his first race, the Circuit of Belfiore, riding a Harley-Davidson.

Soon he began to be noticed and joined the Indian team, where he found himself in confrontation with another ambitious young Italian, Achille Varzi, who was making a name for himself on Sunbeams. In 1925 Nuvolari joined Bianchi, winning four races that year, but by now he had also entered a few car races, which made him determined to move from two wheels to four. To his great joy he was allowed to try a P2 Alfa Romeo at Monza, during practice for the Italian Grand Prix. All went well until the gearbox seized and the car flew off the road. Battered but unbowed, Tazio was carted off to hospital where he was told that he would have to spend at least a month in bed. Ten days later, having ordered his doctors to strap him up in a riding position, he was lifted onto his Bianchi and won the Italian motorcycle GP!

His crash in the Alfa did nothing to dampen his determination to race cars, but clearly there was no place for him—as yet—on the Alfa team. He decided to buy a Bugatti, as the French équipe itself did not race in Italy. He put the idea up to his family and some friends, who included Achille Varzi, and all agreed that it made sense, but where was the money coming from? Tazio took the plunge and suggested selling some of the land that was due to him. His father and uncle agreed to this and Varzi agreed to buy a Bugatti himself and join forces with Nuvolari.

The team was quite successful—at least, as far as Nuvolari was concerned—for in 1927 he won two races with the Bugatti and collected a second and a third also. In 1928 he won four, but Varzi was not happy at having to play second fiddle to his team mate, although, of course, it was his team. Varzi left and bought himself a P2 Alfa and the rivalry which had started on motorbikes was continued.

For 1930 Nuvolari joined Alfa Romeo—and so did Varzi. They did not stay together long. Their first race was the Mille Miglia and this event has passed into legend for the way Nuvolari, allegedly driving without lights, crept up on an unsuspecting Varzi and passed him a few miles from the finish to win. Like many legends, this one doesn't bear close scrutiny, as Count 'Johnny' Lurani revealed in his history of the Mille Miglia.

Nuvolari was at an immediate advantage over Varzi because he started ten minutes after him, so at each control he learned just how far ahead his rival was. The race began at 11 am on 16 April and Varzi arrived in Rome 11 minutes ahead of Nuvolari so he led him in the race by one minute. On the way back to Bologna Varzi suffered two punctures and he passed through that control only three minutes before Nuvolari, who had now made up seven minutes on him and was well in the lead. Clearly, by now Varzi would have been given information to this effect and must have known the race was lost, unless his rival's car failed. Shortly after passing Feltre (only 195 km [120 miles] from Brescia) on his way to Arsie, Varzi recognized the three headlamps in-line on Nuvolari's car behind him and made no effort to hold him off. Tazio may well have switched his lights off as he caught Varzi on the approach to Brescia, but as it would have been getting on towards 5 am that April morning he would not have had too much need of them anyway. Certainly, Varzi was not taken by surprise when Nuvolari passed him, determined to beat his opponent on the road as well as on time. However, headlamps or no headlamps, it was a sensational victory.

Varzi had his revenge a few weeks later when he won

Nuvolari with Wilhelm and Ludwig Sebastian

the Targa Florio and in August he beat Nuvolari to the punch by leaving the Alfa Romeo GP team and buying one of the new and very fast Maseratis. The P2 Alfa was now being outclassed by both the Maserati and Bugatti, but while Nuvolari worried about the situation Varzi dealt with it, and promptly won the Coppa Acerbo on his new mount.

For 1931 Vittorio Jano produced his glorious Alfa 8C 2300 sports car, which also came in Grand Prix form, when it was known as the Monza (the scene of its first victory). Nuvolari had a pretty good season, winning the Targa Florio, the Italian GP (with Campari—it was a ten-hour race), the Coppa Ciano and the Circuito di Tre Province, in which he beat Enzo Ferrari by a few seconds. The Monza was a fine car, but Jano obviously regarded it as only an interim model, for in 1932 he delivered another masterpiece, the Type B Monoposto, which became better known as the P3. However, this car did not appear until

the Italian GP in June, so for the Monaco and Eifel GPs the Alfa drivers had to 'make do' with the Monzas—and they won both!

For this new season the already very strong Alfa Romeo team was considerably reinforced by the addition of Rudolf Caracciola, Mercedes-Benz having withdrawn from racing due to financial difficulties. Nuvolari won the Targa Florio and the Italian and French GPs before having to give way to Caracciola at the Nürburgring. Rudi had already won the Eifel race and Alfa Romeo considered it good business that he should win his own Grand Prix, too. Nuvolari reluctantly agreed to this, but later that month won the Coppa Ciano and in August, the Coppa Acerbo. Having decreed that their German driver should win the German GP, Alfa Romeo made no similar stipulation for the final race of the year, the Monza Grand Prix. It was every man for himself and Caracciola won both his heat and the final.

And that, for the time being, was the end of the P3 Alfas. Early in 1933 the company was nationalized and withdrew from competition. The racing equipment was handed over to Enzo Ferrari, but the fabulous P3s were not—Scuderia Ferrari would have to make do with the 'old' Monzas for Grand Prix racing. On the brighter side, the Scuderia also inherited two of Alfa Romeo's drivers—Nuvolari and Borzacchini.

It was a tremendous year for Tazio, who won no less than ten races—six of them with the Ferrari Alfas. He began his winning streak at Tunis, where he beat Borzacchini by 0.2 sec. and he then won the Mille Miglia for the second time. At Monaco he lost to his great rival, Achille Varzi, after one of the most exciting and hard-fought races ever seen, which lasted for 99 of the 100 laps, until an oil pipe fractured on Nuvolari's Alfa. A week later Tazio won the Bordino Cup at Alessandria, but then Varzi won at Tripoli and Avus in quick succession. That, however, was the end of his challenge for the season, really, as his works Bugattis proved uncompetitive and the promised new model was not forthcoming.

Nuvolari's success continued with wins in the Eifel and Nimes GPs, but in the French at Montlhéry the Ferrari Alfas came badly unstuck and the race was won by Giuseppe Campari in the new 3-litre, 8C Maserati, which proved to be very fast indeed. Nuvolari was aware that the Monza Alfas were now outclassed and the speed and reliability of the Maserati did not go unnoticed.

The next weekend Tazio was at Le Mans for the first time, where he shared Raymond Sommer's 8C Alfa Romeo in a sensational victory, passing Luigi Chinetti (winner the previous year, with Sommer) on the last lap to win by just ten seconds!

Then it was back to Scuderia Ferrari, which had a hectic fortnight with races on successive weekends and it was the team's failure in the first two of these—the Penya Rhin and Marne GPs—which caused a frustrated and furious Nuvolari to leave the Scuderia, breaking his contract. He signed with Maserati and rubbed salt in Enzo Ferrari's wounds by winning the next race—the Belgian GP—in a Maserati that was actually entered by Scuderia Ferrari, Enzo not having broken *his* side of their contract! Tazio

then compounded the felony by going on to win the Coppa Ciano and the Nice GP for his new team.

All this caused a sensation in Italy and reflected very badly on Alfa Romeo. Not long after Nuvolari's departure, six P3s were sent from Milan to Modena! Meanwhile the man himself went to Belfast, where, driving an MG, he won the Ulster Tourist Trophy for the second time in four years. Then it was back to Monza for the Italian GP. After a tremendous battle with Fagioli and Chiron on P3 Alfas, Tazio was robbed of victory on his Maserati when a tyre burst with only two laps to go.

That was frustrating indeed, but stark tragedy was to follow. Later in the day, during the Monza GP, the great Giuseppe Campari was killed, along with Baconin Borzacchini, in a multiple crash during the second heat. Then, in the final, Count Czaikowski lost his life at almost exactly the same spot on the track. It was the blackest day in Italian motor racing history and a distraught Nuvolari spent the night with the widows of the three men, keeping vigil over the coffins at Monza Hospital.

Very shaken by these events, Nuvolari missed the Masaryk GP, but was back in the cockpit for the Spanish at San Sebastian three weeks later, and that race very nearly ended fatally for him, too. He had a very big crash when his Maserati rolled twice and finished up on the bank of a river. Nuvolari suffered only minor head injuries and was able to go straight home to Italy, but that September had provided an altogether dismal ending to an otherwise excellent year.

By the time Mercedes-Benz and Auto Union entered the arena in 1934, Tazio Nuvolari was 41 years old and gener-

Nuvolari first tried an Auto Union during practice for the Spanish GP at Lasarte in September 1934

ally acknowledged as the finest racing driver in the world. His only serious rival was Achille Varzi, as Rudolf Caracciola was still recovering from his terrible Monaco crash. This being so it really is surprising that neither of the German teams should have sought his services for their first season in modern Grand Prix racing. Having walked out on Scuderia Ferrari, Tazio could only look forward to the new season as an independent.

Bugatti offered him his latest 2.8-litre car for the Monaco GP, but it was no match for the Ferrari Alfas and he could only finish fifth. He entered the Mille Miglia in an Alfa, but had to give best to 'the old enemy', Achille Varzi, whose Ferrari Alfa had better tyres for coping with the very wet conditions.

Two weeks later Nuvolari had a very big accident in pouring rain during the Bordino GP on the Alessandria circuit. His broken right leg in plaster, he was sent home to recuperate, and while he was fretting away in Mantua Varzi was winning again! Early in May he won the Tripoli GP and two weeks later he was victorious in the Targa Florio. All this was too much for Tazio who decided that— plaster cast or no plaster cast—he would race at Avus. And

he did. He had the pedals of his Maserati altered so that he could actuate them all with his left foot—and he finished fifth!

The plaster was finally removed in time for the Penya Rhin GP at Barcelona but, of course, the leg was by no means back to full strength. Nonetheless, Nuvolari gave Varzi, Chiron and Lehoux in the Scuderia Ferrari cars a very good fight until his Maserati packed up. He finished third in the Coppa Ciano and second in the Coppa Acerbo, but had to retire in the Swiss GP. In the Italian Grand Prix he had a fine duel with Varzi for a while, but then his brakes began to fade until they disappeared altogether. Nuvolari managed to finish fourth and after the race it was discovered that, in order for the Maserati to weigh in under the 750 kg limit, *all* the fluids—even the brake fluid—had been drained before the race, and someone had forgotten to refill the brake fluid tank!

In the Spanish GP Nuvolari could do nothing about the Mercedes of Fagioli and Caracciola, but he finished a fine third, this time in a Type 59 Bugatti. In the final GP of the season, at Brno, he finished third again (now back with Maserati), but then had the great satisfaction of beating

Varzi and the Ferrari cars in two Italian races, at Modena and Naples, thus ending a very poor season on a high note.

His year as an independent had, frankly, been a failure, so it was only natural that Nuvolari should think of joining a factory team for 1935. He was not keen to go back to Scuderia Ferrari, feeling that he had been let down badly in 1933 and, for his part, Enzo Ferrari had not forgotten that Tazio had walked out on his contract!

Nuvolari decided to look to Germany for his next drive. As Mercedes already had one Italian on their books—Fagioli—it was hardly likely that German nationalism would allow another, so Tazio approached Auto Union. Unfortunately, Achille Varzi had got there first. . . . Precisely when Nuvolari made his approach is not known, but Varzi tested the car at Monza in August 1934, and this may well have prompted Tazio to get on the phone. What is certain is that—almost unnoticed—he did a few laps in an Auto Union during practice for the Spanish GP at Lasarte at the end of September. A week later, at Brno, he was out in the car again, and this time everyone noticed! But it was Varzi who got the contract for 1935.

By the time he tested the car at Monza, Varzi had already won seven races that season and, at the age of 30, must have seemed a very good bet to Auto Union. Nuvolari, on the other hand, was 42, and following his very unsuccessful year there were many who were ready to write off the great man as a spent force. Auto Union were clearly not included here, for as late as mid-October Dr Voelter was corresponding with Nuvolari about the very real possibility of him joining the team for 1935. But then came his letter of 4 December, and his reference to the 'certain other drivers' who didn't want him.

As he refers to 'drivers'—in the plural—this could only mean Hans Stuck and Achille Varzi, for none of the others who had driven for Auto Union in 1934 carried enough clout to prevent the firm from signing any driver, let alone one of Nuvolari's stature. Stuck, however, was close to Professor Porsche, had achieved a great deal for the team in 1934 and had recently turned down the offer of a Mercedes contract for 1935.

For his part, Varzi had long ago made it clear that he would never again drive in the same team as Nuvolari. They were still on good terms socially, but in racing—like oil and water—they just did not mix. Varzi was always very quick to make up his mind and once he had come to an agreement with Auto Union he would have been in a strong position to keep Nuvolari out. With Stuck weighing in, too, the Mantuan never really had a chance.

Once Auto Union's door was closed there was really only one place he could go—Modena—and now Mussolini took a hand. The idea of two French drivers (Louis Chiron and René Dreyfus) leading Italy's premiere racing team did not go down at all well with *Il Duce* and he made it clear that he wanted Nuvolari to join Scuderia Ferrari. To make the point he put up a first prize of 50,000 lire for the Italian Drivers' Championship, which was open only to Italian drivers driving Italian cars. Money did not mean a great deal to Nuvolari (who lived in a fairly modest manner, despite his great success), so he may not have been too impressed by Mussolini's ploy, but he was a patriot, and so when Ferrari and Jano talked to him about his 'patriotic duty', he agreed to join the Scuderia once again.

Having got him back in the fold, Ferrari really put Nuvolari to work and by the year's end he had started in 19 races and won eight, the plum, of course, being the German Grand Prix, on which Tazio put his mark for ever.

By the time the teams assembled at the Nürburgring, Mercedes had won seven races and Auto Union one. Nuvolari had won four for Scuderia Ferrari, but they were minor (though lucrative) events which the Germans hadn't entered, so Mercedes can be forgiven if they were confident of victory in their own Grand Prix that July. That confidence was to be shattered in the dying moments of the very last lap.

ABOVE LEFT **Hans Stuck (*left*) and Achille Varzi conspired to keep Nuvolari out of the Auto Union team for 1935. Between them is Auto Union's Italian representative, Ugo Ricordi**

RIGHT **Varzi and Nuvolari were rivals for years. Here Achille leads Tazio in the 1936 Coppa Acerbo at Pescara**

To begin with Caracciola led fairly easily, challenged only by Rosemeyer. Nuvolari, for the most part, was down in sixth position, but then proceeded to drive faster and faster, moving up to third place on lap 7 and second on lap 9, before passing Caracciola into the lead on lap 10! The order was now Nuvolari, Caracciola, Rosemeyer and von Brauchitsch and to the huge delight of everyone in the packed grandstand, all four drivers came in to refuel on lap 12. Mercedes dealt with Caracciola in 67 seconds and von Brauchitsch in 47, whereas Rosemeyer was at his pit for 75 and poor Nuvolari was stationary for 2 minutes 14 seconds. This was due to the fact that the pressure pump for refuelling packed up and the petrol had to be poured in from churns. When Tazio finally got away, he had dropped from first to sixth place. His next lap must have truly been something to see, for he flung the P3 Alfa round the 'Ring to such purpose that when he passed the pits again he was *second*, having passed Stuck, Caracciola, Rosemeyer, and Fagioli! It was a staggering performance, but it must have seemed to most people that the Alfa Romeo simply couldn't stand up to such ferocious driving and with von Brauchitsch well in the lead now, Mercedes must have been pretty happy.

Von Brauchitsch, too, was driving superbly, determined to win his own Grand Prix, but Nuvolari had the bit between his teeth and was really flying. Over the next few laps the gap between the two went as follows: lap 14—1 min. 26 sec.; lap 15—1 min. 27 sec.; lap 16—1 min. 17 sec.; lap 17—63 sec.; lap 18—47 sec.; lap 19—43 sec.; lap 20—32 sec. Well advised of the danger by Neubauer's pit signals, von Brauchitsch pulled back three seconds on the penultimate lap, going into the 22nd round 35 seconds ahead of Nuvolari. Not even Tazio could make up that amount of time in one lap, so the quarter of a million Germans around the circuit prepared themselves for a famous victory by Manfred von Brauchitsch in his Mercedes.

But the drama was not yet over. Von Brauchitsch was a fast and capable driver, especially on the 'Ring, but smoothness wasn't part of his style and he was notoriously hard on tyres. Neubauer knew this full well and although he could see the rear tyres on the Mercedes deteriorating with every passing lap, he dare not bring Manfred in. Half-way round the very last lap, the left rear tyre flew apart and a wretched von Brauchitsch saw his greatest prize snatched from his grasp.

Nuvolari took the chequered flag in a thunderous silence—the sight of his red Alfa crossing the line with the Mercedes nowhere to be seen being met with disbelief by everyone in the start and finish area (not least by Major Hühnlein, who was going to have to explain this highly embarrassing all-Italian victory in the German Grand Prix to his *Führer*!). Indeed, so confident of a Mercedes win were the authorities that they hadn't bothered to dig out a record of the Italian national anthem, and for a while there was a very embarrassing silence from the loud-speakers. Once again, though, they were outsmarted by Nuvolari, who always brought his own copy of the *Marcia Reale* to the circuits for good luck. So the anthem was played and, to their credit, the Germans gave Tazio a huge reception, for the little man was tremendously popular and

he had won a truly astounding victory.

Nuvolari went on to win three more races that season, but none of the major *Grandes Epreuves*, although he did finish second (in Dreyfus' Alfa) in the Italian GP and again at Brno, where Bernd Rosemeyer scored his first victory. At the end of the year he must have taken considerable satisfaction from his successes, especially since Varzi had only won two races for Auto Union.

For 1936 Tazio stayed with Scuderia Ferrari and although he didn't win any of the major European races in a season which was dominated by Bernd Rosemeyer and Auto Union, he nonetheless scored some noticeable successes. He put up a marvellous fight in the rain at Monaco, leading Caracciola in the early laps after the sensational second-lap crash at the chicane. At the time his eldest son, Giorgio, was very ill and although desperately worried, Nuvolari drove like the master he was, to take the lead from Caracciola on lap 10. He extended his lead to over ten seconds by lap 20, but then his brakes began to play up and Caracciola caught him quickly and soon went by. Rudi won and Tazio managed to finish fourth.

He had yet another of his famous crashes at Tripoli, when a tyre burst on the Alfa. Nuvolari was thrown out and wound up in hospital, once again in a plaster cast, due to some broken ribs. Forbidden to race by the doctors, he naturally turned up at the pits the next day and took part in the Grand Prix, finishing seventh. The winner was Varzi. . . . In deference to medical opinion, Nuvolari then took a month off, before returning to the cockpit in the Penya Rhin GP which he won in the new V-12 Alfa, beating the Mercedes and Auto Unions fairly and squarely.

Not even he, however, could do anything about Bernd Rosemeyer's extraordinary ability to see through the fog that descended upon the Nürburgring during the Eifel GP, although the Alfa led at half distance and finally finished second behind the remarkable German. A week later Tazio reversed the order in the Hungarian GP at Budapest after a masterly drive in which he soundly thrashed the German teams to such effect that all three Mercedes retired! Achille Varzi finished third and optimistically perhaps, persuaded Auto Union to let him have a car for the Milan GP the following weekend. Varzi put up a great fight, but on the short, twisty circuit in Sempione Park the Auto Union was outfumbled by Nuvolari's 12-cylinder Alfa and Tazio won by nine seconds.

No doubt the hundreds of thousands who flocked to the Nürburgring for the German Grand Prix were hoping for another sensational drive by Nuvolari, after his miraculous victory there the previous year. They were to be disappointed, as he retired when holding second place. The next weekend, however, thousands of Italian racegoers were witness to one of the little man's greatest victories when he won the Coppa Ciano—for the fifth time!

Within seconds of the start, Nuvolari's V-12 Alfa broke its rear axle. Furious, he parked it and stormed back to the pits, loudly demanding another car, in particular Carlo Pintacuda's 8C. The Scuderia showed little enthusiasm for this, for although Mercedes had given the race a miss after their disastrous display in the German GP, Auto Union were there in force and there seemed little chance of even

Nuvolari making up time on the likes of Rosemeyer, Stuck and Varzi, who were now well in the lead.

Tazio dismissed this argument and threatened to leave the team if he didn't get the car he wanted. So, at the end of lap 3 Pintacuda was called in and Nuvolari set off in the 8-cylinder Alfa. For the first time, the Coppa Ciano was being held on the new Livorno circuit and its narrow, twisty nature seemed to suit Nuvolari perfectly. Driving with a sustained fury in front of his adoring countrymen, many of whom were almost weeping with joy and excitement, Nuvolari caught the leaders one by one and eventually led the Alfas home to a brilliant one-two-three. It was one of Tazio Nuvolari's most outrageous victories. He nearly did it again in the Coppa Acerbo two weeks later, but after leading for the first four laps his 12C Alfa dropped a valve and he had to retire.

Nuvolari came second behind Rosemeyer (who else in 1936?) in the Italian GP and then finished his European season off nicely with a win in Modena. Early in October he sailed for New York with team mates Brivio and Farina, where they took part in the revived Vanderbilt Cup. Run on the new and exceedingly twisty Roosevelt Raceway, the race was something of a fiasco, as the American cars (which naturally made up most of the 45 starters) were completely outclassed by the Europeans and Nuvolari won by over 11 minutes!

In spite of his lack of real success in major European races, Tazio had done very well financially (his win in New York was worth $20,000), his six wins putting him at the top of the prize money list and making him Italian Champion for the third time. For 1937 he signed again with Scuderia Ferrari.

The year turned out to be a bad one for Nuvolari. To begin with, Ferrari was in some disarray as Alfa Romeo decided to get back into racing by buying a large chunk of the Scuderia. The cars were completely outclassed by the new Mercedes-Benz W125s and the Auto Unions and Nuvolari was able to score only one minor win during the whole season. On top of that, he had a very big accident in April, when he crashed his V-12 Alfa heavily during practice for the Circuit of Turin. He also had two shattering family bereavements, when first of all his father died and then, while he was on his way to America for the Vanderbilt Cup, his beloved son Giorgio also passed away (he had suffered a heart problem all his life). Tazio learned the terrible news on board the *Normandie*, shortly before he arrived in New York. He gamely went through with the race, but his Alfa 12C threw a rod. He took over Farina's car, but that packed up, too.

For some time, Vittorio Jano had been working on a new version of the V-12 Alfa, but when it at last appeared at Pescara for the Coppa Acerbo it was a terrible disappointment. After four laps Nuvolari brought it into the pits and Farina took over. The race marked the return to the circuits of the Alfa Romeo factory and the cars were now entered by Alfa Corse, not Scuderia Ferrari, which no longer existed, although Enzo Ferrari was still running the team. But Alfa's return was too late for Nuvolari, who was fed up with having to compete against the ultra-fast German cars with inferior machinery and although he was to drive

for Alfa Romeo again, the Coppa Acerbo marked the beginning of the end of his relationship with the team.

As early as May 1937, Professor Porsche had been in touch with Nuvolari, to see if he would be interested in joining Auto Union. There was no Varzi to bar his way now, and Rosemeyer—a great admirer—welcomed the idea so, after the Pescara débâcle, Tazio was invited to drive an Auto Union at Bern. He accepted the invitation and his appearance in the silver car in practice caused a sensation. He admitted that he found it difficult to adjust to the demands of the mid-engined machine and in the race did only six laps before being called in to hand over to Rosemeyer. Later, when the ailing Fagioli stopped for fuel, Tazio took over from him and finally finished seventh.

In spite of such a brief acquaintance with the German car, Nuvolari was very impressed by its speed and when the Alfa Romeo failed him yet again in the Italian Grand Prix the thought of signing with Auto Union for 1938 must have been very tempting. In January Bernd Rosemeyer was killed and his death left a great void in the Auto Union team, for not only had they lost their most gifted and charismatic driver but, at the end of the previous season they had fired Hans Stuck! Suddenly, they were in desperate need of a top class driver. In February, Ugo Ricordi met with Nuvolari and tried to persuade him to sign with the Zwickau concern, but although very fed up with Alfa Romeo, Tazio felt honour-bound to give the home team another chance and was under considerable pressure from the Italian press and the public. He did, however, agree to test the new 3-litre, V-12 Auto Union at Avus early in the year, which gave him a good chance to see how it was shaping up and, at the same time, let Enzo Ferrari and Alfa Romeo know just where he would be going if the promised new Alfa failed to deliver the goods.

It failed. During practice for its first race, the Pau GP, the new car—dubbed the 308—caught fire when chassis-flexing caused the fuel tank to rupture. Nuvolari baled out of the flaming car and suffered burns to his legs. Happily, they were not serious, but he was furious with Alfa Romeo for giving him such a badly built car and for once he was clearly very shaken by the incident. He vowed never to drive an Alfa Romeo again and, shortly afterwards, announced his retirement! This was something of a bombshell, and although many people had for some time been suggesting that he should quit, nobody actually believed him. He seemed to have made up his mind, however, and as if to emphasize the point he took his wife on a long trip to America.

Back in Europe, the new Auto Unions made their debut in the French GP at Reims and it was one of the briefest debuts on record, as both cars crashed on the first lap! Now without Rosemeyer and Stuck, the team had no drivers of real calibre and with the German Grand Prix on the horizon, drastic measures were called for. The company made its peace with Hans Stuck and invited Nuvolari to join him in the team at the Nürburgring. Refreshed by his trip to the States, Tazio doubtless felt that he and Auto Union could be of mutual benefit, so he agreed. He had, of course, only driven the car up and down the Avus *autobahn*, but it seemed reasonable to expect that the new 3-litre V-12 with its de Dion rear end would be less of a handful than the V-16. Anyway, it was a challenge, and one that Tazio Nuvolari could not resist.

He got a tremendous ovation as he walked to his car for the Grand Prix. With all eyes upon him and driving on a circuit where he had worked his magic three years before, Nuvolari must have dearly wanted to put on a good show. Alas, it was not to be, for on the very first lap he went off the road at Brünnchen. One report said that he had been distracted while wiping some oil from his windscreen, another that he was just going a mite too fast and had been caught out by the mid-engined car. Whatever the reason, Nuvolari rejoined the race in last-but-one position, but the car was damaged and he had to retire. When H. P. Müller stopped at half-distance, he sportingly handed over to Tazio, who brought the Auto Union home fourth, nine and a half minutes behind the winner, Dick Seaman.

Still dissatisfied with the performance of their cars, Auto Union skipped the Coppa Ciano, but turned out in force for the Coppa Acerbo. All three cars retired, apparently suffering from fuel starvation. Things were no better in the Swiss GP, where they were in and out of the pits throughout the race and Nuvolari finally staggered home in ninth place. His marked lack of success in the first three races with the German team must have given Tazio 'that old feeling' he had experienced far too often with Alfa Romeo, but happily, everything came good on his home ground at Monza, where he beat Mercedes handsomely to win the Italian Grand Prix. His countrymen were only fairly ecstatic about his victory, for although he was still their adored favourite, Nuvolari's rightful place was not in a silver Auto Union, but in a bright red Alfa Romeo!

He then rounded off the year with another superb victory in the Donington Grand Prix, where he showed that, at the ripe old age of 46, he simply had no peers. Singlehanded, he had put Auto Union right back at the top of the Grand Prix tree, in a manner the team hadn't known since Rosemeyer's great season of 1936. They must have rued the day they turned him down in 1934, in favour of Achille Varzi....

Furious with the French for supporting the Spanish Royalists in their fight against Fascism, early in 1939 Mussolini banned all Italians from racing in France, so Auto Union refused to send any cars to Pau. As the Italians had also restricted all their races to 1500 cc cars, Tripoli was out, too, and the team's first race was the Eifel GP where, although he drove brilliantly, Nuvolari could do nothing about young Hermann Lang in his Mercedes. Conditions were so appalling in the Belgian GP at Spa that both Nuvolari *and* Caracciola spun off!

The Spanish Civil War ended in April, so Nuvolari was allowed to race in the French GP. For the first six laps he and Hermann Lang enjoyed a tremendous duel on the high-speed straights of Reims, until the Auto Union's engine expired. Tazio had set up a victory for his team mates, though, as all three Mercedes blew up, allowing H. P. Müller and newcomer Schorsch Meier to finish one-two. But it was Mercedes' year at the 'Ring and Caracciola won the German GP, although Nuvolari gave him a good fight until his engine blew again. The Swiss GP was dominated by

the three Mercedes and Tazio could only finish fifth behind team mate Müller.

There remained one more Grand Prix before war put a stop to everything, and it was fitting that that event—the Yugoslav GP in Belgrade—should be won by Tazio Nuvolari, the man who had virtually dominated European motor racing for the previous decade and a half. Rudolf Caracciola may have won more major races but—and this in no way diminishes the great German's phenomenal skills—he was invariably given superior machinery to drive. Nuvolari, however, almost made a career out of winning with inferior cars and this extraordinary ability was just one of a number of facets about the man which made him the best-loved racing driver of his time—perhaps of all time. His mode of dress was another. Early on in his career he settled on a 'uniform', which he donned almost religiously for every race—a yellow, short-sleeved woollen shirt with his initials, TN, on the left breast, and light blue linen trousers. If it was cold, he would wear a leather waistcoat over his shirt. His lucky charm was a little tortoise shell, given to him by the Italian poet, Gabriele d'Annunzio, for luck. He kept this at home in his study, but bought a tortoise brooch, which he often pinned to the neck of his yellow shirt.

And he was not just colourful to look at, his whole attitude to life, death and motor racing made him a hero to millions—his passion for racing; his absolute refusal to know when he was beaten and his oft-stated belief that the only acceptable death for him would be at the wheel of a racing car. He had numerous crashes, indeed his career

might well be called a chapter of accidents punctuated by victories and those accidents often left him with broken bones and covered in plaster, yet he had the endearing habit of treating his injuries as a reason for *leaving* hospital when there was another race to be run. . . .

His driving style was all his own—indeed, no-one else would have wanted it! The Great Little Man was only 1.6 m (5 ft 3 in.) tall and all skin and bone and as soon as he started racing cars he found that he simply hadn't the strength to force them round corners—it was far easier to use the engine and the steering wheel to make the car slide and then drive it round on the throttle. For this he generally gets the credit for inventing the four-wheel drift. All this meant that he was an incredibly busy driver, with his elbows flashing up and down, often as high as his ears as he urged his car to greater efforts. W. F. Bradley likened him to 'a jockey whipping a tired horse', contrasting him with his great contemporary, Caracciola, whom he described as 'making a fast run for the pleasure of the thing'. Spectators could not fail to admire Caracciola's smoothness and precision, but Nuvolari's jack-in-the-box technique made him excitement personified—the man was charisma on wheels.

Surely, the advent of war should have signalled his retirement but, incredibly, when racing resumed in 1946, Tazio Nuvolari was there. Perhaps it was inevitable rather than incredible, for racing was as necessary to him as the air he breathed, and breathed with increasing difficulty as his lungs began to develop an incurable ailment apparently brought about by years of inhaling exhaust and petrol fumes. To try to combat this he wore a surgical mask when racing, but his condition got worse, not better. Even before the war, when he was in his prime, there were those who firmly believed that Nuvolari had a death wish and his return to racing seemed to indicate that his expectation of dying in a racing car was now an ambition. If so, that ambition was not to be fulfilled, but for the second time death struck him and Carolina a cruel blow by taking their younger son, Alfredo, at the age of 18. Nuvolari raced on.

In that first year after the war, he won the Albi GP, finished second in the Circuit of Mantua and fourth in the GP des Nations in Geneva. The next year he put up a truly astonishing performance in the Mille Miglia, driving an open, 1500 cc Cisitalia in which he very nearly won, having led most of the way until delayed by the appallingly wet conditions which swamped his car's little engine. He still managed to finish second behind Clemente Biondetti's 3-litre Alfa Romeo. Afterwards Biondetti gallantly stated that Nuvolari was the true winner. He, Biondetti, had merely finished first. In 1948 Tazio was reunited with Enzo Ferrari, now building his own cars, and drove a Ferrari for the first time in the Mille Miglia. Again he led, but then the chassis broke up under him and he had to retire.

His last race was actually a hillclimb, at Monte Pellegrino, and he won his class and came fifth overall in an 1100 cc Abarth. Three years later, on 11 August 1953, the Great Little Man died, not in a racing car, but in his own bed, at home. His last wish was that he should be buried in his uniform—his blue trousers, yellow shirt and leather wind helmet. And so he was.

Tazio won a great victory in front of his home crowd in the Italian GP at Monza in 1938. Here he negotiates a chicane, something which Zehender's Maserati evidently failed to do!

July 25, 1939. 997 *The* **Motor**

Caracciola Wins German Grand Prix

Extraordinary Race; Only One Mercedes-Benz and One Auto Union Left Running. Maserati Third, a Lap Behind. New Lap Record

THE German Grand Prix, last Sunday, was an extremely queer race. Practice periods had suggested a race at record speed, but the event had hardly started before the Mercedes team was decimated and Auto Unions lost all but one car.

In the end only one Mercedes and one Auto Union were left, a lap ahead of anyone else. Auto Unions seem to have found more speed and power but are more fragile, whilst Mercedes had carburation trouble which affected plugs and pistons.

Lang led off on the first lap with a huge lead and almost immediately went out of the race. Nuvolari then led until the road after 12 laps and Hasse did the same thing at the same time.

Caracciola won by 58 secs. at 75.18 m.p.h., Muller was second and Pietsch third, a lap behind.

The Race

From " Grande Vitesse " by Telephone.
ADENAU, *Sunday.*

RACE day for the German Grand Prix on the Nurburg Ring last Sunday dawned with typical uncertain Eifel Mountain weather. Heavy, low clouds hung in the grey skies and there were mists over the forests. This year the crowds which flocked to the circuit

RESULTS

22 laps—312 miles
1. **Caracciola** (Mercedes-Benz), 4 hrs. 8 mins. 41.8 secs. (121 k.p.h. = 75.18 m.p.h.).
2. **Muller** (Auto Union), 4 hrs. 9 mins. 39.6 secs.
3. **Pietsch** (Maserati), 1 lap behind, 4 hrs. 12 mins. 46.6 secs.
4. **Dreyfus** (Delahaye), 2 laps behind, 4 hrs. 20 mins. 16.4 secs.
5. **" Raph "** (Delahaye), 3 laps behind, 4 hrs. 11 mins. 43.8 secs.
6. **Mazaud** (Delahaye), 3 laps behind, 4 hrs. 11 mins. 44 secs.
7. **Joa** (1,500 Maserati), 3 laps behind, 4 hrs. 14 mins. 33.4 secs.
Fastest lap.—Caracciola, 20th lap, 81.66 m.p.h.

LIST OF STARTERS AND THEIR CARS

Nuvolari.—3-litre V12 Auto Union with two superchargers.
Stuck.—3-litre V12 Auto Union with two superchargers.
Muller.—3-litre V12 Auto Union with two superchargers.
Hasse.—Auto Union with single supercharger.
Meier.—Auto Union with single supercharger.
Caracciola.—3-litre V12 Mercedes.
Brauchitsch.—3-litre V12 Mercedes.
Lang.—3-litre V12 Mercedes.
Brendel (instead of Hartmann).—3-litre V12 Mercedes.
Sommer.—3-litre 8-cylinder Alfa-Romeo, 1938 type.
Dreyfus.—4½-litre V12 Delahaye unsupercharged two-seater, 1938 type.
" Raph."—4½-litre V12 Delahaye unsupercharged two-seater, 1938 type.
Mazaud.—3½-litre 6-cylinder Delahaye Le Mans two-seater.
Villoresi.—3-litre 8-cylinder Maserati, 1939 type.
Pietsch.—3-litre 8-cylinder Maserati, 1939 type.
Mandirola.—3-litre Maserati, old type.
Joa.—1,500 c.c. 6-cylinder Maserati, old type.

were much smaller than usual, but there were at least 250,000 people all round the 14-mile circuit.

There had been activity in both Mercedes and Auto Union camps until a

PLAN VIEW of the Mercedes-Benz V12 3-litre engine. The two superchargers are out of sight under the cowling in front of the engine. There are twin camshafts to each bank of cylinders, and four valves per cylinder—as in the antecedent 5¼-litre straight-eights.

he, too, had pit stops and eventually blew up. Then Caracciola led to the end—except when displaced whilst he changed wheels—with Muller's Auto Union on his tail all the way.

Sommer's Alfa blew up at two laps. Stuck's Auto Union at two laps. Lang at three laps. Brendel ran off the road after four laps, having done the fastest lap, not beaten until Caracciola went even faster just before the finish.

Villoresi (Maserati) was very rapid, but he went into a ditch after seven laps. " Raph " retired with a leaky tank after six laps. Mandirola was disqualified after 10 laps. Meier went off

• • •

HERMANN LANG, fastest driver in the Mercedes team, made this face specially for our photograph—and wore his helmet thus in honour of the occasion.

The Motor   998   *July 25, 1939.*

LOOKING DOWN on the Auto Union, with its engine at the rear. The unit is a V12, 3-litres, now with two blowers, one camshaft on each cylinder bank for the exhausts and a central camshaft between the V opening the inlets left and right. This car has the turret of four carburetters, but several modifications to this system were in use at Nurburg.

GERMAN GRAND PRIX .

had repeated stops until he retired after 100 miles, going backwards into a ditch and retiring at the pits later.

Right from the start the race went crazy. Nothing seemed to go according to plan. Troubles smote all and sundry.

Maserati Surprises Them

First of all, on the second lap, Pietsch passed nearly everyone and went up into second place and sat just behind Lang, the Maserati emitting a beautiful scream. Then, as they swept on to the plateau at the start, Lang stopped for plugs. Pietsch flashed past into the lead and there, on his tail, sat Nuvolari, shaking his fist and bursting himself to get by.

" Raph " also stopped for plugs and was away again before Lang, who rejoined the rest after a 2½-minute stop. When he restarted Lang did not waste any time.

Nuvolari duly got past Pietsch in

• • •

WHEN SECONDS MATTER: mechanic applying the electric starter to the rear engine of an Auto Union at a pit stop, turning on the power immediately the fuel hose is cut off.

late hour the night before the race. Nuvolari's Auto Union had burst into flames on his last lap in practice, when a fuel pipe broke; he jumped clear and was unhurt. That night eight mechanics slaved on the car, completely dismantling and rebuilding the engine in five hours. Meier, also at the end of the last practice lap, burst his engine and kept the mechanics busy.

The Auto Union " Power Bulges "

The mystery of the new bulges on the Auto Union cowlings is now revealed; there are, on the latest cars, two superchargers (blowing at higher pressures than before) and a very complicated carburation system. Nuvolari, Stuck and Muller had this type in the race. There was one change in the Mercedes team when Brendel was substituted for Hartmann and thus had the excitement of competing in a race for the first time. His excellent practice time of 10 mins. 9 secs. put him in the second row at the start.

Thanks to his record lap in 9 mins. 43 secs. (87.4 m.p.h.), Lang was in the best position; Caracciola and Brauchitsch alongside with laps in 9 mins. 56 secs. and 9 mins. 51 secs. respectively. Then came Brendel and Muller and, in the third row, Pietsch, Stuck and Nuvolari.

One Record——

Lang's practice lap of 87.4 m.p.h., by the way, is the highest speed ever done on the Ring and even beat Rosemeyer's old record with the 6-litre Auto Union.

Instantly, at the start, Brauchitsch darted into the lead, with Stuck, Lang and Caracciola flat out behind him. As they swirled round the South Curve

and tore back up the return road behind the pits, Lang slammed past into the lead, Brauchitsch next, then Stuck and Muller, and all the cars strung out, evenly spaced, as they tore down the valley into the forest on their first lap.

——Now Another

Lang went like a streak and had a lead of 28 secs. on the first lap, which must be a record in itself; Brauchitsch next, then Muller, and, surprisingly, Pietsch, handling a big car for the first time and going like a master, leading Caracciola; behind roared Nuvolari and Stuck. The standing lap was done at 79.6 m.p.h.

Naturally, the unsupercharged French sports cars were somewhat outclassed by the horde of German cars—four Mercedes and five Auto Unions—but Pietsch's Maserati was well in amongst them. Villoresi, on the sister car, stopped after one lap for plugs and

the next few miles and led the race, so that the order was—Nuvolari, Muller, Caracciola, Pietsch.

Lang Out

Sommer blew up. Villoresi stopped again, and, lo, on the next time round, Lang came slowly in and retired with engine trouble. Just after three laps the Mercedes, rather as happened at Rheims, were in great trouble—one car left in 100 per cent. trim, driven by the champion Caracciola, and another, in the inexperienced hands of the cadet Brendel, running fifth. Nor did the Auto Unions escape unscathed, for Stuck broke a fuel connection and retired; Stuck came into the pits on the back of Sommer's limping Alfa.

For the next few laps Nuvolari held a bare 5 secs. lead, but behind him Caracciola passed Muller into second place, Brendel surprisingly fourth and going well.

. . . . Contd.

The circuit was in an extremely dangerous state, with slight rain at some parts and dry roads at others, so that the drivers did not know what they were up against at any given corner. As soon as Lang had blown up Neubauer shot a mechanic off up the course to flag Brendel in, so that Lang could take over the machine and start all over again, but Brendel did the fastest lap of the day so far in 10 mins. 28 secs. at 81.16 m.p.h. and did not see the signal.

Off he went to do another lap, and this time had the fright of his life when Pietsch spun round just beside him and Brendel went off the road on a wet patch and came to an abrupt stop. This disaster left only Caracciola's Mercedes, with four Auto Unions, but Meier's car had plug trouble, too, and fell right back.

Nuvolari Loses Lead

Amidst all this excitement Nuvolari led for five laps (72 miles) and then stopped at his pit, too, so that Caracciola went past into the lead. The little Italian was at rest for over a minute while they inspected his engine but did not do anything to it. He went off again, fourth in the race, only to stop next lap for rear tyres and fuel—a rest of 1½ minutes.

Thus the order at six laps became Caracciola, leading by 18 secs., Hasse, Muller, Nuvolari, Pietsch, Dreyfus, Meier, Joa, "Raph," Mazaud and Mandirola.

Villoresi retired on the next lap after an excursion off the road; Brauchitsch split his fuel tank and retired as well. The leak was in the scuttle tank and dripped on to the magneto—a rather dangerous business.

On the eighth lap Caracciola's car began to sound flat and detuned, and Muller crept to within 10 secs. at 75.5 m.p.h., Hasse close behind, and then Nuvolari. Dreyfus's Delahaye broke its frame.

Putting the Merc. Right

At nine laps (129 miles) Caracciola and Muller both refuelled and changed rear tyres at the same time. The two gangs of mechanics slaved like maniacs to the cheering of the crowds. Muller went off in 44 secs. but they played about with Caracciola's plugs and he was 1 min. 23 secs. at rest. Thereafter, however, Caracciola's car went as it should. During these alarums Hasse went by and led by 35 secs. and had time to stop for tyres and fuel and to get away again in 37 secs. without losing his lead.

At this juncture Mandirola, having passed his pit, chose to refuel from the back of it on the return road and was summarily disqualified for his trouble.

Rain and the slippery circuit kept the race speed down to between 70 and 75 m.p.h. and no lap records were possible.

Half-distance—Hasse Leads

At half-distance (11 laps) the order

Nurburg Ring; 14.17 Mi'es and 174 Corners

THE Nurburg Ring is a winding, normal-width, normally surfaced mountain road running in a wide loop through the Eifel Mountains, just this side of the Rhine, and was built between 1925 and 1927 at a cost of 15,000,000 marks. It is on private ground and, like Donington, is not open to traffic.

The lap measures 14.17 miles and starts on a high plateau 2,000 ft. above sea level near the ancient ruins of the Nurburg Castle. The grandstand is nearly 180 yds. long and holds 2,500 spectators. Opposite, across a concrete area on which the cars start and finish, is the line of concrete pits, with a promenade on top. From the start the cars run almost at once to the wide, slightly banked sweep of the Sudkhere (South Curve), and back behind the pits, before diving off round the Tribunen Curve downhill through the forested valley of Hocheichen, with many twists and turns.

Next comes a run uphill into more open country with several twists, followed by the downhill plunge into the Fuchsrohr, and up the other side to Adenau Forest. From here the road runs dangerously fast through curves and downhill to Adenau Gate, uphill past the cliff side of the mountains of Bergwerk, and along a valley to the climb towards the Karussel Corner.

This corner is almost a semi-circle, with a concrete-banked ditch, one-car wide, on the inside. From here the road climbs to Hohe Acht and dives down, twisting all the way to Brunchen and Wipperman Curves, round a fast bend at the Pflanzgarten into the Swallow Tail Curve, so called from the shape of the corners.

Finally comes the short home straight—1½ miles—over hump-backed bridges, the 120 m.p.h. curve under the Antonius Bridge, and so back on to the Startplaz again.

There are 174 corners of all types—89 to the left, 85 to the right.

Last year's Grand Prix was won by the late Dick Seaman (Mercedes) at 80.75 m.p.h., and he put up the fastest lap at 83.76 m.p.h.

was: Hasse leading by 15 secs. at 71.14 m.p.h., Muller, Caracciola 25 secs. behind leader, Nuvolari 2 mins. 43 secs. behind leader, Pietsch, Meier, Dreyfus, Joa, "Raph" and Mazaud.

On the next lap Caracciola overhauled Muller and on the next took the lead from Hasse and got 32 secs. away in front at an average of 73.52 m.p.h. and then, as Meier came down the Fuchsrohr at 140 m.p.h., the front stub axle snapped so that Meier was very busy indeed until he ended up off the road. Hasse tried to catch Caracciola and overdid it and he ended up in a ditch as well.

Caracciola steadily drove away now, Muller over half a mile to the bad and Nuvolari, unable to make up any ground, in third place; he had a 30-sec. stop for fuel at 16 laps, as well. By this time Pietsch, whose car went remarkably quickly between rather too many stops, was a lap behind and the Delahayes were two laps behind. At

18 laps (256 miles) Caracciola took on a little fuel in only 18 secs. and was off again still leading easily at 74.33 m.p.h., 13 secs. ahead of Muller, with Nuvolari 2½ mins. behind.

Exit Nuvo., and "Carach" Makes Fastest Lap

On the next lap Nuvolari blew up good and proper, the engine hidden in clouds of steam. Thus, of the happy gang that started, each German team had only one man left. At 20 laps, with two to go, Muller refuelled and was off in 15 secs., 38 secs. behind Caracciola now and, just to show willing, Caracciola did the fastest lap of the day at 81.66 m.p.h. and piled up more lead.

He finished his two laps without any trouble and won his fifth German Grand Prix victory by nearly 58 secs. from Muller, Pietsch a lap behind. Dreyfus and "Raph," who, with Mazaud, had done amazingly well, their sports cars fast and reliable, finished three laps later.

BRAKING SYSTEMS OF MODERN GRAND PRIX CARS.

(Right) Rear brake of the Auto Union, an exceptionally wide drum, copiously drilled. The brakes are two-leading-shoe Lockheed hydraulics.

(Below) Front anchor of the Mercedes-Benz, also the two-leading-shoe hydraulic type, with specially ribbed drum and well-slotted back plate for air to escape.

(Above) Front brake of the 4½-litre unsupercharged Delahaye—a cable operated modified Bendix system with generous air vents

THE YEAR IN PICTURES

Caracciola set the last
records of the era on the
wide open spaces of Dessau
with the 3-litre Mercedes

BELOW Hermann Lang disappears into the distance at the start of the 1939 Tripoli GP, which provided a one-two win for the sensational 1½-litre Mercedes

RIGHT Mercedes at rest during practice for the Eifel GP at the 'Ring. Dick Seaman has his back to camera on the right

ABOVE **Black day at Spa. The grid assembles in the rain for the Belgian GP, in which Dick Seaman lost his life. In the foreground are Lang's Mercedes and Farina's Alfa Romeo** (*right*)

RIGHT **Caracciola on his way to victory in the German GP—the final win of his remarkable career**

The marvellous duel at Reims between Nuvolari and Lang in the French GP. They both retired

BELOW Caracciola in a beautiful four-wheel drift as he crosses the line in the Swiss GP at Bern. Hermann Lang won the race

RIGHT **Hermann Lang** not only won the European Championship, but also the *Deutsche Bergmeisterschaft*, which he clinched with victory at Grossglockner

Pau

LENGTH: 2.77 km (1.72 miles)
RACE: Pau GP (1938, 1939)

The French GP was held at Pau in 1930, but on a 15.83 km (9.83 mile) circuit just out of the town. It was called the *Grand Circuit Permanent de Pau*, so naturally it was never used again! In 1933 a new circuit was laid out in the town and the first Pau GP was held that year. Unfortunately, the organizers chose to run the race in February and on the day Pau was unexpectedly snow-bound, making racing somewhat difficult!

With the demise of the Monaco GP in 1938 Pau became the only round-the-houses race in the calendar and Mercedes-Benz decided to use it in 1938 and 1939 as an early test for their new cars. In the first year they suffered a humiliating defeat at the hands of René Dreyfus in his Delahaye and after the race Dreyfus complained again about the exhaust fumes of the Mercedes, just as he had done at Spa in 1935.

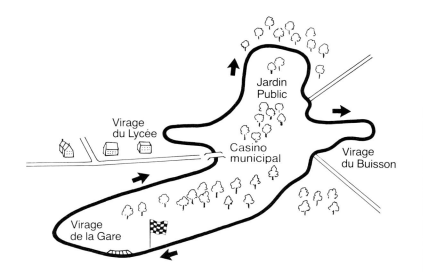

Caracciola leads von Brauchitsch and Lang up the hill at Pau during the 1939 GP, which Lang won

Reims

LENGTH: 7.83 km (4.86 miles)
RACE: French GP (1938, 1939)

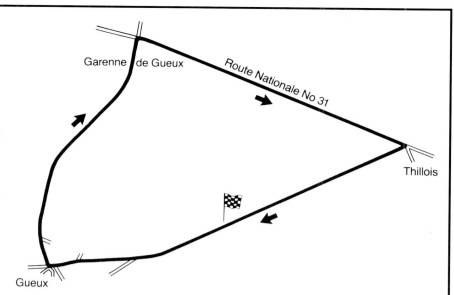

After the sports car nonsense of the previous two years, the French came to their senses in 1938 and made the French Grand Prix for Grand Prix cars once again. For 1938 and 1939, however, the race was given to the AC de Champagne and their very fast, triangular road circuit just outside the cathedral town of Reims. The AC de Champagne was a very wealthy club and had put a great deal of money into its circuit, building a magnificent permanent grandstand opposite the equally magnificent permanent pits. From the higher tiers of this grandstand spectators could look over the pits and across the golden cornfields to watch the cars streaking downhill on the Route Nationale N31 as they raced from Garenne to the Thillois hairpin. There they would turn almost through 180 degrees before screaming down the 3.37 km (2.1 mile) pit straight which led to the little village of Gueux and its tight right-hander which, in turn, led to the trickiest part of the course—the winding, uphill road to Garenne.

Racing began at Reims in 1925, with the GP de Marne (the local *département*). The French GP was first held there in 1932, not to return until 1938, when it became something of a farce, as the Auto Unions both fell out

on the first lap and for the last three-quarters of the race there were only four cars running—three Mercedes and a Darracq, which finished ten laps behind the winner!

Reims vied strongly with Spa for the 'honour' of being the fastest road circuit in Europe and, in order to keep ahead of the opposition, before the 1938 race the AC de Champagne cut down many of the trees which had lined the beginning of the Garenne-Thillois straight and widened and resurfaced the road. In addition, the Club announced plans to demolish some of the houses on the slow right-hander in the village of Gueux,

claiming that this would make the corner safer. No-one could remember a car crashing into any of these houses and clearly the authorities were simply bent on making the circuit faster still. In the event none of the houses was demolished, but nonetheless, many observers felt that the Club's quest for more and more speed was destroying the character of the place.

Reims, 1938 and Hermann Lang leads his team mates Rudolf Caracciola and Manfred von Brauchitsch (the eventual winner) through the village of Gueux

Belgrade

LENGTH: 2.79 km (1.73 miles)
RACE: Yugoslav GP (1939)

This Grand Prix had the sad distinction of being the last to be run until after World War II, being held on the very day England declared war on Germany. Only a fraction longer than Pau, the circuit was roughly triangular in shape and ran round a large park. The Grand Prix was a near farce, with only five contestants.

Due to the outbreak of war, details of the race (such as it was) proved hard to come by for the Press and these communication problems gave rise to a story that Hermann Lang had crashed, receiving injuries from which he later died in Vienna. Happily, this proved to be quite untrue.

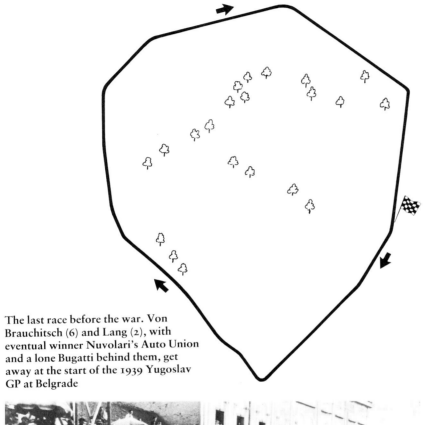

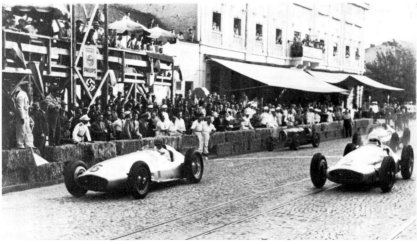

The last race before the war. Von Brauchitsch (6) and Lang (2), with eventual winner Nuvolari's Auto Union and a lone Bugatti behind them, get away at the start of the 1939 Yugoslav GP at Belgrade

Spa-Francorchamps

LENGTH: 14.86 km (9.29 miles)
14.50 km (9.06 miles) (1939)
RACE: Belgian GP (1934, 1935, 1937, 1939)

Generally considered to have been one of the greatest of all road circuits, Spa was a narrow, tree-lined road running in a roughly triangular shape around the Eau Rouge valley some 40 km (25 miles) south-east of Liège. Very fast, it comprised several long, sweeping curves, the long Masta Straight (where Hermann Lang's W154 Mercedes was reported to have reached 310 km/h (193 mph) during practice for the 1939 Belgian GP) and a hairpin at two of its three 'corners'—La Source and Stavelot. The circuit was unique in that its start and finish was on a steep hill, flanked by permanent wooden grandstands and pits, with a spectator gallery above the latter. At the end of the 1934 race this gallery collapsed and, according to Rodney Walkerley, 'shot showers of Belgians onto the heads of the pit personnel below'.

Spa made its debut with the first Belgian Motorcycle GP in 1921 and the first Grand Prix for GP cars (as opposed to touring cars) was held in 1925. Sports and touring car races continued, but the GP was not held again until 1933. In 1934 both Mercedes-Benz and Auto Union withdrew before the race when the Belgian Customs demanded 180,000 francs duty on the 3000 litres (660 gall.) of special fuel they wanted to bring into the country! The following year Mercedes won and René Dreyfus complained bitterly that the German fuel forced him to retire, as he had become ill when following von Brauchitsch for a while. Dreyfus claimed that he had been gassed by the exhaust fumes of the Mercedes, although only a few weeks earlier von Brauchitsch himself had followed Caracciola very closely for many laps in the French GP, without any ill-effects. In 1936 and 1938 Spa hosted a 24-hour Sports Car race instead of a GP, but the Belgian GP was held again in 1937 and 1939, Auto Union winning the former and Mercedes the latter.

Although Spa couldn't compete with the phenomenal lap speeds achieved at Tripoli, the Belgian authorities were determined that theirs should be the fastest road circuit in Europe. To this end the sharpish right-hander at

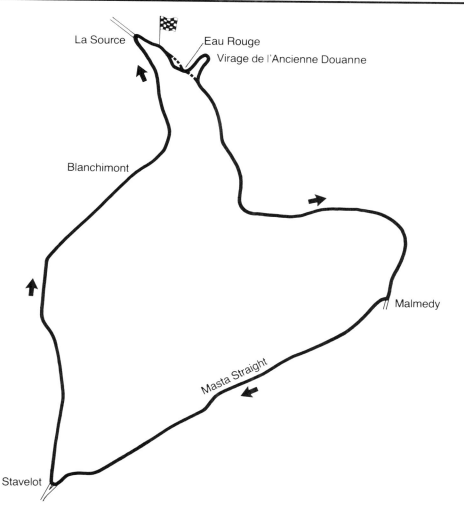

La Source

Eau Rouge

Virage de l'Ancienne Douanne

Blanchimont

Malmedy

Masta Straight

Stavelot

Malmedy was eased considerably in 1934 and in 1939 the hairpin at the Virage de l'Ancienne Douanne, which followed the Eau Rouge left-hander after the start, was by-passed completely, giving the cars a very fast run up the hill to Les Combes and on to Malmedy. This reduced the circuit length by 364 m (398 yds) and was expected to increase lap speeds considerably. However, the 3-litre Mercedes and Auto Unions lacked the sheer power of their 1937 predecessors and although Lang managed 5 min. 3.2 sec. in the dry on the first day of practice for the 1939 event, this was still only two seconds faster than his fastest lap in 1937, set with the 5.6-litre W125 Mercedes. Lang was unable to approach these times in the race, which was run in appallingly wet conditions and is remembered, sadly, for the tragic death of Dick Seaman, who crashed when in the lead.

BELOW LEFT **Hermann Lang turns left at Eau Rouge and heads towards the Ancienne Douanne hairpin at Spa in 1937**

BELOW **Hans Stuck (Auto Union) leads Hermann Lang (Mercedes) round the Ancienne Douanne hairpin at Spa in 1937. This corner was by-passed completely for the 1939 race**

RESULTS

1934

April 2   MONACO GP   100 laps—318 km (197.6 miles)
1 Guy Moll (Alfa Romeo)
   3 hr. 31 min. 31.4 sec. 90.20 km/h (56.05 mph)
2 Louis Chiron (Alfa Romeo) 3 hr. 32 min. 33.4 sec.
3 René Dreyfus (Bugatti) 1 lap behind
4 Marcel Lehoux (Alfa Romeo) 1 lap behind
5 Tazio Nuvolari (Bugatti) 2 laps behind
6 Achille Varzi (Alfa Romeo) 2 laps behind
FASTEST LAP: Felice Trossi (Alfa Romeo)—
   2 min. 02.0 sec. 95.38 km/h (58.28 mph)
Mercedes-Benz and Auto Union did not enter.

May 6   TRIPOLI GP (Mellaha)   40 laps—526.6 km (326.6 miles)
1 Achille Varzi (Alfa Romeo)
   2 hr. 48 min. 53.8 sec. 186.1 km/h (115.7 mph)
2 Guy Moll (Alfa Romeo) 2 hr. 48 min. 54.0 sec.
3 Louis Chiron (Alfa Romeo) 2 hr. 49 min. 07.0 sec.
4 Phi-Phi Etancelin (Maserati) 2 laps behind
5 Clemente Biondetti (Maserati)
6 René Dreyfus (Bugatti)
FASTEST LAP: Chiron—200.35 km/h (124.52 mph)
Mercedes-Benz and Auto Union did not enter.

May 27   AVUS GP   15 laps—294.43 km (182.95 miles)
1 Guy Moll (Alfa Romeo)
   1 hr. 26 min. 03 sec. 205.24 km/h (127.56 mph)
2 Achille Varzi (Alfa Romeo) 1 hr. 27 min. 30 sec.
3 August Momberger (Auto Union) 1 hr. 27 min. 48 sec.
4 Earl Howe (Maserati) 1 hr. 35 min. 18 sec.
5 Tazio Nuvolari (Maserati)
6 Paul Pietsch (Alfa Romeo)
FASTEST LAP: Moll—207.56 km/h (129.0 mph)
Mercedes-Benz withdrew before the race.

June 3   EIFEL GP (Nürburgring)   15 laps—347.15 km (215.7 miles)
1 M. von Brauchitsch (Mercedes-Benz)
   2 hr. 47 min. 36.0 sec. 122.47 km/h (76.12 mph)
2 Hans Stuck (Auto Union)
3 Louis Chiron (Alfa Romeo)
4 Paul Pietsch (Alfa Romeo)
FASTEST LAP: not known

June 17   PENYA RHIN GP (Barcelona)   70 laps—265.3 km (164.85 miles)
1 Achille Varzi (Alfa Romeo)
   2 hr. 33 min. 06.0 sec. 104.0 km/h (64.64 mph)
2 Louis Chiron (Alfa Romeo) 2 hr. 34 min. 23.0 sec.
3 Marcel Lehoux (Alfa Romeo) 2 hr. 35 min. 19.0 sec.
FASTEST LAP: Chiron—2 min. 08.0 sec. 106.59 km/h (66.25 mph)
Mercedes-Benz and Auto Union did not enter.

July 1   FRENCH GP (Montlhéry)   40 laps—500 km (310.4 miles)
1 Louis Chiron (Alfa Romeo)
   3 hr. 39 min. 14.6 sec. 136.88 km/h (85.05 mph)
2 Achille Varzi (Alfa Romeo) 3 hr. 42 min. 31.9 sec.
3 F. Trossi/G. Moll (Alfa Romeo) 3 hr. 43 min. 23.8 sec.
4 Robert Benoist (Bugatti) 4 laps behind
FASTEST LAP: Chiron—
   5 min. 06.0 sec. 147.11 km/h (91.41 mph)
All Mercedes-Benz and Auto Unions retired.

July 15   GERMAN GP (Nürburgring)   25 laps—570.25 km (354.25 miles)
1 Hans Stuck (Auto Union)
   4 hr. 38 min. 19.1 sec. 122.93 km/h (76.39 mph)
2 Luigi Fagioli (Mercedes-Benz) 4 hr. 40 min. 26.1 sec.
3 Louis Chiron (Alfa Romeo) 4 hr. 46 min. 32.4 sec.
4 Tazio Nuvolari (Maserati) 4 hr. 55 min. 10.1 sec.
5 Hanns Geier (Mercedes-Benz) 4 hr. 59 min. 05.3 sec.
6 Ulrich Maag (Alfa Romeo) 5 hr. 04 min. 49.4 sec.
FASTEST LAP: Stuck—
   10 min. 44.2 sec. 127.6 km/h (79.75 mph)

July 22   COPPA CIANO (Montenero)   12 laps—241.2 km (149.9 miles)
1 Achille Varzi (Alfa Romeo)
   2 hr. 49 min. 52.2 sec. 84.77 km/h (52.67 mph)
2 Guy Moll (Alfa Romeo) 2 hr. 50 min. 01.2 sec.
3 Tazio Nuvolari (Maserati) 2 hr. 53 min. 53.4 sec.
4 Felice Trossi (Alfa Romeo) 2 hr. 58 min. 48.0 sec.
5 Nando Barbieri (Alfa Romeo) 2 hr. 59 min. 07.0 sec.
FASTEST LAP: Moll—86.83 km/h (53.97 mph)
Mercedes-Benz and Auto Union did not enter.

August 15   COPPA ACERBO (Pescara)   20 laps—516 km (320.6 miles)
1 Luigi Fagioli (Mercedes-Benz)
   3 hr. 58 min. 56.8 sec. 129.57 km/h (80.51 mph)
2 Tazio Nuvolari (Maserati) 4 hr. 03 min. 35.0 sec.
3 Antonio Brivio (Bugatti) 4 hr. 05 min. 07.6 sec.
4 A. Varzi/P. Ghersi (Alfa Romeo) 4 hr. 05 min. 27.6 sec.
5 Wilhelm Sebastian (Auto Union) 1 lap behind
6 Ernst Henne (Mercedes-Benz) 1 lap behind
FASTEST LAP: Guy Moll (Alfa Romeo)—
   10 min. 51 sec. 143.36 km/h (89.1 mph)
(Moll later crashed and was killed)

August 26 **SWISS GP (Bern)** *70 laps—*
509.6 km (316.6 miles)
1 Hans Stuck (Auto Union)
  3 hr. 37 min. 51.6 sec. 140.35 km/h (87.21 mph)
2 August Momberger (Auto Union) 3 hr. 37 min. 54.4 sec.
3 René Dreyfus (Bugatti) 1 lap behind
4 Achille Varzi (Alfa Romeo) 1 lap behind
5 Louis Chiron (Alfa Romeo) 1 lap behind
6 Luigi Fagioli (Mercedes-Benz) 2 laps behind
FASTEST LAP: Momberger—151.94 km/h (94.42 mph)

September 9 **ITALIAN GP (Monza)** *116 laps—*
499.9 km (310.6 miles)
1 R. Caracciola/L. Fagioli (Mercedes-Benz)
  4 hr. 45 min. 47 sec. 105.18 km/h (65.37 mph)
2 H. Stuck/H. zu Leiningen (Auto Union)
  4 hr. 47 min. 25 sec.
3 F. Trossi/F. Comotti (Alfa Romeo) 2 laps behind
4 Tazio Nuvolari (Maserati) 3 laps behind
5 G. Comotti/A. Marinoni (Alfa Romeo) 3 laps behind
6 Louis Chiron (Alfa Romeo) 3 laps behind
FASTEST LAP: Stuck—
  2 min. 13.6 sec. 116.79 km/h (75.59 mph)

September 23 **SPANISH GP (San Sebastian)** *30 laps—*
519.45 km (322.78 miles)
1 Luigi Fagioli (Mercedes-Benz)
  3 hr. 19 min. 40 sec. 156.3 km/h (97.1 mph)
2 Rudolf Caracciola (Mercedes-Benz) 3 hr. 20 min. 23 sec.
3 Tazio Nuvolari (Bugatti) 3 hr. 20 min. 47 sec.
4 H. zu Leiningen/H. Stuck (Auto Union)
  3 hr. 21 min. 03 sec.
5 Achille Varzi (Alfa Romeo) 3 hr. 21 min. 49 sec.
6 Jean-Pierre Wimille (Bugatti) 1 lap behind
FASTEST LAP: Stuck—
  6 min. 20 sec. 164.09 km/h (101.96 mph)

September 30 **CZECH GP (Brno)** *17 laps—*
495.4 km (307.84 miles)
1 Hans Stuck (Auto Union)
  3 hr. 53 min. 27.9 sec. 127.32 km/h (79.1 mph)
2 Luigi Fagioli (Mercedes-Benz) 3 hr. 56 min. 24.5 sec.
3 Tazio Nuvolari (Maserati) 3 hr. 57 min. 14.1 sec.
4 Hermann zu Leiningen (Auto Union)
  4 hr. 02 min. 05.2 sec.
5 Achille Varzi (Alfa Romeo) 4 hr. 04 min. 08.9 sec.
6 E. Henne/H. Geier (Mercedes-Benz) 1 lap behind
FASTEST LAP: Fagioli—
  13 min. 16.2 sec. 133.25 km/h (82.80 mph)

1935

April 22 **MONACO GP** *100 laps—318 km*
(197.6 miles)
1 Luigi Fagioli (Mercedes-Benz)
  3 hr. 23 min. 49.8 sec. 93.60 km/h (58.16 mph)
2 René Dreyfus (Alfa Romeo) 3 hr. 24 min. 21.3 sec.
3 Antonio Brivio (Alfa Romeo) 3 hr. 24 min. 56.2 sec.
4 Phi-Phi Etancelin (Maserati) 1 lap behind
5 Louis Chiron (Alfa Romeo) 3 laps behind
6 Raymond Sommer (Alfa Romeo) 6 laps behind
FASTEST LAP: Fagioli—
  1 min. 58.4 sec. 96.69 km/h (60.08 mph)
Auto Union did not enter.

May 5 **TUNIS GP (Carthage)** *40 laps—*
504 km (313.2 miles)
1 Achille Varzi (Auto Union)
  3 hr. 05 min. 40.2 sec. 162.87 km/h (101.2 mph)
2 Jean-Pierre Wimille (Bugatti) 3 hr. 09 min. 29.8 sec.
3 Phi-Phi Etancelin (Maserati) 2 laps behind
4 Gianfredo Comotti (Alfa Romeo) 3 laps behind
5 Giuseppe Farina (Maserati) 5 laps behind
6 R. Chambost (Maserati) 5 laps behind
FASTEST LAP: Varzi—
  4 min. 28.4 sec. 169.25 km/h (105.17 mph)
Mercedes-Benz did not enter.

May 12 **TRIPOLI GP (Mellaha)** *40 laps—*
525.6 km (326.6 miles)
1 Rudolf Caracciola (Mercedes-Benz)
  2 hr. 38 min. 47.6 sec. 197.99 km/h (123.03 mph)
2 Achille Varzi (Auto Union) 2 hr. 39 min. 54.2 sec.
3 Luigi Fagioli (Mercedes-Benz) 2 hr. 41 min. 03.8 sec.
4 Tazio Nuvolari (Alfa Romeo) 2 hr. 47 min. 36.4 sec.
5 Louis Chiron (Alfa Romeo) 2 hr. 49 min. 14 sec.
6 René Dreyfus (Alfa Romeo) 2 hr. 49 min. 15 sec.
FASTEST LAP: Caracciola—
  3 min. 34.0 sec. 220.17 km/h (136.8 mph)

May 26 **AVUS GP**
Heat 1—5 laps 97.85 km (60.8 miles)
1 Hans Stuck (Auto Union)
  23 min. 44.8 sec. 249.39 km/h (155.0 mph)
2 Luigi Fagioli (Mercedes-Benz) 24 min. 17.0 sec.
3 René Dreyfus (Alfa Romeo) 26 min. 52.4 sec.
4 Hanns Geier (Mercedes-Benz) 27 min. 05.0 sec.
Heat 2—5 laps 97.85 km (60.8 miles)
1 Rudolf Caracciola (Mercedes-Benz)
  24 min. 47.0 sec. 238.13 km/h (148.0 mph)
2 Achille Varzi (Auto Union) 25 min. 41.3 sec.
3 M. von Brauchitsch (Mercedes-Benz) 26 min. 29.3 sec.
4 Louis Chiron (Alfa Romeo) 27 min. 21.5 sec.
Final—10 laps—196.56 km (122.14 miles)
1 Luigi Fagioli (Mercedes-Benz)
  49 min. 13.2 sec. 238.5 km/h (148.2 mph)
2 Louis Chiron (Alfa Romeo) 50 min. 48.4 sec.

3 Achille Varzi (Auto Union) 51 min. 27.4 sec.
4 Hans Stuck (Auto Union) 51 min. 36.4 sec.
5 M. von Brauchitsch (Mercedes-Benz) 53 min. 18.4 sec.
6 René Dreyfus (Alfa Romeo) 54 min. 24.4 sec.
FASTEST LAP: Stuck—
    4 min. 31.1 sec. 260.65 km/h (162.0 mph)

June 16   EIFEL GP (Nürburgring)   11 laps—
250.8 km (155.84 miles)
1 Rudolf Caracciola (Mercedes-Benz)
    2 hr. 08 min. 02.3 sec. 117.45 km/h (73.00 mph)
2 Bernd Rosemeyer (Auto Union) 2 hr. 08 min. 04.2 sec.
3 Louis Chiron (Alfa Romeo) 2 hr. 09 min. 34.4 sec.
4 Luigi Fagioli (Mercedes-Benz) 2 hr. 12 min. 44.2 sec.
5 Hermann Lang (Mercedes-Benz) 2 hr. 13 min. 48.3 sec.
6 Paul Pietsch (Auto Union) 2 hr. 14 min. 49.0 sec.
FASTEST LAP: Rosemeyer—
    11 min. 05 sec. 126.5 km/h (78.6 mph)

June 23   FRENCH GP (Montlhéry)   40 laps—
500 km (310.4 miles) (3 chicanes added)
1 Rudolf Caracciola (Mercedes-Benz)
    4 hr. 00 min. 54.6 sec. 124.57 km/h (77.40 mph)
2 M. von Brauchitsch (Mercedes-Benz)
    4 hr. 00 min. 55.1 sec.
3 Goffredo Zehender (Maserati) 2 laps behind
4 Luigi Fagioli (Mercedes-Benz) 3 laps behind
5 Achille Varzi (Auto Union) 5 laps behind
6 Raymond Sommer (Maserati) 5 laps behind
FASTEST LAP: Tazio Nuvolari (Alfa Romeo)
    5 min. 29.1 sec. 136.78 km/h (84.99 mph)

June 30   PENYA RHIN GP (Barcelona)   70 laps—
265.3 km (164.85 miles)
1 Luigi Fagioli (Mercedes-Benz)
    2 hr. 27 min. 40 sec. 107.82 km/h (66.99 mph)
2 Rudolf Caracciola (Mercedes-Benz) 2 hr. 28 min. 28 sec.
3 Tazio Nuvolari (Alfa Romeo) 2 hr. 29 min. 15 sec.
4 Antonio Brivio (Alfa Romeo) 2 laps behind
5 Goffredo Zehender (Maserati) 3 laps behind
6 Giorgio Soffietti (Maserati) 6 laps behind
FASTEST LAP: Caracciola—
    2 min. 03.6 sec. 110.95 km/h (68.94 mph)
Auto Union did not enter.

July 14   BELGIAN GP (Spa-Francorchamps)   34 laps—
505.24 km (313.95) miles)
1 Rudolf Caracciola (Mercedes-Benz)
    3 hr. 12 min. 31 sec. 157.5 km/h (97.87 mph)
2 L. Fagioli/M. von Brauchitsch (Mercedes-Benz)
    3 hr. 14 min. 08 sec.
3 Louis Chiron (Alfa Romeo) 3 hr. 14 min. 47 sec.
4 R. Dreyfus/A. Marinoni (Alfa Romeo)
    3 hr. 17 min. 54 sec.
5 Robert Benoist (Bugatti) 3 laps behind
6 Marcel Lehoux (Maserati) 3 laps behind
FASTEST LAP: von Brauchitsch—
    5 min. 23 sec. 165.66 km/h (102.94 mph)
Auto Union did not enter.

July 28   GERMAN GP (Nürburgring)   22 laps—
501.8 km (311.8 miles)
1 Tazio Nuvolari (Alfa Romeo)
    4 hr. 08 min. 40.2 sec. 121.1 km/h (75.25 mph)
2 Hans Stuck (Auto Union) 4 hr. 10 min. 18.8 sec.
3 Rudolf Caracciola (Mercedes-Benz)
    4 hr. 11 min. 03.3 sec.
4 Bernd Rosemeyer (Auto Union) 4 hr. 12 min. 51.0 sec.
5 M. von Brauchitsch (Mercedes-Benz)
    4 hr. 14 min. 17 sec.
6 Luigi Fagioli (Mercedes-Benz) 4 hr. 15 min. 58 sec.
FASTEST LAP: von Brauchitsch—
    10 min. 32.0 sec. 129.6 km/h (80.53 mph)

August 4   COPPA CIANO (Montenero)   12 laps—
241.2 km (149.9 miles)
1 Tazio Nuvolari (Alfa Romeo)
    2 hr. 42 min. 08.8 sec. 88.8 km/h (55.18 mph)
2 Antonio Brivio (Alfa Romeo) 2 hr. 44 min. 06.0 sec.
3 Felice Trossi (Alfa Romeo) 2 hr. 48 min. 23.2 sec.
4 René Dreyfus (Alfa Romeo) 2 hr. 49 min. 08.2 sec.
5 L. Magistri (Alfa Romeo) 3 hr. 00 min. 03.0 sec.
FASTEST LAP: Nuvolari—
    13 min. 15.8 sec. 90.47 km/h (56.21 mph)
Mercedes-Benz and Auto Union did not enter.

August 15   COPPA ACERBO (Pescara)   20 laps—
516 km (320.6 miles)
1 Achille Varzi (Auto Union)
    3 hr. 43 min. 45.0 sec. 139.4 km/h (86.62 mph)
2 Bernd Rosemeyer (Auto Union) 3 hr. 47 min. 07.0 sec.
3 Antonio Brivio (Alfa Romeo) 3 hr. 52 min. 20.0 sec.
4 Gianfranco Comotti (Alfa Romeo) 1 lap behind
5 Mario Tadini (Alfa Romeo) 1 lap behind
6 Carlo Pintacuda (Alfa Romeo) 1 lap behind
FASTEST LAP: Varzi—
    10 min. 35 sec. 146.25 km/h (90.9 mph)
Mercedes-Benz did not enter.

August 25   SWISS GP (Bern)   70 laps—
509.6 km (316.6 miles)
1 Rudolf Caracciola (Mercedes-Benz)
    3 hr. 31 min. 12.2 sec. 144.7 km/h (89.9 mph)
2 Luigi Fagioli (Mercedes-Benz) 3 hr. 31 min. 38. sec.
3 Bernd Rosemeyer (Auto Union) 3 hr. 32 min. 20.0 sec.
4 Achille Varzi (Auto Union)
5 Tazio Nuvolari (Alfa Romeo)
6 Hermann Lang (Mercedes-Benz)
FASTEST LAP: Caracciola—
    2 min. 44.4 sec. 160.7 km/h (99.87 mph)

September 8 **ITALIAN GP (Monza)** *73 laps—503.7 km (312.9 miles)*
1 Hans Stuck (Auto Union)
   3 hr. 40 min. 09 sec. 138.7 km/h (86.2 mph)
2 R. Dreyfus/T. Nuvolari (Alfa Romeo)
   3 hr. 41 min. 50 sec.
3 P. Pietsch/B. Rosemeyer (Auto Union) 3 laps behind
4 Attilio Marinoni (Alfa Romeo) 5 laps behind
5 Piero Taruffi (Bugatti) 14 laps behind
FASTEST LAP: Nuvolari—
   2 min. 49.8 sec. 146.9 km/h (91.3 mph)

All four Mercedes failed to finish.

September 22 **SPANISH GP (San Sebastian)** *30 laps—519.5 km (322.8 miles)*
1 Rudolf Caracciola (Mercedes-Benz)
   3 hr. 09 min. 59.4 sec. 164 km/h (101.9 mph)
2 Luigi Fagioli (Mercedes-Benz) 3 hr. 10 min. 42.4 sec.
3 M. von Brauchitsch (Mercedes-Benz)
   3 hr. 12 min. 14.2 sec.
4 Jean-Pierre Wimille (Bugatti) 3 hr. 12 min. 53.8 sec.
5 Bernd Rosemeyer (Auto Union) 3 hr. 17 min. 35.0 sec.
6 Robert Benoist (Bugatti) 1 lap behind
FASTEST LAP: Achille Varzi (Auto Union)—
   5 min. 58 sec. 173.8 km/h (108.0 mph)

September 29 **CZECH GP (Brno)** *17 laps—495.4 km (307.84 miles)*
1 Bernd Rosemeyer (Auto Union)
   3 hr. 44 min. 10.6 sec. 132.6 km/h (82.39 mph)
2 Tazio Nuvolari (Alfa Romeo) 3 hr. 50 min. 48.4 sec.
3 Louis Chiron (Alfa Romeo) 3 hr. 50 min. 52.8 sec.
4 Antonio Brivio (Alfa Romeo) 3 hr. 52 min. 57.0 sec.
5 Laszlo Hartmann (Maserati) 2 laps behind
FASTEST LAP: Achille Varzi (Auto Union)—
   12 min. 45.0 sec. 137.13 km/h (85.21 mph)

Mercedes-Benz did not enter.

1936

April 13 **MONACO GP** *100 laps—318 km (197.6 miles)*
1 Rudolf Caracciola (Mercedes-Benz)
   3 hr. 49 min. 20.4 sec. 83.19 km/h (51.69 mph)
2 Achille Varzi (Auto Union) 3 hr. 51 min. 09.5 sec.
3 Hans Stuck (Auto Union) 1 lap behind
4 Tazio Nuvolari (Alfa Romeo) 1 lap behind
5 Giuseppe Farina (Alfa Romeo) 3 laps behind
6 Jean-Pierre Wimille (Bugatti) 3 laps behind
FASTEST LAP: Stuck—
   2 min. 07.4 sec. 89.87 km/h (55.86 mph)

May 10 **TRIPOLI GP (Mellaha)** *40 laps—525.6 km (326.6 miles)*
1 Achille Varzi (Auto Union)
   2 hr. 31 min. 25.4 sec. 207.63 km/h (129.0 mph)

2 Hans Stuck (Auto Union) 2 hr. 31 min. 29.8 sec.
3 Luigi Fagioli (Mercedes-Benz) 2 hr. 33 min. 38.4 sec.
4 Rudolf Caracciola (Mercedes-Benz)
   2 hr. 34 min. 56.4 sec.
5 Carlo Pintacuda (Alfa Romeo) 1 lap behind
6 Mario Tadini (Alfa Romeo) 1 lap behind
FASTEST LAP: Varzi—
   3 min. 27.4 sec. 227.4 km/h (141.3 mph)

May 17 **TUNIS GP (Carthage)** *30 laps—381.4 km (237.0 miles)*
1 Rudolf Caracciola (Mercedes-Benz)
   2 hr. 22 min. 44.6 sec. 160.32 km/h (99.62 mph)
2 Carlo Pintacuda (Alfa Romeo) 2 laps behind
3 Jean-Pierre Wimille (Bugatti) 2 laps behind
4 Raymond Sommer (Alfa Romeo) 5 laps behind
FASTEST LAP: Bernd Rosemeyer (Auto Union)—
   4 min. 34.0 sec. 167.0 km/h (103.8 mph)

Both Auto Unions retired.

June 7 **PENYA RHIN GP (Barcelona)** *80 laps—303.2 km (188.4 miles)*
1 Tazio Nuvolari (Alfa Romeo)
   2 hr. 43 min. 07 sec. 111.65 km/h (69.37 mph)
2 Rudolf Caracciola (Mercedes-Benz) 2 hr. 43 min. 12 sec.
3 Giuseppe Farina (Alfa Romeo) 4 laps behind
4 Ernst von Delius (Auto Union) 5 laps behind
5 Bernd Rosemeyer (Auto Union) 5 laps behind
6 Louis Chiron (Mercedes-Benz) 5 laps behind
FASTEST LAP: Nuvolari—
   1 min. 58 sec. 115.65 km/h (71.86 mph)

June 14 **EIFEL GP (Nürburgring)** *10 laps—228.1 km (141 miles)*
1 Bernd Rosemeyer (Auto Union)
   1 hr. 56 min. 41.2 sec. 117.1 km/h (72.76 mph)
2 Tazio Nuvolari (Alfa Romeo) 1 hr. 58 min. 54.0 sec.
3 Antonio Brivio (Alfa Romeo) 1 hr. 59 min. 30.4 sec.
4 Giuseppe Farina (Alfa Romeo) 1 hr. 59 min. 58.6 sec.
5 Hermann Lang (Mercedes-Benz) 2 hr. 02 min. 28.4 sec.
6 Louis Chiron (Mercedes-Benz) 2 hr. 03 min. 33.0 sec.
FASTEST LAP: Rosemeyer—
   11 min. 25.0 sec. 120.3 km/h (74.76 mph)

June 21 **HUNGARIAN GP (Budapest)** *50 laps—250 km (155.4 miles)*
1 Tazio Nuvolari (Alfa Romeo)
   2 hr. 14 min. 03.0 sec. 111.9 km/h (69.5 mph)
2 Bernd Rosemeyer (Auto Union)
   2 hr. 14 min. 17.0 sec.
3 Achille Varzi (Auto Union) 2 laps behind
4 Mario Tadini (Alfa Romeo) 3 laps behind
5 H. Stuck/E. von Delius (Auto Union) 4 laps behind
6 Austin Dobson (Alfa Romeo) 5 laps behind
FASTEST LAP: Nuvolari—
   2 min. 35.6 sec. 115.7 km/h (71.89 mph)

All three Mercedes-Benz retired.

June 28   MILAN GP (Sempione Park)   60 laps— 156 km (96.9 miles)
1 Tazio Nuvolari (Alfa Romeo)
   1 hr. 35 min. 56.2 sec. 97.7 km/h (60.7 mph)
2 Achille Varzi (Auto Union) 1 hr. 36 min. 05.1 sec.
3 Giuseppe Farina (Alfa Romeo) 1 hr. 37 min. 07.1 sec.
4 Antonio Brivio (Alfa Romeo) 1 hr. 37 min. 11.1 sec.
5 Mario Tadini (Alfa Romeo) 1 hr. 37 min. 14.2 sec.
6 Clemente Biondetti (Alfa Romeo) 1 hr. 37 min. 46 sec.
FASTEST LAP: Varzi—100.2 km/h (62.3 mph)

Mercedes-Benz did not enter.

July 26   GERMAN GP (Nürburgring)   22 laps— 501.8 km (311.8 miles)
1 Bernd Rosemeyer (Auto Union)
   3 hr. 48 min. 39.5 sec. 131.65 km/h (81.80 mph)
2 Hans Stuck (Auto Union) 3 hr. 52 min. 36.2 sec.
3 Antonio Brivio (Alfa Romeo) 3 hr. 57 min. 05.0 sec.
4 Rudolf Hasse (Auto Union) 3 hr. 59 min. 13.1 sec.
5 L. Fagioli/R. Caracciola (Mercedes-Benz) 1 lap behind
6 Ernst von Delius (Auto Union) 1 lap behind
FASTEST LAP: Rosemeyer—
   9 min. 56.4 sec. 137.6 km/h (85.53 mph)

August 2   COPPA CIANO (Livorno)   30 laps— 216.6 km (134.6 miles)
1 Tazio Nuvolari (Alfa Romeo)
   1 hr. 44 min. 40 sec. 120.35 km/h (74.8 mph)
2 Antonio Brivio (Alfa Romeo) 1 hr. 44 min. 57.8 sec.
3 René Dreyfus (Alfa Romeo) 1 hr. 46 min. 10.4 sec.
4 Hans Stuck (Auto Union) 1 hr. 47 min. 44.2 sec.
5 Giosue Calamai (Alfa Romeo) 3 laps behind
FASTEST LAP: not known

Mercedes-Benz did not enter.

August 15   COPPA ACERBO (Pescara)   16 laps— 412.8 km (256.5 miles)
1 Bernd Rosemeyer (Auto Union)
   2 hr. 57 min. 04.0 sec. 139.2 km/h (86.5 mph)
2 Ernst von Delius (Auto Union) 3 hr. 04 min. 18.0 sec.
3 Achille Varzi (Auto Union) 3 hr. 05 min. 01.3 sec.
4 Antonio Brivio (Alfa Romeo) 3 hr. 05 min. 06.4 sec.
5 Hans Ruesch (Alfa Romeo)
FASTEST LAP: Varzi—144.27 km/h (89.64 mph)

Mercedes-Benz did not enter.

August 23   SWISS GP (Bern)   70 laps— 509.6 km (316.6 miles)
1 Bernd Rosemeyer (Auto Union)
   3 hr. 09 min. 01 sec. 161.7 km/h (100.48 mph)
2 Achille Varzi (Auto Union) 3 hr. 09 min. 39 sec.
3 Hans Stuck (Auto Union) 2 laps behind
4 L. Fagioli/H. Lang (Mercedes-Benz) 2 laps behind
5 Rudolf Hasse (Auto Union) 4 laps behind
FASTEST LAP: Rosemeyer—
   2 min. 34.5 sec. 170.0 km/h (105.64 mph)

September 13   ITALIAN GP (Monza)   73 laps— 503.7 km (312.9 miles)
1 Bernd Rosemeyer (Auto Union)
   3 hr. 43 min. 25 sec. 135.4 km/h (84.1 mph)
2 Tazio Nuvolari (Alfa Romeo) 3 hr. 45 min. 30.6 sec.
3 Ernst von Delius (Auto Union) 3 laps behind
4 René Dreyfus (Alfa Romeo) 3 laps behind
5 Carlo Pintacuda (Alfa Romeo) 5 laps behind
6 Piero Dusio (Maserati) 14 laps behind
FASTEST LAP: Rosemeyer—
   2 min. 59.6 sec. 140.3 km/h (87.2 mph)

Mercedes-Benz did not enter.

October 12   VANDERBILT CUP (New York)   75 laps— 480 km (298.3 miles)
1 Tazio Nuvolari (Alfa Romeo)
   4 hr. 32 min. 44.4 sec. 106.7 km/h (65.99 mph)
2 Jean-Pierre Wimille (Bugatti) 4 hr. 41 min. 41.9 sec.
3 Antonio Brivio (Alfa Romeo) 4 hr. 45 min. 44.4 sec.
4 Raymond Sommer (Alfa Romeo) 4 hr. 46 min. 59.5 sec.
5 F. Trossi/F. McEvoy (Maserati) 4 hr. 57 min. 25.8 sec.
6 Mauri Rose (Burd Piston Spl) 4 hr. 57 min. 35.2 sec.
FASTEST LAP: not known

Mercedes-Benz and Auto Union did not enter.

1937

January 1   SOUTH AFRICAN GP   (East London)   18 laps—340.2 km (211.4 miles)
1 Pat Fairfield (ERA)
   2 hr. 13 min. 37 sec. 143.47 km/h (89.17 mph)
2 B. Meyer (Riley) 2 hr. 34 min. 00 sec.
3 F. Chiappini (Riley) 2 hr. 36 min. 48 sec.
4 Hans Ruesch (Alfa Romeo)
5 Bernd Rosemeyer (Auto Union)
6 Earl Howe (Bugatti)
FASTEST LAP: Rosemeyer—
   5 min. 46.4 sec. 181.8 km/h (112.97 mph)

Mercedes-Benz did not enter.

January 16   GROSVENOR GP (Cape Town)   45 laps—333.9 km (207.4 miles)
1 Ernst von Delius (Auto Union)
   2 hr. 31 min. 14.2 sec. 129.31 km/h (80.37 mph)
2 Bernd Rosemeyer (Auto Union) 2 hr. 31 min. 39.4 sec.
3 Earl Howe (ERA)
4 Pat Fairfield (ERA)
5 Hans Ruesch (Alfa Romeo)
6 Kay Petre (Riley)
FASTEST LAP: Rosemeyer—
   134.72 km/h (83.73 mph)

Mercedes-Benz did not enter

Note: Both these South African races were handicap events.

May 9   TRIPOLI GP (Mellaha)   40 laps—
525.6 km (326.6 miles)
1 Hermann Lang (Mercedes-Benz)
   2 hr. 27 min. 57.67 sec. 216.28 km/h (134.42 mph)
2 Bernd Rosemeyer (Auto Union) 2 hr. 28 min. 07.32 sec.
3 Ernst von Delius (Auto Union) 2 hr. 29 min. 11.85 sec.
4 Hans Stuck (Auto Union) 2 hr. 29 min. 39.59 sec.
5 Luigi Fagioli (Auto Union) 2 hr. 29 min. 42.58 sec.
6 Rudolf Caracciola (Mercedes-Benz)
   2 hr. 29 min. 53.2 sec.
FASTEST LAP: Stuck—
   3 min. 25.7 sec. 229.22 km/h (142.44 mph)

May 30   AVUS GP

Heat 1—7 laps—136.99 km (85.12 miles)
1 Rudolf Caracciola (Mercedes-Benz)
   32 min. 29.3 sec. 250.34 km/h (155.59 mph)
2 Bernd Rosemeyer (Auto Union) 32 min. 30.0 sec.
3 Ernst von Delius (Auto Union) 32 min. 37.2 sec.
4 Richard Seaman (Mercedes-Benz)
Heat 2—7 laps—136.99 km (85.12 miles)
1 M. von Brauchitsch (Mercedes-Benz)
   31 min. 29.3 sec. 258.03 km/h (160.37 mph)
2 Rudolf Hasse (Auto Union) 31 min. 50.4 sec.
3 Hermann Lang (Mercedes-Benz) 31 min. 51.0 sec.
4 Laszlo Hartmann (Maserati)
5 Giorgio Sofietti (Maserati)
Final—8 laps—156.56 km (97.28 miles)
1 Hermann Lang (Mercedes-Benz)
   35 min. 30.2 sec. 261.63 km/h (162.61 mph)
2 Ernst von Delius (Auto Union) 35 min. 32.2 sec.
3 Rudolf Hasse (Auto Union) 36 min. 06.2 sec.
4 Bernd Rosemeyer (Auto Union)
5 Richard Seaman (Mercedes-Benz)
6 Laszlo Hartmann (Maserati)
FASTEST LAP: Rosemeyer—
   276.32 km/h (171.74 mph)

June 6   RIO DE JANEIRO GP (Gavea)   25 laps—
279.0 km (173.37 miles)
1 Carlo Pintacuda (Alfa Romeo)
   3 hr. 22 min. 01 sec. 82.7 km/h (51.4 mph)
2 Hans Stuck (Auto Union) 3 hr. 22 min. 09 sec.
3 Antonio Brivio (Alfa Romeo) 3 hr. 29 min. 08 sec.
FASTEST LAP: Pintacuda—
   7 min. 10.5 sec. 87.24 km/h (54.21 mph)
Mercedes-Benz did not enter.

June 13   EIFEL GP (Nürburgring)   10 laps—
228.1 km (141 miles)
1 Bernd Rosemeyer (Auto Union)
   1 hr. 42 min. 11.5 sec. 113.5 km/h (82.95 mph)
2 Rudolf Caracciola (Mercedes-Benz)
   1 hr. 43 min. 01.8 sec.
3 M. von Brauchitsch (Mercedes-Benz)
   1 hr. 43 min. 56.8 sec.
4 Rudolf Hasse (Auto Union) 1 hr. 45 min. 46.0 sec.
5 Tazio Nuvolari (Alfa Romeo) 1 hr. 46 min. 25.0 sec.

6 Hermann Lang (Mercedes-Benz) 1 hr. 48 min. 06.0 sec.
FASTEST LAP: Rosemeyer—
   9 min. 58.8 sec. 137 km/h (85.13 mph)

June 20   MILAN GP (Sempione Park)   70 laps—
168 km (104.4 miles)
1 Tazio Nuvolari (Alfa Romeo)
   1 hr. 37 min. 15.0 sec. 103.6 km/h (64.4 mph)
2 Giuseppe Farina (Alfa Romeo) 1 hr. 39 min. 19.0 sec.
3 Hans Ruesch (Alfa Romeo) 1 lap behind
4 Rudolf Hasse (Auto Union) 1 lap behind
5 Felice Trossi (Alfa Romeo) 3 laps behind
6 G. Minozzi (Alfa Romeo) 4 laps behind
FASTEST LAP: Nuvolari—
   1 min. 20.6 sec. 107.2 km/h (66.6 mph)
Mercedes-Benz did not enter.

July 5   VANDERBILT CUP (New York)   90 laps—
482.4 km (299.76 miles)
1 Bernd Rosemeyer (Auto Union)
   3 hr. 38 min. 17 sec. 132.87 km/h (82.56 mph)
2 Richard Seaman (Mercedes-Benz) 3 hr. 39 min. 07 sec.
3 Rex Mays (Alfa Romeo) 3 hr. 44 min. 57 sec.
4 Ernst von Delius (Auto Union) 3 hr. 48 min. 25 sec.
5 Giuseppe Farina (Alfa Romeo) 3 hr. 51 min. 30 sec.
6 J. Thorne (Alfa Romeo) 3 hr. 59 min. 56 sec.
FASTEST LAP: Rudolf Caracciola (Mercedes-Benz)—
   135.96 km/h (84.5 mph)

July 11   BELGIAN GP (Spa-Francorchamps)   34 laps—
505.24 km (313.9 miles)
1 Rudolf Hasse (Auto Union)
   3 hr. 01 min. 22 sec. 167.2 km/h (103.89 mph)
2 Hans Stuck (Auto Union) 3 hr. 02 min. 04 sec.
3 Hermann Lang (Mercedes-Benz) 3 hr. 04 min. 07 sec.
4 Christian Kautz (Mercedes-Benz) 3 hr. 04 min. 29 sec.
5 Raymond Sommer (Alfa Romeo) 2 laps behind
FASTEST LAP: Lang—
   5 min. 05 sec. 175.6 km/h (109.1 mph)

July 25   GERMAN GP (Nürburgring)   22 laps—
501.82 km (311.8 miles)
1 Rudolf Caracciola (Mercedes-Benz)
   3 hr. 46 min. 00.1 sec. 133.2 km/h (82.77 mph)
2 M. von Brauchitsch (Mercedes-Benz)
   3 hr. 46 min. 46.3 sec.
3 Bernd Rosemeyer (Auto Union) 3 hr. 47 min. 01.4 sec.
4 Tazio Nuvolari (Alfa Romeo) 3 hr. 50 min. 04.2 sec.
5 Rudolf Hasse (Auto Union) 3 hr. 51 min. 25.1 sec.
6 Christian Kautz (Mercedes-Benz)
   3 hr. 52 min. 10.3 sec.
FASTEST LAP: Rosemeyer—
   9 min. 53.4 sec. 137.68 km/h (85.57 mph)
Note: Ernst von Delius died following a crash in this race.

August 8   *MONACO GP*   *100 laps—318 km*
(197.6 miles)
1 M. von Brauchitsch (Mercedes-Benz)
   3 hr. 07 min. 23.9 sec. 101.82 km/h (63.27 mph)
2 Rudolf Caracciola (Mercedes-Benz)
   3 hr. 08 min. 48.2 sec.
3 Christian Kautz (Mercedes-Benz) 2 laps behind
4 H. Stuck/B. Rosemeyer (Auto Union) 3 laps behind
5 Goffredo Zehender (Mercedes-Benz) 3 laps behind
6 Giuseppe Farina (Alfa Romeo) 3 laps behind
FASTEST LAP: Caracciola—
   1 min. 46.5 sec. 107.49 km/h (66.79 mph)

August 15   *COPPA ACERBO (Pescara)*   *16 laps—*
412.8 km (256.5 miles)
1 Bernd Rosemeyer (Auto Union)
   2 hr. 55 min. 39.05 sec. 141.0 km/h (87.62 mph)
2 M. von Brauchitsch (Mercedes-Benz)
   2 hr. 57 min. 20.9 sec.
3 H. P. Müller (Auto Union) 3 hr. 01 min. 49.86 sec.
4 Luigi Fagioli (Auto Union) 1 lap behind
5 R. Caracciola/R. Seaman (Mercedes-Benz) 1 lap behind
6 V. Belmondo (Alfa Romeo) 1 lap behind
FASTEST LAP: Rosemeyer—
   10 min. 36 sec. 145.2 km/h (90.22 mph)

August 22   *SWISS GP (Bern)*   *50 laps—*
364 km (226.2 miles)
1 Rudolf Caracciola (Mercedes-Benz)
   2 hr. 17 min. 39.3 sec. 158.6 km/h (98.55 mph)
2 Hermann Lang (Mercedes-Benz) 2 hr. 18 min. 28.7 sec.
3 M. von Brauchitsch (Mercedes-Benz)
   2 hr. 18 min. 45.7 sec.
4 Hans Stuck (Auto Union) 2 hr. 18 min. 46.8 sec.
5 T. Nuvolari/B. Rosemeyer (Auto Union)
   2 hr. 19 min. 00.5 sec.
6 Christian Kautz (Mercedes-Benz) 1 lap behind
FASTEST LAP: Rosemeyer—
   2 min. 31.6 sec. 168.1 km/h (104.45 mph)

September 12   *ITALIAN GP (Livorno)*   *50 laps—*
361 km (224.3 miles)
1 Rudolf Caracciola (Mercedes-Benz)
   2 hr. 44 min. 54.4 sec. 131.3 km/h (81.58 mph)
2 Hermann Lang (Mercedes-Benz) 2 hr. 44 min. 54.8 sec.
3 Bernd Rosemeyer (Auto Union) 2 hr. 46 min. 59.4 sec.
4 Richard Seaman (Mercedes-Benz) 1 lap behind
5 Hermann Müller (Auto Union) 1 lap behind
6 Achille Varzi (Auto Union) 1 lap behind
FASTEST LAP: Caracciola and Lang—
   3 min. 11.2 sec. 135.9 km/h (84.4 mph)

September 26   *CZECH GP (Brno)*   *15 laps—*
437.1 km (271.6 miles)
1 Rudolf Caracciola (Mercedes-Benz)
   3 hr. 09 min. 25.3 sec. 138.4 km/h (86.0 mph)
2 M. von Brauchitsch (Mercedes-Benz)
   3 hr. 10 min. 01.7 sec.

3 H. P. Müller/B. Rosemeyer (Auto Union)
   3hr. 10 min. 07.1 sec.
4 Richard Seaman (Mercedes-Benz) 3 hr. 10 min. 43.8 sec.
5 Tazio Nuvolari (Alfa Romeo) 1 lap behind
6 Antonio Brivio (Alfa Romeo) 1 lap behind
FASTEST LAP: Caracciola—
   11 min. 59.3 sec. 145.9 km/h (90.66 mph)

October 2   *DONINGTON GP*   *80 laps—*
402.24 km (249.9 miles)
1 Bernd Rosemeyer (Auto Union)
   3 hr. 01 min. 02.5 sec. 133.3 km/h (82.86 mph)
2 M. von Brauchitsch (Mercedes-Benz)
   3 hr. 01 min. 40.0 sec.
3 Rudolf Caracciola (Mercedes-Benz)
   3 hr. 02 min. 18.8 sec.
4 H. P. Müller (Auto Union) 3 hr. 04 min. 50.0 sec.
5 Rudolf Hasse (Auto Union) 3 hr. 09 min. 50.0 sec.
6 B. Bira (Maserati) 2 laps behind
FASTEST LAP: Rosemeyer and von Brauchitsch—
   2 min. 11.4 sec. 137.76 km/h (85.62 mph)

1938

April 10   *PAU GP*   *100 laps—277 km (172 miles)*
1 René Dreyfus (Delahaye)
   3 hr. 08 min. 59 sec. 87.9 km/h (54.62 mph)
2 R. Caracciola/H. Lang (Mercedes-Benz)
   3 hr. 10 min. 50 sec.
3 Gianfranco Comotti (Delahaye) 6 laps behind
FASTEST LAP: Caracciola—
   1 min. 47.0 sec. 93.18 km/h (57.9 mph)
Auto Union did not enter.

May 15   *TRIPOLI GP (Mellaha)*   *40 laps—*
525.6 km (326.6 miles)
1 Hermann Lang (Mercedes-Benz)
   2 hr. 33 min. 17.14 sec. 205.10 km/h (127.5 mph)
2 M. von Brauchitsch (Mercedes-Benz)
   2 hr. 37 min. 55.64 sec.
3 Rudolf Caracciola (Mercedes-Benz)
   2 hr. 38 min. 20.76 sec.
4 Raymond Sommer (Alfa Romeo)
   2 hr. 46 min. 52.82 sec.
5 Piero Taruffi (Maserati) 2 hr. 57 min. 47.14 sec.
6 Giovanni Rocco (Maserati) 2 hr. 57 min. 56.03 sec.
FASTEST LAP: Felice Trossi (Maserati)—
   3 min. 35.41 sec. 218.9 km/h (136.0 mph)
Auto Union did not enter.

July 3   *FRENCH GP (Reims)*   *64 laps—*
501.12 km (311.2 miles)
1 M. von Brauchitsch (Mercedes-Benz)
   3 hr. 04 min. 38.5 sec. 162.76 km/h (101.13 mph)
2 Rudolf Caracciola (Mercedes-Benz)
   3 hr. 06 min. 19.6 sec.

3 Hermann Lang (Mercedes-Benz) 1 lap behind
4 René Carrière (Darracq) 10 laps behind
FASTEST LAP: Lang—
  2 min. 45.3 sec. 170.17 km/h (105.74 mph)
Both Auto Unions retired.

July 24 **GERMAN GP (Nürburgring)** *22 laps—*
501.82 km (311.8 miles)
1 Richard Seaman (Mercedes-Benz)
  3 hr. 51 min. 46.1 sec. 129.8 km/h (80.6 mph)
2 R. Caracciola/H. Lang (Mercedes-Benz)
  3 hr. 55 min. 06.1 sec.
3 Hans Stuck (Auto Union) 4 hr. 00 min. 42.3 sec.
4 H. P. Müller/T. Nuvolari (Auto Union)
  4 hr. 01 min. 19.1 sec.
5 René Dreyfus (Delahaye) 1 lap behind
6 Paul Pietsch (Maserati) 1 lap behind
FASTEST LAP: Seaman—
  10 min. 09.1 sec. 134.9 km/h (83.82 mph)

August 7 **COPPA CIANO (Livorno)** *40 laps—*
232 km (144.2 miles)
1 Hermann Lang (Mercedes-Benz)
  1 hr. 40 min. 35.2 sec. 138.4 km/h (86.0 mph)
2 Giuseppe Farina (Alfa Romeo) 1 hr. 41 min. 23.2 sec.
3 J-P. Wimille/C. Biondetti (Alfa Romeo) 1 lap behind
4 V. Belmondo (Alfa Romeo) 2 laps behind
5 René Dreyfus (Delahaye) 3 laps behind
FASTEST LAP: Lang and M. von Brauchitsch—
  2 min. 25.4 sec. 143.6 km/h (89.2 mph)
Auto Union did not enter.

August 14 **COPPA ACERBO (Pescara)** *16 laps—*
412.8 km (256.5 miles)
1 Rudolf Caracciola (Mercedes-Benz)
  3 hr. 03 min. 45.6 sec. 134.8 km/h (83. 75 mph)
2 Giuseppe Farina (Alfa Romeo) 3 hr. 07 min. 11.6 sec.
3 V. Belmondo (Alfa Romeo) 3 hr. 12 min. 20.7 sec.
4 Gianfranco Comotti (Delahaye) 1 lap behind
FASTEST LAP: Luigi Villoresi (Maserati)—
  10 min. 57 sec. 141.4 km/h (87.8 mph)
Auto Union did not enter.

August 21 **SWISS GP (Bern)** *50 laps—364 km*
(226.2 miles)
1 Rudolf Caracciola (Mercedes-Benz)
  2 hr. 32 min. 07.8 sec. 143.56 km/h (89.20 mph)
2 Richard Seaman (Mercedes-Benz) 2 hr. 32 min. 33.8 sec.
3 M. von Brauchitsch (Mercedes-Benz)
  2 hr. 33 min. 11.6 sec.
4 Hans Stuck (Auto Union) 2 laps behind
5 Giuseppe Farina (Alfa Romeo) 2 laps behind
6 Piero Taruffi (Alfa Romeo) 3 laps behind
FASTEST LAP: Seaman—
  2 min. 50.8 sec. 153.44 km/h (95.34 mph)

September 11 **ITALIAN GP (Monza)** *60 laps—*
419.4 km (260.6 miles)
1 Tazio Nuvolari (Auto Union)
  2 hr. 41 min. 39.6 sec. 155.73 km/h (96.77 mph)
2 Giuseppe Farina (Alfa Romeo) 3 laps behind
3 R. Caracciola/M. von Brauchitsch (Mercedes-Benz)
  3 laps behind
4 Clemente Biondetti (Alfa Romeo) 3 laps behind
5 Felice Trossi (Maserati) 4 laps behind
6 Pietro Ghersi (Alfa Romeo) 13 laps behind
FASTEST LAP: Hermann Lang (Mercedes-Benz)—
  2 min. 34.2 sec. 163.26 km/h (101.44 mph)

October 22 **DONINGTON GP** *80 laps—*
402.24 km (249.95 miles)
1 Tazio Nuvolari (Auto Union)
  3 hr. 06 min. 22 sec. 129.5 km/h (80.49 mph)
2 Hermann Lang (Mercedes-Benz) 3 hr. 08 min. 00 sec.
3 Richard Seaman (Mercedes-Benz) 1 lap behind
4 H. P. Müller (Auto Union) 1 lap behind
5 M. von Brauchitsch (Mercedes-Benz) 1 lap behind
6 Arthur Dobson (ERA) 6 laps behind
FASTEST LAP: Nuvolari—
  2 min. 14.4 sec. 134.68 km/h (83.71 mph)

1939

April 2 **PAU GP** *100 laps—277 km (172 miles)*
1 Hermann Lang (Mercedes-Benz)
  3 hr. 07 min. 25.2 sec. 88.66 km/h (55.09 mph)
2 M. von Brauchitsch (Mercedes-Benz)
  3 hr. 07 min. 42.0 sec.
3 Phi-Phi Etancelin (Talbot) 2 laps behind
4 Raymond Sommer (Alfa Romeo) 5 laps behind
FASTEST LAP: von Brauchitsch—
  1 min. 46.8 sec. 94.07 km/h (58.45 mph)
Auto Union did not enter.

May 7 **TRIPOLI GP (Mellaha)** *30 laps—*
394.2 km (244.9 miles)
1 Hermann Lang (Mercedes-Benz)
  1 hr. 59 min. 12.36 sec. 197.8 km/h (122.8 mph)
2 Rudolf Caracciola (Mercedes-Benz)
  2 hr. 02 min. 49.64 sec.
3 Emilio Villoresi (Alfa Romeo) 1 lap behind
4 Piero Taruffi (Maserati) 2 laps behind
5 Armand Hug (Maserati) 3 laps behind
FASTEST LAP: Lang—
  3 min. 43.77 sec. 211.67 km/h (131.53 mph)
Auto Union did not enter. Race limited to s/c 1500 cc cars.

May 21　**EIFEL GP (Nürburgring)**　*10 laps—*
228.1 km (141 miles)
1　Hermann Lang (Mercedes-Benz)
　　1 hr. 40 min. 57.1 sec. 135.5 km/h (84.14 mph)
2　Tazio Nuvolari (Auto Union) 1 hr. 41 min. 08.3 sec.
3　Rudolf Caracciola (Mercedes-Benz)
　　1 hr. 41 min. 28.4 sec.
4　M. von Brauchitsch (Mercedes-Benz)
　　1 hr. 42 min. 53.0 sec.
5　Rudolf Hasse (Auto Union) 1 hr. 42 min. 56.1 sec.
6　Ulli Bigalke (Auto Union) 1 hr. 44 min. 52.1 sec.
FASTEST LAP: Lang—
　　9 min. 52.2 sec. 138.5 km/h (86.06 mph)

June 26　**BELGIAN GP (Spa-Francorchamps)**　*35 laps—*
507.5 km (315.36 miles)
1　Hermann Lang (Mercedes-Benz)
　　3 hr. 20 min. 21.0 sec. 152 km/h (94.45 mph)
2　Rudolf Hasse (Auto Union) 3 hr. 20 min. 37.9 sec.
3　M. von Brauchitsch (Mercedes-Benz)
　　3 hr. 22 min. 14.0 sec.
4　Raymond Sommer (Alfa Romeo) 3 laps behind
FASTEST LAP: Lang—
　　5 min. 19.9 sec. 163.2 km/h (101.39 mph)

Richard Seaman died following a crash in this race.

July 9　**FRENCH GP (Reims)**　*51 laps—*
399.33 km (248.14 miles)
1　H. P. Müller (Auto Union)
　　2 hr. 21 min. 11.8 sec. 169.38 km/h (105.25 mph)
2　Georg Meier (Auto Union) 1 lap behind
3　René Le Begue (Talbot) 3 laps behind
4　Phi-Phi Etancelin (Talbot) 3 laps behind
5　Raymond Sommer (Alfa Romeo) 4 laps behind
6　Hans Stuck (Auto Union) 4 laps behind
FASTEST LAP: Hermann Lang (Mercedes-Benz)—
　　2 min. 32.9 sec. 182.46 km/h (113.38 mph)

All three Mercedes-Benz retired.

July 23　**GERMAN GP (Nürburgring)**　*22 laps—*
501.82 km (311.8 miles)
1　Rudolf Caracciola (Mercedes-Benz)
　　4 hr. 08 min. 41.8 sec. 121.9 km/h (75.74 mph)
2　H. P. Müller (Auto Union) 4 hr. 09 min. 39.6 sec.
3　Paul Pietsch (Maserati) 1 lap behind
4　René Dreyfus (Delahaye) 2 laps behind
5　'Raph' (Delahaye) 3 laps behind
6　R. Mazaud (Delahaye) 3 laps behind
FASTEST LAP: Caracciola—
　　10 min. 24.0 sec. 131.6 km/h (81.77 mph)

August 20　**SWISS GP (Bern)**　*30 laps—*
218.4 km (135.7 miles)
1　Hermann Lang (Mercedes-Benz)
　　1 hr. 24 min. 47.6 sec. 154.6 km/h (96.08 mph)
2　Rudolf Caracciola (Mercedes-Benz)
　　1 hr. 24 min. 50.7 sec.
3　M. von Brauchitsch (Mercedes-Benz)
　　1 hr. 25 min. 57.5 sec.
4　H. P. Müller (Auto Union) 1 hr. 27 min. 01.3 sec.
5　Tazio Nuvolari (Auto Union) 1 hr. 27 min. 08.6 sec.
6　Giuseppe Farina (Alfa Romeo) 1 lap behind
FASTEST LAP: Lang—
　　2 min. 38.4 sec. 165.0 km/h (102.5 mph)

September 3　**YUGOSLAV GP (Belgrade)**　*50 laps—*
140 km (86.99 miles)
1　Tazio Nuvolari (Auto Union)
　　1 hr. 04 min. 03.8 sec. 130.7 km/h (81.22 mph)
2　M. von Brauchitsch (Mercedes-Benz)
　　1 hr. 04 min. 11.4 sec.
3　H. P. Müller (Auto Union) 1 hr. 04 min. 34.4 sec.
4　Milenkowitsch (Bugatti) 19 laps behind
FASTEST LAP: Nuvolari and von Brauchitsch—
　　1 min. 14.0 sec. 135.1 km/h (83.9 mph)

Rudolf Caracciola was one of the greatest racing drivers
of all time and the most successful of the 1934–39 era. He
scored 15 outright victories for Mercedes-Benz, (including
the 1938 Coppa Acerbo at Pescara, *right*) and was three
times European Champion

All the Winners

The accompanying tables are concerned only with races from 1934–39 in which Mercedes-Benz and/or Auto Union took part at least once.

Alfa Romeo withdrew from racing at the end of 1932 and from 1934–38 Scuderia Ferrari provided the only serious opposition to the German teams, so the three of them are shown in all races they entered, the winning team (where appropriate) underlined with the winning driver initialled below. In 1938 the Alfa Romeo factory returned to Grand Prix racing and, for a while, Scuderia Ferrari ceased to exist.

Key to teams:
MB — Mercedes-Benz
AU — Auto Union
SF — Scuderia Ferrari
AR — Alfa Romeo
DEL — Delahaye

Key to drivers:
RC — Rudolf Caracciola
LF — Luigi Fagioli
HS — Hans Stuck
GM — Guy Moll
AV — Achille Varzi
LC — Louis Chiron
MvB — Manfred von Brauchitsch
TN — Tazio Nuvolari
BR — Bernd Rosemeyer
CP — Carlo Pintacuda
HL — Hermann Lang
EvD — Ernst von Delius
RH — Rudolf Hasse
RS — Richard Seaman
HPM — H.P. Müller
RD — René Dreyfus

	1934	1935	1936	1937	1938	1939
Monaco	SF(GM)	MB(LF)　　SF	MB(RC) AU SF	MB(MvB) AU SF		
Tripoli	SF(AV)	MB(RC) AU	MB AU(AV) SF	MB(HL) AU SF	MB(HL)　　AR	MB(HL)
Tunis		AU(AV) SF	MB(RC) AU SF			
Avus	AU SF(GM)	MB(LF) AU SF		MB(HL) AU		
Eifel	MB(MvB) AU SF	MB(RC) AU SF	MB AU(BR) SF	MB AU(BR) SF		MB(HL) AU
Penya Rhin	SF(AV)	MB(LF)　　SF	MB AU SF(TN)			
French	MB AU SF(LC)	MB(RC) AU SF			MB(MvB) AU	MB AU(HPM)
German	MB AU(HS) SF	MB AU SF(TN)	MB AU(BR) SF	MB(RC) AU SF	MB(RS) AU AR	MB(RC) AU
Coppa Ciano	SF(AV)	SF(TN)	AU SF(CP/TN)		MB(HL)　　AR	
Coppa Acerbo	MB(LF) AU SF	AU(AV) SF	AU(BR) SF	MB AU(BR) SF	MB(RC) AU AR	
Swiss	MB AU(HS) SF	MB(RC) AU SF	MB AU(BR) SF	MB(RC) AU SF	MB(RC) AU AR	MB(HL) AU AR
Italian	MB(RC/LF) AU SF	MB AU(HS) SF	AU(BR) SF	MB(RC) AU SF	MB AU(TN) AR	
Spanish	MB(LF) AU SF	MB(RC) AU SF				
Czech	MB AU(HS) SF	AU(BR) SF		MB(RC) AU SF		
Hungary			MB AU SF(TN)			
Milan			AU SF(TN)	AU SF(TN)		
Belgian	SF	MB(RC)　　SF		MB AU(RH) SF		MB(HL) AU AR
Rio			SF	AU SF(CP)	AR	
Vanderbilt Cup			SF(TN)	MB AU(BR) SF		
Pau		SF(TN)			MB DEL(RD)	MB(HL)
Donington				MB AU(BR)	MB AU(TN)	
Bucharest						AU(HS)
Belgrade						MB AU(TN)
East London				AU		
Cape Town				AU(EvD)		

Starts and Wins—Teams

Mercedes-Benz

Year	Starts	Wins	Percentage
1934	8	4	
1935	11	9	
1936	8	2	
1937	12	7	
1938	9	6	
1939	8	6	
TOTAL	56	34	60.71%

Auto Union

Year	Starts	Wins	Percentage
1934	9	3	
1935	11	4	
1936	12	6	
1937	16	6	
1938	6	2	
1939	7	3	
TOTAL	61	24	39.34%

Scuderia Ferrari

Year	Starts	Wins	Percentage
1934	14	6	
1935	15	3	
1936	14	5	
1937	12	2	
TOTAL	55	16	29.09%

Alfa Romeo

Year	Starts	Wins	Percentage
1938	7	0	
1939	3	0	
TOTAL	10	0	

Silver Arrows

Mercedes-Benz and Auto Union competed against each other on 47 occasions. The only one of these races not won by either team was the 1935 German GP, when Nuvolari was victorious on the Scuderia Ferrari Alfa Romeo.

MERCEDES-BENZ 47 STARTS 28 WINS 59.57%
AUTO UNION 47 STARTS 18 WINS 38.29%

The Drivers

Driver	Starts	Wins	Percentage
1) B. Rosemeyer	33	10	30.30
2) R. Caracciola	52	15.5	29.80
3) G. Moll	7	2	28.57
4) H. Lang	32	9	28.13
5) T. Nuvolari	55	11.5	20.90
6) L. Fagioli	28	5.5	19.60
7) A. Varzi	34	6	17.60
8) H. Stuck	41	5	12.19
9) E. von Delius	13	1	7.69
10) M. von Brauchitsch	45	3	6.66
11) R. Seaman	15	1	6.66
12) H. P. Müller	18	1	5.55
13) R. Hasse	20	1	5.00
14) L. Chiron	31	1	3.22

Note:
Caracciola's 15.5 wins include one shared victory—the 1934 Italian GP—with Fagioli.

Nuvolari started 43 races for Scuderia Ferrari (8.5 wins) and 12 for Auto Union (3 wins). He shared victory with Pintacuda in the 1936 Coppa Ciano.

Fagioli started 24 races for Mercedes-Benz and 4 for Auto Union. All his wins were with Mercedes.

Varzi started 12 races for Scuderia Ferrari (3 wins) and 22 for Auto Union (3 wins).

Chiron started 24 races for Scuderia Ferrari (1 win) and 7 for Mercedes-Benz.

*　　　*　　　*

Guy Moll was killed at Pescara (Coppa Acerbo) in 1934.

Ernst von Delius was killed at the Nürburgring (German GP) in 1937.

Bernd Rosemeyer was killed in a record attempt on the Frankfurt-Darmstadt *autobahn* in 1938.

Dick Seaman was killed at Spa (Belgian GP) in 1939.

The Last Word

'By the time these gems of prose appear in print everything I have written about future motor racing may read as so much nonsense, what with politics and one thing and another. I merely hope that I shall be here to write and you to read these notes next week.'

Rodney Walkerley,
The Motor, 29 August 1939

Bibliography

BEINHORN, Elly, *Mein Mann der Rennfahrer*, Deutsche Verlag, Berlin, 1938. *My Husband the Motor-Racer*, Massie Publishing Co Ltd, London, 1939. *Allein Flug—Mein Leben*, Langen Müller, Munich, 1977.

BRAUCHITSCH, Manfred von, *Kampf um Meter und Sekunden*, Verlag der Nation, Berlin, 1953.

BRETZ, Heinz, *Bernd Rosemeyer—Ein Leben für den Deutschen Sport*, Wilhelm Limpert Verlag, Berlin, 1938.

CANCELLIERI, Gianni, DE AGOSTINI, Cesare and SCHRODER, Martin, *Auto Union, Die Grossen Rennen, 1934–9*, Schroder & Weise GmbH, Hannover, 1980.

CARACCIOLA, Rudolf, *Mein Leben als Rennfahrer*, Deutsche Verlag, Berlin, 1939. *A Racing Driver's World*, Cassell & Co Ltd, London, 1963.

CHAKRABONGSE, Prince Chula, *Dick Seaman, Racing Motorist*, G. T. Foulis & Co Ltd, London, 1948.

CLUTTON, Cecil, POSTHUMUS, Cyril, and JENKINSON, Denis, *The Racing Car—Development and Design*, B. T. Batsford Ltd, London, 1962.

COURT, William, *Power and Glory*, Macdonald, London, 1966.

DREYFUS, René and KIMES, Beverly Rae, *My Two Lives*, AZTEX Corp, USA, 1983.

DUGDALE, John, *Great Motor Sport of the Thirties*, Wilton House Gentry Ltd, London, 1977.

EARL, Cameron C., *Investigation into the Development of German Grand Prix Racing Cars between 1934 and 1939*. British Intelligence Objectives Sub-Committee, His Majesty's Stationery Office, London, 1949.

EYSTON, George and LYNDON, Barré, *Motor Racing and Record Breaking*, B. T. Batsford Ltd, London, 1935.

FERRARI, Enzo, *Le Mie Gioie Terribili*, Cappelli Editore, Italy, 1962.

FRANKENBERG, Richard von, *Porsche, the Man and his Cars*, G. T. Foulis & Co Ltd, London, 1954.

GEORGANO, Nick, *The Encyclopaedia of Motor Sport*, Ebury Press and Michael Joseph Ltd, London, 1971.

HODGES, David (ed), *Great Racing Drivers*, Temple Press Ltd, London, 1966. *The Monaco Grand Prix*, Temple Press Ltd, London, 1964.

HORNICKEL, Ernst, *Wer wusste das von Rosemeyer?*, Verlag Karl und Alfred Walder, Stuttgart, 1937.

HORNUNG, Thora, *50 Jahre Nürburgring*, Görres-Verlag, Koblenz, 1985.

HULL, Peter, *Alfa Romeo*, Ballantine Books Inc, New York, 1971.

JENKINSON, Denis, *The Grand Prix Mercedes-Benz Type W125, 1937*, Lionel Leventhal Ltd, London, 1970.

KIRCHBERG, Peter, *Grand Prix Report Auto Union, 1934–1939*, Motorbuch Verlag, Stuttgart, 1982.

KNITTEL, Stefan, *Auto Union Grand Prix Wagen*, Verlag Schrader & Partner GmbH, Munich, 1980.

LANG, Hermann, *Grand Prix Driver*, G. T. Foulis & Co Ltd, London, 1953.

LUDVIGSEN, Karl, *Mercedes-Benz Racing Cars*, Bond/Parkhurst Books, USA, 1971.

LURANI, Count Giovanni, *Racing Round the World*, G. T. Foulis & Co Ltd, 1948. *Nuvolari*, Cassell & Co Ltd, London, 1959.

LYNDON, Barré, *Grand Prix*, John Miles Ltd, London, 1935.

MAYS, Raymond, *Split Seconds*, G. T. Foulis & Co Ltd, London, 1951.

MOLTER, Günther, *German Racing Cars and Drivers*, Floyd Clymer, USA, 1950.

MONKHOUSE, George, *Motoraces*, George Newnes Ltd, London, 1937. *Motor Racing with Mercedes-Benz*, George Newnes Ltd, London, 1938. *Grand Prix Racing, Facts and Figures*, G. T. Foulis & Co Ltd, 1950. *Mercedes-Benz Grand Prix Racing 1934–1955*, White Mouse Editions & New Cavendish Books, London, 1984.

NEUBAUER, Alfred, *Männer, Frauen und Motoren*, Schweizer Druck- und Verlaghaus A.G., Zurich, 1958. *Speed Was My Life*, Barrie & Rockliff, London, 1960.

ORSINI, Luigi and ZAGARI, Franco, *The Scuderia Ferrari*, Osprey Publishing Ltd, London, 1981.

POMEROY, Laurence, *The Grand Prix Car*, Vols 1 & 2, Temple Press Ltd, London, 1949.

PORSCHE, Ferry and BENTLEY, John, *We At Porsche*, Doubleday, USA, 1976.

POSTHUMUS, Cyril, *The German Grand Prix*, Temple Press Ltd, London, 1966. *Classic Racing Cars*, The Hamlyn Publishing Group Ltd, London, 1977. *The 16-cylinder GP Auto Union*, Profile Publications, Surrey, UK, 1967.

SCHEUER, Luki, *Nürburgring, Tradition und Fortschritt*, Rhenania- Fachverlag GmbH, Koblenz, 1984.

SCHRADER, Halwart and DEMAND, Carlo, *The Supercharged Mercedes*, Patrick Stephens Ltd, Cambridge, UK, 1979.

SCOTT-MONCRIEFF, David, *The Three-Pointed Star*, Gentry Books Ltd, London, 1979.

SEBASTIAN, Ludwig, *Hinter Dröhenden Motoren*, Verlag Carl Ueberreutter, Vienna, 1952.

SHIRER, William L., *The Rise and Fall of the Third Reich*, Secker & Warburg, 1959. *The Nightmare Years, 1930–1940*, Bantam Books, New York, 1985.

SMITH, Norman, *Case History*, Autosport, London, 1958.

STUCK, Hans, *Tagesbuck eines Rennfahrers*, Moderne Verlags–GmbH, Munich, 1967.

STUCK, Hans and BURGGALLER, Ernst, *Motoring Sport*, G. T. Foulis & Co Ltd, London, 1935.

WALKERLEY, Rodney, *Grands Prix 1934–1939*, Motor Racing Publications Ltd, London, 1948. *Automobile Racing*, Temple Press Ltd, London, 1962. *Motor Racing Facts and Figures*, B. T. Batsford Ltd, London, 1961.

Periodicals
The Motor; *The Autocar*; *Speed*; *Motor Sport*; *Automobile Quarterly*.

Photographic acknowledgements

The author and the publisher are grateful to the following for permission to reproduce their photographs on the pages indicated:

Alfa Romeo page 203 (bottom); Daimler-Benz pages 8, 18–19, 28, 37, 39, 40, 41, 42, 45, 50 (bottom), 52 (top), 55, 57, 58, 59, 68 (bottom), 71, 72, 74, 75, 77, 79, 80, 81, 83, 85, 87, 88, 89, 90, 91, 96 (bottom), 97, 98 (bottom), 99 (bottom), 100 (top), 103 (left), 105, 116–117, 120, 132–133, 142, 143, 148, 156, 159 (top), 160, 162 (top), 163 (bottom), 174, 181, 182, 184, 186 (bottom), 187, 188, 189, 190–1, 193, 194, 195, 197, 198, 201, 203 (top), 205, 210, 213, 214–215, 222, 223, 224, 225, 226 (top), 229, 230–231, 238 (bottom), 240, 241, 242 (bottom), 245, 249, 252, 257, 258–259, 262–263, 265, 266, 267 (top), 268, 276, 277, 278, 279 (bottom), 280, 281, 282, 285, 292, 293, 295, 297, 299, 300, 317, 318, 320, 320–321, 322, 323, 324, 325, 327 (left), 337; Christoph Eberan-Eberhorst pages 33, 50 (top), 137, 147, 162 (bottom), 212, 233, 307; Jochen & Barbara Essers 161, 185, 251 (bottom), 253; Hanns & Brigitte Geier pages 68 (top), 69 (bottom), 99 (top), 183, 196; Ernst Henne pages 27, 29; Dieter Jochisch pages 51, 96 (top), 106–107, 165, 172, 176–177, 208, 228, 237, 267 (bottom), 303; Ghislaine Kaes pages 23, 24, 25, 52 (bottom), 110, 111, 113 (both), 117 (top), 141; Louis Klementaski 127–128, 226 (bottom), 279 (top), 283 (top), 321 (top); La Meuse page 301; Chris Nixon pages 22, 26, 64, 67, 110 (top), 114, 167 (top), 179, 186, 242 (top), 244, 247, 291, 302; Paul Pietsch pages 65, 66, 133 (bottom); Porsche AG page 112; Cyril Posthumus pages 56, 60–61, 104, 119, 129, 135, 145 (top), 158, 261 (top), 264, 383 (bottom), 326; Elly Beinhorn Rosemeyer pages 124, 144, 151, 284; Lothar Rubelt pages 54, 221, 234, 235; Halwart Schrader pages 146 (bottom), 175, 209, 236, 309, 319; Martin Schroder pages 103 (right), 125, 130–131, 250–251, 286, 312–313; Ludwig Sebastian pages 34, 69 (top & centre), 73, 78, 115, 121, 123, 145 (bottom), 146 (top), 154, 159 (bottom), 238 (top), 261 (bottom), 288–289, 306; Hans Joachim Stuck pages 31, 53, 100 (bottom), 101, 150, 202, 207, 227, 254, 308, 327 (right); Rupert Stuhlemmer pages 164, 167 (bottom).

Cover photographs, front: Daimler-Benz; back: Daimler-Benz (top, centre & bottom left), Rupert Stuhlemmer (centre right), Martin Schroder (bottom right).

Index